Foundations of the Vocational Rehabilitation Process

Foundations of the Vocational Rehabilitation Process

Sixth Edition

Stanford E. Rubin
and
Richard T. Roessler

pro·ed
An International Publisher

8700 Shoal Creek Boulevard
Austin, Texas 78757-6897
800/897-3202   Fax 800/397-7633
www.proedinc.com

An International Publisher

© 1987, 1995, 2001, 2008 by PRO-ED, Inc.
8700 Shoal Creek Boulevard
Austin, Texas 78757-6897
800/897-3202   Fax 800/397-7633
www.proedinc.com

Library of Congress Cataloging-in-Publication Data

Rubin, Stanford E.
  Foundations of the vocational rehabilitation process / Stanford E. Rubin and Richard T. Roessler.
— 6th ed.
      p. cm.
  Includes bibliographical references and index.
  ISBN-13: 978-1-4164-0251-0
  ISBN-10: 1-4164-0251-9
1. Rehabilitation counseling.   2. Vocational rehabilitation.   I. Roessler, Richard, 1944– II. Title.
  HD7255.5.R823 2008
  362'.0425—dc22

                                                                    2007003081

Art Director: Jason Crosier
Designer: Sandy Salinas
This book is designed in Bembo and Futura.

Printed in the United States of America

1 2 3 4 5 6 7 8 9 10   11 10 09 08 07

To our wives,
Nancy and Janet;
our children,
Penelope, Jenny, Allison,
Jennifer, and Kristin;
and our parents,
Ruth and Frank
and
Kathryn and Ralph

Contents

Preface ⚘ **ix**

Chapter 1
Historical Roots of Modern Rehabilitation Practices ⚘ *1*

Chapter 2
Current Rehabilitation History ⚘ *41*

Chapter 3
The Americans with Disabilities Act:
Major Mandates and Ambiguities ⚘ *91*

Chapter 4
Philosophical and Economic Considerations in Regard to Disability Rights
and Support for Rehabilitation Programs ⚘ *143*

Chapter 5
Sociological Aspects of Disability ⚘ *167*
Charles Maria V. Arokiasamy, Stanford E. Rubin, and Richard T. Roessler

Chapter 6
Societal Values and Ethical Commitments That Influence
Rehabilitation Service Delivery Behavior ⚘ *197*
Eugenie Gatens-Robinson and Stanford E. Rubin

Chapter 7
Rehabilitation Clients and Their Needs ⚘ *215*

Chapter 8
The Role and Function of the Rehabilitation Counselor ⚘ *267*

Chapter 9

The Vocational Rehabilitation Process: Evaluation Phase ⟡ *287*

Chapter 10

Planning the Rehabilitation Program ⟡ *337*

Chapter 11

Utilizing Rehabilitation Facilities and Support Services ⟡ *365*

Chapter 12

Job Placement ⟡ *399*

Chapter 13

Assistive Technology: Prospects and Problems ⟡ *427*

Chapter 14

Women with Disabilities: Special Issues in Rehabilitation ⟡ *459*
Walter Chung and Stanford E. Rubin

Chapter 15

Independent Living ⟡ *483*

Chapter 16

Rehabilitation in the Private-for-Profit Sector:
Opportunities and Challenges ⟡ *501*
Martin G. Brodwin

References ⟡ **525**

Author Index ⟡ **585**

Subject Index ⟡ **597**

About the Authors ⟡ **603**

Preface

The sixth edition of *Foundations of the Vocational Rehabilitation Process* is the culmination of a 30-year joint effort to learn and teach about the vocational rehabilitation process. Since the first edition in the mid-1970s, our text has gradually grown to span over 3 decades of advances in our field. We have learned a great deal; we hope our readers will have the same experience.

Like its predecessors, the sixth edition of *Foundations of the Vocational Rehabilitation Process* provides the historical, philosophical, legislative, and sociological foundations for the habilitation/rehabilitation of persons with disabilities. These foundations are found primarily in Chapters 1 through 6, 14, and 15. In Chapters 7 through 13 and 16, we provide a comprehensive overview of the workings of rehabilitation. Our understanding of these foundations and procedures has evolved through teaching the introductory rehabilitation course to graduate students in rehabilitation education and through active research in rehabilitation. As our experience has grown, so too has the scope and depth of *Foundations*.

This edition addresses mandates presented in the major pieces of disability legislation influencing the practice of rehabilitation. This legislation emphasizes not only vocational, independent living, social, and educational rehabilitation services, but also the removal of environmental barriers and the civil rights of people with disabilities. Only through this dual focus on individual and environment can rehabilitation maximize participation of people with disabilities in mainstream American society. As in the previous edition, the right to this accessibility is the essential message of this edition. Throughout the 16 chapters of the book, the reader encounters this groundswell movement, initiated and nurtured by people with disabilities and their advocates, for equal access to public services, transportation, accommodations, and telecommunications, as well as to economic and educational opportunities. Any environmental barriers to such freedom and responsibility, whether physical or attitudinal, are unacceptable. We believe that disability often places people with disabilities in our society in negative situations and that these situational factors are often far more limiting than are any medical, intellectual, or emotional conditions.

Current legislation calls for (a) greater involvement of individuals with severe disabilities, (b) alternative approaches to vocational placement, (c) provision of independent living services, (d) expansion of rehabilitation/habilitation services for individuals with developmental disabilities, and (e) protection of the civil rights of people with disabilities. The many implications of recent legislation are still in the process of being fully understood and acted upon by the field. Hence, the reader will find that this book provides both theoretical and practical information to help rehabilitation professionals translate legislative mandates into practice.

The reader will find many changes in the sixth edition. More than 1,200 references are incorporated into the text, over 350 of which are new references. We have updated and moved the fifth-edition chapter titled "Overcoming Environmental Barriers to Employment Through Reasonable Accommodation in the Workplace" to the fourth edition of *Case Management and Rehabilitation Counseling* (Roessler & Rubin, 2006) because we believe that students in case management will be better prepared to apply information about job accommodation. We have added a new chapter, Chapter 14, on women with disabilities. By including this chapter, we stress the importance of rehabilitation counselor awareness of the unique challenges faced by many women with disabilities in regard to employment inequality, health needs, sexuality and intimacy, motherhood, and abuse. We are very appreciative of Dr. Walter Chung's major efforts as the senior author of Chapter 14.

Chapter 2, "Current Rehabilitation History," is expanded and updated. We provide a new section on the Ticket to Work and Work Incentives Improvement Act of 1999. The chapter discusses governmental and legislative efforts to reduce disincentives to employment for people with disabilities who are receiving benefits from programs such as Social Security. As in the past, Chapter 2 traces the history of post-1970 legislation pertaining to accessibility of public transportation by persons with disabilities. Civil rights implications of Title V (Sections 501–504) of the Rehabilitation Act of 1973 are discussed, as are perspectives comparing the treatment of persons with disabilities with that of other minority groups. Chapter 2 describes the critical differences between the minority group model and the functional limitations model.

Chapter 3, "The Americans with Disabilities Act" (ADA), provides an updated discussion of how the ADA prohibits discrimination on the basis of disability in employment, public accommodations, public services, and telecommunications. We wish to thank Jenny Rubin for her capable assistance in helping us find many of the law library resources necessary for developing the content of Chapter 3.

Chapter 4 continues to discuss timeless issues related to the philosophical underpinnings of rehabilitation, incorporating disability rights topics as well as the traditional arguments for rehabilitation services. We have added three new brief sections to Chapter 4 (e.g., "The Effect of Advances in the Science of Molecular Genetics on the Right to Equal Access to Employment for Those with Disabilities"). Many interesting class debates can be planned using the issues presented in Chapter 4, including the right to medical treatment, the meaning and relevance of "quality of life" as a consideration in the service provision determination process, and viable arguments for independent living and vocational rehabilitation services. Over the years students have conducted many heated arguments over the pros and cons of the economic, moral/ethical, and human rights arguments in support of rehabilitation.

Chapter 5, "Sociological Aspects of Disability," addresses the attitudinal and environmental features of handicapism in society. It analyzes the history of society's responses to persons with disabilities to illuminate the major determinants of such treatment. In so doing, Chapter 5 explains the roots of attitudinal barriers that block full integration of persons with disabilities into society.

Chapter 6 discusses how certain basic values of rehabilitation professionals and of others in American society can be expected to be compatible since both groups are products of the same socialization process. These values, such as perception of physical attractiveness, can limit what rehabilitation professionals see as possible and logical goals for persons with disabilities, as well as limit the opportunities of persons with disabilities to participate fully in everyday life. Chapter 6 also discusses how the ethical principles of beneficence, autonomy, and justice shape rehabilitation professionals' philosophy of helping by influencing their interpretation of the scope of their moral responsibility to their clients.

New information and updated references were added on the four disability types—physical disabilities, emotional disorders, mental retardation, and learning disabilities—previously discussed in Chapter 7, "Rehabilitation Clients and Their Needs." As always, we thank Nancy Rubin and Joseph Ashley for their excellent contributions to the learning disabilities section. We also draw the reader's attention to the new section added to Chapter 7 on visual impairments and blindness. Much of the information on all five areas of disability contained in Chapter 7 should be of great value to rehabilitation counselors as they communicate to employers the many benefits of hiring people with disabilities.

Although containing many new references and much new information in Chapters 8 through 13 and Chapter 16, the sixth edition retains the strengths of previous editions in coverage of the role of the rehabilitation counselor and the four-stage rehabilitation process—evaluation, planning, treatment, and placement. Chapter 13, which was added to the textbook in 1987, has been updated with some new references and additional information on assistive technology. Recognizing the fact that information of that sort is constantly changing, we remind readers of their continuing responsibility to stay abreast of technological advances.

At the same time, Chapter 13 introduces readers to a procedure that never goes out of date, namely the application of the problem-solving process in the use of technology. To help people with disabilities take advantage of technology, counselors must first and foremost be good problem solvers. They must also be well informed and creative as they apply these problem-solving steps to enhancing an individual's productivity and independence through assistive technology. In closing, Chapter 13 presents a review of social attitudes and governmental policies that influence the development of assistive technology. The instructor is encouraged to devote at least one class session to exploring technology-related issues and new technological devices. Much of what is referred to as the "handicapping condition" can be removed by creative applications of assistive technology.

The many opportunities available in private sector rehabilitation continue to require a chapter on private sector rehabilitation. An experienced rehabilitation educator, Dr. Martin Brodwin has an extensive work history in private sector rehabilitation. In Chapter 16, he discusses the functions of the private provider in worker's compensation, insurance rehabilitation, disability management, forensic, and life planning roles. He compares and contrasts the skills needed to perform in these jobs with those required in the public sector. Dr. Brodwin's chapter is an excellent introduction to the private sector for students, helping them decide whether and in what ways they might wish to work in that dynamic part of rehabilitation.

In closing, we call the reader's attention to the outdated sexist and disability language in several of the quotes used in the sixth edition (e.g., "disabled persons"). Because these quotes were taken from "another time and place," they do not reflect an editorial sensitivity to appropriate language. Rather than paraphrase these quotes, we include them as originally written, but we do point out here the problem associated with them.

Foundations of the Vocational Rehabilitation Process is designed for the introductory course at the master's level or a senior-level course in an undergraduate program on vocational or independent living rehabilitation. Like the fifth edition, the sixth edition provides the groundwork for further study of the rehabilitation counseling process as described in the fourth edition of our textbook *Case Management and Rehabilitation Counseling* (Roessler & Rubin, 2006). When combined in a yearlong study of the rehabilitation process, this two-volume set covers (a) the history and philosophy of rehabilitation, (b) sociological aspects of disability, (c) the characteristics of clients with disabilities, (d) rehabilitation counseling, (e) case management, (f) the rehabilitation process, and (g) descriptions of rehabilitation services.

In terms of in-service applications, *Foundations* offers valuable information to practicing counselors who are dedicated to staying abreast of developments in the field. *Foundations* is also a valuable resource for those newly entering the profession who are preparing to become Certified Rehabilitation Counselors (CRCs). Finally, we hope that the sixth edition will assist in-service training directors in their efforts to develop informative training programs for their staff members.

As always, many people have made it possible for the new edition to be written. Although we have dedicated this volume to our families, we again offer it in the hope that it will contribute to the efforts of rehabilitation professionals to meet the pressing needs of individuals with severe disabilities. We also wish to recognize the individuals who have contributed to this book. Special thanks go to Charles Maria V. Arokiasamy, Martin Brodwin, Walter Chung, and Eugenie Gatens-Robinson for their contributions. We owe a great deal to Linda Patrick and her staff (Ashley Charvat, Melissa

McMahan, Missy Moore, and Sherri Wieland) of the Operations Support Center in the College of Education and Human Resources at Southern Illinois University–Carbondale for their careful word processing and general handling of the manuscript. Having managed the word processing responsibilities for the second, third, fourth, fifth, and now sixth editions, Linda Patrick has our unending gratitude.

Chapter 1

Historical Roots of Modern Rehabilitation Practices

The history of rehabilitation of people with disabilities focuses on the treatment of individuals who deviate negatively from the majority of society in regard to one or more of the following: physical appearance, physical functioning, intellectual functioning, and behavior. Society's willingness at any point in time to attend to the needs of persons with disabilities has been greatly determined by the perceived cause of the disability, the perceived threat of the disability group to the nondisabled community, the prevailing economic conditions, the existing medical knowledge, and the prevailing sociocultural philosophy. The influence of these factors will become apparent as the history of the treatment of people with disabilities unfolds in the subsequent sections of this chapter.

Greek and Roman Eras

Early attitudes toward persons with physical disabilities were far from compassionate. The Greek philosophy of the unity of body and soul, with a blemish on one signifying a blemish on the other (Dickinson, 1961), could not have helped but predispose the Greeks to a negative attitude toward persons with disabilities. The extreme manifestation of that negative attitude was found in Sparta, where "the immature, the weak, and the damaged were eliminated purposefully" (Nichtern, 1974, p. 14). Spartan children were considered more the property of the state than of their parents. Whether a newborn child was to be raised or exposed to die was determined "within the first week following birth" by a council of city elders who had closely inspected the child (Preen, 1976, pp. 8–9).

The Spartans, however, had no monopoly on the practice of infanticide in ancient Greece. In the 4th century B.C., an overpopulated Athens used exposure of infants with physical disabilities as one means of population control (Preen, 1976). Both Plato and Aristotle sanctioned infanticide—"the former for eugenic,… the latter for economic reasons" (A. Deutsch, 1949, p. 334).

Centuries later, in Rome, persons with disabilities fared no better. Romans could legally exterminate puny or deformed children because a newborn child had no rights until officially entering a household 10 days after birth. At that point, the infant was brought to the father, who decided whether to admit the child into the family. If rejected, the child "was taken away to be killed or exposed in some lonely place—baskets for this very purpose were offered for sale in the marketplace" (Sand, 1952, p. 350). Some of those unwanted Roman children were disposed of "in sewers located, ironically, outside the Temple of Mercy" (Garrett, 1969, p. 31).

In early Greece, mental illness was considered the result of "divine or demoniacal visitations." Greek mythology contains many references "to madness set down upon human beings by angry and displeased deities" (A. Deutsch, 1949, p. 5). Because the treatment was logically based on the perceived cause, numerous healing shrines were established and staffed by priest–physicians claiming descent from the gods (A. Deutsch, 1949).

The supernatural etiology was later rejected by Hippocrates (460 to 370 B.C.), the Greek physician, in favor of a brain pathology and environmental hypothesis. Hippocrates' thesis was at least partially accepted by the Greeks who developed first-rate sanitariums in Alexandria, Egypt, where individuals with mental illness received humane treatment. These sanitariums provided a pleasant setting where recovery from a mental illness was augmented by the provision of "constant occupation, entertainment, and exercise" (Coleman, 1964, pp. 26–27).

Treatment of persons with mental illness in Rome was dependent on social class. Well-to-do individuals were likely to receive humane treatment similar to that found in the sanitariums of Greece. However, the remaining Romans who suffered from mental illness were more likely to be treated with brutal methods, including "chaining, flogging, semi-starvation diet, and the application of terror and torture" (Sand, 1952, p. 101). Members of the poorer classes with mental illness in both Greece and Rome may have met an even less fortunate fate—being "put to death as undesirable or intolerable burdens, in the absence of public provision for their care" (A. Deutsch, 1949, p. 11).

From ancient history, little more can be derived than the fact that individuals with mental retardation existed. For all practical purposes, there was a total absence of organized efforts to provide for the "shelter, protection, or training" of persons with mental retardation in Greek or Roman society (Kanner, 1964, p. 3). The only occupation reported for persons with mental retardation in ancient literature was that of the "fool" or "jester" kept in some wealthy Roman households for entertainment purposes (Kanner, 1964, p. 5).

Middle Ages Through the 17th Century

During the Middle Ages, the world was viewed as a battleground where the angels of God and the infernal demons of Satan fought for the souls of men (see A. Deutsch, 1949). Dr. Johann Weyer identified over 7 million demons in the world ready "to cripple, maim, confuse, and destroy men and women" (Obermann, 1965, p. 56). Because disability was frequently seen as either God's punishment or the result of demonic possession, it is not surprising that persons with disabilities "were feared, hated, and often persecuted and tortured as collaborators of the Evil One and bringers of all kinds of misfortune to their towns and their fellow men" (Safilios-Rothschild, 1970, p. 6). The state of medical knowledge did little to ameliorate the situation. Physicians were poorly trained and relatively ineffective. Surgery, which was held in general disrepute, was often conducted by barbers. Progress in medical knowledge was extremely difficult to achieve due to strong public opposition to the dissection of human bodies for anatomical study. "As late as 1750 European medical schools which engaged in this practice were in danger of destruction by irate mobs" (E. Burns & Ralph, 1958, p. 49).

Mental illness during the Middle Ages was also seen as the result of possession "by the Evil One." Therefore, individuals with a mental illness were treated by monks and priests rather than by physicians (A. Deutsch, 1949, pp. 16–17). Treatment was located in monasteries, where, during the early

Middle Ages, gentle and humane methods—such as exorcism via the gentle "laying on of hands"—were used. However, as the Middle Ages progressed, cruel treatment methods, such as starving, whipping, and immersion in hot water, were more typically applied to make the body of a person with mental illness a very unpleasant place for a self-respecting devil to reside (Coleman, 1964, pp. 31–32).

By the 16th century, the belief that mental illness resulted from possession began to be replaced by the belief that those with mental illness were sick (Coleman, 1964). As a result, persons with mental illness were more likely to be sent to asylums than to monasteries and prisons. Unfortunately, the treatment in these early asylums was often far from therapeutic. It was not unusual for patients to be found chained to the wall in dark cells. In the 16th century, at the London asylum known as "Bedlam," the "more violent patients were exhibited to the public for one penny a look" (Coleman, 1964, p. 37). Overall, the asylums for persons with mental illness during the 16th, 17th, and 18th centuries were more like prisons than hospitals.

Some of the earliest recorded rehabilitation attempts occurred during this period. A deaf pupil was taught to write in the 15th century. During the 16th century, deaf pupils were taught "to speak, read, write and understand arithmetic" (Obermann, 1965, p. 64), and "the much more difficult task of teaching a blind deaf-mute by forming the letters on his arm" was achieved (Sand, 1952, p. 409). The 17th century saw the development of a controversial two-handed means of communication for individuals who were deaf (Obermann, 1965).

Education and training for persons with mental retardation during this period were precluded by society's view of mental retardation as inherited and, therefore, incurable. With the prevailing belief being "once retarded, always retarded" (L. M. Dunn, 1961, p. 14), there was an almost total absence of reference to individuals with mental retardation in the medical literature during this period (Kanner, 1964, p. 7).

Rehabilitation in Early America

The energies of colonial Americans were devoted primarily to survival. These already overburdened settlers preferred to avoid assuming responsibility for those incapable of self-support in this highly challenging environment. "Laws in the Thirteen Colonies excluded settlers who could not demonstrate an ability to support themselves independently. Immigration policy forbade people with physical, mental, or emotional disabilities to enter the country" (U.S. Commission on Civil Rights, 1983, p. 18). However, immigration laws do not eliminate the presence of persons with disabilities in a society. Children with disabilities were born in the colonies, and some colonists acquired disabilities through illness or injuries. Unfortunately, the outlook for most of these persons with a disability was far from rosy (U.S. Commission on Civil Rights, 1983, p. 18).

With the typical colonist barely able to scratch out a living from the soil and with disability perceived as the result of God's punishment, conditions were not ripe in colonial America for the development of rehabilitation programs. Additionally, medical practices in the colonies precluded much hope of medical, let alone vocational, rehabilitation. For example, colonial physicians, many of whom were self-trained, would commonly try to drive out of the patient's body diseases such as dysentery, influenza, diphtheria, typhoid fever, yellow fever, scarlet fever, and consumption by inducing nausea via the ingestion of terrible concoctions. Other remedies included bleeding and blistering. Physicians were even known to prescribe "the swallowing of a leaden bullet for 'that miserable Distemper which they called the Twisting of the Guts'" (J. C. Miller, 1952/1966, pp. 240–244). Colonial physicians who read the popular medical books of the period were not likely to increase their effectiveness. The inquiring doctor could very likely find a medical book that suggested using "the famous 'Spirit of Skull' ... concocted from an elaborate preparation of 'moss from the skull of a dead man unburied who had died a violent death,' mixed with wine" (A. Deutsch, 1949, p. 27).

It was not until 1752 that the Quakers, with the aid of Benjamin Franklin, set up the first colonial general hospital in Philadelphia (J. C. Miller, 1952/1966). The establishment of this and other early hospitals had little immediate effect on upgrading the quality of medical care. However, by serving as laboratories in which the ineffectiveness of existing medical practices was demonstrated, they laid a foundation for improved medical care in the future (Grob, 1973).

Although the first three American medical schools opened between 1765 and 1783, improved medical practice was not observed in the latter part of the 18th century. It has been said that in order to effect a cure, the American physician at the end of the 18th century depended on "10 percent knowledge, 40 percent pseudoscientific surmise, [and] 50 percent bedside manner" (Furnas, 1969, pp. 336–337). Unfortunately, medical practices based on "pseudoscientific surmise" may have contributed more to the deterioration than the cure of the patient. The early practices of Dr. Benjamin Rush, who practiced medicine from 1769 to 1813 and who also trained approximately 3,000 doctors, provide some support for that conclusion. He believed cure was promoted when the physician attempted to drive out disease from the body in the same way that evil was expelled from human society. As a result, Rush "freely resorted to the use of mercury in its various forms to purge patients of certain 'morbific' or disease-making substances that were supposed to lurk in their bodily fluids" (Weisberger, 1975, p. 40). In the latter half of his career, Rush became a strong advocate of "bleeding" the patient who suffered from fever (Weisberger, 1975, pp. 45–47, 98).

The type of treatment afforded to persons with mental illness in the American colonies was dependent on two factors: (a) the socioeconomic status of the person's family and (b) whether the mental illness manifested itself in a violent or nonviolent way. Members of well-to-do families were usually kept at home. If "violent or troublesome," they were "locked up and chained by their families in strong-rooms, cellars, and even in flimsy outhouses" (A. Deutsch,

1949, p. 40). If nonviolent, they were sometimes allotted a certain amount of freedom of movement, but even some nonviolent persons were locked away for years in attics by their families. Paupers who were mentally ill experienced a harsher plight. Those viewed as harmless were treated like paupers. If violent, they were treated as common criminals and incarcerated in jails if any existed in the community. In localities where the jail was nonexistent, "the pillory, the whipping post and the gallows—all placed conveniently near the courthouse—afforded simple and inexpensive means" of rapid punishment (A. Deutsch, 1949, p. 49). The dismal picture painted of the treatments of people with mental illness was not unique to the American colonies, but rather emerged from, "and reflected, conditions in the Old World" (A. Deutsch, 1949, p. 54).

Rehabilitation Advances in 19th-Century America

Advances in rehabilitation in 19th-century America occurred with a minimum of financial support from state governments and almost no support from the federal government. The role of federal government in America was shaped during this period by the Jeffersonian–Jacksonian philosophy of limited government. A flavor of that philosophy can be gleaned from Jefferson's first inaugural address, in which

> he called for "a wise and frugal government, which shall restrain men from injuring one another, *which shall leave them otherwise free to regulate their own pursuits of industry and improvement* [italics added], and shall not take from the mouth of labor the bread it has earned." (Hofstadter, 1948, p. 38)

Therefore, programs for persons with disabilities looked to sources other than the federal government for financial support during the 19th century.

Fortunately, for at least some persons with disabilities, the 19th-century American was the product of a humanitarian religious background that stressed the responsibility of the successful to help the unfortunate. In addition, because they lived in a rapidly developing country where even the most ambitious agricultural and industrial development goals were often surpassed, 19th-century Americans became incurable optimists (Commager, 1950). That humanitarianism and optimism generated a receptive environment for the initiation of programs designed to meet the needs of persons with disabilities. Those who were deaf or blind were especially less likely to be held accountable for their misfortune.

Unfortunately, good intentions and a receptive societal attitude toward helping persons with disabilities were insufficient to significantly minimize the plight of those with physical disabilities. The paucity of knowledge about human anatomy and physiology limited surgical practice to the excision of kidney stones and superficial cancers and the amputation of limbs (Furnas, 1969).

Because attempts to reduce or splint a compound fracture typically led to death from infection, amputation was not rare in America during the early decades of the 19th century. During this pre–antiseptic surgery era, the high incidence of one-armed and peg-legged Americans probably resulted more from large numbers of such operations than from high success rates (Furnas, 1969). In fact, as late as the Franco-Prussian War, reports indicated that over 75% of the amputation cases in French field hospitals died (Sand, 1952).

The improved environment for persons with disabilities almost immediately affected those who were deaf or blind, and a little later it benefited those who were mentally retarded or mentally ill. Thomas Gallaudet, Samuel Gridley Howe, and Dorothea Dix emerged as effective advocates for society's responsibility to meet the needs of persons with disabilities in the United States. Thomas Gallaudet became the champion of those with hearing impairment. Dr. Samuel Gridley Howe carried the banner for both those who were blind and those with mental retardation. Dorothea Dix led the fight for reform in the treatment of persons with mental illness.

Rehabilitation of Persons with Hearing Disabilities

Upon graduation from Yale, Thomas Gallaudet went to Andover to complete his theological studies. While there, his health deteriorated to the point that employment as a preacher became impossible. While recuperating at his home in Hartford during the winter of 1814–1815, Gallaudet became interested in "the young deaf-mute daughter of Dr. Mason F. Cogswell. With infinite patience, but nothing to guide him save his own intelligence, he managed to 'impart to her a knowledge of many simple words and sentences'" (Holbrook, 1957, p. 262). Greatly impressed, Dr. Cogswell spearheaded an effort by influential Hartford citizens to found a school for children who were deaf. Realizing that knowledge of effective methods for educating persons who were deaf was not present in America, they sent young Gallaudet to Europe to learn the latest deaf education methods (Holbrook, 1957). Soon after his departure, a survey revealed the existence of at least 400 children who were deaf in New England. With the need documented, $5,000 was raised to set up the first school for persons who were deaf in the United States. Congress also provided a land grant in support of the new institution, which took the name of the American Asylum. Gallaudet returned from Europe in 1816 with his new knowledge of deaf education. He was accompanied on his return home by Laurent Clerc, a senior teacher at the National Institute for Deaf Mutes in Paris. With the assistance of Clerc, Gallaudet established the American Asylum, which opened in Hartford in 1817, and became its first director (Groce, 1992; Tyler, 1962). This school, which proved to be very successful, used the manual method of instruction. The manual method thereafter became the dominant method used in American schools (Obermann, 1965).

During his visit to Europe, Gallaudet likely heard of the effective public relations efforts of Jacob Rodgriques Pereire. Having successfully taught a person who was deaf to read and speak, Pereire was invited to demonstrate the results of his work at the Court of King Louis XV in 1749. The impressed king "granted him an annual pension of 800 francs as a token of esteem" (Kanner, 1964, p. 11). The excitement generated by Pereire's success no doubt facilitated the founding in Paris of the first public school for deaf persons in 1760. Following Pereire's lead, Gallaudet "took his most accomplished pupils on tours, visiting state legislatures and giving exhibitions in churches" (Tyler, 1962, p. 296). Gallaudet's public relations efforts were very successful. In addition to stimulating the congressional land grant already mentioned, funds were appropriated by Massachusetts and New Hampshire for sending 30 pupils to Hartford (Holbrook, 1957). By the time of his death in 1851, institutions for educating individuals who were deaf had opened in 13 other states. In 1857 the first college program for deaf persons was set up in the nation's capital (Tyler, 1962). By 1880 graduates of that college had been placed as "teachers, journalists, lawyers and draftsmen" (LaRue, 1972, p. 20).

Rehabilitation of Persons Who Were Blind

Early attempts at educating children and youth who were blind date back to at least 1784, when Valentin Hauy, "influenced by the revolutionary ideas about the rights of man," founded a school and workshop in Paris for individuals who were blind (Lowenfeld, 1973; Nelson, 1971, p. 25). Pupils in Hauy's school were taught to read via a system of raised type. Both general education and technical education were provided in this school (Sand, 1952). Hauy's goal was to provide persons who were blind, through training for employment, with the skills necessary for supporting themselves in the community. Although Hauy failed to achieve his industrial objective of vocational rehabilitation of persons who were blind, his effort was one of the earliest positive attempts at vocationally rehabilitating persons with disabilities. Between 1791 and 1827, "six institutions for the blind were started in the United Kingdom" (Nelson, 1971, pp. 25–26). Two of those institutions had workshops.

By the time the first school for persons who were blind, the New England Asylum for the Blind, opened in the United States in 1832, institutions for teaching persons who were deaf could be found as far west as Ohio and as far south as Virginia (Holbrook, 1957). The success of the New England Asylum, which later became known as the Perkins Institute, has been largely attributed to the man chosen to be its first director, Dr. Samuel Gridley Howe. Rather than practicing medicine upon graduation from Harvard, this highly unusual man went to

> Greece to fight the invading Turks. For six years this knight-errant Bostonian fought guerilla-style on land, served as a surgeon on a Greek warship,

and at war's end hurried home to raise money and return to the devastated country with a shipload of clothing and food. In 1830, loaded with malaria, plus a chevalier's ribbon of the Greek Order of the Redeemer, and a helmet that had been worn by Lord Byron, he returned to Boston. (Holbrook, 1957, p. 269)

Prior to accepting the position of director of the New England Asylum for the Blind, this "born crusader" had no interest in either individuals who were blind or their education. Fortunately for those who were blind, this man who "was out to change the world" was in need of a new crusade when he was asked to become director of the school for the blind (Holbrook, 1957, pp. 269–270).

Howe believed that persons who were blind could be prepared to "participate in the economic and social life of their home communities" (Lenihan, 1977, p. 23). Therefore, he designed the school's program to be as similar as possible to the education received by other children. However, music and crafts received greater emphasis in Howe's school (Sink, Field, & Gannaway, 1978).

In less than a year, Howe had exhausted the funds provided for the school. Although critical of the French Blind Schools for using students in public demonstrations of their educational gains, necessity forced him to adopt their fundraising method. In 1833 he had his two most outstanding pupils, "Abby and Sophia Carter, six and eight years old," demonstrate their ability to read aloud "with their fingers" both before the Massachusetts state legislature and in a Boston theater for the ladies of Boston. The latter group was sufficiently impressed to organize a 4-day fund-raising fair for the school. Over $11,000 was raised (Holbrook, 1957, p. 271).

Howe apparently never forgot the effectiveness of "public demonstrations" as a fund-raising technique. In an attempt to increase public support for his educational efforts, he later toured various states with his blind students, who demonstrated their educational gains (Lenihan, 1977, p. 23). Howe's public relations efforts had a definite impact: Schools for persons who were blind existed in 19 states by 1869 and in over 30 states by 1887 (Holbrook, 1957; Obermann, 1965).

Howe was also interested in providing persons who were blind with the vocational skills necessary for living in their home communities. That goal led him in 1837 to set up the first workshop in the United States at the Perkins Institute and to import "a blind instructor from the Edinburgh Institute for the Blind, John Pringle," as its first director. Under Pringle's supervision, "the shop manufactured mattresses, cushions, pillows, brushes, brooms, chair bottoms (caning) and floor mats," all of which found a market. While Howe saw the workshop as preparing persons who were blind for work in their home communities, most "preferred to remain in the shop where they could work and live under the same roof." Although he successfully "established a separate shop a few blocks away from the school" in 1851 where persons who were blind worked while living in the community, they "still failed generally to find jobs in private industry" (Nelson, 1971, pp. 26–27). Following the Perkins example, schools for persons who were blind in several other states established workshops during the latter half of the 19th century. These ventures tended to be short-lived because of financial problems. The Perkins workshop managed to overcome its financial problems until 1951, when it was forced to close (Nelson, 1971).

The year 1874 marked the beginning of a movement to set up workshops for persons who were blind that were independent of their schools. The first such "independent" workshop was "established by Hinman Hall at Philadelphia in 1874." That workshop, the Pennsylvania Working Home for Blind Men, deviated from Howe's idea of having workers live in the community and come to the workshop only to work, by combining "the ideas of a workshop and a home into a working home." While present-day attitudes tend to support Howe's "antidenormalization" position, the "working home" concept dominated during the end of the 19th and the beginning of the 20th centuries (Nelson, 1971, pp. 27–28).

Rehabilitation of Persons with Mental Retardation

Interest in persons with mental retardation began growing in the French medical community around the turn of the 19th century (Nichtern, 1974). At the beginning of the 19th century, the French physician Jean Itard, influenced by the teachings of John Locke and Jean-Jacques Rousseau, "took charge of a boy of twelve, captured in the forests of Aveyron and diagnosed by the great physician Pinel as severely retarded" (L. M. Dunn, 1961, p. 15). When he came to Itard, the boy was literally a "wild" and totally unsocialized human being. He was "mute, walked on all fours, drank water while lying flat on the ground, and bit and scratched everyone interfering with his actions" (Kanner, 1964, p. 16). He also did not consider location when answering the "calls of nature." Itard worked with the boy intensively for 5 years (Kanner, 1964), emphasizing sense and motor training (L. M. Dunn, 1961). Although he failed to accomplish his independent living goal with the boy, Itard's educational achievements with the "wild boy of Aveyron," who came to prefer civilization to the wild, were seen as remarkable by fellow French scientists. At the end of the 5-year period, the boy "had learned to recognize objects, identify letters of the alphabet, comprehend the meaning of many words, apply names of objects and parts of objects [and] make 'relatively fine' sensory discriminations" (Kanner, 1964, p. 16). Such results undermined the incurability hypothesis for mental retardation and thereby opened the door for the development of habilitation efforts with that disability group.

As was the case for rehabilitation of individuals who were deaf or blind, progress in Europe with persons with mental retardation was soon reflected in rehabilitation activities in the United States. In 1848 Harvey Wilbur opened a residential school in his home in Barge, Massachusetts, for "defective" children. His first student was "the seven year old son of a distinguished lawyer" (Kanner, 1964, p. 39). Shortly thereafter, Wilbur went on to become the superintendent of an experimental school in Albany, New York. Never believing that he could make persons with mental retardation normal, Wilbur's goal was the greatest potential development and utilization of their "dormant faculties" for useful purposes (M. Rosen, Clark, & Kivitz, 1977, p. 5).

In 1848 the Massachusetts state legislature provided what could be considered the first research and demonstration grant. With strong encouragement from Samuel Gridley Howe, who had experienced educational gains with persons who were mentally retarded and blind (Kanner, 1964, p. 40), the Massachusetts legislature appropriated $2,500 per year for 3 years "for an experimental school for the training of ten pauper idiots" (Obermann, 1965, p. 81). Howe became the school's first director (Lenihan, 1977). At the end of the 3-year period, the project was judged a success by the Massachusetts legislature. As a result the first permanent residential school for students with mental retardation in the United States was established in Boston (Kanner, 1964).

Twenty-four institutions for persons with mental retardation were in existence in the United States by 1898 (LaRue, 1972). Unfortunately, during the second half of the 19th century, the orientation in these residential schools changed from one of training and education to that of custodial care (Nichtern, 1974). This change occurred in spite of a Federal Bureau of Education report in 1880 indicating that a small proportion of residential school students with mental retardation "may be made self-supporting, that a further larger proportion may be trained to do some useful work" (LaRue, 1972, p. 20). However, the proselytizing style of persons like Howe had led people to expect more dramatic results. The unfulfilled expectations generated a public pessimism "that was to last many decades" (M. Rosen et al., 1977, p. 5). Overall, as the practices of such institutions for persons with mental retardation changed from training and education to custodial care, these institutions grew in population and rapidly evolved into detention units for such individuals (Nichtern, 1974). That change paralleled a shift in rehabilitation philosophy regarding persons with mental retardation "from the desire, between 1850 and 1880, to 'make the deviant undeviant,' to a concern from 1870 to 1890, to 'shelter the deviant from society,' to alarm between 1880 and 1900 over 'protection of society from the deviant'" (M. Rosen et al., 1977, p. 5). By the turn of the century, public perception of persons with mental retardation as a "menace" was being reinforced by the inappropriate application of the expanding science of genetics for explaining the cause of mental retardation as hereditary and the invalid, but popularly accepted, linking of mental deficiency and criminality. With such prevailing negative societal attitudes toward persons with mental retardation, it is not surprising that these individuals were denied access to government-supported vocational rehabilitation services until the 1940s.

Rehabilitation of Persons with Mental Illness

In both Europe and America, the basic medical attitude during the 18th century was that mental illness was incurable. However, a minority of physicians in both Europe (e.g., Dr. Phillippe Pinel) and America did not accept the incurability position and advocated the value of humane treatment. In America, at the turn of the 19th century, the most significant spokesperson for humane treatment of persons with mental illness was Dr. Benjamin Rush, whose prescriptions included "pleasant surroundings, useful occupation, [and] the conversation of others when feasible" as the road to cure. Rush also suggested that persons with mental illness be provided opportunities "to unburden their distressed minds by writing out their fantasies for discussion, [thereby] vaguely foreshadowing psychoanalysis" (Weisberger, 1975, p. 99).

Unfortunately, Rush's attitudes had very little impact on the prevailing negative societal treatment of persons with mental illness, who were usually tightly secured in (a) the home of their family, (b) an almshouse, (c) the local jail, or (d) a mental hospital. The living conditions found in the latter would make some of the worst present-day jails and prisons look like country clubs in comparison. Things began to change with the arrival on the scene of Dorothea Dix, "a tall, sickly, nervous, and excessively shy New England spinster." In 1841, at the approximate age of 40, she visited a house of correction to teach a Sunday school class. Following that visit, which provided her first encounter with the plight of people with mental illness, she seemed to change from a genteel governess and schoolteacher into the most effective champion of persons with mental illness in 19th-century America. "What Miss Dix had seen was the condition of four insane persons … kept in one dark, airless room the walls of which … were shimmering white with frost" (Holbrook, 1957, p. 227).

Between 1844 and 1854 Dorothea Dix visited hundreds of locations where persons with mental illness were incarcerated. She made these visits to accumulate data for her effective appeals for reform to both state and federal legislators. By 1860 many state legislatures had appropriated funds for the building of new mental hospitals that were to dispense more humane treatment (Tyler, 1962). Dorothea Dix's activity almost produced federal government financial support. In 1854 Congress legislated land grants to the states for the financing of mental hospitals. The same legislation also provided for land grants for purposes of financing facilities for those who had hearing impairments, had visual disabilities, or were mute. Unfortunately, President Franklin Pierce, an advocate of the philosophy of limited federal powers and the "States' Rights" position, vetoed the measure. That "veto became a landmark precedent limiting federal intervention in welfare matters for the next half century" (Lenihan, 1977, pp. 21–22).

Dorothea Dix's views reflected a cultural renaissance that took place in New England during the 30-year period that preceded the Civil War.

> This new Renaissance retained the old religious intensity of Puritanism but substituted, in the concept of man's relationship with God, the ideal of love for that fear. That new ideal was extended into the field of man's relationship with his fellow men.... Like the eighteenth century Enlightenment, with which it had much in common, the New England movement involved a new sense of duty toward humanity, particularly the weaker and more needy sections of it—a sense of duty that had been hitherto almost exclusively reserved for "God." (A. Deutsch, 1949, pp. 163–164)

Rehabilitation of Persons with Physical Disabilities

Prior to the latter part of the 19th century, individuals with physical disabilities were either cared for by their families or placed in an almshouse (Lenihan, 1977). Due to limitations in medical knowledge and/or resources, rehabilitation opportunities were extremely rare. However, medical advances in the latter half of the 19th century increased the potential for both the survival and the medical restoration of persons with physical disabilities. Antiseptic surgery was introduced by Joseph Lister in 1865. Medical progress also was made in orthopedic surgery in the latter half of the 19th century. After 1880 a much larger number of "articles on the care and treatment of cripples" began appearing in medical journals, "and the *American Journal of Orthopedic Surgery* was founded in 1902" (LaRue, 1972, p. 21). Paralleling the increased medical knowledge was the development of new medical treatment facilities for persons with physical disabilities. Between 1863 and 1884, three hospitals for the care of people with physical disabilities (whether wealthy or poor) were established in New York and Philadelphia (Obermann, 1965). The origin of the modern-day rehabilitation center could be seen in the founding of the Cleveland Rehabilitation Center in 1889. Its program was initially restricted to services for children with physical disabilities, but it gradually expanded to include adults with physical disabilities (Allan, 1958). Many modern restorative medical procedures, such as "reconstructive surgery, exercise, and massage, use of heat, water, and other therapy procedures, and bracing of limbs and back" had their origins in these early hospitals for children with physical disabilities (Allan, 1958, p. 41).

Near the end of the 19th century, greater public support was being given to the education and training of children with physical disabilities. Many states either established state-supported schools or provided state aid to school districts for purposes of educating these children. In 1893 the Boston Industrial School for Crippled and Deformed opened. It was the first American school for children with physical disabilities, and its purpose was vocational training (MacDonald, 1944).

Movements Affecting Persons with Disabilities in Post–Civil War 19th-Century America

During the latter half of the 19th century, America changed from a primarily rural, agrarian society to an urban, industrial society. By 1890 there were already 28 cities in the United States with populations over 100,000. In that same year only 43% of U.S. workers were engaged in farmwork (Tishler, 1971). By 1900 the value of manufactured products exceeded the total value of farm products by 2.5 times (S. Fine, 1956), and the United States had emerged as one of the world's leading industrial nations (Tishler, 1971). The economic instability resulting from that transition, highlighted by major depressions in 1873 and 1884–1885, clearly challenged the validity of both the prevailing societal attitude that dependency was the result of "individual moral failings" (LaRue, 1972, p. 13) and the popular Jeffersonian–Jacksonian liberalism principle of "'the less government the better'" (S. Fine, 1956, p. 24).

Unfortunately, the prevailing social climate still seemed to produce more interest in theories of selective breeding than in the development of rehabilitation programs (Obermann, 1965). During this period, the "science" of eugenics was founded, the competing Social Darwinism and Social Gospel movements came into existence, the validity of laissez–faire economic theory was challenged by a new breed of economists, the charity organization movement developed, states adopted compulsory education laws and established special education programs, and vocational education became a part of American public education.

The Science of Eugenics

The latter half of the 19th century provided ripe conditions for Sir Francis Galton's theory of eugenics. Galton defined "eugenics (a term coined by him) as 'the science which deals with all influences that improve the inborn qualities of a race'" (Kanner, 1964, p. 128). Galton's fears were reinforced by publications such as Richard Louis Dugdale's *The Jukes: A Study in Crime, Pauperism, Disease and Heredity* in 1877. The implications of that report of a genealogical survey of the Juke family "were to link crime and pauperism to the heredity transmission of mental deficiency" (Nichtern, 1974, p. 19). Such literature laid the groundwork for the development of eugenics movements in American society. The goal of such movements was the colonization and sterilization of all undesirable subgroups in American society, one of which was the population of persons with mental retardation.

By the mid-1890s, half the states already had laws that made it legally impossible for those with intellectual or emotional impairments to marry. These laws were passed not "on eugenic grounds but on the grounds that such persons were unable to make a contract" (Haller, 1963, p. 47). This situation changed in 1896, when

> Connecticut became the first state to regulate marriage for breeding pur-poses. A law of that year provided that "no man and woman either of whom is epileptic, or imbecile, or feebleminded" shall marry or have extra-marital relations "when the woman is under forty-five years of age," and set a minimum penalty of three years imprisonment for violation. Connecticut was immediately extolled as an example for other states to follow and many legislatures discussed bills to forbid marriage to a variety of persons: the feebleminded, insane, syphilitic, alcoholic, epileptic, and certain types of criminals. Kansas in 1903, New Jersey and Ohio in 1904, and Michigan and Indiana in 1905, joined the ranks of states with eugenic marriage laws. (Haller, 1963, p. 47)

Marital restriction laws for controlling breeding achieved public accep-tance and support prior to sterilization as an acceptable means to the same end. This was due largely to the radical castration medical procedures (surgical removal of the male's testes and female's ovaries) used to achieve sterilization prior to the beginning of the 20th century. In addition to sterilization, these procedures produced major hormonal changes, which inhibited public support. However, the attitude of the public toward these early methods of sterilization did not always prevent their use on those with mental disabilities. For example, in "the third quarter of the 19th century the superintendent of the Winfield Kansas State Home for the Feebleminded castrated 44 boys and 14 girls before being forced to stop for medical (not legal) reasons" (Pfeiffer, 1994, p. 482). Both the elimination of these medical practices and the greater acceptability of the practice of sterilizing individuals with mental disabilities occurred by the late 1890s with the development of two new surgical procedures to achieve sterilization without negative residual hormonal effects: "salpingectomy—the cutting and tying of the fallopian tubes" of a woman, and "vasectomy—the cut-ting and tying of the *vas deferens* through a slit in the scrotum" of a man (Haller, 1963, p. 49). Armed with knowledge of these more "humane" sterilization procedures, the eugenics movement laid the groundwork for society's general acceptance of sterilization during the first quarter of the 20th century as a means for eliminating the presence of mental illness, mental retardation, and criminal behavior from future generations.

The first sterilization law was passed by the Indiana state legislature in 1907 and signed by a governor who was a strong advocate of racial purity. The law "made mandatory the sterilization of confirmed criminals, idiots, imbe-ciles, and rapists in state institutions when recommended by a board of experts" (Haller, 1963, p. 50). By 1926 laws permitting the sterilization of members of such groups "had been enacted in twenty-three states ... and ... declared constitutional by the highest courts in Idaho, Kansas, Michigan, Nebraska, Oklahoma, Utah, and Virginia, and on May 2, 1928, by the Supreme Court of the United States" (Kanner, 1964, p. 136). These laws likely had the support of the American Breeder's Association, a eugenics group, which in 1911 set up a committee to study methods for reducing the number of persons with mental retardation in American society. The ultimate goal of that association was to eliminate defective genetic strains from the race via segregation and/or sterilization (Kanner, 1964).

The continued success of the eugenics movement in the United States between the 1920s and 1960s is evidenced by the fact that by 1938 sterilization laws existed in 33 states and that between 1921 and 1964 an estimated 63,000 individuals were involuntarily sterilized for genetically related reasons (Pfeiffer, 1994). Some of the eugenics-based, involuntary sterilization practices that occurred in the first half of the 20th century were still supported in the latter part of the 20th century by the existence of laws in 22 states (Pfeiffer, 1994). This practice of involuntary sterilization is based on the doctrine of *parens patriae,* which loosely means "father power." "That is, fathers—both biological and legal—know what is in the best interest of the 'child' and can force the 'child' to comply even if the 'child' is an adult who happens to have a disability" (Pfeiffer, 1994, p. 484).

Given the prevailing social attitudes in the second half of the 19th century, it is little wonder that the residential training schools that opened during that period for persons with mental retardation quickly moved toward a *custodial-only* position. A habilitation philosophy oriented toward helping persons with mental retardation adjust within the mainstream of American life was simply incompatible with the overpowering isolationist philosophy advanced by the "eugenics scare" groups.

Social Darwinism

As might be expected during an era of "dog-eat-dog" business competition, honors were heaped upon the successful, with contempt being the reward for the unsuccessful (Obermann, 1965, p. 61). Therefore, the writings of the English philosopher Herbert Spencer, who developed the theory of Social Darwinism, found much acceptance in the United States during the latter part of the 19th century. Spencer's theory saw society progressing toward a higher level of morality via the natural selection of the fittest—those who were capable of adapting to a changing society. For such a system to truly work, Spencer advocated the necessity of a laissez-faire philosophy of government, with state responsibilities limited to police and military functions (Morison, 1965). Spencer saw all other government intervention as interfering with the purification process whereby the unfit were eliminated. From Spencer's point of view, it was far better for society to allow the poor and weak to perish than to sustain their existence and encourage their multiplication through government-supported public relief and health programs (S. Fine, 1956). Such a philosophy was obviously incompatible with the well-being of individuals with disabilities.

Spencer's Social Darwinism philosophy had a strong influence on late 19th-century American social and economic thought. By 1900 U.S. sales of

Spencer's books, *Social Statics* and *Principles of Biology,* approximated 350,000 copies—"a fantastically high figure for sociological and philosophical works" (Hofstadter, Miller, & Aaron, 1959, p. 290). Many Americans considered Spencer "to be the greatest thinker of the age" (S. Fine, 1956, p. 41). Spencer's influence reached right into the chambers of the U.S. Supreme Court, where his laissez-faire theory of government was almost worshipped during the last few decades of the 19th century. "So deep did Spencer's theories penetrate American thought that Justice Holmes, in a dissenting opinion of 1905, felt obliged to remind his fellow jurists that *Social Statics* was not embodied in the Constitution of the United States" (Morison, 1965, p. 83).

Fortunately for persons with disabilities, the influence of the strict interpretation of self-reliance began to permanently wane near the turn of the 20th century. The negative social effects of the Industrial Revolution appeared to be greatly responsible for this outcome (Tishler, 1971).

Social Gospel Movement

Paralleling the Social Darwinism and eugenics movements was the Social Gospel movement, which developed in the United States during the last 20 years of the 19th century. That religious movement stressed social reform as a significant role of religion. The ministers at the forefront of the Social Gospel movement openly "wrote and preached against the economic philosophy of the Social Darwinists" (Hofstadter et al., 1959, p. 276).

The Social Gospelers strongly disagreed with Spencer's position that a laissez-faire government philosophy that facilitates unrestricted competition would eventually lead to an ideal society (S. Fine, 1956). To the Social Gospelers, a society that cherished the "survival of the fittest" doctrine would tend to reinforce the selfish behavior of its members. It would be "a cruel society" absent of "elements of kindness and compassion" (S. Fine, 1956, p. 177). Such a society would be operating in opposition to the teachings of the Bible—that is, the Golden Rule.

One leading member of the Social Gospel movement, Washington Gladden, saw Social Darwinism as based on an unnatural rather than a natural foundation. Gladden stated that "the law of brotherhood is the only natural law. The law of nature is the law of sympathy, of fellowship, of mutual help and service" (cited in Commager, 1950, p. 172). Such teachings were compatible with improved societal attitudes regarding society's responsibility for the rehabilitation of persons with disabilities.

Unfortunately for persons with disabilities, the Social Gospelers were not in the majority. In fact, the majority of both the Protestant clergy and American churchgoers in general were supportive of the concept that personal misfortune was the result of defects in the individual rather than defects in society. Thus, the philosophy of Social Darwinism was simply more compatible with the preachings of the majority of the Protestant clergy at that time, which stressed the relationship of sin and poverty (Hofstadter et al., 1959). This attitude began to change, however, around the turn of the century.

Orthodox Economic Thought Challenged

Although the laissez-faire position was the predominant economic theory of the latter part of the 19th century, it was challenged in the mid-1880s by a new breed of scholar represented by economists such as Thorstein Veblen and Richard T. Ely (Hofstadter et al., 1959). In viewing the exercise of power by the state as a legitimate means of improving society, their position was in opposition to the Social Darwinists and was more compatible with the Social Gospelers. Veblen strongly attacked the theories of Social Darwinism as an explanation of success in business. For Veblen, rather than being the most "biologically fit" and the most "socially useful," the self-made businessman was more aptly described by the characteristics of "'cupidity, prudence, and chicane.'" The American Economic Association, founded in 1885 under the leadership of Richard T. Ely, declared the doctrine of laissez faire to be "unsafe in politics and unsound in morals" and "declared itself in favor of 'the positive assistance of the state'" (Hofstadter et al., 1959, pp. 295–296).

American Charity Organization Movement

By the last quarter of the 19th century, interest was growing in the development of organizations whose goal was the alleviation of poverty. American charity organizations were created by middle-class Americans to attack the problem of poverty. The first such organization, the Buffalo Charity Organization Society, was founded in 1877. By 1892 ninety-two such societies existed in U.S. cities (Lubove, 1965).

These new charity organizations seemed to be more influenced by the Social Darwinists than by the members of the Social Gospel movement. Some historians have, in fact, interpreted their underlying philosophy as "virtually socially Darwinian in outlook" (Tishler, 1971, p. 31). These organizations operated from the premise that poverty had moral roots and that, "more than alms, the poor needed supervision to help them avoid the snares of intemperance, indolence, and improvidence" (Lubove, 1965, p. 3). Personal service rather than material relief was stressed by these new societies (Lubove, 1965, p. 4). They felt that giving anyone anything that was obtainable via their own labors reduced their incentive to work and contributed to their moral deterioration. Therefore, the practices of these groups could have been construed as "benevolent stinginess" (Lubove, 1965, p. 9). The attitude of the charity organizations merely reflected the general attitude toward the poor seen in the press during the last quarter of the 19th century: "that wealth was the product of individual initiative, hard work and thrift, and that poverty except as temporary incentive, was the hell to which moral and mental defectives were consigned" (Tishler, 1971, p. 16).

This whole movement was based on a concept referred to as "scientific charity." The charity organizations stressed comprehensive investigation and treatment designed to meet the needs of the individual case. An army of middle-class volunteers ("friendly visitors") comprised the social service work force of these organizations. The diagnosis was usually moral degradation, and the goal of the friendly visitor was promotion of moral insight in poverty-stricken individuals. Judge (1976) pointed out that the operation of these early charity organizations was guided by the philosophical precept that "man is a spiritual being and, if he is to be helped, it must be by spiritual means" (p. 6). It was basically felt that the morally superior (i.e., the well-to-do) could help the morally inferior (the poverty-stricken).

Although these early charity organizations misdiagnosed the problems of their clients and may not have been very effective, they did demonstrate a rehabilitation rather than a maintenance orientation. Therefore, they represented the first widespread vocational rehabilitation movement. Their emphasis on the extensive investigation of the background of each case and, in theory, the use of a differential treatment approach (Lubove, 1965) created a structure not only for future social work practices but also for vocational rehabilitation casework.

By the 1890s the charity organizations began recognizing the relationship between economic and social conditions and dependency (Judge, 1976). In spite of their Social Darwinism tendencies, their records were more congruent with the Social Gospel position. Such records showed that misfortune rather than misconduct was identified as the cause of poverty in approximately 80% of their cases (Tishler, 1971).

Compulsory Education and the Rise of Special Education Programs

The first state to pass a compulsory school attendance law was Massachusetts in 1852. By 1890 most states had passed such laws (Sarason & Doris, 1979). Although initially these early laws were unenforced or unenforceable, they began to be strengthened and enforced in the early years of the 20th century (Sarason & Doris, 1979). The active enforcement of these laws contributed to the rise of special education programs in the public schools. Although it would be nice to believe that these programs were established primarily out of humanitarian concerns over meeting the educational needs of children with mental and other disabilities, this was apparently not the case. Rather, the programs appear to have been born out of the prevailing segregationist attitudes (i.e., the desire to separate the "deviant" from the "normal") once children with disabilities were legally unable to drop out of school after a short period of attendance. That the establishment of special programs in the public schools for children with mental retardation was primarily stimulated by segregationist considerations finds support in an article prepared by Van Sickle for the Psychological Clinic (1908–1909):

> If it were not for the fact that the presence of mentally defective children in a school room interfered with the proper training of the capable children, their education would appeal less powerfully to boards of education and the tax-paying public. It is manifestly more expensive to maintain small classes for backward and refractory children, who will profit relatively little by the instruction they receive, than to maintain large classes for children of normal powers. But the presence in a class of one or two mentally or morally defective children so absorbs the energies of the teacher and makes so imperative a claim upon her attention that she cannot under these circumstances properly instruct the number commonly enrolled in a class. School authorities must therefore greatly reduce this number, employ many more teachers, and build many more school rooms to accommodate a given number of pupils, or else they must withdraw into small classes these unfortunates who impede the regular progress of normal children. The plan of segregation is now fairly well established in large cities, and superintendents and teachers are working on the problem of classification, so that they may make the best of this imperfect material. (cited in Sarason & Doris, 1979, p. 263)

Vocational Education Movement

During the last part of the 19th century, educational practices were being refined, and educational opportunities were beginning to be considered more as the right of every citizen. Such developments laid a necessary foundation for the later advent of vocational rehabilitation programs whose viability was dependent on the existence of effective vocational education programs.

Between 1870 and 1910 the number of public high schools in the United States grew from 500 to 10,000. In 1870 only about 7 million U.S. children attended either elementary or high school, but by 1910 that figure exceeded 17 million. During that same period, per-capita pupil expenditures more than doubled (Hofstadter et al., 1959).

Between 1865 and 1890 the curriculum of public education was expanded with the addition of literature, history, vocational, and commercial courses. In fact, by the 1870s Massachusetts and New York had laws requiring public schools to include some type of vocational training in their curriculum. By 1881 five other states had manifested a definite interest in industrial training within their public school systems. One of those states, New Jersey, "passed an act for the establishment of industrial training schools" (LaRue, 1972, p. 27). Support for the expansion of industrial training opportunities came from the private sector as well. By 1885 two private industrial schools, "The Working-man's

School of New York City and the Boston Manual Training School," were in operation (LaRue, 1972, p. 27).

The Emergence of Significant Political Movements

Near the end of the 19th century, increasing acknowledgment of the effect of social conditions on the individual was manifested in two political movements emphasizing government responsibility for dealing with societal problems. The Populists were the first to reject the existing laissez-faire philosophy of government in favor of government intervention for purposes of serving the public interest (Hofstadter et al., 1959). Although the Populist Party had few followers in the more industrialized areas of the country, their message called for government intervention to right many of the social evils being produced by the rapid increase in industrialization. This concern was readily seen in the preamble to the Populist Party platform for the election of 1892, which indicated that the nation was in a moral, political, and economic crisis, with land concentrated in the hands of capitalists and with laborers abused, impoverished, and "denied the right to organize for self-protection" (Commager, 1950, pp. 50–51).

Emphasizing the responsibility of government for the control of social evils, the Progressives were active during the presidencies of Theodore Roosevelt, Taft, and Wilson (until about 1916). According to the Progressives, changes in the economic structure of society invalidated earlier social laws that suggested people would succeed as a result of their abilities and hard work and would fail in their absence. Therefore, they stressed the necessary role of government in ensuring most Americans a "fair shake" in a society marked by the accumulation of power and wealth in the hands of a few. The Progressives disagreed with the Jeffersonian viewpoint that government was a necessary evil whose primary role was the provision of police protection. They saw government more as an "affirmative agency of national progress and social betterment" (A. M. Schlesinger, 1957, pp. 18–19).

Progressives such as Theodore Roosevelt were not interested in creating a social welfare state. Rather than wanting government to provide a "square meal" for everyone, they wanted to guarantee a "square deal" to all. A *square deal* could be defined as the restoration of America to a "land of opportunity" for the average citizen. Those opportunities would be restored when government was capable of diminishing the excessive power concentrated in the hands of a relatively small number of very wealthy men. For the national government to do its job, its strength had to exceed that of any private group (A. M. Schlesinger, 1957, p. 20).

In addition to regulating big business for purposes of restoring the individual's ability to compete, and thereby expanding economic opportunities, the Progressives believed that government had a responsibility to help those who became "casualties" of the rapidly changing society. In the latter belief, they were clearly influenced by the "teaching of the Social Gospel" (A. M. Schlesinger, 1957, p. 22). By stressing the position that the federal government should both guarantee economic opportunity and help the "casualties" of the system, the philosophy of the Progressives could be seen as compatible with federal government responsibility for establishing vocational rehabilitation programs for Americans with disabilities.

Acknowledging responsibility is one thing; assuming responsibility is another. The latter required access to greater financial resources than available to a government almost totally financed by tariffs, sale of public lands, and excise taxes. An additional major source of revenue was made available to the federal government in 1913 via a new amendment to the Constitution that authorized the collection of income taxes. In that same year, Congress passed a law authorizing the collection of an income tax that ranged from 1% to 6% of annual earnings, depending on income (Carson, 1973).

The federal income tax opened the door to significant future government and private financial backing of vocational rehabilitation in the United States. First, income tax revenue made possible the establishment of federally supported rehabilitation programs for both veterans and civilians. Second, it provided a tax write-off incentive to wealthy individuals and corporations to provide financial support for rehabilitation endeavors. The presence of an income tax also allowed for the development of the economic argument for governmental support of rehabilitation programs. After 1913 many persons with disabilities who were rehabilitated could actually repay the government for the cost of their rehabilitation through taxes.

It would be nice to think that Congress in 1913 was stimulated to enact an income tax to establish a revenue base by which government could meet its humanitarian responsibility to its people. That was not the case. Instead, Congress wanted to ensure the availability of federal revenues for "paying for wars past, present, or future." Rather than for support of social programs, revenues from the income tax were solicited for patriotic reasons (Carson, 1973).

Legislation: To World War II

Workers' Compensation Laws

Acquiring a disability at the turn of the 20th century was a sure ticket to poverty. Vocational rehabilitation programs and workers' compensation laws did not yet exist in the United States. Although industrial workers who were injured could sue their employers, such lawsuits were extremely difficult to win. The law was stacked against the injured workers. They could not expect to receive any compensation from their employers if their injuries resulted from personal negligence or the negligence of a fellow employee. The ultimate unfairness in the law was found in the fact that "if the dangerous conditions were present when the worker took the job, he could be assumed to have accepted the risk and the possibility of injury [and] could not collect" (Obermann, 1967, p. 13).

It is not surprising that workers' compensation laws were absent in the United States in the late 19th century. They were certainly not encouraged by the prevailing laissez-faire and Social Darwinism philosophies. American businessmen opposed any legislation that would increase production costs. State legislators feared that the enactment of such laws could drive industry to states without workers' compensation insurance in order to decrease operating costs (Safilios-Rothschild, 1970, p. 19).

With the ushering in of the Progressive Era at the turn of the century, the time was ripe for the passage of workers' compensation legislation. President Theodore Roosevelt led the way with a message to Congress in 1908 in which he "laid down a general pattern for workers' compensation legislation.... Acting upon the President's recommendation, Congress enacted the Civil Employees Act in 1908 and later on the Federal Employer's Liability Act to cover employees of 'common carriers'" (Safilios-Rothschild, 1970, p. 19).

The first compulsory state workers' compensation law in the United States was passed in New York in 1910. By 1921 workers' compensation legislation had been passed in 42 states (Faulkner, 1931). With the passage of a workers' compensation law by Mississippi in 1948, all states had some type of workers' compensation legislation (Safilios-Rothschild, 1970).

While early workers' compensation laws made no specific provisions for vocational rehabilitation (Obermann, 1965), they had an indirect positive effect on the funding of vocational rehabilitation programs. Although muckrakers such as Upton Sinclair had publicized the health hazards faced by the industrial worker, workers' compensation programs resulted in statistics that clearly demonstrated the extent of one of the negative by-products of the expanding Industrial Revolution—the large numbers of persons disabled as a result of industrial accidents. In fact, workers' compensation programs demonstrated "for the first time ... that civilian living was more dangerous than life in the army during a war" (Obermann, 1965, p. 124). As a result, legislators became more aware of the need for civilian vocational rehabilitation programs.

1917: Smith-Hughes Act

Relatively early in the history of organized labor, its leaders realized the need for vocational education programs. All too many cases had been observed where the skills of workers performing only one isolated industrial operation suddenly became obsolete (Kessler, 1953). It also became evident that vocational training was needed by the large numbers of unskilled, rural youths who were flocking to cities during the early part of the 20th century. The realization of the retraining needs of dislocated industrial workers as well as the training needs of migrating rural youths led to federal action in 1917 in the form of the

Smith-Hughes Act. That act made federal monies available to each state on a matching basis for vocational education programs. It also created the Federal Board for Vocational Education, which later administered both the veteran and the civilian vocational rehabilitation programs. Under the act, all participating states had "to designate or create a state board for vocational education which should have the necessary power to cooperate with the Federal Board in the administration of the act" (MacDonald, 1944, p. 17).

During World War I, the idea of extending vocational education to persons with disabilities gained acceptance. The purpose of the training was to help individuals with a disability develop "residual capacities" needed for vocational effectiveness. Government officials and society leaders were beginning to realize that a person with a disability could be vocationally rehabilitated by training around the impairment. These developments, paired with the large number of veterans returning from the war with disabilities, led to much interest in federal legislation for the vocational rehabilitation of the returning wounded.

1918: The Soldier's Rehabilitation Act

The first U.S. federal program for vocational rehabilitation of persons with disabilities was initiated in 1918. Representing breakthrough legislation for rehabilitation, the program was designed to rehabilitate veterans with disabilities. Veterans of all early U.S. wars, dating back to the Revolution, were compensated for their war-related disabilities via government pensions. Although medical care for acute conditions was sometimes provided, vocational rehabilitation was an unknown entity.

Under the Soldier's Rehabilitation Act, the Federal Board for Vocational Education was given the primary responsibility for developing vocational rehabilitation programs for veterans with disabilities. The act authorized vocational rehabilitation services for all veterans with disabilities resulting from military service that presented a handicap to employment. Employment as a result of vocational rehabilitation training had to be a feasible possibility (Obermann, 1965).

As could be expected in any new, large-scale venture, planning problems arose. Medical advances that improved the survival rate for wounded veterans resulted in more veterans with disabilities returning to the United States than the program was designed to serve. In addition, the agency responsible for determining veterans' eligibility for the vocational rehabilitation program, the Bureau of War Risk Insurance, proved to be a bottleneck. The agency's inability to rapidly process compensation claims resulted in a rehabilitation program waiting list of 4,000 veterans by the end of the program's first year. To correct this problem, Congress passed a law that charged the Federal Board for Vocational Education with the sole responsibility for establishing eligibility for vocational rehabilitation services. By late summer of 1921, the program was going full blast, with nearly 236,000 veterans with disabilities being trained for jobs (Obermann, 1965).

During the congressional hearings on the Soldier's Rehabilitation Bill, serious consideration was given to including a civilian vocational rehabilitation provision in the bill (Whitten, 1957). Dr. R. M. Little of the U.S. Employee's Compensation Commission argued before Congress for such a provision on the grounds that it was even a larger national problem "than the rehabilitation of disabled soldiers" (MacDonald, 1944, p. 23).

Congressional opposition to including a civilian component in the final bill existed for several reasons. First, the implementation of a program for veterans would have been delayed while details were being worked out related to the inclusion of a civilian measure in the bill (Whitten, 1957). In addition, existing facilities were inadequate for even rehabilitating all eligible veterans. Congress also opposed the civilian measure on the grounds "that the states should bear some of the financial burden of a civilian rehabilitation scheme" (MacDonald, 1944, p. 26).

There was far from overwhelming congressional support for the passage of a civilian rehabilitation act in the 66th Congress (1918–1919). Although some congressmen viewed such legislation as both "humanitarian" and "visionary," others saw such a federal grant program as a violation of states' rights, paternalistic, and socialistic. One senator even referred to such legislation as "2 percent Bolshevist" (MacDonald, 1944, pp. 49–55). It was therefore not surprising that the first civilian vocational rehabilitation bill, introduced 3 months after the passage of the Soldier's Rehabilitation Act, failed to pass (Whitten, 1957). Almost 2 more years elapsed before a federally subsidized civilian vocational rehabilitation program became a reality. During that interim, eight states (Massachusetts actually passed a law before passage of the Soldier's Rehabilitation Act) passed laws establishing civilian vocational rehabilitation programs. In six of those states, effective programs were already operating prior to the passage of the federal Civilian Vocational Rehabilitation Act (or Smith-Fess Act) (MacDonald, 1944). In fact, one of the states—New Jersey—passed a law in April 1919 that set up a rehabilitation program that allowed for more comprehensive services to persons with disabilities than did the subsequent federal Civilian Vocational Rehabilitation Act passed in June 1920. The New Jersey law contained provisions for providing surgery to persons with disabilities if it could be expected to increase physical functioning. A comparable provision was not included in the federal civilian rehabilitation legislation until 1943 (Kessler, 1953).

1920: The Smith-Fess Act

With the passage by the 67th Congress of the Smith-Fess Act, or the Civilian Vocational Rehabilitation Act, on June 2, 1920, the civilian vocational rehabilitation program in the United States was launched. This initial vocational reha-bilitation legislation was very similar to the earlier vocational education legisla-tion. It was, in fact, primarily an extension of the vocational education legis-lation to individuals with physical disabilities. With that realization, it is not surprising that the Federal Board for Vocational Education was given the re-sponsibility of administering the act at the federal level.

The Smith-Fess Act provided $750,000 of federal funds the first year and $1 million for each of 2 subsequent years to be used for the rehabilitation of persons with physical disabilities who were either "totally or partially inca-pacitated for remunerative occupation." It was temporary legislation and had to be extended by additional legislation in 1924. The amount of the total federal appropriations allocated to a state under the act was determined by the ratio of its population to the total U.S. population, based on the most current census figures. However, even the smallest state could receive a minimum allotment of $5,000. Because the act provided federal funds to states on a 50–50 matching basis, it provided a strong incentive for states to pass similar legislation.

The funds could be used to provide vocational guidance, vocational edu-cation, occupational adjustment, and placement services. Provision of place-ment services as the only service to a client was not within the spirit of the act, which primarily mandated vocational training opportunities for persons with disabilities. Although the act was not oriented toward the provision of physical restoration services, a client with a disability could be provided with a prosthe-sis if it could be justified as a necessary "supply" for the successful completion of training. Although not specified in the act, the Federal Board for Vocational Education set the minimum age of legal employability, 16, as the minimum age for qualifying for services. Because home economics was considered a legiti-mate training program under the vocational education legislation, the Federal Board considered homemaking as an appropriate occupation for which to pro-vide training to a client with a disability (Lassiter, 1972).

A Sluggish Beginning

By May 1924 twelve states had still not passed the necessary legislation for participating in the federal–state rehabilitation program (MacDonald, 1944). It was also evident that the federal legislation had only minimally affected the problem. It was estimated that in 1924 only about 5% of the eligible civilian population with disabilities received services from state rehabilitation agencies (Bowers, 1930). Therefore, as the 1920 legislation was nearing its expiration date, its primary purpose of promoting and stimulating "state activity was in-complete." Withdrawal of federal support would have led to the demise of the civilian vocational rehabilitation program (MacDonald, 1944, p. 84). In 1924 additional federal legislation was passed that extended and amended the origi-nal 1920 legislation. The new federal legislation continued the federal grants for the civilian vocational rehabilitation program for 6 more years. Federal funding of slightly more than $1 million per year was authorized by the legislation.

As the 1924 legislation approached its end, all state rehabilitation agencies were still very small. In 1930 only 143 rehabilitation workers were spread across the staffs of state rehabilitation agencies in the 44 participating states (Lamborn, 1970). That was about as adequate for dealing with the problem of rehabilitating the large numbers of persons with disabilities as a peashooter would be for hunting bear. In 1930 alone there were 10 million nonfatal accidents in the United States, many of which resulted "in temporary or permanent disability" (Pegg, 1947, p. 453). The problem of limited resources was even more evident when persons with developmental disabilities and those who acquired a disability through disease were added to the above accident figure.

What could have restricted the expansion of the federal–state vocational rehabilitation program during the 1920s, a decade marked by prosperity? A brief view of the public attitudes, concerns, and behaviors of the decade can provide some potential insights.

By 1920 Americans had tired of idealistic crusades. During the previous 30 years, they had been involved in the Populist and Progressive movements, as well as in the "crusade to make the world safe for democracy" (Goldston, 1968, p. 15). When Americans did attach to a cause in the 1920s, it was usually one with a negative orientation, such as the Ku Klux Klan or immigration restriction movements (Rothman, 1972). Overall, the 1920s was a decade of personal indulgence. Goldston (1968) pointed out that its "symbols were the hip flask, the raccoon coat, short skirts, the Ford roadster, the saxophone, and the dollar sign.... Domestically, the burning political issue of the decade was ... whether or not people had a constitutional right to get drunk" (pp. 11–13).

The 1920s were also characterized by two ineffective American presidents. Warren Harding demonstrated more interest in playing poker, bridge, and the stock market than in the responsibilities of the presidency. His successor, Calvin Coolidge, "firmly believed the President governed best who governed least" (Goldston, 1968, pp. 16–17). Neither president could have been expected to expand the role of the federal government.

By 1929 signs of the coming economic calamity were on the horizon. Investment in construction had constricted by nearly $1 billion from 1928 to 1929. Inventories were rising, levels of production were declining, and unemployment rates were increasing. Finally, the financial house of cards built by buying stocks on margin collapsed on Black Thursday, October 24, 1929, ushering in the Great Depression.

One would not have expected much expansion in the federal–state vocational rehabilitation program during Herbert Hoover's presidential administration (1929–1933). Hoover embraced a philosophy of rugged individualism. To Hoover, any programs that smacked of socialism would not have been in the best interests of the country. Although not opposed to rehabilitation, Hoover would have seen financial support for such programs coming, more appropriately, from the local level.

The 1930s

To meet the devastating economic conditions of the 1930s, widespread expansion of vocational rehabilitation was needed more than ever. As MacDonald (1944) pointed out, vocational rehabilitation, at best, was serving only about one third to one fifth of those who needed services. Need for expansion of rehabilitation was recognized by congressmen such as Representative Bankhead, who introduced a bill in 1932 to expand the funding of rehabilitation and to put rehabilitation on a somewhat permanent status with Congress. Interestingly, at this point, rehabilitation leaders, such as Dr. R. M. Little of the New York Vocational Rehabilitation Department, blocked the efforts of Bankhead because they believed that a permanent federal rehabilitation program would lessen the determination of states to make a significant contribution to the rehabilitation movement. Others opposed to the permanency of a federal vocational rehabilitation program viewed it as a significant incursion into states' rights. Representative McDuffie "viewed with great alarm such federal activities, believing they opened the door to state medicine and a federal department of education, and, he asked, 'if these come, what next?'" (MacDonald, 1944, p. 75).

In 1932 Franklin Delano Roosevelt was swept into office on a platform of governmental responsibility for the state of the nation and the economy and for the relief of the starving and homeless individuals struggling under the burdens of a depressed economy and unemployment. Roosevelt had firsthand experience with the problems of disability, having contracted polio in 1921 at the age of 39. He was to suffer tremendously in the ensuing years from the effects of the disease. In 1924 he began his famous visits to the therapeutic mineral waters of Warm Springs, Georgia. Because there were neither doctors nor a formal rehabilitation program during his early visits to Warm Springs, Roosevelt personally supervised the activities. "In 1927 he purchased the Springs and set up the Warm Springs Foundation as a nonprofit center for the treatment of polio victims" (Goldston, 1968, pp. 100–101). In spite of his personal experience with disability, Roosevelt placed no special governmental emphasis on the needs of persons with disabilities. Instead of focusing on the needs of a single group, he concentrated on dealing with the massive general problems of inadequate food, housing, and employment faced by the nation as a whole. Indeed, in 1933 Roosevelt called for a 25% reduction in funding for vocational rehabilitation, a cut that was never implemented. In fact, vocational rehabilitation secured extra funds for a short period from one of the New Deal projects, the Federal Emergency Relief Administration, which in October 1933 allocated $70,000 a month to vocational rehabilitation for individuals on public relief (MacDonald, 1944).

Before the federal–state vocational rehabilitation program could expand, it had to be converted from an experimental to a permanent program. That change occurred in 1935 with the passage of the Social Security Act, which contained breakthrough legislation for the vocational rehabilitation program as a permanent program. After 1935 the program could be discontinued only by congressional action. In establishing the permanency of rehabilitation, Congress acknowledged vocational rehabilitation of persons with disabilities as "a matter of social justice, a permanent on-going public duty that should not depend on periodic determination of deservability" (Lenihan, 1977, p. 57). Unfortunately, the "conscience of Congress" was only slightly visible when appropriations were determined. Federal funding for the federal–state vocational rehabilitation program was increased only to approximately $2 million by the act (MacDonald, 1944, p. 82). By 1939 rehabilitation still found itself with minimal funding (federal appropriation of $3.5 million) to accomplish a tremendous task.

Legislation Concerning Individuals with Visual Disabilities

A prevailing assumption in the 1920s and early 1930s was that persons with visual disabilities had little potential for competitive employment; hence, they received very little benefit from early legislative developments in rehabilitation. Individuals who were blind were maintained in stereotyped occupations and were expected to work in either sheltered workshops or home industry settings (Risley & Hoehne, 1970). However, with the passage of the Randolph-Sheppard Act of 1936 and the Wagner-O'Day Act of 1938, opportunities began to expand. The thrust of the Randolph-Sheppard Act was to enable individuals who were blind to operate vending stands on federal property. That act also mandated a survey to identify other feasible types of work for individuals with visual handicaps (Risley & Hoehne, 1970). The increased emphasis on the rehabilitation of individuals with visual disabilities brought about by the Randolph-Sheppard Act represents the only significant program expansion for rehabilitation between 1920 and the start of World War II.

The Social Security Act of 1935, which committed the federal government to support efforts to develop and expand a stable market for products made by persons who are blind, laid a foundation for the subsequent Wagner-O'Day Act of 1938. This latter act made it mandatory for the federal government "to purchase designated products from workshops for the blind" (Nelson, 1971, pp. 29–30). As a result, more persons who were blind could find employment in these workshops. "To funnel the government orders into the shops, a private non-profit organization, the National Industries for the Blind, was created" (Nelson, 1971, p. 30).

The Randolph-Sheppard Act of 1936 and the Wagner-O'Day Act of 1938 helped to clear up many misperceptions regarding the abilities of individuals who are blind. Both acts expanded opportunities for these individuals to demonstrate their abilities. Job opportunities made available at a federal level for persons who were blind, via administration of the two acts, also created an increased awareness in the civil service system of the potential of employees with that disability (Risley & Hoehne, 1970).

World War II and the Rehabilitation Movement

In contrast to the inhibiting effects of the Depression of the 1930s, World War II resulted in significant growth of the rehabilitation movement. The war created an increased demand for industrial products necessary to maintain the war effort, while drawing 12 million persons into the military who might otherwise have been workers in the civilian labor force (Levitan, Mangum, & Marshall, 1976). The resulting labor shortage during that period afforded persons with disabilities an opportunity to demonstrate to thousands of employers that the presence of a disability did not necessarily handicap a person's performance if the person were placed in an appropriate job. The pressing labor shortage also made increased participation of persons with disabilities in the labor force a national necessity. Therefore, it is not surprising that federal legislation in the form of the Barden–LaFollette Act was passed in 1943, which both extended federal–state rehabilitation program services to persons with mental retardation or mental illness and expanded the types of physical restoration services that could be provided for persons with physical disabilities. However, there was far from a carte blanche legislative mandate for the latter. Physical restoration services could be provided only "to those with static defects" (Kessler, 1953, p. 229). In addition, because Congress wished to avoid the issue of socialized medicine, the legislation specifically stipulated that rehabilitation agencies could "expend funds for medical and surgical care and hospitalization costs" only for those in need of financial assistance (Kessler, 1953, pp. 228–229). Financial need also had to be demonstrated before a client could receive maintenance funds while being rehabilitated (R. Thomas, 1970). Only "physical examination, vocational counseling, training and placement" could be "provided without cost irrespective of the economic status of the individual" (Kessler, 1953, p. 230).

In providing the first federal–state rehabilitation program support for rehabilitation of persons who were blind (Switzer, 1969), the Barden–LaFollette Act of 1943 stands out as a major piece of legislation for blind rehabilitation services. Federal support went either to the vocational rehabilitation agency or to separate agencies serving persons who were blind, which had previously been set up under a state commissioner for the blind or a similar agency structure. Rapid growth in vocational rehabilitation services for persons who were blind and a vast increase in the number of such clients who were rehabilitated followed. For example, in 1936 two clients who were blind were rehabilitated by vocational rehabilitation, whereas in 1969 there were 8,884 rehabilitated clients who were blind (Risley & Hoehne, 1970).

Significant medical advances made during World War II positively affected the rehabilitation movement. "Wonder drugs" developed during the war made possible the combating of "surgical shock, infection, and other post-injury complications" (Allan, 1958, p. 8). Battle casualties involving spinal cord injuries, "complete or partial paralysis, multiple amputation, severe burns of the body surface, or sucking wounds of the chest no longer died within days or months of the injury as the result of shock or other complications" (Allan, 1958, p. 8). This was, unfortunately, not the case for many of the wounded World War I veterans, whose survival was dependent upon orthopedic surgery methods that dated back to the Victorian era. Medical treatment for paraplegic patients left much to be desired at the end of World War I. Kessler (1968) pointed out that they "were allowed to lie in a bed of sawdust, treated almost like animals. The theory was that if their bowel and bladder could not be controlled, at least the bed could be kept clean by removing the sawdust" (Kessler, as cited in Groce, 1992, pp. 13–14). Not surprisingly, over 96% of the "400 men who became paraplegics in World War I died in less than a year" (Rusk, 1972, p. 424). By contrast, "75% of the 2500 World War II American combat paraplegics would still be alive twenty years later, and of these survivors 1400 would be holding down jobs" (Rusk, 1972, p. 424). With so many new cases requiring long-term medical management, the American Medical Association (AMA) began to see comprehensive rehabilitation as the third phase of medical care, the first two being preventive and curative. As a result of the increasing emphasis on the third phase of medicine, the 1940s saw the establishment of 21 new rehabilitation centers, as well as the development of rehabilitation programs in a number of general hospitals (Allan, 1958, p. 10).

The development of physical medicine as a medical specialty could be considered to have resulted from needs growing out of World War II. In 1944 the AMA established the Council on Physical Medicine. By 1947 the AMA had created a specialty Board of Physical Medicine, whose name was changed to the Board of Physical Medicine and Rehabilitation in 1949 (Allan, 1958).

World War II yielded some strong professional advocates for expanding the federal support of rehabilitation services. One of the most significant was Dr. Howard Rusk (Switzer, 1969). After his Air Force discharge in 1945, Rusk accepted the challenge of organizing the first department of physical medicine and rehabilitation at the New York University medical school. He also personally undertook a public relations campaign to promote this new field of medicine. Rusk spoke to any group that would listen about the successful rehabilitation efforts with disabled fighting men that he had observed while in the Air Force.

Legislation: 1954–1972

Significant growth in vocational rehabilitation activity occurred from 1954 to 1965. During that period, annual funding for the federal–state rehabilitation program more than quadrupled, to over $150 million by 1965. Increases in funding were indicative of the strong support that vocational rehabilitation received from Congress and from the administrations of Presidents Eisenhower, Kennedy, and Johnson. Because of the expansion that occurred in rehabilitation services during this period, many have called it the Golden Era of Rehabilitation (Rusalem, 1976). Through the 1965 and 1972 amendments to the Social

Security Act, Congress once again demonstrated its interest in and willingness to provide support for advancing the vocational rehabilitation movement. That interest and support was further manifested in the passage of the Vocational Rehabilitation Act Amendments of 1965.

Vocational Rehabilitation Act Amendments of 1954

As a result of his wartime observations of the contributions of persons with disabilities in the civilian workforce and the effectiveness of vocational rehabilitation programs with disabled World War II veterans, President Eisenhower was clearly predisposed to be a strong supporter of the vocational rehabilitation movement. That support was manifested in January 1954 when, "for the first time in our history, a president [devoted] an entire special message to the Congress to the subject of the health needs of the nation, with a major portion of the message being directly concerned with rehabilitation" (Allan, 1958, p. 11). The president urged Congress to draft legislation for meeting the rehabilitation needs of the nation. Congress responded with the Vocational Rehabilitation Act Amendments of 1954, Public Law (P.L.) 565, which increased the federal funding share of the federal–state vocational rehabilitation program from 50% to $3 for every $2 of state funds. This legislation also authorized $30 million in 1955 to the states for rehabilitation purposes and appropriated an expansion in the annual funding to $45 million in 1956, $55 million in 1957, and $65 million in 1958 (Obermann, 1967). The significance of these figures in the overall growth of vocational rehabilitation can easily be seen by contrasting them with the congressional authorization of $750,000 in 1921 and $3.5 million in 1940.

P.L. 565 also resulted in the expansion of services to a larger number of persons with mental retardation or mental illness. Although the 1943 Vocational Rehabilitation Act Amendments enabled state rehabilitation agencies to serve both groups, little progress was made in that direction until the late 1950s. In 1945 state rehabilitation agencies reported that a total of only 106 persons with mental retardation were rehabilitated. For the year 1955, that total had climbed to only 531. Services were expanded to persons with mental illness somewhat more rapidly; yet, for fiscal year 1953 that group represented less than 5% of the persons rehabilitated by state rehabilitation agencies (Parker, Thoreson, Haugen, & Pfeifer, 1970).

Three significant provisions of P.L. 565 for expanding services to individuals with mental retardation or mental illness were (a) research and demonstration grants, (b) extension and improvement grants, and (c) rehabilitation facility development. Research and demonstration grants were provided to either state rehabilitation agencies or nonprofit organizations for projects directed at discovering new knowledge for vocational rehabilitation (Obermann, 1965). Extension and improvement grants allowed state agencies to expand into new geographic areas, to serve new disability groups, and to develop new aspects of their rehabilitation programs. Many states used this money to hire rehabilitation counselors to work with specialized caseloads (e.g., persons with mental retardation or mental illness). By July 1, 1956, a total of 104 extension and improvement grant projects had been initiated (Whitten, 1957). Funds authorized for rehabilitation facility development enabled state rehabilitation agencies to remodel and expand buildings to be used for sheltered workshops or other rehabilitation services. These funds could also be used for equipment. In the case of rehabilitation facilities, the funds could be used to cover initial staffing costs. The result was "a substantial upswing in the number of facilities and in the quality of services they provided" (Lamborn, 1970, pp. 11–12). By expanding the number of rehabilitation facilities and workshops, P.L. 565 underscored the significance of the work personality in regard to vocational adjustment. As a result, state rehabilitation agencies moved in the direction of working with greater numbers of persons with mental illness and mental retardation.

The long-range effect of P.L. 565 on services to persons with mental retardation or mental illness can be seen in the increased number of such persons rehabilitated by state rehabilitation agencies in subsequent years. For the year 1963 the number of persons with mental retardation who were rehabilitated had expanded to almost 6,000 (Wolfensberger, 1967). By 1973 that number had grown to 41,000 (Posner, 1974). For fiscal year 1969 a total of 55,303 individuals with mental illness (or 23.3% of the total persons rehabilitated by state rehabilitation agencies) were rehabilitated through the federal–state vocational rehabilitation program (R. Thomas, 1970). P.L. 565 also authorized grants to colleges and universities for the training of professional rehabilitation workers. As a result, master's degree training programs for rehabilitation counselors became widespread, with students being provided federal fellowships. This training provision, paired with the research and demonstration provision, provided a foundation for the professionalization of the rehabilitation counselor.

Social Security Act Amendments (1956–1972)

The passage of the Social Security Act Amendments of 1956 authorized Social Security disability allowances for individuals with disabilities. Those amendments provided disability income allowances for any permanently disabled "injured" person age 50 or older who was considered incapable of returning to competitive employment (Erlanger & Roth, 1985). Although the 1956 amendments afforded income protection for many individuals with disabilities, it was not until the passage of the Social Security Act Amendments of 1965 that Social Security became directly involved with vocational rehabilitation.

Several provisions of the 1965 amendments to the Social Security Act have direct relevance to the federal–state vocational rehabilitation program. Through those amendments, Congress made clear that cash benefits are "not the sole objective of the disability insurance program" (Popick, 1967, p. 11). The vocational rehabilitation of the greatest number of applicants for the Social Security Disability Insurance (SSDI) program was also an objective. To achieve the latter objective, Congress mandated SSDI funds to cover the cost of rehabilitating "selected disability beneficiaries" through state rehabilitation agency services. The funds available for that endeavor for any given year were to be "equal to one percent of the total disability benefits paid nationally in the preceding year" (Popick, 1967, p. 11). The program was expected to be cost-effective, with SSDI rehabilitation funds restricted to beneficiaries with disabilities who were feasible for competitive employment and whose vocational rehabilitation costs would not exceed the cost of maintaining the individual indefinitely on the SSDI roles (Popick, 1967).

The 1972 amendments to the Social Security Act made beneficiaries with disabilities eligible for "Medicare health coverage, though a waiting period of 29 months after application for disability benefits was enacted to intentionally limit the eligible population and the budget outlays of Medicare" (Verville, 1979, p. 50). Total federal expenditure of Medicare funds "for all forms of health care" for beneficiaries with disabilities approximated $3 billion in 1978 (Verville, 1979, p. 50).

Vocational Rehabilitation Act Amendments of 1965

In addition to the Golden Era's being characterized by increasing appropriations of federal funds for (a) client services, (b) training of personnel, (c) facility development, and (d) rehabilitation research, the era also marked the beginning of an independent living rehabilitation movement. In the early 1960s the National Rehabilitation Association (NRA) lobbied for the addition of an independent living amendment to the rehabilitation legislation. NRA helped write an unsuccessful congressional bill in 1961 that "contained a separate title on independent living services ... which would have authorized 15 million dollars in the first year and 25 million dollars in the second year for independent living rehabilitation services" (DeJong, 1979b, p. 17). Although the Department of Health, Education, and Welfare (HEW) was sympathetic to NRA's objectives, they felt that the time was not right. There still existed a "large backlog" of individuals with disabilities with vocational potential to be rehabilitated (Straus, 1965, p. 22). However, HEW proposed that state rehabilitation agencies be allowed to accept persons with disabilities with obscure potential, "provide services for a limited period of time, observe the response to services, and then decide whether" they could be rehabilitated into employment (cited in Straus, 1965, p. 22). Because an extended evaluation component was contained in the Vocational Rehabilitation Act Amendments of 1965 (P.L. 333), Congress apparently viewed that proposal positively. P.L. 333 established 6- and 18-month extended evaluation services for the purposes of determining the employment potential of some applications for services. As a consequence, since 1965 the state rehabilitation agency counselor has been permitted to extend the evaluation of the vocational rehabilitation potential of an applicant with a disability for up to 18 months.

The 1965 amendments also expanded the definition of disability to include behavioral disorders diagnosed by a psychologist or psychiatrist. Behavioral disorders were described as manifested social behaviors that were deviant and that likely resulted from factors such as abnormal environmental, cultural, or educational experiences that could impair one's ability to develop normal relationships with family members or others in the community. As was the case with other disabilities, however, a behavioral disorder must create a substantial handicap to employment for a person with employment potential in order for the counselor to determine the individual eligible for rehabilitation services. Individuals could not be deemed eligible simply because they belonged to certain "sociological" categories, such as public offender, and/or because they possessed backgrounds characterized by social disadvantagement, chronic poverty, illiteracy, educational deficit, or long-term unemployment. Although diagnosis of a behavioral disorder had to be made by either a psychologist or a psychiatrist, it should be noted that the term *behavioral disorder* originated with the Rehabilitation Services Administration as an agency term. It did not designate a psychiatric diagnosis of a type of mental illness (e.g., behavior disorder) (Seventh Institute on Rehabilitation Services, 1969).

The Vocational Rehabilitation Act Amendments of 1965 also mandated the following:

1. An increase to $3 of federal funds for each state dollar (this 75–25 ratio was further increased by legislation in 1968 to 80–20) and a doubling of the federal appropriation for the federal–state program.
2. Elimination of economic need as a prerequisite for the provision of any vocational rehabilitation services. States could, however, require economic need tests for some services (i.e., training and physical restoration).
3. Provision of federal funds to help construct new rehabilitation centers and workshops (matching funds, with the federal share ranging from one third to two thirds).
4. Provision of special statewide planning grants to help states develop service delivery systems that would reach all handicapped citizens in the state.

Concluding Statement

With a few exceptions, the treatment of persons with disabilities prior to the 19th century tended to range from benign neglect to extreme abuse. The 19th century saw a significant increase in interest in the development of programs for rehabilitating individuals with disabilities. That interest resulted in the implementation of educational programs for individuals who were blind, deaf, or mentally retarded, and medically based restoration programs for persons who were mentally ill or had a physical disability. Although most of those 19th-century rehabilitation activities were on a relatively small scale, their demonstrated success suggested the viability of the larger scale programs that were implemented in the 20th century. The growth of large-scale rehabilitation programs in the latter part of the 19th century was at least partly prevented by the popularity of such political, economic, and social philosophies as laissez-faire economics and Social Darwinism. During that same period, however, a foundation was being laid for the later expansion of rehabilitation activities in the United States. Education was beginning to be viewed as the right of every American, and vocational education programs became more widespread. Additionally, significant medical advances were made, and casework practices were being developed.

The seeds of a large-scale vocational rehabilitation program in the United States were sown in the 19th century. The 20th century then saw the "growth of the plant," resulting from nourishment received through private, federal, and state financial support. During the first four decades of the 20th century, the role of the federal government in providing for the social needs of the "American public" became clearly established through

> Theodore Roosevelt and his New Nationalism, Woodrow Wilson and his New Freedom and Franklin D. Roosevelt and his New Deal. Out of these three great reform periods there emerged the conception of a social welfare state in which the national government had the express obligation to maintain high levels of employment in the economy, to supervise standards of life and labor, to regulate the methods of business competition and to establish comprehensive patterns of social security. (A. M. Schlesinger, 1962, p. 68)

With such a role established, it was predictable that the federal government would emerge as the primary provider for the needs of persons with disabilities and the champion of their rights.

Because of the negative by-products of industrialization, the tragedies of World War I, and a growing humanitarian philosophy, the U.S. government began to accept responsibility for the vocational rehabilitation of both disabled veterans and civilians with disabilities. The first federal laws directed at establishing federally supported veteran and federal–state-supported civilian rehabilitation programs were enacted in 1918 and 1920, respectively. At its initiation in 1920, the federal–state civilian rehabilitation program was a $1-million-per-year experimental adventure directed at the rehabilitation of civilians with physical disabilities. Although the program had grown substantially by the end of the 1940s, it still represented a minimal federal commitment by modern standards.

Little growth or modification occurred in the federal–state program prior to World War II. The lack of growth in the 1920s appeared to stem from general public disinterest in social problems and the dominance of a political philosophy that opposed the role of the federal government in addressing the social needs of the people. There is little doubt as to why the 1930s saw little expansion in government-supported vocational rehabilitation services for persons with disabilities. It could be chalked up to a combination of the following reasons: (a) The country was not prospering and unemployment was high; (b) the public was primarily interested in the problem of large numbers of poor created by the economic depression; and (c) the energies of liberals were being consumed by more pervasive social measures, such as unemployment insurance, social security pensions for the elderly, and national health insurance (which failed to be realized).

Things began to change in the 1940s. New federal rehabilitation legislation in 1943 resulted in an expansion of services—and an extension of program services to persons with mental retardation or mental illness. Employment opportunities for persons with disabilities created by the World War II labor shortage provided a large-scale demonstration of their work potential. In addition, medical advances made during the war greatly extended the long-term, postinjury survival rate for persons with disabilities.

The period following World War II revealed a clear conflict in public attitudes toward persons with disabilities. On the one hand, they were seen as incapable of "competing" in the job market while, on the other hand, they were seen as having a "right" to vocational rehabilitation services. Whereas the public had become more aware of the ability of persons with disabilities to function in the competitive labor market during the war, those attitudes began to move in a negative direction when the war ended. Workers with disabilities, who were being replaced by returning veterans in the competitive job market, found themselves back in the secondary job market, where "a burgeoning sheltered workshop movement" was developing. "While one hand pulled and kept disabled workers out of the competitive labor market, the other hand built vocational rehabilitation as a sizeable peacetime industry" (Vash, 1982, p. 199).

As the 1950s approached, medical advances, an expansion in the number of rehabilitation facilities, and the presence of potent advocates for expanded support of rehabilitation services laid a foundation for the upcoming growth period. Reflecting the philosophy of dynamic conservatism, the Eisenhower administration strongly supported vocational rehabilitation in its efforts to grow as a service program for individuals with disabilities. The 1956 Social Security Amendments provided disability income allowances. Then in 1965 Social Security added coverage for the cost of vocational rehabilitation of unemployed individuals with disabilities who were supported solely by SSDI.

The time period covering the Eisenhower, Kennedy, and Johnson administrations has been referred to by some as the "Golden Era of Rehabilitation." It was a time of increased funding for client services, expanded training opportunities for rehabilitation personnel, further development of rehabilitation facilities, and implementation of many significant rehabilitation research projects. Although actual legislation had to await the 1970s, this period also saw an emergence of interest in serving severe disability populations as well as in independent living rehabilitation programming. However, the first major piece of rehabilitation legislation in the 1970s, the Rehabilitation Act of 1973, could not be enacted until the independent living provision was removed from the bill. As will be seen in Chapter 2, it was not until 1978 that a major independent living rehabilitation services provision was added to rehabilitation legislation.

Chapter 2

Current Rehabilitation History

As with most government-funded social programs, the Golden Era of Rehabilitation began to wane as the 1970s approached. The philosophy of extending vocational rehabilitation services to all citizens with disabilities was now being questioned on rational grounds. In 1973, for example, the

> eminent economist, Eli Ginzberg, of Columbia University declared in a lead article in the *Teachers College Record* that the expenditure of public funds to rehabilitate severely disabled persons was a policy of dubious validity in an era of marked unemployment among the nondisabled. (Rusalem, 1976, p. 35)

In spite of the major growth in federal financial support for vocational rehabilitation services in the 1950s and 1960s, the attitude reflected by Ginzberg toward vocational rehabilitation services was closer to the pre-1970s public policy on disability in the United States than to the belief that comprehensive vocational rehabilitation services should be extended to all persons with disabilities. Rather than being focused on their integration into the mainstream of society, public policies before the 1970s were primarily oriented toward income maintenance payments to persons with disabilities (Erlanger & Roth, 1985).

In the 1970s a new force—the rapidly emerging disability consumer movement—exerted a significant influence on rehabilitation legislation. The large-scale growth in the size of the disability population that occurred between 1940 and 1970 provided a foundation on which to build a major disability consumer movement. Much of that increase could be attributed to the large number of veterans with disabilities who, as a result of advances in medical technology (e.g., new medications and surgical techniques), survived World War II, the Korean War, and the Vietnam War, and the expansion in the "number of elderly people in American society, many of whom have physical disabilities" (Scotch, 1984, pp. 6–7).

This new consumer movement had effective models of social activism to copy. The frequent demonstrations for minority and women's rights, along with the widespread protests against the Vietnam War during the middle and late 1960s, contributed to the acceptance of social activism as a legitimate tool for producing social change in the eyes of the American public. Therefore, by observing the strategies of minorities and women in achieving greater civil rights in the 1960s, persons with disabilities learned not only the value of overtly demanding their rights but also the techniques needed to influence government legislation.

One conclusion that disability consumer groups may have drawn from the civil rights activities of minorities and women was the limited ability of the courts to remove social barriers to the acquisition of civil rights without government legislation to guarantee those rights. For example, although the United States Supreme Court declared segregation unconstitutional in the landmark 1954 *Brown v. Board of Education of Topeka, Kansas,* by "late 1964 only about two percent of the black school children in the 11 southern states were attending integrated schools" (Dye, 1978, pp. 48–50). The federal judiciary acting alone simply lacked the formal power to enforce the law of the land. On the other hand, the passage of the Civil Rights Act of 1964 significantly reduced segregation. By 1970, "58.3 percent of black pupils in the South were attending school with whites" (Dye, 1978, p. 52). Unlike the 1954 Supreme Court decision, the Civil Rights Act of 1964 had a clearly observable threatening set of sharp teeth.

> It provided that every federal department and agency must take action to end segregation in all programs or activities receiving federal financial assistance. It was specified that this action was to include termination of financial assistance if states and communities receiving federal funds refuse to comply with federal desegregation orders. (Dye, 1978, p. 52)

In the 1970s the disability consumer organizations wisely channeled their energies toward encouraging Congress to produce a set of "sharp teeth" to stimulate the necessary social changes for promoting their rights as citizens.

The consumer rights movement that pervaded American society in the 1960s (e.g., "Naderism") also provided a valuable lesson to persons with disabilities. They learned that they did not have to be passive recipients of rehabilitation services. They became more aware of their rights as a group to participate in the formulation of the public policies that could affect the satisfaction of their needs, as well as of their right to participate in the planning of their own rehabilitation programs. Individuals with severe disabilities were losing confidence in the ability or desire of rehabilitation professionals to unilaterally "champion" what was best for them. For example, disability consumer groups were asking why state rehabilitation agencies were allocating so little of their resources to the rehabilitation of persons with severe disabilities, such as those with spinal cord injuries. Therefore, they lobbied for legislation that would provide them a greater say (e.g., through appointments on advisory boards) about who was to be served and in the determination of the type and quality of rehabilitation services that society would provide to meet the rehabilitation needs of persons with disabilities. To assure quality services, consumers wanted a more comprehensive system for evaluating the effectiveness of these programs, and they wanted to play a role in that evaluation (e.g., client satisfaction measures).

The disability consumer groups rejected the notion that separate but equal programs and facilities were acceptable and demanded that persons with disabilities become fully integrated into the mainstream of American life. They began to successfully lobby for mainstreaming in regular classrooms (shared with nondisabled students) with necessary supplemental services as a replacement for special education at segregated schools. Rather than participation in "sheltered workshops for the construction of handicrafts and repair of discards," persons with disabilities demanded greater participation in the mainstream labor market. They stressed that persons with disabilities should not be provided "separate arrangements for transportation, recreation, and access to public facilities, but equal access to facilities and services used by the general public" (Scotch, 1984, p. 10).

The disability consumer groups also wanted legislation passed that would provide for a comprehensive program of both independent living and vocational rehabilitation services. Rather than seeing independent living and vocational rehabilitation as distinct programs with different goals, they saw the two as integrated parts of an optimal program of services for persons with severe disabilities. Consumer groups have traditionally rejected "the conception of independent living and employment as competing policy goals." Because that concept subtly placed a self-fulfilling "arbitrary upper limit to the goals" persons with disabilities might set for themselves, it was seen as "potentially sinister" (DeJong, 1979b, p. 21).

The compatibility of independent living and vocational rehabilitation goals was being reinforced by the growing realization that if advances in medical and rehabilitation technology were paired with increases in the accessibility of buildings and transportation systems to persons with disabilities, vocational goals would become more feasible for larger and larger percentages of the community of individuals with severe disabilities. Therefore, after 1970 rehabilitation legislation began to emphasize environmental accessibility and the provision of independent living rehabilitation services, as well as increased support for rehabilitation research.

As was suggested above, as the 1970s approached, environmental barriers were being considered a significant contributor to the *de facto* denial of equal rights to employment, education, and government services for those with severe disabilities. Such barriers were seen as communicating a clear discriminatory message to persons with severe disabilities. For example, Hull (1979) stated, "As clearly as 'No Irish allowed' and 'White only,' the stairways, narrow doors, and sidewalk curbs of our society indicate to handicapped persons their exclusion from the centers of our social life" (p. 65). Therefore, as the 1970s approached, the need for government legislation to address major accessibility problems and civil rights issues was becoming more evident.

Ready to become their own champions, beginning in the early 1970s, people with disabilities started to fight for laws guaranteeing their rights to effective rehabilitation services and to an accessible environment. They sought

> to reshape laws, institutions, environments, and practices that have barred the handicapped from many aspects of life; to insist that service providers and policy makers consult the disabled on all decisions that affect them, whether these pertain to individual services or to the creation of new federal policies and programs; and to infuse into … the nondisabled public the idea that a handicap need not mean the end of worthwhile life and does not justify second class or unequal treatment. (A. Asch, 1984, p. 534)

These goals began to be addressed through the legislation discussed in the remainder of this chapter and in Chapter 3.

The Rehabilitation Act of 1973 and Its Subsequent Amendments Through 1986: An Overview

The Rehabilitation Act of 1973 (Public Law [P.L.] 93-112) has been called the "billion-dollar program," which it certainly approximated when state matching funds were added to the $650 million and $680 million federal appropriation for 1974 and 1975, respectively. Retaining the 80–20 ratio for federal and state dollars established by the Vocational Rehabilitation Act Amendments of 1968 (P.L. 90-391), the 1973 legislation continued to reflect a major congressional commitment to rehabilitation. However, that commitment became more focused on target groups and target services. For example, Congress felt that the act should reflect a greater commitment to the traditional meaning of the term *handicapped*—that is, to serving clients with severe physical, intellectual, and professionally diagnosed emotional disorders—while removing the 1965 and 1968 congressional mandates to serve behavioral disorders (LaVor & Duncan, 1976).

The Rehabilitation Act Amendments of 1974 and 1976 essentially extended the 1973 authorizations for rehabilitation. The next extensive legislative statement came in 1978 in the Rehabilitation, Comprehensive Services, and Developmental Disabilities Amendments (P.L. 95-602). These amendments called for a federal allocation of $808 million to rehabilitation for the fiscal year ending September 30, 1979, and for $972 million for the fiscal year ending September 30, 1982. These 1978 Amendments to the Rehabilitation Act of 1973 further expanded the emphasis on serving persons with severe disabilities. For example, it mandated the establishment of an independent living rehabilitation program for those persons with disabilities without work potential who could be brought to independent living status through the provision of rehabilitation services.

The Rehabilitation Act Amendments of 1986 contained provisions that further increased the probability that the services of the federal–state rehabilitation program would be directed at persons with severe disabilities and would promote their greater integration into the everyday life of society. Although the Rehabilitation Act Amendments of 1984 (P.L. 98-221) had, in addition to other provisions, mandated that each state rehabilitation agency have a client assistance program, the 1986 amendments constituted a more extensive legislative statement. Its new provisions mandated increased use of rehabilitation engineering services with persons with disabilities served by state rehabilitation agencies. The 1986 amendments also authorized state rehabilitation agencies to provide supported employment services (described in Chapter 12) for individuals with severe disabilities for whom competitive employment had not been traditionally available (A. Jones, 1988).

Although numerous congressional mandates can be found in the Rehabilitation Act of 1973 and its subsequent amendments, five most clearly stand out as reflecting the "spirit of the times": (a) Serve individuals with severe disabilities, (b) promote consumer involvement, (c) stress program evaluation, (d) provide support for research, and (e) advance the civil rights of persons with disabilities. Each is fully discussed in the remainder of this section, with further discussion of the civil rights mandate in Chapter 3.

Serve Individuals with Severe Disabilities

Reemphasizing rehabilitation's traditional emphasis on employment goals, the Rehabilitation Act of 1973 mandated federal–state rehabilitation programs to serve people with severe disabilities. With gainful occupation as the goal, states were required to provide services to persons with more severe disabilities before serving those with less severe disabilities.

Opposed to the provision for establishing an independent living rehabilitation program in two rehabilitation bills passed by Congress in 1972, President Nixon vetoed both bills (Whitten, 1973). The message in those vetoes resulted in the omission of a provision for independent living rehabilitation in the subsequently passed Rehabilitation Act of 1973. The Nixon administration did, however, agree to a compromise—a Comprehensive Needs Study (CNS; Section 130 of the act) to determine the rehabilitation needs of individuals who "cannot reasonably be expected to be rehabilitated for employment but for whom a program of rehabilitation would improve their ability to live independently or function normally within their family and community" (P.L. 93-112). Conclusions from the Comprehensive Needs Study were the following:

1. An independent living rehabilitation program was a crucial need of many individuals with disabilities.
2. Individuals surveyed in the CNS needed vocational, transportation, and medical services.
3. Accessibility was the chief concern of many individuals. Barriers inside the home, in public transportation, and in public facilities were identified as major handicapping factors.

Section 130 in the 1973 act also authorized six independent living rehabilitation (ILR) demonstration projects, which were subsequently located in Seattle, Washington; New York City; Peoria, Illinois; Salt Lake City, Utah; San Antonio, Texas; and Berkeley, California. The Peoria Project was subsequently discontinued. Of the remaining five projects, two (Seattle and New York City) concerned themselves with physical restoration services; two (Salt Lake City and San Antonio) emphasized the role of state agencies in ILR; and one (Berkeley) was a consumer-based and consumer-operated ILR program.

These independent living rehabilitation activities were clearly compatible with the mandate of the 1973 act to place a high priority on serving people with severe disabling conditions.

A study of these projects by the Urban Institute (Muzzio et al., n.d.) resulted in the following conclusions (Rehab Brief, 1979):

1. Clients with severe disabilities can benefit from independent living rehabilitation services.
2. ILR clients have many basic needs that are diverse and change over time. Counselors need to develop highly specialized individualized written programs and to reevaluate clients and revise these programs continually.
3. Transportation and architectural barriers are a major problem, and most service delivery programs have little direct control over these environmental barriers. More work needs to be done in these areas.
4. Sound ILR eligibility criteria must be developed to avoid placing into ILR programs persons with severe disabilities who can best benefit from vocational rehabilitation (VR) services.
5. Some clients with severe disabilities need to be in an ILR program indefinitely.
6. ILR costs are higher than VR costs. Higher ILR costs are partly a function of the length of time in the program; the average client stays in VR programs only 2 years, whereas many ILR cases remain unclosed after 3 years.
7. Further exploration of alternative service delivery methods in ILR is needed. There are many possible ways of serving the ILR population, and more research is needed to identify the more effective methods (Rehab Brief, 1979).

Title VII of the Rehabilitation Act of 1978 authorized the addition of an ILR program to the federal–state rehabilitation program. Title VII contained three parts:

1. Part A authorized comprehensive services to individuals with severe disabilities who were severely limited in their ability to engage or continue in employment or their ability to function independently in family or community. *Comprehensive services* were defined as any services intended to improve the ability of people with disabilities to function in employment or live independently in the home or community. The state rehabilitation agency was designated as the one to establish comprehensive services.

2. Part B of Title VII authorized the Commissioner of Rehabilitation Services to make grants to state rehabilitation agencies for "the establishment and operation of independent living centers, which shall be facilities that offer a broad range of services." These services included attendant care, independent living skills training, peer counseling, and assistance with housing and transportation. These centers were to make maximum use of other resources available to individuals with severe disabilities

(e.g., Medicaid, social services, housing assistance). Funding has since been provided for a large number of these centers designed to provide new opportunities for individuals with severe disabilities to live more independently in the community and in housing of their choice.

    3. Part C authorized program funds from which the Commissioner of Rehabilitation Services could make grants to state vocational rehabilitation agencies to provide independent living services to older blind individuals. Services covered were specific to blindness and included optical aids, brailling services, and reader services.

Promote Consumer Involvement

Along with the strong emphasis on clients with severe disabilities, the Rehabilitation Act of 1973 stressed joint client–counselor involvement throughout the rehabilitation process (Randolph, 1975). According to the act, this joint involvement should pervade the evaluation and rehabilitation planning period (i.e., the time for determining client eligibility for services and for developing the rehabilitation program).

    If eligible for services, the client should jointly participate with the counselor in the service planning process by completing an Individualized Written Rehabilitation Program (IWRP). All vocational rehabilitation goals must be spelled out in the IWRP. In addition to the vocational objective, key subobjectives must be identified in the areas of physical restoration, counseling, educational preparation, work adjustment, and vocational training. The IWRP also calls for identification of the evaluation criteria for determining progress toward both the vocational goal and the intermediate program objectives.

    When ruling a person ineligible for rehabilitation services, the counselor must clearly explain to the individual the reasons for ineligibility. The person has the right to appeal this decision regarding ineligibility. The act also required each state rehabilitation agency to prepare a system to review annually each ineligible case. Through the annual case review, the agency could determine whether changes in the person's life situation might result in eligibility for services.

    Although the intent of Congress to (a) increase the involvement of clients in the rehabilitation planning process and (b) increase clients' ability to question any decision of their ineligibility for rehabilitation services was clear, Congress realized that certain difficulties might present themselves in the process of attempting to achieve these goals. Two of these difficulties that were discussed in the 1972 hearings on the then-proposed Rehabilitation Act were that some people would have problems "understanding the Vocational Rehabilitation program requirements, and [the] specific services that rehabilitation agencies could provide or the reasons such services were not provided" (J. B. Patterson & Woodrich, 1986, p. 49). Congress attempted to address these problems by authorizing competitive grants for up to 20 client-assistance pilot projects under the Rehabilitation Act of 1973 (18 such projects were actually funded in 1974 and 1975). P.L. 93-112 stated that these projects were

> to provide counselors to inform and advise all clients and client applicants in the project area of all available benefits under this Act and, upon request of such client or client applicant, to assist such clients or applicants in their relationships with projects, programs, and facilities providing services to them under this Act. (cited in J. B. Patterson & Woodrich, 1986, p. 49)

In addition to removing the limit on the number of Client Assistance Projects (CAPs) authorized by the act, the responsibilities of the CAPs were expanded by the Rehabilitation Act Amendments of 1978 to include "'assistance in pursuing legal, administrative or other appropriate remedies to insure the protection of the rights of ... individuals under the Act'" (cited in J. B. Patterson & Woodrich, 1986, p. 49). However, prior to turning to administrative or legal solutions, CAPs were still expected to utilize mediation procedures to the greatest degree possible (J. B. Patterson & Woodrich, 1986).

Congress further strengthened the Client Assistance Program via the 1984 Rehabilitation Act Amendments. That legislation "changed CAP from discretionary, competitive grant *projects* to formula state grant *programs* with each state required to have a Client Assistance Program ... in effect by October 1, 1984" (J. B. Patterson & Woodrich, 1986, pp. 49–50). The amount of federal funds for the CAP for which each state was eligible was determined by the size of the state's population, with "a minimum allotment of $50,000 per state and $30,000 per territory" (J. B. Patterson & Woodrich, 1986, p. 50).

The Rehabilitation Act of 1973 also mandated consumer involvement in state rehabilitation agency policy development. The rationale for consumer involvement in agency policy development was clear. By drawing upon the experience of consumers, state agencies could improve the effectiveness of their rehabilitation services (Bowe, Fay, & Minch, 1980).

Consumer involvement has occurred at the federal level as well. The 1978 Rehabilitation Act Amendments mandated the reconfiguration of the Architectural and Transportation Barriers Compliance Board to include at least five individuals with disabilities. These same amendments also established the National Council on the Handicapped (later renamed the National Council on Disability), a broad-based group appointed by the president. The purposes of the council (Purposes 3, 4, and 5 were added by the Rehabilitation Act Amendments of 1986) include to

1. establish general policies for and review the operation of the National Institute of Handicapped Research (P.L. 95-602) (later renamed the National Institute on Disability and Rehabilitation Research);
2. provide advice to the commissioner with respect to the policies and conduct of the Rehabilitation Services Administration (P.L. 95-602);
3. "review and evaluate policies, programs, and activities concerning in-

dividuals with handicaps assisted by Federal departments and agencies, including programs under the [Rehabilitation] Act or under the Developmental Disabilities Assistance and Bill of Rights Act" (A. Jones, 1988, p. 32);

4. "review and evaluate all [laws] pertaining to Federal programs which assist such individuals with handicaps" (A. Jones, 1988, p. 32); and

5. "assess the extent to which such policies, programs, and activities provide incentives or disincentives to the establishment of community-based services for individuals with handicaps, and promote the full integration of such individuals and contribute to the independence and dignity of such individuals" (A. Jones, 1988, p. 32).

At least 5 of the council's 15 members must be individuals with disabilities. Other individuals on the council may be representatives of national organizations concerned with individuals with disabilities, individuals engaged in conducting medical or scientific research related to individuals with disabilities, and business or labor leaders. In 1986 and 1988 the National Council on Disability published thorough reviews of recent rehabilitation laws and programs titled, respectively, *Toward Independence* and *On the Threshold of Independence*. Through a series of policy recommendations, *Toward Independence* outlined an important agenda for rehabilitation for the remainder of the century. Among its many recommendations, the report called for passage of a broad-based bill ensuring the rights of individuals with disabilities (National Council on Disability, 1986). Passed in 1990, that legislation is called the Americans with Disabilities Act, which is comprehensively discussed in Chapter 3.

Stress Program Evaluation

Program evaluation was another key theme of the Rehabilitation Act of 1973. The act called for development of a set of standards by which the impact of rehabilitation services could be assessed. This mandate, as subsequently interpreted (*Federal Register,* 1974, 1975), meant that state rehabilitation agencies would be held accountable for providing information on (a) the percentage of the existing target population being served, (b) the timeliness and adequacy of their services, (c) the suitability of the employment in which clients are placed and their retaining of that employment, and (d) client satisfaction with rehabilitation services.

The legislation's extensive accountability mandate resulted in a large-scale expansion of state rehabilitation agency program evaluation activities. The sufficiency of these evaluation efforts for accurately assessing the effectiveness of rehabilitation services was hampered by a limited evaluation technology in the 1970s (S. E. Rubin, 1977). However, evaluation technology was significantly expanded in the 1980s and 1990s (Cronbach, 1982; Patton, 1997; Rossi & Freeman, 1982).

Support Research

The Rehabilitation Act of 1973 continued the long-standing tradition of providing support for rehabilitation research that could include both vocational and independent living emphases. The importance of research could be seen in the provisions for innovation and expansion grants and for the continuation of research and training centers, rehabilitation engineering research centers, and other related projects and demonstrations. The act also called for special programs emphasizing research with severe disability groups (e.g., clients with end-stage renal disease, spinal cord injury, or deafness). To further increase the impact of rehabilitation research, the Rehabilitation Act Amendments of 1978 established the National Institute of Handicapped Research (NIHR).

The NIHR was established to direct the research thrust in rehabilitation, in particular that of the Rehabilitation Research and Training Centers. Special charges to NIHR included to (a) disseminate information on ways to increase the quality of life of individuals with disabilities; (b) educate the public about ways of providing for the rehabilitation of individuals with disabilities; (c) conduct conferences concerning research and engineering advances in rehabilitation; and (d) produce and disseminate statistical reports and studies on the employment, health, and income of individuals with disabilities. The name of NIHR was changed in the mid-1980s to the National Institute on Disability and Rehabilitation Research (NIDRR).

Research directed at understanding disability and determining how to most optimally meet the needs of persons with disabilities has historically focused primarily both on describing the characteristics of persons with disabilities and on the development of treatment directed at reducing the disability-related limitations experienced by these individuals. This orientation has clearly located the responsibility for the social problem of handicap with the person rather than with the environment or the attitudes and systems that control that environment. This research focus has operated primarily from a *functional limitations model* of handicapping aspects of disability, which locates the responsibility for the handicap primarily within the individual. Hahn (1985b) questioned the capability of the functional limitations model to provide a sufficient explanation for the inability of persons with disabilities to fully participate in American society. He suggested that the primary research focus in the future should be on investigating the effect of public attitudes on the design of the environment and on the assumed physical, intellectual, and emotional characteristics necessary to optimally participate in activities of everyday life in society. Through such research, Hahn (1985b) predicted that a more valid explanation for the limited participation of persons with disabilities in social and vocational activities can be developed.

As a contrast to the traditional functional limitations model, Hahn (1985a) described in detail the importance of the *minority group model* in rehabilitation research. The perspective of the functional limitations model on disability "stresses methods of improving the physical and economic skills of disabled individuals to enable them to cope with the existing environment" (Hahn,

1985a, p. 53). Whereas the functional limitations model considers problems associated with disability as residing in the individual, the minority group model proposes that the major problems confronting persons with disabilities should be attributed primarily to a disabling environment that contains both physical and attitudinal obstacles to the individuals' full participation in daily life (Hahn, 1985a, 1987). Hahn (1987) suggested that the attitudinal obstacles produce even greater restrictions on persons with disabilities than do the physical barriers. He commented that any research evidence that reveals "a deep seated and pervasive antipathy or aversion toward people with disabilities" suggests that the "restrictions imposed by the built environment and by social institutions" are not "simply accidental or coincidental" (pp. 187–188).

Public attitudes can be seen as greatly responsible for the handicapping environment confronted by persons with disabilities. This is because the structure of the environment has been "fundamentally determined by public policy," and public policy tends to be greatly influenced by public attitudes (Hahn, 1988b, p. 40). Hahn (1988b) elaborated on these causal associations:

> The present forms of architectural structures and social institutions exist because statutes, ordinances, and codes either required or permitted them to be constructed in that manner. These public policies imply values, expectations, and assumptions about the physical and behavioral attributes that people ought to possess in order to survive or to participate in community life. (p. 40)

Rehabilitation research focused on the minority group model would also indirectly further investigate the validity of the functional limitations model. It would do so by helping determine the manner in which and the degree to which extent of handicap can be attributed to environmental and attitudinal barriers. It would also test the wisdom of disability community demands for a reallocation of public funds from "programs which have compelled them to fit the requirements of the existing environment" to programs "designed to adopt external surroundings to meet the needs and desires of citizens with disabilities" (Hahn, 1985a, p. 62). The following statement by Hahn (1985a) further illuminates the issues in regard to barriers to employment:

> Serious analyses must be conducted, for example, to determine the appropriateness of functional requirements and physical examinations which have been established as preconditions for many types of jobs. While some of these prerequisites might appear to be justified by the demands exerted on human beings by the configurations of the existing environment, others may reflect stereotypical perceptions of disability or an unwillingness to modify the job or the worksite to fit the capabilities of workers with disabilities. Perhaps the clearest evidence of the irrelevance of functional requirements to employment was provided by experience during World War II when, in the face of severe labor shortages, the stipulations were waived to permit the hiring of workers with disabilities and other minorities who

lost their jobs after the war when the requirements were reimposed to facilitate the employment of nondisabled veterans. (p. 63)

In being compatible with the functional limitations model, the focus of past rehabilitation research has also been compatible with the *person-blaming approach* (Caplan & Nelson, 1973), which addresses person change rather than system change. A number of purposes are served by the person-blaming approach that do not serve the interests of people with disabilities. First, "government and primary cultural institutions" are freed from blame for the handicap and, therefore, from responsibility for its removal as well (Caplan & Nelson, 1973, p. 210). Caplan and Nelson further stated,

> Person-blame interpretations reinforce social myths about one's degree of control over his own fate, thus rewarding the members of the great middle class by flattering their self-esteem for having "made it on their own." This in turn increases public complacency about the plight of those who have not "made it on their own." (p. 210)

Advance the Civil Rights of Persons with Disabilities

As the disability rights movement emerged during the 1970s and early 1980s, the population with disabilities began to more fully realize the similarity between their situation and the situation experienced by other minority groups—that is, as stigmatized as biologically inferior and as victims of "stereotyping,… bias, prejudice, segregation, and discrimination" (Hahn, 1985b, p. 300). Their rights to employment have been suppressed as a result of being stereotyped as either unemployable or feasible for only certain types of jobs. Many employment roles have been seen historically by society as "unnatural, inappropriate, or impossible" for persons with disabilities (Vash, 1982, p. 199). Like other minority groups, they have been confronted by inaccessible polling places, which have infringed on their voting rights, as well as "rigid patterns of segregation in education, transportation, housing, and other areas of life" (Hahn, 1985b, p. 300).

As the disability population became aware of their minority status and the associated discrimination, they began to manifest a more militant stance against it. Persons with disabilities started to realize that they have been limited less by their disabilities than by the effect of societal attitudes and environmental barriers. Therefore, the disability community actively lobbied for the incorporation of civil rights provisions in the Rehabilitation Act of 1973. These provisions are found in Sections 501, 502, 503, and 504 of Title V.

It is important to note that persons covered under the Rehabilitation Act of 1973 were initially defined as those whose disability limited their employability and who could reduce that limitation through vocational rehabilitation services (Feldblum, 1991). However, because that definition tended to suggest that Title V addressed only discriminatory practices in employment, another definition was established for coverage, under Section 504 in 1974, which addressed discriminatory practices in housing, health care, and education programs, as well as in employment. That 1974 definition, which has remained in effect since, defines a person covered under Section 504 of the Rehabilitation Act as someone who

1. Has a physical or mental impairment that substantially limits that person in one or more major life activities, or
2. Has a record of such a physical or mental impairment, or
3. Is regarded as having such a physical or mental impairment. (Feldblum, 1991, pp. 83–84)

Speaking to the second and third prongs of the definition of disability, Feldblum (1991) stated,

The second prong ... is designed to extend protection to an individual who had a physical or mental impairment at some point in the past, who has recovered from that impairment, but who nevertheless experiences discrimination based on the *record* of having the impairment. Examples of such discrimination would include individuals who have recovered from cancer or from a mental illness, but who experience discrimination because of the stigma or the fear associated with such disabilities....

The third prong ... is designed to extend protection to a person who may not have any impairment at all, or to a person who has some relatively minor impairment, but who is regarded by others as having a physical or mental disorder serious enough to limit him or her in some major life activity. For example, a person may have a significant physiological cosmetic disorder, such as a large birthmark on a cheek, that does not, in fact, substantially limit the person in any way. An employer, however, may view that disorder as substantially limiting that person's ability to work and to interact with others, and may discriminate against the person on that basis. (p. 85)

The U.S. Commission on Civil Rights (1983) provided further elaboration on this definition by abstracting the definitions of *physical impairment, mental impairment,* and *major life activities* found in Health and Human Services (HHS) regulations for Section 504 of the Rehabilitation Act of 1973 as follows:

The regulations explain that "physical impairment" refers to any physiological disorder or condition, cosmetic disfigurement, or anatomical loss affecting an important body system ... [and] mental impairments are "any mental or psychological disorder, such as mental retardation, organic brain syndrome, emotional or mental illness, and specific learning disabilities." ...

The regulations also define "major life activities" to mean such functions as caring for one's self, performing manual tasks, walking, seeing, hearing, speaking, breathing, learning, and working. (pp. 7–8)

The civil rights legislation for persons with disabilities passed in 1973 was clearly needed to increase their employment opportunities. Even though vocational rehabilitation services had greatly expanded between the early 1950s and early 1970s, a large percentage of the disability population was unemployed. The scope of the existing unemployment problem in the early 1970s is driven home by the major unemployment problem that still existed almost a decade after the passage of Title V in 1973. The U.S. Census Bureau *Current Population Survey* figures for 1985 showed that only "slightly over one-third of American adults with disabilities worked full- or part-time, all or part of the year during 1984" (Bowe, 1985, p. 5).

Section 501: Affirmative Action in Federal Hiring

Section 501 mandated "nondiscrimination by the federal government in its own hiring practices" (Bayh, 1979, p. 58) and called for each federal department, agency, and instrumentality (e.g., the U.S. Postal Service) to submit "an affirmative action program plan for the hiring, placement, and advancement" of individuals with disabilities to the U.S. Civil Service Commission (P.L. 93-112). The most important feature of Section 501 has been its effort to establish the federal government as a model agency for promoting the recruiting, hiring, and advancing of workers with disabilities. Section 501 required all federal agencies and the Postal Service to establish annual written affirmative action plans in which they specified goals for the hiring and promotion of persons with disabilities in their workforce. They were also required to develop special programs for recruiting persons with disabilities, as well as goals and time tables for making their facilities accessible. In addition, Section 501 required those federal agencies with more than 500 employees to "establish numerical goals for employment of persons with targeted disabilities," such as those who are deaf, blind, mentally retarded, mentally ill, paraplegic, or quadriplegic (U.S. Commission on Civil Rights, 1983, pp. 55–56). The early impact of Section 501 was minimized by the absence of active enforcement of its mandate between 1973 and 1978. Even in the early 1990s, the ability of Section 501 to increase numbers of jobs for persons with disabilities remained unclear.

Section 502: Accessibility

Although no concerted national effort to eliminate architectural and transportation barriers existed before 1959, the next decade was one of significant progress. To initiate steps toward accessibility, such groups as the President's Committee on Employment of the Handicapped, the National Society for Crippled Children and Adults, and the American Standards Association combined their resources to develop standards and codes and to sponsor a national institute on architectural barriers. In 1968 Congress passed the Architectural Barriers Act (P.L. 90-480). That act recommended that the General Services Administrator (GSA), the Secretary of Housing and Urban Development (HUD), and the Secretary of the Department of Defense (DOD)—in consultation with the Secretary of Health, Education and Welfare—develop accessibility standards for their respective agencies "for the design, construction, and alteration of [their] buildings to insure whenever possible that physically handicapped persons will have ready access to, and use of, such buildings" (P.L. 90-480). By 1970, GSA, HUD, and DOD had published their own accessibility standards. Following publication those standards covered each agency's buildings that were constructed, designed, or significantly altered. Transportation facilities, including train terminals, bus terminals, and airports, built since 1970 with federal funds were covered by the GSA accessibility standards. The elimination of architectural and transportation barriers is important because of the social segregation role they play in limiting the mobility and, therefore, the opportunities of persons with physical disabilities to participate in many normal daily activities. Nugent (1976) provided a cogent argument for accessibility:

> How frustrating it is to handicapped individuals when their great investments of time, effort, and money to achieve independence and self-sufficiency are negated because of inaccessible facilities which were supposedly built for everyone. Handicapped people must have access if they are to pursue their aspirations, develop their talents and exercise their skills in all areas of endeavor. (p. 65)

Physical aspects of structures that deny access are commonplace and for the most part have often gone unnoticed by people without disabilities. For example, Edgar (1975) provided the following partial list of such barriers:

> revolving doors, doors less than 32 inches wide, unnecessary steps, too small parking stalls, too high drinking fountains, too small toilet cubicles or location of the toilet fixture itself, elevator controls out of reach, automatic elevator doors that close in less than seven seconds, wall mounted telephones, slippery or uneven floor surfaces, lack of handrails, inadequate lighting, warning buzzers the deaf cannot hear, or warning lights the blind cannot see. (p. 6)

Such architectural barriers contribute to the insecurity of persons with disabilities. Thoreson and Kerr (1978) drove this point home:

> Reverse the situation and imagine for a moment the outlook of the able-bodied person as he starts out to work if he knew that the steps of the bus might be five feet high, that the seats might be without backs, that his office might turn out to be ten miles from the bus station, that the controls of the elevator might be ten feet above the floor, and that he might be unable to hear his employer. (p. 24)

Section 502 of the Rehabilitation Act of 1973 established the Architectural and Transportation Barriers Compliance Board (ATBCB) to enforce the accessibility standards established in response to the Architectural Barriers Act of 1968 (P.L. 90-480). In 1976 the Architectural Barriers Act of 1968 was amended by P.L. 96-541, Temporary Tax Provision extension. Those amendments did the following:

1. required that the U.S. Postal Service develop accessibility standards and
2. mandated that newly leased buildings or lease renewals had to meet the accessibility standards of the leasing government (or quasi-government) agency.

The U.S. Postal Service published their accessibility standards in 1978. Thus, in 1978 four different sets of accessibility standards were in effect. HUD's standards covered public housing. DOD's standards covered defense buildings intended for use by the public. The U.S. Postal Service's standards covered all postal buildings. GSA's standards covered virtually all other buildings or facilities owned or leased by the federal government.

Initially, the impact of the ATBCB was minimal due to both insufficient funds and board membership limited to government officials. The membership of the original ATBCB comprised the head (or his or her designated assistant secretary) of five federal departments (HEW, Transportation, HUD, Labor, and Interior) and the GSA, the U.S. Postal Service, and the Veterans Administration. The realization that the limited action of the board during its first year of existence may have resulted partially from a situation in which the government was overseeing itself in regard to accessibility led to expansion of board membership through the 1978 amendments to the following 21 members (later changed to 22 members due to the division of HEW into the Department of Health and Human Services and the Department of Education):

A. Eleven members "appointed by the President from the general public" (five must be individuals with disabilities).
B. The heads (or their designated assistant secretary) of each of the following federal departments or agencies:
    (i)   Department of Health, Education and Welfare
    (ii) Department of Transportation
    (iii) Department of Housing and Urban Development
    (iv) Department of Labor
    (v)   Department of Interior
    (vi) Department of Defense
    (vii) Department of Justice
    (viii) General Service Administration
    (ix) Veteran's Administration

(x) United States Postal Services. (Rehabilitation, Comprehensive Services, and Developmental Disabilities Amendments of 1978, P.L. 95-602)

By 1980 the impact of the Architectural Barriers Act of 1968 and the 1973 establishment of the ATBCB on the removal of architectural barriers still appeared to be minimal. A major reason for that minimal impact was that the act applied only to those "federal buildings or buildings built or remodeled with federal assistance" after the act was passed, even though government services and agencies were frequently housed in older buildings. In addition, the act did not cover private and most state facilities (Weicker, 1984, p. 521). A 1980 study in Maryland of the state-owned buildings that housed

> services and programs available to the general public ... found 76 percent of the buildings physically inaccessible and unusable for serving handicapped persons, even when taking into account the option of moving programs and services to other parts of the buildings or otherwise restructuring them. (U.S. Commission on Civil Rights, 1983, p. 39)

In addition to expanding ATBCB membership, Congress, via the 1978 amendments, mandated the board to develop minimum guidelines and requirements for standards issued by the four standard-setting agencies. Considerable controversy followed, with several different versions developed before a set of minimum guidelines and requirements was issued by the board and made effective on September 3, 1982. As a result, all federal departments or agencies were required by law to use the board's regulations or to make their regulations consistent with the board's regulations. "The Board can enforce these Federal accessibility regulations through administrative proceeding as well as litigation" (U.S. Commission on Civil Rights, 1983, p. 62).

The legislative activity focusing on architectural and transportation barriers since the late 1960s clearly demonstrates the relationship between the content of public policy and the design of environments. Because environmental design is greatly shaped by public policies implemented in the form of "statutes, ordinances, codes, and regulations" (Hahn, 1985b, p. 56), it is only logical that environmental change will result from the same process. Hahn (1985b) argued that such legislative mandates are reflections of public "values and attitudes about the personal capabilities which human beings ought to possess in order to be accepted as participating members of the community" (p. 56). Hahn (1985a) stated,

> Thus policy-makers must devote serious attention to the possibility that features of the environment which have an adverse effect on persons with disabilities may reflect a pervasive, deep-seated aversion to these people. As policies are increasingly changed to produce an environment which would permit citizens with disabilities to be treated in an impartial manner, many prevailing myths about the alleged biological inferiority of persons with disabilities are almost certain to be eradicated. (p. 56)

Section 503: Affirmative Action by Federal Contract Recipients

Section 503 of the Rehabilitation Act of 1973 prohibits discrimination in employment on the basis of physical or mental handicaps and requires affirmative action on the part of all federal contract recipients and their subcontractors who receive annual federal contracts exceeding $10,000. "It typically applies to defense contractors, space program contractors, construction companies and firms which might sell equipment or supplies to the federal government" (Bayh, 1979, p. 58). Firms subject to this provision are required to make reasonable modifications in work settings and work facilities to increase accessibility to persons with disabilities. Furthermore, they must assure the federal government that policies of nondiscrimination are followed in the recruiting, hiring, and promoting of workers. A written affirmative action plan is required of contractors with the federal government having 50 or more employees or a federal contract exceeding $50,000 (U.S. Commission on Civil Rights, 1983, p. 54).

The Department of Labor's Office of Federal Contract Compliance Programs has been responsible for enforcing the affirmative action provisions of Section 503 (U.S. Commission on Civil Rights, 1983, p. 54). The Employment Standards Administration of the Department of Labor reviews noncompliance in regard to Section 503 and helps employers understand the regulations and develop outreach programs to recruit qualified employees with disabilities. By 1978 nearly 100 workers had been awarded an approximate total of $330,000 in back pay as the result of Section 503–based decisions by the Department of Labor (Spellane, 1978). Some of the more common violations of Section 503 by federal contractors included (a) an inaccessible personnel office and/or worksite, (b) applicant requirements for a job that are clearly unrelated to the successful performance of the job, and (c) failure to use appropriate recruitment sources for informing individuals with disabilities of the job (Bowe, 1980).

Section 504: Equal Opportunities

Section 504 of the Rehabilitation Act of 1973 prohibits the exclusion, based on disability, of otherwise qualified persons with disabilities from participation in any federal program or activity, or from "any program or activity receiving federal financial assistance" (U.S. Commission on Civil Rights, 1983, p. 49). Examples of the latter include "school districts, colleges and universities, day care centers, hospitals, nursing homes or public welfare offices" (Bayh, 1979, p. 58). Strongly emphasizing accessibility of buildings and programs for persons with disabilities, Section 504 has tremendous implications because of the many social institutions receiving some type of federal assistance. It is also important to note that under Section 504 a person with a disability cannot "be found unqualified without considering whether a reasonable accommodation would render the individual qualified" (U.S. Commission on Civil Rights, 1983, p. 162).

Section 504 was not implemented until 1977, when, under strong pressure via nationwide demonstrations coordinated by citizens with disabilities, U.S. Department of Health, Education, and Welfare (HEW) Secretary Califano signed it into effect (Bowe et al., 1980; Fields, 1977). The American Coalition of Citizens with Disabilities helped organize demonstrations throughout the country to pressure HEW "to promulgate regulations implementing Section 504 of the 1973 Rehabilitation Act" (DeJong, 1979b, p. 17).

The need for a government mandate for equal access to higher education opportunities for persons with disabilities was brought home by the results of a pre–Section 504 implementation study. Fonosch (1980) summarized the results of a 1974 survey of a thousand 4-year colleges and universities as follows:

> 18 percent rejected the blind, 27 percent refused admittance to students in wheelchairs, and 22 percent rejected deaf students. Although approximately 75 percent of the institutions would accept handicapped students, only 25 percent provided special facilities and services. (p. 165)

Once implemented in 1977, Section 504 directly attacked this discriminatory situation. Otherwise-qualified individuals with disabilities can no longer be denied admission to institutions of higher education because of their disability. Although colleges and universities receiving federal funds can request information on disability from applicants for admission, they can no longer demand it. Admission quotas for students with disabilities and discriminatory admission tests are also no longer acceptable (Fonosch, 1980, p. 163).

A controversial 1979 Supreme Court decision reinforced the significance of the term *qualified individual with a disability*. Reversing an earlier decision by the 4th U.S. Circuit Court of Appeals, the Supreme Court ruled unanimously in *Davis v. Southeastern Community College* that educational institutions were not obligated to substantially modify their standards to admit those with disabilities. The case in point was a 46-year-old woman (Davis) with severe hearing loss who had been trained as a practical nurse and sought further training at Southeastern Community College (Whiteville, North Carolina) to become a registered nurse. Stating that any candidate for the registered nurse degree must be able to perform in all nursing situations so as to ensure the safety of the patient, the school did not admit Davis. The school pointed out that her reliance on lip-reading would be of little benefit in the "operating room or in intensive care or post-natal units, where doctors wore surgical masks" (Brubaker & Wright, 1979, p. 2). Interpretations of the significance of the decision were mixed. Some claimed that the decision represented a serious blow to rights of persons with disabilities, whereas others saw it as upholding the basic meaning of nondiscriminatory treatment—that is, that the person with a disability be "otherwise qualified" for the position, which, from their point of view, the complainant in this case was not. Fonosch (1980) pointed out that "the *Davis v. Southeastern Community College* case reaffirms that the intent of Section 504 is providing equal opportunity rather than affirmative action" (p. 167).

Rather than negate the requirement for reasonable accommodation under Section 504, the *Davis* decision helped define that requirement. In their 1985

Alexander v. Choate decision, the U.S. Supreme Court reinforced that point by further elaborating on the *Davis* decision as follows:

> We held that the college was not required to admit Davis because it appeared unlikely that she could benefit from any modifications that the relevant HEW regulations required ... and because the further modifications Davis sought—full-time, personal supervision whenever she attended patients and elimination of all clinical courses—would have compromised the essential nature of the college's nursing program.... Such a "fundamental alteration in the nature of a program" was far more than the reasonable modifications the statute or regulations required. (cited in N. L. Jones, 1991, p. 31)

N. L. Jones (1991) pointed out that in the *Choate* case the court "went on to conclude that Section 504 required a balancing approach between the rights of persons with disabilities to be integrated into society and the legitimate interests of grantees in preserving the integrity of their programs" (p. 31).

Section 504 guidelines mandate that institutions of higher education provide "educational auxiliary aides," such as taped texts, talking calculators, and tape recorders, if their absence will hinder the educational performance of persons with disabilities. Readers for those who are blind and interpreters for those who are deaf are also mandated (Fields, 1977).

Because Section 504 involves all agencies that disburse federal funds, the Department of Justice has responsibility for coordinating enforcement activities. "Section 504 can also be enforced by aggrieved handicapped persons through lawsuits" (U.S. Commission on Civil Rights, 1983, p. 51). Unlike Section 504, Section 503 is not enforceable through "private lawsuits brought by aggrieved" persons with disabilities (U.S. Commission on Civil Rights, 1983, p. 54).

Reasonable Accommodation

The regulations for both Sections 503 and 504 require employers to make reasonable accommodations for employees with disabilities, such as making facilities accessible to them, restructuring jobs, modifying work schedules, or providing interpreters or readers (Bayh, 1979). Griffin Bell, attorney general during President Carter's administration, suggested that Sections 503 and 504 were not intended to "require the impossible." Therefore, factors such as fiscal restraints have been considered when determining an appropriate degree of compliance by an employer (Bayh, 1979, p. 60). However, to claim cost as a factor, the institution must show that the modifications as required would "impose an undue hardship on the operation of its program" (Hull, 1979). Factors affecting extent of hardship depend on the program's resources, its type of operation, and the extent of the modifications recommended (Hull, 1979). Overall, reasonable accommodation has been a central concept in disability antidiscrimination law because it provides a realistic midpoint between nonaction and doing everything to assist persons with disabilities (U.S. Commission on Civil Rights, 1983, p. 2).

Initial reactions to Section 504 regulations tended toward overexaggerations of the cost of complying. For example, architects for the Kaiser Aluminum Company estimated that a barrier-free environment would cost $160,000; however, consultant architects from Mainstream, Inc., determined that "reasonable accessibility" for the industry would cost more like $8,000. Poorly planned and hence wasteful responses to the Section 504 regulations also occurred. For example, one company in California spent $40,000 lowering all of its drinking fountains when all that was required was the installation of paper cup dispensers, at a cost of $1.60 per water fountain (J. Moore, 1979). In addition to the installation of paper cup dispensers, the U.S. Commission on Civil Rights (1983) has provided the following examples of types of accommodations that could be provided at reasonable cost with significant benefits to persons with disabilities:

- Adding inexpensive Braille or raised letter and number tabs to doors and elevator control panels;
- Changing desktops and tables to appropriate heights for persons who are very short or who use wheelchairs;
- Providing concrete, step-by-step instructions for mentally retarded people;
- Providing a wooden pointer for reaching the upper buttons on an elevator control panel;
- Moving a program or service to an accessible part of a building so that a handicapped person can participate;
- Using alternative testing procedures for students with visual impairments, learning disabilities, or orthopedic impairments that interfere with reading or writing ability;
- Providing seating priority for mobility impaired persons for whom standing would be difficult. (p. 2)

In the early 1980s, the federal courts ruled in favor of plaintiffs with disabilities in a number of cases based on Section 504. Examples include

the provision of sign language interpreters for deaf college students,... provision of an extended school year for mentally retarded pupils,... permission for a deaf applicant to use hearing aids or telephone amplification devices during testing for Federal employment,... and provision of different ways of administering tests to a job applicant with dyslexia. (U.S. Commission on Civil Rights, 1983, p. 53)

Access to Transportation

Federal assistance for transportation for persons with disabilities dates back "to 1944 when the Social Security Act was amended to provide transportation assistance to the elderly, blind, and disabled" (Poister, 1982, p. 6). However, it was not until 1970, when the Urban Mass Transportation Assistance (UMTA) Act of 1964 was amended by the insertion of Section 16, that a national policy was established for elderly persons and persons with disabilities to "have equal status with other persons in being able to utilize mass transit facilities and services" (Poister, 1982, p. 7). The enactment of Section 16 was probably greatly stimulated by the growing awareness of the size of the problem. In 1970 it was estimated that about half of the 26.4 million elderly persons and persons with disabilities in the United States had difficulty using existing transportation services (Fielding, 1982).

The public policy on transportation services for persons with disabilities was further strengthened by Section 504 of the Rehabilitation Act of 1973, "which stated that no individual was to be discriminated against in programs receiving federal assistance solely on the basis of a handicap" (Poister, 1982, p. 7). Because the UMTA Act and its subsequent amendments provided federal funds for urban mass transit systems, its awards could be affected by the Section 504 antidiscrimination mandate after 1973. Further strengthening of that public policy resulted through the 1975 amendments to the UMTA Act, which required "that all new fixed transportation facilities, and, to the extent possible, all new buses ... be accessible to" elderly persons and persons with disabilities (Poister, 1982, p. 7). Department of Transportation (DOT) regulations published in 1976 (*Federal Register,* 1976) allowed the secretary of transportation to waive the requirements for all new buses to be accessible in local areas where alternative specialized transportation services were being provided at moderate prices for elderly persons and persons with disabilities. This gave the DOT "discretionary authority over what type of service to require" at that time (Poister, 1982, p. 7). That flexibility was removed in 1979, when new DOT regulations that superseded the 1976 DOT regulations were published. The 1979 regulations removed the acceptability of the specialized demand-responsive services option and mandated that regular transit systems (e.g., regular bus service) be made accessible to persons with disabilities. The 1979 DOT regulations were more compatible with Section 504 implementation standards than were the previous 1976 DOT regulations. Poister (1982) stated,

> The major point of departure of these ... regulations from the earlier "special efforts" requirements concerned wheelchair accessible buses; all new buses purchased with federal assistance must be accessible and within ten years, one-half of a local operator's bus fleet must be wheelchair accessible. Local transit authorities were required to use lift equipment until the preferred low-floor Transbus became available. (p. 7)

The validity of the 1979 DOT regulation was challenged in *American Public Transit Association v. Lewis,* heard by the District of Columbia Circuit Court of Appeals in 1981. The challenge was to the authority of Section 504 in regard to actions taken by the DOT in accord with Section 16 of the UMTA where "massive expenditures" would be required to make all mass transit accessible (Rothstein, 1984, p. 165). As a direct result of that court decision, DOT issued new regulations in 1981 that superseded the 1979 regulations and basically made the DOT's policy similar to that reflected in its 1976 regulations "in requiring special efforts … rather than setting a goal of accessibility with a timetable for achieving it." The 1981 regulations simply mandated that recipients must certify that special efforts to provide usable transportation to persons with disabilities are being made (Rothstein, 1984, pp. 166–167). *Special efforts* were described as follows in the 1981 regulations:

> The term "special efforts" refers both to service for handicapped persons in general and specifically to service for wheelchair users and semiambulatory persons. With regard to transportation for wheelchair users and others who cannot negotiate steps, "special efforts" in planning means genuine, good-faith progress in planning service for wheelchair users and semiambulatory handicapped persons that meets a significant fraction of the identified transportation needs of such persons within a reasonable time period. Particular attention should be given to those handicapped persons who are employed or for whom the lack of adequate transportation constitutes the major barrier to employment or job training. (*Federal Register,* 1981)

New DOT regulations were proposed in 1983 in the *Federal Register* for the purpose of soliciting comments. Over 650 comments were subsequently received from a variety of sources, including individuals with disabilities and groups representing persons with disabilities, local transit authorities, transportation providers, state departments of transportation, human service agencies, congressional representatives, and private citizens. With the aid of these comments, the DOT drafted new final regulations concerning requirements for urban mass transit (UMT) systems receiving DOT funds. Those regulations, which were published in the *Federal Register* in 1986, allowed UMT systems that receive DOT financial assistance to meet their accessibility obligations by providing any of the following: a special service such as a dial-a-ride or taxi voucher system; a bus system (regularly scheduled or on-call); or a mixed system comprised of elements of both an accessible bus system and a special service. Therefore, the 1986 DOT regulations continued the DOT policy reflected in the 1976 and 1981 DOT regulations, which provided each UMT system with the final decision-making authority concerning the specific characteristics of its program for making accessible transportation available to persons with disabilities.

The 1986 DOT regulations attempted to resolve the "undue burdens" problem that led the District of Columbia Circuit Court of Appeals in 1981 in *American Public Transit Association v. Lewis* to strike down the 1979 regulations that removed the flexibility from local areas to provide alternative specialized transportation in lieu of making their regular bus service accessible to persons with disabilities. The regulations did so by indicating that a transit system did not have to spend more than 3% of its budget in its attempt to provide adequate transportation service for persons with disabilities (Katzmann, 1991). The specific "cost cap" had a short life. In 1989, in *ADAPT v. Skinner*, the "United States Court of Appeals for the Third Circuit concluded ... that, although the department could take costs into consideration ... the 3 percent cost cap was arbitrary" (Katzmann, 1991, pp. 218–219).

The specifics of the U.S. public policy on transportation for persons with disabilities in the 1970s and 1980s were the focus of debate among interested parties. On the one hand, the American Public Transit Association (APTA), which represents the transit industry, was strongly opposed to any regulations requiring

> accessible buses on all systems.... According to the industry viewpoint, the objective of policy in this area should be to provide adequate *mobility* for the individual around the urban area rather than accessibility to certain vehicles. Its preferred means of achieving this objective is through a combination of standard vehicles, specialized small vehicles and demand responsive services. (Poister, 1982, p. 8)

On the other hand, disability consumer groups argued for full accessibility to regular transportation services as a civil rights issue. Poister (1982) elaborated:

> This lobby is morally and philosophically committed to barrier free, accessible transportation. The rallying point for these groups has been the struggle to gain full accessibility to regular, fixed route transit service. Their major goal has been fully accessible buses on fixed routes, by far the most widespread type of transit service in the country, and they have rejected alternative specialized services on the basis that it really represents "separate but equal" treatment. Their position is that such specialized separate services "only reinforce the negative image of the handicapped as dependent individuals who are more of a burden on society rather than fully functioning productive citizens." (p. 8)

The effectiveness of the resistance of the transportation industry to the removal of transportation barriers was reflected in the results of a 1982 General Accounting Office survey of public transportation systems. That survey

> found that 36 percent of the systems with rail service did not have a single station accessible to wheelchair users; another 36 percent reported that fewer than 10 percent of their stations were accessible. More than one-third of the surveyed transit systems offering bus service did not have a single bus with a lift mechanism to provide access for wheelchairs. Some

of these transit systems offered paratransit services—special demand-responsive systems (such as "dial-a-bus" programs). But 84 percent reported that, because of eligibility criteria and limited resources, they were periodically unable to comply with requests for transportation, and one-third of the systems maintained waiting lists of persons who wanted, but were not yet permitted, to use the paratransit service for daily commuting. (U.S. Commission on Civil Rights, 1983, p. 39)

The debate on accessibility of public transportation for individuals with disabilities in the 1970s and 1980s resembled debates over access that occurred during the "heyday" of the African American civil rights movement (Fielding, 1982; Poister, 1982). In addition, it paralleled the mainstreaming issues regarding the rights of children and adults with disabilities to access education.

Movement Toward an Action Orientation

Title V of the Rehabilitation Act of 1973 demonstrated a distinct change in public policy in regard to the civil rights of people with disabilities from "passive benevolence" to "active reinforcement" of those rights. Previously, public policy recognition of the employment rights of individuals with disabilities was limited to providing federal funds to states for rehabilitation programs and to "imploring and beseeching" the public to provide persons with disabilities with equal access to employment and to the benefits of federally supported programs. However, no federal law was in effect to enforce the rights of persons with disabilities (Hull, 1979, p. 21). What brought about the change in the national policy? The change in the public policy was greatly stimulated by the militancy of persons with disabilities themselves, who "sought to adapt, to their own needs, the success of the American civil rights movement of the 1960s" (Hull, 1979, p. 22). Therefore, it is not surprising that the wording in Section 504 was "patterned after, and is almost identical to, the antidiscrimination language of Section 601 of the Civil Rights Act of 1964 … and Section 901 of the Education Amendments of 1972" (Hull, 1979, p. 25).

Although the intent of Title V was sound, its sufficiency for addressing the problem was still being questioned in the mid-1980s. Pati (1985) questioned whether the affirmative action and antidiscrimination provisions of the Rehabilitation Act of 1973 had produced any more than token change in regard to job opportunities for persons with disabilities. He saw many U.S. employers still doing little or nothing in regard to hiring persons with disabilities. Pati (1985) suggested that little change can occur in this situation until legislation mandates a "quota system" for the employment of qualified persons with disabilities to which all employers would be required to adhere, with heavy fines imposed on those who fail to do so. Such quota system models for generating employment opportunities for persons with disabilities already existed by the 1970s in some other countries, including Austria and Japan.

Other Relevant Legislation Initiated in the 1970s

Two other acts passed in the 1970s provided federal support for persons with disabilities. They were the Developmental Disabilities Assistance and Bill of Rights (DDA) Act of 1976 (P.L. 94-103; subsequently reauthorized, but not renamed, in 1984 by P.L. 98-527) and the Education for All Handicapped Children Act of 1975 (P.L. 94-142). The DDA Act is a response to the needs of over 3 million people in the United States with developmental disabilities (Administration on Developmental Disabilities, 1994). In the act, *developmental disabilities* were defined as those disabilities

> attributable to mental or physical impairments that cause substantial functional limitation in three or more of the following life activities: self-care, receptive and expressive language, learning, mobility, self-direction, capacity for independent living, and economic sufficiency. The disability must start before a person reaches the age of 22 and be likely to continue indefinitely. To be considered developmentally disabled a person must also need extended, individually planned and coordinated, interdisciplinary care or treatment. (U.S. Commission on Civil Rights, 1983, p. 59)

The purpose of the act is to help states assure access to culturally competent services for persons with developmental disabilities and their families in order to augment the productivity and independence of those with developmental disabilities, as well as their integration and inclusion in the community (Administration on Developmental Disabilities, 1994). The act further specifies goals consistent with the overarching mission of promoting productivity and inclusion. Policies and programs contained in the act should enable people with developmental disabilities to

> 1. make informed choices and decisions,
> 2. live in homes and communities in which they can exercise their full rights and responsibilities as citizens,
> 3. pursue productive lives,
> 4. contribute to society,
> 5. make and maintain friendships, and
> 6. achieve personal goals consistent with individual preferences and capacities. (Administration on Developmental Disabilities, 1994)

Through this act, grants are provided

> to states for developmental disabilities councils (DD Councils), university-affiliated programs (UAPs), and protection and advocacy activities for persons with developmental disabilities (PADD). Grants to UAPs include grants for training projects with respect to assistive technology services for

the purpose of assisting university-affiliated programs in providing training to personnel who provide, or will provide, assistive technology services and devices to individuals with developmental disabilities and their
families. Such projects may provide training and technical assistance to
improve access to assistive technology services for individuals with developmental disabilities and may include stipends and tuition assistance for
training project participants. (A. M. Cook & Hussey, 2002, p. 13)

Under the DDA act, each state is required to have a network of protection and
advocacy organizations that are independent of agencies that provide services.
"They advocate for and represent the rights of persons with developmental
disabilities, in addition to providing information and referral services" (West,
1991, p. 18).

Following passage of P.L. 94-142 in 1975, the law has been reauthorized
and amended five times, with the latest reauthorization being the Individuals
with Disabilities Education Improvement Act of 2004 (IDEA) (Heward, 2006).
This special education legislation was initially stimulated by "congressional concern and dissatisfaction with the complete exclusion of millions of handicapped
children from the Nation's public schools and with the inappropriateness of
educational programs available to additional millions of handicapped children"
(U.S. Commission on Civil Rights, 1983, p. 56). In the IDEA amendments of
2004 (P.L. 108-446), Congress stated that, prior to the passage of P.L. 94-142
in 1975,

the educational needs of millions of children with disabilities were not being fully met because

(A) the children did not receive appropriate educational services;

(B) the children were excluded entirely from the public school system
and from being educated with their peers;

(C) undiagnosed disabilities prevented the children from having a successful educational experience; or

(D) a lack of adequate resources within the public school system forced
families to find services outside the public school system. (P.L. 108-
446, 118 STAT. 2469)

P.L. 108-446 states that the purposes of IDEA are

(1) (A) to ensure that all children with disabilities have available to
them a free appropriate public education that emphasizes special
education and related services designed to meet their unique
needs and prepare them for further education, employment, and
independent living;

(B) to ensure that the rights of children with disabilities and parents
of such children are protected; and

(C) to assist States, localities, educational service agencies, and Federal agencies to provide for the education of all children with disabilities;

(2) to assist States in the implementation of a statewide, comprehensive, coordinated, multidisciplinary, interagency system of early intervention services for infants and toddlers with disabilities and their families;

(3) to ensure that educators and parents have the necessary tools to improve educational results for children with disabilities by supporting system improvement activities; coordinated research and personnel preparation; coordinated technical assistance, dissemination, and support; and technology development and media services; and

(4) to assess, and ensure the effectiveness of, efforts to educate children with disabilities. (P.L. 108-446, 118 STAT. 2651)

For a state to qualify for federal grants under IDEA, it must implement procedures for identifying, locating, and evaluating all its children with disabilities and for assuring that children with disabilities are educated with children without disabilities to the greatest extent possible (B. P. Tucker, 1998). In addition, IDEA requires that an Individualized Education Program (IEP) be developed for each child (Heward, 2006). The IEP must contain, at a minimum, the following: current performance levels; measurable annual goals and short-term instructional objectives; services and aids to be provided to achieve annual goals; a rationale for any time away from the regular classroom; required modifications in assessment and testing; timelines, frequency, and location for services; a statement of transition-from-school-to-adult-life services not later than age 16; and procedures for determining educational progress and notifying parents (Annino, 2005; Heward, 2006; B. P. Tucker, 1998).

During the 2003–2004 school year, the number of students with disabilities ages 3 to 21 in educational programs that received federal funds under IDEA exceeded $6 million (Annino, 2005; Heward, 2006). Moreover, consistent with themes in the 1992 and 1998 amendments to the Rehabilitation Act, IDEA stressed the importance of school-to-work transition planning and services for students with disabilities. Schools are required to include in students' IEPs a transition plan that must be acted upon for them no later than age 16 (Heward, 2006). A transition plan in the IEP describes the activities required to enable a student to achieve postschool outcomes, which may fall into areas such as selection of an employment goal, vocational training, postsecondary education, financial support, independent living, transportation and mobility, social relationships, recreational activities, health and safety, self-advocacy, and future planning (Cronin, Patton, & Lock, 1997). "This portion of the student's IEP is called an Individualized Transition Plan (ITP) [and] outlines actions, events, and resources that will affect and support [the student's] move from school to adulthood" (Heward, 2006, p. 600).

The 1980s: A Decade of Uncertainty

The 1980s began with Ronald Reagan becoming president of the United States and concomitantly with his attempt to implement his philosophy of government. That philosophy stressed a limited role for the federal government in meeting the needs of disadvantaged persons and persons with disabilities. The potential implementation of his philosophy, therefore, presented a direct challenge to the maintenance of the civil rights and benefit rights achieved by the disability community during the 1970s.

Based on statements made and actions taken by Reagan when he was governor of California, the challenge to persons with disabilities should already have been evident when he entered the presidency. In his book *On Reagan: The Man and His Presidency,* Dugger (1983) described some of Reagan's positions as follows:

> Bothered by criticism that as governor he lacked compassion, he said in a letter: "I'm sure everyone feels sorry for the individual who has fallen by the wayside or who can't keep up in our competitive society, but my own compassion goes beyond that to those millions of unsung men and women who get up every morning, send the kids to school, go to work, try to keep up the payments on their house, pay exorbitant taxes to make possible compassion for the less fortunate, and as a result have to sacrifice many of their own desires and dreams and hopes. Government owes them something better than always finding a new way to make them share the fruit of their toil with others." (p. 293)

As governor of California, Reagan cut back Medi-Cal (California Medicaid) services to the 1.5 million eligible poor, which included many persons with disabilities. "California courts, holding that the cuts violated welfare statutes and were not required by shortages in available funds, canceled them" (Dugger, 1983, p. 293).

Given the above manifestation of the Reagan philosophy when he was governor of California, the following observations by Dugger (1983) on Reagan's first presidential term were not surprising:

> For two years, the administration made plans to reduce requirements that federal grant recipients accommodate the physically disabled in the construction of new facilities. Proposals of the Office of Management and Budget, leaked to the press, stated that in some cases the recipients of grants could weigh the cost of accommodation against the "social value" of the handicapped person concerned. Organizations of the disabled rallied and lobbied; the administration dropped the effort. (pp. 311–312)

> Social Security and Supplemental Security Income (SSI), the program for needy aged, blind, and disabled persons, pay benefits to about seven mil-

lion disabled citizens. Reagan's preelection hint that he would go after disability benefits materialized. (p. 60)

Under Reagan, then, the Social Security headquarters in Baltimore started
the scheduled review ten months early (two months after Reagan took
office) and began sending out about 30,000 cases a month for review. In
the first thirteen months, 175,000 people receiving disability benefits were
cut off—40 percent of the cases reviewed. Law required people thrown off
disability rolls to prove they had been wronged, so people who were too ill
or too poor to get a lawyer or gather the evidence themselves just lost out.
Representative Claude Pepper (D. Fla.) said that there was "a wholesale
purge of the disability rolls." (pp. 60–61)

During the early 1980s the U.S. Supreme Court handed down several
decisions that provided a conservative interpretation of civil rights provisions
of the disability legislation enacted during the 1970s. For example, in regard to
the Developmental Disabilities Assistance and Bill of Rights Act of 1976, the
U.S. Supreme Court in *Pennhurst State School and Hospital v. Halderman* "concluded that Congress did not intend in the bill of rights sections of the Act to
create enforceable obligations upon the states to provide habilitation in the least
restrictive setting" (U.S. Commission on Civil Rights, 1983, p. 61).

Although the 1980s were a conservative political period during which
the federal government was attempting to reduce its obligation as a provider
of benefit rights and enforcer of civil rights for persons with disabilities, some
laws directed at reducing unjust discrimination against persons with disabilities
were enacted during that period. Examples include the Voting Accessibility
for the Elderly and Handicapped Act of 1984, the Air Carrier Access Act of
1986, and the Fair Housing Act Amendments of 1988. The Voting Accessibility for the Elderly and Handicapped Act "required that registration and polling
places for federal elections be accessible to persons with disabilities" (West,
1991, p. 18). The Air Carrier Access Act of 1986 made clear that Congress
intended that Section 504 also pertain to the actions of air carriers operating at
federally funded airports. This act prohibited all carriers from discriminating
against persons with disabilities and gave the Department of Transportation the
responsibility for enforcement (West, 1991). By extending the federal protections against discrimination in housing to persons with disabilities, the Fair
Housing Act Amendments of 1988 became the first federal law to extend "the
antidiscrimination mandate for persons with disabilities ... into the private sector"—that is, to housing, which has been the recipient of no federal subsidies
or funds (West, 1991, p. 18). These amendments mandated standards for accessibility for all new multifamily housing construction and ensured persons with
disabilities the right "to adapt their dwelling place to meet their needs" (West,
1991, p. 19).

In addition to the above-noted antidiscrimination laws passed in the 1980s,
federal legislation passed in that decade was directed at increasing the potency

of vocational rehabilitation programs for persons with disabilities. This included the Rehabilitation Act Amendments of 1984 (already discussed in regard to client assistance programs), the Social Security Disability Amendments first enacted during the 1980s (to be discussed later in this chapter), and the Rehabilitation Act Amendments of 1986.

The 1986 Amendments to the Rehabilitation Act of 1973

While the Rehabilitation Act Amendments of 1986 (P.L. 99-506) continued in effect the provisions found in the Rehabilitation Act of 1973 and its subsequent pre-1986 amendments, it contained a number of new mandates. These mandates tended to reflect both advances in technology related to the needs of persons with disabilities and the need to either strengthen old programs or provide new programs directed at increasing the employability of persons with disabilities and facilitating their fuller participation in everyday life.

The 1986 amendments emphasized the need for state rehabilitation agencies to expand the use of rehabilitation engineering services to meet the needs of persons with disabilities. In addition to other required content, each state rehabilitation agency plan was required to describe how rehabilitation engineering services were to "be provided to assist an increasing number of individuals with handicaps" (A. Jones, 1988, p. 8). Consistent with that mandate, when appropriate, the Individualized Written Rehabilitation Program developed between the state agency rehabilitation counselor and the client with a disability was required to contain a "statement of the specific rehabilitation engineering services to be provided" (A. Jones, 1988, pp. 10–11). Rehabilitation engineering was defined in P.L. 99-506 as follows:

> the systematic application of technologies, engineering methodologies, or scientific principles to meet the needs of and address the barriers confronted by individuals with handicaps in areas which include education, rehabilitation, employment, transportation, independent living, and recreation.

P.L. 99-506 authorized, in Title VI, Part C, grants to assist states in developing "collaborative programs with appropriate public and nonprofit organizations for training and employment services leading to supported employment for individuals with severe handicaps" (A. Jones, 1988, p. 43). Supported employment was defined in P.L. 99-506 as

> competitive work in integrated settings ... (a) for individuals with severe handicaps for whom competitive employment has not traditionally occurred, or (b) for individuals for whom competitive employment has been interrupted or intermittent as a result of a severe disability, and who,

because of their handicap, need on-going support services to perform such work. Such term includes transitional employment for individuals with chronic mental illness. (Section 103)

That the intent of supported employment was to integrate persons with severe disabilities into regular places of employment can be observed in its definition in the 1984 Amendments to the Developmental Disabilities Assistance and Bill of Rights Act (P.L. 98-527):

> paid employment which (i) is for persons with developmental disabilities for whom competitive employment at or above the minimum wage is unlikely and who, because of their disabilities, need ongoing support to perform in a work setting; (ii) is conducted in a variety of settings, particularly work sites in which persons without disabilities are employed; and (iii) is supported by any activity needed to sustain paid work by persons with disabilities, including supervision, training, and transportation. (cited in Rusch & Hughes, 1990, p. 9)

Jenkins, Patterson, and Szymanski (1992) also spoke to the motivation for authorizing supported employment services in the Rehabilitation Act Amendments of 1986:

> Special educators and advocates for people with severe disabilities (especially people with mental retardation) had been concerned that traditional, workshop-based rehabilitation services did not provide suitable employment or opportunities for community integration.... Supported employment addressed many of these concerns with a new alternative that provided training and ongoing support for persons with severe disabilities employed in integrated settings. (pp. 12–13)

Rusch and Hughes (1990) described individuals eligible for supported employment services under P.L. 99-506 as "those who cannot function independently in employment without intensive on-going support services and require these on-going support services for the duration of their employment" (p. 9).

Finally, it is important to note that P.L. 99-506 mandated a gradual reduction in the federal share of support for the federal–state rehabilitation programs beginning in fiscal year 1989, when it was to be reduced to 79%. It was to be further reduced through fiscal year 1993 as follows: "78 percent for fiscal year 1990, 77 percent for fiscal year 1991, 76 percent for fiscal year 1992, and 75 percent for fiscal year 1993" (P.L. 99-506, Section 103).

Rehabilitation Act Amendments of 1992

Signed into law on October 29, 1992, by President George H. W. Bush, the Rehabilitation Act Amendments of 1992 (P.L. 102-569) had many philosophical and practical implications for the field of rehabilitation (Thompson, 1992). Important philosophical tenets in the amendments included a restatement of the priority placed on employment outcomes for people with disabilities, a continuing commitment to independent living services, and a strengthening of client involvement in the entire rehabilitation process, from individual program development to overall direction of agency programming. In regard to involvement in agency programming, the 1992 amendments required state rehabilitation agencies to establish Rehabilitation Advisory Councils to provide guidance in the development of agency policies and procedures. The majority of councilmembers must be people with disabilities who are members of the community at large or of disability service or advocacy organizations.

Section 105 of the amendments described the functions of the Rehabilitation Advisory Council. Serving in a reviewing, analyzing, and advising capacity to the state rehabilitation agency, the council addressed topics such as eligibility determination (including order of selection); the extent and scope of services; issues pertaining to administrative planning and program evaluation, which includes the evaluation of consumer satisfaction with agency services; and the establishment and coordination of a working relationship among the council, state agency, statewide Independent Living Council, and centers for independent living operating within the state. The role of the council was to ensure that people with disabilities achieved their rehabilitation goals and objectives consistent with the provisions of the Rehabilitation Act Amendments of 1992.

Client involvement, an important theme in the Rehabilitation Act of 1973, is promoted in the 1992 amendments in several ways. For example, the 1992 amendments indicate that the state rehabilitation agency's plan for vocational rehabilitation services must "describe the manner in which individuals with disabilities will be given choice and increased control in determining their vocational rehabilitation goals and objectives" (Section 101). Section 102 of the amendments stresses the importance of empowering people with disabilities to be involved in selecting their own career goals and developing their own written rehabilitation programs. As spelled out in Section 102, elements of the Individualized Written Rehabilitation Program (IWRP) must include

1. an employment objective of the individual, "consistent with the unique strengths, resources, priorities, concerns, abilities, and capabilities of the individual";
2. "a statement of the long-term rehabilitation goals based on the assessment for determining eligibility and vocational rehabilitation needs ..., including an assessment of career interests, for the individual, which goals shall, to the maximum extent appropriate, include placement in integrated settings";
3. "a statement of the intermediate rehabilitation objectives related to the attainment of such goals, determined through such assessment carried out in the most individu-

alized and integrated setting (consistent with the informed choice of the individual)";

4. "a statement of the specific vocational rehabilitation services to be provided, and the projected dates for the initiation and the anticipated duration of each such service";

5. "the entity or entities that will provide the vocational rehabilitation services and the process used to provide or procure such services"; and

6. "a statement by the individual, in the words of the individual (or, if appropriate, in the words of a parent, a family member, a guardian, an advocate, or an authorized representative, of the individual), describing how the individual was informed about and involved in choosing among alternative goals, objectives, services, entities providing such services, and methods used to provide or procure such services." (P.L. 93-112, Section 102)

Calling for annual reviews of IWRPs, the amendments stipulate that the client with a disability or his or her parents or guardians must participate in the review and may modify the program at that time. Modifications made in the program are not binding until the person seeking the services or a representative of the person (e.g., parent, family member, guardian, advocate, or other authorized representative) agrees to them and signs the new program.

As was the case prior to 1992, eligibility for rehabilitation services was based on two factors: (a) the presence of a physical or mental disability that presents a significant barrier to employment and (b) the assumption that the person with a disability could benefit from rehabilitation services. The state agency's role, therefore, was to serve all people with severe disabilities, unless the agency could clearly demonstrate that the person will not benefit. Although the amendments supported the position that the presence of a severe disability, coupled with the assumption that the person could benefit from services, was the basis for eligibility, they enabled each state to establish an order of selection. Based on criteria developed by each state, the order of selection specified the procedures by which agency resources were allocated among individuals on the caseload. The principle underlying the order-of-selection process was that those individuals who experience the greatest functional limitations as a result of disability would have first access to agency resources.

Other policy changes in the 1992 amendments have had a bearing on the eligibility process. Agencies had 60 days to respond to an application from a person with a disability for rehabilitation services and to determine whether the person is eligible or ineligible. In this determination, agencies could also use existing evaluation data—that is, information collected by other agencies or schools that is pertinent to the person's rehabilitation potential and needs. In cases where counselors were uncertain as to whether individuals would benefit from VR services, they could, with permission from clients, schedule an extended evaluation period of 18 months. During extended evaluations, counselors were expected to follow up on the client's progress every 90 days.

Strong endorsement of new service programs and of what were previously viewed as experimental service programs was apparent in the 1992 amendments as well. For example, Section 103 of the amendments mandated that state rehabilitation agencies provide (a) "transition services that promote or facilitate the accomplishment of long-term rehabilitation goals and intermediate rehabilitation objectives"; (b) "on-the-job or other related personal assistance services ... while an individual with a disability is receiving vocational rehabilitation services"; and (c) "supported employment services."

Meeting a real need of many people with severe disabilities, personal assistance services were available through rehabilitation programs for both on- and off-the-job needs (Nosek & Fuhrer, 1992). Personal assistance services are directed at enabling the person to better meet the demands of daily living activities. One or more individuals could provide such services, and the assistance was expected to increase the control that the individual with a disability has over his or her life. Research indicates that many people with severe disabilities prefer to acquire such services from a full-time assistant on a fee-for-service basis (Nosek, 1990). Describing personal assistance as a "linchpin service" for people with severe functional limitations, Nosek (1990, p. 5) stated that "productivity is impossible without it."

The 1992 amendments expanded access to rehabilitation services for individuals with disabilities through a renewed commitment to interagency collaboration. This mandate for collaboration was directed at encouraging written interagency agreements as exemplified in those between school systems and state rehabilitation agencies in the habilitation of students with disabilities. For example, Section 101 of the 1992 amendments stated that each state rehabilitation agency was mandated to enter

> into formal interagency cooperative agreement ... with education officials responsible for the provision of a free appropriate public education to students who are individuals with disabilities ... designed to (A) facilitate the development and accomplishment of (i) long-term rehabilitation goals; (ii) intermediate rehabilitation objectives; and (iii) goals and objectives related to enabling a student to live independently before the student leaves a school setting, to the extent ... [they] ... are included in an individualized education program of the student, ... [and] ... (B) facilitate the transition from the provision of a free appropriate public education under the responsibility of an educational agency to the provision of vocational rehabilitation services under the responsibility of the ... [state rehabilitation agency].

The 1992 amendments also authorized resources for the generation of new knowledge and strategies to address important barriers to the rehabilitation of people with disabilities. Research and development funds were available to examine such topics as transportation alternatives to meet the needs of people with disabilities who live in rural areas, strategies for improving the vocational placement outcomes of people with severe disabilities, demonstration of early intervention programs for working adults with disabilities, evaluation of programs to improve the transition from medical rehabilitation facilities to community independent living programs, model programs for providing personal care assistance, and procedures for increasing the participation in rehabilitation of underserved groups, such as people with disabilities from minority backgrounds.

Given that the ethnic and racial profile of the U.S. population is rapidly changing, ethnic and racial minorities have a disproportionately higher rate of disabling conditions, and minority populations have been traditionally underserved by state rehabilitation agencies, the 1992 amendments directed the Commissioner of the Rehabilitation Services Administration to develop a policy for preparing more people from minority groups for careers in rehabilitation in order to attempt to eliminate these inequities. That policy was implemented by providing financial support to many colleges and universities with minority enrollments of "at least 50% to prepare ... students for careers in vocational rehabilitation and other related service careers" (Rehabilitation Services Administration, 1993, p. 6).

One should also note that the 1992 amendments increased the federal share of support for the federal–state rehabilitation program beginning fiscal year 1993 from 75% to 78.7%. This increase suggested a clear continuation of the federal government's commitment to helping meet the rehabilitation needs of individuals with disabilities, who were defined in Section 7 of the amendments as including any individual who has a physical or mental impairment that constitutes a substantial impediment to employment and who can benefit in terms of an employment outcome from vocational rehabilitation services.

The Workforce Investment Act (WIA) and the Rehabilitation Act Amendments of 1998

Signed into law by President Clinton on August 7, 1998, the Workforce Investment Act (WIA; P.L. 105-220) represented a major change in vocational rehabilitation legislation. For the first time, the Rehabilitation Act Amendments were combined with enabling legislation for a number of other major federal workforce and employment programs. In fact, over 60 separate job training programs (e.g., Employment Services, Postsecondary Vocational Education, Veterans Employment and Training Programs, and Vocational Rehabilitation) were combined into three block grants in the areas of adult employment and training, disadvantaged youth employment and training, and adult education and family literacy. Overall, the purpose of the act was to meet the needs of America's employers for well-trained employees and America's citizens for improved access to employment services.

The concept of the "one-stop delivery system" or "one-stop shop" was the centerpiece of the WIA. Established in each local workforce investment area in a state, the one-stop shop or Workforce Development Center coordinates programs and services from federally funded vocational training programs in a single organizational entity. Hence, the one-stop shop had the distinct advantage of helping people with disabilities use a wide variety of workforce programs (The Arc, 1999). Services in one-stop shops may include vocational assessment, information on vocational training programs and employment projections, assistance in filing claims for unemployment insurance, and placement counseling and assistance (U.S. Workforce, 1999).

At the same time, the federal–state vocational rehabilitation (VR) program retained its independent identity via Title IV of the WIA (i.e., the 1998 Amendments to the Rehabilitation Act of 1973). Reinforcing themes from rehabilitation legislation from 1973 to 1992, the 1998 amendments contained strong emphases on comprehensive vocational and independent living rehabilitation services, employment outcomes, supported employment, and client assistance projects. In addition to these traditional priorities, the amendments also called for increased client control of the vocational planning process, improved linkages between vocational rehabilitation and other federal workforce programs, expanded access to services, outreach to traditionally underserved populations, and service provision by qualified personnel. Title IV also continued the federal share of funding at 78.7%, which had been set by the 1992 amendments.

Increased Client Control of the Vocational Planning Process

Continuing the "informed choice" initiatives of prior rehabilitation legislation, the Rehabilitation Act Amendments of 1998 put the client squarely in control of the Individualized Plan for Employment (IPE), formerly referred to as the Individualized Written Rehabilitation Program (IWRP). The 1998 amendments mandated far more than client sign-off or even client coauthorship of vocational plans. People with disabilities receiving vocational rehabilitation services had the right to develop some or all of their vocational plans with or without input from the rehabilitation counselor (The Arc, 1999). In an analysis of this change, the United Cerebral Palsy Association (1999) described the role of the counselor as one of "facilitator," rather than "developer," of the vocational plan. In facilitating plan development, counselors were directed to use services and settings that were in the "most integrated setting appropriate" (PACER Center, 1999, p. 1).

Improved Linkages Between Vocational Rehabilitation and Other Federal Workforce Programs

The Workforce Investment Act created an opportunity for unprecedented access to employment services for people with disabilities. This "improved linkages" mandate in the 1998 amendments was the impetus for both coordination and collaboration among workforce programs. According to the United Cerebral Palsy Association (1999), this language in the WIA meant that people with disabilities would be served "throughout the entire State workforce system, not only through the State VR program" (p. 3). In the amendments, federal workforce programs such as VR were also required to establish interagency agreements with public entities beyond the purview of the WIA, such as postsecondary educational institutions. At the same time, organizations specifically named in the WIA were expected to develop cooperative agreements to improve the coordination of their services to all citizens. Cooperative agreements could address such activities as "staff training, technical assistance regarding vocational rehabilitation services and eligibility, common customer service procedures such as intake and human services hot lines, common dispute resolution procedures, and electronic links to share employment statistics and employment opportunities" (United Cerebral Palsy Association, 1999, p. 3).

Expanded Access to Services

The 1998 Rehabilitation Act Amendments enumerated several ways that VR would participate in expanding services to people with disabilities. First, VR became an active participant in developing and implementing cooperative agreements with agencies covered by and related to the WIA. Second, VR established formal linkages and roles with the one-stop service delivery settings that brought together multiple programs serving the employment development needs of all citizens. Third, VR addressed expansion of services through its own internal procedures. Examples included greater efforts by VR agencies to perform the information and referral function for individuals with disabilities who might not receive a high priority for services in states operating under order of selection standards. As The Arc (1999) noted, this provision increased the probability that people with disabilities who were not severely disabled, and thus who did not receive a high priority for "paid-for" services, would connect with the "generic workforce investment system" for help finding a job or securing vocational training (p. 4). Expanded options for employment and services to achieve those options constituted another example of broadening service access. The 1998 amendments placed a strong emphasis on vocational outcomes involving telecommuting, self-employment, and small business options, which included the availability of technical consultation services in support of those objectives (PACER Center, 1999).

Outreach to Traditionally Underserved Populations

Recognizing the growing diversity of America's population, Title IV of the WIA stressed the need for increased outreach efforts to minorities. These outreach efforts addressed both serving a clientele and hiring a professional workforce consistent with the racial and ethnic composition of the nation. The 1998 Rehabilitation Act Amendments noted that the number of individuals from minority backgrounds is increasing rapidly and that this group experiences a higher disability rate than the majority population.

Service Provision by Qualified Personnel

The Rehabilitation Act Amendments of 1998 reiterated the importance of moving into the future with services from qualified rehabilitation providers. Consistent with the 1992 amendments, rehabilitation legislation in 1998 stressed the importance of both preservice and in-service training. In discussing the goals of comprehensive personnel development, the 1998 amendments referred to the concept of the "qualified vocational rehabilitation counselor." Criteria for such a designation should include the capacity to demonstrate knowledge and skills acquired by earning a master's degree in rehabilitation and passing a professional certification examination such as that administered for the title of Certified Rehabilitation Counselor (CRC).

Numerous other recommendations were made in the 1998 amendments for innovations in service provision that would result in improved outcomes for people with disabilities. For example, the rehabilitation counselor's role in transition planning for students with disabilities continued, with the expectation that much of that planning would be contained in the student's Individualized Education Program (IEP) so that the student did not need to develop a separate Individualized Plan for Employment (IPE). In other provisions of the amendments, VR counselors could involve people with severe disabilities in real work settings to determine their vocational readiness, as well as continue services to individuals in supported employment who were not receiving minimum wage but were projected to do so as part of their IPE (PACER Center, 1999). With respect to assessment and eligibility determination, the amendments stressed the concept of *presumptive eligibility*; thus, the counselor had the burden of documenting that a person was not eligible for services. Presumptive eligibility applied also in the case of Supplemental Security Income (SSI) and Social Security Disability Insurance (SSDI) recipients who were considered as having passed a more stringent eligibility test than the one required by the federal–state vocational rehabilitation program (The Arc, 1999, p. 4). The subject of heated debate during the early years of the 21st century, provisions of the Workforce Investment Act and Title IV of the act continue to guide the delivery of VR services in the United States.

Social Security Disability Legislation: Promoting Fuller Participation in Employment

The Social Security Disability Insurance (SSDI) program (Title II of the Social Security Act) was established in 1954 to provide eligible persons with disabilities (i.e., insured workers who have been judged to be "totally and permanently disabled") with monthly income benefits and Medicare insurance (for the spouse and dependent children, including disabled adult children, as well as the worker with a disability) (Shrey, Bangs, Mark, Hursh, & Kues, 1991; Walls, Dowler, & Fullmer, 1990, pp. 257–258). The SSDI program defines a disabled "adult child" beneficiary as an individual age 18 years or older who was "disabled before age twenty-two, and is the son or daughter of [a] covered former worker who is disabled, retired, or deceased" (Walls et al., 1990, p. 258).

To be eligible for SSDI benefits, a person must (a) "have worked and paid Social Security taxes ... for enough years to be covered under Social Security; some of the taxes must have been paid in recent years"; (b) "be considered medically disabled"; and (c) "not be working or working but earning less than the substantial gainful activity level" (Social Security Administration, 1991, pp. 5, 9) (i.e., in 2006, less than $860 per month for beneficiaries who are not blind and $1,450 per month for SSDI beneficiaries who are blind) for at least 5 months after onset of disability. Increases in substantial gainful activity (SGA) level occur regularly and are paced with the rising cost of living (Sheldon & Trach, 1998). In 1999, about 4.7 million workers with disabilities and their dependents received SSDI benefits. The average SSDI monthly payment was $773 for an individual beneficiary, placing the person's income at about the poverty level (Social Security Administration, 1999). By 2005 the number of workers with disabilities and their dependents receiving benefits under SSDI had risen to 8.3 million (Social Security Administration, 2006a), an increase that clearly illustrates the mounting pressure on Social Security Trust Fund resources.

Somewhat counter to its income maintenance orientation for persons who have been judged as incapable of working due to their disability, the SSDI program is also legislatively mandated to attempt, through referral for vocational rehabilitation (VR) services, to rehabilitate as many persons on the SSDI rolls "as possible and return them to the work force" (Walls et al., 1990). Although the maintenance and VR philosophies have coexisted for many years in the SSDI program, the latter has tended to have a very minimal effect. One major reason is that only 10% to 15% of all beneficiaries "are thought to be realistic prospects for rehabilitation" (Walls et al., 1990, p. 258). In addition, research has shown that a very small percentage of those who are seen as feasible for VR leave the SSDI rolls and return to work (Shrey et al., 1991), partly because many people considered feasible for VR appear to lack incentives for employment (Walls et al., 1990). Their low motivation may be due to their having had to prove that they cannot work in order to get on the SSDI rolls, their fear of losing much-needed financial and medical benefits if suspected of having potential to work, and their uncertainty of their ability to hold a job for a long period of time.

The Social Security Administration has recognized that fear of loss of benefits creates a major disincentive for SSDI beneficiaries to try to return to work (Sheldon, 2002). Consequently, the Social Security Administration attempted to reduce that disincentive for SSDI beneficiaries and thereby encourage employment participation by developing "specific Work Incentives under the Social Security Disability Amendments of 1980 and subsequent revisions" (e.g., 1986, 1989, 1990) (Shrey et al., 1991, p. 258) and via the Ticket to Work and Work Incentives Improvement Act of 1999 (discussed later in this chapter). Those work incentives are (a) a trial work period, (b) impairment-related work expenses, (c) an extended period of eligibility, and (d) continuation of Medicare coverage. Each is described below.

The Trial Work Period

The trial work period covers a total of 9 months (not necessarily consecutive) during which SSDI beneficiaries can try working or running a business without their disability benefits being affected. During the 9-month trial period, the beneficiary continues to receive a benefit check every month no matter how high earnings are (Sheldon, 2002). If the work during the trial period does not meet the earnings criteria for "substantial gainful activity, SSDI benefits continue" (Social Security Administration, 1991, p. 31). If, however, at the end of that trial work period the individual is considered to be able to work (i.e., the work done during that trial period met the earning criteria for SGA), cash benefits will automatically continue for 3 more months (a grace period), after which the individual will still be entitled to an SSDI check in any month in a subsequent 33-month period during which wages are at or below the SGA level (Sheldon, 2002). The 36-month period following the 9-month trial work period is referred to as an extended period of eligibility.

Impairment-Related Work Expenses

Impairment-related work expenses comprise items and services needed by the SSDI beneficiary in order to work. In figuring substantial gainful activity during the trial work period, one can deduct these expenses from earnings when (a) "the cost of the item or service is paid by the person with the disability"; (b) "the person has not been, nor will be, reimbursed for the expense"; (c) "the expense enables a person to work"; (d) "the person, because of a severe physical or mental impairment, needs the item or service for which the expense is incurred in order to work"; and (e) "the expense is reasonable—that is, it represents the standard charge for the item or service in the person's community"

(Social Security Administration, 1991, pp. 19–20). Examples of expenses likely to be deductible are (a) attendant care services performed to help the person prepare for work (e.g., bathing, dressing, cooking, eating) or get to and from work; (b) "the cost of structural or operational modifications to a vehicle, which the person needs in order to drive to work or be driven to work, even if the vehicle is also used for non-work purposes"; and (c) "expenses for a person who serves as a reader for a visually impaired person" (Social Security Administration, 1991, pp. 21–23).

Extended Period of Eligibility

As noted above, for a consecutive 36-month period beginning at the end of the trial work period, cash benefits are "reinstated for any month the person does not work at the SGA (substantial gainful activity) level" (Social Security Administration, 1995, p. 27). This is referred to as a reentitlement period, during which eligibility for monthly SSDI benefits can be reestablished "without either a new application for benefits or an application for expedited reinstatement, if work activity ceases or is significantly diminished" (Sheldon, 2002, p. 13).

Continuation of Medicare Coverage

For a period of 93 months following the trial work period, during which time a person is engaging in substantial gainful activity, despite a continuing disability, SSDI beneficiaries can continue to receive Medicare medical insurance coverage. Therefore, although the SSDI beneficiary may not receive SSDI cash benefits due to being employed during this time period, the continuation of health insurance is still guaranteed (Sheldon, 2002).

Other Important Social Security Legislation

In 1972 the Social Security Administration made provisions for financial support and medical assistance for individuals with disabilities with low incomes and little or no coverage through SSDI (Crimando & Riggar, 1996). Financed through the general funds of the U.S. Treasury, this important source of support is referred to as the Supplemental Security Income program, or SSI (Title XVI). Available for people who are blind or disabled, SSI requires both income and resource tests. In addition to financial assistance, SSI provides medical insurance through Medicaid. SSDI and SSI have many of the same work incentives that are designed to encourage recipients to attempt a return to work as soon as feasible. Examples of the types of work incentives available through SSI include expedited return to benefits following an unsuccessful attempt to return to work, impairment-related work expenses, the Plan for Achieving

Self-Support (PASS Plan), and continued medical insurance through a Medic-aid buy-in even if working (Roessler, 2002).

The Ticket to Work and Work Incentives Improvement Act of 1999 (TWWIIA)

On December 17, 1999, President William Clinton officially signed the Ticket to Work and Work Incentives Improvement Act into law. Known as TWWIIA, this major piece of Social Security legislation was intended to further encourage individuals receiving SSDI or SSI to return to work, thereby relieving the Social Security Administration (SSA) of some of its financial obligations under SSDI and SSI. Incentive-oriented provisions in the legislation made it possible for individuals to retain their medical insurance and partial financial benefits even if they returned to work. Projections regarding the long-term availability of disability benefits provided by the Social Security Administration substantiated the need to strengthen return-to-work incentives in order to encourage individuals to leave the benefit rolls.

The primary mechanism for enabling more individuals to resume work is the Ticket to Work (TTW), which is a major component of the SSA Ticket to Work and Self-Sufficiency Program (Kriegal, O'Mara, & West, 2003; Silverstein, 2001). The ticket program is entirely voluntary, and individuals may choose their own vendor for rehabilitation services. Referred to as members of the Employment Network or ENs, these vendors may include both public and private providers such as the federal–state rehabilitation program or private rehabilitation companies or counselors. SSA contracted with MAXIMUS, Inc., to screen potential providers and to oversee the quality of services provided. These services are specified in an Individual Work Plan developed between the ticket holder and the EN (McManus, 2001). Payments to the ENs for their services are based on one of two methods: either (a) payment for accomplishing certain program milestones, such as completion of 3 or 6 months of employment, or (b) payment for securing and holding employment for a 60-month period, at which time the EN would receive compensation at the rate of 40% of the average monthly SSDI or SSI benefit for every month the person did not receive benefits due to earnings from work.

The rationale for TWWIIA was self-evident; previously, work incentive initiatives to improve return-to-work rates for people with SSA benefits provided insufficient protection to beneficiaries in regard to loss of financial benefits, continuation of medical insurance, and continuation of program eligibility (Marini & Reid, 2001).

According to research, prior attempts to encourage work had failed to include sufficient incentives (Shrey et al., 1991). Marini and Reid (2001) empirically demonstrated this fact in evaluations of SSA return-to-work programs implemented prior to the TWWIIA. In their evaluation of one such program, they found that only .3% of the individuals (5 of approximately 1,446) contacted for return-to-work services ever secured employment. According to the U.S. General Accounting Office in 1997, SSA could save approximately $3 billion if only 1% of those receiving SSI or SSDI benefits returned to work. Other information provides a strong rationale for the implementation of return-to-work programs. For example, in a reanalysis of data from SSDI beneficiaries completed in 1995, Reno (2004) reported that the rate of returning to work could be as high as 6.2% when the sample included only those individuals who were living and not on retirement rolls. Others have been even more optimistic regarding return-to-work potential. Mead (2004) estimated that as many as 20% of eligible ticket holders have the potential to return to work under improved work incentives.

To realize improved rates of employment, SSA must overcome certain real and perceived barriers in the minds of people receiving assistance through SSDI or SSI. These barriers pertain to the very incentive conditions mentioned previously that consumers apparently perceived as insufficient for risking removal from the SSDI or SSI roles. Recognizing this fact, SSA implemented through TWWIIA a new "package" of work incentives to combine with its existing ones (the result of which has also been somewhat described in the previous section). For example, SSA continued to offer a 9-month trial work period during which a person's benefits are not affected regardless of the amount of money earned. The trial work period is followed by a 3-month grace period, which, in effect, provides individuals with a 12-month period in which their benefits are not affected by level of earnings. In addition, TWWIIA provisions for SSDI beneficiaries and SSI recipients contain extended medical coverage through Medicare (up to 93 months following the trial work period) or Medicaid (more liberal buy-in options) even if the person began working. These provisions also call for an expedited reinstatement of benefits should the work attempt fail and the guarantee that the person will not have a review of his or her disability status during the time of ticket use (i.e., a continuing disability review). Individuals can retain more of their financial benefits by subtracting impairment-related work expenses from earned income or by reducing earned income by placing it in a "set-aside" account to be used for work-related expenses for education or training. To communicate these new benefits to consumers and to overcome their fears about losing eligibility, financial support, and medical insurance, SSA funded new programs at the state level for advocacy and protection services and for benefits planning, assistance, and outreach counseling (Roessler, 2002; Silverstein, 2001).

Initial evaluations of the Ticket to Work program indicate that ticket utilization has lagged behind hoped-for outcomes for several reasons. First, only a small number of individuals with disabilities connected with Employment Networks in their local communities. For example, only 36% of the ENs in 2004 had accepted tickets (386 of 1,064 ENs) (Ticket to Work and Work Incentives Advisory Panel, 2004), and these service providers only served a limited number of clients (Ticket to Work and Work Incentives Advisory Panel, 2003). Second, most of those individuals seeking to assign tickets continued to use the federal–state rehabilitation program. For example, 86% of the ticket holders utilized the federal–state rehabilitation program in 2003 (Ticket to Work Advisory Panel, 2003), a pattern that had not changed through February 2006, when only 8,928 tickets out of 121,267 had been assigned to ENs outside the federal–state rehabilitation system (Social Security Administration, 2006b).

Major Initiatives for the 21st Century

As the first decade of the 21st century draws to a close, the federal–state rehabilitation system finds itself at a crossroads in terms of support. This first decade of the century has been one of tenuous economic conditions in the nation stemming in part from significant tax cuts, the ongoing costs of the Iraq war effort, rising energy costs, and a growing national deficit. For the foreseeable future, power struggles might occur in Congress between those advocating cuts in health and human service programs and those advocating government's obligation to individuals in need. The impact of the country's financial position was easily seen in debates over the proposed $7 billion budget cuts for health and human service programs revealed in comparisons between 2005 and 2007 levels.

Other significant historical events merit mention. For example, as of 2006, the reauthorization of the 1998 Amendments to the Rehabilitation Act (Title IV), which were contained in the Workforce Investment Act (WIA), has been delayed long past what policymakers and planners in rehabilitation expected. Arguments have continued as to whether rehabilitation was simply another workforce training program that should be blended in with similar types of programs in the U.S. Department of Labor. Supporters of rehabilitation have feared that the historic mandates for improving services for people with disabilities would be weakened as a result and that the hard-won separate identity of the program would be lost via consolidation in other workforce programs and services included in the WIA. Similarly, supporters of rehabilitation have reacted with concern regarding rumors that funding for rehabilitation might be combined into block grants to the states under the control of governors' offices. In such a case, state legislators might place lower priorities on disability services than on other human service initiatives at the state level. Consequently, advocacy continues among supporters of the federal–state rehabilitation program for the program's integrity and identity.

Many other challenges remain, and no challenge is greater than the need to improve the employment outcomes of people with disabilities. Statistics reported by the National Organization on Disability (1998, 2002, 2004) clearly indicate the gravity of the situation. For the past 20 years, approximately two out of every three adults with disabilities have been unemployed, with unemployment rates ranging from 65% to 71%. Certainly, these statistics bear witness to the need to emphasize employment as the ultimate outcome of rehabilitation services, a theme strongly underscored in the 1992 Amendments to the Rehabilitation Act and in Title IV of the WIA.

The hoped-for improvement in rates of employment for people with disabilities is not unfounded. Experts in human resource management (Schramm & Burke, 2004) project a significant labor shortage in the coming years, which could work to the advantage of people with disabilities. Further, political efforts such the New Freedom Initiative of the Bush administration and protections against discrimination in the Americans with Disabilities Act (ADA), if they result in greater legislative support, have the potential to create conditions conducive to the employment of people with disabilities (Batavia & Schriner, 2001; Blanck, 2004; D. Cohen & Shields, 2005).

At the same time, many familiar barriers stand in the way of achieving improved employment outcomes for people with disabilities in the 21st century. These long-standing physical and attitudinal barriers reflect the need for continued vigilance and effort on the part of rehabilitation professionals. Examples of some of the negative forces that must be overcome include stereotypes and fears among coworkers regarding disability and chronic illness, erroneous employer opinions about the work potential of people with disabilities, resistance to the provision of reasonable accommodations, the lack of adequate health insurance and financial and emotional support for people with disabilities to remain at work, and perceived and real work disincentives in federal benefit programs (Blanck, Schur, Kruse, Schwochau, & Song, 2003; Hernandez, Keys, & Balcazar, 2000; Roessler, Rumrill, et al., 2003; Schur, Kruse, & Blanck, 2005). The agenda is set.

Concluding Statement

As the 1970s approached, the Golden Era of Rehabilitation waned. Suddenly, rehabilitation programs were in competition with many other government-funded programs for diminishing resources. At the same time, like African Americans and women had done in the 1960s, persons with disabilities stood ready to fight for their equal right to life, liberty, and the pursuit of happiness. They were no longer willing to accept "second-class citizenship." Disability consumer groups played a significant role in campaigning for legislation that emphasized vocational rehabilitation and independent living services, consumer involvement in rehabilitation service planning, service provider accountability, relevant rehabilitation research, and the promotion of the civil rights of persons with disabilities.

The 1970s and early 1980s also saw increased interest in removing environmental barriers to the full participation of persons with disabilities in American society. No longer did the rehabilitation movement focus almost entirely on changing the person with a disability. Emphasis was also placed on breaking down those societal barriers that could be more handicapping to the person with a disability than the disability itself. However, by the end of the 1980s, a balance had yet to be achieved between progress made in increasing the functional capacity of persons with disabilities and progress in the environmental barriers area. Norman Acton (1982), secretary general of Rehabilitation International, elaborated on this point:

> Magnificent achievements have been recorded in surgery, in physical medicine, in prosthetics and orthotics, in speech therapy and in other interventions upon the impairment; progress in ensuring full participation in the environments of living and learning and working has been less satisfactory. Thanks to the dedication and skill of the professions, a quadriplegic person can operate with one breath a motorized wheelchair or other complicated mechanism. But we have not been able to guarantee the social integration of that person. (p. 146)

The current environmental design, which contains many barriers to the full participation of persons with disabilities in society, "has not been decreed by natural law" (Hahn, 1985b, p. 297). Environments can be modified to be "friendlier" to all members of society, including those with functional limitations. This "is not a utopian vision" (Hahn, 1985b, p. 297). Public policy had moved to some extent in this direction through laws such as the Rehabilitation Act of 1973 and its amendments, the Education for All Handicapped Children Act of 1975 and its amendments, the Architectural Barriers Act of 1968 and its amendments, the Developmental Disabilities Assistance and Bill of Rights Act of 1976, and selected transportation legislation. Unfortunately, by the end of the 1980s, the "attack" had still been piecemeal rather than comprehensive. The result was "token" progress in the removal of environmental barriers. While not ideal, public policy in the 1970s and 1980s appeared to be more positive in regard to establishing programs to provide "medical care, financial support, and vocational skills" to persons with disabilities (Hahn, 1985b, p. 295). Therefore, in the late 1980s society appeared more willing to provide services to maintain or change persons with a disability than to significantly change the environment that they must negotiate. This tended to deny the reality that extent of limitation for persons with disability is a product of the interaction between the characteristics of the person and the characteristics of the environment.

While having an obvious impact on the furthering of disability rights, the work of the disability consumer group movement in that regard was far from finished by the end of the 1980s. Hahn (1985a) saw the achievements of the disability consumer group movement as having been limited by its inability "to organize a political constituency comparable to the power of other minorities" (p. 59). Hahn (1985a) attributed the lack of sufficient unity in the disability consumer group movement "to the impact of a medical model that encourages both nondisabled and disabled observers to focus their attention on separate diagnostic categories rather than on the generic characteristics of disability" (p. 59). Hahn (1985a) suggested a unifying concept:

> From a perspective that stresses the reactions evoked by visible or identifiable disabilities rather than personal limitations, persons with disabilities

might be able to recognize the similar experiences which unite them rather than the functional differences which divide them ... to the extent that people with various types of disabilities can begin to realize that their problems stem from prejudice and discrimination rather than from functional limitations, they may develop a sense of cohesion that could provide the foundation for a powerful and growing political movement. (p. 59)

Although its passage in 1990 places the Americans with Disabilities Act (ADA) within the current history period of this chapter, its significance as a major legislative initiative for the removal of environmental barriers to the full participation of persons with disabilities in society and the comprehensiveness of its coverage in that regard warrant a separate chapter. Therefore, the ADA is comprehensively discussed in the next chapter.

Clearly, the 21st century begins with a stronger emphasis than ever on improving the employment outcomes of people with disabilities as well as the control that people with disabilities exert over their own vocational planning. Moreover, this emphasis on employment services and outcomes involves contributions from a wide range of federal workforce programs, rather than expecting a single agency to meet the employment needs of people with disabilities, with the proviso being that vocational rehabilitation service must retain its own unique and individual identity. Moreover, people with disabilities and rehabilitation professionals and advocates must unite to achieve goals for the 21st century that were very much a part of the agenda for rehabilitation at the turn of the century. These goals include improving the employment rate of people with disabilities to that of the general population; expanding health care coverage for people with disabilities; and implementing tax incentives that facilitate return to work for people with disabilities through support for assistive technology, accessible transportation, and personal assistance services (F. Kirk, 1999; National Organization on Disability, 2004).

Chapter 3

The Americans with Disabilities Act: Major Mandates and Ambiguities

Political debate in the United States preceding all major disability legislation in the 20th and 21st centuries has demonstrated a conflict between "the rhetoric of rights" and "the reality of economics" (E. D. Berkowitz, 1992, p. 2). This conflict between political liberals and fiscal conservatives in the legislative process has tended to be resolved in favor of establishing beneficial programs for persons with disabilities. That outcome has resulted from the ability of liberals, who see such programs as necessary social services, to portray their implementation as long-range cost-saving actions. The federal–state rehabilitation program, which dates back to 1920 and which has been supported by both political groups, provides a classic example. It has been regarded as "a vitally needed social service" by liberals and as "an investment in the productivity of persons with disabilities" by conservatives (E. D. Berkowitz, 1992, p. 4).

The Americans with Disabilities Act of 1990 (ADA; P.L. 101-336) broke that historical tradition because it was passed in spite of many conservative politicians and businesspeople seeing it as increasing rather than decreasing costs. In fact, instead of ameliorating the "conflict between the rhetoric of rights and the reality of economics," the political interaction that preceded the passage of the ADA seemed to exacerbate it (E. D. Berkowitz, 1992, p. 7).

Why, then, did the ADA pass in spite of being perceived as a very costly piece of legislation? First, during the period when the ADA was being drafted and considered for passage, Congress was exposed to a staggering amount of evidence on the effect of unjust discrimination on the lives of people with disabilities and on the economy of the country (Mikochik, 1991). Second, by not creating new government programs but instead mandating private actions to equalize opportunities for persons with disabilities, the law did not result in additional government spending. Third, it was championed by key senators such as Tom Harkin, Lowell Weicker, and Ted Kennedy, all of whom have a family member with a disability. Fourth, President George H. W. Bush backed the ADA (E. D. Berkowitz, 1992). Fifth, a legislative foundation for the ADA was laid by several earlier major federal antidiscrimination/disability rights laws directed at promoting equal opportunity, economic self-sufficiency, and full participation in society for persons with disabilities. These laws included the Architectural Barriers Act of 1968, the Urban Mass Transportation Act Amendments of 1970, Title V of the Rehabilitation Act of 1973, the Education for All Handicapped Children Act of 1975 (currently titled the Individuals with Disabilities Education Improvement Act), the Developmental Disabilities Assistance and Bill of Rights Act of 1975, the Civil Rights of Institutionalized Persons Act of 1980, the Voting Accessibility for the Elderly and Handicapped Act of 1984, the Air Carriers Access Act of 1986, and the Fair Housing Act Amendments of 1988 (Colker, 2005). Both individually and in combination, they created a strong precedent in the public policy on disability for the passage of the ADA (Pfeiffer & Finn, 1997; West, 1991). Sixth, support for the ADA was obtained from the results of the Louis Harris survey in 1986 of 1,000 Americans with disabilities. Those results suggested that the disability community considered the above-noted antidiscrimination/disability rights laws to have helped expand their opportunities. However, 75% of the survey's respondents also saw a need to strengthen federal antidiscrimination laws (West, 1991). The latter was compatible with the survey data documenting the limited participation of persons with disability in many major activities of society (Taylor, Kagay, & Leichenko, 1986). It was also compatible with unemployment statistics in the 1970s and 1980s, which showed a decline from 1970 to 1988 in the percentage of persons with disabilities employed from 41% to 33%. Furthermore, the August 1989 Census Bureau report indicated "that the income of people with disabilities dropped—for men by as much as 13% and for women by as much as 7%—from 1981 to 1988" (L. Smart, 1990, p. 20).

Of the preceding antidiscrimination legislation, Section 504 of the Rehabilitation Act of 1973 most closely approximated the content of the ADA. On the basis of an analysis of 10 years of enforcement of that antidiscrimination legislation, B. P. Tucker (1990) concluded that while it "unlocked the door for handicapped persons to enter the mainstream of society, it ... failed in its goal of opening that door wide" (p. 915). The realization in the late 1980s that the opportunities for persons with disabilities were still greatly limited also helped provide a stimulus for the passage of the ADA.

As was noted above, while the ADA was being drafted, Congress collected a tremendous amount of information on the ways that persons with disabilities were segregated and discriminated against in our society, through research such as the 1986 survey of Americans with disabilities by Louis Harris and Associates (Taylor et al., 1986). During that period, testimony was also obtained on the then proposed ADA at 11 public hearings by the House of Representatives and at three Senate hearings. In addition, much information pertaining to the need for the ADA was revealed at public forums held in every state (T. M. Cook, 1991). On the basis of vast amounts of testimony on the experiences of persons with disabilities in American society, Congress concluded the following in one of the opening sections (42 U.S.C. § 12101) of the ADA:

1. Some 43,000,000 Americans have one or more physical or mental disabilities, and this number is increasing as the population as a whole is growing older;
2. historically, society has tended to isolate and segregate individuals with disabilities, and, despite some improvements, such forms of discrimination against individuals with disabilities continue to be a serious and pervasive social problem;
3. discrimination against individuals with disabilities persists in such critical areas as employment, housing, public accommodations, education, transportation, communication, recreation, institutionalization, health services, voting, and access to public services;
4. unlike individuals who have experienced discrimination on the basis of race, color, sex, national origin, religion, or age, individuals who have experienced discrimination on the basis of disability have often had no legal recourse to redress such discrimination;

5. individuals with disabilities continually encounter various forms of discrimination, including outright intentional exclusion, the discriminatory effects of architectural, transportation, and communication barriers, overprotective rules and policies, failure to make modifications to existing facilities and practices, exclusionary qualification standards and criteria, segregation, and relegation to lesser services, programs, activities, benefits, jobs, or other opportunities;

6. census data, national polls, and other studies have documented that people with disabilities, as a group, occupy an inferior status in our society, and are severely disadvantaged socially, vocationally, economically, and educationally;

7. individuals with disabilities are a discrete and insular minority who have been faced with restrictions and limitations, subjected to a history of purposeful unequal treatment, and relegated to a position of political powerlessness in our society, based on characteristics that are beyond the control of such individuals and resulting from stereotypic assumptions not truly indicative of the individual ability of such individuals to participate in, and contribute to, society;

8. the Nation's proper goals regarding individuals with disabilities are to assure equality of opportunity, full participation, independent living, and economic self-sufficiency for such individuals; and

9. the continuing existence of unfair and unnecessary discrimination and prejudice denies people with disabilities the opportunity to compete on an equal basis and to pursue those opportunities for which our free society is justifiably famous, and costs the United States billions of dollars in unnecessary expenses resulting from dependency and nonproductivity.

Based on those conclusions, in that same opening section (42 U.S.C. § 12101), Congress provided the following clear set of purposes for the ADA:

1. to provide a clear and comprehensive national mandate for the elimination of discrimination against individuals with disabilities;

2. to provide clear, strong, consistent, enforceable standards addressing discrimination against individuals with disabilities;

3. to ensure that the Federal Government plays a central role in enforcing the standards established in this Act on behalf of individuals with disabilities; and

4. to invoke the sweep of congressional authority, including the power to enforce the Fourteenth Amendment and to regulate commerce, in order to address the major areas of discrimination faced day-to-day by people with disabilities.

Disability Defined Under the ADA

It has been estimated that more than 900 disabilities are covered by the ADA (L. Davis, 1994). *Disability* under the ADA is defined in the same three-pronged manner as has been the case for Section 504 of the Rehabilitation Act since 1974: (a) "a physical or mental impairment that substantially limits one or more of the major life activities of such individual; (b) a record of such an impairment; or (c) being regarded as having such an impairment" (Colker, 2005, p. 101). The definition of *disability* under the ADA is highly significant because whether an individual has the rights to the ADA's protections in the legal system is a factual question (i.e., Does the person have a disability that fits the ADA's definition of disability?) that must be addressed in each individual court case (897 F. Supp. 423). According to Bruyére (2000),

> The definition of *disability* is considered one of the more contentious aspects of disability law and sets the ADA apart from previous civil rights legislation.... Civil rights litigation based on race or gender discrimination seldom starts out with a challenge regarding whether the complainant is really a member of a racial minority or of a specific gender. Cases brought under the ADA, however, often raise questions about whether the claimant is eligible to be covered by the protective umbrella of the statute. This question becomes particularly significant when the disability is invisible or is an impairment that requires more refined diagnostic assessment, such as psychiatric disability. In these cases, the determination of whether a claimant is protected may require documentation of the level of impairment that exists and whether there is a substantial impact on the person's major life functions. (p. 22)

Major life activities referred to under the definition of disability in the ADA include walking, sitting, seeing, hearing, standing, breathing, reaching, learning, speaking, concentrating, sleeping, performing manual tasks, working, lifting, caring for oneself, and interacting with others (Edmonds, 2002; U.S. Equal Employment Opportunity Commission [EEOC], 1996; "What Is a Disability?," 1997). As indicated in the definition, a person has to have a physical or mental impairment that substantially limits one or more of these major life activities. For purposes of the ADA, "substantially limits" indicates either an inability to perform the major life activity or a significant restriction

> as to the condition, manner, or duration under which an individual can perform a particular major life activity as compared to the condition, manner or duration under which the average person in the general population can perform the same major life activity. (U.S. EEOC, 1996, p. B-9)

Therefore, a person who could walk for only "very brief periods of time would be substantially limited in the major life activity of walking" (Golden, Kilb, & Mayerson, 1994, p. 11). Golden et al. (1994) clarified this point with the following examples:

> An individual who had once been able to walk at an extraordinary speed would not be substantially limited in the major life activity of walking if, as a result of a physical impairment, he was only able to walk at an average speed, or even at a moderately below average speed. As another example, if an individual experienced severe leg cramps after walking ten miles, the individual is not substantially limited in the major life activity of walking because the average member of the general population is likely to experience severe leg cramps after walking ten miles. On the other hand, the individual who experiences severe leg cramps after walking fifty yards is substantially limited because the average member of the general population would be able to walk that distance without experiencing severe leg cramps. (pp. 11–12)

As noted previously, working is considered a major life activity under the ADA. For the purposes of coverage under the ADA, a substantial limitation in the major life activity of working has been defined by the EEOC. That definition has been subsequently validated by many court cases in which employees have charged employers with discrimination against them by terminating their employment on the basis of their impairment. The EEOC definition states that

> the term "substantially limits" means significantly restricted in the ability to perform either a class of jobs or a broad range of jobs in various classes as compared to the average person having comparable training, skills, and abilities. The inability to perform a single, particular job does not constitute a substantial limitation in the major life activity of working. (U.S. EEOC, 1996, p. B-10)

The following two cases demonstrate the point, with the plaintiff in the first case being seen as not substantially limited and the plaintiff in the second case as being substantially limited in the major life activity of working.

In *McKay v. Toyota Motor Manufacturing* (TMM), the plaintiff, a 24-year-old woman who developed carpal tunnel syndrome that prevented her from continuing to use vibratory tools or lift significant weight while employed in the body welding division of a TMM factory, "alleged that her employment with TMM … was terminated in violation of the Americans with Disabilities Act" (878 F. Supp. 1013). The defendant (TMM) claimed that McKay was terminated because of excessive absences from work and that she did not have a disability covered by the ADA. In addition, TMM claimed that prior to the termination, they had taken several actions directed at attempting to accommodate to McKay's disability. Specifically, TMM alleged that

> it engaged in the following efforts to help McKay: granting her a medical leave of absence; placing her in modified light duty jobs; placing her in two rehabilitative work conditioning programs; referring her to TMM's job placement committee; extending her initial evaluation period because of her medical leave of absence; providing her with several work reintroduction periods; and approving her transfer to the job of her choice. (878 F. Supp. 1014)

In its move to have the case dismissed, the defendant disputed McKay's claim that she was a "qualified individual" under the ADA due to substantial limitations in the major life activity of working (878 F. Supp. 1014). The plaintiff had a college degree and was working toward a teaching certificate (Coil & Shapiro, 1996; M. Lee, 1997; "What Is a Disability?," 1997). The district court concluded that given the plaintiff's age and educational background, she was qualified for numerous alternative job opportunities that did not use the skills she learned while working as an automobile assembler (M. Lee, 1997; "What Is a Disability?," 1997). Therefore, in ruling in favor of the defendant and dismissing the case, the judge concluded that the plaintiff was not significantly limited in the major life activity of working or in any other major life activity and, therefore, was not covered by the ADA.

In *Smith v. Kitterman Inc.* the plaintiff filed suit on May 26, 1994, alleging that Kitterman Plastics terminated her employment in violation of the ADA (897 F. Supp. 424). In a pretrial hearing in which the defendant attempted to have the case dismissed, Kitterman argued that the plaintiff was

> not a "qualified individual with a disability" because she does not have, she does not have a record of having, nor is she regarded by Kitterman as having, a physical or mental impairment *which substantially limits one or more of the major life activities.* On the other hand, Plaintiff argued that she is a "qualified individual with a disability" because she is substantially limited in the major life activity of "working." (897 F. Supp. 425–426)

While the defendant argued that the plaintiff was not "qualified" to do the job from which she was terminated, the plaintiff argued that she could have done the job with reasonable accommodations that the defendant did not see fit to make (897 F. Supp. 424). The court ruled that the 42-year-old plaintiff—who, after 25 years of employment at Kitterman in jobs requiring repetitive motions, had been fired from her job upon developing carpal tunnel syndrome resulting in an inability to use tools requiring sustained strong gripping or repetitive grasping—was in fact significantly limited in the major life activity of working under the ADA. Unlike the plaintiff in the *McKay* case, the plaintiff in the *Smith* case had neither completed high school nor acquired any formal vocational training (M. Lee, 1997; "What Is a Disability?," 1997). Without mandating any formal evaluation of Smith's potential for other employment, "the *Smith* court drew the common sense inference that the plaintiff's circumstances could constitute a substantial restriction on her ability to perform a class or broad range of jobs" (M. Lee, 1997, p. 168). Therefore, the judge ruled against the defendant's motion to dismiss the case.

The ADA's definition of disability also covers people with a contagious disease (N. L. Jones, 1991, p. 33). Although such individuals would be covered under the first prong of the definition of disability, as are persons with other types of disabilities, they are only protected under the law in employment situations where they do "not pose a 'direct threat' to the health or safety of others" (Feldblum, 1991, p. 86).

Under the second prong of the definition, the ADA also affords protection against discrimination to individuals with a record of disability. These are individuals who have "had, but may no longer have, an actual disability" (Gilbert, 2001, p. 660), such as those who once had a substance abuse problem but entered a rehabilitation program in the past and are no longer substance abusers (Feldblum, 1991), or those who were once considered to have a disability but no longer do, such as individuals with a record of cancer that is now in remission (Colker, 2005). The individual with a history of mental illness has been used frequently as the model example of the type of person covered by the second prong of the definition (Adams, 1991).

The second prong is also directed at protecting from discrimination those individuals who may have been erroneously classified as having a disability in the past. For example, individuals whose educational records may contain an erroneous diagnosis of learning disability and are thereby vulnerable to discrimination by employers as a result of that invalid historical record are covered by the ADA under the second prong of its definition of disability (Gilbert, 2001). "Therefore, an employer who makes a vocational judgement based upon misclassification of disability risks liability even though it relied upon a literal document" (Gilbert, 2001, p. 670).

For an individual to be covered by the second prong of the definition, there must be a clearly documented historical record of a disability that contains (a) a description of the way the individual's impairment limited him or her in one or more major life activities and (b) a diagnostic label for the disability. Having "an undocumented history of substantially limiting impairment is not enough for coverage under the 'record of' prong" (Gilbert, 2001, p. 664).

EEOC's regulations indicate that under the third prong of the ADA—that is, "being regarded as having an impairment"—an individual is covered if he or she

- has an impairment that does not substantially limit major life activities but is treated by a covered entity as constituting such limitation,
- has an impairment that substantially limits major life activities only as a result of the attitudes of others toward such impairment, or
- has no impairment but is treated by a covered entity as having a substantially limiting impairment. (U.S. EEOC, 1998, TAB-C, p. 3-4)

Whereas the first two prongs of the definition of disability under the ADA

require that an individual actually have either an impairment that substantially limits major life activities or a record of such impairment, the third prong focuses on the beliefs and acts of the employer. Thus, an individual could be considered disabled even though he or she does not have, nor has ever had, any physical or mental impairment. ("What Is a Disability?," 1997, p. 3-82.6)

For example, having a severe facial burn or a huge facial birthmark would not limit a person in any physical sense, but the person's opportunities might be limited by the attitudes of others, such as employers who refuse to hire the individual because of the effect they believe the person's physical appearance will have on others ("What Is a Disability?," 1997). In other cases, such as when employers discriminate by not hiring individuals who are obese, the courts might be less likely to provide the ADA's protection. Obesity would be less likely to be covered to the extent that it was considered to be self-imposed or volitional. There appears to be some judicial bias against providing the same antidiscriminatory protections for persons with disabilities that are seen as self-imposed as for individuals whose disabilities are the result of the lottery of life. The appeal of this distinction may stem from the fact that "there is no other protected class in civil-rights law that an individual can 'will' him- or herself to join" (N. L. Jones, 1991, p. 44). Colker (2005) noted that the courts have rarely extended "disability status" to individuals under the third prong of the ADA.

Certain conditions or states of mind are not protected from discrimination by the ADA. These include bisexuality, homosexuality, transvestism, voyeurism, transsexualism, pedophilia, exhibitionism, gender identity disorders not resulting from physical impairments, and other sexual behavior disorders, as well as pyromania, compulsive gambling, and kleptomania (Devience & Convery, 1992; B. P. Tucker, 1998). Also not covered are having a prison record; pregnancy; advanced age; or behaviors or personality traits such as quick temper, irritability, poor judgment, stress, or chronic lateness where those traits or behaviors are not symptoms of underlying mental or psychological disorders ("What Is a Disability?," 1997).

With some exceptions, such as drug abuse where the individual is currently engaging in illegal drug usage, the mental or psychological disorders found in the *Diagnostic and Statistical Manual of Mental Disorders—Fourth Edition* (*DSM–IV*; American Psychiatric Association [APA], 1994) are recognized as mental impairments covered by the ADA ("What Is a Disability?," 1997). However, as was noted in the discussion of the first prong of the definition of disability under the ADA, the disability has to *substantially limit* the individual in one or more major life activities. *Substantially limit* has been defined by the EEOC as an impairment-related limitation that lasts longer than several months (McDonald & Rosman, 1997). Therefore, by definition, adjustment disorders described in the *DSM–IV* (APA, 1994, pp. 623–627), because of their short duration, would also typically be excluded as impairments covered by the ADA. Consequently, employees diagnosed with an adjustment disorder would not be eligible for reasonable accommodations under the ADA (McDonald & Rosman, 1997). Adjustment disorders are described as follows in the *DSM–IV* (APA, 1994):

> The essential feature of an Adjustment Disorder is the development of clinically significant emotional or behavioral symptoms in response to an identifiable psychosocial stressor or stressors. The symptoms must develop within 3 months after the onset of the stressor(s).... By definition, an Adjustment Disorder must resolve within 6 months of the termination of the stressor (or its consequences). (p. 623)

Although current illegal drug use is expressly excluded as a covered disability under the ADA, "current" unfortunately was not defined in the ADA. However, the definition was addressed to some degree by the Ninth Circuit in *Collings v. Longview Fibre Co.* (1995), in which the court held

> that an individual who has used drugs illegally in the weeks or months preceding an allegedly discriminatory employment action may be engaged in "current, illegal drug use," even though the individual was drug-free on the day of the challenged employment action. (Coil & Shapiro, 1996, p. 9)

Courts have been allowed much latitude for interpreting disability under the ADA. Much of this latitude relates to the court's interpretation of whether the plaintiff's disability limits the individual in one or more of the previously noted major life activities, such as walking, standing, seeing, and caring for oneself. In its Interpretive Guidance on the ADA, published soon after enactment of the ADA, the EEOC indicated that any determination of a limitation in a major life activity (i.e., an impairment) should be made without consideration of mitigating measures such as assistive or prosthetic devices or medicines (Frierson, 1997).

In clarification of this position in supplemental interpretive guidance on the ADA published in March 1995, the EEOC (1998) stated,

> Individuals with impairments (such as epilepsy or diabetes) that substantially limit major life activities are individuals with disabilities, even if medication controls the effects of the impairment.... Accordingly, an individual who received dialysis treatments for polycystic kidney disease had a substantially limiting impairment even though the disease was adequately treated through dialysis.... ("We are inclined to view persons whose kidneys would cease to function without mechanical assistance or whose kidneys do not function sufficiently to rid their bodies of waste matter without regular dialysis, as substantially limited in their ability to care for themselves.") (pp. 902-35, 902-36)

However, a number of judges claimed that the EEOC's interpretive guidance was found in the appendix to the ADA regulations and therefore did not have the force of law since it was not located in the regulations themselves (Frierson, 1997). As a result, some courts dismissed cases of disability discrimination by employers brought on the basis of the ADA because medical intervention for persons with disabilities such as "diabetes, multiple sclerosis, mental illness, and asbestosis" allowed individuals with such disabilities to perform major life activities (Frierson, 1997, p. 428). Of course, the basic assumption in the rulings in these cases was that the person did not have a disability covered by the ADA and therefore could not be protected against discrimination on the basis of disability by employers. Frierson pointed out that the above restrictive (current limitations in one or more major life activities) definition of disability was "used by at least thirteen different U.S. District Courts and seven of the twelve U.S. Courts of Appeals" to dismiss disability discrimination suits (p. 429). An example can be seen in the ruling of the Court of Appeals for the Fifth Circuit in the case of *Robinson v. Global Marine Drilling Co.* (1996).

William Robinson was employed as a rig engineer and rig mechanic for 10 years by Global Marine before being laid off in 1992 along with most of the rest of the crew on *Adriatic IV,* a Global Marine drill ship that was taken out of service as a result of losing its drilling contract. Robinson had notified his employer that he had asbestosis as soon as he was diagnosed with the condition in 1986. The condition resulted in lung capacity of less than 50%. After the layoff in 1992, all members of the crew were hired back except Robinson, even though "Global Marine had 20–25 openings for which he was qualified" (*Robinson,* 1996). According to Frierson (1997),

> At trial, a jury determined that the employer had violated the ADA by refusing to rehire Robinson, and it awarded him $49,000 in back pay and $50,000 in punitive damages. However, the Court of Appeals held that

Robinson was not disabled because he was not substantially limited in any major life activity.

The court found that the only current effect of the disease was shortness of breath when climbing stairs, and that climbing stairs is not a major life activity. Although the court accepted the fact that Robinson's lung capacity was less than 50% of normal, it stated that "the fact of a lower lung capacity is not evidence of a disability." ... Because the court found no disability it reversed judgement for Robinson without further considerations of the facts. Therefore, even though Robinson was currently qualified to work, and even if the company intentionally refused to rehire him because he had asbestosis, there was no legal remedy. (p. 423)

The conclusion in the *Robinson* case unfortunately illustrates how the legal outcome in some cases in the mid-1990s ignored the spirit of the ADA (Frierson, 1997). In these cases, even though the employer's reason for actions such as refusing to hire or discharging has been "based on the individual's asbestosis, cancer, epilepsy, diabetes, or other serious and chronic health condition," the courts did not find an ADA violation (Frierson, 1997, p. 423). Therefore, the ADA, which was passed to discourage disability discrimination against qualified individuals, appeared to allow such discrimination via the rulings of some courts in the mid-1990s. However, there has also been a legislative history on the ADA found in House and Senate committee reports, as well as court cases in the mid-1990s such as *Canon v. Clark* and *Harris v. H & W Contracting Co.,* that supported the EEOC's interpretive guidance that the "existence of an impairment is to be determined without regard to mitigating measures such as medicine, or assistive or prosthetic devices" (Frierson, 1997, p. 424).

In *Canon v. Clark,* the plaintiff Elizabeth Canon brought suit under the ADA in 1995 in U.S. District Court against John K. Clark in his official capacity as tax collector of Palm Beach Courts, Florida. Canon worked in the Palm Beach Tax Collector's Office from 1979 to 1993, when she alleged she was terminated because of her diabetes. Canon's diabetes was considered by the court to be covered by the ADA since "she is forced to rely on medical assistance to perform major life activities and to survive and she would lapse into a coma without insulin" (*Canon v. Clark,* 1995, p. 734).

In *Harris v. H & W Contracting Co.* (1996), the 11th Circuit Court supported the EEOC's interpretive guidance with the following statement:

At first glance, it is difficult to perceive how a condition that is completely controlled by medication can substantially limit a major life activity. However, the appendix to the applicable federal regulations provides explicit guidance on this point ... [citing EEOC interpretive guidance stating that a disability should be judged on a case-by-case basis without regard to mitigating measures such as medicines or assistive or prosthetic devices]. The Supreme Court has long recognized that an agency's interpretation of a statute it is entrusted to administer should be given "considerable weight" and should not be disturbed unless it appears from the statute or legislative history that Congress intended otherwise ... There is not direct conflict between the interpretation contained in the appendix to the regulations and the language of the statute itself. There is nothing inherently illogical about determining the existence of a substantial limitation without regard to mitigating measures such as medicines or assistive or prosthetic devices [and] the appendix ... is firmly rooted in the legislative history. (Cited in Frierson, 1997, pp. 425–426)

As the above discussion suggests, the courts should protect under the ADA persons with disabilities who are substantially limited in a major life activity after medical treatment. However, in the mid-1990s it was difficult to predict whether a particular court would or would not protect an individual with a disability who was not substantially limited in a major life activity after medical treatment.

In June 1999, via rulings on three cases—*Sutton v. United Airlines, Murphy v. UPS,* and *Albertsons Inc. v. Kirkingburg*—the U.S. Supreme Court eliminated the confusion regarding whether persons with disabilities who were not substantially limited in a major life activity after medical treatment were covered by the ADA. Chemerinsky (1999) pointed out that

all three cases involved people who were denied employment because of physical conditions. In each instance, the condition was corrected or controlled so that there was no claim that it would interfere with job performance. Each of the plaintiffs claimed that the denial of employment because of the condition was discrimination based on disability in violation of the ADA. Each of the defendants argued that the individuals were not disabled because their conditions were corrected and did not interfere with any major life activities. (p. 88)

Greenhouse (1999) pointed out that in the decisions on those three cases,

the Supreme Court ruled ... that people with physical impairments who can function normally when they wear their glasses or take their medicine generally cannot be considered disabled and therefore do not come within the law's protection against employment discrimination. (p. 1A)

Keen (1999) pointed out that via those three decisions

the court ruled that a disability is a disability only if it is an uncorrectable disability. The intent of the ruling seemed to be to prevent a flood of litigation ... [that it was] feared might result if the Americans with Disabilities Act were interpreted as protecting the 100 million Americans who wear eyeglasses and the 50 million who have high blood pressure. (p. 1)

In *Sutton v. United Airlines* (1999), twin sisters who were regional airline pilots, with uncorrected visual acuity of 20/200 in one eye and 20/400 in the other eye (Colker, 2005) and 20/20 when wearing glasses, were rejected for employment by United Airlines because they did not meet United Airlines' "minimum vision requirement which was uncorrected visual acuity of 20/100 or better" (p. 2143). The twin sisters filed a lawsuit under the Americans with Disabilities Act, claiming that United Airlines "discriminated against them when it rejected their applications as pilots because their eyesight without glasses [was] worse than 20/100 that the airline requires of pilots" (Keen, 1999, p. 23). The complaint was dismissed by the lower courts because the twin sisters could fully correct their visual impairments and, when corrected, their visual disability did not substantially limit them in any major life activity. Basically, in concurring with the decisions of the lower courts in the *Sutton v. United Airlines* case, the U.S. Supreme Court concluded that individuals with correctable disabilities are not covered by the ADA because, when corrected, the disability does not substantially limit a major life activity. In writing the opinion of the court, Justice O'Connor concluded that Congress intended that the ADA should cover only disabilities that substantially limit a major life activity, not those that " 'might,' 'could,' or 'would' be substantially limiting if mitigating measures were not taken" (119 S.CT. 2146). Furthermore, that "the ADA's coverage is restricted to only those whose impairments are not mitigated by corrective measures" is evidenced by the fact that the number of persons who need corrective glasses to see properly exceeds 100 million in the United States while, in the ADA, Congress estimated there to be 43 million individuals with a disability (119 S.CT. 2149) who would benefit from the ADA. Justice O'Connor assumed that if, in drafting the ADA, Congress had wanted to cover persons with correctable disabilities such as nearsightedness, diabetes, or high blood pressure who, after medical treatment, were not substantially limited in the carrying out of a major life activity, Congress would have estimated in the ADA legislation that the number of persons with disabilities was approximately 160 million rather than 43 million (Chemerinsky, 1999).

The U.S. Supreme Court decisions in the other two cases mentioned above, *Murphy v. UPS* (1999) and *Albertsons Inc. v. Kirkingburg* (1999), also supported the conclusion that persons with correctable disabilities were not protected against discrimination by the ADA if after medical treatment they were not substantially limited in a major life activity (Fleisher & Zames, 2001). Therefore, in June 1999, the U.S. Supreme Court resolved the previously debatable issue of whether an individual with a disability who after medical correction was not substantially limited in a major life activity was protected against discrimination by the ADA. The answer from the court was a clear "No."

According to the Supreme Court's rulings, then, unlike Title VII of the Civil Rights Act of 1964, which "prohibits employers from considering race and sex when making employment decisions," the ADA only prohibits discrimination against some individuals with a disability (Travis, 2002, p. 493). The determination of who is protected by the ADA has been "complicated by the fact that unlike race and sex, physical and mental impairment falls along a vast continuum" (Travis, 2002, p. 494).

The ADA contains five titles. Through those five titles, the ADA prohibits discrimination on the basis of disability in employment (Title I), public services (Title II), public accommodations (Title III), and telecommunications (Title IV). Title V contains miscellaneous provisions, such as access to historic sites and hiring practices of the federal government. The content of each of these titles of the ADA is comprehensively discussed below.

Title I: Prohibition of Discrimination in Employment Practices

The purpose of Title I of the ADA is to ensure equal access to employment opportunities for qualified individuals with a disability. It is directed at promoting equal access to a major aspect of the American dream, "a stable and fulfilling job" (Feldblum, 1991, p. 82). It prohibits employers from discriminating against a qualified individual with a disability because of the disability in such aspects of employment as hiring, job training, promotion, or the discharge process (Adams, 1991; A. B. Kaplan, 2001). For employers of 25 or more employees, Title I became effective on July 26, 1992. It became effective for employers of 15 or more employees on July 26, 1994. Because there are businesses with fewer than 15 employees, Title I does not cover all employers. However, it covers approximately 80% of all businesses in the United States (Schall, 1998).

Title I contains several terms and procedural guidelines that must be comprehended before the extent of its protections against discrimination on the basis of disability in employment practices can be understood sufficiently. These include terms such as *essential functions of the job, reasonable accommodation,* and *undue hardship* and procedural guidelines in regard to the job application process, contractual relationships, and enforcement of Title I.

Essential Functions of the Job

The ADA defines a qualified person with a disability as an individual who can perform the essential functions of the job held or desired with or without reasonable accommodations (Dispenza, 2002; Muther, 1996). The regulations for Title I of the ADA indicate that a job function can be considered essential for several reasons. Three such reasons stated in the regulations are:

(i) The function may be essential because the reason the position exists is to perform that function.

(ii) The function may be essential because of the limited number of employees available among whom the performance of that job function can be distributed.

(iii) The function may be highly specialized so that the incumbent in the position is hired for his or her expertise or ability to perform the particular function. (U.S. EEOC, 1996, p. B-19)

Although the employer's conception of which job functions are essential is considered neither conclusive nor presumptive by the ADA, courts have generally been unwilling to challenge such claims by employers "unless the employee comes up with specific and compelling proof that the job is different than the employer states" (M. Lee, 1997, p. 170). M. Lee provided the following summary of *Kuehl v. Wal-Mart Stores Inc.* (1995) as an example of the predisposition of courts to defer to employer judgments on the issue of essential functions:

> *Kuehl* involved the request of an employee who worked as a door greeter at a Sam's Wholesale Club store to be able to work sitting on a stool to accommodate her chronic tibula tendinitis. Wal-Mart contended its door greeters needed to be mobile in order to greet customers, check membership cards, give directions, place stickers on return items and monitor the entryway.... Observing that "Wal-Mart wants its door greeters to act in an 'aggressively hospitable' manner" and that "Wal-Mart does not believe that a door greeter sitting on a stool would convey the desired image or would be able to adequately greet the customers," ... the court agreed that standing for a full shift was an essential function of the job.... Significantly, the court flatly dismissed plaintiff's disagreement with the store's definition of essential functions as insufficient. (M. Lee, 1997, p. 171)

The issue of "whether regular or dependable attendance may constitute an essential function of a job" has been addressed in many court cases, with the judicial opinion usually being that it does (Coil & Shapiro, 1996, pp. 16–17). However, each such case must be addressed separately in regard to the possibility that deviations from regular attendance can be dealt with via reasonable accommodations in the form of unpaid or available paid leave (e.g., sick days or vacation days). The EEOC considers granting such leave for treatment or recovery related to a covered disability to qualify as a reasonable accommodation (Befort, 2002; U.S. EEOC, 1996). The courts have generally concurred with this position of the EEOC by interpreting "reasonable accommodations" to include those actions that enable an employee to, either currently or in the immediate future, perform those functions of the job considered as essential (Befort, 2002). In elaborating on this point, Befort (2002) stated,

> One court [Garcia-Ayala, 212 F.3d at 655] posited that leave should qualify as a reasonable accommodation if it fulfills two requirements: (1) it must effect or advance a change in the employee's disabled status such that he or she will be enabled to perform their job, and (2) "the employee's return to work must be relatively proximate in a temporal sense." (pp. 459–460)

In regard to the former, an employee requesting such leave must obtain a medical opinion that it could be plausible to expect the leave period to "enable the employee satisfactorily to perform the job upon return to work" (Befort, 2002, p. 461).

Even though "the EEOC maintains that a request for a leave of indefinite absence is a reasonable accommodation," many courts have ruled indefinite leave to be unreasonable (Befort, 2002, p. 463). In coming to this conclusion, many courts have noted "that the purpose of an accommodation is to assist the employee in performing the job, not to protect the employee who cannot perform the job" (McDonald & Rosman, 1997, p. 23).

A currently unresolved issue is, when does the amount of unpaid leave requested become judged as unreasonable (i.e., what is the maximum amount of time an employee with a disability may remain on leave)? Befort (2002) pointed out that the courts are likely to consider a leave request as a reasonable accommodation when its length "is consistent with documented employer leave policies" (p. 461). Request for leaves beyond such periods of time would be considered unreasonable if they created an undue hardship on the employer by interfering with the operation of his or her business. It should also be noted that the burden of proof rests on the employer for showing how an unpaid leave creates an undue hardship (McDonald & Rosman, 1997). However, "courts generally have found leave requests for periods beyond one year in duration to be unreasonable" (Befort, 2002, p. 463).

Employees are entitled to up to 12 weeks of unpaid leave annually by the Family and Medical Leave Act (FMLA) for serious medical problems that prevent them from performing the essential functions of their job. However, employees who have "taken 12 weeks of FMLA leave for a disability may be entitled to additional unpaid leave as an accommodation under the ADA" (Coil & Shapiro, 1996, p. 23). Befort (2002) elaborated on this double coverage:

> Regulations adopted by the Department of Labor suggest that an employer must allow an employee in this situation to take leave under the FMLA first, so as not to jeopardize the employee's full statutory protection, although it is permissible for the two types of leave to run concurrently. (p. 467)

Essential functions of the job cannot automatically be determined by reading the job description. According to the EEOC the determination of the essential functions of a job "occurs on a case by case basis" (Schall, 1998, p. 194). In addition to the previously stated criteria for a job function to be considered essential, Schall indicated that the following can be used to help employers identify the functions that are essential for a particular job: "whether employees in the position actually perform the function; if removing the function would significantly and fundamentally change the job" (p. 194).

Essential functions of the job do not include tasks marginal to the job involved (M. Lee, 1997). For example, an employer who refused to hire a person with epilepsy for a clerical position where the basic job is filing because that individual stutters when performing the nonessential or tangential job function of answering the telephone could be considered as being in violation of Title I of the ADA. Adams (1991) pointed out that an "example of a non-essential function cited in the legislative history of the ADA is the requirement imposed by many employers that an employee have a driver's license, even though the job does not entail driving" (p. 36). Although the employer could consider the possession of a driver's license as enabling a worker to "run an occasional errand or [be] more likely [to] arrive at work on time," such considerations alone would not justify the requirement of a driver's license (Adams, 1991, p. 36).

Kopelman (1996) provided the following example showing how a person with a double amputation could not be denied a job because of inability to perform nonessential job tasks:

> Suppose that a veteran who lost both legs in a war can work as a cashier in a certain restaurant. Cashiers in this establishment, however, usually are required to get things off high shelf tops or help out in the kitchen when times are slow, tasks that this man cannot complete. He would probably be protected under the ADA because he seems to meet all three necessary conditions: he is disabled, but can perform the essential functions of the job; the non-essential functions of this job could be reassigned, while he could assume others, such as routine paperwork, with no undue burden to the restaurant. (p. 190)

Schall (1998) provided the following hypothetical example to show how an employer could be in violation of the ADA by considering a person with a visual disability unqualified for a job based on his or her inability to perform a nonessential function of the job:

> A hypothetical employer denied a prospective employee with vision impairment a job as a social worker. The employer reasoned that the individual, while qualified as a social worker, did not have a driver's license and could not drive to the homes of clients. That is a violation of the ADA because driving is a marginal function of the job and the individual could get to clients' homes in other ways. (p. 194)

It is important to note that a job applicant with a disability who could perform the essential functions of a job with or without reasonable accommodations but who is not hired for the position due to an inability to meet the standard of performance for the essential functions set by the employer is not viewed as a victim of discrimination by the ADA. Muther (1996) explained this point as follows:

> The ADA protects the employer from having to quantitatively or qualitatively justify the standards imposed on the employees. Employers may place more stringent standards on their workers in order to improve production or reduce costs. These higher standards must be uniformly

applied to avoid scrutiny by the EEOC. This is a valuable understanding for employers, because the ADA attempts to preserve employers' decisions concerning productivity in the workplace. (p. 19)

Therefore, even if a job applicant with a disability can perform the essential functions of the job, an employer is not required to hire that individual if there is another individual applying for the job with or without a disability who is more highly qualified (Muther, 1996).

Reasonable Accommodations

Employers are required by Title I of the ADA to provide reasonable accommodations for applicants with disabilities for employment or employees who are qualified individuals with disabilities, unless doing so would cause undue hardship. "In general, an accommodation is any change in the work environment or in the way things are customarily done that enables an individual with a disability to enjoy equal employment opportunities" (U.S. EEOC, 1999, pp. 2–3). According to Dispenza (2002), such accommodations can fall into any of the following three categories:

> modifications to the job application process, accommodations designed to permit an employee to perform the "essential functions" of his or her job, and accommodations that permit individuals with disabilities to share equally in the attendant benefits and privileges of employment. (p. 162)

Part-time as well as full-time employees with a disability are entitled to reasonable accommodations. "Generally, the individual with a disability must inform the employer that an accommodation is needed" (U.S. EEOC, 1999, p. 3). Once the employer has been so informed, he or she should ask the individual with a disability relevant questions such as those regarding the nature of the disability, the associated functional limitations, the existing workplace barriers that need to be addressed, and the type of accommodations that may solve the problem (knowledge of which the individual with a disability may or may not possess). However, when

> the disability and/or the need for accommodations are not obvious, the employer may ask the individual for reasonable documentation about his or her disability and functional limitations. The employer is entitled to know that the individual has a covered disability for which he or she needs a reasonable accommodation. (U.S. EEOC, 1999, p. 7)

Refusal by an employer to make reasonable accommodations for a qualified job applicant with a disability that results in denial of an employment opportunity constitutes unlawful employment discrimination. Furthermore, the duty to provide reasonable accommodations is not always a one-time responsibility. The duty to provide reasonable accommodations is ongoing and may need to be acted upon "any time that a person's disability or job changes" (Golden et al., 1994, pp. 21–22).

Several modifications have been listed in the ADA as falling within the boundaries of reasonable accommodation. These include the following:

1. Modifying the physical environment of a workplace such as a lunch-room, a meeting room, or a restroom to make it accessible to persons with disabilities (U.S. EEOC, 1992).
2. Restructuring a job so that its essential functions can be performed by an individual with a disability (Befort, 2002; Feldblum, 1991). This could include part-time or modified work schedules for those persons with disabilities incapable of working a traditional-length workday or workweek (such as might result from fatigue problems or an ongoing medical treatment regimen) (Feldblum, 1991, p. 93; U.S. EEOC, 1999). In regard to an ongoing medical treatment regimen, Golden et al. (1994) provided the example of an accountant who needed 2 hours off twice a week to see a psychiatrist. The accountant "was permitted to take longer lunch breaks and to make up the time by working later on those days" (p. 23). Also considered reasonable within job restructuring would be the reallocation or redistribution by an employer of "nonessential, marginal job functions, that a qualified individual is unable to perform" (Befort, 2002, p. 444).
3. Provision of devices or equipment (such as providing a telephone handset amplifier for a person with a hearing impairment) (Adams, 1991).
4. Modifying the job application process (e.g., administering a job application examination orally to a person with dyslexia) (Feldblum, 1991, p. 93).
5. Modifying company policies (e.g., allowing a person with a disability to bring a service dog or guide dog into the workplace) (Befort, 2002; Feldblum, 1991).
6. Provision of qualified readers or interpreters (Befort, 2002; U.S. EEOC, 1992).
7. Providing an individual with a psychiatric disability "a private place to work to alleviate stress" (Kopelman, 1996, p. 190).
8. Providing an individual with a disability with a leave of absence. Although not listed in the ADA, a leave of absence that may enable an employee with a disability, "through rest and/or rehabilitation, to return to productive work" has been recognized "as an additional type of reasonable accommodation" by both the courts and the EEOC (Befort, 2002, p. 445).
9. Reassigning an individual with a disability to a vacant position (Befort, 2002; U.S. EEOC, 1999).

In regard to the last example in the previous list, the EEOC stressed that reassignment should be considered by employers as a last-resort reasonable accommodation. It should be resorted to only if no available reasonable accommodation will enable the individual with a disability to perform his or her current job or if any other reasonable accommodation will produce an undue hardship on the employer (Befort, 2002).

The ADA also requires that employers provide reasonable accommodations that are necessary for employees with disabilities to enjoy the benefits and privileges of employment to an extent equal to that "enjoyed by similarly-situated employees without disabilities" (U.S. EEOC, 1999, p. 13). Types of benefits and privileges of employment listed by the U.S. EEOC as covered by the reasonable accommodation provision of Title I of the ADA include "employer sponsored: (1) training, (2) services (e.g., employee assistance programs ..., credit unions, cafeterias, lounges, gymnasiums, auditoriums, transportation), and (3) parties or other social functions (e.g., parties to celebrate retirements and birthdays, and company outings)" (p. 13). Where a reasonable accommodation is needed for an employee with a disability to have equal opportunity to access such benefits and privileges of employment, the ADA mandates that it must be provided unless it results in an undue hardship (U.S. EEOC, 1999). On the other hand, employers are not required to provide, as reasonable accommodations, personal-use items such as a wheelchair, a hearing aid, or a prosthetic limb if the device is also needed off the job for accomplishing daily activities (U.S. EEOC, 1999).

The failure of an employer to make a reasonable accommodation requested by an otherwise qualified job applicant or employee with a disability that would be in accordance with the provisions of the ADA is considered to be discrimination on the basis of disability. This aspect of the ADA has been referred to as discrimination in favor of persons with disability. Such *pro-discrimination* reasonable accommodations are not available through civil rights laws that bar discrimination against minorities and women, even though for some jobs some women or members of a minority group who lack a disability covered by the ADA could be viewed as otherwise qualified with the provision of a reasonable accommodation. For example, for a job that requires the reading of a variety of documents and the preparation of reports, an employer may be required by the ADA to accommodate an otherwise qualified blind worker with a reader. This would not be the case for an African American employee who, as a result of receiving an inferior education in underfunded *de facto* segregated schools, "lacks adequate reading comprehension and writing skills. Even if he could certainly understand the documents if they were read to him and could communicate his reports orally," he would not be considered to have a disability and therefore would have no legal claim to an accommodation from an employer for his impairment (Karlan & Rutherglen, 1996, p. 4).

The concept of reasonable accommodation as an affirmative action in the ADA differentiates the ADA from preexisting employment discrimination law. As opposed to the rationale for affirmative action in the latter, the mandate for employers to make reasonable accommodations for persons with disabilities in the workplace is not based on any "finding of prior wrongful discrimination as the predicate for affirmative relief for identified individuals, and imposes a duty to accommodate without a prior finding of wrongdoing. Thus the ADA imposes a kind of liability without fault" (Karlan & Rutherglen, 1996, p. 41).

Undue Hardship

The requirement to provide a reasonable accommodation is not unlimited (N. L. Jones, 1991). Employers are not required to make accommodations that would create an undue hardship on them. *Undue hardship* is defined by the ADA as any action that creates "significant difficulty or expense" for an employer given "the size of the employer, the resources available, and the nature of the operation" (U.S. EEOC, 1992, p. III-12). Since the determination of undue hardship must take into account the financial resources of the employer and the structure and operations of the workplace, it is a relative standard. Therefore, an accommodation considered reasonable for one employer might be considered unreasonable for another employer (Adams, 1991). Golden et al. (1994) elaborated on this differentiation with the following example:

> If a medium sized computer company employs a deaf computer programmer, it may well not be an undue hardship for such an employer to hire a sign-language interpreter to assist the deaf programmer in conversations with co-workers and in staff meetings. However, if a deaf individual applied for work at a small restaurant and asked the restaurant to hire a full-time sign language interpreter as an accommodation, that could be an undue hardship. (p. 33)

The availability of outside funding to cover the cost of an accommodation by an employer can reduce the likelihood that an accommodation would create an undue hardship on the employer. Therefore, it is important for employers to be aware of such outside funding resources. For example, a state rehabilitation agency might be able to cover the cost of a job coach for a person with mental retardation who is much more likely to successfully learn how to perform the essential functions of the job via an extended period of individualized on-the-job training (Fielder, 1994).

Some accommodations for employees with a disability, such as the acquisition of a speech recognition device, a special computer monitor, or a portable reading machine, can be quite costly (Dispenza, 2002). However, many companies report that, assuming "cooperation between employers and employees, the majority of accommodations cost less than $100" (Muther, 1996, p. 19). Reinforcing the point that the costs of accommodations tend to be rather modest, the President's Committee on Employment of People with Disabilities reported that company expenses for reasonable accommodations were less than $500 in approximately 70% of cases examined (Samuelson, 1999). An additional 12% of job accommodations reportedly cost between $501 and $1,000. Therefore, the available data suggested that four out of five job accommodations cost less than $1,000 (Bruyére, 2000). Further evidence for the low cost of accommodations can be found in the experiences of Sears, Roebuck and Co., which reported that the average cost of accommodations for Sears employees with disabilities from 1993 to 1997 was under $45 (Blanck, 2000). In addition, the results of a 1995 Harris poll of over 400 executives showed that the "median direct cost for accommodations was $233 per covered employee" (Blanck, 2000, p. 217). Finally, the Job Accommodation Network, which provides consultation on accommodations, has found that the provision of accommodations for employees with disabilities can result in substantial monetary savings for many employers in the form of "lower job training costs and insurance claims, increased worker productivity, and reduced rehabilitation costs after injury on the job" (Blanck, 2000, p. 217). Still, the uncertainty in regard to compliance costs associated with the reasonable accommodation mandate is what worries employers most in regard to the ADA (Muther, 1996).

The cost of a proposed accommodation is not the only factor in determining whether an undue hardship would be placed on the employer. "The impact of the accommodation on the operation of the facility that is making the accommodation" can also be considered as a relevant factor in determining undue hardship (U.S. EEOC, 1996, p. III-12). Such effects can "include the impact … on the facility's ability to conduct business" (U.S. EEOC, 1996, p. III-12). For example, the EEOC has cited a low-cost request that a nightclub "install bright lighting to accommodate an applicant for a position as waiter whose visual impairment prevents him from seeing well in dimmed lighting" as an example of undue hardship because its effect on the operation of the facility would be too substantial (Adams, 1991, p. 39).

Several courts have taken the effect of an accommodation for an employee with a disability on other employees as a relevant consideration in determining undue hardship (Coil & Shapiro, 1996). For example, Coil and Shapiro (1996) pointed out that in *Milton v. Scrivner Inc.* (1995)

> the court held that the ADA does not require an employer to implement an accommodation that would result in other employees having to work harder or longer hours…. [And] in *Barth v. Gelb* [1993] … the District of Columbia Circuit held that the impact on the morale of nondisabled employees may be taken into account in determining whether an accommodation imposes an undue hardship, particularly when the workforce is small. (p. 27)

Employers would have preferred a very specific definition for undue hardship in the ADA so that the exact accommodations required under the law would have been clearly indicated. However, the drafters of the ADA saw the various alternatives to the flexible undue hardship standard as potentially restricting the opportunities of people with disabilities as well as the flexibility that employers might need to comply with the law in the most efficacious manner (Feldblum, 1991). Feldblum provided examples of some of those more specific alternatives to the current flexible definitions of undue hardship in the ADA and clarified why they are less desirable. For example, if some employers incur heavy expenses in a particular year while others do not, a requirement that 10% of the gross income of each employer be available for reasonable accommodations would be unfair. The problem would not necessarily be resolved by requiring employers to spend 10% of their net income on accommodations because that requirement "would allow employers to allocate all of their income to other expenses (including discretionary expenses) before any resources would be considered for accommodations" (Feldblum, 1991, p. 95). Another alternative discussed by Feldblum was tying the amount an employer must pay for accommodations to the salary of an employee:

> An approach that tied the accommodation limit to a certain percentage of an employee's salary would mean that a wide range of accommodations, which would be perfectly reasonable to expect large employers to provide, would not be required simply because the person with a disability was in a low paying job. (p. 95)

Situations can arise where an existing collective bargaining agreement, such as one in which seniority is given priority in requests by employees for reassignment, causes what typically might be viewed as an appropriate request by an employee with a disability for a reasonable accommodation to be viewed as an undue hardship by the employer. For example, consider a situation in which the following two employees request reassignment to the only vacant file clerk's job: a loading-dock worker with 4 years of seniority who has developed a deteriorated disc condition and is no longer able to perform the functions of that job and a cross-country truck driver without a disability with 6 years of seniority who wants to have more time at home with his family. It might be viewed as an undue hardship on the employer in that situation to violate the union contract and reassign the employee with the disability, as a reasonable accommodation, to the vacant file clerk's job. To avoid such confusing conflicts between the contents of collective bargaining agreements and the duty of employers to provide reasonable accommodations, employers might find it helpful to seek a provision in such agreements that permits them to use reassignment to a vacant position as a reasonable accommodation for employees with a disability even when such an action is incompatible with the seniority rights of employees without a disability. Because the ADA does not address the issue of "whether or not employers must act contrary to a collective bargaining agreement in order to comply with the Act" (J. Beale, 2002, p. 818), such provisions in collective bargaining agreements can have much utility for avoiding confusion. These provisions can also increase the likelihood that reassignment to a vacant position is used as a reasonable accommodation in more employment situations.

Given the silence of the ADA on this issue, National Labor Relations Act case law has

> created a per se rule that reasonable accommodation did not require employers to violate the seniority rights of employees who are not disabled.... In addition, many ADA cases have held that employers are not required to violate a collective bargaining agreement or bona fide seniority system in order to reassign a disabled employee. (J. Beale, 2002, p. 818)

One selling point for the ADA with Congress was that it would have a cost-saving effect; that is, it would save society billions of dollars by reducing the dependency and increasing the productivity of many individuals with a disability. Therefore, to avoid exchanging one set of costs for another without a sufficient associated benefit, the courts have indicated that whether an accommodation is considered reasonable—and therefore required of an employer—is somewhat dependent on the consequences produced by it. Therefore, in *Mohamed v. Marriott International Inc.* (1995), the judge stated that "an accommodation is reasonable only if its costs are not clearly disproportionate to the benefits it will produce" (cited in "What Is a 'Reasonable Accommodation'?," 1996, p. 6-16).

Therefore, while the intent of the ADA was to promote equal opportunity for persons with disabilities, it was not intended to do so regardless of the economic burden created on society in general. Kopelman (1996) provided some extreme examples to reinforce this point:

> Someone with severe mental disabilities might be able to perform the essential functions of her job if her therapist came to work with her daily and sat at her elbow at the institution's expense. This would be as unreasonable as insisting that the aspiring pilot with narcolepsy be provided with an extra qualified pilot in attendance in anticipation of those occasions when she loses consciousness. (p. 195)

In effect, the undue hardship provision in the ADA indicates that society is not yet ready to underwrite the total cost of providing equal opportunity to persons with disabilities. Therefore, no matter how aspirational or inspirational the congressional rhetoric was regarding the need for and purposes of the ADA, "as a practical matter the equality that will be attained under the ADA is a rough approximation, rather than an exact reproduction, of the employment options and choices open to the most fortunate or proficient individuals in the labor market" (Karlan & Rutherglen, 1996, p. 29).

The primary hope for changing this partial-equality-of-opportunity situation may rest on the possibility of an increased awareness that any of us who do not currently have a disability could acquire one in the future simply in accordance with the lottery of life. We simply lack the knowledge of what that lottery will afford us in the future in regard to disability status. It is that veil of ignorance that could result in society's willingness to provide greater equal employment opportunity for persons with a disability in the future by underwriting the insurance costs for compensatory employment subsidy programs that will make that possible. For example, tax-supported insurance programs could be established that provide full financial coverage (a) for persons with disabilities to cover extra disability-related work expenses, including aids that would allow them to be more productive at work, and (b) for reimbursing potential employers for the greater costs of employing some individuals with a disability (Karlan & Rutherglen, 1996).

Although the lottery of life argument can be a major motivator for society to further break down barriers to employment for persons with a disability, some barriers may currently be immune to the effect of that argument. For example, because the performing of many essential functions of good-paying jobs has become dependent on the use of advanced technologies, more and more individuals with disabilities may lack the reasonable accommodations protections of the ADA for securing desired employment. This is because the technological accommodations that could be viewed as reasonable accommodations for persons with disabilities for such jobs are often "not widely and readily available to businesses" (Dispenza, 2002, p. 166). The source of this problem is that the technology companies often "assume that they cannot afford to invest in the research and development efforts that would make their products accessible" because the costs of such activities are seen as greatly outweighing any potential profits that could result (Dispenza, 2002, p. 167). Since court cases (*Flemmings v. Howard University,* 1995; *Humphrey v. Memorial Hospitals Association,* 2001; *Kimbro v. Atlantic Richfield Co.,* 1989) have held that an unavailable accommodation cannot be considered as a potential reasonable accommodation, companies "are not statutorily required [to], and indeed cannot, provide [such] technological accommodations to individuals with disabilities" (Dispenza, 2002, p. 167). This employment barrier problem is further exacerbated by the overall difficulty that people with disabilities have gaining experiences with new computer-based technologies. For example, statistics show that "individuals without disabilities are four times more likely to use the Internet regularly compared to individuals with disabilities.... Nearly sixty percent of individuals with disabilities have never used a personal computer" (Dispenza, 2002, p. 166).

Job Application Process Guidelines

The ADA spells out detailed requirements regarding medical exams and medical inquiries in the job application process. These specific requirements are designed to protect both job applicants with a disability and employers. They protect the former from being denied a job because of their disability when that disability, without or with reasonable accommodation by the employer, would not prevent them from performing the essential functions of the job. Employers are protected from having to hire applicants incapable, even with reasonable accommodation, of performing the essential functions of the job because of their disability (Feldblum, 1991). To provide these protections, the ADA has established "a two step process for medical examinations and inquiries of job applicants" (Feldblum, 1991, p. 98).

Step 1 occurs during the initial job application stage, before a job offer is made. During that stage employers can ask job applicants about their educational and professional qualifications for the job and their ability to perform essential functions of the job (e.g., "drive a car, lift 50 pounds, or answer the telephone"; Feldblum, 1991, p. 98). However, during the initial job application phase, the employer may not ask questions pertaining to the "applicant's health, past medical history, and worker's compensation claims" (Devience & Convery, 1992, p. 43). The U.S. EEOC (1992) provided the following examples of questions pertaining to medical history that *cannot* be asked by employers either on job application forms or in job interviews during the initial job application phase:

> Have you ever been treated for any of the following conditions or diseases? (Followed by a checklist of various conditions and diseases.)
>
> Have you ever been hospitalized? If so, for what condition?
>
> Have you ever been treated by a psychiatrist or psychologist? If so, for what conditions?
>
> How many days were you absent from work because of illness last year?
>
> Are you taking any prescribed drugs? (pp. v–6, v–7)

In addition, during the initial application phase, the applicant cannot be required to undergo any medical examinations (Feldblum, 1991). However, tests that would not be perceived as a medical examination can be administered to job applicants in the initial stage of the job application process. Examples include "physical agility tests in which applicants demonstrate their ability to perform actual or simulated job-related tasks" and "physical fitness tests that measure applicants' performance on physical criteria" (e.g., strength, running) as long as typical medical measurements such as blood pressure or heart rate are not taken during or after the test (Coil & Shapiro, 1996, p. 34).

Although an employer can ask an applicant during the initial job application stage whether he or she drinks alcohol or engages in the illegal use of drugs (Coil & Shapiro, 1996), the employer may not ask an applicant whether he or she is a drug addict or an alcoholic, or has ever been treated for those conditions (Golden et al., 1994). However, a test to determine the illegal use of drugs can be given to a job applicant at any point during the job application process. Because such tests can often reveal the use of legal as well as illegal drugs, they can reveal the presence of a disability such as epilepsy to an employer before any conditional job offer has been made. Therefore, it is wise for employers to refrain from giving drug tests until after they have made a conditional job offer (i.e., based on the individual's being drug free). That practice will help employers avoid being accused of discriminating against persons with disabilities in the job application process based on pre–conditional job offer knowledge of a disability via drug tests (Golden et al., 1994).

If the employer wants to hire the person based on the information collected during the initial job application phase, and makes a conditional job offer, the employer can then move to the second step of the process. If such testing is required of all applicants for that job category, the employer may then "require the applicant to undergo a medical examination or respond to medical inquiries, and may condition the final offer of employment on those medical tests or inquiries" (Feldblum, 1991, p. 98). However, the conditional job offer cannot be withdrawn unless the results of the medical exam indicate that the applicant lacks the physical or emotional capability, even with reasonable accommodation, to perform the essential functions of the job. Feldblum (1991) provided the following example:

> Assume, for example, that a necessary qualification for a job was to lift 50 pounds on a regular basis. If the examination or inquiry revealed that the applicant, even with reasonable accommodation, could not fulfill the necessary requirement of the job, then the results of the exam could legitimately be used to withdraw the conditional job offer. By contrast, if the exam revealed that the person had Hodgkin's cancer in remission, or some other disability that did not affect the person's lifting ability, the conditional job offer could not legitimately be withdrawn. (p. 99)

Several examples of employer actions that are prohibited or required by the ADA have been provided by the American Bankers Association (1992). For example, employers must be certain that any employment agency from which they receive employee referrals does not discriminate in its "selection of candidates to be sent for interviews" (American Bankers Association, p. 4). Employers cannot reject a person with a child with a disability for employment because they "fear that the employee would miss too much work. (The employee will be held to the same standards of attendance as other employees)" (American Bankers Association, p. 4). Employment tests that are biased against job applicants with a disability are not to be used with that population. For example, employers "may not require that paper and pencil employment tests be administered to a dyslexic applicant unless it can be demonstrated that ability to read the test measures an essential job function" (American Bankers Association, p. 5).

Insurance cost or coverage considerations cannot be used to evade the requirements of Title I of the ADA. For example, the ADA prohibits employers from refusing to hire qualified individuals with a particular disability because their present health insurance plan lacks coverage for that disability or because their insurance costs would increase (N. L. Jones, 1991). For example, a person with diabetes could not be denied a job by an employer because of the cost of health insurance coverage for that individual (Feldblum, 1991).

The ADA also prohibits the exclusion of an individual with a disability from a particular job based on the employer's general, and insufficiently substantiated, fear that performing the job would pose a threat of substantial harm to the individual (e.g., a fear of exacerbating the disability due to job-induced stress) or to "others that cannot be eliminated or reduced by reasonable accommodation" (A. B. Kaplan, 2001, p. 399). For such an exclusion to not violate Title I of the ADA, it must be based on enough evidence from *both* the individual's work history and medical history that "employment of that individual would pose a reasonable probability of substantial harm" (Adams, 1991, p. 36). Adams further elaborated, "It is not enough that the individual presents an elevated risk of injury nor for the determination to be based on the employer's subjective evaluation or, in most cases, medical reports alone" (p. 36).

It should also be pointed out that there has been a significant dispute in the case law regarding whether the "direct threat" provision in the ADA pertains to the individual with a disability as well as to others in the workplace. For example, in *Moses v. American Nonwovens Inc.*, the Court of Appeals for the Eleventh Circuit in 1997 found that an

> employee's uncontrolled seizures made him a direct threat to himself, because his assigned tasks all involved working in close proximity to dangerous equipment.... Because Moses presented no evidence that he was not a direct threat or that any reasonable accommodation could be made, the court

ruled in favor of the employer—that is, that the employer could fire an employee with epilepsy whose behavior on the job could be construed as a direct threat only to the employee himself (and to no one else). In a similar case, *LaChance v. Duffy's Draft House Inc.* (1998), the Court of Appeals for the Eleventh Circuit ruled in favor of an employer who fired an employee with "a history of complex partial seizures with secondary generalization" from a job as a cook who had to cook "on a gas flat top grill, use a 'fryolater' filled with hot grease, and use slicing machines" because the employee was unable to provide evidence that performing the job in question did not pose a direct threat to his health and safety "or that the employer could have provided a reasonable accommodation for his disability" (A. B. Kaplan, 2001, pp. 403–404).

Contrary to the above rulings by the Court of Appeals for the Eleventh Circuit, in the case of *Echazabal v. Chevron USA Inc.* (2000), the Court of Appeals for the Ninth Circuit ruled in favor of the plaintiff. Greenburg (2002) partially summarized the case as follows:

> Mario Echazabal, who has hepatitis C ... wanted a permanent job in one of Chevron's California oil refineries even though company doctors had said chemical exposure there could destroy his damaged liver. After Chevron refused to hire him, Echazabal sued the company under the Americans with Disabilities Act, arguing it should be his decision whether to take the risk and that he was being discriminated against because of his liver condition. (p. 4)

Although the federal district court ruled in favor of the oil refinery, the Court of Appeals for the Ninth Circuit reversed that decision "and held that the ADA's 'direct threat' defense is not applicable to disabled individuals who pose a direct threat to themselves" (A. B. Kaplan, 2001, p. 406).

The divergent views of the circuit courts in regard to the direct threat defense for employers can be attributed to a conflict between what the ADA states in that regard and how the EEOC interpreted the meaning of that provision of the ADA. In regard to the direct threat defense, the ADA states only that "an individual shall not pose a direct threat to the health and safety of *other individuals* in the workplace" (A. B. Kaplan, 2001, p. 408) [italics added]. However, the EEOC's interpretive regulation expanded the direct threat provision's meaning to include "the disabled individual himself within the provision's reach" (A. B. Kaplan, 2001, p. 408). A. B. Kaplan suggested that Congress clearly limited the ADA's direct threat provision to others in the workplace in order to prevent employers, in the hiring process, from acting on their prejudices and preconceptions regarding what is best for individuals with disabilities rather than focusing on whether those individuals possess the true qualifications for the job.

To resolve the conflict in the lower courts regarding the direct threat provision of the ADA, the U.S. Supreme Court agreed to hear an appeal to the Ninth Circuit's ruling on the *Echazabal* case. On June 10, 2002, the U.S. Supreme Court "ruled unanimously ... that employers do not have to hire disabled workers for jobs that could hurt or kill them" (Greenburg, 2002, p. 4), thereby supporting the EEOC's expanded interpretation of the direct threat provision. Although the U.S. Supreme Court might appear to have demonstrated wisdom in its decision, that decision can also be seen as undermining the antidiscrimination protection of the ADA by considering employers to have a right in the hiring process to overrule what individuals with disabilities who can perform the essential functions of a job might consider to be their right to self-determine what is and is not in their best interests.

While the ADA was intended to provide the same type of protections for those with psychiatric disabilities as it has for those with physical disabilities, the realizing of such equal protection for both groups as a result of the ADA has been seriously questioned (J. Campbell, 1994). This can be especially observed in regard to the requirement that employers provide reasonable accommodations for persons with psychiatric disabilities while at the same time prohibiting employers from requesting job applicants to reveal their disability. Whether to reveal one's psychiatric disability to a potential employer can be an anguishing decision for an individual "who may want to keep this information private because of the stigma attached" (Pollett, 1995, p. 167). In fact, it is not uncommon for rehabilitation counselors to encourage their clients with psychiatric disabilities to withhold information from potential employers about their prior hospitalizations (J. Campbell, 1994). This clearly can become a problem since employers are not required to provide reasonable accommodations for job applicants or employees with disabilities of which the employer is not aware.

According to Dalgin (2001), when a client with a psychiatric disability wishes to disclose in order to acquire a reasonable accommodation, the client should ask a rehabilitation counselor to help in preparing for such an interaction with the employer.

> Questions about what will be told, what disability information will be shared and what accommodations will be requested should all be reviewed thoroughly prior to the client/employer interaction. "Depending on individual needs, disclosure of such information may include emphasis on the availability of assistance from the rehabilitation provider for support as needed." (Dalgin, 2001, p. 49)

Unfortunately, the person with a psychiatric disability is not necessarily provided with reasonable accommodations after informing an employer of a psychiatric disability. This is because the employer may perceive the individual with a psychiatric disability, often incorrectly, as a significant risk to the health and safety of other individuals in the workplace. The employer might, based on stereotypical beliefs about the association of psychiatric disability and violent behavior, consider him- or herself to be exempt from the requirement to provide reasonable accommodation based on the direct threat exclusion allowed by the ADA (Dalgin, 2001). The direct threat exclusion "exempts employers from the requirement to provide reasonable accommodation to a person with disabilities if that person poses a significant risk to the safety of others" (J. Campbell, 1994, p. 133). However, as Gostin (1991) pointed out, "Disability law has been thoughtfully crafted to replace reflexive actions based upon irrational fears, speculation, stereotypes or pernicious mythologies,... with carefully reasoned judgments based upon well-established scientific information" (pp. 276–277). Therefore, before the person with a psychiatric disability is not considered to be protected under the ADA,

> health officials must identify the specific conduct and provide credible evidence that the person is likely to engage in dangerous behavior. For example, if a person with mental illness ... were to be excluded from ... a job because he or she posed a "direct threat," health officials must present objective evidence that a recent dangerous act was committed. (Gostin, 1991, p. 277)

As a result of three 1999 U.S. Supreme Court cases discussed earlier in this chapter (*Sutton v. United Airlines, Murphy v. UPS,* and *Albertsons v. Kirkingburg*)—in which the court ruled that individuals with disabilities who were not substantially limited in a major life activity after medical treatment were not covered by the antidiscrimination protections of the ADA—many individuals with psychiatric disabilities who are taking medication to overcome the functional limitations associated with their disability may not be protected by the ADA from discrimination by employers. This is because they would not meet the definition of a covered disability. However, Dalgin (2001) pointed out that the "Bazelon Center for Mental Health Law has recently issued strategies on how to best meet the ADA definition, which include considering the side effects of medications as additional impairments" (p. 46). The Bazelon Center has also stressed the importance of considering any limitations associated with the psychiatric disability that are not sufficiently eliminated by the medical treatment being received (Dalgin, 2001). Furthermore, the Bazelon Center has stressed the need to expand the list of major life activities in which limitations could be experienced under the ADA definition to include activities "such as learning, concentrating, thinking, [and] interacting with others" (Dalgin, p. 46). Persons with psychiatric disabilities could be experiencing limitations in any of those activities even after treatment for the disability is considered to have a major ameliorating effect, but at the same time be able to perform the essential functions of many jobs. However, when filing a discrimination complaint against an employer, it is often difficult for the individual with a psychiatric disability to convince the court that he or she is substantially limited by the disability in spite of receiving effective medical treatment and still being capable of performing the job (e.g., *Castorena v. Runyon,* 1994; *Mackie v. Runyon,* 1992; *Milton v. Scrivner Inc.,* 1995).

Contractual Relationships Must Comply with the ADA

The ADA prohibits employers from entering into contractual relationships that result in discrimination against their employees with disabilities (Adams, 1991). If discriminatory situations occur through such contractual relationships, the employer is responsible for eliminating the problem. The following example has been provided by the U.S. EEOC (1992):

> Suppose a company with which an employer has contracted proposes to conduct training at an inaccessible location. The employer is responsible for providing an accommodation that would enable an employee who uses a wheelchair to obtain this training. The employer might do this by: requiring the training company to relocate the program to an accessible site; requiring the company to make the site (including all facilities used by trainees) accessible; making the site accessible or providing resources that enable the training company to do so; or providing any other accommodation (such as temporary ramps) that would not impose an undue hardship. If it is impossible to make an accommodation because the need is only discovered when an employee arrives at the training site, the employer may have to provide accessible training at a later date. (p. VII-6)

Enforcement of Title I

Title I of the ADA covers the same employers and provides the same administrative and judicial remedies to persons discriminated against on the basis of disability as "are provided under Title VII of the Civil Rights Act of 1964 for individuals who are discriminated against on the basis of race, sex, religion or national origin" (Feldblum, 1991, p. 104). As in Title VII, persons with disabilities claiming employment discrimination under Title I of the ADA complete the same administrative process of the EEOC as had been previously established for review of alleged discrimination on the basis of race, sex, religion, or national origin (Feldblum, 1991). (Parties interested in filing a Title I complaint can call the EEOC at 800/669-4000 [voice] or 800/669-6820 [TTY] to reach the field office in their area.)

Also as with Title VII, under Title I, once a person with a disability files a charge of discrimination against an employer with the EEOC, he or she also has the right to file a private lawsuit. The U.S. EEOC (1992) has elaborated on the process of acting on this right as follows:

> The charging party can request a "right to sue" letter from the EEOC 180 days after the charge was first filed with the Commission. A charging party will then have 90 days to file suit after receiving the notice of right to sue. If the charging party files suits, EEOC will ordinarily dismiss the original charges filed with the Commission. "Right to sue" letters also are issued when EEOC does not believe discrimination occurred or when conciliation attempts fail and EEOC decides not to sue on the charging party's behalf. (p. x-5).

When passed in 1990, Title I of the ADA allowed for the same remedies as Title VII of the Civil Rights Act of 1964 to be provided through private lawsuits charging employment discrimination (Richter, 2002). These remedies included hiring, reinstatement in a job, back pay, and attorney fees. However, those remedies were expanded to include compensatory and punitive damages by amendments to Title VII of the Civil Rights Act of 1964 via the Civil Rights Act of 1991. In so doing, it made compensatory and punitive damages available for private lawsuits under Title I of the ADA as well (Bleyer, 1992). The maximum amount of those damages is determined by the employer's size. Bleyer delineated those caps as follows: "The maximum award for employers with 15–100 employees is $50,000, with 101–200 employees is $100,000, with 201–500 employees is $200,000, and with more than 500 employees is $300,000" (p. 348).

The first verdict in a private lawsuit claiming employment discrimination under Title I of the ADA was decided in March 1993 by a federal court jury in Chicago. That jury found for the plaintiff, Charles H. Wessel, a 59-year-old "executive who was fired after being diagnosed with terminal cancer," and awarded him $572,000 in back pay and compensatory and punitive damages (designated to be reduced to $222,000 because of the limits set by the law). His employer, AIC Security Investigation Ltd. of Chicago, fired him "on July 29, 1992 three days after the ADA went into effect" (Flannery, 1993, p. 1E).

Within the first 3 years after Title I of the ADA became effective, over 50,000 job discrimination complaints had already been filed with the EEOC

(Coil & Shapiro, 1996). By March 31, 1997, over 81,000 charges of discrimination under Title I of the ADA had been filed with the EEOC ("Region V News," 1997). By 1999 the total number of charges of discrimination since implementation of the act had risen to over 100,000 (J. Beale, 2002). Unfortunately, by 1999, almost a decade after the passage of Title I of the ADA, the results for persons with disabilities seeking the protection against employment discrimination were disappointing. By 1999, in 93% of the cases filed in the lower courts based on alleged violations of ADA protections against employment discrimination, the defendant (i.e., the employer) prevailed (Chemerinsky, 1999). The prevalence of prodefendant (i.e., employer) decisions is higher in ADA case law than in other related areas of litigation such as that associated with Title VII of the Civil Rights Act (Colker, 2005).

The reasons for this tremendous imbalance in ADA-related litigation outcomes in favor of the employer could arise from concepts found in the ADA law itself, in its regulations, or in its associated case law that favored the defendant (employer) in cases filed under Title I of the ADA, according to a study by the American Bar Association's Commission on Mental and Physical Disability Laws (Mainstream, Inc., 1998). First, it is difficult for plaintiffs (employees) to prove that they have a very severe disability but that it is not "so severe that they are unable to do the job competently" (Mainstream, Inc., 1998, p. 10). Second, when employees with a disability have filed a claim for Social Security disability or workers' compensation benefits, "which require applicants to assert that they are unable to work," and then subsequently sue their employers for disability discrimination, "some courts have concluded that these employees are not otherwise qualified to carry out essential job functions" (Mainstream, Inc., 1998, pp. 10–11). Therefore, some individuals with disabilities who lose jobs due to disability discrimination may have to choose between filing "a discrimination suit, which may take a long time to resolve and in the interim … leave them without income, or [filing] for disability benefits and risk undermining their discrimination claims" (Mainstream, Inc., p. 11). Third, even when the previously mentioned obstacles are overcome, the employer still may have access to the defense that he or she "could not reasonably accommodate the individual with a disability without creating an undue administrative or financial burden on the company" (Mainstream, Inc., p. 11).

The scope of the antidiscrimination protections in employment for persons with disabilities was further eroded by the U.S. Supreme Court's 2001 decision in *Board of Trustees of the University of Alabama v. Garrett*. The primary reason that the U.S. Supreme Court heard the case was to resolve the issue of whether states were immune from private suits seeking monetary damages under the ADA in federal court because of protections from such provided them by the Eleventh Amendment. A split among several federal appellate courts in cases dealing with that question had left the issue unresolved (Richter, 2002). Patricia Garrett, a plaintiff in the case that was eventually heard by the U.S. Supreme Court, had filed suit based on violations of her right under the ADA to not be discriminated against in employment because of her disability.

Richter (2002) briefly described the claimed discrimination and effect in that case as follows:

> Patricia Garrett, a registered nurse, sued the University of Alabama in Birmingham because the university hospital had removed her from her position as Director of Nursing after she took a substantial leave to treat breast cancer.... As a result she was forced to take a lower paying job. (p. 887)

In a far from unanimous decision by the nine justices (5 to 4) in that case, the U.S. Supreme Court held that the 11th Amendment provided immunity to states against suits for monetary damages in federal court based on violations of the ADA (Richter, 2002). As a result of that decision, one might conclude that the teeth were pulled from the antidiscrimination protections for persons with disabilities in state employment situations.

Title II: Nondiscrimination on the Basis of Disability in State and Local Government Services

Taking effect on January 26, 1992, Title II of the ADA contains two subtitles, A and B. Subtitle A extends the Section 504 of the Rehabilitation Act of 1973 prohibition of discrimination on the basis of disability in the programs and activities of state and local governments (public entities) receiving federal financial assistance to all activities of state and local governments including those not receiving federal funds (B. P. Tucker, 1998; U.S. Department of Justice, 1992, U.S. EEOC, 1991, p. II-1). Examples of state and local government operations that do not receive federal funds and are, therefore, beyond the reach of Section 504 include courts, licensing bureaus, and legislative facilities (U.S. Department of Justice, 1992, p. 1).

Subtitle A stresses that individuals with disabilities must have equal opportunity to access the services and benefits of public entities (U.S. Department of Justice, 1992). An illustration of not providing such equal opportunity would be failure to provide an interpreter at a city council meeting for individuals who are deaf (U.S. Department of Justice, p. 9). Another example would be locating an office where property owners apply for a special property tax rebate on the second floor of an old municipal building without an elevator.

As suggested by these two illustrations, Subtitle A of Title II requires public entities to make reasonable modifications in their "policies, practices, or procedures to avoid discrimination" (U.S. Department of Justice, 1992, p. 13). An example of a reasonable modification would be a city's allowing a pharmacy to install a ramp to its front entrance even though it would violate by 3 feet a municipal zoning ordinance that "requires a set-back of 12 feet from the curb in the central business district" (U.S. Department of Justice, p. 13). Another illustration would be simplifying the application process for (or providing individualized assistance to) individuals with mental disabilities who need to complete a very long and complex application for the benefits of a county general relief program that "provides emergency food, shelter, and cash grants to individuals who can demonstrate their eligibility" (U.S. Department of Justice, p. 13).

Another example of a reasonable modification under Subtitle A of Title II would be to modify eligibility rules for participation in interscholastic sports for students with a disability receiving special education or related services, in order to allow them to participate beyond the traditional maximum age of 18. In accordance with the ADA, such students can remain in school through their 22nd birthday. Such eligibility rules for interscholastic sports competition are typically established by an interscholastic sports association, which would be an independent regulatory body in which schools in a particular area have membership. Such associations are considered to be covered under the ADA. In *Dennin v. Connecticut Interscholastic Athletic Conference* (CIAC; 1995), the court viewed the failure to modify such arbitrary rules of exclusion—thereby denying otherwise qualified persons with disabilities enrolled in high school the opportunity to participate in or benefit from a sports program—to be an act of discrimination on the basis of disability (Berliner, 1996). Dennin was a 19-year-old student with a diagnosis of mental retardation whose Individualized Education Program stipulated that he would participate on the high school swim team. His request for a waiver of the age rule in order to allow that participation had been denied by the CIAC.

> The *Dennin* Court found that the plaintiff was an otherwise qualified individual with a disability under ... the ADA titles,... and ... that a waiver of the age rule would not create an undue burden for the CIAC ... since "granting him a waiver would not [fundamentally] alter the nature of the swimming program."... Accordingly, the court granted plaintiff's request for injunctive relief. (Berliner, 1996, p. 542)

Subtitle A of Title II prohibits a public entity from denying individuals with disabilities "the benefits of its programs, activities, and services" because it has an inaccessible facility. Under Subtitle A the programs of public entities were required to be accessible by January 26, 1992, to persons with disabilities unless structural changes were needed. Where structural changes were required to achieve program accessibility, those modifications were required to be made no later than January 26, 1995 (U.S. Department of Justice, 1992).

A public entity is not automatically required to make all of its existing facilities accessible (U.S. Department of Justice, 1992, p. 19). For example, persons with disabilities must be provided access by a municipality to any public activity in an existing building. However, the city is only required to make the location of the activity accessible rather than all areas of the building. An example would be a situation where all civil suits have been tried on the second floor of a courthouse without an elevator. For a defendant in a civil suit who cannot climb stairs because of a respiratory condition, the proceedings could be relocated to an accessible site in the same or another building rather than making the second floor courtroom accessible (U.S. Department of Justice, 1992). Telephones and bathrooms should also be accessible to the participants of a public activity (U.S. Department of Justice, 1992, p. 19).

There are other ways that public entities can achieve program accessibility in addition to structural alterations of existing facilities and construction of new facilities. The U.S. Department of Justice (1992) has provided the following illustration of an acceptable nonstructural method for providing program accessibility:

> A public library's open stacks are located on upper floors having no elevator. As an alternative to installing a lift or elevator, library staff may retrieve books for patrons who use wheelchairs. The aides must be available during the operating hours of the library. (p. 20)

When a choice among methods for achieving program accessibility is available, the method that provides for the most "normal" experience for persons with disabilities should be given priority. The U.S. Department of Justice (1992) provided the following illustration to demonstrate the point:

> A rural, one-room library has an entrance with several steps. The library can make its services accessible in several ways. It may construct a simple wooden ramp quickly and at relatively low cost. Alternatively, individuals with mobility impairments may be provided access to the library's services through a bookmobile, by special messenger service, through use of clerical aides, or by any other method that makes the resources of the library readily accessible. Priority should be given, however, to constructing a ramp because that is the method that offers library services to individuals with disabilities and others in the same setting. (p. 20)

Although several court decisions in the 1980s indicated that Section 504 did not disallow the provision of services to persons with disabilities in segregated settings (e.g., *Barnett v. Fairfax County School Board,* 1989; *Pinkerton v. Moge,* 1981; *St. Louis Developmental Disabilities Treatment Center v. Mallory,* 1984), the interpretations of Section 504 in these decisions were rejected by Congress, which made clear that the intent of Title II of the ADA was to disallow public entities from developing such segregationist policies (T. M. Cook, 1991). For example, T. M. Cook pointed out that the House Judiciary Report in 1990 on the ADA stressed

> that "[n]othing in the ADA is intended to permit ... discriminatory treatment on the basis of disability, even when such treatment is rendered under the guise of providing an accommodation, service, aid or benefit to the individual with disability." ... Then for example, under the ADA a state Medicaid agency that spends its funds on auxiliary aids and services for persons with disabilities only in segregated settings such as nursing homes

and other institutions, without providing those same programs, aids, and services in regular community settings, plainly runs afoul of the ADA. Moreover, under the ADA, "[n]o longer will children be subjected to forced busing to programs outside of their neighborhoods because that is where the 'handicapped' program is located." (p. 430)

Subtitle A of Title II also prohibits discrimination by state and local governments "against individuals or entities because of their known relationship or association with persons who have disabilities" (U.S. Department of Justice, 1992, p. 15). For example, under Subtitle A of Title II it would be illegal for the director of a county recreation center to "refuse admission to a summer camp program to a child whose brother has HIV disease" or for a municipal government to not "allow a theater company to use a school auditorium on the grounds that the company has recently performed at an HIV hospice" (U.S. Department of Justice, 1992, p. 15).

Many complaints filed with the U.S. Department of Justice under Subtitle A of Title II have been resolved without a lawsuit, by means of formal written settlement agreements between the Department and the violating party. Seven cases resolved via formal written settlement agreements during late 1997 were summarized by the U.S. Department of Justice (1997). These cases provide examples of the types of complaints about violations of Title II by units of state and local governments that have been dealt with by the Department of Justice. These cases also suggest that, even in government entities, there has not necessarily been a *natural inclination to open the door* to full participation by persons with disabilities in the absence of an effective mechanism to enforce the legal mandate. The seven cases were summarized by the U.S. Department of Justice as follows:

> *New Hampshire Sweepstakes Commission, Concord, New Hampshire*—The Department signed a settlement agreement with the New Hampshire Sweepstakes Commission that will ensure program accessibility in the State's lottery program. The agreement resolved a complaint charging that establishments that sell lottery tickets were inaccessible to persons with mobility impairments. New Hampshire will evaluate the accessibility of lottery sales in the 1300 retail establishments participating in the lottery program, the geographical dispersal of accessible facilities, the ratio of accessible to inaccessible sites in each town and county, and the rate of use of each retailer. It will then develop and implement a plan to ensure that the lottery program as a whole is accessible to people with mobility impairments. The Department will review and approve the Commission's actions. Because of the large number of facilities participating in the lottery program, the settlement promises to substantially increase the overall accessibility of public accommodations and State facilities throughout New Hampshire. (p. 5)

> *Newaygo County, Michigan*—Newaygo County agreed to adopt a written policy stating that persons with disabilities may bring their service animals

to any county building or county-sponsored activity. Under this policy persons may be asked if an animal is a service animal and may be asked to describe the service the animal provides and the training the animal has received. However, they may not be required to document their own disability or show identification or certification of the service animal's status. The policy statement will be distributed to all county board members, posted in county buildings, and made available to the public on request. (p. 6)

Twin Falls, Idaho—The Department concluded a settlement agreement with the Fifth Judicial District of the Idaho State court system to provide effective communication in court proceedings. The agreement resolves a complaint by a deaf individual alleging that he was not provided with effective communication during a small claims court hearing. The individual complained that the small claims judge appointed a county employee to interpret at the proceeding who was unable to translate properly, rather than appoint a qualified sign language interpreter. Under the agreement, the Fifth Judicial District agreed to provide appropriate auxiliary aids and services to ensure effective communication and to train judges and court clerks on this policy. (p. 6)

Jackson, Mississippi—The Mississippi Coliseum, one of the largest stadiums in that State, will be made accessible to people with disabilities under an agreement with the Mississippi Fair Commission and the Mississippi Department of Finance and Administration. As part of an ongoing renovation of the 10,000-seat coliseum, the State will make one percent of the seating accessible to people with wheelchairs and provide companion seating. The agreement calls for the accessible seats to be dispersed throughout the coliseum with lines of sight over standing spectators. The State will also provide accessible restrooms, concession stands, and parking lots; institute new ticketing policies for accessible seating; train paid and volunteer staff on the requirements of the ADA; and appoint ADA coordinators to assist people with disabilities. (p. 6)

Kingstree, South Carolina—The Town of Kingstree agreed to make public documents available on tape at the request of individuals who are blind or who have impaired vision. The tapes will be provided at no cost and within three days of the request. Kingstree agreed to adopt and post a written policy statement on making reasonable modifications in policies, practices and procedures for people with disabilities. In addition, Kingstree will adopt and publish a procedure for providing prompt and equitable resolution of ADA complaints. (p. 7)

Court of Common Pleas, Philadelphia, Pennsylvania—Prospective jurors with disabilities will now be able to request accommodations prior to proceedings in open court under an agreement between the Department and the

Philadelphia Court of Common Pleas. The complaint alleged that the only available means for requesting accommodations for a disability was during voir dire in open court. This procedure resulted in the unnecessary public disclosure of information about prospective jurors' disabilities and the unwarranted exclusion of some prospective jurors because of this information. Under the agreement the court will include information about requesting accommodations in the initial jury summons. It will also adopt and publish procedures for evaluating requests and maintaining the confidentiality of such requests. If an accommodation is not available for a particular court date, the court will reschedule the juror for a time when the accommodation can be provided. The court also agreed to designate an ADA coordinator and to post publicly its policy on making reasonable modifications in policies, practices, and procedures. (p. 7)

Denver, Colorado—The City and County of Denver Election Commission will take steps to ensure program accessibility in voting. The agreement resolves a complaint alleging that the commission was ignoring its own procedures for providing an effective voting process in precincts with inaccessible voting machines. It requires the election commission to publish accessibility procedures and to ensure that at least two election judges are present to assist voters who are unable to use inaccessible voting machines. It also requires the commission to provide training for all election judges on the accessibility procedures, to secure a signed statement from each judge stating that he or she will follow the procedures, and to discipline any election judge who fails to follow them. (pp. 7–8)

Subtitle B of Title II of the ADA clarifies what Section 504 requires of public transportation systems receiving federal financial assistance. It also extends those antidiscrimination requirements to public transportation systems not receiving federal financial assistance (U.S. Department of Justice, 1992).

Subtitle B of Title II requires that any new buses, purchased or leased by a public transportation system for use on a fixed route, be accessible to persons with disabilities, including those using wheelchairs (P.L. 101-336). The requirement does not apply to the purchase or lease of used buses. However, when purchasing or leasing used buses, the public transportation system must make a good faith effort to purchase used buses that are accessible. Public fixed-route bus systems are also not required to make accessible those existing buses in their fleet. However, public entities that operate a fixed-route bus system are required to provide paratransit and other special transportation services to persons who, because of a disability, are unable to use the regular vehicles on the fixed route (P.L. 101-336). Nevertheless, paratransit and other special transportation services are only required to the extent that such provision does not create an undue financial burden on the public entity. Katzmann (1991) discussed the issue of the difficulty of "determining what constitutes an 'undue financial burden' under the ADA" in this regard (p. 230). For example, should it be determined by the percentage that the fares on the entire transit system would have to be increased "to cover the costs of supplemental paratransit" (p. 230)? Or, should it be determined by how the transit system's "overall ridership would be affected by service cutbacks brought on by the paratransit costs" (p. 230)? Possibly it could be determined by the extent that the transit system's "deficit would be increased, on an overall per rider basis" by paratransit costs (p. 230). Regardless of which criterion is chosen, the problem still exists of determining the size of the effect (e.g., percentage of fare increase) that should be involved before an undue financial burden can be seen as being imposed on the transit system (Katzmann, 1991).

Subtitle B of Title II requires that new facilities constructed for public transportation services be accessible to persons with disabilities. It also mandates that any alteration to existing public transportation facilities should be done in a way that "the path of travel to the altered area and the bathrooms, telephones, and drinking fountains serving the altered area, are readily accessible to and useable by individuals with disabilities" (P.L. 101-336, § 227).

Subtitle B of Title II mandates that all rail systems, including rapid rail, light rail, inner city rail, and commuter rail transit have at least one car per train "that is accessible to individuals with disabilities ... as soon as practical," but no later than January 26, 1997 (P.L. 101-336, § 228). In addition, rail stations designated as "key" commuter stations by the Secretary of the Department of Transportation (DOT) were to be accessible to persons with disabilities no later than January 26, 1995, unless extraordinarily expensive structural changes were required (Katzmann, 1991). When the latter was the case, the time period for making necessary structural changes for accessibility could be extended by the secretary of the DOT up to the year 2022 (Katzmann, 1991). "All existing inner city rail stations are to be readily accessible to individuals with disabilities" no later than 2010 (Katzmann, 1991, p. 222).

The U.S. Department of Justice is responsible for the enforcement of Title II of the ADA. Complaints about violations of Title II by units of state and local government should be filed with the U.S. Department of Justice (950 Pennsylvania Avenue NW; Civil Rights Division—Diversity Rights Section; New York Avenue Building, Room 4023; Washington, DC 20530; see http://www.ada.gov/enforce.htm)

Title III: Nondiscrimination in Public Accommodations and Commercial Facilities

Title III of the ADA, which took effect on January 26, 1992, covers private entities that are places of public accommodation, commercial facilities, as well as private entities offering "examination and courses related to applications, licensing, certification or credentials for secondary or post secondary education, professional, or trade purposes" (U.S. Department of Justice, 1992, p. 1). Title III also covers any fixed route or demand responsive transportation system operated by a public accommodation that is not primarily engaged in the business of transporting people. Examples include airport shuttle services operated by hotels, customer bus or van services operated by shopping centers, transportation systems at colleges and universities, and transport systems in places of recreation, such as those at stadiums, zoos, and amusement parks. (U.S. Department of Justice, 1992, p. 36)

Title III prohibits discrimination on the basis of disability that would prevent persons with disabilities from having the full and equal enjoyment of the "goods, services, facilities, privileges, advantages or accommodations" (American Bankers Association, 1992) of entities such as hotels, restaurants, bars, theaters, bowling alleys, golf courses, libraries, lawyers' offices, auditoriums, laundromats, dry cleaners, grocery stores, insurance offices, museums, funeral parlors, parks, zoos, private schools, gas stations, gymnasiums, day-care centers, banks, hospitals, and professional offices of health care providers (Devience & Convery, 1992; N. L. Jones, 1991; B. P. Tucker, 1998; U.S. Department of Justice, 1992). Courses and examinations for licensing and certification must be offered by a private entity "in a place and manner accessible to persons with disabilities," or accessible alternatives must be provided for such individuals (Golden et al., 1994, p. 86). In regard to this aspect of Title III, the U.S. Department of Justice stated,

> A private entity offering an examination covered ... is responsible for selecting and administering the examination in a place and manner that ensures that the examination accurately reflects an individual's aptitude or achievement level or other factor the examination purports to measure, rather than reflecting the individual's impaired sensory, manual, or speaking skills (except where those skills are the factors that the examination purports to measure).
>
> Where necessary, an examiner may be required to provide auxiliary aids or services, unless it can demonstrate that offering a particular auxiliary aid or service would fundamentally alter the examination or result in an undue burden. For individuals with hearing impairments, for example, oral instructions or other aurally delivered materials could be provided through an interpreter, assistive listening device, or other effective method. For individuals with visual impairments, providing examinations and answer sheets on audio tape, in large print or Braille, or providing qualified readers or transcribers to record answers, may be appropriate. Also, some individuals with learning disabilities may need auxiliary aids or services, such as readers, because of problems in perceiving and processing written information. (p. 39)

The roots of the public accommodation aspect of Title III of the ADA can be found in the opinion of Justices Goldberg and Douglas in the 1964 U.S. Supreme Court case of *Bell v. Maryland*.

> Justice Goldberg declared his belief that all Americans are guaranteed "the right to be treated as equal members of the community with respect to public accommodations" and Justice Douglas stated that "the right to be served in places of public accommodations is an incident of national citizenship." (Burgdorf, 1991, p. 184)

Those opinions were endorsed shortly thereafter in Title II of the Civil Rights Act of 1964, which prohibits discrimination in public accommodations based upon race, color, religion, or national origin. In 1988 the *Washington Post* reported a disturbing example of discrimination against persons with disabilities that dramatically demonstrated the need to extend the coverage of Title II of the Civil Rights Act of 1964 to persons with disabilities. A New Jersey zookeeper refused to admit children with Down syndrome to the zoo because of fear that they would upset the chimpanzees (Burgdorf, 1991).

Although Title III mandates the removal of architectural, communication, and other barriers to the full and equal enjoyment by persons with disabilities of the "goods, services, facilities, privileges, advantages or accommodations" of any of the entities mentioned above, it does so to a lesser extent than Title I, which mandates reasonable accommodations that do not place an undue hardship on the employer (N. L. Jones, 1991, p. 38). For example, under Title III, failure to remove architectural barriers and communication barriers does not violate the nondiscrimination mandate unless the removal of such is readily achievable. The undue hardship standard was intended by Congress to place a much higher demand for modifications on employers than the readily achievable standard would on managers of public accommodations and commercial facilities (N. L. Jones, 1991; B. D. Tucker, 1998). *Readily achievable* refers to barrier removal that can be accomplished without much expense or difficulty (Burgdorf, 1991; B. P. Tucker, 1998). The U.S. Department of Justice (1992) provided the following 21 examples of modifications that could be viewed as readily achievable under Title III of the ADA:

1. Installing ramps;
2. Making curb cuts in sidewalks and entrances;
3. Repositioning shelves;
4. Rearranging tables, chairs, vending machines, display racks, and other furniture;
5. Repositioning telephones;
6. Adding raised markings on elevator control buttons;
7. Installing flashing alarm lights;
8. Widening doors;
9. Installing offset hinges to widen doorways;
10. Eliminating a turnstile or providing an alternative accessible path;
11. Installing accessible door hardware;
12. Installing grab bars in toilet stalls;

13. Rearranging toilet partitions to increase maneuvering space;
14. Insulating lavatory pipes under sinks to prevent burns;
15. Installing a raised toilet seat;
16. Installing a full-length bathroom mirror;
17. Repositioning the paper towel dispenser in a bathroom;
18. Creating designated accessible parking spaces;
19. Installing an accessible paper cup dispenser at an existing inaccessible water fountain;
20. Removing high pile, low density carpeting; or
21. Installing vehicle hand controls. (pp. 30–31)

Burgdorf (1991) provided the following example to demonstrate the ADA policy on readily achievable barrier removal:

A real-estate agency doing business with the general public at a three-story walk-up office would not be required to install an elevator to provide access to the upper floors. The agency would be required, however, to install a simple ramp over a few steps to its entrance, in order to provide its services to customers with mobility impairments in the first-floor accessible offices. (pp. 195–196)

Modifications under Title III that would be considered readily achievable appear to require less massive changes than do those required as reasonable accommodations under Title I. Changes that would fundamentally alter the nature of a program service, facility, or accommodation, and thereby undermine its viability or jeopardize its effectiveness, exceed what would be seen as readily achievable under Title III. The American Bankers Association (1992) provided the following two modifications that would be seen as readily achievable by banks and therefore necessary under the Title III mandate:

It would not be necessary for a bank to have all its applications, policy forms and so forth available in braille, as long as someone was available to read these documents to a visually impaired customer. (p. 13)

A bank could provide braille overlays with directions for using its ATMs as an auxiliary aid without fundamentally changing the ATM. (p. 14)

The American Bankers Association (1992) provided the following list of examples of actions by banks that would be prohibited by Title III of the ADA:

A bank may not refuse to interview a disabled individual for a loan and may have to provide an interpreter or reader to facilitate the interview and provide a private location for the interview if the loan officer's office is not accessible. (p. 12)

A bank cannot require that a person with a disability be accompanied by a non-disabled person when entering the safety deposit box area (in fact, the bank needs to ensure that the safety deposit area is accessible or provide comparable service in an accessible location). (p. 12)

A wheelchair user cannot be required to make a withdrawal in a location other than the bank lobby where tellers serve other customers. A desk may be provided for this purpose rather than constructing a lower teller window. (p. 12)

A blind individual could not be denied access to a financial planning seminar offered by the bank, even though audio cassettes of the program are available. Goods and services should be provided in the most integrated setting even if separate programs exist. (p. 13)

A teller cannot require a driver's license as identification from individuals whose disabilities prevent them from driving. (p. 13)

The bank cannot refuse a loan to a qualified health professional who cares for AIDS patients. (p. 13)

The U.S. Department of Justice is responsible for the enforcement of Title III of the ADA. Complaints about violations of Title III by public accommodations and commercial facilities should be sent to the U.S. Department of Justice (950 Pennsylvania Avenue NW; Civil Rights Division—Disability Rights Section; New York Avenue Building, Room 4023; Washington, DC 20530; see http://www.ada.gov/enforce.htm). The Department of Justice must first attempt to settle disputes through negotiations. If negotiations have been unsuccessful at achieving a formal settlement agreement, the U.S. Department of Justice can file a lawsuit in federal court to enforce Title III of the ADA. A number of Title III–based lawsuits and negotiated formal settlement agreements have been described by the U.S. Department of Justice. In late 1997 a federal district court judge gave the Department of Justice permission to pursue a lawsuit (*United States v. Ellerbe Beckett*) against one of the largest U.S. architectural firms that violated Title III by failing to comply with ADA accessibility standards in the construction of new sports arenas. "In denying Ellerbe Beckett's motion to dismiss, the court found that architects can be held liable" under Title III for failing "to provide wheelchair seating locations with a line of sight over standing spectators" in newly constructed arenas (U.S. Department of Justice, 1997, p. 2).

During the same period a formal settlement agreement was reached between the U.S. Department of Justice, two private plaintiffs, and the "Arizona

Shuttle Service, which operates a fixed route shuttle service between Tucson and Phoenix International Airport" (U.S. Department of Justice, 1997, p. 8).

> The two complaints investigated by the Department alleged that the Arizona Shuttle Service violated the ADA by refusing to transport an individual with her service animal because the animal was not a "seeing eye dog" and by purchasing two new vans that were not accessible to people with disabilities, including people who use wheelchairs. Just before entering the agreement, Arizona Shuttle purchased two accessible vans for its fleet. The agreement requires the company to maintain its accessible vans and to post and implement a service animal policy and a written reservations policy that meet the nondiscrimination requirements of the ADA. The agreement requires Arizona Shuttle to pay $10,000 in compensatory damages to the individual who was denied access because of her service animal. Another wheelchair user and a disability group in Arizona who jointly sued the company for having inaccessible buses and vans will each receive $2,500 in damages. Arizona Shuttle will also pay $5,000 in civil penalties to the United States. (U.S. Department of Justice, 1997, pp. 8–9)

Title III of the ADA can also be enforced through private lawsuits brought by an individual plaintiff. According to Tucker (1998),

> Any person who is subjected to discrimination on the basis of disability in violation of Title III, and any person who has "reasonable grounds" for believing that he or she is "about to be subjected to discrimination" in violation of the provisions relating to the construction or alteration of places of public accommodations, may file suit under the Act. (B. P. Tucker, 1998, p. 156)

Title IV: Increased Access to Telecommunications

Via the Communications Act of 1934, Congress mandated that to the greatest extent possible, all people in the United States have access to telephone and radio communications at reasonable cost. That congressional objective has a chance of being realized for persons with hearing disabilities and speech impediments through the Americans with Disabilities Act (Strauss, 1991).

By amending Title II of the Communications Act of 1934, Title IV of the ADA mandated the availability of a dual-party relay service system for intrastate and interstate telephone service by July 26, 1993 (N. L. Jones, 1991; Strauss, 1991). As a result, individuals who use a TDD (telecommunication device for the deaf) for communicating via the telephone can now call an operator for assistance in relaying the communication to a third party who uses a conventional telephone.

"A TDD is a device with a keyboard, resembling a small typewriter," used to transmit written messages to and receive written messages from others who have a TDD (Strauss, 1991, pp. 239–240). Therefore, without the relay service, a TDD user cannot independently carry out many simple tasks, such as making a reservation for dinner or calling a plumber, which require telephone communication with persons who have a conventional telephone. Without a relay service, such tasks can end up either requiring a special trip across town or a friend's assistance with the telephone call (Strauss, 1991).

Title IV of the ADA mandates that the relay services be sufficient to create a functional equivalence between the telephone service available to those who are deaf, hard of hearing, and speech impaired and those who are not. The Federal Communications Commission has the responsibility for establishing minimum standards for that relay service. Examples of such minimum standards required by the ADA are (a) 24-hour-per-day availability of relay services, (b) no restrictions on the length or content of calls that are assisted by relay services, (c) confidentiality maintained by relay operators about the context of all calls they handle, and (d) same rates for relay service and regular service calls (Strauss, 1991).

By the time the ADA was signed into law in July 1990, 40 states already had statewide dual-party telephone relay services available or a concrete plan formulated for beginning that service within the following 18 months. Even before the passage of the ADA, many of the states that had already implemented a relay system had experienced a high rate of usage of their systems. For example, California implemented a relay system in early 1987 that was designed to receive 50,000 calls per month. That number was exceeded by 37,511 calls in its first month of operation. By the summer of 1988, nearly 250,000 calls were being handled by the California relay system each month (Strauss, 1991).

Because the extra cost associated with the provision of a telephone relay service cannot be charged to the users of that service, it has typically been covered by three methods of funding: state appropriations, a surcharge on all telephone users in a state, and integration of costs into the normal operating expenses of the telephone company and recovery of the additional costs by increasing the rates for all telephone services. The majority of the states that had relay programs in 1990 funded them through a surcharge on all telephone subscribers that ranged from 3 to 20 cents per telephone access line (Strauss, 1991).

The Federal Communications Commission has the overall authority for enforcing Title IV of the ADA. However, that authority can be delegated to a state in which a complaint was filed if that state has established "adequate enforcement procedures and remedies to address violations of the Act" (Strauss, 1991, p. 255).

The mandate for the dual-party relay system in Title IV has direct implications for the reasonable accommodation or reasonable modification requirements in the other titles of the act. For example, with the existence of a dual-party national relay system, denying employment to a person with a hearing or speech impairment in a job that required using the telephone periodically would be considered employment discrimination on the basis of disability under Title I of the ADA (Strauss, 1991). The availability of that same national relay system tends to expand the definition of discrimination under Title III of the ADA. For example, hotels without a TDD to accept telephone reservations from people who are deaf or speech impaired may be required to have a TDD as well as to prepare their employees to efficiently process reservations made through a relay system (Strauss, 1991). To not do so would be to discriminate against persons with disabilities and therefore be in violation of Title III of the ADA.

Title IV also mandates that all television public service announcements that are produced with the assistance of federal funds must "include closed captioning of the verbal content of the announcement" (N. L. Jones, 1991, p. 39). Closed captioning is the use of printed words on the screen to communicate the "audio portions of television and video programming" (Peterson, 1998, p. 18). Parallel legislation, the Television Decoder Circuitry Act of 1990 (P.L. 101-431), addresses the electronic composition of future television sets to allow for the viewing of closed captions. That act amended the Communications Act of 1934 to "require as of July 1, 1993, that all televisions with screens of 13 inches or wider have built-in decoder circuitry for displaying closed captions" (U.S. EEOC, 1991, p. III-4). Subsequent to the passage of the ADA, Section 713 of the Telecommunications Act of 1996 also attempted to address the needs of persons with disabilities for greater access to video services. It

> mandates the video services be accessible to individuals who are hearing impaired and/or visually impaired. It requires the FCC to study the level to which video programming is closed-captioned and then to establish a timetable for closed captioning requirements. Section 713 also directs the FCC to study the use of video description in order to assure broad accessibility of this service to persons with visual impairments. (Peterson, 1998, p. 18)

Video description is defined as the auditory description of a visual element of a video program for those with visual impairments. These descriptions are "inserted in the natural pauses of a program's dialogue and may be used to describe visual elements such as body language, settings and actions" (Peterson, 1998, p. 18).

Title V: Miscellaneous Provisions

Title V contains a number of miscellaneous provisions. For example, it "prohibits retaliation and coercion against an individual who has opposed an act or practice made unlawful by the ADA" (N. L. Jones, 1991, p. 40). It also requires the Architectural and Transportation Compliance Board to issue procedural guidelines for making historic buildings and facilities accessible to persons with disabilities (N. L. Jones, 1991). In addition, for the first time in the history of the United States, Congress, under Title V of the ADA, "covered its own hiring practices by prohibiting discrimination in employment based upon disability" (Hearne, 1990, p. 77).

Compliance with the ADA

Pfeiffer and Finn (1997) summarized several of the more in–depth evaluations of compliance with the ADA. For example, National Council on Disability hearings in 1993 and 1995 resulted in a positive assessment regarding the responses of federal officials, people with disabilities, and trade associations. Testimony in the hearings underscored several benefits resulting from the ADA, such as "greater access, more communication, and more mobility" for people with disabilities (Pfeiffer & Finn, 1997, p. 755). These gains were made at reasonable costs and reflected a willingness to cooperate among different entities.

Results from site visits and surveys conducted by the U.S. General Accounting Office (GAO) back up this positive perspective. In those site visits, GAO raters reported compliance with ADA criteria at 67% and 74% in two studies. Furthermore, survey results supported the conclusion that the ADA promoted initial compliance via barrier removal (Pfeiffer & Finn, 1997). Room for improvement does, of course, exist. On the basis of its hearings, the National Council on Disability concluded that more educational and technical assistance efforts are needed and that specific groups of people (whether grouped by disability types or racial/ethnic backgrounds) were not receiving adequate protection. Evidence from site visits indicated that some employers were not maintaining their barrier removal efforts following their initial push to do so following the passage of the act (Pfeiffer & Finn, 1997).

Concluding Statement

DeJong and Batavia (1990) described the ADA as both a major achievement on the road to expanded human rights and a confirmation that most prior governmental efforts directed at helping individuals with disabilities to enter the mainstream of society had failed. The latter was based on the fact that after almost 20 years of pre-ADA government legislation directed at the removal of environmental and employment barriers for persons with disabilities, "only a quarter of work-age Americans with disabilities [were] employed full-time" and many "places of employment, vehicles of public transportation, and places of public accommodation [were still] inaccessible to people with disabilities" (p. 66).

Putting the ADA in the context of the entire public policy on disability, DeJong and Batavia (1990) questioned the ability of the ADA to significantly increase the employment rate for persons with disabilities unless there are also changes in other areas of the public policy that could counteract any of its potential effect. For example, efforts to promote the employment rights of persons with disabilities on Social Security Disability Insurance (SSDI) could prove futile unless counterincentives in the SSDI income maintenance and medical benefits policies that reduce their motivation to seek work are also sufficiently addressed. Once SSDI recipients have demonstrated their total inability to work in order to receive the income maintenance and associated Medicare benefits, they are often "hesitant to seek gainful employment for fear they will lose program eligibility they have fought hard to establish" (DeJong & Batavia, 1990, p. 68). As discussed in Chapter 2, although Congress removed "several of the work disincentives associated with the SSDI" program in the 1980s, many persons with disabilities remain "hesitant to risk losing their program eligibility through employment, even if they are assured that they will probably be able to regain eligibility in the future if necessary" (DeJong & Batavia, 1990, pp. 68–69).

The ADA was clearly a legislative breakthrough in the establishment of disability rights. Through the ADA, civil rights protections analogous to those found in the Civil Rights Act of 1964, as amended, have been extended to persons with disabilities in an attempt to bring them "into the mainstream of American life" (DeJong & Batavia, 1990, pp. 66–67). Therefore, the ADA established "long-awaited parity in federal civil rights laws between people with disabilities and other minorities and women" (Feldblum, 1991, p. 83). In signing the ADA into law, President George H. W. Bush kept a promise made at his inauguration: "I'm going to do whatever it takes to make sure that the disabled are included in the mainstream. For too long they have been left out, but they are not going to be left out anymore" (cited in Hearne, 1990, p. 76). The emphatic directive by then President Bush on the day of the signing of the ADA into law—"Let the shameful walls of exclusion finally come tumbling down"—neatly encapsulated the simple yet long-overdue message of the ADA: that 43 million Americans with disabilities are full-fledged citizens and as such are entitled to legal protections that ensure them equal opportunity and access to the mainstream of American life (U.S. EEOC, 1991, p. 1).

While the ADA has certainly been a progressive piece of legislation that has further opened up the door to equal opportunity in employment to persons with disabilities, due to the overall conservative posture taken by the courts in ADA cases that tend to clarify ambiguities in the ADA, that progress has not been overly exciting. Some examples of this conservative posture by the courts are as follows:

> Courts have rarely scrutinized employer claims of inability to accommodate in terms of actual cost, the overall financial resources of the enterprise, the size of the business, or the other the factors enumerated in the statute.... In addition, an accommodation generally strikes courts as reasonable only when it will involve modest cost and will not entail a significant change in the job or the normal course of workplace operation. Courts have been particularly reticent to demand [that] employers explore the option of reassignment to a vacant position. The burden of showing that other jobs are

available has been placed primarily on plaintiffs, even though that kind of information is often known only to employers. (M. Lee, 1997, p. 195)

That conservative posture was also reflected in the 1999 decisions of the U.S. Supreme Court in the cases of *Sutton v. United Airlines, Murphy v. UPS,* and *Albertsons Inc. v. Kirkingburg.* Those decisions limited the coverage of the ADA to only those individuals with disabilities who were limited in a major life activity with or without medical corrections. Whether intentionally or not, those decisions sent out a message that it is acceptable to discriminate against those individuals with a disability if they are not limited in a major life activity after medical corrections (e.g., a person whose epilepsy is controlled by medication). They also sent a message to all those individuals with genetic markers for a yet-to-emerge disability that they can be discriminated against on the basis of genetic markers until the disability actually manifests itself (D. Kaplan, 2000). The conservative posture of the U.S. Supreme Court was also reflected in its decisions on the "direct threat" provision of the ADA and on the right of persons with disabilities to sue states for monetary damages where discrimination in employment on the basis of disability occurs. In both cases the antidiscrimination protections of the ADA for persons with disabilities were somewhat eroded.

Chapter 4

Philosophical and Economic Considerations in Regard to Disability Rights and Support for Rehabilitation Programs

The population of persons with disabilities is an extremely heterogeneous group. People became part of this population for various reasons:

> Some are unable to get around without wheelchairs; others learn at a slower rate than most people; some experience abnormal electrical discharges in their brains called seizures; and still others have malformed or disfigured facial features. People are termed handicapped because they "talk funny" or "walk funny"; because they cannot hear or cannot see; because their reasoning thought processes do not work in conventional ways; because their limbs are missing or malformed; because they have learning disabilities, such as dyslexia …; because they have disorders like kidney disease, arthritis, heart disease, diabetes, or cancer; or even because they once had certain conditions, such as mental illness, cancer, or seizures, from which they have since recovered. (U.S. Commission on Civil Rights, 1983, p. 4)

Approximately 50 million people in the United States have disabilities, based on data from the U.S. Census Bureau (Head & Baker, 2005). A school-age subset of this population was estimated in 2002 to approximate 6 million (i.e., students with disabilities in the age range of 6–21 receiving special education services) (U.S. Department of Education, 2002). Another subset of this population, Americans between the ages of 16 and 24 with disabilities that affect their capacity to work, has been estimated to exceed 21 million (Waldrop & Stern, 2003). Given these statistics, it is safe to say that millions of Americans currently in and soon to be in the workforce would be good candidates for vocational rehabilitation services as a result of meeting the following criteria:

1. Their disability presents a substantial handicap to employment.
2. It can reasonably be expected that vocational rehabilitation services would enable them to engage in a gainful occupation.

The estimate of the number of persons with disabilities who can benefit from rehabilitation services is even greater when those persons capable of benefiting from independent living rehabilitation services (but with little potential for competitive employment) are also considered.

Is American society willing or able to underwrite the cost of rehabilitating the large number of persons with disabilities? The answer would be a qualified "yes," given the fact that rehabilitation services are being provided to only a small percentage of the population of persons with disabilities. Results from a survey conducted by the Council of State Administrators in Vocational Rehabilitation indicated that state rehabilitation agencies serve only 1 of every 20 eligible people with disabilities (Rehab Action, 1993). Given that a 2004 survey conducted by Louis Harris and Associates showed that "78 percent of the nondisabled population of working age are employed compared to only 35 percent of people with disabilities" (National Organization on Disability, 2004), a major expansion in the amount of resources allocated to help meet the employment needs of persons with disabilities seems warranted. Furthermore, given the fact that the majority of "Americans with disabilities who are employed hold only marginal jobs" (Fleischer & Zames, 2001, p. 111), the real suggested level of neglect of the rights to employment for persons with disabilities may be somewhat underestimated by even the above-noted 35% employment rate. But even if that employment rate figure is an accurate reflection of the right to employment for persons with disabilities, it is nothing to cheer about. What rights do persons with disabilities have to an improved situation?

A Right to What?

Americans in general and Americans with disabilities in particular consider themselves to have certain rights. For example, it is not unusual for Americans to claim a constitutional guarantee of the right to life, liberty, and the pursuit of happiness. Those rights imply the right to normal opportunities, that is, to have opportunities whose sum falls within the "normal opportunity range." Daniels (1981) defined the normal opportunity range for a given society as "the array of 'life-plans' reasonable persons in it are likely to construct for themselves" (p. 158). Compatible with the right to normal opportunity would be a guarantee that persons with disabilities have the right to restoration services and to accessible environments in order to make the opportunities of persons with and without disabilities more equal. Such a guarantee provides a powerful rationale for federal and state tax-based financial support for rehabilitation programs and environmental barrier removal.

A society that values equal opportunity will attempt to distribute its discretionary resources in a way that increases the likelihood that the basic needs of all will be met. Such a society would provide persons with disabilities a larger share of the health care resources commensurate with the greater difficulty they experience in achieving a level of "normal-species" functioning. Such a society would also commit sufficient resources to the design of environments for increasing the likelihood that persons with and without disabilities have equal freedom of movement for acquiring basic satisfactions.

A statement such as "the right to life, liberty, and the pursuit of happiness" gains further clarity when translated into specific rights, such as rights to medical care, education, or employment. However, such rights statements might be misleading because they imply that all persons have an "absolute" right to either an equal or a necessary share of medical care, education, or employment. Fried (1983) provided a definition of a right that clearly demonstrates the danger of loosely using the term without qualification:

> A right is more than an interest that an individual might have, a state of affairs, or a state of being which an individual might prefer. A claim of right invokes entitlement; and, when we speak of entitlement, we mean not those things which it would be nice for people to have, or which they would prefer to have but which they must have, and which if they do not have they may demand, whether we like it or not. (p. 491)

Legislation since the early 1970s, discussed in Chapters 2 and 3, contains a "bill of rights" for persons with disabilities. Rather than extending any open-ended right, that legislation provides a right to what society would consider as a necessary minimum amount of education, medical care, income, and employment, given available resources. It also enables people with disabilities who have adequate discretionary funds to have equal access to greater amounts of necessary or desired social and educational services. This would be more acceptable than an open-ended right in a democratic capitalistic society, which "considers that inequalities of wealth and income are morally acceptable—acceptable in the sense that the system that produces these inequalities is in itself not morally suspect" (Fried, 1983, p. 494). Furthermore, a prevailing belief in U.S. society is that members have a right to a "decent" level of nutrition, health care, education, and legal assistance, and when that level has been provided for, "all that exists in the way of rights has been accorded.... Were we to insist on equality beyond this minimum, we would have committed ourselves to political philosophy which is not the dominant one in our society" (Fried, 1983, p. 494).

The Questionable Right to a Guaranteed Minimum: Health Care as an Example

Although legislation since the early 1970s established a so-called Bill of Rights for people with disabilities, the disability community cannot assume that a consensus exists among all Americans in regard to those rights. One of the "hotter" issues in American society is what "right" Americans have to health care.

Perusal of the professional medical journals clearly shows that not all physicians consider health care as a right. In an article published in the *Journal of Medical Ethics,* Shelton (1978) pointed out that a major portion of the health delivery system in the United States has operated on the basis that health care is "a commodity to be bought and sold, rather than a right to be claimed, guaranteed and protected" (p. 167). In an article in the *New England Journal of Medicine* titled "Medical Care as a Right: A Refutation," Sade (1971) stated,

> Medical care is neither a right nor a privilege: It is a service that is provided by doctors and others to people who wish to purchase it. It is the provision of this service that a doctor depends upon for his livelihood, and is his means of supporting his own life. If the right to health care belongs to the patient, he starts out owning the services of the doctor without the necessity of either earning them or receiving them as a gift from the only man who has the right to give them: the doctor himself. (p. 1289)

Was Sade without support in his opposition to the doctrine of health care as a right? Not according to Dr. F. J. Ingelfinger, then editor of the *New England*

Journal of Medicine. Personally opposed to Sade's position, Ingelfinger (1972) was surprised at the positive response Sade received from the medical community:

> Within three weeks he had received 200 commendatory letters and over 1000 reprint requests. At least seven groups (including a state medical journal, two county medical societies and the officers of a state medical society) ... requested permission to reprint the article. (Ingelfinger, 1972, p. 487)

At present, no clear integrated public policy exists on health care and rehabilitation benefit rights for persons with disabilities. Also, no constitutionally guaranteed right is afforded persons with disabilities to all medical care and rehabilitation services needed. In the absence of both, persons with disabilities cannot claim a legal right to *sufficient* medical care and rehabilitation services. The presence of government support for medical care and rehabilitation services for persons with disabilities is not necessarily synonymous with there being a legal right to sufficient medical care and rehabilitation services (Fleischer & Zames, 2001).

The plight of persons with severe disabilities without a legal right to costly, but available medical services, as well as the moral problem associated with the failure of society to guarantee that right, was reflected in a nurse's letter to the editor of the *Southern Illinoisan* newspaper pertaining to the predicament of a 7-year-old leukemia victim named Jeff. An abstract of that letter follows:

> Jeff needs a bone marrow transplant; his insurance company won't pay; hospitals that provide this service require $125,000 to $150,000 "up front" to consider him a candidate. Therefore, his parents must appeal to the public to help raise funds to give their son a chance.... Somewhere along the way, our health care system has taken the wrong road. Why should parents of a seriously ill child have to plead with society for his right to live? Why do hospitals have the right to demand astronomical fees "up front" before accepting such a child? ... No health care person, team, equipment or facility can possibly be worth one day of a child's life. There is no argument to justify this practice. This child and others like him should not have to wait one minute for a chance to live. (Hindman, 1985, p. 8)

In today's society, where the size of the population of persons with severe disabilities continues to expand annually as a result of both lifesaving and life-lengthening medical advances, ethical problems related to access to medical care and rehabilitation services are encountered. Limited access to medical care did not present a major problem prior to the 20th century, because medical care at that time conferred no real advantage in terms of health or survival (Abram & Wolf, 1984). Today, as a result of the existence of expensive high-technology treatment options, society is sometimes confronted with the problem of determining criteria for selection of persons for treatment. That decision-making problem exists to the degree that U.S. society is both unwilling and unable economically to "pay the bill" for all in need of accessing such advanced medical and rehabilitation techniques. Because treating everybody optimally given the available technology is economically impossible, decisions are made regarding who receives treatment. Such decisions are incompatible with the existence of an absolute right to treatment.

The issue of the right of persons with disabilities to medical treatment was faced in the Baby Doe case. Baby Doe was born in Bloomington, Indiana, on April 9, 1982, with "Down's Syndrome, plus esophageal atresia with associated tracheoesophageal fistula" (Weir, 1983, p. 661). As a result of a decision not to provide surgery or intravenous feeding because of the severity of the medical problems, Baby Doe was allowed to die from starvation. The resulting public furor stimulated an action by the federal government to prevent recurrences by drafting regulations based on Section 504's prohibition against discrimination on the basis of handicap. On July 5, 1983, the "Department of Health and Human Services issued proposed rules to ensure that handicapped newborns, no matter how severe their handicaps, receive all possible life-sustaining treatment, unless imminent death is considered inevitable or the risks of treatment are prohibitive" (Angell, 1983, p. 659). Both public support and opposition to this federal action followed. In a September 15, 1983, editorial in the *New England Journal of Medicine,* Dr. Marcia Angell expressed her opposition to the federal action on the basis of its failure to recognize quality of life as a consideration in medical treatment decisions for infants with severe disabilities. Angell suggested that reasonable people would consider their lives as intolerable in the absence of a "certain" minimum level of intellectual or physical functioning and, therefore, not want them prolonged in spite of availability of the medical technology to do so. Arras (1984) pointed out that a major limitation in basing an argument on the type of life that reasonable people might not prefer to death is that "reasonable" is basically defined from a "normal" adult's point of view. Arras (1984) stated, "It is only natural to expect that, were the questions put to them, many normal adults, having grown accustomed to the social and intellectual satisfactions that normalcy makes possible, would rather die than live without these basic human capacities" (p. 30). What about the point of view, however, of the infant with severe mental or physical disabilities? Would that child, "who has never known the satisfactions and aspirations of the normal world,... prefer nothing to what he or she has" (Arras, 1984, p. 30)?

The type of medical nonaction taken in the case of Baby Doe is referred to in the medical literature as *selective nontreatment* or *passive euthanasia* (Harris, 1981). Another example of its application occurred in 1971 at Johns Hopkins University Hospital, where an infant born "with Down's Syndrome and operable duodenal atresia was allowed to die, apparently because it could never achieve some semblance of normality" (C. Cohen, 1983, p. 125). The literature suggests that these practices have not been unusual, especially in the case of severe congenital disabilities such as spina bifida. Harris (1981) discussed a report of nontreatment by Dr. John Lorber in a hospital in England where nontreatment was reported as a success because none of the first 41 infants with spina bifida selected for nontreatment survived beyond 8 months, with 60%

dying before they were 1 month old. In defending his practice of selective non-treatment in a reply to Harris (1981), Lorber (1981, p. 121) stated that his own "point of view has been supported by churchmen in the highest offices from various Christian denominations and other religions," as well as by the ethics committee of his hospital. Lorber (1981) went on to say,

> I know that [a] policy of selective non-treatment is a very long way from ideal and may be attacked on principle for many reasons, but we live in a practical world and I believe that this is the only practical and humane way in which one can deal with these virtually impossible situations where truly good solutions do not exist. (p. 121)

Arras (1984) would question the medical ethics of Lorber's practices on the ground that Lorber would be incapable of reliably predicting the characteristics of the lives of many of those infants with disabilities if they were allowed to survive. Arras (1984) stated,

> The mere presence of Down Syndrome or of spina bifida does not by itself indicate how disabled a child will be.... The problem is that, except for a few classes of disease, physicians cannot accurately predict the degree of a child's eventual impairment. This problem is compounded by our ability to diminish a child's eventual degree of disability by some means of vigorous medical and education interventions. (p. 27)

In the Baby Doe, Johns Hopkins, and Lorber cases, right to health care decisions were made for infants with disabilities on the basis of other people's judgment of the potential quality of their lives. However, *quality of life* is a difficult concept to delineate. Its definition cannot be argued in the absence of subjective judgments. Although there may be objective criteria on which quality of life can be measured (P. A. Murphy & Williams, 1999), those same criteria cannot be used to determine what is intolerable, or what life is not worth living, for a given individual. For example, is it possible that the same person might at 21 years of age see death as preferable to suffering "the imagined ignominy of a nursing-home" but at age 85 be "only too grateful to accept the nursing-home bed and warm meal" (Haliker, 1983, p. 718).

The problem is complicated by the fact that "quality of life" has no universally accepted subjective, let alone objective, definition (C. Cohen, 1983). Quality-of-life positions can address the potential "happiness" of the individual, the potential net worth of the individual to the society in which he or she lives, or a combination of both. In regard to the happiness of the individual, Arras (1984) questioned how reasonable adults could "compare the advantages of life, even with severe disabilities, against the state of nonbeing initiated by death" without having experienced the latter (p. 26).

As major technological advances continue to be made in the areas of biological and genetic engineering, the bioethical dilemmas reflected in the Baby

Doe, Johns Hopkins, and Lorber cases will surface more and more in discussions of the rights of fetuses with disabilities. Given access to these technologies, how many prospective parents will determine the right to life of fetuses with discernible disabilities such as cystic fibrosis, Down syndrome, or sickle cell anemia? Do parents' rights to have a "normal" child trump the right of the fetus with a disability to life? Do expectant parents play into the distorted vision of the eugenicist when they draw upon the technological "capacity to create designer offspring—with predetermined characteristics, intelligence quotients, or personality traits" (Fleischer & Zames, 2001, pp. 159–160)? How will the ethical and pragmatic problems associated with the conflict between the rights of parents and those of fetuses be resolved (Fleischer & Zames, 2001)?

As medical costs continue to escalate with the development of more advanced medical treatment technologies, greater emphasis is being placed on extent of potential benefit and quality-of-life criteria in determining right-to-treatment issues. What are the implications of that emphasis for persons with severe disabilities? Which persons with severe disabilities will receive treatment? What expensive medical procedures will be done?

"Providing expensive technology in the management of one patient's medical problem may mean that another patient's needs have to be ignored" (Leaf, 1984, pp. 718–719). Leaf (1984) pointed out that while the costs of providing high-tech treatments to everyone are very high for low-incidence diseases such as end-stage renal disease, they become prohibitive for high-incidence diseases such as cardiovascular disease. He called for much more specificity in regard to both the proportion of the national wealth that should be allocated for health care and the distribution of that allocation across competing health care needs.

When the public policy on the right to medical care tends to be designed in a way that significantly limits the right to employment of individuals falling into certain categories, such as those who are unemployed and have a chronic disability, the rights to employment for persons with disabilities supposedly being championed by the public policy reflected in Title V of the Rehabilitation Act and Title I of the ADA tend to be unintentionally short-circuited. Fleischer and Zames (2001) discussed the effect of these unsynchronized rights as follows:

> The disincentives resulting from the nexus between jobs and health care for people with disabilities have presented a major obstacle to the employment of potential workers with disabilities who can and want to work. Since Medicaid—the sole source of reimbursement for long-term services and supports—has been available only to people who are not working, many people with disabilities have been forced to remain unemployed. In order to remain on Medicare by 1999, recipients of Social Security Disability Insurance were precluded from earning more than seven hundred dollars a month.... In addition, because of "preexisting condition exclusions, limits on benefits, and caps on payment," most health insurance companies do not adequately cover people with disabilities.... Consequently, many

workers with disabling conditions, no longer covered by health insurance companies, have been forced to become Social Security beneficiaries on Medicare or Medicaid rather than employees. (pp. 129–130)

Recognition of the need to decouple medical insurance benefits and employment is increasingly evident in the literature (Growick, 2004; Marini & Reid, 2001) and in major Social Security legislation such as the Ticket to Work and Work Incentives Improvement Act of 1999 (TWWIIA) (Roessler, 2002). The TWWIIA provision that calls for the extension of Medicare for 9.5 years following employment is one example of ways to reduce disincentives related to returning to work.

Are Rights Related to Cause of Disability?

To a large degree, congenital disabilities, as well as many noncongenital disabilities, can be considered the result of a "natural lottery." A just society might distribute its discretionary resources to help equalize the lifetime opportunities afforded the victims of the natural lottery and those of persons without disabilities. Resources would be distributed to equalize access to education, employment, health care, and the physical environment.

Would a just society accept the same responsibilities for those individuals whose disabilities do not result from a natural lottery, but are rather the result of taking voluntary risks to their health? Examples of such voluntary risk-taking behaviors could include "smoking, skiing, playing professional football, compulsive eating, omitting exercise, exposing oneself excessively to the sun, skipping needed immunization, automobile racing, and mountain climbing" (Veatch, 1980, p. 50). Should persons whose disabilities result from taking such voluntary risks have less of a right to health care and rehabilitation services than those persons with disabilities who are victims of the natural lottery? If the answer is "yes," then what are the rights of the professional firefighter and the police officer who acquire disabilities while performing their jobs? They took a voluntary risk when they entered those professions. If this example is seen as a nonsensical comparison with the other examples, then what rights should the professional athlete who becomes seriously injured have if his or her alternative to entering that profession may have been a life of poverty or crime? Veatch (1980) comprehensively addressed the complexity of attempting to determine differential rights to health care on the basis of the cause of the disability.

The Interaction of Medical Advances and the Rights of Persons with Disabilities

From an absolute moral position, an individual has the right to life, liberty, and the pursuit of happiness regardless of the extent of functional limitation resulting from a disabling condition. On the other hand, from a resource allocation position, the rights of the individual can be in conflict with the rights of the group. This conflict between individual and group rights pervades history. In ancient Roman society, it was clearly evident that the rights of the group were paramount—the head of the household could decide if a baby was to live or die 10 days following birth. Today, 1-day-old children have the legal right to life regardless of their physical or mental state. Costs, monetary or otherwise, are not considered acceptable as the primary factor in any life-sustaining determination decisions. Consequently, it appears that, as a society, Americans have a more humane attitude toward persons with disabilities than did the citizens of ancient Rome.

Medical advances, however, have laid a foundation for recreating situations somewhat comparable to the "10th-day" Roman situation. A good example would be the development of amniocentesis as a relatively safe and accurate diagnostic procedure for identifying fetuses with Down syndrome and a number of other abnormalities that can be identified via analysis of the amniotic fluid. Although the technological development itself can be discussed without considering society's attitude toward persons with disabilities (e.g., its diagnostic information can prepare parents psychologically for the birth of a child with Down syndrome), few high-risk parents (e.g., pregnant women over 40 years old) opt for the procedure without entertaining abortion as an option (Graham, 1981, p. 267). Therefore, by allowing for amniocentesis, as well as abortion when the results indicate Down syndrome, is U.S. society manifesting an attitude toward persons with disabilities that differs from that of the Romans? Do Americans consider it acceptable to destroy a fetus only because of the identified imperfection?

Continued technological advances in medicine, paired with the growing realization of the limited financial resources available, confront society with difficult moral challenges. As medical and rehabilitation service costs continue to escalate with the development of more advanced medical technologies, what criteria should be used in determining right-to-treatment issues? Will the criteria be primarily economic in nature?

What is the most just criterion for the allocation of health care resources in American society? The resolution of the problem of allocation of health care resources is fraught with complexities when questions of individual rights and social justice are simultaneously considered. Which society is more just? Is it the society that allocates its resources to "remove serious impairments of opportunity for a few people" or the one that allocates its resources to "remove significant but less serious impairments" for many (N. Daniels, 1981)?

Many difficult moral issues were posed in the preceding paragraphs. Regardless of the ambiguity associated with those issues, U.S. society, as evidenced by the Americans with Disabilities Act (ADA) and amendments to the Rehabilitation Act, appears to be increasingly committed to ensuring that people with severe disabilities have access to vocational and independent living services. One may argue, however, that society is not sufficiently putting its money where its mouth is.

Does U.S. Public Policy on the Right of Persons with Disabilities to Employment Suggest a State of "Upside-Down Welfarism"?

The pervading orientation of social welfare policy in the United States has been to initiate programs that socioeconomically uplift those with a disability with the greatest needs least and those with a disability with lesser needs most. Such a policy perspective has been referred to as "upside-down welfarism" (Walz & Boucher, 2000, p. 432). It has been hypothesized that this orientation is the result of the contents of American social welfare policy being greatly influenced by market forces. As a result of that influence, laws that provide for "various kinds of public assistance, support, and civil protections" are greatly directed at helping those individuals with disabilities who are most capable of functioning positively in the current market economy (Walz & Boucher, 2000, p. 432). For example, while definitely opening doors to competitive employment and positively affecting the lives of some persons with disabilities, in general the Americans with Disabilities Act and subsequent associated case law decisions can be viewed as being compatible with a social welfare policy that reflects a state of upside-down welfarism and that is beneficial to a market economy (Walz & Boucher, 2000).

In reflecting the upside-down welfarism in the public policy on disability, the ADA seems to have been constructed to address primarily the needs of a preferred and privileged group of people with disabilities while systematically slighting others with more severe disabilities and thereby not meeting many of their significant needs (Walz & Boucher, 2000). Walz and Boucher (2000) pointed out that members of the preferred group tend to be "the better educated, more work experienced, higher social class persons within the disability community" (p. 433) whereas the members of the slighted group tend to be those who, historically, have been seen as having minimal potential to function in competitive employment. Therefore, they tend to be those who would require the type of accommodations to function in a competitive labor market job that, under the ADA, would allow employers to claim that the accommodations cause an "undue hardship." Consequently, U.S. public policy tends to divert these individuals "into social service sheltered employment (e.g., Goodwill Industries)," where they usually "earn a substandard wage" (Walz & Boucher, 2000, p. 434). According to Walz and Boucher (2000), "most systematically slighted persons have one or more developmental disabilities. Included are persons who have experienced moderate to severe mental retardation or autism, mental illness, and physical impairments, or dual diagnoses of the aforementioned" (p. 434).

The public policy on disability as reflected in the ADA can be very unfair to those with a history of mental illness in regard to failing to facilitate their employment in jobs in the competitive labor market. Fleischer and Zames (2001) pointed out that individuals with

> psychiatric disabilities have limited recourse under the employment discrimination laws because if their impairment is treated successfully, they are considered non-disabled under the ADA; yet if their symptoms persist, they may be considered unable to perform the essential function of the job. (p. 115)

Therefore, it is not surprising that the estimated unemployment rate for persons with psychiatric disabilities is 85% (W. Wilkinson & Frieden, 2000).

Can You or Can You Not Discriminate Against Certain Persons with Disabilities in Employment? That Is the Question.

American society is still trying to determine which individuals with disabilities can be discriminated against in employment. This is exemplified in the case of individuals with Type I insulin-dependent diabetes. Such diabetes is controlled by continuously maintaining a delicate balance between the amount of food ingested and the amount of insulin injected. When the balance is maintained, such individuals with diabetes are not protected from discrimination by Title I of the ADA because they are not seen as substantially limited in a major life activity (for further discussion of this criterion, see Chapter 3). When the balance is not maintained, however, the individual would be seen as incapable of performing many of the functions of jobs in the competitive labor market, or the accommodations needed to do so would often be viewed as creating an undue hardship on employers. This issue regarding the right to employment for persons with Type I diabetes was demonstrated in the case of Rebecca Ann Fraser, who has Type I diabetes and who claimed she was unjustly fired by United States Bancorp due to her disability. Fraser filed suit in U.S. District Court and lost, then won on appeal in the Ninth Circuit Court, only to have the bank petition the U.S. Supreme Court to take the case (Kilpatrick, 2004).

In his column "Diabetes and Disabled Act," James Kilpatrick (2004) described this case, which originated from a firing in March 1999 and which was yet to have a final resolution in February 2004. According to records of the court, Fraser's supervisor, Jeff Erwin, in November 1998,

> ordered her not to eat at her desk. On the day in question, her blood sugar level had precipitately dropped to 34. She had food in her desk and begged permission to eat it. "Erwin," the court remarked, "told her to come back when she had an intelligent question to ask." She became disoriented. She ate some candy from a vending machine, but to no avail. Eventually she

passed out in the lobby of the bank building. With her husband's assistance she finally made it home and injected glucagon.

Things went rapidly downhill at the office. She complained to Erwin's supervisor, and then was harassed for filing the complaint. She was subjected to changes in her assignment and workstation. Her evaluations declined. In March 1999 she was fired. (Kilpatrick, 2004, p. 2E)

In its petition to the U.S. Supreme Court to hear the case, the defendant argued that the plaintiff was not disabled under the ADA based on any substantial limitation in a major life activity. The plaintiff had claimed that she was limited by her disability in the major life activity of eating, which the defendant argued was not the case because her disability "does not restrict her ability to engage in the physical act of eating" (Kilpatrick, 2004, p. 2E). In writing the decision for the Ninth Circuit's overturning of the District Court's decision, the judge declared that the plaintiff was limited in the major life activity of eating because the timing of her meals and daily shots must be so carefully attended to

that it is not safe for her to live alone. She must also have certain foods available in case her blood sugar drops or skyrockets. She cannot skip or postpone a snack or meal without cautiously studying her insulin and glucagon levels. She must "constantly, faithfully and precisely monitor her eating, exercise, blood sugar and other health factors, and even this is no guarantee of success." (Kilpatrick, 2004, p. 2E)

Will the U.S. Supreme Court agree to hear this case? If they do, what will they decide? Will that decision strengthen or weaken the rights of individuals with disabilities to protection against discrimination in employment?

The Effect of Advances in the Science of Molecular Genetics on the Right to Equal Access to Employment for Those with Disabilities

The genetic research revolution characterized by the Human Genome Project promises to provide future diagnostic tools to physicians that should increase the effectiveness of medical services. However, those same diagnostic tools could be used to provide information to employers that may result in discrimination against people who do not currently have a disability, but who have a genetic marker for potentially developing one in the future, on the basis of that potential future disability (Olick, 2000). Thus far, neither the ADA nor the courts have spoken to the reach of the ADA in regard to its potential for preventing genetic discrimination (Olick, 2000). There have been enough examples of past employment discrimination on the basis of disability to warrant serious attention to the question of the ADA's ability to "battle" genetic discrimination. If the ADA allows genetic testing as part of medical exams to identify genetic markers for possible future illnesses, employers will have the possibility to practice genetic discrimination (Olick, 2000). This is because of the type of information genetic markers can provide. For example, genetic markers can be used as

> predictors of an employee's future years on the job, need for sick leave, and consumption of health and disability benefits; as indicators of an individual's ability to perform a particular job; as signals of hypersusceptibility to workplace injury (e.g., the employee with respiratory sensitivity to the work environment); or as evidence of a (potential) threat to coworkers or to the public at large (the air traffic controller with the gene for Alzheimer's disease). (Olick, 2000, p. 286)

Further exacerbating the current level of unfairness associated with genetic discrimination is the present realization that, with only a few exceptions such as Huntington's disease or Tay-Sachs disease, genetic markers can only "identify *predispositions* to develop certain illnesses, diseases, or conditions. Genetic prediction is 'probabilistic … not deterministic'" (Olick, 2000, p. 291). However, future development in the science of molecular genetics could undermine the validity of this current perception (Olick, 2000).

Title I of the Americans with Disabilities Act is directed at reducing discrimination in the workplace on the basis of disability. Employment statistics reported elsewhere in this book suggest that that goal may have only been chipped away at thus far rather than achieved. One possible reason for the slow progress that has been made is the attitudinal barriers that result in the tendency of persons without disabilities to socially distance themselves from those with disabilities. According to Hahn (1988b), this social distancing is largely the result of discomfort that is stimulated in those without a disability by the presence of those with disabilities. He referred to this discomfort as stemming from two types of anxiety: *aesthetic anxiety* and *existential anxiety*. Hahn (1988b) described these terms as follows:

> The term *aesthetic anxiety* refers to the fears engendered by persons whose appearance deviates markedly from the usual human form or includes physical traits regarded as unappealing. These fears are reflected in both the propensity to shun those with unattractive bodily attributes and the extraordinary stress that modern society devotes to its quest for supernormal standards of bodily perfection.
>
> *Existential anxiety* refers to the threat of potential loss of functional capabilities by the nondisabled. The existential anxiety triggered by disabilities occasionally may become the subject of conscious attention. Sometimes these concerns are evident in the silent thought that "there, but for the grace of God [or luck or fate or other fundamental beliefs], go I." At other times, these worries may be verbalized in statements such as,

"I would rather be dead than live as a paraplegic [or as blind, deaf, or immobilized]." In fact, the threat of a permanent and debilitating disability, with its resulting problems, can even outrank the fear of death, which is, after all, inevitable. (pp. 42–43)

In the absence of the implementation of effective nondiscrimination safeguards in employment law, and as the science of molecular genetics continues to progress, this fear of being in the presence of those with disabilities makes all those who may not currently have a disability, but who possess a genetic marker for the onset of one in the future, potentially the future victims of discrimination by employers who are predisposed to the above-described aesthetic and existential anxiety. Possibly this realization will stimulate additional legislation to guarantee everyone, including those with disabilities, the right to equal access in employment. It will be very interesting if many of the potential unintended consequences from the advances in molecular genetics are both addressed and defused in future public policy debates on disability. Even more interesting could be the future manifestation of a positive unintended consequence in the form of a significant reduction in negative devaluing and social distancing attitudes toward disability as a result of advances in the science of molecular genetics. Greater acceptance of differences could occur, as molecular genetics points out that there are 5,000 heritable disorders and, "if the prophets of genetics are correct, each of us possess [sic] some small number of 'disease genes,' and each of us is potentially vulnerable to genetic discrimination" (Olick, 2000, p. 309). As progress in the science of molecular genetics continues, will it be altruism or self-interest that will, in the end, substantially remove the barriers to the full participation of persons with disabilities in society?

Arguments for Rehabilitation Services

Many reasons can be provided for support of rehabilitation services as a federal and state government funding priority. These reasons can be grouped as either economic or moral arguments. However, dangers associated with a total dependence on either argument suggest the viability of a rationale that combines the two. Each argument, the associated dangers, and the balancing of the two arguments for gaining public support for rehabilitation services are discussed in the following sections.

The Economic Argument

Most persons with disabilities receiving rehabilitation services are unemployed at referral. Their unemployment status is often the result of their inability to produce on a job an amount of output that equals or exceeds the wages associated with the position. The vocational rehabilitation process is designed "to improve the value of the client's potential contribution to the employer's output.... The change can be made either by improving the client's functioning, or by making job accommodations, or both" (M. Berkowitz, 1984, pp. 354–355). Rehabilitation services have helped many unemployed individuals with disabilities enter or reenter the competitive labor market, with the result being both increased lifetime earnings and the eventual repayment of the cost of their rehabilitation in tax dollars.

From an economic point of view, it can be argued that lack of government financial support for rehabilitation programs makes little sense. In fact, rehabilitation programs have traditionally argued for government support on the grounds of being a good investment. Senator Robert Dole (2004) clarified just how cost-effective rehabilitation is in commenting that rehabilitants pay back their annual costs for rehabilitation in 2 to 4 years. Studies conducted in the early 1970s yielded benefit–cost ratios of approximately 10 to 1 for money expended on vocational rehabilitation (Levitan & Taggert, 1982, p. 114), a figure supported by the Office of Management and Budget, which reported that the government earns $11 in taxes for every $1 spent on the rehabilitation program (Rehab Action, 1993). Compatible with that ratio, the fiscal year 1981 annual report of the Rehabilitation Services Administration estimated that

> lifetime earnings for persons rehabilitated in fiscal year 1980 would improve by $10.40 for every dollar spent on services. Those persons were expected to pay federal, state, and local governments an estimated $211.5 million more in income, payroll, and sales taxes than they would have paid had they not been rehabilitated. (Weicker, 1984, p. 521)

Similar benefit–cost ratios were found by Nowak (1983) for fiscal year 1975 rehabilitants of the New Jersey State Vocational Rehabilitation Program who ranged in age from 35 to 44 and who had 12 years of education. However, Nowak found more modest benefit–cost ratios of 4 or 5 to 1 for fiscal year 1975 rehabilitants of the same agency who had fewer than 12 years of education and who were less than 25 or more than 54 years of age. Therefore, size of the return on investment in vocational rehabilitation programs may depend on the characteristics of the client served.

Major increases in the total maintenance cost underscore the need for rehabilitation services. Between 1970 and 1977, federal disability transfer program payments increased from $8.4 billion to $26.5 billion (M. Berkowitz & Berkowitz, 1985). In 1979, in addition to losses in productivity and taxes, it cost the American public $29 billion for income payments to persons with disabilities "under all Federal disability income support programs" (Verville, 1979, p. 49). By 1982 the federal income support cost for people with disabilities had increased to approximately $36 billion (Office of Technology Assessment, 1983). Those costs likely exceed $100 billion today (Marini & Reid, 2001). These figures clearly support inclusion of reduced government maintenance costs in the economic rationale for vocational rehabilitation.

The economic argument can also be used in support of independent living rehabilitation services. This can be demonstrated by examining the situation of the 231,000 people a year who survive a stroke, in many cases with significant functional limitations (Eazell & Johnston, 1981). Studies show that provision of comprehensive rehabilitation services following completion of acute medical care services results in a higher rate of people who have had a stroke living outside of institutions such as nursing homes. Via data from these studies, estimates could be derived of the additional number of stroke patients who could return home if provided comprehensive rehabilitation services. Using those estimates, plus estimates of (a) the average added cost for comprehensive rehabilitation services for people who have survived a stroke and (b) the cost savings for a stroke patient living at home rather than in a nursing home, Eazell and Johnston (1981) computed a cost–benefit ratio of 1.769 to 1. They concluded the following from this ratio:

> Considering the national picture, if only half of the 231,000 known persons who survive stroke each year in the United States were to receive comprehensive rehabilitation, total national savings would be $740 million. If 80% could receive rehabilitation, saving would be $1.18 billion in 1980 dollars. (p. 18)

The savings of 1.18 billion in 1980 dollars would probably exceed $2 billion in current dollars.

Eazell and Johnston (1981) summarized other research that suggests that independent living rehabilitation services make economic sense even when stroke patients are likely to reside permanently in an extended care facility. That research has shown that the amount of functional independence is strongly related to "costs in extended care facilities. Improvement of a patient from total dependence to partial dependence has been found to reduce care cost by 65%. A further improvement of partial independence saved 40% more" (Eazell & Johnston, 1981, p. 19).

The cost to society of failing to address the vocational or independent living rehabilitation needs of persons with developmental disabilities is even more staggering. For example, DeOre (1983) estimated that a child born with a disability "who is institutionalized in Illinois will cost taxpayers $1,898,000 over a 65 year lifespan [$80 a day times 65 years], that's $29,200 per year" (p. 13). That cost per child would also be much greater today.

The Achilles' heel of the economic argument is that it can be attacked as well as supported by data. For example, of the 25% of the population of persons with disabilities who had received rehabilitation service at some time according to the 1972 Social Security survey of persons with disabilities, "only 11 percent claimed that they got a better job as a result, and only 8 percent that they were enabled to do their job better" (Levitan & Taggert, 1982, p. 93). M. Berkowitz and Berkowitz (1985) also pointed out a "weak spot" in the economic argument: "Rehabilitation programs have not stopped the growth of income maintenance programs" (p. 414). More recent survey data continue to indicate that more people with disabilities live in poverty than do people in the nondisabled population (National Organization on Disability, 2004).

Published figures such as these suggest the danger of overzealous dependency on the economic argument by supporters of the rehabilitation movement. In fact, it could be hypothesized that until there has been optimal removal of architectural, transportation, and attitudinal barriers to the employment of persons with disabilities in U.S. society, economists will always be able to generate figures that throw doubt on the economic viability of public support for vocational rehabilitation services.

Although the economic argument tends to be logically appealing, those who live totally by the economic argument can also "die" by the economic argument. Some years ago, Talbot (1961) urged us not to forget that our ancestors were using an economic rationale when they left persons with disabilities on a mountaintop. Therefore, to stress the need for rehabilitation services from a return-on-investment standpoint potentially sets the stage for total withdrawal of public support for rehabilitation services if they stop making economic sense. Because what makes economic sense is relative to the "payoff" from other potentially competing uses of public funds, rehabilitation services can stop making economic sense in spite of positive cost–benefit ratios.

One need only go back to 1939 in Nazi Germany to observe the negative application of the economic argument by a society. The Nazi euthanasia program drew upon the Hegelian philosophical principle of "rational utility." To save money for society as a whole, the medical profession in Nazi Germany embraced the Hegelian utilitarian principle as a justification for carrying out a program of mass extermination of persons unable to work due to severe chronic disabilities, such as mental retardation, psychosis, and organic neurological disorders (L. Alexander, 1949). L. Alexander (1949) described the operation of the euthanasia program initiated in 1939 as follows:

> All state institutions were required to report on patients who had been ill five years or more and who were unable to work, by filling out questionnaires giving name, race, marital status, nationality, next of kin, whether regularly visited and by whom, who bore financial responsibility and so forth. The decision regarding which patients should be killed was made entirely on the basis of this information by expert consultants, most of whom were professors of psychiatry in the key universities. These consultants never saw the patients themselves.... A parallel organization devoted exclusively to the killing of children was known by the similarly euphemistic name of "Realm's Committee for Scientific Approach to Serve Illness Due to Heredity and Constitution." (p. 39)

The beginnings of the crimes against humanity by the German physicians under the Nazis can be traced to a subtle emergence of an attitude among these physicians "that there is such a thing as a life not worthy to be lived" (L. Alexander, 1949, p. 44).

The Moral Argument

American culture has reached a point at which value themes, such as enabling others to lead quality lives and to exercise self-determination, provide potent reasons for rehabilitation. Rather than "luxuries to be indulged in as long as they pay," rehabilitation programs should be considered a humane necessity; Americans are, in fact, each others' "keepers," responsible for providing the means necessary for the rehabilitation of persons with disabilities (Busse, 1973; Talbot, 1961).

A growing sense of social responsibility manifested during the 1960s lent support to the humanitarian argument for rehabilitation. Mary Switzer, one-time commissioner of vocational rehabilitation and a significant figure in the rehabilitation movement, saw society in the early 1960s moving toward greater acceptance of the necessity of rehabilitation programs on moral grounds. Switzer characterized public attitudes toward persons with disabilities as evolving historically "through three stages—compassion without action, followed by willingness to act for economic reasons, followed by willingness to act for social reasons," with public attitudes in the 1960s being in transition from acting for economic reasons to acting for social reasons (cited in McGowan & Porter, 1967, p. 4). That transition in attitudes was furthered during the 1970s via increased public awareness of the needs of persons with disabilities as a result of magazine articles (Kleinfield, 1977) and feature-length films, such as *The Other Side of the Mountain* (Peerce, 1975), *Ice Castles* (Wrye, 1978), and *Coming Home* (Ashby, 1978).

This shift in public attitudes toward acting for social reasons was paralleled by developments, within the population of persons with disabilities, of a strong advocacy position. During the 1970s through the 1990s, individuals with disabilities began to more fully assert their rights to freedom of choice and independence (Fleischer & Zames, 2001). This exercise of human rights, fueled by the continued strength of the consumer movement, has been played out in recent years against the backdrop of decreased societal resources. With an increasing national debt in recent years, it is even more critical for society to recognize its obligation to protect the basic rights of individuals with disabilities.

Research has shown that adult Americans value opportunities to (a) develop close relationships with other people, (b) participate in community activities, (c) participate in educational and employment activities, and (d) participate in recreational activities (Flannigan, 1982). It would appear that if persons with and without disabilities are considered to have an equal right to access these sources of life's satisfactions and if rehabilitation services are considered necessary for such access for persons with disabilities, then the availability of such services could be argued for on that basis.

Assuming that American society is pervaded by values that are both decent and humane, focusing *extensively* on rights issues in regard to access to health and rehabilitation services as well as in regard to environmental accessibility can be both inflammatory and counterproductive. This is evidenced in the medical literature, where "arguments" for patients' rights seem to stimulate "counterarguments" for health providers' or society's rights, and vice versa. Would not a decent and humane society feel an obligation to increase the likelihood that persons with disabilities can meet their own needs? Would a non-humane society be affected by disability rights rhetoric? Does answering "yes" to both questions negate the value of an active push for disability rights by disability consumer groups? The answer would likely be "no" as long as that rhetoric is directed at increasing society's awareness of the needs of persons with disabilities without contributing to a "guilt reaction" in society that results in arguments directed at rationalizing the status quo.

Overemphasis on the rights of persons with disabilities, as opposed to adequate emphasis on the obligations of a just society to all its members, can stimulate compensating arguments stressing the duty of all Americans to lead healthy lives and avoid all risks to health in order to keep down society's health costs. Siegler (1980) pointed out that

> freedom to pursue unhealthy practices and to squander one's health may be sacrificed for a societal guarantee of health care unless society decrees that resources for health care are unlimited. This vision of a coercive state and a decline in human liberty may seem inordinately pessimistic. However, a right to health care could make this jeremiad a reality. (pp. 1595–1596)

Although the moral argument tends to have natural appeal, sole dependence on it can backfire. This can be the case where policymakers find themselves capable of providing for only a portion of the needs of the community of persons with disabilities due to a competition for scarce resources among public programs. If "bombarded" by the moral argument, such handcuffed policymakers could experience guilt and, in order to avoid such, not deal with the problems at all.

A Balanced Approach

Support for rehabilitation has rested in the past, and will rest in the future, on a blend of moral and economic themes. Such a blend should further facilitate the expansion of rehabilitation toward both vocational and independent living emphases.

A focus on the moral justification for rehabilitation services is not necessarily incompatible with a focus on the economic necessity for such services. In fact, it makes little sense to attack an economic rationale that stresses the importance of enabling individuals with disabilities to secure competitive employment. Emphasis on competitive employment as an outcome of rehabilitation services has led to promotional campaigns for employers to recruit and employ people with disabilities, as well as to employment protections in Sections 501, 503, and 504 of Title V of the Rehabilitation Act of 1973 and in Title I of the Americans with Disabilities Act. This emphasis on employment contributes to a decrease in the stigmatization of persons with disabilities. Through placement in competitive employment, individuals with disabilities become more socially integrated into the mainstream of U.S. society. As a result, individuals without disabilities also have an opportunity to develop a more realistic perception of people with disabilities (Dembo, 1968).

Emphasis on employment as the only purpose for providing rehabilitation services can, however, create an elite among individuals with disabilities by justifying rehabilitation services only for those having definite employment potential (Dembo, 1968; Walz & Boucher, 2000). What about those individuals with severe disabilities capable of more independent functioning but not employment? By not making provisions for serving individuals with severe disabilities with minimal or no immediate vocational potential, rehabilitation finds itself working against one of its own key sources of philosophical support—the moral or humanitarian argument for rehabilitation. Data presented in an earlier part of this chapter suggest that it is also economically unwise to ignore the needs of this group.

Concluding Statement

Is society faced with a choice between moral bankruptcy and financial bankruptcy when dealing with the development of a health care and rehabilitation policy for persons with disabilities? Can a national disability policy be based on both egalitarian and utilitarian principles? Or are the two incompatible?

Noble (1984) wrote that utilitarianism, which advocates the greatest good for the greatest number rather than fairness based on egalitarianism, is the prevailing moral philosophy embraced in the United States. Therefore, our "utilitarian society is easily disposed to sacrifice the interests of the severely disabled individual for the aggregate good" (Noble, 1984, p. 12).

A good example of how the applications of a utilitarian moral philosophy to policymaking can affect persons with disabilities can be seen in a 1980 policy decision on heart transplants made by the 12 lay trustees of Massachusetts General Hospital:

> These trustees voted not to permit heart transplants at that institution "at the present time" (1980) because "in an age where technology so pervades the medical community, there is a clear responsibility to evaluate new procedures in terms of the greatest good for the greatest number." They decided that the resources necessary for heart transplantation could be deployed elsewhere to greater advantage. (Beauchamp & Childress, 1989, p. 27)

Ironically, in a utilitarian society, the effective moral and economic arguments may have very similar content. This is the case because the society that embraces a utilitarian moral philosophy would "try to maximize rehabilitation services and environmental accessibility for" persons with severe disabilities only if it can be shown that society's aggregate utility would be maximized as a result (Noble, 1984, p. 13).

Contemporary U.S. society seems most accurately portrayed as stressing the importance of the self-sufficiency and productivity of each individual. The typical American citizen would strongly support the assertion that independence and personal productivity are far superior to dependence and idleness. Most Americans also tend to believe that a person's level of self-satisfaction is directly tied to whether the person is a member of the workforce. Hence, the values of most Americans would be compatible with the goals of programs that emphasize the importance of helping individuals use their resources maximally to achieve productive, independent, and fulfilling lives.

Americans greatly value freedom of choice. Freedom of choice is highly determined by the individual's level of independence. A disability that reduces a person's independence can, therefore, impair that freedom of choice. For example, a person with a severe disability "can choose only the school or home that happens to be accessible" (DeLoach, Wilkins, & Walker, 1983, p. 4). It is likely that the majority of Americans would view programs designed to provide or restore a reasonable amount of freedom of choice to persons with disabilities as compatible with the values of U.S. society.

Because American society is both a pragmatic and a humanitarian one, support can be expected for both vocational and independent living rehabilitation programs in the future. Public support reflects not only belief in the values espoused by rehabilitation but also faith in society's ability to progressively solve the problems of individuals with disabilities. In the past few decades, Americans have witnessed the elimination of polio; the application of space-age technology to the needs of persons with disabilities; and the addition of years to the lives of individuals suffering from cancer, heart disease, head injury, and spinal cord injury as a result of advances in medical and surgical techniques. Government funding, both federal and state, must continue to stimulate comparable advances in rehabilitation techniques in the future. The public's commitment to the same objective is dramatically demonstrated by the millions of dollars raised annually by charity drives such as the muscular dystrophy fund-raising campaign.

Whether resting on an egalitarian or a utilitarian foundation, the ultimate goal should be to establish a public policy that guarantees the legal right of persons with disabilities to those habilitation or rehabilitation services necessary for them to restore, or to an "optimal degree" compensate for the loss or absence of, normal species functioning in an environment reasonably free of attitudinal, architectural, transportation, and communication barriers. If the goal is achieved, American society will be a just society for persons with disabilities.

Much of the rehabilitation legislation passed and implemented since the early 1970s suggests that U.S. society is becoming a more just place for persons with disabilities. Surveys of the public attitude on the government's responsibility for health care also suggest movement toward a just society. An analysis of public opinion expressed in nationwide polls during the late 1970s and early

1980s suggests that a popular mandate exists for government support for meeting the health care needs of the people (Navarro, 1982).

Although public attitudes appear to support the expenditure of government funds to provide necessary health and medical services (Navarro, 1982) as well as vocational services to persons with disabilities, it is difficult to predict the limits of the public's willingness to guarantee the right to comprehensive health, medical, and vocational services to persons with severe disabilities. Clearly, the debate on the breadth of health care and employment rights for persons with disabilities will continue through the latter half of the first decade of the 21st century.

Unfortunately, a sufficient number of persons with disabilities may not actively participate in that debate because only a very limited number of individuals in the disability community tend to be politically active or even aware of empowering legislation such as the ADA. The number becomes even more limited when criteria of empowerment, such as understanding rights mandates such as the ADA or possessing the resources to act upon those mandates effectively, are taken into consideration (W. Wilkinson & Frieden, 2000). Perhaps this limited base for self-advocacy within the disability community

> can be attributed, in part, to the nature of the legislative mandates with which people with disabilities are most familiar. The programs most people with disabilities have traditionally had access to are entitlement programs in nature, design, and perception. They have imbued many individuals with disabilities with a sense of powerlessness over their destiny. People with disabilities are faced with a tremendous learning curve. For years they have been conditioned to accept second-class citizenship. Individuals who have been segregated and who have existed at the lowest rungs of society for years cannot be expected to be able to develop a "civil rights conscience" overnight. Many may be afraid to exercise their civil rights for fear of losing access to the very programs that sustain them and provide them with access to medical care and related support services. (W. Wilkinson & Frieden, 2000, p. 75)

Chapter 5

Sociological Aspects of Disability

Charles Maria V. Arokiasamy,
Stanford E. Rubin,
and
Richard T. Roessler

From early civilizations to the present day, negative attitudes toward persons with disabilities have persisted (Altman, 1981; Bowe, 1978, 1980; A. Deutsch, 1949; Longmore & Umansky, 2001). The poor treatment of persons with disabilities throughout history has been considered to stem from such negative social attitudes toward them (Bowe, 1978, 1980; DeJong & Lifchez, 1983; Hahn,1982, 1983, 1985a; Szasz, 1977). Reflected in all forms of communication and media, from the Bible to comic books (Gartner, 1982; Kokaska, 1984; Kokaska, Woodward, & Tyler, 1984; Kriegel, 1982; Nunnally, 1961), these negative attitudes have existed within most cultures and nations (Albrecht, 1981; Bhatt, 1963; Rosenbaum & Katz, 1980; Safilios–Rothschild, 1981).

Historical and contemporary reviews of the literature on attitudes toward persons with disabilities suggest the following as major determinants of societal responses: (a) the perceived cause of the disability, (b) the perceived responsibility for the disability, (c) the perceived threat of the disability, (d) the prevailing economic conditions within society, and (e) the prevailing sociocultural milieu. Cutting across time and cultures, these factors have been, and continue to be, crucial, basic, and consistent determinants of societal responses toward persons with disabilities. Chapter 1 provided many examples of the operation of one or more of these determinants from ancient Greece and Rome, through the Middle Ages, and up to colonial and 19th- and 20th-century America. This chapter provides a detailed examination of these five determinants of societal attitudes toward persons with disabilities.

Perceived Cause

Societal attitudes and responses toward persons with disabilities are determined less by the actual cause of a disability than by what society *perceives* as the cause of the disability. These perceptions are themselves shaped at different times by different forces, such as religious beliefs and advances in medicine.

Supernatural Causes

The supernatural, particularly demonic possession, was the earliest recorded explanation of disability. Although, historically, this cause was most often applied to mental disorders, it has also been attributed to diseases such as epilepsy and even sensory disabilities, such as blindness and deafness (Braddock & Parish, 2001). Many societies tended to think of people who behaved or thought differently to be evil or possessed by demons (Bikenbach, 1993; Winzer, 1997). Such perceptions often led to beatings, killings, imprisonment, exile, and exorcisms. Ancient Egyptian and Greek civilizations saw demonic possession as the dominant explanation of mental illness. The early Greeks also added the notion of divine visitation—hence, the famous Greek saying, "Whom the Gods would destroy, they would first make mad."

Demonic possession has been the oldest and the most lasting among perceived causes of mental disorders (Deutsch, 1949). The Christian gospels, for instance, provide many accounts of demonic possession as causal explanations for deviant behavior (Matthew 8:28–34; Mark 5:1–20; Luke 8:26–36), dumbness and blindness (Matthew 9:32–33; Matthew 12:22–23; Mark 9:17; Luke 11:14), and epilepsy (Matthew 17:14–18; Mark 9:16–27). In the Western Christian world, possession remained the primary explanation of mental disorders during the Middle Ages and in the period that followed. Witch-burning became a common extermination procedure, and many thousands of those allegedly possessed by evil spirits were killed. Many of these were actually persons who had a mental illness. Joan of Arc, who heard voices directing her to liberate France from the English, was perhaps the most celebrated victim of this abuse. Neither the Renaissance nor the Protestant Reformation brought reform or relief in the treatment of people with mental illness. Witch-hunting raged undiminished through the Renaissance, and the Reformation "had the effect of throwing added fuel on the witch-pyres, as Protestant vied with Catholic in bringing the Devil's agents to judgment" (A. Deutsch, 1949, p. 19).

Persons with mental retardation during the Renaissance and Reformation did not suffer as harshly as those in earlier times. However, they were also subject to superstitious explanations of their condition either as "children of God" or as "children of the devil" (A. Deutsch, 1949, p. 336). The latter perception usually led to harsh treatment. Even Martin Luther and John Calvin considered "idiots" to be children of the devil. According to A. Deutsch (1949), Luther once advised the parents of a child who was mentally retarded to throw the child into a river and "rid their house of the presence of a demon" (pp. 334–336).

Punishment by God was a popular causal hypothesis for physical disabilities. The book of Job is primarily a series of arguments that deal with the divine punishment hypothesis. Eliphaz, Bildad, and Zophar vainly attempt to convince a recalcitrant Job, who is covered with sores, that his sufferings are a divine punishment for his sins—an argument that Job rejects absolutely, especially because he knows that he has not sinned. Up to 142 illnesses and physical defects are mentioned in the Old Testament and by later Talmudists as marks of sin that disqualify a priest from officiating (B. Wright, 1983, p. 66). Not only are people believed to be punished for their own sins, but even the sins of their ancestors could be visited on them—hence, the biblical phrase, "The fathers have eaten sour grapes and their children's teeth are set on edge" (Ezekiel 18:2).

A positive variant of supernatural cause is the notion of divine involvement as a blessing or selection for a higher purpose. Disability and suffering in general, particularly in Catholic cultures, were sometimes seen as a mark of selection by God to suffer for the sins of the world. Foucault (1965) mentioned a medieval recipient of divine punishment who was told to be grateful because such punishment was a mark of divine attention. The Church of Vienne used a ritual of expulsion for lepers that read, "My friend, it pleaseth Our Lord that thou shouldst be infected with this malady, and thou hast great grace at the hands of Our Lord that he desireth to punish thee for thy iniquities in this world" (Foucault, 1965, p. 6). According to Levitas and Reid (2003), mental retardation was sometimes seen as divinely inspired or a blessing by God. The divine visitation hypothesis engendered positive responses, such as healing shrines.

The possession and punishment hypotheses have been very resistant to extinction throughout history and continue to survive in their original and many variant forms in modern times (A. Deutsch, 1949), shaping contemporary society's treatment of persons with disabilities. Even today some fundamentalist Christian groups associate suffering with sin, and many deviant behaviors are attributed to demonic possession. Deliverance and exorcism still sometimes occur. An example of the punishment hypothesis in the United States is the public reaction to AIDS, which is seen by some as God's way of punishing homosexuals for their sinful behavior ("AIDS Fears," 1986, p. 2).

These hypotheses, however, are not the exclusive province of Judeo-Christian tradition. Similar hypotheses have existed and continue to exist in all cultures and in the popular practice of many religions. The Hindu concept of Karma (Dharma) attributes suffering in the present life to sin in the former life. Indian medical practices before 800 B.C. were based on the Hindu scriptures, the Vedas, which held that "sin is the cause of disease, confession is the healing rite, and demons are to be fought with exorcism, spells and hymns" (Rosenbloom, 1972, p. 38). These beliefs have existed side by side with impressive sophistication in surgery, the use of prosthetics, inoculation, and medical training (Rosenbloom, 1972). Even in advanced, modern countries with sophisticated and well-developed medical systems, such as Malaysia and Singapore, many psychiatric problems and even physical ailments are referred first to traditional healers (Gwee, 1969, 1971; Rosenbloom, 1972; Strange, 1973; Tan & Wagner, 1971). Gwee (1969) found that about 90% of the Chinese patients in an acute general hospital ward in Singapore had seen traditional healers before seeking treatment at the hospital. Tan and Wagner (1971) found a similar percentage across all ethnic groups for psychiatric patients at the University of Malaya Medical Centre. A mere 35 years ago, the senior author of this chapter was treated for migraine by Hindu mediums who performed rites ranging from cutting lemons on his head to providing the spirits with a full-course meal. He was also treated for a heart condition by Muslim healers whose ministrations included periodic spreading of egg yolk on his chest and regular drinking of *ayer tawar* (blessed water).

Medical Causes

During the later part of the Greek era, Hippocrates (460–370 B.C.) posited a humoral pathology for mental illness. He believed that mental illness was caused by imbalances in the black bile, yellow bile, mucus, and blood (A. Deutsch, 1949, p. 8). Even in the Middle Ages, Hippocrates' explanation found a home in the Eastern Muslim world, leading to a far less harsh treatment of people with mental illness. At the same time in the Christian West, with its demonic possession hypothesis, these individuals were being burned at stakes. A. Deutsch (1949) described the situation in the East:

> Nowhere during the medieval period did the mentally ill find more understanding and better treatment than at the hands of the "heathen" Moslems.... In the Mohammedan East the torch of medical science lit by Hippocrates was still held aloft, dispelling the darkness of superstition in the treatment of mental and physical diseases. (p. 15)

During the 18th and 19th centuries in the West, there emerged hundreds of competing medical explanations of the psychic and somatic causes of mental disorders. Among the psychic causes recorded by Kraepelin (1962) were

> love and jealousy ... grief, resentment, and worry ... pride, greed, ambition, avarice, conceit, arrogance and fanaticism ... debauchery, alcoholism and gluttony ... disappointment in love ... excessive elation like that associated with winning a lottery or a happy marriage ... relaxation of judgment ... deep persistent thinking ... and reading of novels too zealously (applicable only to women). (Kraepelin, 1962, pp. 38–50)

Masturbation was a popularly held cause of mental problems—a belief that extended to the mental hygiene movement of 20th-century America (A. Deutsch, 1949; Kraepelin, 1962). As Kraepelin (1962) said, "Chronic illness, imbecility, dessication of the spinal marrow, paralysis, and death were believed to result from onanism (masturbation)" (p. 51).

Taking pride in their superior medical training, those of the somatic school sharply disagreed with their colleagues of the psychic school. Recalling Hippocrates' teaching that the brain was the seat of psychic processes, many laid the blame for mental disturbances squarely on that organ. Others included the lungs, liver, intestines, heart, spleen, kidneys, blood vessels, skin, muscles, and bones among the organs responsible for mental disorders. Fluids, such as the neural fluid and blood, were also believed to cause mental disorders.

Consonant with these causes were the assumptions that mental illness (a) resulted from weakness of character and (b) was incurable (Kraepelin, 1962, pp. 21–25). Adherence to the idea of psychic causation reinforced the myth that mental disorders were due to weakness of character and hence justified whipping, beating, starving, chaining, and forced labor. The somatic school tended to promote the incurability assumption, which was used to justify physically restraining people with mental illness in deplorable conditions in institutions.

Natural Causes

During the later part of the Greek era, some Greek medical pioneers raised the possibility of natural causation of mental illness. Pioneers such as Asclepiades of Prusa during the 2nd century B.C. and Soranus of Ephesus around the 2nd century A.D. pushed for humane sanatoriums with proper lighting, temperature control, sanitation, comfort, and little restraint (A. Deutsch, 1949, pp. 9–10). Although these humane traditions were continued by people such as Alexander of Tralles and Paulus Aegenita in 6th- and 7th-century Rome, they did not gain popularity until the 18th century, when Philippe Pinel, having studied the methods of the Greek pioneers, advocated humanitarian treatment of those suffering from mental illness at a time when persons with mental illness throughout Europe were often kept in prisonlike institutions, chained to walls, beaten, and starved. Violent reactions by inmates to such brutality were met with worse treatment and physical restraints, strengthening the view that persons with mental illness were violent, base, and intemperate creatures. Passive acceptance of this ill treatment, however, fed the myth that they felt no pain or hunger and needed little food, clothing, or comfort (Kraepelin, 1962, pp. 10–19). John Conolly recounted a situation in which a single towel was deemed enough for an institution of 176 patients (Kraepelin, 1962, p. 19). Against this morass of ill treatment and despondency came Pinel's unchaining of the inmates of Bicetre in 1792 in Paris—a bold and radical move that inaugurated the new "moral treatment" of persons with mental illness and gave birth to the asylum movement. For a short while, during the 18th century, the natural causes hypothesis of Pinel and William Tuke, with their "moral treatment" and humane asylums, brought fresh hope and optimism for persons with mental illness (Dain, 1964; Foucault, 1965; Kraepelin, 1962).

Pinel rejected somatic causes as contrary to anatomical fact and replaced prevailing medical practices with a humanitarian approach to individual patient needs (Dain, 1964; A. Deutsch, 1949; Kraepelin, 1962; Ray & Gosling, 1982; Rothman, 1971). The moral treatment approach was "based on the assumptions that disturbed behavior was caused either by ignorance or incorrect understanding—that is, a remediable cognitive lack—and that it could be modified by manipulation of social and psychological variables" (Rabkin, 1972, p. 154). The dramatic success of Pinel's bold unchaining of the "insane"—they did not go berserk and kill everyone in sight as many expected—and the subsequent replay of this drama in other parts of Europe, such as Conolly's removal of restraints at Hanwell (England's largest asylum) in 1839 (Kraepelin, 1962, p. 136), provided impetus for psychiatric reform. This reform resulted in an explosion of state-financed asylums in quiet, restful environments in Europe and the United States (A. Deutsch, 1949; Rabkin, 1972; Ray & Gosling, 1982; Rothman, 1971). In the United States, as noted in Chapter 1, prodding by people such as Dorothea Dix led to the establishment, by 1860, of one or more such institutions in almost every state (Ray & Gosling, 1982). During this era 90% to 100% cure rates were reported for new cases, the so-called "cult of curability" (Achenbach, 1982; A. Deutsch, 1949; Ray & Gosling, 1982).

By the 1860s, however, many factors combined to bring about the demise of these humane movements. The most commonly mentioned of these factors is the resurgence of the somatic school, especially the development of neurology (Bockhoven, 1963, 1971; Dain, 1964; A. Deutsch, 1949; Grob, 1973; Rabkin, 1972; Rothman, 1971). Despite Pinel's rejection of the organic lesion hypotheses, belief in organic lesions of the brain as the cause of mental illness was firmly entrenched in society during the mid-1800s. This reversion from Pinel's moral treatment to organic causes negatively affected the treatment of individuals with mental illness. Societal expectations of cure fizzled, and the notion of curability was replaced by a pessimistic emphasis on heredity and incurability. Custodial care replaced attempts at active rehabilitation, and the asylums became warehouses for persons with mental illness waiting for some medical breakthrough in the future. The conditions in these asylums quickly degenerated to rival those in the institutions of what Foucault (1965) called the "Great Confinement" era of the 17th century.

Society as Cause

Not until the mid-20th century were causes for mental illness sought in the external environment—that is, in society, its institutional forms, and the interaction among its members. The writings of R. D. Laing, Thomas Szasz, David Rosenhan, Erving Goffman, Michel Foucault, Albert Deutsch, and Robert Perrucci contributed to this new understanding of mental illness.

Laing blamed society, capitalism, and social institutions such as the family for mental illness. He theorized that schizophrenia was caused by undesirable interactions within the family (Laing & Esterson, 1970). Szasz considered madness to be a sociohistorical myth used by society to justify victimization of individuals who caused it unacceptable problems (Szasz, 1961, 1966, 1973, 1977). This social control and victimization hypothesis has received much support from sociological and psychosocial studies on the effect of labeling (Gove, 1970; Lemert, 1951; J. M. Murphy, 1976; Piner & Kahle, 1984; Scheff, 1966; R. Scott, 1969). Rosenhan's (1973) famous study "On Being Sane in Insane Places" provided empirical support for the victimization claim and strongly attacked the arbitrariness of psychiatric diagnosis and labeling (see also Rosenhan, 1975).

During the 1960s institutionalization itself came under heavy attack. Goffman (1961), in his classic book *Asylums: Essays on the Social Situation of Mental Patients and Other Inmates,* was perhaps the first to make the point that institutions, no matter how well intentioned, were inherently harmful to those who resided within them (Ray & Gosling, 1982). He was soon joined by many others, such as Foucault, Rothman, and Szasz. This attack on institutionalization was fueled by A. Deutsch's (1948) famous exposé of the appalling conditions in American asylums in his book *The Shame of the States.* Perrucci (1974), after a study of mental hospitals, bluntly concluded that "the mental hospital functions primarily as a system of justification for a commitment process which cannot openly be admitted to be what it is; namely, a victimization process" (p. 36). The writings of these muckraking advocates for the rights of those with mental illness facilitated the development of the deinstitutionalization, normalization, and independent living movements; the least restrictive environment and right-to-treatment doctrines; and the community mental health movement.

Perceived Responsibility

People often believe that suffering and punishment, like joys and rewards, are deserved (S. E. Asch, 1952; Heider, 1958). The pride associated with achieving something by the "sweat of the brow" and the popular sentiment "success has a price" are manifestations of the belief that rewards must be earned. Conversely, suffering is often seen as the result of wrongdoing or of "not paying the price." In the case of disability, society often assumes that "someone has to be blamed, for disability is all too easily perceived as having its source in wrongdoing" (B. Wright, 1983, p. 65). Even when the cause of the disability has been established, people find it difficult to shake the notion that the condition was somehow deserved. Often people with disabilities themselves may believe that they were somehow responsible.

Historically, much of the responsibility for disability has been attributed directly to the individual. Personal responsibility is implicit in the perception of divine punishment as a cause of disability. In more recent times, especially in the last two centuries, medical advances have led to an emphasis on external agents such as germs and viruses. Within the last century, society itself has been seen as at least partly responsible for disability. All these developments have important implications for the way persons with disability are treated.

Personal Responsibility

Whomever a society holds responsible for a disability is likely to be treated badly by that society. The person with a disability who is seen as culpable can expect less compassionate concern than the individual whose disability is perceived to be due to circumstances beyond his or her control (Aubert & Messinger, 1965; DePoy & Gilson, 2004; Friedson, 1966; Orcutt & Cairl, 1979; T. Parsons, 1951; Stiker, 2000; Stoll, 1968). Thus, obese people, alcoholics, sex offenders, people with AIDS, and criminals generally elicit more negative responses from society than, for example, persons who are blind or deaf, those with congenital disabilities, and war veterans with disabilities.

The role that personal responsibility plays in shaping societal responses toward people with disabilities is highlighted by the verdicts in the well-known insanity trials of Charles Guiteau, the assassin of President James Garfield in the 19th century (C. Rosenberg, 1968), and John Hinckley, convicted of the attempted assassination of President Ronald Reagan more than 80 years later (Bulmash, 1982; Ray & Gosling, 1982). The defense for each man argued strenuously for the organic and hereditary basis of insanity, and therefore the absence of personal responsibility for his actions. In Guiteau's case, the judge instructed the jury that "indifference to what is right is not ignorance of it, and depravity is not insanity, and we must be careful not to mistake moral perversion for mental disease" (Bulmash, 1982, p. 286). Guiteau was found guilty and executed. In Hinckley's case, the jury refused to ascribe personal responsibility to the act. They held the defendant to be insane and acquitted him. Guiteau's trial took place during the last days of the moral treatment era, which rejected organic or medical etiology and maintained personal responsibility for individual actions. Hinckley's trial occurred at a time when medical explanations of insanity were tenable.

Society reacts unfavorably not only to those considered personally responsible for their disability but also to those perceived as shirking the responsibility to cope with or overcome that disability (Shurka, Siller, & Dvonch, 1982; J. Smart, 2001; B. Wright, 1983). In a 1982 study, Shurka et al. manipulated two variables: (a) coping with the disability and (b) responsibility for the disability. Subjects were shown videotapes of a person in a wheelchair depicting one of the following conditions: (a) coping but not responsible for the disability, (b) coping and responsible for the disability, (c) succumbing to but not responsible for the disability, or (d) succumbing to and responsible for the disability. Coping/not responsible received the most favorable rating, followed, in descending order, by coping/responsible, succumbing/not responsible, and succumbing/responsible.

Societal Responsibility

Over the years handicappism has become attributed less to physical or mental impairment than to the environment and societal attitudes toward persons with a disability (Arokiasamy, 1993a; A. Asch, 1984; Bowe, 1978, 1980; Bury, 1979; DeJong, 1979a; DeJong & Lifchez, 1983; Fagen & Wallace, 1979; Hahn, 1982, 1985a; Hamilton, 1950; B. Wright, 1983). The theories of Goffman, Laing, Szasz, Rosenhan, Scheff, and others thrust the responsibility for mental illness on society. Similarly, part, if not most, of the handicap associated with physical disability is nowadays thought to be caused by societal attitudes; economic, social, and political structures; and environmental barriers (Arokiasamy, 1993a). Contemporary social scientists in the main believe the "root cause of dysfunction often associated with disability" to be "attitudes, stereotypes and prejudices (including self-defeating attitudes and behaviors of some disabled persons)" (Fenderson, 1984, p. 527). Some definitions of disabilities distinguish between disability and handicap and reflect society's role in turning a disability into a handicap (Bury, 1979; Fagen & Wallace, 1979; Hamilton, 1950; Kailes, 1985; Urban Institute, 1975). Thus, a person with a physical disability may be handicapped not simply because he or she uses a wheelchair, but because society has decided to use stairs instead of elevators or ramps. He or she may be unemployed not because of physical limitations, but because of employer prejudices and stereotypes. As personal responsibility for disability has been downplayed over the years and more responsibility for its associated functional limitations has been ascribed to society, less negative attitudes and more humane treatment of persons with disabilities have become possible.

Perceived Threat

Fear is a powerful motivating force among human beings. Historically, persons with disabilities have been seen as a threat in at least two ways: a threat to personal safety and to economic well-being. These perceptions have influenced the way societies and individuals respond to persons with disabilities.

Threats to Personal Safety

Threats to personal safety include contagion and physical violence. Leprosy provides an excellent example of the threat of contagion. In the past, leprosy could be neither cured nor adequately contained. Society reacted by isolating lepers in leprosaria or lazar houses. The book of Leviticus in the Old Testament, which is sacred to Christians, Jews, and Muslims alike, devotes two entire chapters to detailed descriptions of the diagnosis of leprosy and rules of conduct for lepers and society (Leviticus 13–14). Among its prescriptions is a firm injunction for the isolation of lepers:

> A man infected with leprosy must wear his clothing torn and his hair disordered; he must shield his upper lip and cry, "Unclean, unclean." As long as the disease lasts he must be unclean; and therefore he must live apart; he must live outside the camp. (Leviticus 13:45–46)

The fear of contagion was an important element in modern society's reaction to persons with AIDS. Among the issues on California ballots in 1986 was Proposition 64, which would have permitted mandatory physical quarantine of persons suspected of having AIDS. An Iowa poll in 1986 revealed that 16% of Iowans believed that schoolchildren with AIDS should be locked out of public schools ("AIDS Fears," 1986, p. 2). Frustrated by unsuccessful attempts to garner support from clergy and others for a prayer vigil for persons with AIDS, Reverend Reid Christensen, the pastor of a church for homosexuals in Carbondale, Illinois, said, "Society is not worried that homosexuals are dying. They're worrying that it might spread to them" ("Public Called Callous," 1986, p. 1). As disabilities stemming from infectious diseases, leprosy and AIDS serve to illustrate clearly the effect of perceived threat of contagion on people's behavior.

Other types of fear of contagion also affect the attitudes and behavior of people toward individuals with disabilities. Behavioral contagion is demonstrated by parents who object to locating group homes or halfway houses in their neighborhood for fear that their children may pick up the behaviors of the residents of these homes. Hitler's programs to eliminate people with disabilities illustrate another kind of fear of contagion, namely, the fear of contaminating the gene pool. Both Plato and Aristotle sanctioned the killing of infants with mental retardation—Plato for eugenic reasons and Aristotle for economic reasons (A. Deutsch, 1949, p. 334). The fear of contaminating the gene pool inspired laws in the United States in the late 1800s to restrict the marriage and procreation rights of people with disabilities (Haller, 1963; Pfeiffer, 1994).

The second perceived threat to personal safety, as noted above, is the threat of physical violence. The hardening of societal attitudes in recent years toward persons with alcohol dependence illustrates the perceived threat of physical violence. Mounting evidence of the role of alcohol in accidents (Filkins et al., 1970; Holcomb, 1938; Neilson, 1967, 1969; Waller, King, Neilson, & Turkel, 1969) has led to stiffer laws and sentences for DWI (driving while intoxicated) and DUI (driving under the influence) and to the emergence of anti-alcohol groups, such as MADD (Mothers Against Drunk Driving).

Societal responses have almost always been more negative toward persons with mental than physical disabilities (Altman, 1981; Chan, McMahon, Cheing, Rosenthal, & Bezyak, 2005; Davies, 1995; DePoy & Gilson, 2004; Freed, 1964; Furnham & Pendred, 1983). Persons with mental illness are often perceived as irrational, and therefore unpredictable and dangerous. The witch mania observed during the Middle Ages in Europe and in the trials at Salem, Massachusetts, during the 17th century is an extreme example of the effect of such perceptions (A. Deutsch, 1949; Lea, 1957). Also, sensationalized stories in news and movies about serial killers such as Jeffrey Dalmer have reinforced the notion of people with mental illnesses as dangerous. Furthermore, through characters such as Captain Hook, Long John Silver, and the Hunchback of Notre Dame, the media and literature have perpetuated the stereotype of persons with physical disabilities as dangerous (Arokiasamy, 1996; Bogden, Biklen, Shapiro, & Spelkoman, 1982; Gartner, 1982; Greer, 1996; Kriegel, 1982).

> By linking ugliness and physical and mental differences with murder, terror and violence, the media creates, at the same time as it perpetuates, society's prejudices—prejudices that result in fear of the handicapped and ultimately in their systematic, intentional exclusion from society. (Bogden et al., 1982, p. 32)

Threat to Economic Well-Being

The perceived threat to economic well-being may manifest itself at the national level, as fear of a "welfare drain" on the national economy, and at an individual level, as in the case of employers who consider workers with disabilities as economic liabilities. Calls for cuts to social programs almost always portray those receiving services as a drain on resources (Roybal, 1984). When it comes to hiring people with disabilities (see Chapter 12), employers fear increases in worker's compensation rates, increased absenteeism, and the costs of modifying the workplace or providing extra safety precautions. These concerns are generally unfounded, but they play to employers' perceptions of a threat to the profitability of their business or their economic well-being (Allan, 1958; Ellner & Bender, 1980; Pati & Adkins, 1981; Unger, Campbell, & McMahon, 2005).

Perceived threats, however, can benefit persons with disabilities by stimulating positive social responses, such as prevention and rehabilitation efforts. Benefit–cost studies, such as those discussed in Chapter 4 (Conley, 1969; Eazell & Johnston, 1981; Hammerman & Maikowski, 1981; Levitan & Taggert, 1982), have shown societal investment in rehabilitation to be economically wise and desirable. Estimates of the cost of disability to society are frequently used to prompt legislation establishing new programs. Often, such estimates highlight the cost of not addressing a problem.

Justification by Fear or Perceived Threat

Many historic responses toward persons with disabilities would strike the contemporary person as blatantly cruel and morally inadmissible. How does society justify the casting of people with mental illness as witches and burning them at stakes or locking them away in horrific institutions? How did Nazi Germany justify its systematic program of eliminating people with disabilities? According to Szasz (1977), one common mechanism portrays society as the potential victim of the person with a disability. Thus, Hitler portrayed persons with disabilities (and Jews and gypsies) as threats to social order, to the integrity of the gene pool, and hence to the physical and mental constitution of society and the economic well-being of the German nation. The gassing of more than 275,000 persons with mental or physical disabilities (A. Deutsch, 1949, p. 376) rested on that justification.

A second way to justify immoral treatment of persons with disabilities has been to represent them as threats to themselves (Szasz, 1977). Throughout history, society has tended to abrogate the rights of persons with disabilities to self-determination and arrogate to itself the role of protector (Foucault, 1965; Kittrie, 1973; Szasz, 1961, 1965, 1977). Society has often justified even blatantly cruel treatment of persons with disabilities under the guise of acting in their best interests. Albert Camus accurately, albeit somewhat harshly, described society's penchant for the paternalistic role: "The welfare of the people in particular has always been the alibi of tyrants, and it provided the further advantage of giving the servants of tyranny a good conscience" (Camus, 1960, p. 101).

Despite gains in the last 30 years, such as the right to the least restrictive environment, the Americans with Disabilities Act, and federal legislation requiring the direct involvement of clients in planning their treatment (e.g., Individualized Plans for Employment [IPE] and Individualized Education

Programs [IEPs]), society has not relinquished its paternalistic role and persists in protecting "the weak" (Bowe, 1978; DeJong, 1979a; Hahn, 1982; Kamieniecki, 1985; Kittrie, 1973; Szasz, 1965, 1977; U.S. Catholic Bishops Conference, 1978). Hahn (1982) stated that paternalism

> has allowed the nondisabled to act as the protectors, guides, leaders, role-models, and intermediaries for disabled individuals who, like children, are often assumed to be helpless, dependent, asexual, economically unproductive, physically limited, emotionally immature, and acceptable only when they are unobtrusive. (p. 388)

In a similar vein, the 1978 pastoral of the U.S. Catholic Bishops Conference stated, "When we think of handicapped people in relation to ministry, we tend automatically to think of doing something for them. We do not reflect that they can do something for us and with us" (U.S. Catholic Bishops Conference, 1978, p. 2).

This paternalism and perceived dependency, especially of persons with physical disabilities, can be explained by the sociological construct of "the impaired role" (DeJong, 1979a; G. Gordon, 1966; Siegler & Osmond, 1973), a derivative of the "sick role" first articulated by Talcott Parsons in 1951. The sick role offered patients exemption from usual activities and responsibilities in return for the obligation to acknowledge the sickness as an undesirable state and to actively seek competent help in getting better. The sick role is a temporary role that all people slip in and out of when ill. Because disability is permanent, however, the impaired role—an extension of the sick role to disability—can provide a permanent exemption from usual activities and responsibilities, thereby placing the person with a disability in a permanently dependent state. Even the obligation to get well is removed because society does not expect the person with a disability to recover (DeJong, 1979a). Thus, although persons with physical disabilities are not perceived as a direct threat to themselves or others, they are often seen as quite incapable of taking care of themselves and, hence, as needing paternalistic protection from others. "In return for this childlike status, they are allowed to spend their days as children do, playing card games, taking up hobbies, having meals served to them, playing with each other, or most often, doing nothing at all" (Siegler & Osmond, 1973, p. 53).

The negative effects of paternalism resulting from the perception of persons with disabilities as a threat to themselves are clearly visible in societal attitudes toward persons with mental disabilities. Szasz (1965) complained that when a person is labeled schizophrenic, especially in a courtroom, "everybody all of a sudden wants to help.... Everybody is protecting you ... the so called patient has no enemies" (p. 34). One of the ways contemporary American society has tried to be friend and protector to people with disabilities is through the judiciary. In a thoughtful comparison of civil and criminal commitment procedures, Hochstedler (1982) found the protections afforded those under civil commitment (by which persons with mental illness are institutionalized) to be seriously deficient and dangerously unconstitutional.

> The compelled psychiatric exam in civil commitment constitutes an arrest, search and interrogation. The court may authorize all three of these serious intrusions on the basis of a single petition.… In contrast, the criminal procedure requires one judicial review for arrest and search, while custodial interrogation of a suspect may never be authorized by a court. (Hochstedler, 1982, pp. 268–270)

Typically, civil commitment procedures do not provide the protections of the Fourth Amendment against unreasonable search and seizure, the Fifth Amendment against self-incrimination, and the Sixth Amendment of right to counsel. According to R. D. Miller (1982), nine U.S. states allow judicial personnel other than judges (magistrates, clerks of court, etc.) to authorize involuntary commitment. In his study of such a system in North Carolina, R. D. Miller (1982) found that the magistrates had insufficient knowledge or experience in mental health to make such determinations. According to R. D. Miller (1982), there were 10,000 such commitments a year in North Carolina (p. 499).

It is important to note that judicial procedures are almost always motivated by good intentions. That is the essence of paternalism. In 2002 the Supreme Court made it unconstitutional to execute anyone with mental retardation regardless of the seriousness of his or her crime (DePoy & Gilson, 2004). Is it a sensitive and fair response to assume that people with mental retardation are incapable of understanding the consequences of their behavior and therefore should not be held accountable for such effects, or is it demeaning? Most states have laws protecting people with mental illnesses or mental retardation from being sexually exploited by nondisabled persons. Again, is this compassionate protection of such persons from predators or a demeaning declaration that they are not capable of even giving consent?

In sum, many practices have been permitted and continue to be supported because of the perception of persons with mental illness as being a threat to others or themselves. The latter affords society what Camus, Szasz, and many others have referred to as the added advantage of a clear conscience by paternalistically designating itself as friend and protector to persons with disabilities. Persons with disabilities may well be justified in asking, "With friends like these, who needs enemies?"

Prevailing Economic Conditions

Economics is a science born out of the realization that resources are limited while needs and wants are unlimited. The problem of stretching finite resources to meet infinite needs and wants forces hard decisions about which needs and wants to satisfy and to what extent. Hence, the economic conditions at a particular time can significantly affect the responses of a society toward its members with disabilities. First, the state of the economy, whether good or bad, determines the amount of resources available to meet the needs of groups such as individuals with disabilities. Second, the level of economic development of the society determines which of its many needs and wants a society can afford to meet. In third-world countries, for example, attempting to meet fundamental requirements, such as basic education, food production, and primary health care, leaves few resources to meet the needs of persons with disabilities. Third, the economic philosophy of the society influences how its needs will be met.

State of the Economy

Rodgers (1968) listed surplus economic resources as one of the prerequisites for the development of social services. "Developing countries often face this problem [of lack of surplus] and frequently have to make decisions between competing social services, all of which are needed" (Rodgers, 1968, p. 4). It also follows that the greater the amount of resources available, the more needs and wants that can be satisfied. History shows us that economies go through waves of growth and recession. During economic upswings, a society has more resources available to meet its needs. More goods and services are being produced, more people are earning money, and more businesses are reaping greater profits. These periods are often marked by societal largesse in meeting the special needs of disadvantaged groups, such as persons with disabilities. For example, the Golden Era of Rehabilitation mentioned in Chapter 1 occurred during the prosperous decades of the 1950s and 1960s both in the United States and internationally. In Great Britain, arguments against the provision of social services fell away "as economic expansion of the latter fifties and early sixties made itself felt" (Rodgers, 1969, p. 57). As Coudrouglou (1990) succinctly wrote, "the best rehabilitator would be a full-employment economy" (p. 207). On the other hand, during economic downswings, resources are limited and services to disadvantaged groups tend to be cut back.

Apart from the overall state of the economy, fluctuations in specific components of the economy, including (a) demand for labor, (b) level of inflation, and (c) government revenue, can have a very direct and potent impact on societal responses toward persons with disabilities. The impact of these elements on the well-being of persons with disabilities is discussed in the sections following.

Demand for Labor

By siphoning off able-bodied manpower and by increasing the demand for industrial goods, wars cause sudden and reversible change in the employment picture of a society. Therefore, they provide excellent opportunities to study the effects of unemployment rates on societal responses toward persons with disabilities. World War II created a huge demand for workers in the U.S. economy, thereby opening many jobs to persons with disabilities. However, sudden and artificial situations such as labor shortages and demand for increased output created by war are double-edged swords. The return of servicemen after World War II to reclaim their former jobs forced workers with disabilities out of the postwar competitive job market into the newly created sheltered workshops.

Times of peak demand for labor—whether created artificially by war or as a natural consequence of a fast-growing economy—are generally thought to be good times for people with disabilities, as well. However, conventional wisdom that labor shortages may lead to considering people with disabilities as an untapped source of labor may only be wishful thinking. Based on years of study of labor force participation of persons with disabilities, Yelin (1991) concluded that even in times of increased participation, the hiring rate of persons with disabilities usually lagged that of their nondisabled peers. Conversely, periods of labor decline always resulted in sharper declines for those with disabilities than those without. These rates were worse for minorities with disabilities. Although demand for labor is a factor that influences how readily people with disabilities will be received by the workforce, it would be too simplistic to see it as a simple cause–effect variable. Instead, there is a complex interplay of factors that affect how people with disabilities are treated by the labor force.

Level of Inflation

Although inflation increases the amount of money available, it decreases its value. The higher the inflation, the less that money will buy, making materials and services to meet the needs of persons with disabilities more expensive. Inflationary times are also accompanied by wage and cost-of-living increases. Social services such as rehabilitation tend to be labor intensive. Consequently, during inflationary times, the cost of services increases considerably without a corresponding increase in the quantity or quality of that service. Hence, inflationary times often result in cutbacks to social welfare services (Rusalem & Malikin, 1976; Taylor-Gooby & Dale, 1981).

Government Revenue

The amount of available governmental financial resources strongly influences policymakers' decisions regarding appropriations for social services. A principal source of revenue for the government is taxes. The tax structure of the society influences public and private treatment of persons with disabilities. Tax write-off incentives, for instance, may increase private funding for social programs. They can also be used to encourage businesses to provide employment or on-the-job training for persons with disabilities. Tax reforms that threaten tax write-offs could thus negatively affect the level of private support for social programs.

Level of Economic Development

Viewed from the perspective of per-capita income, the nations of the world form a continuum from the very rich to the very poor. In comparing social security spending of 64 countries in 1966, Wilensky (1975) divided these nations into four quartiles from the richest 16 to the poorest 16 on the basis of per-capita gross national product (GNP) figures. The average percentage of GNP spent on social security (welfare) showed a steady decrease for each quartile from 13.8% for the richest quartile to 2.5% for the poorest quartile (p. 19). The position a society occupies on that continuum appears to determine the amount of resources it will allocate for the care of its members who are disadvantaged or have a disability. That position may, in fact, be the best predictor of the level of public expenditure on welfare (Aaron, 1967; Cutright, 1965; Pryor, 1968; Wilensky, 1975).

Most of the poorer nations of the world are commonly referred to as third-world countries. Persons with disabilities within these countries have been aptly referred to as the "third world within the third world." Because these societies are preoccupied with basic necessities, such as food, clothing, shelter, and defense, they view rehabilitation of persons with disabilities as a luxury only the West can afford (Safilios-Rothschild, 1981; D. Wilson, 1963). Even when third-world nations make a concerted push to provide health care, they focus primarily on prevention and acute care services. Rehabilitation is almost an afterthought (Albrecht, 1981). Thus, in societies at a lower level of economic development, rehabilitation services for persons with disabilities, while badly needed, may not be economically feasible. Conversely, in rich countries, according to Wilensky (1975), welfare programs automatically emerge as a result of economic growth.

Prevailing Economic Philosophy

The prevailing economic philosophy of a society can be expected to influence the way it allocates its resources to meet its social needs and wants. Indeed, history shows that this is the case. The following brief examination of the impact of the three most significant economic philosophies of the last three centuries illustrates the effect of economic philosophy on societal responses and public policies affecting persons with disabilities.

Laissez-Faire Economics

The late 18th and early 19th centuries were the heyday of Adam Smith's laissez-faire or free enterprise capitalism. For Smith, the recipe for social harmony and economic prosperity was full and free interplay of the market forces of demand

and supply without any form of government intervention. His vision called for the freedom of individuals to pursue their own self-interest. "To each according to his ability" was his battle cry. Inevitably, under such a system, people who were poor, ill, or disabled were seen as losers in open competition.

The social climate of the laissez-faire society has spawned and supported theories such as the theory of population of Thomas Malthus, another 18th-century economist. Malthus's theory bore even more frightening implications for persons with disabilities. He argued that population increased by geometric progression while economic activity, such as food production, grew only by arithmetic progression. Naturally, the exponential population growth was bound to outstrip food production. In the past, the theory suggested, a balance was maintained by natural catastrophes, such as wars, famines, and disease, which slowed down the growth of population. Any attempt to interfere with these natural processes could dangerously upset the balance between population and resources. Taken to its logical conclusions, Malthus's reasoning would condemn social action such as welfare, immunization, or rehabilitation as unwarranted interference in this natural process. The late 18th and early 19th centuries in Great Britain were therefore characterized by (a) opposition to central government's involvement in social action, (b) belief in the "sacredness" of the free market, (c) opposition to legislation or help for disadvantaged people, and (d) the tendency to blame persons with disabilities as both the victims and the causes of their own sufferings.

The influence on U.S. public policy and societal attitudes of laissez-faire capitalism and its concomitant political philosophy of Jeffersonian–Jacksonian liberalism can be seen in President Franklin Pierce's veto of the 1854 bill seeking to establish land grants for mental hospitals (Lenihan, 1977), in congressional opposition to a civilian rehabilitation act in 1919 on grounds that it was socialistic (MacDonald, 1944), and in the widespread public acceptance of Herbert Spencer's Social Darwinism and the eugenics movement at the turn of the 20th century (Morison, 1965). To this day, the idea of a welfare state is very unpopular in the United States, and the enactment of welfare programs is met with great political outcry. Workers' compensation came into being at the beginning of the 20th century, and it was not until 1964, far later than any other affluent country of the time, that the United States "moved gingerly toward health insurance with the passage of Medicare" (Wilensky, 1975, p. 10). Wilensky's description of welfare efforts in the United States highlights the sociological and attitudinal influence of the country's prevalent laissez-faire philosophy:

> It is true that the United States is more reluctant than almost any other rich country to make a welfare effort appropriate to its affluence. Our support of national welfare programs is halting; our administration of services for the less privileged is mean. We move toward the welfare state, but we do it with ill grace, carping and complaining all the way. (p. 32)

Socialist Economics

Rising principally in reaction to the immense miseries that laissez-faire economics had engendered by allowing huge disparities in wealth between the rich and the poor, socialism caused a shifting of public opinion in mid-19th century Great Britain. The growing awareness that economic growth did little to shrink urban poverty helped create a reaction against laissez-faire economics and for socialism. The development and spread of socialist thought laid the foundation for the welfare states of Europe. "Social reformers were increasingly willing to countenance a more positive role for the state in the making of social policy" (M. E. Rose, 1981, pp. 30–31). As early as 1906, moves for a national insurance scheme were begun in Great Britain. By 1914, it had become a fully established system (Hay, 1978; Rodgers, 1968; M. E. Rose, 1981), which laid the foundation for the modern British welfare state (Hay, 1978). Similar schemes had been instituted as early as the 1870s in other European countries, notably Germany (Rodgers, 1968; Taylor-Gooby & Dale, 1981), which under Bismarck pioneered the welfare state (Wilensky, 1975). By the 1880s Austria was already providing workers' compensation and maternity benefits (Wilensky, 1975).

Keynesian Economics

Even though contemporary government and society lean fervently toward the free enterprise philosophy, the United States has some of the largest and most expensive welfare programs in the world. While avowedly antisocialist, the government freely uses socialist tools such as taxation to finance these programs. What or who is responsible for such contradictions? Developments such as these in laissez-faire economies are due largely to the brilliant economist John Maynard Keynes, whose influence produced the "Keynesian Revolution," which dominated 20th-century economics and society. The era of Keynesian economics coincided with the Golden Era of Rehabilitation of the 1950s and 1960s. While a member of the laissez-faire school, Keynes provided the rationale for state intervention in society and in the marketplace to promote social good. He demonstrated that government intervention in many areas of the economic and social life of a society was necessary and beneficial.

Keynes's strong recommendation for increased government spending during depressions figured largely in President Franklin Roosevelt's launching of the New Deal program during the Great Depression. As mentioned earlier, one of the prerequisites for the provision of social services is the condition of economic surplus (Rodgers, 1968). Keynes's (1964) *The General Theory of Employment, Interest and Money* provided the rationale for government spending and even deficit spending (i.e., spending more than the government earns). This appears to negate Rodgers's (1968) prerequisite of surplus economic resources for the establishment of welfare programs. If the government did not have surplus resources, it could now borrow the resources it did not have. As a result of such borrowing, U.S. government budget deficits and national debt grew rapidly during the Keynesian years. Although the Vietnam War accounted for massive increases in government expenditures during the mid-1960s, with defense expenditures rising nearly $25 billion, or 50%, in 2 short years from the third quarter of 1965 to the third quarter of 1967 (W. G. Branson, 1979, p. 8), the social programs of the Kennedy and Johnson years accounted for no small increases in federal spending. Although Keynes did not fashion his general theory with people with disabilities in mind, his economic philosophy demanded, as an economic and moral imperative, that laissez-faire governments and societies reduce the huge disparities of wealth that had become prevalent (Keynes, 1964). He, therefore, defended direct taxation as a valid tool for financing social programs.

The Prevailing Sociocultural Milieu

Encompassing the four other determinants, the prevailing sociocultural milieu is the broadest and most basic of the five determinants of societal responses toward persons with disabilities. The prevailing sociocultural milieu is shaped by two factors: (a) sociocultural values and (b) sociocultural trends.

Sociocultural Values

Attitudes and behaviors do not happen in a vacuum. They occur within a context. Societies have their own characteristic social, cultural, moral, legal, political, and economic values that provide this context. Many societies throughout history have greatly valued physical perfection, functional ability, logical reasoning, and sensory acuity. (See Chapter 1 for examples of harsh treatment of persons who deviated from these cultural ideals.) The Spartans and Athenians, as well as the Romans centuries later, practiced infanticide of children with physical or mental disabilities. Contemporary society also appears to place a high value on bodily form, order, functional ability, logical reasoning, mobility, and sensory acuity. Accordingly, Western societies today describe disabilities and persons with disabilities in terms of deviations from these values (e.g., *de*-formed, *dis*-ordered, *dys*-functional, *in*-sane, *in*-valid).

However, not everyone holds these values in high esteem. Many African tribes, for instance, intentionally disfigure their children for purposes of tribal identification and wear these scars with pride. Maisel (1953, as reported in B. Wright, 1983, pp. 444–446) compiled anthropological data on more than 50 tribes or societies, many of which react very differently from the early Greek or contemporary Western societies to persons with mental or physical disabilities. For example, the Chagga tribe of East Africa and the Ponape of the Eastern Carolines treat their members with disabilities well (B. Wright, 1983, p. 445). In Dahomey, West Africa, "state constables are chosen from persons with physical disabilities" (B. Wright, 1983, p. 445). Among the Wogeo of New Guinea, "children with obvious deformities are buried alive at birth, but children crippled in later life are looked after with loving care" (B. Wright, 1983, p. 445).

Ancestor worship and deep filial respect, the hallmarks of Chinese cultures, encourage members of these societies to care for their elderly at home rather than in institutions. In Chinese societies, elderly persons, even those with disabilities, frequently maintain moral authority and decision-making power within the family or clan. Catholicism tends to value suffering, in some cases rendering a disability as a mark of divine favor—a sign of being chosen to suffer for the sake of the world. It is noteworthy that whatever the cultural context or societal values, deviance from those values is often punished and consonance with those values rewarded.

What is important to keep in mind is that values are not static and can change over time. In 2004 DePoy and Gilson recommended using "atypicality" to refer to disability. Also, disability itself is a value judgment (DePoy & Gilson, 2004). For example, many deaf persons see themselves not as disabled but simply as using a different mode of communication or language. From some modern perspectives, such as the independent living perspective, the limitations associated with disability are not attributed to a medical condition but simply result from oppression, lack of political power, discrimination, and marginalization (Mackelprang & Salsgiver, 1999).

Sociocultural Trends

As noted in Chapter 1, the early 19th century in America was a time of general optimism (Commager, 1950). This "climate of optimism helped to spread the belief that a better society was at hand and fired the public willingness to fund the construction of asylums" (Ray & Gosling, 1982, p. 138). The optimism was reflected in what historians of mental illness called the "cult of curability," fueled by announcements of 100% and 90% cure rates (A. Deutsch, 1949, pp. 132–157; Grob, 1966, p. 256; Ray & Gosling, 1982, pp. 139–143), and in the establishment of facilities for persons who were blind or mentally retarded.

At other times in U.S. history, sociocultural trends have negatively affected societal treatment of persons with disabilities. As described in Chapter 1, during the second half of the 19th century, a number of such trends emerged that resulted in a return to maltreatment of persons with disabilities. With the advent of Social Darwinism, many people supported the idea of survival of the fittest and opposed government involvement in social welfare or rehabilitation efforts. They proposed that persons with disabilities be allowed to perish, in keeping with the natural selection process that allowed only the strong and worthy to survive. The "eugenics scare" stimulated the passage of laws restricting marriage by persons with mental illness or mental retardation.

Chapter 1 described sociocultural developments that influenced rehabilitation throughout the first half of the 20th century, such as the rising rate of permanent disabilities from industrial accidents in a rapidly industrializing United States and medical advances in saving lives, especially of those injured in World War I and World War II. These developments helped lay a foundation for the Golden Era of Rehabilitation during the 1950s and 1960s.

Thus, it can be seen that various sociocultural trends in the past affected the way people with disabilities were treated by society. The rest of this section examines three current sociocultural trends that influence societal attitudes toward persons with disabilities: (a) the Civil Rights movements, (b) professionalization, and (c) multiculturalism.

Civil Rights Movements

Since the 1960s some important trends in American society have dramatically changed societal attitudes toward persons with disabilities. The Civil Rights and the feminist movements of the 1960s and 1970s dealt primarily with issues of racial and gender equality, as well as with disability rights issues. The movements highlighted the need for persons with disabilities to assert themselves in demanding their civil and benefits rights and demonstrated effective ways to do so (DeJong, 1979a). Following in the footsteps of the African American and women's rights movements, persons with disabilities organized to fight for their rights. Attempts to present persons with disabilities as a minority group lobbying for disability rights legislation to fight discrimination (Bowe, 1978; DeJong & Lifchez, 1983; Dexter, 1964; Gellman, 1959; Hahn, 1985b; B. Wright, 1983; Yuker, 1965) and the use of protest movement tactics, such as sit-ins and demonstrations to demand implementation of such legislation (DeJong, 1979a; Hahn, 1985a), drew their inspiration from the preceding civil rights activities. Hence, portions of the Rehabilitation Act of 1973 were patterned after the Civil Rights Act of 1964 and were therefore directed at providing civil rights protections for persons with disabilities. The Americans with Disabilities Act passed in 1990 further strengthened and expanded civil rights of persons with disabilities.

Just as racial segregation and discrimination were seen as depriving African Americans of their civil rights, persons with disabilities began to insist that architectural and transportation barriers as well as attitudinal barriers were jeopardizing the exercise of their civil rights. As DeJong (1979a) said,

> The black movement that eventually grew out of the civil rights movement ... saw the issue as one of racism ... and beyond the scope of simple legal remedies. The IL (Independent Living) movement has come to recognize that prejudice against disability is rooted in our culture's attitudes about youth and beauty, and in the able-bodied person's fear of vulnerability to physical disability. The black movement has inspired the IL movement to search more deeply for the sources of attitudes and behavior toward persons with disabilities. (p. 439)

Persons with disabilities also clearly realized that civil rights without concomitant benefits rights were insufficient for breaking down barriers to their full participation in society. Without income assistance and attendant care benefits, many persons with disabilities would be involuntarily confined to long-term care facilities (DeJong, 1979a, p. 438). These rights movements also inspired inquiry into the language of society and the role of mass media as transmitters of prejudice and stereotypes (Arokiasamy, Strohmer, Guice, Angelocci, & Hoppe, 1994; Kailes, 1985; La Forge, 1991; Manus, 1975; Mullins, 1979; J. B. Patterson & Witten, 1987; B. Wright, 1983). Hence, changes have occurred in terminology and descriptors from the *disabled* to *persons with disabilities* and from *wheelchair bound* to *wheelchair user* (Kailes, 1985, pp. 68–69).

Professionalization

Illich (1976) noted that "the specialties recognized by the American Medical Association have steadily increased.… Within each of these fields a fiefdom has developed with specialized nurses, technicians, journals, congresses" (p. 246). In the last 35 years, the field of rehabilitation also has seen a multiplication of specializations, in both number and type. Presently, specialists exist in rehabilitation nursing, rehabilitation counseling, rehabilitation administration, vocational evaluation, job placement, independent living, and so on.

This proliferation of professionals and specialists has been accompanied by growth in the power and pervasiveness of their influence in society. In general, professionals act as gatekeepers of information and services; help define appropriate behaviors, goals, strategies, and treatment for clients; influence the reactions of the family and significant others; shape societal reactions; affect the beliefs and behaviors even of persons with disabilities themselves; and are the respected gurus of public opinion and policy (Altman, 1981; Arokiasamy, 1993c; R. Branson, 1973; Friedson, 1970; Illich, 1976; Safilios-Rothschild, 1976; D. A. Stone, 1979; Szasz, 1963). Professionals have been and still are highly influential participants in debates on involuntary confinement, involuntary euthanasia, involuntary sterilization, the right to treatment, the right to refuse treatment, and other issues that affect persons with disabilities (Noble, 1984; Preston & Jansen, 1982; Stevens & Conn, 1976; Walmsley, 1978). Professional autonomy can degenerate into what Illich (1973, 1976) called a "radical monopoly." Societal acceptance of professionalization, especially in the highly medicalized West, continues to allow the professional to be the primary, sometimes sole, determiner of what is illness or deviance and what should be done about it. "Only doctors now 'know' what constitutes sickness, who is sick, and what shall be done to the sick and to those whom they consider at a special risk" (Illich, 1976, p. 47). In analyzing the independent living movement, DeJong (1979a) said,

> Today, most public policy with respect to disability requires some type of professional medical presence, whether in the acute stages of disability, in the determination of eligibility for income maintenance benefits, or in long-term institutional care. The IL movement asserts that much of this medical presence is both unnecessary and counterproductive. (p. 440)

A more subtle and perhaps the most negative aspect of professionalization is *paternalism* (Bowe, 1978, 1980; Fitting, 1986; Hahn, 1982, 1983; Jackman,

1983; Kamieniecki, 1985; U.S. Catholic Bishops Conference, 1978). Jackman (1983) called paternalism "enemy number one" (p. 23) in the fight by persons with disabilities for independence. In the rehabilitation process, a counselor or any other rehabilitation professional is automatically in a one-up position vis-à-vis the client. The professional is the help giver, the one with superior knowledge and training. It becomes easy in both obvious and subtle ways to keep the client dependent. The Rehabilitation Act of 1973 and especially its more recent amendments try to reverse this by giving clients a much stronger voice in decisions regarding their treatment through such doctrines as the informed choice doctrine.

Paternalism can often be confused with caring. What the counselor believes is best for the client can get in the way of true respect for the client's autonomy and independence (Arokiasamy, 1993a, 1993c). If a client with emphysema, knowing full well the dangers of smoking, decides not to give up cigarettes, should the counselor respect that decision or attempt to change it? If a client who received a $5 million settlement from the automobile accident that landed him in the rehabilitation center decides to forgo the arduous task of extended physical and vocational rehabilitation and be dependent, should the rehabilitation professional persistently encourage him to "maximize his potential"? The goal of "making" the client as independent as possible contains an inherent contradiction if the client is denied the freedom to choose not to be independent. Professional and medical approaches toward persons with disabilities emphasize changing the client. Persons with disabilities, especially those in the independent living movement, are opposed to client change as the primary focus. Rather, they urge that the rehabilitation effort be greatly focused on changing the society.

Multiculturalism

Another current major sociocultural trend is the multicultural movement, which has begun to influence the helping philosophy of those professionals who provide services to persons with disabilities. Before one can define *multiculturalism, culture* must be defined. Defining culture is not an easy task. Some prefer a narrow definition based on race, ethnicity, historic origin, or nationality (C. C. Lee, 1991; Triandis, 1972; Triandis, Bontempo, Leung, & Hui, 1990), whereas others include factors such as age, gender, socioeconomic status, place of residence, lifestyle, level of education, and affiliations (Brislin, 1990; Fukuyama, 1990; Locke, 1990). Too narrow a concept of culture can exclude many cultural subgroups, such as the gay community, baby boomers, and midwesterners, but too broad a definition could include all those who consider themselves different and thereby make the definition meaningless.

Multiculturalism suggests that the concept of the *melting pot* in our society has to give way to a newer concept, such as the *mosaic* or the *salad bowl,* which reflects cultural pluralism. Reverend Jesse Jackson, for instance, has used the term *Rainbow Coalition.* The emerging view of society is one in which a variety of cultures coexist while maintaining their respective cultural identities and integrity instead of surrendering to a cultural homogeneity with the majority. In fact, it may be argued that diversity is itself a cultural trait of American society ("Culturally Sensitive Rehabilitation," 1993).

Multiculturalism has become an important force in the counseling and rehabilitation counseling professions (Alston, 1996; Alston & Bell, 1996; Arokiasamy, 1993b; Cartwright, 2001; E. L. Davis & Rubin, 1996). Certain developments during the last 30 years have greatly increased the recognition of the importance of an emphasis on multiculturalism in counseling professions. Among these developments were the discoveries that (a) minorities were generally underserved by the counseling profession; (b) current counseling methods operating out of the majority cultural perspective lacked efficacy with minority clients; (c) minority clients, therefore, were more prone to avoid or drop out earlier from counseling; and (d) counseling was sometimes viewed as a way of maintaining the status quo of oppression and control of minorities (Alston & Bell, 1996; Capella, 2002; C. C. Lee & Richardson, 1991; C. L. Moore, Feist-Price & Alston, 2002; Olney & Kennedy, 2002; Pedersen, 1991; President's Committee on Mental Health, 1978; Sue & Sue, 1990; Vontress, 1971; K. B. Wilson, Alston, Harley, & Mitchell, 2002). In addition, more often than with White clients, minority clients found themselves in situations where they were forced into counseling, giving rise to the statement that the White client "seeks" counseling while the minority client is "brought into" counseling. Examples of such mandatory counseling are court-ordered or school-referred counseling. An examination of the New York State Office of Vocational Rehabilitation's database for fiscal years 1982 and 1983 revealed that the reason most often cited for closure of the majority of White clients was "refused services," whereas for African American clients it was "failure to cooperate" (Rehab Brief, 1987).

As counseling came under greater scrutiny, it became clear that, as in many other areas of life, minorities were clearly being excluded from counseling services. This has become evident both in the rehabilitation counseling literature and in rehabilitation legislation. The consensus within the rehabilitation counseling literature has been that compared with their Caucasian counterparts, ethnic and racial minorities with disabilities (a) have had a disproportionately higher rate of rejection for rehabilitation services and (b) when accepted, have been provided less effective services, with poorer rehabilitation outcomes being the result (Alston & Mngadi, 1992; Atkins, 1988; Atkins & Wright, 1980; Capella, 2002; Dziekan & Okocha, 1993; Herbert & Cheatham, 1988; Olney & Kennedy, 2002; Walker, Akpati, Roberts, Palmer, & Newsome, 1986; K. B. Wilson, 2000; K. B. Wilson et al., 2002; T. J. Wright, 1988). For example, in their study on the application and acceptance rates of racial and ethnic minorities in public vocational rehabilitation services, Dziekan and Okocha (1993) reported that racial and ethnic minority individuals with disabilities applied for vocational rehabilitation services at a rate higher than their representation within the general population but were accepted for services at lower rates than majority applicants. The state of inequality reported in the rehabilitation literature was clearly reflected in the Rehabilitation Act Amendments of 1992. That act stated that compared with White Americans, African Americans are less often accepted for services, and a higher percentage of those accepted are closed not rehabilitated, with the inference being that less service money is spent on them.

Principles of multicultural counseling are directed at trying to counteract these negative trends in the treatment of persons with disabilities from minority cultures. One of these principles is that the counselor should consider cultural variables as very real and very important. A second principle is that these cultural variables affect both the counselor and the client. Traditional counseling usually assumed the counselor to be the expert and focused on the client's differences and issues. Often, the way the client differed from the norm, which happened to be the norms of the White majority, became deviancies to address or "cure." Multiculturalism forces counselors to look at possible errors in such assumptions. A third principle is that counselors must become aware of their own cultural baggage. They need to become more cognizant of their own values, beliefs, attitudes, worldviews, and perspectives. Being unaware of their own cultural baggage could lead to many mistakes or false assumptions by counselors. They also need to become aware of how their beliefs, values, attitudes, and worldviews affect their counseling and their clients. A fourth principle of multiculturalism is that counselors should respect the culture of the client. They need to become aware of any unique cultural characteristics of the client and learn to value these characteristics.

The realization of the above four principles clearly demonstrates that the counseling process is not as value free and objective as previously thought. Multiculturalism holds value-free counseling to be a myth, because both counselors and clients bring their own cultural values into the counseling interaction. These differences are always interacting with each other and affecting the process and outcomes of counseling. Therefore, effective multicultural counseling requires that the counselor be sensitive to the client's cultural values and perspective in the counseling process.

Concluding Statement

This sociohistorical analysis of society's treatment of persons with disabilities shows that societal responses appear to be greatly determined by what is the perceived cause of the disability, who is perceived to be responsible for the disability, and to what extent the disability is seen as a threat. Additionally, responses toward persons with disabilities have been influenced by internal conditions within the society, such as the prevailing economic conditions and the prevailing sociocultural milieu.

During the second half of the 20th century, for the first time in history, society began to accept in a systematic and concerted manner some responsibility for disability and handicap. Only in recent decades have people begun to realize that part, if not a great deal, of the handicap arising out of disability, may be caused by society itself—its attitudes; economic, social, and political structures; and the physical environment. Society has begun to perceive itself as at least partly responsible not only for causing disability but also for making disability a handicap. As Ted Kennedy, Jr. (1986), echoing the thoughts of many persons with disabilities, said, "Ours is not the disability of accident or birth, but the one created by a society insensitive to the needs of millions" (p. 5).

Throughout history persons with disabilities have frequently been seen as a threat to society. However, in recent decades an awareness has emerged that society poses a serious threat to persons with disabilities through its indifference, condescension, segregation, stigmatization, and discrimination. As never before, persons with disabilities have began organizing into autonomous constituencies. Whereas in the past they depended on nondisabled champions, such as religious reformers or concerned professionals, to speak for them, they have now become their own spokespersons. Whereas historically myths of the biological inferiority or incompetence of persons with disabilities were occasionally undermined by rare heroes such as Beethoven or Helen Keller, over the last 30 years there has been a growing number of persons with disabilities, such as Harlan Hahn, Frank Bowe, Lex Friedan, and Ted Kennedy, Jr., who are part of the educated elite of society. The growth of such an elite is crucial for the articulation and defense of the needs and rights of persons with disabilities.

Also for the first time, the rehabilitation of persons with disabilities is being recognized as an economically profitable enterprise for service providers in the private sector. There have been instances in the past when individuals or groups were paid to set up private homes to care for individuals with disabilities, especially people with mental illness or mental retardation (Parry-Jones, 1972), but never before has society had the technological expertise or the financial tools, such as governmental and private insurance, to make rehabilitation a large-scale activity in the private-for-profit sector of the economy. Previous approaches to disability care stressed only the least costly effort and private charity. By contrast, contemporary society is seeing the rise of rehabilitation as a burgeoning private-for-profit business (see Chapter 16) and as an enterprise that contributes to the growth of the economy of the state.

The evolution of social policy regarding disability is such that the time has finally arrived when it is in some instances desirable to be considered disabled (DePoy & Gilson, 2004). Requiring people with the most severe disabilities to be served first, as is required by the 1992 amendments of the Rehabilitation Act of 1973, is an invitation to persons with disabilities to show their disability in the worst possible light in order to increase their chances of receiving state rehabilitation services in states where those with the most severe disabilities are served first. DePoy and Gilson (2004) pointed out that in *Atkins v. Virginia* (2002) the Supreme Court outlawed execution of anyone with mental retardation regardless of the seriousness of his or her crime invites many on death row to claim mental retardation. The insanity defense is another example. Even pressure on corporations and government agencies to hire more people with disabilities may actually make it advantageous to claim disability in particular instances. Coveting disabled parking is perhaps the easiest example of this. It will be interesting to see how all this affects attitudes toward those with disabilities in the future.

Current technological progress also carries the promise that (a) many disabilities may be prevented or eliminated, as in the case of polio; (b) the functional limitations caused by other disabilities can be reduced, compensated for, or wiped out through medical advances; (c) the environment can become more accessible (e.g., through the use of accessible mass transit systems); (d) the perceived threats posed by some disabilities can be minimized or eliminated, as in the case of the pharmacologic control of violent symptoms of mental disorders; and (e) social integration of persons with disabilities will be achieved through full inclusion in education, employment, and recreational activities.

Historically, medical advances have had the net effect of increasing the prevalence of disability rather than decreasing it. As medicine keeps more people living longer, the size of the population of those with disabilities will expand. After all, any person who lives long enough will likely acquire a disability. It will be interesting to see the effect of this greater prevalence of disability on American society, especially regarding its sociocultural milieu and economics. The higher the prevalence of disabilities, the more of a mass market people with disabilities become. In Singapore, for instance, the rapid increase in its aging population has forced the revamping of thousands of high-rise buildings. Where previously elevators stopped every four floors, the elevators are now being converted to stop at every floor.

Contemporary society, as never before, has the tools to store, process, and transmit attitudes and information. Films made in the United States can impact the attitudes of the public in Botswana, and innovations in rehabilitation in Sweden can be shared with persons with disabilities in Sri Lanka. As the world becomes a smaller and smaller place because of advances in communication, the way society attends to persons with disabilities in the future is bound to change.

Chapter 6

Societal Values and Ethical Commitments That Influence Rehabilitation Service Delivery Behavior

Eugenie Gatens-Robinson
and
Stanford E. Rubin

The values people hold are a product of socialization and enculturation (White House Conference on Handicapped Individuals, 1977). As part of the socialization and enculturation process, the great majority of Americans have learned to highly value "attractive" physical appearance, a range of appropriate behaviors, independence, self-sufficiency, productivity, and competitive employment. To be considered "normal," Americans must be perceived as either falling or being capable of falling within certain boundaries on those characteristics. Persons falling outside those boundaries tend to be perceived as being less capable of contributing to the common good of society or achieving an acceptable quality of life.

Rehabilitation professionals are a product of the same basic socialization process that has shaped the values of other members of U.S. society. Therefore, their basic values can be expected to mirror those of others in U.S. society.

A substantial minority of the population of the United States comprises individuals who, either temporarily or permanently, fall outside traditional norms in regard to physical appearance; physical, intellectual, or emotional capacity; or behavior (Bowe, 1978). Many of these individuals seek assistance from rehabilitation professionals who draw upon a specialized system of services directed at helping those with disabilities enter more fully into the mainstream life of the community. In negotiating that service system, rehabilitation professionals must make many decisions that affect the future lives of the clients with disabilities being served. Although those decisions are typically considered to be rational and scientific, their objectivity is inherently susceptible to influence from the values of the decision maker.

While value-laden decisions and rational decisions are often considered to be antithetical, many people have argued against this incompatibility between rationality and valuation and see facts and values as interacting or even mutually defining each other in a rational decision-making process (e.g., Agich, 1982). For example, a client's scores on an intelligence test constitute a fact, but how a particular counselor interprets the relevance of those scores for future planning with the client is a complex clinical judgment influenced by the values of the counselor as well as the empirically based objective meaning of the test scores.

As suggested above, the life experiences of rehabilitation professionals prior to their entering the profession can have a significant influence on their basic values and, concomitantly, on their definition of a "valuable" human life. Therefore, those experiences and resulting values can somewhat shape the way professionals judge the value and potential of persons with disabilities. This chapter discusses some of those socialized values that influence what is perceived as appropriate levels of autonomy for, fair treatment of, and genuine benefit for persons with disabilities by rehabilitation professionals. That discussion should stimulate current and aspiring rehabilitation professionals to explore their own values and biases, as well as any preconceived notions about people with disabilities. It should stimulate them to think about how those values, biases, and preconceived notions might influence their responses to and judgments about persons with disabilities. Achieving that self-awareness can help rehabilitation professionals prevent those values, biases, and preconceived notions from inhibiting their optimal effectiveness with their clients (Sue, Arredondo, & McDavis, 1992).

Prominent Societal Values That Influence the Behavior of Rehabilitation Professionals

Independence and Self-Sufficiency

In the competitive, individualistic culture of the United States, dependency of any kind is usually perceived negatively. Our cultural myths, embedded in everything from television commercials to movies, honor the rugged individual, the self-made person. The model for maturity within U.S. culture is to become self-sufficient and independent from family and governmental support. Even though much of the quality of our lives is dependent on the support of others, "Americans generally believe that they are quintessentially the architects of their lives" (Stubbins, 1988, p. 32).

The moral is clear: Dependency always ought to be minimized and self-sufficiency maximized. This general mandate is supported by the pervasiveness of freedom, autonomy, and independence as cherished values in the United States (Fowler & Wadsworth, 1991). Although these are positive values that have promoted much good in our society, they can result in condemnation of those in a state of permanent dependency, such as many individuals with severe disabilities, to an irredeemably devalued state (Wendell, 1989). When disability is seen as synonymous with helplessness, incompetence, dependence, and passivity, and when individuals with disabilities are perceived as always being recipients of support and never as capable of being providers of support, contributors to society, or sources of pleasure to those around them, a sense of devaluation is likely to be felt by them (M. Fine & Asch, 1988).

To what extent is the ideal of total autonomy attainable or even desirable? Some of the most apparently "independent" individuals within our society, the business executive or the physician, can often be incompetent when it comes to some ordinary activities, such as washing their clothes, cooking, or caring for a child. Each person must decide which of the potential pool of skills that can be developed are most important to develop, and which should be delegated to others so that time and energies can be spent in more desired ways.

Any absolute position on independence held by rehabilitation professionals should be open to careful examination of the situation at hand to avoid forcing persons with disabilities into more independent settings than they might prefer. When such situations occur, to what extent have they resulted because counselors perceived the individuals as incapable "of making any choices regarding their lives" and felt a strong need to push them toward normalization (Perrin & Nirje, 1985, p. 72)? But would it not be more normalizing to encourage and assist such individuals to express "their own preferences and [make] their own choices" in a context where they are provided opportunities for different types or levels of independent living (Perrin & Nirje, 1985, p. 72)?

Should there be more concern with making people with disabilities appear normal or with promoting their self-determination and equality of opportunity "without having to deny or hide their uniqueness" (Perrin & Nirje, 1985, p. 72)? Which approach moves them more toward a quality-of-life–enhancing kind of normalization?

Wendell (1989) argued that in a culture that valued interdependencies, or even acknowledged the appropriateness of interdependencies in certain adult relationships, the tremendous amount of energy people with disabilities put into becoming independent in what are essentially trivial ways might be put to far better use. Many people with disabilities will always be dependent to some degree on the help of others in ways that people without a disability are not. How should people with a disability interpret that dependency? How vigorously should maximum independence be pushed?

Independence as a rehabilitation goal is central to the design of publicly supported programs and services for persons with disabilities. However, when independence is seen as the only desirable state by rehabilitation professionals, provision of rehabilitation services to those persons with disabilities judged to be incapable of achieving that state will be viewed by rehabilitation professionals as both unjustified and not cost-beneficial. This could be the case in spite of a realization by rehabilitation professionals that such individuals are capable of becoming more independent via such services. Rehabilitation professionals can be predisposed to embrace a minimum feasibility-to-benefit criterion as a primary justification for denial of services. This is likely to be true to the extent that the professionals are a product of a society that believes that without a minimum level of independence and self-sufficiency, life lacks sufficient value to warrant certain investments of resources or time.

Work and Productivity

In U.S. society, labor and productivity are often used as measures of social worth. It is generally felt that people should do their fair share. Individuals who do not work are seen as not doing their fair share and, therefore, as having less social value than those who do.

Cultures hold various beliefs about the value of work and productivity that influence what is considered to be just or fair. Some believe that the goods of society ought be shared only by those who make a contribution to that society (Buchanan, 1990). The most visible contributions are those paid activities within the public sphere. Unpaid activities, such as care for children or the ill and aged, are much less valued (except perhaps rhetorically) than paid labor, which generates revenues and goods and services. Cultures that do not share this central dedication to the virtue of paid work and the image of "time as money" are seen as "lazy" or primitive, or perhaps unreliable.

This attitude that ability to acquire remunerative employment is a measure of an individual's social worth can influence the practices of rehabilitation professionals in both appropriate and inappropriate ways. That attitude has had a rather pervasive effect on the practice of rehabilitation as far back as the Smith-Fess Vocational Rehabilitation Act of 1920. That early legislation authorized rehabilitation services for those individuals with a disability for whom future employment was feasible. This criterion for eligibility for services ignored the rehabilitation needs of those persons with disabilities lacking potential for employment. It, in effect, categorized people with disabilities who lack employment potential as permanent failures. That categorization is compatible with the attitudinal foundation for the income maintenance and associated medical benefits programs that comprise the safety-net component of U.S. public policy on disability. Eligibility for those programs rests on an assumption of vocational limitations and seems "to equate disability with unemployability or an 'inability to engage in substantial gainful activity'" (Hahn, 1987, p. 182).

The degree of devaluation of those with little possibility for competitive employment has lessened over the years, especially with the advent of the independent living movement and its emphasis on improving the quality of life of those with disabilities with or without placement in employment. However, the values reflected in the policies of the 1920s are still evident in the current goals of many state rehabilitation agency programs in which the number of clients' cases closed in competitive employment is taken as the primary measure of success (Kuehn, 1991, p. 10). It seems legitimate to be concerned over the effect of such policies on the attitudes of rehabilitation professionals toward persons with severe disabilities.

Physical Appearance

Attractiveness is a highly valued attribute in U.S. society. The very term *attractive* has a connotation of both interpersonal magnetism and sexual appeal. In many social contexts, those with either physical deformities or behavioral abnormalities are often responded to as unattractive individuals, even to the point of their bodily presence being ignored. They become either "invisible" or the object of rude stares. This leads many of those with disabilities to avoid public places. Research has shown that a much larger percentage of those with disabilities than those without disabilities do not go to movies, restaurants, cultural events, sports events, or grocery stores (Taylor, Kagay, & Leichenko, 1986).

Americans place much value on keeping in condition, dressing for success, and sexual attractiveness. The standard for female beauty is set in accordance with the models in many magazines, including the *Sports Illustrated* annual swimsuit issue, and the standard for male attractiveness is presented as tall, athletically built individuals with rugged faces. Such values are so deeply ingrained in the American mentality that most members of U.S. society "feel, in varying degrees, that [they] must at least approach [that physical state] to be happy" (Vash, 1981, p. 29). This is so much the case that those who deviate from a societal desired appearance norm are frequently discriminated against in the employment sector. Using weight problems as an example, Kolata (1993) provided the following support for this point:

> Studies have found that fat people are less likely to be admitted to elite colleges, are less likely to be hired for a job, make less money when they are hired, and are less likely to be promoted. One study found that businessmen sacrifice $1,000 in salary for every pound they are overweight. (p. 1)

Little wonder that so many Americans suffer from anorexia and bulimia. Little wonder also that the desire of many people to approximate the physically perfect image and to avoid the anxiety produced by the belief of the impossibility of that achievement has created a multibillion dollar market for "an awesome range of products that promise to improve attractiveness" (Hahn, 1988a, p. 30).

Wendell (1989) commented that the idealization of a certain kind of body image is self-destructive for able-bodied people as well as those with disability because it prevents everyone from loving his or her real body. No matter how closely individuals can approximate the so-called ideal body, if their acceptance of their body is dependent on that association, it will be a short-lived illusion because that body status can only be temporary.

The idealization of the body tends to correspond with a desire to control the body and the belief that those who cannot are failures. However, there are limits to which anyone can control his or her body (Wendell, 1989). Unfortunately, the belief that those who are incapable of controlling their bodies are of low value eventually undermines the self-concept of most people because those who perpetuate that myth will frequently become its victim by reason of the aging process alone. As Wendell (1989) pointed out,

> Unless we die suddenly, we are all disabled eventually. Most of us will live part of our lives with bodies that hurt, that move with difficulty or not at all, that deprive us of activities we once took for granted or that others take for granted, bodies that make daily life a physical struggle. (p. 108)

The *de*valuing effect on many persons with disabilities of the *over*valuing of a very limited range of physical attributes is obvious. Keeping a positive self-image and maintaining self-esteem for a person whose appearance deviates from the norm is indeed a challenge, especially in U.S. culture. Admiration for physical fitness, grace, and certain ideals of masculine and feminine beauty are often unconsciously incorporated into our responses to others. We appraise and evaluate with our eyes.

Hahn (1988b) attributed much avoidance of persons with disabilities by nondisabled persons to two types of anxiety: *existential anxiety* and *aesthetic anxiety*. The existential anxiety triggered in the nondisabled by contact with persons with disabilities is the threat that comes from the realization of the fragility of the body, the possibility of experiencing pain, and the "potential loss of functional capacities … deemed necessary to the pursuit of a satisfactory life" (Hahn, 1988b, pp. 42–43; see also Wendell, 1989). When faced with a visible disability in another, those without a disability are often made conscious of the inevitable weakness or fragility of their own body. Thus, they are made painfully aware of their inability to totally control their state of health. For this reason, they tend to avoid such encounters and consider people with disabilities as radically different from themselves, possibly even to the point of seeing them as a different "species" (Wendell, 1989). Wendell (1989) discussed the effect of existential anxiety from the standpoint of the threat of possible pain as follows:

> If someone tells me she is in pain, she reminds me of the existence of pain, the imperfection and fragility of the body, the possibility of my own pain, the inevitability of it. The less willing I am to accept all these, the less I want to know about her pain; if I cannot avoid it in her presence, I will avoid her. I may even blame her for it. I may tell myself that she could have avoided it, in order to go on believing that I can avoid it. I want to believe I am not like her; I cling to the differences. Gradually, I make her "other" because I don't want to confront my real body, which I fear and cannot accept. (p. 113)

The presence of existential anxiety can help explain the irrational resistance of some employers to hiring persons with disabilities. These employers can be so influenced by the perceived tragedy of the disability and the associated existential anxiety they experience that they cannot see how the work environment can be modified to eliminate any handicap to effective functioning on the job.

Aesthetic anxiety triggered by contact with persons with disabilities can take the form of worries by the nondisabled about their own appearance or potential loss of attractiveness. Such thoughts can be very bothersome to individuals living in a society that places "extraordinary stress on beauty and attractiveness" and the "quest for supernormal standards of bodily perfection" (Hahn, 1988b, pp. 42–44). Those thoughts can easily stimulate avoidance of persons with disabilities.

The idealization of the body helps to marginalize people with disabilities and actually gets them to participate in this marginalization of themselves (Wendell, 1989). In this way, it tends to undermine any positive self-image possessed by a person with a disability.

In U.S. culture, which puts high value on conformity in appearance and on good physical condition, rehabilitation professionals may see their task as helping individuals with disabilities to achieve some closer approximation to a "normal" appearance in order to increase self-esteem and allow for better social mobility (S. Thomas & Wolfensberger, 1982). However, when such an effort produces a kind of self-rejection by the person with a disability, it can be defeating and destructive.

Ethical Principles That Shape Rehabilitation Professionals' Philosophy of Helping and Guide Their Responses to Clients

The ethical principles that shape rehabilitation professionals' philosophies of helping greatly influence their interpretation of their moral responsibility to their clients. These responsibilities have been defined via the ethical principles of beneficence, autonomy, and justice for medical practice by Beauchamp and Childress (1989) and for rehabilitation practice by Howie, Gatens-Robinson, and Rubin (1992). They can be briefly described as follows:

- *Beneficence*—acting in a manner that promotes the well-being of others through both actions that provide positive benefits and actions that prevent harm (Beauchamp & Childress, 2001)
- *Autonomy*—respect for the freedoms of choice and action of the individual to the extent that those freedoms do not conflict with similar freedoms of others (Kitchener, 1984, p. 46)
- *Justice*—"treating persons fairly, which implies treating equal persons equally and nonequal persons differently if the inequality is relevant to the issue in question" (Welfel, 1987, p. 10)

The positive guidance provided by these principles ensures that the behavior of society members positively affects their shared life together. They also guide the behavior of rehabilitation professionals who embrace the beliefs that they ought to treat their clients fairly, promote their well-being, and respect their freedom of choice. A brief discussion of how each principle relates to the obligations of rehabilitation professionals is presented in the following section.

The Obligation of the Rehabilitation Professional to Be Beneficent

It is often difficult to define the extent of professionals' obligations to actively promote the welfare of others. Rehabilitation professionals know that they ought not actively bring harm to their clients. What rehabilitation professionals are less certain about is the *extent* of their obligation to help clients (Gatens-Robinson, 1992; Howie et al., 1992). Put in a societal context, how many and what type of services should society be obligated to provide to meet the needs of persons with disabilities? Wendell (1989) described that obligation as being greatly determined by what the majority of Americans can see themselves as needing at some point. For example, short-term medical care would be considered a societal obligation because most people can anticipate their need for it. On the other hand, because few people can imagine themselves with a severe disability, they would not typically be inclined to feel that the environment should be modified to allow persons with disabilities to more fully participate in the everyday activities of society (Wendell, 1989). Even though demographic trends indicate that most Americans will experience a disability during the course of their lives (DeJong & Lifchez, 1983), there is a lack of a beneficent orientation toward persons with disabilities reflected in the present environment (Wendell, 1989). If the majority of Americans could perceive a likelihood of acquiring a physical disability during their lifetime, the physical world would be greatly restructured.

The nature of their professional position places a role-based obligation on rehabilitation professionals to go to extraordinary lengths to help persons with disabilities. Howie et al. (1992) provided three reasons for why rehabilitation counselors have that strong obligation to their clients:

1. *Special Knowledge.* Through training, education, and practical experience, the counselor has acquired a well-developed knowledge of the special needs and risk conditions of a certain group of individuals. Therefore, they are in a unique position to help and to be able to assess the risks and benefits associated with different client actions.

2. *Control of Benefits.* The counselor has the power to dispense or withhold resources and/or information that could promote the welfare of the client. Indeed, the counselor may at times be the client's sole access to needed information and resources.

3. *Societal Expectations of the Profession.* There is an implicit covenant within the client/counselor relationship that the counselor will act to promote the interests of the client. By entering the relationship, the counselor has given the client reason to have this expectation. Furthermore, the nature of the relationship allows the counselor special access to the intimate details of the client's life. The client provides the counselor with a picture of his or her needs and desires, strengths and weaknesses with the understanding that appropriate help can be given. This access to private information not only increases the counselor's ability to help, but also increases his or her obligation to use this information in the helping process. The fact that the counselor is paid to help the client in specific ways further adds to the obligation. (p. 44)

The current attitudes of most rehabilitation professionals, like those of the majority of the citizenry, have been greatly influenced by differences, which they directly observed or believed to be the case during their developmental years, between persons without disabilities and those with disabilities. As a result, many individuals enter the rehabilitation profession with more ability to feel sympathy than empathy for persons with disabilities (Wendell, 1989). No matter how beneficent they wish to be, insufficient empathy by rehabilitation professionals for persons with disabilities will greatly moderate what they define as needed and will, therefore, place potential limits on what they consider as the scope of their obligations to beneficence for persons with disabilities. This can be understood by considering potential differences between the perceptions of persons with severe disabilities and those of persons without disabilities of the acceptability of specific costs and benefits associated with habilitation and rehabilitation services directed at having a significant effect on an individual's quality of life. The person with the disability and the nondisabled professional service provider could have very different perceptions of the real value of a specific service for a particular individual and the level of cost deemed acceptable for producing it.

Take the example of two 11-year-old boys with cerebral palsy who cannot ambulate without a wheelchair, cannot stand, and must use diapers as a result of lack of bladder control. One child, Bob, is capable of dressing himself and the other, Joe, is not. Through surgical intervention, both children can achieve bladder control. Following surgery, Bob will function independently in regard to toileting; however, Joe will still require the help of a personal attendant to assist him with his clothes during toileting. Although, like most of the general public, the great majority of rehabilitation professionals might lean toward providing the operation for Bob because the result will be independent toileting, both groups might tend to see less value in providing Joe with the operation because he will still be incapable of independent toileting. However, although the rehabilitation professional might not view the operation as equally warranted for Bob and Joe because of the pain and risks associated with it for both, as well as its inability to produce independent toileting for Joe, Joe might view it as having a very significant positive effect on his quality of life and, therefore, assess its value differently.

The nature of their position requires rehabilitation professionals to have enough self-understanding and understanding of their clients to be sensitive to any incompatibility between their own values and the values of their clients. For example, rehabilitation professionals should be aware of what they have been conditioned to perceive as constituting a significant improvement in the quality of life of persons with disabilities, as well as what their clients would find acceptable or desirable, be willing to work toward, and accept the risks to achieve. When that level of understanding is present, rehabilitation professionals are more likely to consider the point of view of their clients when determining which benefits they should be helped to realize. There will be a clear relationship between that level of understanding by rehabilitation professionals and their perception of which of their potential actions are compatible with their obligation to beneficence.

The Obligation of the Rehabilitation Professional to Respect Client Autonomy

By respecting the prerogatives of clients to make independent decisions and take actions accordingly, rehabilitation professionals show their respect for client autonomy (Howie et al., 1992). By refraining "from unnecessary interference in the client's independence in choice making and action" and providing the client with "relevant knowledge upon which necessary choices can reasonably be made," the rehabilitation professional respects the client's autonomy (Howie et al., 1992).

Client competence is a key assumption, however, underlying the rehabilitation professional's belief that the client's freedom of choice and action should be both respected and facilitated. Howie et al. (1992) discussed the relationship between client incompetence and the appropriateness of the rehabilitation professional's respect for the client's autonomy:

> Clients who cannot utilize relevant knowledge for a reasonable choice, or who lack understanding of the knowledge needed to assess a situation and to plan and execute an action, are incapable of autonomous decision making. On the ground of beneficence or nonmaleficence, the autonomy of such persons may be restricted. If beneficence is the ground, then their autonomy is restricted to keep their actions beneficial to themselves. If nonmaleficence is the ground, then their autonomy is restricted to keep them from harming themselves or others. (p. 48)

As is obvious, many situations are possible in which the likelihood that a rehabilitation professional will respect the autonomy of persons with disabilities will be determined by the professional's perception of the level of competence of these persons. A rehabilitation professional's perception of client competence can be influenced by the valued characteristics discussed earlier in the chapter. To the extent that those values have been incorporated into the professional's value system, the likelihood could be diminished for the professional's respecting the freedom of choice and action of some persons with disabilities who are without those characteristics but who are in fact competent.

The ultimate test of respect for autonomy can be found in the degree to which professional service providers are willing to honor the right of individuals to refuse treatments that service providers strongly believe are necessary for their welfare. Much of the medical ethics literature related to this issue focuses on the right of patients or clients to control their own body, including refusing treatment that might be required to sustain their life. (Beauchamp & Childress, 2001).

A good example of the conflicts that manifest themselves within the framework of this issue can be found in the case of Elizabeth Bouvia, a 25-year-old college graduate with cerebral palsy who had a lifelong condition of almost total paralysis. She had enough control of her hands to operate a wheelchair and of her facial muscles to speak, eat, and smoke. She married, conceived, and subsequently miscarried. Her husband left her, and her parents refused to support her. Her attempts to find employment were frustrated, and one of the employees in the rehabilitation program from which she sought services told her she was too severely handicapped to work. Finally, she checked herself into a California hospital and declared her intention of starving to death (Steinbock & Lo, 1986). She expressed a need to be free of her disability and the tremendous struggle to go on living.

In Bouvia's judgment, the quality of her life was so poor and the likelihood of improvement so remote that death seemed a reasonable escape. Neither the hospital nor the judge who handled the case was willing to cooperate with her plan. She was force-fed. The organization Advocates for the Developmentally Handicapped held a candlelight vigil outside the hospital, claiming that if she was allowed to die, it would cause other people with disabilities to follow her example (Steinbock & Lo, 1986).

Although Bouvia had struggled and worked to achieve a certain quality of life, she was unable to attain it. The causes of this failure are not easily gleaned from the available reports. Her personal support system seems to have crumbled, and the rehabilitation services received seem to have been inadequate or even incompetent, if Bouvia's account is accurate. The responses of both the medical and the disability communities may have been more self-serving than focused on the needs of Bouvia. The medical establishment was threatened by her challenge to their values by choosing to die under their roof. The disability community was disturbed that she refused to be more heroic in her struggle against the tremendous physical and psychological odds and was thus setting a bad example to others facing equally difficult and painful lives. Although both sides had valid concerns, Bouvia's quality of life was not improved as a result of this debate, and her autonomy was seriously violated on numerous occasions.

What was at stake here? It has been an ongoing struggle for those with disabilities and their advocates to establish the concept of the inherent value of their lives. The discrimination against people with disabilities has often involved some judgments about their capacity for a "good life." Such judgments about quality of life are often biased and made by individuals lacking sensitivity to the range of possibilities for or preferences of people with severe disabilities.

Bouvia may not have been allowed the right to die or to refuse treatment for the most part *because* she had a severe disability. If her action was some last-ditch effort to effect some control of her life, which it may well have been, she failed. When she bit through the feeding tube, she was tied down and her mouth held open in order to continue the feeding. Would this be classified as battery in most other cases? One must be curious as to why those who, on general principles of autonomy, would defend any competent patient's right to refuse treatment, even if that resulted in death, in this case did not see such considerations as valid. Was it because Bouvia was not seen as competent to decide whether she wanted to continue living? Would she have been perceived as incompetent to make that decision if she had characterized her action not as assisted suicide, but as a hunger strike in protest against an environment that isolated and disempowered her? If hunger strike was the case, would the reaction of at least the disability community have been different?

The Obligation of the Rehabilitation Professional to Be Just

Justice is another principle relevant for guiding the actions of the rehabilitation professional. For the rehabilitation professional, justice generally applies to the fair distribution of a finite amount of caseload monies and service provider time among clients to meet their rehabilitation needs. The principle of justice becomes very useful when ethical problems of distribution arise as a result of competition for scarce resources. "In such a situation, who gets what and why is a lingering ethical issue" (Howie et al., 1992, p. 49).

What rehabilitation professionals perceive as just resource allocations in regard to persons with disabilities is greatly determined by what they categorize as beneficial. The boundaries of that category for any particular client would be greatly influenced by what rehabilitation professionals perceive any reasonable person as desiring or finding acceptable. That perception could be greatly influenced by the societal values discussed earlier in this chapter. For example, what the rehabilitation professional perceives as an acceptable quality of life will influence what services may or may not be provided to certain clients. Therefore, client-requested services that the rehabilitation professional does not anticipate as making a significant difference in that client's quality of life will probably not be provided. The rehabilitation professional would not consider the decision to deny those services as being unfair because no denial of benefit would be seen as associated with it. In this case, the interpretation of beneficence and justice interact.

Many of the service delivery decisions of rehabilitation professionals are influenced by their belief of what ought to be, by the clients' beliefs about what ought to be, and by what the professionals see as cost-beneficial. With the tendency toward utilitarian thinking in U.S. society, the greatest influence on the service provision decisions of rehabilitation professionals is probably the perceived cost–benefit associated with an action. That economic index obviously is greatly influenced by the amount of benefit perceived in the anticipated outcome from the service delivery action (cost incurred). Therefore, when a particular service is requested by a client, the likelihood that the rehabilitation professional will adhere to the principle of autonomy (i.e., respecting the client's right to choose) will be greatly determined by the benefit perceived by the rehabilitation professional in the anticipated outcome from the service delivery action. This point can be further reinforced by the following question: In our utilitarian society, how many rehabilitation professionals will financially support the desire to attend college by a client who has the intellectual capacity to learn but who, even with reasonable accommodations in the employment setting, lacks many of the necessary capabilities to work?

Because of the utilitarian influence on American thought, the behavior of rehabilitation professionals is predominantly controlled by what they perceive as being fair (i.e., the effective use of scarce resources). Given the above discussion, denying services requested by persons with disabilities will be perceived neither as unjust nor as violating the principle of autonomy when that denial is not perceived by the rehabilitation professional as violating the principle of beneficence. It might also not be seen as violating the principle of autonomy, because the client's choice might be viewed as irrational, or at best unrealistic, and possibly even the decision of an incompetent person (i.e., a person viewed as incapable of using available information to make the decision).

Justice requires employing a relevant criterion as a basis for distributing resources. Examples of such criteria include "to each person an *equal* share,… to each person according to free-market exchanges, and to each person according to fair opportunity" (Howie et al., 1992). Allocating rehabilitation services according to the *equal-share criterion* would clearly provide access to those services to the greatest possible number of persons with disabilities. However, because differences among disabilities produce major differences in the amount of rehabilitation services required for rehabilitation, the equal-share criterion would be dysfunctional.

The *free-market exchange criterion* would make rehabilitation services available to any individual with a disability willing and able to purchase them. The cost of such services would be determined by the laws of supply and demand, which would be "allowed to operate in an unimpeded manner" (Howie et al., 1992, p. 50). As is obvious, the free-market exchange criterion would produce such a major compromise of the ethical principle of beneficence, in regard to the large number of persons with severe disabilities for whom vital rehabilitation services would be too costly to purchase, that it would be considered morally unacceptable to most Americans as a criterion for the distribution of resources.

Howie et al. (1992) described the *fair opportunity rule* as follows:

> This rule functions in two ways. It prevents persons from being granted social benefits on the basis of undeserved advantaging properties and insists that persons should not be denied social benefits on the basis of undeserved disadvantaging properties. In effect this rule requires that retarded persons, individuals with reading difficulties, or low IQs should receive more of society's resources and services to offset their disadvantaging properties. For these persons to have fair opportunities (in competition with those not disadvantaged) the disadvantages they have received in the lottery of life must be counterbalanced. Not to correct (within the limits of our resources) or to ignore these disadvantages (while being aware of their presence) is to lend them our approval. (p. 50)

The fair opportunity rule is probably the best criterion for determining the just obligations of U.S. society in regard to both what portion of its resources should be allocated to meet the needs of the disability population and how those allocated resources should be distributed among the disability population to meet the needs of its members in a fair manner. However, even the fair opportunity rule has its limitations as a criterion for just allocation of resources because the decisions made will be greatly influenced by the decision maker's perceptions of what are "worthwhile" benefits for persons with disabilities to achieve.

In our utilitarian-oriented society, the application of the fair opportunity rule will likely be limited to those persons with disabilities who are seen as capable of having the "playing field leveled" for them by being considered eligible for a greater share of the resources of society than are persons without disabilities. Those who are not seen as capable of having the playing field leveled, regardless of the amount of resources provided to meet their needs, are more likely to be seen as not eligible for a greater share of society's resources. They are more likely to be seen as dependent on voluntary charity to meet any needs beyond basic ones such as food, clothing, and shelter. Thus, as suggested earlier, filling the request of an individual with a disability for public funds for a college education that may enhance his or her life, but without augmenting future entrance into competitive employment, might not be viewed as justified under the fair opportunity rule in a utilitarian society. However, in such a circumstance, cause might be found to reflect on how prevailing values, such as those discussed above, act to restrict the moral imagination of both rehabilitation service providers and formulators of public policy on disability about what is possible within a particular life, and what kind of help is justified in achieving it.

Concluding Statement

Independence, self-sufficiency, health, productivity, work, physical beauty, and certain types of behavior are values embraced by the great majority of the U.S. public. Rehabilitation professionals should be aware that their attitudes are shaped not only by professional training and work experience, but by these dominant societal values as well. They should also understand that the unquestioned embracing of these dominant values as traditionally defined can negatively influence their responses to the goals of their clients.

Rehabilitation professionals are faced with the challenge of moving persons with disabilities into the mainstream of U.S. society. That goal may be achieved by an individual with a disability without mirroring the quality-of-life standards of persons without disabilities. Helping the individual with a disability achieve a "good life"—a good living situation in which he or she can maintain self-esteem, find pleasure, and lead a reasonably fulfilling life—and helping the individual with a disability lead a "normal life," as defined by the norms and values of society, are not always compatible. In "a world that was planned and constructed almost exclusively for the non-disabled" (Hahn, 1987,

p. 192), this latter goal might require incredible effort, and promote frequent failures and loss of self-esteem.

Both the client and the rehabilitation professional may perceive a clear association between having a "good life" and having certain personal characteristics, such as being competitively employed and independent, as well as being physically and behaviorally similar to the great majority. However, both parties must be able to envision the attainment of a good life without these qualities. To do so, rehabilitation professionals must be able to examine the validity and the implications of these deeply held and largely unexamined beliefs regarding absolute requirements for the good life. Through that process, they can achieve self-awareness about the extent to which they personally embrace those values and how that might affect their service delivery behavior.

It can be argued that the ethical principles of *beneficence* (helping others fulfill their basic needs), *autonomy* (respecting the choices of others), and *justice* (making fair decisions regarding distribution of scarce resources) greatly help define ethical behavior by rehabilitation professionals. Many factors affect how or how well individuals apply these ethical principles within various situations. For example, rehabilitation professionals must actively engage in analyzing the interpretation of their commitments to ethical principles within particular situations. Each professional has an obligation to benefit clients; however, what is perceived as a *benefit* by a rehabilitation professional in a specific context may be colored by the values discussed earlier in this chapter. The professional also has an obligation to facilitate the client's freedom of choice and action; therefore, promoting autonomy can come to be seen as the primary goal to be maximized above others. However, that possibility is influenced by the extent to which a client is viewed as capable of rational choice. Finally, the professional has an obligation to be just; however, what is considered to be a fair allocation of resources for a particular client is greatly dependent on the rehabilitation professional's perception of how much the client can benefit from that allocation. That perception is also influenced by the values discussed earlier in this chapter.

The practice of rehabilitation is directed at assisting people with disabilities to structure their lives in ways that actually benefit them. However, because the rehabilitation professional is frequently an individual without a disability, or at least not the same sort of disability as the client's, significant realms of experience are not shared by the rehabilitation professional and the client. Because of this difference, it seems particularly important to heighten the awareness that what is perceived as a benefit or as of value to an individual is greatly determined by culture. The values considered valid by the great majority of people within a culture may not be easily applicable in a positive manner to many of those individuals with severe disabilities who have been excluded from participation in the validation of those values. Several of those values often held by rehabilitation professionals as a result of their being socialized in U.S. society can interact in a negative way with their judgments about client welfare or autonomy or fair treatment.

Rehabilitation professionals are involved in an inherently moral practice because their actions can directly affect the well-being of their clients. Their judgments are influenced by their beliefs of what ought to be. However, their actions can be greatly controlled by their beliefs about what can be and what is cost-beneficial. Thus, it is crucial for rehabilitation professionals to achieve a self-awareness of those forces that can potentially shape their beliefs and thereby influence their decisions and actions.

Chapter 7

Rehabilitation Clients and Their Needs

I ndividuals with disabilities have long struggled with situations ranging from outright rejection to subtle prejudice and devaluation. Many historical examples of this can be found in the earlier chapters of this book. The following examples further drive home the "second-class citizenship" endured by people with disabilities throughout American history.

> The 1872 civil procedure code of the County of Los Angeles prevented persons who were deaf, blind, and physically handicapped from serving on juries. The reason was that such persons were considered, according to the code, to be "decrepit and lacking in all their natural faculties." (Pfeiffer, 1994, p. 489)

According to Pfeiffer (1994), those attitudes were still being reflected by the opposition of two county judges in 1976 to a measure being considered by the Los Angeles County Supervisors to repeal the provision. The judges' opposition was based on the belief that the "blind would have difficulty in determining the credibility of witnesses" without being able to observe their demeanor (p. 489). Overall, the stereotypes that have resulted from perceived functional limitations have contributed to a history of devaluation and discrimination against persons with disabilities. Indeed, the labels applied to people with functional limitations of a physical, emotional, or intellectual nature clearly reflect this socially imposed inferior status (e.g., the *de*-formed, the *dis*-eased, the *dis*-ordered, the *ab*-normal, the *in*-valid, and most particularly, the *dis*-abled; Zola, 1981). It is not unusual for any of these nouns to be used interchangeably with the term *handicapped,* thereby causing the person with functional limitations to be viewed as nonfunctional.

Perceptive analyses of the effects of disability on the individual are resulting in broader acceptance of the notion that the psychology of disability "is the study of normative responses from (psychologically) normal organisms to abnormal stimuli" (Vash, 1981, p. xiii). Furthermore, one should recognize that interventions to enable individuals to "take care of the chores of living with a disability" (Hohmann, 1981, p. ix) must concentrate as much on removing environmental barriers (Shontz, 1977) as on helping people with disabilities "cope with, adapt to and adjust to those barriers" (Vash, 1981, p. xiv). It is our intention that this chapter *not* be a clinical and potentially dehumanizing view of the person with a disability. Rather, the reader is encouraged to remember throughout this discussion Vash's (1981) admonition: "The fact is, human beings are more alike than different, regardless of variances in their physical bodies, sensory capacities, or intellectual abilities" (p. xiii).

Terminology

A basic distinction must first be made regarding terminology. As numerous authors have noted, *disability* and *handicap* are not synonymous (Bowe, 2000; Hamilton, 1950; B. Wright, 1983). Depending on an individual's vocation and life situation, a disability may or may not constitute a handicap. B. Wright

(1983) distinguished between the terms *disability* and *handicap* in the following way:

> *Disability:* ... a limitation of function that results directly from an impairment at the level of specific organ or body system.
>
> *Handicap:* ... the actual obstacles the person encounters in the pursuit of goals in real life, no matter what their source. (p. 11)

Therefore, *disability* is generally defined as a medically diagnosable physical or mental impairment that limits the individual's functioning. Whether this limitation imposes obstacles to the person's goal attainment (i.e., whether this limitation is vocationally relevant) depends on numerous factors. For example, a below-the-knee amputation of the right leg might not result in a vocationally relevant functional limitation for a receptionist or a disc jockey, but it would for a bricklayer or a professional hockey player.

Hershenson (1974) pointed out that the handicapping aspect of a functional limitation can be manifested in an indirect manner, "as in the case of a salesman who suffers a facial disfigurement. He may still do his job in exactly the same way as before, but customers may react to him differently" (p. 480).

There are also situations in which the handicapping nature of a physical disability is lessened through lateral vocational movement by the individual. For example, a vocational education (woodworking shop) teacher who cannot return to the classroom following the surgical removal of his cancerous larynx could find equally well-paying employment as a cabinetmaker. The degree of vocational handicap for such an individual would be greatly related to the strength of his predisability identification with the teaching profession.

As is evident, the extent of handicap is affected by a number of factors, such as the individual's previous occupational role and other aspects of the individual's vocational and social environment. Therefore, handicap must be understood in terms of an interaction between the impairment or the disability and the characteristics of both the person with a disability and his or her architectural, attitudinal, legal, and social environments (B. Wright, 1983). A disability represents a significant handicap to the degree that it causes the individual to become economically, emotionally, socially, and/or physically dependent on others.

Factors Affecting Extent of Vocational Handicap

Three factors affecting the extent of a vocational handicap associated with a disability include the individual's (a) physical capacity, (b) acquired vocational skills and skill acquisition potential, and (c) psychological functioning. To understand the effects of disability on individuals, one must consider the disability in relation to each of the three areas.

Physical Capacity

Questionable physical capacity becomes a significant concern in the consideration of types of work for which the individual is otherwise emotionally, intellectually, and skill-wise suited. Hershenson (1974) suggested that it would be a mistake to ignore the "fairly consistent functional limitations associated with particular chronic conditions" in regard to vocational choice (p. 488). The following examples demonstrate the point:

> Individuals confined to wheelchairs must work in locations with appropriate access and toilet facilities; those with degenerative diseases must assume a decreasing supply of energy and range of activity in planning their vocational future; and those whose conditions may be worsened by stress (for example, some tubercular cases, ulcer and colitis cases, certain epileptics, and emotional problems) should seek job roles which minimize this factor. (Hershenson, 1974, p. 488)

Acquired Vocational Skills and Skill Acquisition Potential

Skill acquisition, real or potential, as a result of either formal education, formal vocational training, or on-the-job training experiences is a significant employability factor. The focus is on being able to perform or learn specific tasks through which income can be acquired. The identification of such acquired skills could facilitate rapid reentry (or initial entry) into the labor market in positions for which the individual with a disability is otherwise suited psychologically and physically.

The basic intellectual capacity of a client is also a significant consideration (Hamilton, 1950). For example, an unskilled laborer with limited intellectual capacity who acquires a severe physical disability is limited in regard to postdisability vocational choices. On the other hand, another unskilled laborer with an equally severe physical disability may have a much wider range of vocational choices because of an above-average IQ. In the latter case, skills necessary for reentering the labor market might be easily acquired through appropriate vocational training.

Psychological Functioning

Psychological functioning, a significant employability factor, can either restrict or enhance the level of employment suggested by the individual's physical capacity and acquired vocational skills. Using the example of a deaf student in an airplane mechanics course, Hamilton (1950) effectively illustrated the significance of psychological adjustment:

> Despite considerable counsel on the problem, he still had difficulty arising out of his feeling that persons whose conversation he could only partially hear were talking about him.... One day, ... he became convinced that an instructor and the student at the next bench were talking about him. Without previous warning, he raised the drawing board on which he had been working and brought it down over the head of the instructor. Obviously, until such psychological problems were dealt with, this student would not have been employable as an airplane mechanic. (p. 30)

Although the three functional areas discussed above are common considerations in determining the extent of handicap associated with any type of disability, there is knowledge regarding the differential effects of a variety of physical, emotional, and intellectual disabilities. Hence, the material to follow profiles several disability groups: persons with (a) physical, (b) emotional, (c) intellectual, (d) learning, or (e) visual disabilities.

Physical Disabilities

As pointed out earlier, not every medically diagnosable physical condition necessarily results in a vocational handicap. For example, Burk (1975a) pointed out that although "atherosclerotic plaques may line our blood vessels ... (and) opposing surfaces of our joints ... show evidences of early degeneration," we would not consider ourselves as handicapped unless the physiological aberrations interfered in some way with our daily functioning (p. 22). Burk (1975a, pp. 22–24) also observed that although a diagnostic label such as cardiovascular disease or diabetes mellitus locates the difficulty anatomically, it provides few real clues as to the severity of the condition or the extent of functional limitation. Bowe (2000) has spoken to this point in regard to spinal cord injury (SCI):

> The extent of the effects of SCI vary according to (1) the type of injury (e.g., complete vs. incomplete) and (2) the level of the injury (e.g., C5 vs. T9). For example, someone with a complete injury at the C5 level could achieve some control over the shoulders and biceps but not usually over the wrists, hands, or fingers. An individual with an incomplete T9 injury, on the other hand, could control the abdominal muscles well and achieve good seating posture; the arms, wrists, hands, and fingers would not be affected by the injury. (p. 120)

Devins (1989) discussed the devastating effect of end-stage renal disease (ESRD). In dealing with ESRD, individuals who have not yet received a kidney transplant inevitably face the realization that their life spans are reduced and that they are "dependent on medical machinery and personnel" (p. 11). Following transplant, individuals with ESRD are still in a state of uncertainty as to whether the operation will be successful. They also encounter significant side effects from the immunosuppressive medications they must take to avoid organ rejection.

Reactions to Disability

Siller (1969) identified the following long-term defensive reactions to physical disability: denial, overdependency, passivity/withdrawal, aggression and identification/compensation. Denial is a common defense soon after onset of disability in cultures such as the United States where great significance is placed on health and physical appearance. It is characterized by lack of acceptance of the implications of the disabling condition. In its more obvious forms, denial manifests itself in such statements as "This is not happening to me" and "This is not going to be permanent; I will get better." It is not unusual for individuals with spinal cord injury to "talk about walking out of the hospital," or to ask repeatedly, "When will I be able to move my legs?" (Trieschmann, 1984, p. 126). Refusal to acknowledge limitations imposed by onset of disability often has damaging consequences. A typical example would be a dockworker who develops a chronic back problem. Although ordered to change occupations by his physician, in an attempt to act and feel normal, he returns to the dock job and exacerbates his back injury (Safilios-Rothschild, 1970).

Resistance to the alteration of body image through denial is not unusual if such alterations are perceived by individuals with a disability as "negative, disagreeable, and devaluative to … their self-esteem" (Safilios-Rothschild, 1970, p. 95). An example of denial would be a person with an amputation experiencing phantom limb in an attempt to "keep the body image and body sensation intact" (Safilios-Rothschild, 1970, p. 96). Referring to denial of changes in functional capacity following the onset of disability as an "ostrichlike reaction," Himler (1958) pointed out that apparently such a person finds "some comfort in his unrealistic insistence that he has not lost his normal ability" (p. 441). This is reminiscent of the denial of the mentally ill woman who insists, "It isn't me that should be here, Doctor, but my husband" (Himler, 1958, p. 441). One theory holds that the greater the significance of the afflicted part to the person's self-concept, the more likely it is that the person will deny the disability.

Some clinical research suggests that denial can play a positive role in the acute recovery stages of cardiac disease. Providing a means of diminishing emotional stress and related physiological reactions, denial represents an effective short-term defense "which is remarkably efficient as a buffer" (Brammell,

McDaniel, Roberson, Darnell, & Niccoli, 1979, p. 37). However, Brammell et al. (1979) also emphasized that denial becomes "counterproductive in terms of long-term rehabilitation objectives" (p. 37).

In cases of invisible disability (e.g., diabetes, epilepsy, cardiovascular disease), denial may blend into a reaction referred to as nonacceptance. Nonacceptance is a situation in which the person recognizes the limitations of the disability but consciously disregards its implications for his or her performance. This denial of limitations causes the person to fear discovery and, therefore, to be both resistive to rehabilitation efforts and prone to further personal injury (Falvo, Allen, & Maki, 1982).

In response to a perceived threat from their conditions (Devins, 1989), some individuals with physical disabilities may be tempted to quickly accept the changes in body image. Such overacceptance or overdependency can result in unnecessary self-imposed limitations that preclude the use of remaining physical capacities. Secondary gains from having dependency needs met and from attributing failures to disability serve to reinforce the overaccepting reaction. W. Gordon, Bellile, Harasymiw, Lehman, and Sherman (1982) reported results indicating that the tendency to attribute control of one's life to external factors was related to poorer skin-care practices in individuals with spinal cord injuries. Overall, individuals who tend to overaccept the limitations of disability and to attribute control of their lives to outside forces may make slower progress in rehabilitation because they have "the perfect alibi" for not succeeding.

Some individuals with a physical disability may withdraw from social contacts and activities (J. Smart, 2001). Lack of response, or passivity (Siller, 1969), may reflect a fear-of-failure syndrome; the individual does not try to respond to the disability for fear of not making a successful response. Individuals manifesting such a reaction are likely to place excessive demands on those around them.

Some individuals with physical disabilities may also respond in an aggressive or passive-aggressive way. Aggressive responses, tempered by social convention, are less likely to take a physical form than a "constructive" criticism form. For example, the individual may criticize aspects of his or her rehabilitation program and use those criticisms as excuses for not participating more fully. Passive-aggressive responses take such subtle forms as "misinterpreting" instructions and "forgetting" to take medication (Siller, 1969).

It is not surprising that some individuals with physical disabilities resort to defense mechanisms such as denial, overdependency, withdrawal, and aggression in an attempt to preserve their self-esteem. One can explain the presence of defensiveness as an initial response both to the shock of disability and to the extreme negative social reactions of others. D. L. Berry and Catanzaro (1992) enumerated some of the social barriers that workers with a history of cancer encounter, such as "dismissals, failure to hire, reduction in salary or failure to receive due increases, changes in hours or work location that isolated the worker ..., and reduction of group health or life insurance coverage" (p. 42). Defensive reactions to such discriminatory treatment come as no surprise. Nevertheless, it is hoped that such individuals will eventually move toward use of defense mechanisms, such as identification and compensation, which signal a positive acceptance of the disability (Cull, 1972; Siller, 1969).

Identification reactions are evident when individuals with disabilities join forces with an outside group or cause that provides them with feelings of social and psychological adequacy. For example, they can readily identify with a disability consumer group. Identification with a group having needs in common with their own provides a basis for new compensatory behaviors (Cull, 1972). Through compensation, the individual with a physical handicap overcomes feelings of inferiority by finding ways to reach newly desired goals; avenues toward these goals were probably demonstrated by members of the new identification group. For example, individuals might complete vocational training in areas different from their previous occupations in order to achieve some of the same monetary and social objectives possible through participation in an earlier occupation. According to Cull (1972), identification and compensation go together in the adjustment process:

> When a client starts using these two defenses, he is at a point where he may adequately adjust to the new body image and to his new role in life. As the individual experiences successes, he will become less preoccupied with anxieties relating to disability and his lack of productivity. (p. 432)

The process of adjustment to disability has also been described as a developmental sequence. Krueger (1984) described adjustment to disability as involving a progression through the following stages or "passages": shock, denial, depressive reaction, reaction against independence, and adaptation. Kerr (1961, 1977), who had earlier used slightly different stage labels within a five-stage adjustment to disability sequence, saw such stages as a conceptual convenience rather than "discrete categories" that universally describe the road to client acceptance of disability. In this regard, Kerr (1961, p. 16) observed orthopedic patients in a large rehabilitation center progressing through the following phases:

1. *Shock*—"This isn't me."
2. *Expectancy of Recovery*—"I'm sick, but I'll get well."
3. *Mourning*—"All is lost."
4. *Defense A* (Healthy)—"I'll go on in spite of it." *Defense B* (Neurotic)—Marked use of defense mechanisms to deny the effects of the disability.
5. *Adjustment*—"It's different, but not 'bad.'"

The validity of the above sequential stages as a description of the adjustment to disability process has not gone unchallenged (Cushman & Dijkers, 1991). According to Trieschmann (1984, 1988), stages in the process of adjusting to disability have not received significant empirical support. Indeed, based on a review of research with people with spinal cord injuries, D. Cook (1998) concluded that acceptance of spinal cord injury is not necessarily preceded by feelings of depression or mourning.

Coping with Physical Disability

Due to the stigmatizing effect of disability, one must be very careful not to equate acceptance of disability with acceptance of helplessness and inferiority (Wolfensberger & Tullman, 1982). Acceptance also suggests an end or state that, once reached, is forever maintained (J. Smart, 2001). This could be considered an unrealistic goal for individuals with a disability. Those with a disability are more likely to be participating in an ongoing process throughout their lifetime in which they are coping with their disability and making adjustments (J. Smart, 2001). Consequently, *"acceptance is not a one time event"* (J. Smart, 2001, p. 229).

In discussing response to disability, Vash (1981) isolated a number of factors that affect the process. Initially, one must realize that coping with disability occurs in a context having both social and disability-related aspects. For example, such factors as the "type of disability, its severity, its stability, the person's sex, inner resources, temperament, self-image, self-esteem, the presence of family support, income, the available technology, and government funding trends" are a few factors influencing the effect of the disability on the person (Vash, 1981, p. 3).

Dealing with the disability necessitates a modification in self- and body image in the direction of acknowledging limitations, relying on others without excessive anxiety, and developing greater congruence between physical abilities and personal expectations (Geis, 1972; L. Levine, 1959). Regarding coping with disability, B. Wright (1960, 1967, 1983) emphasized the importance of developing new interests, enlarging the scope of one's values, reducing the value placed on "body beautiful," enhancing the ability to compare oneself with certain internalized functional standards rather than with standards based on what others are able to do, and resisting a view of oneself as disabled in all ways because of certain discrete limitations (i.e., spread of effect). Evidence of a clinical nature (Mayer & Andrews, 1981) supports Wright's position. Individuals who were successfully coping with disability-related problems were more likely to view disability as a "challenge or facilitator of growth" rather that as an "obstacle they could not overcome" (p. 137).

With respect to fuller participation in life, particularly involvement in employment, Gulick (1992) stated that counselors must understand how the stress-coping process affects adjustment to disability. Speaking of people with chronic illnesses, she wrote that adaptational outcomes such as resumption of employment were, in part, a function of the person's interpretation (appraisal) of the disability and its impact and of the adequacy of the individual's coping mechanisms. In other words, the meaning the person attributes to the effects of disability or chronic illness—such as disruption of one's schedules, gait and motor disturbance, fatigue, and other health crises—directly affects his or her cognitive and behavioral coping responses. She noted that two types of coping responses significantly improve the person's chances of resuming and retaining work. One set of work "enhancers" includes the environmental modifications suggested by the Americans with Disabilities Act, such as flexible work schedules, job modification, and use of adaptive equipment. The other set of work "enhancers" consists of personal qualities of the individual, such as "a positive attitude, humor, faith and hope, and control of stress" (Gulick, 1992, p. 271).

Physical Disability and Sexuality

The impact of disabling conditions on sexual desire and behavior has received much attention in the rehabilitation literature (Burling, Tarvydas, & Maki, 1994; Connine, 1984; Maddox, 2003; Robbins, 1985). Prior to the 1970s rehabilitation counselors were not expected to address the sexual concerns of their clients with severe disabilities during interviews (Sawyer & Allen, 1983). That attitude began to change by the end of that decade. For example, the results of a survey of vocational rehabilitation agency administrators in the late 1970s showed that they saw discussion of client sexual concerns as an appropriate service for rehabilitation counselors to provide during individual rehabilitation counseling sessions (Sawyer & Allen, 1983).

The complexity of the subject becomes clear when one considers that sexual desire and behavior are affected in different ways by different disabilities (S. Keller & Buchannan, 1984; Maddox, 2003). Rather than attempt to comprehensively address the subject of disability and sexuality, the following discussion will demonstrate its complexity and reiterate the need for sex education and counseling during the rehabilitation process.

Physiological impairment of sexual functioning can complicate psychological adjustment to conditions such as multiple sclerosis, diabetes, renal disease, and spinal cord injury (Berkman, 1975; H. S. Kaplan, 1974; Stewart, 1981). For example, degeneration in the spinal cord in multiple sclerosis can cause erectile and organic disorders (H. S. Kaplan, 1974; Keller & Buchannan, 1984). Juvenile diabetes has been found to produce retrograde ejaculation or impotence in males, whereas females with juvenile diabetes are particularly prone to miscarriage (Gregg, 1980; J. B. Stone & Gregg, 1981). "Renal disorders, which impair detoxification and excretion of metabolic products and estrogen, are especially likely to be accompanied by diminished sexual interest" (H. S. Kaplan, 1974, p. 77).

According to Singh and Magnes (1975), spinal cord injury for females causes loss of physical feeling but not loss of function. Indeed, females with paraplegia are capable of conceiving children and delivering babies normally (S. Keller & Buchannan, 1984; Sandowski, 1976). Singh and Magnes (1975) also cited evidence that neither sexual desire nor activity decreased in females after onset of disability.

Research suggests that few males with paraplegia are able to ejaculate; however, the majority are capable of erection even though they may not be capable of sustaining it long enough to have intercourse (Maddox, 2003). Erection can sometimes be achieved or prolonged via the use of special devices or therapies (Diamond, 1974; Maddox, 2003; Sandowski, 1976). These include penile injection therapy, medicated urethral system erection, and penile implants (Maddox, 2003). With penile injection therapy, a drug such as papavarine or alprostadil is injected into the side of the penis and produces "a hard erection that can last for an hour or two" (Maddox, 2003, p. 109). With medicated urethral system erection, a medicated pellet containing the drug alprostadil "is placed into the urethra for absorption into the surrounding tissue [causing] the blood vessels to relax," with the result being an erection as blood fills the penis (Maddox, 2003, p. 109). Both penile injection therapy and medicated urethral system erection have a number of potential side effects, such as infection (Maddox, 2003). Farrow (1990) described two types of penile implants that have been developed through medical research for assisting men with spinal cord injuries to achieve erections.

> One type of penile implant involves a semirigid rod that can be straightened manually for intercourse and then placed to the side when not in use. The second type is a more complicated device that consists of two cylinders, a balloon type reservoir, and an external pump. When an erection is desired, the external pump is used to force liquid into the cylinders, which creates an erection. A serious disadvantage of both types of implants is that the devices may cause serious damage to the surrounding tissue if not monitored closely. (p. 257)

The decision to use prostheses or devices to enhance sexual satisfaction is, of course, a personal consideration for the individual with a disability and his or her spouse. Although they can give no simple answers, rehabilitation professionals can provide accurate information and an atmosphere that encourages individuals to discuss their sexuality and sexual desires in order to "clarify their feelings and values and make informed choices" (Ames & Boyle, 1980, p. 175). In sexual counseling with a person with a disability, the counselor must consider the person's attitudes toward sexuality and predisability patterns of sexual behavior. Therapeutic efforts must include the partner of the individual with a disability "since both must learn new patterns of behavior" (Trieschmann, 1975, p. 10). As Shontz (1977) noted, "Teaching persons with spinal cord injuries to find new means to gain sexual satisfaction or intimacy often restores emotional balance, even though it does not remove or alter the physical disability" (p. 209).

Considering a person's attitude toward sexuality and predisability patterns of sexuality also calls for recognition that sex and sexuality are two different matters. As Burling et al. (1994) pointed out, sex "is one of the four basic human drives.... Sexuality is a multidimensional and intricate area of human function and includes such components as gender, sex acts, and the psychosocial aspects of sexuality including emotions, attitudes, and relationships" (p. 10). Hence, counselors must understand that diverse types of relationships and practices are possible as people seek to meet their needs for intimacy and affection. For example, McAllan and Ditillo (1994) described how counselors, regardless of their own sexual orientation, can become more sensitive to the needs of lesbian and gay clients with disabilities. They reminded counselors to reexamine both their beliefs and their behaviors in order to "create a place for all clients to feel safe, free of discrimination, and free of fear" (p. 32).

Rehabilitation Potential

Some of the self-imposed and socially imposed factors affecting realization of the rehabilitation potential of the person with a disability have previously been discussed. Manifestation of such potential requires adjusting to one's disability psychologically and learning to cope with architectural and transportation barriers as well as negative social attitudes. If individuals with disabilities are not able to surmount psychological and social barriers, society will lose the considerable contributions they can make. Support for that conclusion can be found in the literature (G. Murphy & Athanasou, 1994; M. Siegel, 1969). For example, based on a review of the results of 17 postinjury employment follow-up studies of those who sustained a severe spinal cord injury resulting in paraplegia or quadriplegia, G. Murphy and Athanasou (1994) concluded that such individuals had significant potential to return to the workforce. G. Murphy and Anthanasou (1994) found that

> 1441 or 40.3% of all the 3568 subjects sampled in the 17 studies returned to work post-injury. For subjects who were followed-up less than five years post-injury, the average return to work rate was 37.9%; for subjects who were followed up at periods exceeding five years post-injury, the return to work rate was higher at 48.6%. (p. 47)

A follow-up survey of Institute of Rehabilitation Medicine clients, which predated the studies reviewed by G. Murphy and Athanasou (1994), demonstrated that about 80% of those with quadriplegia admitted to the institute in a 5-year period were employed or would eventually be employed. Successful because of their individual determination and comprehensive rehabilitation services, these clients would typically be found working in "professional, technical, managerial, sales and clerical areas" (M. Siegel, 1969).

Vocational potential should not be thought of as a direct function of the severity of the disability. In fact, severity of disability is not a "reliable index of vocational potential" at all. "Vocational potential, the capacity to attain successful performance in a job, is a function of ability, not of residual disability" (M. Siegel, 1969, p. 713). The issue is not one of medical and functional limitations so much as it is one of what abilities remain and what skills the individuals can learn.

Pimentel (1995) provided an illuminating analysis of vocational potential and the factors affecting it in his discussion of the transitional employment plan that he recommends for industry-based return-to-work programs. He described the different reactions to impairments related to spinal cord and back injuries in two individuals. One individual was a veteran dealing with quadriplegia. The other person experienced continual back pain, although no medical indications existed. The veteran with quadriplegia called Pimentel to excitedly report that he received a job offer and would start work within a month. The person with back pain received a rating of "totally disabled" in a worker's compensation hearing and never returned to work.

In considering which of the two men was more severely disabled, Pimentel (1995) concluded that factors other than the objective nature of the disability affected the vocational potential of each person. From the perspective of disability management procedures in business, Pimentel concluded that the ways in which the two cases were managed had a great deal to do with the final outcome. For example, he noted that negative or positive responses by the rehabilitation counselor, employer, claims personnel, and medical professionals create or remove barriers to returning to work. Most of these barriers, according to Pimentel, eventually are internalized psychologically, causing the person to become unresponsive in the return-to-work process. For example, unsupportive and insensitive actions of others create feelings of fear, isolation, hostility, frustration, and negativity on the part of the person with a disability.

Many examples have appeared in the literature over the years that indicate how employers can help people with disabilities continue to realize their vocational potential. For example, Kenny (1998) reported findings indicating that people with disabilities were more likely to return to work when employers were supportive in terms of attending to workplace safety issues and providing assistance and information.

Dow Chemical Company of Midland, Michigan, reported on a cost-effective and supportive Special Services rehabilitation program that focused on postdisability residual abilities (Lanhann, Graham, & Schaberg, n.d.). The Special Services program used a selective placement committee to evaluate the skill levels, functional abilities, and training needs of the person with a disability, as well as the demands of potential jobs. If a match existed without worker retraining, the individual was placed in the position. However, individuals who had not yet gained the abilities to return to their previous job or to a new job received special training in the Special Services "base work" program. Performing valuable work for Dow, individuals in the training program were involved in work consisting of the

> salvage of scrap materials and repair of pipe fittings, gauges, steam traps, instrument motors, rotameters, instrument heaters, electrical fittings, flanges and pallets. Product packaging of commercial items, tying saran liners, assembling bromine bottles, fabrication and repair of infrared cells

and vinyl chloride monitoring tubes, and cleaning safety equipment [were] ... all done within the work complex. (Lanhann et al., n.d., p. 4)

Needed training was provided by the unit at an overall cost savings to Dow because of the valuable salvage, handling, and repair work being completed. Lanhann et al. (n.d.) reported that the Dow program was a successful rehabilitation venture. During an 18-year period, 159 Dow employees with disabilities were helped by the program to return to their previous job ($N = 79$) or to move into a job suitable to their existing abilities ($N = 80$). Performance of the workers in the areas of safety and attendance was outstanding.

Unfortunately, many nondisabled employers tend to view people with disabilities as having little or no vocational potential. When they contemplate hiring workers with disabilities, employers expect to have "extra costs" far outweighing the benefits (Michaels & Risucci, 1993). Extra costs to interview, screen, and test are anticipated, as are problems of absenteeism, accidents, getting along with coworkers, increased insurance rates, and poor work quality (Reagles, 1981; Satcher, 1992; C. Williams, 1972). Given such attitudes, it is not surprising that studies have shown that those whose disabilities present a substantial activity limitation are "more apt to live at or below 150 percent of the poverty level" and that "only 20 percent of persons requiring assistance with basic activities of daily living have a job" (Danek, 1992, p. 9).

Fortunately, data exist to document the rehabilitation or vocational potential of persons with disabilities (G. Murphy & Athanasou, 1994; Reagles, 1981; Wessman, 1965). For example, in an industrial setting utilizing job modification and restructuring techniques, Yuker, Campbell, and Block (1960) reported that 400 workers with disabilities had safety and attendance records superior to those of nonhandicapped workers in conventional companies. Overall, research comparing the absenteeism of able-bodied workers and workers with disabilities showed either no differences or better attendance for persons with disabilities (Greenwood & Johnson, 1987; Ondusko, 1991). Data supporting the conclusion that the worker with a disability is a safe and regular employee are available in the DuPont survey titled "Equal to the Task II" (DuPont, 1990). Speculations as to the reasons for the positive work records of persons with disabilities include their capacity to deal more effectively with stress on the job because they had met the challenge of their disability and the fact that work has more intrinsic meaning to individuals with disabilities (Wessman, 1965).

Research has shown that, while not totally leveling the playing field for those with a disability, a college education can have a major positive effect on the employment potential of individuals with a disability (DeLoach, 1992). According to DeLoach (1992), Bureau of the Census data from the period 1981 to 1988 indicated that

the percentage of persons who had work disabilities and who were in the workforce ranged from 14.8 percent for those with less than 12 years to 46.5 percent for those with 16 or more years of education. This is compared to 54.1 percent and 82.2 percent, respectively, for those with no work disability. (p. 58)

DeLoach (1992) also reported that Memphis State University alumni with a disability "who graduated with a minimum of a bachelors degree between 1980 and 1986" had a postgraduation employment rate of 62% (p. 58).

DeLoach (1992) reported on a mail survey of highly motivated and qualified individuals with severe disabilities (that predated their entrance to college) who had graduated from the University of Illinois between 1948 and 1988. Over 83% of the 501 individuals who responded to the survey in 1988 reported being currently employed. DeLoach (1992) stressed that this finding shows how "access to higher education can enhance the employability and vocational success of qualified individuals with severe disabilities," as well as how, paired with such access, environmental and academic accommodations at the University of Illinois very likely spared these individuals from "a lifetime of financial dependence" (p. 62).

Psychiatric Disabilities

According to the U.S. Department of Health and Human Services (2000), approximately 40 million individuals in the United States between the ages of 18 and 64 have some type of mental disorder. Estimates suggest that approximately 10% of that population experiences a long-term reduction in the ability to carry out normal activities for their age group, such as working or keeping house (National Institute on Disability and Rehabilitation Research, 1991). Unemployment among this working-age population with severe mental health problems has been estimated to be approximately 75% to 80% (Anthony & Blanch, 1987; J. Cook & Razzano, 2000).

Rutman (1994) identified a number of characteristics associated with psychiatric disorders that can make it more difficult to acquire and maintain employment. These include (a) poor work history and job skills; (b) inability "to establish or maintain a personal support system"; (c) inappropriate social behaviors; (d) difficulties with controlling anxiety and impulse control; (e) "work capacity deficits, such as punctuality, appearance and grooming, task performance, and following directions"; (f) side effects from antipsychotic medications, antidepressant medications, and medications for manic–depressive illnesses, such as "tremor, shuffling gait, drooling, restlessness, stiffness in facial muscles, lightheadedness, blurred vision, low blood pressure, facial twitches and grimacing, loss of coordination and swelling limbs"; and (g) unrealistically high or low vocational aspirations (Rutman, 1994, pp. 19–21). In regard to the latter, Rutman (1994) pointed out that practitioners regularly encounter clients with psychiatric disabilities "who insist on referrals to jobs far beyond their capabilities, or others who, conversely, will accept only lower-level jobs although they readily could handle more challenging work roles" (p. 21).

For most of the 20th century, "serious psychiatric disabilities" were "viewed as irreversible illnesses with increasing disability over time" (Spaniol, 2001, p. 167). However, recent research has tended to contradict the validity of that assumption. That research has "demonstrated that one half to two thirds of people with severe mental illnesses significantly recover over time" (Spaniol, 2001, p. 168). According to Spaniol (2001),

> There is no evidence to support the notion that people with psychiatric disabilities follow a specific inflexible and negative natural history. While the impact of serious mental illness is devastating to those who experience it and to their families, it does not appear that serious mental illness is necessarily a disease of slow and progressive deterioration as was once widely believed.... People with psychiatric disabilities can achieve partial or full recovery from the illness at any point during its course, even in the later stages of life. (p. 168)

The definition of mental illness is based on a traditional system of psychiatric diagnosis. Over the years considerable controversy has raged regarding the diagnostic process itself. The controversy regarding traditional psychiatric diagnoses has focused on both reliability and validity. In terms of reliability, Hersen (1976) quoted a large number of studies that indicate "that when assessments of patients are made by independent clinicians, the resulting inter-rater agreements are of low magnitude" (p. 5). Regarding validity of psychiatric diagnoses, Hersen (1976) quoted research demonstrating that it is extremely difficult to distinguish between diagnostic categories either in terms of their origins as defined by life stressors or in terms of treatment responses necessitated.

Traditional psychiatric diagnoses have also failed to provide meaningful data as to an individual's work potential. For example, in their study of workers in the clothing industry, Weiner, Akabas, and Sommer (1973) found that psychiatric diagnoses were unrelated to the client's level of work potential. They considered the results of their study to offer "evidence to suggest the importance of evaluating the individual, his strengths, potential, and environmental opportunities rather than focusing on diagnostic labels" (Weiner et al., 1973, p. 123). In a study on the effectiveness of a supported employment program for returning individuals with severe psychiatric disability to competitive employment, Trotter, Minkoff, Harrison, and Hoops (1988) found successful outcomes for program participants to be independent of psychiatric diagnosis.

Anthony and others (Anthony, 1980; Anthony, Cohen, & Nemec, 1987) developed a functional approach to diagnosing the rehabilitation needs of persons with psychiatric disabilities. Stressing that skill, or lack thereof, predicts rehabilitation outcome, not psychiatric diagnoses, Anthony (1980) recommended a diagnostic approach that analyzes the individual's physical, intellectual, and emotional strengths and limitations as they interact with the demands of living, learning, and working environments. This skill-by-environment diagnosis is required because individual performance varies from setting to setting. Some persons with psychiatric disabilities are able to live independently but do not have the skills to acquire a job. Others can maintain a job but not social relationships (Trotter et al., 1988).

Rehabilitation Potential

For some individuals with psychiatric disabilities, existing treatment programs are insufficient to overcome the effects of emotional disturbance. For others, treatment may do little beyond what they could do for themselves. Olshansky (1968) concluded that about 40% to 50% of all individuals with severe emotional disabilities find their own jobs and, for all practical purposes, "pass" as normal. The remaining 50% who end up in vocational rehabilitation represent the chronically unemployed. Of that group, Olshansky estimated that about 10% to 20% can profit from vocational rehabilitation services that concentrate on vocational placement and independent living. The rest need more intensive, long-term services.

Olshansky's (1968) estimates are consistent with Kunce's (1970) division of the population of individuals with psychiatric disabilities into thirds. One third of the individuals diagnosed with a psychiatric disability will require rehospitalization and long-term treatment regardless of type of intervention. One third may be able to obtain successful employment and sustain it whether they receive treatment or not. Kunce, therefore, stressed that rehabilitation services can make the most difference with the middle one third as far as "enhancing their ultimate vocational adjustment but not necessarily insuring complete and sustained social independence" (Kunce, 1970, p. 298). Compatible with the estimates of Olshansky (1968) and Kunce (1970), the Rehabilitation Services Administration indicated that many of the unemployed individuals with mental illness have substantial vocational potential and could benefit from vocational rehabilitation services (Skelley, 1980).

The existence of negative social attitudes toward mental illness (Berven & Driscoll, 1981; Fabian & Coppola, 2001; E. E. Jones et al., 1984; Mansouri & Dowell, 1989; Rutman, 1994) obviously explains why so many individuals with a history of emotional disturbance prefer to "pass" rather than admit to having received psychiatric treatment. Even though employers say it is not the case, individuals with such a background feel, for good reason, that they will be discriminated against in employment.

In two studies (Drehmer & Bordieri, 1985; C. I. Stone & Sawatzki, 1980), MBA (master's of business administration) students were asked to evaluate job applicants without disabilities, with physical disabilities, and with psychiatric disabilities on the basis of observation of taped interviews and reported work history (C. I. Stone & Sawatzki, 1980) or a complete résumé containing information on applicant education and work history (Drehmer & Bordieri, 1985). The results of both studies suggested that the MBA students' ratings were influenced by the disability conditions, with job applicants with psychiatric disabilities much less likely to be hired.

In an earlier study, although 90% of a group of 127 employers said they would hire an ex–psychiatric patient if he or she were properly trained, only about 1 in 6 had knowingly done so (Hartlage, 1965). Possibly that discrepancy resulted from the employers' expectations for ex–psychiatric patients as workers. That sample of employers expected ex–psychiatric patient workers to be more prone to violence, impulsiveness, and unpredictability. These workers were also expected to require more supervision, to be able to tolerate little frustration, to be likely to become emotionally ill again, and generally, to be a poor employment risk (Hartlage, 1965). In a more recent study, Kirszner, Baron, and Rutman (1992) found that such employer attitudes may be ameliorated through direct personal experiences with employees with psychiatric disabilities. Kirszner et al. found

> that employers who have had experience with persons with psychiatric disabilities in supported employment and/or transitional employment programs are relatively unconcerned about violence or bizarre behaviors, while employers uninvolved with persons with psychiatric disabilities in prior employment programs exhibit the stereotypical fears. (cited in Rutman, 1994, p. 27)

Although factors of prejudice affect the receptivity of employers to hiring the ex–psychiatric patient, Olshansky and Unterberger (1965) also pointed out that many ex–psychiatric clients simply do not have the educational and vocational skills to be desirable employees. These clients would not be hired even if they did not have a history of psychiatric disability.

Individuals with psychiatric disabilities who have the most difficulty are those with moderate to severe impairment of their adaptational skills (Goldstone & Collins, 1970). Typical work adjustment problems of these individuals include (a) adapting poorly to new situations, (b) producing low-quality work, (c) having inappropriate grooming and dress habits, (d) relating poorly to supervisors and coworkers, (e) losing confidence on the job, (f) having difficulty dealing with time pressure and deadlines, (g) having difficulty initiating interpersonal contact, (h) having difficulty focusing on multiple tasks simultaneously, (i) having difficulty following directions, (j) being adversely affected by criticism, and (k) being ineffective due to fear of being fired (Hamburger & Hess, 1970; Holden & Klein, 1967; Kline & Hoisington, 1981; Mancuso, 1990; Rutman, 1994).

Work adjustment training programs for individuals with psychiatric disabilities can be designed to overcome some of the above-mentioned problems. Such training situations must simulate the roles found in the competitive work environment (Ciardiello & Bingham, 1982). Helping individuals with a psychiatric disability adjust to a work situation unlike a real work situation will probably only prepare them for sheltered employment.

Promising work adjustment programs that approach the "real" work situation have been either described or demonstrated in the rehabilitation literature. Historically, these programs have their roots in hospital-based efforts to involve people with mental illness in productive activity. For example, J. Brown (1970) developed a transitional vocational and social training program that was designed to provide a competitive work environment. Manpower Development Training Act programs for farmhands, maintenance men, cook helpers, and general maids were set up on the grounds of the Vermont State Hospital at Waterbury, and hospital facilities were used for the training. The program deviated from typical mental hospital patient work routines in that competitive work environment conditions, such as quality standards and time deadlines, were stressed. However, work experiences were complemented by social development activities such as group therapy, gripe sessions, and field trips to restaurants. Program participants ranged in age from 16 to 57, with an average hospitalization of 7.5 years. Only individuals who were considered good candidates for discharge were selected for the program. Thirty-seven of the 40 patients who entered the program completed it. When the program results were reported, 22 of the completers were holding jobs and 6 were taking either further training or were in school.

Brennan (1968) described a paid work rehabilitation program at Bedford Veteran's Administration Hospital for people with mental illnesses with the potential for competitive employment. The hospital provided the work space, and private industry provided the equipment and paid the wages for the products. The program had a positive effect on patient self-concept and played a vital vocational rehabilitation role in that it conditioned the participants for entering a competitive work situation at discharge. Brennan stressed the importance of payment of at least the national minimum hourly wage to participants in work rehabilitation programs.

In an early application of the supported employment model, L. Newman (1970) recommended a job contract approach or work rehabilitation transitional program located directly in either a private industry or a public agency. In this regular wage paying system, a certain number of positions would be contracted for, and the employer would be guaranteed that the positions would be competently filled at all times. Worker supervision would be provided by nonprofessional assistants whose work would in turn be supervised by professional rehabilitation counselors. Therefore, the nonprofessional person would be the one in continual contact with the client. If a client did not report for work, the nonprofessional assistant would step in and do the job. L. Newman's (1970) proposed program was designed to provide instant placement opportunities for rehabilitation clients with psychiatric disabilities who have minimal vocational potential (e.g., no special skills, low work motivation, stormy personal life, dependent and fearful behavior, inability to handle ordinary level of interpersonal stress). Newman's strategy was implemented in the transitional employment programs (TEPs) established by many community mental health facilities.

Promising results regarding the employment potential of persons with chronic mental illness (e.g., affective disorder) occurred in a pilot project implemented by the Colorado Division of Mental Health in spring 1986 in Denver. The purpose of the project was

> to train and employ individuals with chronic mental illness to provide case management services to other mental health consumers. The project's goal was to have the four community mental health centers in Denver employ 20 consumers [clients with a chronic mental illness] … who would share ten full-time jobs with the title of consumer case manager aide. (Sherman & Porter, 1991, p. 494)

Twenty five consumers were selected for the project from a pool of 49 nominees with chronic mental illness. They were provided with 6 weeks of formal classroom training that focused on skills such as interviewing, crime intervention, stress management, "acquiring benefits, identifying deficits in independent living skills,… transportation logistics,… identifying crises and analyzing problems, communicating with team members, and supporting peers" (Sherman & Porter, 1991, pp. 495–496). Classroom training was followed by 14 weeks of on-the-job training as a case management aide intern in one of the four community mental health centers (which could never be one in which the aide was receiving treatment). All of the trainees also attended a weekly support group with a counselor, which provided opportunities "to ventilate frustrations; to solve personal, learning, and work problems; and to encourage each other" (Sherman & Porter, 1991, p. 496).

Seventeen of the 25 individuals who entered the training program both completed it and were subsequently employed as consumer case management aides. As of August 1988, 15 of the case management aides "had been continuously employed for 26 months" (Sherman & Porter, 1991, p. 497). During that 26-month period, that entire group of 15 aides required a total of only 2 days of psychiatric hospitalization. Sherman and Porter (1991) reported that the success of the project "had a pronounced effect on the attitudes of staff and consumers in the mental health system in Colorado. The professional mental health community … [was] forced to reconsider its pessimistic prognosis about the potential abilities of clients who have chronic mental illness" (p. 497).

Jacobs, Kardashian, Kreinbring, Ponder, and Simpson (1984) reported promising results in terms of employment outcomes for a Job Club program used with individuals in an inpatient psychiatric hospital. Incorporating two phases, training in job-finding skills and support in the job search, their Job Club program helped the majority of participants to retain employment over 30-, 60-, 90-, and 180-day follow-ups. The authors noted that the individuals in the group had particular need for training in (a) job finding, (b) reconstruction of their work histories, and (c) goal setting and full-day programming.

Trends such as deinstitutionalization and the consequent rise of the community mental health center have changed the approach to treating many persons with emotional problems. Greater emphasis is placed on vocational preparation at the work site through temporary or transitional employment programs. Fountain House in New York City received considerable recognition for programs that integrated community-based employment with a range of other necessary services, such as "transitional living arrangements, group placement, guaranteed completion of jobs under contract, and a system for rapid return into the vocational rehabilitation process of those individuals whose mental illness rendered them unable to participate in employment" (Skelley, 1980, p. 29).

Through a Project with Industry grant, the Menninger Foundation coupled its psychiatric services with a four-phase vocational rehabilitation effort emphasizing job development, client job-readiness preparation, follow-along support after placements, and business and industry liaison and training (Skelley, 1980). Programs such as those at the Fountain House and Menninger Clinic exemplify the psychosocial rehabilitation approach to mental health programming. Stressing the need for functional diagnosis and skill building, psychosocial rehabilitation programs address the broad objective of improving a person's social role functioning as a "spouse, parent, household/family member, friend, neighbor/community member, educational consumer, wage earner, mental health consumer, public services consumer" (Hume & Marshall, 1980, p. 62). As Ten Hoor (1980) stressed, treatment of those with psychiatric diagnoses requires the integration of "practices and principles" from both mental health and rehabilitation.

Many reasonable accommodations can be made at the workplace that could increase the likelihood that persons with psychiatric disabilities will acquire and maintain competitive employment. Many such job modifications would be consistent with mandates found in the Americans with Disabilities Act discussed in Chapter 3. Mancuso (1990) listed the following examples of job accommodations appropriate for persons with emotional disabilities, many of which might simply be viewed as good management practices:

- Arranging for all work requests to be put in writing for a library assistant who becomes anxious and confused when given verbal instructions …
- Training a supervisor to provide positive feedback along with criticisms of performance for an employee re-entering the work force who needs reassurance of his/her abilities after a long psychiatric hospitalization …
- Allowing a worker who personalizes negative comments about his/her work performance to provide a self-appraisal before receiving feedback from a supervisor …
- Scheduling daily planning sessions with a co-worker at the start of each day to develop hourly goals for someone who functions best with added time structure …
- Purchasing room dividers for a data entry operator who has difficulty maintaining concentration (and thus accuracy) in an open work area …
- Arranging for an entry-level worker to have an enclosed office to reduce noise and interruptions that provoke disabling anxiety. (p. 15)

Fabian, Waterworth, and Ripke (1993) conducted a study of the reasonable accommodations (job modifications) made for 30 workers with a serious mental illness (e.g., schizophrenia, schizoid personality disorder, bipolar disorder, personality disorder) who were participants in a supported employment program in Bethesda, Maryland. During the period of the study, the workers held a total of 47 jobs. The majority of the job placements involved were in clerical positions, retail store positions, and unskilled laborer positions, although 4 individuals were placed in semiprofessional or professional positions. All told, 231 job modifications could be identified for the 47 jobs held by the 30 workers in the study. Fabian et al. (1993) found that all but 3 of these modifications could be categorized among the following eight types of accommodations:

Modifying job tasks	e.g., "shifting tasks from one job to another ... or removing job tasks" (p. 167)
Modifying work schedules and time	e.g., "allowing employees to leave early for mental health and/or other appointments related to disability issues; ... allowing the employee 'flex time' in selecting hours of employment" (pp. 167–168)
Providing orientation and training to supervisors to provide necessary assistance	e.g., "including the job coach in supervision, and arranging on-site meetings between job coach, employee, and supervisor" (p. 168)
Modifying work rules and procedures	e.g., "modifications of work procedures such as allowing employees to use the telephone to call the job coach for support, and 'saving' jobs during periods of psychiatric hospitalization" (p. 168)
Modifying job performance expectations	e.g., "changing performance expectations such as allowing employees a longer period to learn a job ... and providing the employee with more time for completion of work tasks" (p. 168)
Modifying non-physical work environment by providing physical assistance at the job site	e.g., "denotes on-site job assistance provided by the job coach to the employee" (p. 168)

| Modifying workplace social norms | e.g., "not expecting the employee to attend weekly lunches ... to accommodate the needs of individuals with psychiatric disabilities" (p. 168) |
| Providing orientation and training to coworkers | e.g., "educating coworkers about mental illness, enlisting their assistance with overseeing client job performance" (p. 168) |

Fabian et al. (1993) also found a significant relationship between the number of accommodations provided for a worker in their sample on a job and the number of months the worker retained the job. Those who received a larger number of accommodations tended to have a longer retention period on their job. These study results suggest that reasonable accommodations made by the employer could be a key factor in the ability of persons with a serious mental illness to retain employment.

Many of the vocational rehabilitation approaches used with individuals with serious mental illness are pervaded by the principle of gradualism (Bond, Dietzen, McGrew, & Miller, 1995). That principle assumes that vocational rehabilitation clients with serious mental illness

> can best improve their work habits and job performance through the process of meeting expectations in successively more demanding work environments, beginning with relatively low demand environments.... Eventually, as clients move through this rehabilitation continuum, their behaviors ostensibly are "shaped" to satisfy community employment standards.... In most psychiatric rehabilitation programs clients spend a substantial amount of time in prevocational training before, and even after, their initial entry into community employment. (Bond et al., 1995, pp. 75–76)

Although the gradualism approach has been perceived as the "state of the art in psychiatric rehabilitation" by many rehabilitation professionals, the validity of that perception has been undermined by a review (Bond, 1992) of 24 experimental evaluations of gradualism-type "programs conducted between 1963 and 1986" (Bond et al., 1995, p. 77). From that review,

> Bond (1992) concluded that, although a variety of vocational rehabilitation approaches did increase clients' level of paid employment in the short term, none demonstrated an effect on long-term competitive employment rates. Bond (1992) also concluded that treatment programs without a specific vocational focus have little chance of affecting employment rates. (Bond et al., 1995, p. 77)

To further investigate the validity of Bond's (1992) conclusions, Bond et al. (1995) compared the effect on 74 clients with serious mental illness (randomly divided between the two approaches) of an *"Accelerated Approach* to supported employment (SE) ... which bypassed traditional prevocational preparation" and "a *Gradual Approach* which consisted of a minimum of 4 months in prevocational preparation followed by SE services" (p. 75). Results at both 1 year and 3 years following the initiation of the study suggested better employment outcomes for those clients with serious mental illness who were served under the Accelerated Approach. Based on the results of their study, Bond et al. (1995) concluded that for the population of persons with serious mental illness, "early entry into competitive employment, with intensive support, is more effective than approaches incorporating prevocational training" (p. 75). They speculated that the Accelerated Approach may be more effective than the Gradual Approach because the Gradual Approach may have the effect of lowering client expectations for the level of employment they can achieve.

Other rehabilitation strategies are needed, however, when community resources are not sufficient to accomplish the Accelerated Approach. Revisiting the traditional concept of homebound employment, Kates, Nikolaou, Baillie, and Hess (1997) described an experimental project in which they brought work contracts to the homes of people with severe mental illnesses. These individuals wanted to participate in work activities but were unable to do so because of the unavailability, or perceived inappropriateness, of local facilities. Individuals in the program completed such work activities as assembling saw and telephone drop wires, making jewelry, and packing screws and beads. They also had access to a monthly luncheon to meet each other and discuss their activities and a monthly newsletter, prepared by participants.

In an evaluation of the program over a 24-month period, Kates et al. (1997) found that program participation contributed to gains in self-esteem and symptom relief. Although the sample size was small, research findings also indicated that participation in work contracts at home encouraged more members of the experimental groups to seek other work groups or to find competitive employment. Touting the benefits of the program, the authors stressed adaptability for many community settings and its low participant cost.

Promising Trends in Mental Health Services: Assertive Community Treatment and Supported Employment

The importance of employment as an outcome for mental health services for the 21st century is clearly stated in agenda-setting documents such as "Healthy People 2010" (U.S. Department of Health and Human Services, 2000). Clarifying priorities for health and human services, the report documents that unemployment of people with mental illness remains a critical national problem that must be solved. After presenting statistics indicating that only 43% of people with mental illness are employed, the report calls for an improvement in that rate to a 51% employment target by 2010. At the same time, the report notes that the 43% employment rate is for all people with mental illness, making it a rather exaggerated figure when individuals with severe mental illness (SMI) are considered. Statistics indicate that employment rates for people with SMI are approximately 20% to 25% in most studies (J. Cook & Razzano, 2000; Crowther, Marshall, Bond, & Huxley, 2001). Consequently, new service delivery models are needed if individuals with severe emotional disabilities are to live more independently in the community.

One promising approach to increase community integration and employment rates for people with severe mental illness is a combination of an intensive case management strategy referred to as Assertive Community Treatment (ACT) and supported employment (Morris & Lloyd, 2004). In ACT, services are provided by a team of professionals including psychiatrists, nurses, social workers, rehabilitation counselors, and representatives of other specialties such as recreation, physical therapy, and occupational therapy. Team members are available on a 24-hour basis to assist individuals with serious emergency situations or maintenance of individualized treatment plan goals (Prince & Gerber, 2005). Services are provided in the person's typical living environment, and the staff-to-client ratio is quite small compared to other approaches (1:10 rather than 1:30 or more; Mueser & McGurk, 2004).

Research on ACT indicates that the program is producing some very positive outcomes for people diagnosed with SMI. ACT participants are reporting fewer days of hospitalization, fewer medication and life crises, improved psychological status, higher levels of subjective quality of life, and greater success in independent living and community integration (B. J. Burns & Santos, 1995; Fekete et al., 1998; Mueser & McGurk, 2004; Phillips et al., 2001). The positive results from ACT underscore the appropriateness of its assumptions about the need for intensive, around-the-clock, long-term case management and professional care in real-life settings if people are to deal with the chronic, unpredictable effects of SMI.

To achieve similar gains in the employment arena, treatment specialists have combined the multidisciplinary ACT approach with supported employment services, sometimes referred to as the Individual Placement and Support Model (IPS) (Garske & McReynolds, 2005; G. Lee, Chronister, Tsang, Ingraham, & Oulvey, 2005). Because supported employment has demonstrated its value in helping people with mental illness find and keep work (Ackerman & McReynolds, 2005; Meisler & Williams, 1998), it is a logical adjunct to comprehensive case management. Keys to the supported employment approach include such practices as expedited job search and placement, situational assessment, behavior modification, job coaching and natural workplace supports, and long-term employment support planning (Morris & Lloyd, 2004). Other practical considerations that are important in supported employment planning include the types of accommodations needed, the intensity of job coaching required, strategies to meet childcare and transportation needs, and benefits planning should wages or salary affect Social Security Disability Insurance or Supplemental Security Income payments. Interestingly, the combination of these improved service strategies, such as ACT and supported employment, is occurring at a time when social policy and legislation (e.g., Title I of the Americans with Disabilities Act) strongly endorse nondiscrimination in the hiring process and provision of reasonable accommodations in the workplace (Rumrill, Roessler, McMahon, & Fitzgerald, 2005).

Given its success in maintaining people with SMI in more independent roles, ACT, when coupled with supported employment, is an appropriate response to the challenge issued by the U.S. Department of Health and Human Services (2000) to improve the employment rate of people with SMI. This combined program is based on certain assumptions that make a great deal of sense. For example, people with SMI are dealing with a chronic condition that requires long-term rather than short-term interventions. Therefore, program planning must emphasize support and recovery rather than cure (Nemec & Gagne, 2005). Similarly, to be effective, employment interventions for people with SMI must be intensive, immediate, and in situ. The ACT approach stresses that acquisition and maintenance of employment by people with SMI require interventions both on and off the job—hence the blending of intensive case management and supported employment (e.g., job coaching) strategies.

Coupling ACT with supported employment is only one side of the coin necessary for improving employment outcomes of people with SMI. As noted, ACT is primarily a case management, rather than an employment, intervention that focuses on helping people maintain an appropriate level of independent living in the community. Although of recognized value as a placement strategy, the supported employment/coaching model tends to focus initially on client behavior and the person's capacity to satisfy job requirements. But it is also important to build employer willingness and ability to maintain people with SMI in the workforce through provision of reasonable accommodations, which may include changes in supervisory styles, flexible scheduling, private break areas, and less distracting work settings (Granger, 2000; Roessler & Rubin, 2006). Clearly, the person with SMI does not bear the total responsibility to change; the workplace must respond to the person as well. Hence, the concept of job–person match refers to a fluid situation in which both parties—employer and employee—are committed to meeting the needs of the other.

Mental Retardation

Mental retardation, a nondescriptive term in regard to etiology or prognosis (N. Robinson & Robinson, 1976), is usually caused by either organic factors (e.g., brain damage) or environmental (cultural or familial) factors. Over 750 causes of mental retardation have been identified (Heward, 2006). Individuals with mental retardation whose etiology is biological or medical are typically thought of as having "clinical or pathological (brain damage) retardation" (Heward & Orlansky, 1992, p. 106). The causes of such organic brain damage include (a) infections such as encephalitis or congenital rubella, (b) trauma resulting from accidents during or after birth, (c) metabolic disorders such as phenylketonuria, (d) hydrocephalus, (e) Down syndrome, and (f) postnatal gross brain diseases such as neurofibromatosis (Drew, Logan, & Hardman, 1992; Heward & Orlansky, 1992). In spite of the large number of medical causes, however, it is estimated that about 75% to 85% of mental retardation cases *cannot* be associated with an organic condition (Drew et al., 1992).

Mental retardation is one of the most prevalent disabilities in the United States. Its prevalence exceeds the combined prevalence of visual impairment, epilepsy, cerebral palsy, and spinal cord injury. Estimates of the prevalence rate for mental retardation in the U.S. population have ranged from 1% to 3%, with the most frequently reported prevalence rate being approximately 3% (Drew et al., 1992; Heward, 2006).

Although there have been at least 23 classification systems for persons with mental retardation in the English language alone (N. Robinson & Robinson, 1976), the definition provided by the American Association on Mental Retardation (AAMR; previously named the American Association on Mental Deficiency) has been the most widely accepted (Westling, 1986). The AAMR has defined *mental retardation* as follows:

> Mental retardation is a disability characterized by significant limitations in both intellectual functioning and in adaptive behavior as expressed in conceptual, social, and practical adaptive skills. This disability originates before age 18. (Luckasson et al., 2002, p. 13)

A diagnosis of mental retardation under the AAMR definition typically requires an IQ standard score of 70 or below on a highly respected individually administered general IQ test such as the *Wechsler Intelligence Scale for Children–Fourth Edition* (Wechsler, 2003). However, an IQ score of 75 or higher can "also be associated with mental retardation if, according to a clinician's judgment, the child exhibits deficits in adaptive behavior thought to be caused by impaired intellectual functioning" (Heward, 2006, p. 143). Although earlier (pre-1992) AAMR diagnostic standards allowed for the sorting of persons with mental retardation among four levels (mild, moderate, severe, and profound), the AAMR diagnostic standard "eschews levels of retardation and instead focuses on the types and intensities of supports needed by the individual, either intermittent, limited, extensive, or pervasive" (Sharp & West, 1996, p. 134).

As indicated above, although previously used terms—*mild* (educable), *moderate* (trainable), *severe* (minimal speech and motor development), and *profound* (needs constant supervision)—are no longer used in the AAMR classification system for severity of mental retardation (American Association on Mental Retardation, 1992), those individuals who have traditionally been diagnosed in the mild group (i.e., those with a measured IQ in the subaverage range of 55 to 70) comprise about 80% to 85% of the population of those with mental retardation (Heward & Orlansky, 1992). The great majority of the mild group have potential for vocational habilitation. According to S. Kirk and Gallagher

(1983), many postschool follow-up studies of individuals who had been identi-fied as mildly mentally retarded as children indicate that "once released from the intellectual demands of ... school ... [they] can be marginally self-sufficient in the community through a variety of unskilled, semi-skilled, and service positions" (p. 140).

Psychosocial Aspects of Mental Retardation

Individuals with mental retardation often manifest psychosocial adjustment problems. That reality was somewhat supported by the results of Foss and Bostwick's (1981) self-report survey of 101 individuals with mental retardation. The respondents indicated the following significant social relationship con-cerns: "Finding or keeping friends," "Talking in a group of people," "Getting parents to allow them more freedom in making decisions," and "Getting along with a boyfriend/girlfriend or husband/wife" (Foss & Bostwick, 1981, p. 70). The psychosocial adjustment problem of persons with mental retardation may stem from limited cognitive ability, which makes it more difficult for them to discriminate among various verbal and nonverbal behavioral cues in social situations. "Consequently, their interpersonal skills may be deficient, and their behavior may seem strange or even offensive in some situations" (E. Lynch & Lewis, 1988, p. 113).

Too often the family environment has a negative effect on the behavior of the individual with mental retardation as a result of parental tendencies toward either overprotection or rejection. Overprotection promotes fear-based avoid-ance "of independent travel, job placement, out of home activities, and unsu-pervised peer relationships," whereas rejection tends to produce unstable and "emotionally scarred" individuals (Malikin & Rusalem, 1976, p. 169). Denial of the disability is also not unusual among parents of individuals with mental retardation. When denying the disability, parents may attempt to attribute the cause of the observed limitations to "laziness, indifference, or lack of motiva-tion" (Drew et al., 1992, p. 368). Such inaccurate attributions can be destruc-tive if they impede the individual's acceptance of limitations or "prevent neces-sary education and therapy" (Drew et al., 1992). Drew et al. (1992) pointed out that denial is an understandable and temporary reaction that professionals can help parents work through:

> Although denial strains the relationship between parents and professionals, professionals should always be aware of the extreme emotional stress placed on the family and realize that, for the time being, this reaction may be the only one possible for the parents. With time, patience, and continued support, professionals may eventually help parents face the reality of their situation. Eventually, parents may realize that the birth of a child with retardation need neither stigmatize their lives nor cast any doubts on their integrity as adequate parents or human beings. (p. 368)

The realization that past experiences have greatly shaped the present behavior of individuals with mental retardation allows for the possibility of changing that behavior through new experiences. For adults with mental retardation, those experiences should include opportunities to (a) develop meaningful relationships, (b) participate in leisure and recreational activities of their choice, and (c) undertake valued work activities. The focus of health, education, and rehabilitation services for adults with mental retardation is typically directed at promoting such opportunities (E. Lynch & Lewis, 1988). E. Lynch and Lewis (1988) characterized that priority as emphasizing "vocational education, movement from sheltered to competitive employment, a range of least restrictive housing options away from the family home, and the use of generic community services for health care, recreation, housing, and employment" (p. 128).

Rehabilitation Potential

Job adjustment problems are common for individuals with mental retardation. Research has identified a number of specific difficulties (Foss & Bostwick, 1981; Peckham, 1951; Wehman, 2001; Wehman, Kregel, & Seyfarth, 1985), including problems with coworkers, problems dealing with supervision, social skills deficits (e.g., inappropriate social and sexual behaviors), unrealistic parental expectations, unrealistic client expectations, inability to utilize available transportation, tardiness, money management problems, lack of initiative, slow work speed, and quitting.

Foss and Peterson (1981) surveyed job placement personnel in 93 sheltered workshops in 11 states regarding the social–interpersonal behavior that would be *most relevant* for retaining a job in competitive employment for individuals with mental retardation. The results suggested that the greater "social-interpersonal concern for mentally retarded workers in the work setting is the relationship between worker and supervisor"—that is, (a) "following supervisor instructions," (b) "responding appropriately to supervisor criticism or correction," and (c) "working independently of direct supervision" (p. 105). The validity of these findings was further supported by the results of a survey of 101 mildly retarded graduates of special education programs in Nevada, California, and Oregon by Foss and Bostwick (1981). The respondents with mental retardation in the latter study saw "Getting along with the boss" as a major concern (p. 70). Other high-ranking concerns pertaining directly to employment found in Foss and Bostwick's (1981) study were (a) "finding a job," (b) "interviewing for a job," and (c) "working fast enough" (p. 70).

In the case of formerly institutionalized individuals with mental retardation, slow work rate and lack of initiative are common work adjustment problems. Such problems are seen as by-products of institutionalization:

> [Persons with mental retardation] have been conditioned to take lots of time to perform a task, there being a limit to the number and kind of tasks to be done at a "home."

> Another difficulty is … lack of initiative. Accustomed to institutional … restriction, they do one thing then wait for permission to do something else. Some have never known that they should ask, "What shall I do, now that I have finished?" (Brainard, 1954, p. 6)

In spite of the prevalence of work adjustment difficulties, it has been estimated that, with proper training, approximately 90% of individuals of working age with mental retardation are employable in either competitive or sheltered work situations (Posner, 1974, p. 231). Although indicating high unemployment rates among individuals with mental retardation (Wehman et al., 1985), research conducted since the mid-1950s suggests that given effective evaluation, training, and on-the-job support, individuals with mental retardation can reach a higher level of work performance than previously thought possible (A. Beale, 1985; Bernstein, 1966; Flexer et al., 1982). Based on a comprehensive literature review, Browning and Irvin (1981) stressed that vocational evaluation and preparation must focus on specific task behaviors involved in a job rather than on broader trait-based variables such as aptitudes, interests, and skills.

Determining how long it takes for a person with mental retardation to learn to consistently perform a task correctly has been addressed via discrimination learning research. Results suggest that it takes persons with mental retardation longer to learn a task, but once that learning has taken place, their task performance accuracy tends to be satisfactory (E. Lynch & Lewis, 1988). For example, E. Lynch and Lewis (1988) pointed out that "in sorting tools to be packaged for sale, it would take longer for retarded students to sort the tools correctly; but once they had learned, their accuracy would approximate that of someone with average intelligence" (pp. 109–110).

Kelly and Simon (1969) interviewed employers in the Greater Denver Metropolitan area regarding their experiences with workers with mental retardation who had been placed in competitive employment situations by the Colorado State Home and Training School at Wheatridge and the Colorado Vocational Rehabilitation Administration. Manufacturing, agricultural, and service industries were represented. Employers evaluated each employee with mental retardation individually in regard to how he or she compared with normal employees. The majority of employees with mental retardation received average or better ratings on each of the following three criteria: successful task completion, speed in performing tasks, and resistance to fatigue. On high-cost factors such as tardiness, absenteeism, quit rate, and accident rate, the majority of employees with mental retardation received better than average supervisor ratings. The primary negative rating seemed to be in the area of job induction. The majority of employees with mental retardation were rated as requiring more than the average amount of training. The training cost factor proved to be well compensated for by other positive aspects of performance, such as the low quit rate.

Strickland and Arrell (1967) looked at the relationship between the type of on-the-job training received by educable mentally retarded youth (1,405 students who had completed training through the Texas Statewide Cooperative

Program of Special Education) and the type of job subsequently obtained. For matching purposes, on-the-job training placements were divided among the following occupational categories: (a) agriculture and horticulture; (b) automobile service; (c) cleaning, pressing, and laundry; (d) construction; (e) domestic service; (f) furniture; (g) homemaking; (h) hotel and restaurant; (i) medical service; (j) personal service; (k) retail trade; and (l) miscellaneous (jobs that could not be classified within the aforementioned occupational categories). The results showed that, following training, 80% of the educable mentally retarded youth in the sample were placed in jobs that fell in the same occupational category in which they received training.

In another study, Brickley and Campbell (1981) found that properly selected and trained individuals with mental retardation could become effective employees for McDonald's restaurants. In a joint project between the Franklin County Program for the Mentally Retarded and a McDonald's company-owned restaurant in Columbus, Ohio, 17 individuals with mental retardation were placed in paid employment (about 20 hours per week) in selective positions (e.g., lot and lobby maintenance, making french fries, grill operations, pies and fish fillets). Counter positions were not involved "because of the money handling, writing, and social skills involved." The results of the 2-year project suggested that individuals with mental retardation would make good McDonald's employees with a lower than average turnover rate.

Halpern, Browning, and Brummer (1975, p. 372) cited several research reports that showed "that moderately retarded … adults can learn surprisingly complex vocational tasks," which included the assembly of (a) "electrical relay panels," (b) "television rectifier units," (c) "14-piece and 24-piece bicycle brakes," (d) "a 52-piece cam switch … which requires the use of five different hand tools," (e) "a 24-piece and 26-piece printhead … for a labeling gun such as the kind used in most grocery stores," (f) "a four-piece electrical cord … involving the use of three different hand tools," and (g) "a six piece battery pack … which requires soldering." A common factor running through all of these training situations was that complex tasks were presented in terms of their subtasks and the steps involved in each of those subtasks. Individuals "were then taught these subtasks, using procedures based on the findings of laboratory research on operant learning, imitation, and discrimination learning" (p. 372).

Halpern et al. (1975) felt that the results of their literature review raised

> new questions about how we should define and measure vocational abilities, since they appear to be a function not only of personal characteristics, but also of task complexity and method of training. One possible and practical approach would be to define level of vocational ability as the amount of time required for training within the context of the type of training employed and complexity of the vocational task. Such a definition would focus attention on the possibility that vocational performance is constantly amenable to change, and can be manipulated effectively through training, even with moderately and severely retarded persons. The question for

evaluation would then become one of predicting training time for a task of given complexity with prescribed training methods, using readily available client characteristics as the predictors. (p. 372)

A logical question would be, How retarded can a person be and still be capable of productive work? Even when focusing on individuals with a very low IQ, the total absence of vocational potential cannot be automatically assumed. Jordan (1972) described the working ability of six males in their 20s with a mean IQ of 33 that clearly demonstrates the difficulty of using an arbitrary IQ cutoff to answer the question.

> At the time of reporting, the six had been producing cardboard-box folders for two-and-a-half years. They had produced 30,000 to 40,000 each week. Such was their satisfaction that they even gained access to the workshop over a weekend and proceeded to produce a morning's output as a way of avoiding boredom. (Jordan, 1972, p. 583)

A number of studies reported in the literature have demonstrated the employment potential of individuals with mental retardation. Brolin, Durand, Kromer, and Muller (1975) conducted a follow-up study between November 1972 and March 1973 of "80 former special education students (educable mentally retarded students) ... randomly selected from a list of the last 400 attending the ten Minneapolis high schools between the years 1966–1972" (p. 145). The former students held over 40 different types of jobs since leaving high school, indicating the large number of jobs potentially feasible for persons with mental retardation. The following types of jobs (using *Dictionary of Occupational Titles* classification) were most frequently reported as being obtained: dishwasher, kitchen help; janitorial work; busboy, waitress; nurse aid; grocery carry-out; gas station attendant; car washer; shop work, assembly; maintenance; shoe repair; laundry work; maid; inventory, stock; phone solicitor; coupon sorting; rag cutter; mechanics aid; construction, carpentry; packaging; file clerk; nursery school aid; presser; cementary work; machine work; and bag liner.

Between December 1983 and May 1984, Wehman et al. (1985) conducted a follow-up study of the employment status of 300 young adults with mental retardation who had left special education school programs in Virginia between 1979 and 1983. Sixty percent of the sample "were labeled mildly retarded, and 40% had been served in programs for students labeled moderately, severely, or profoundly mentally retarded" (p. 93). Although only 35% of the sample were competitively employed at follow-up, they had many different types of jobs, with the most frequent being janitor, food service, farm worker, factory worker, lumberyard worker, construction, office worker, forestry worker, bagger in grocery store, stockroom aide, driver, yard helper, and domestic help.

Studies comparing the attendance records of workers with mental retardation and those of nondisabled workers have shown the former group to have either similar or better attendance records (Adams-Shollenberger & Mitchell,

1996; Martin, Rusch, Tines, Brulle, & White, 1985; National Association of Retarded Citizens, 1986). The results of one study (Adams–Shollenberger & Mitchell, 1996) suggested that where absenteeism rates of those with mental retardation rise, transportation difficulties may be a significant source of the problem. A potential solution suggested for ameliorating the problem was for employers to develop a ride-share program for these employees (Adams-Shollenberger & Mitchell, 1996).

While the literature strongly suggests that individuals with mental retardation make capable workers (Brickley & Campbell, 1981; Brolin et al., 1975; Mithaug, Horiuchi, & Fanning, 1985; Wehman et al., 1985), it also shows very high unemployment rates for this disability group (Hasazi, Gordon, & Roe, 1985; Wehman et al., 1985). The size of the unemployment problem suggests that more effective school-to-work transition programs and job placement efforts for young adults with mental retardation are needed (Wehman et al., 1985). In particular, job placement efforts that include supported employment for people with mental retardation must extend beyond a specific closure date. Pumpian, Fisher, Certo, and Smalley (1997) called for postemployment (long-term) services to both respond to the high turnover rate in this group and initiate "career development" through the job change process. Noting that less than 1% of rehabilitation funding is directed toward postemployment services, Pumpian et al. (1997) saw such services as the only feasible strategy for meeting the job replacement and retraining needs of people with mental retardation.

Learning Disabilities[1]

Learning problems and *learning disability* are not interchangeable terms. Learning problems are viewed as environmentally caused (N. M. Rubin & Ashley, 1983), whereas learning disabilities are considered to have a neurological etiology (i.e., to result from a central nervous system dysfunction) (Getzel & Gugerty, 2001; N. M. Rubin & Ashley, 1983; Turnbull, Turnbull, Shank, & Leal, 1995). Therefore, a learning disability is not seen as resulting from economic disadvantage, ineffective educational practices, or poor child-rearing practices. While the presence of such factors may complicate rehabilitation, "they are not considered to be the cause of the learning disability" (Crystal, Witten, & Wingate, 1982, p. 34). Suggested causes of learning disabilities include "Genetic Defects, Endocrine Gland Dysfunction, Pre-Natal Malnutrition, Obstetrical Complications, Maternal Substance Abuse, Chronic Illness, Lead Poisoning, Brain Damage or Dysfunction, Accidents, and Toxins" (Newill, Goyette, & Fogarty, 1984, p. 36).

---

[1]Some material in this section has been adapted from "Rehabilitation Considerations with Adult Learning-Disabled Individuals," by N. M. Rubin and J. Ashley, in *Foundations of the Vocational Rehabilitation Process* (2nd ed., pp. 219–232), by S. E. Rubin and R. Roessler (Eds.), 1983, Austin, TX: PRO-ED.

According to Heward (2006), the term *learning disabilities* is defined in the Individuals with Disabilities Education Improvement Act of 2004 as follows:

> *In General*—The term "specific learning disability" [SLD] means a disorder in 1 or more of the basic psychological processes involved in understanding or in using language, spoken or written, which disorder may manifest itself in an imperfect ability to listen, think, speak, read, write, spell, or to do mathematical calculations.
>
> *Disorders Included*—Such term includes such conditions as perceptual disabilities, brain injury, minimal brain dysfunction, dyslexia, and developmental aphasia.
>
> *Disorders Not Included*—Such term does not include a learning problem that is primarily the result of visual, hearing, of motor disabilities, of mental retardation, of emotional disturbance, or of environmental, cultural, or economic disadvantage. (p. 182)

Under this definition individuals with learning disabilities such as dyscalculia (inability to perform mathematical calculations), dysgraphia (inability to express oneself in writing), agnosia (inability to recognize and identify known objects through one or more senses), and dysphasia (impairments in language communication through speech) with an intelligence level in the normal range or above would fall into the SLD category and therefore be eligible for state rehabilitation agency services (N. M. Rubin & Ashley, 1983).

The Ninth Institute on Rehabilitation Issues (1982) identified the following three distinct SLD groups: the "pure" hyperkinetic type, the "pure" learning disability type, and the mixed type. The learning difficulties of individuals in the pure hyperkinetic group stem from a symptom triad of hyperactivity, attention deficits, and impulsivity. This group constitutes approximately 5% of the SLD population.

Individuals within the pure learning disability group have complex cognitive/language processing disabilities that result in severe handicaps in areas such as reading, written language, and mathematics. For example, Turnbull et al. (1995) pointed out that those with reading disabilities may "exhibit word recognition errors (omissions, insertions, substitutions, reversals), comprehension errors (difficulty recalling or discerning basic facts, sequence, or theme), and other behaviors such as losing their place while reading in a choppy, halting manner" (p. 147). Written language performance deficits can be observed in areas such as spelling, sentence structure, and thematic development, whereas those in math might involve difficulties such as differentiating numbers, recalling math facts, or solving word problems (Turnbull et al., 1995). Also constituting approximately 5% of the SLD population, individuals in the pure learning disability group show few, if any, of the behavioral symptoms characteristic of the pure hyperkinetic type.

The mixed type constitutes the remainder of the SLD population. "This group exhibits varying combinations of behavioral problems and cognitive/ language processing deficits. However, their symptoms are usually less severe than those experienced by the two 'pure' types" (N. M. Rubin & Ashley, 1983, pp. 221–223).

Although the actual number of adults with SLD in the United States is yet to be determined, the 2004 federal estimate of over 2.8 million students with learning disabilities (LD) in U.S. schools (Heward, 2006) suggests that the size of that adult disability group is likewise substantial. According to Getzel and Gugerty (2001), it has been estimated "that 35% of youth with LD drop out of high school … and that 62% are unemployed a year after graduating. Without proper educational planning and intervention, 56% of those with LD who do drop out will be arrested" (p. 379).

A diagnosis of SLD is made by a psychiatrist, psychologist, or neuro-psychologist familiar with learning disability. At minimum, a valid and reliable intelligence test (e.g., *Wechsler Adult Intelligence Scale–Third Edition;* Wechsler, 1997) and achievement test (*Woodcock-Johnson III;* Woodcock, McGrew, & Mather, 2001) are used to establish the diagnosis. It is also advisable to include a neuropsychological test in the battery (N. M. Rubin & Ashley, 1983), as well as tests of reading comprehension and written language (Turnbull et al., 1995). Overall, "the diagnostician should focus on identifying any discrepancy that might exist between an individual's potential achievement and actual achievement as revealed by … performance on a variety of diagnostic measures" (Simpson & Umbach, 1989).

Psychological Aspects

Friendlessness, social ineptitude, and loneliness are social development patterns that may result from learning disabilities. "As learning disabilities represent disorganization in decoding, memory and encoding of information, such disorganization may be a factor in social inadequacy as well. Organizing the smallest social situation may be so overwhelming that isolation, however painful, is sometimes preferred" (Krishnaswami, 1984, p. 19). Therefore, it is not surprising that the results of some research with the young adult population suggest that these individuals are "more at risk for depression and possibly suicide, than non-disabled youths" (Bender, 1996, p. 274).

Having an invisible disability (i.e., one not immediately obvious to the casual observer), individuals with SLD may be labeled as bright but bored by parents, "lazy" or "dumb" by teachers, "strange" by peers, and incapable of performing a job by prospective employers (T. J. Black, 1976; D. Brown, 1984). Lack of social skills or the presence of soft neurological signs (clumsiness, awkward gait, staring) may make the individual appear strange, leading to rejection by others (D. Brown, 1980). Soft neurological signs are basically the observable results of mild central nervous system dysfunction. Behavioral manifestations of learning disabilities, such as staring, moving in a disorganized manner, inability to make eye contact, and appearing easily startled in a job interview, can lead to rejection of the job applicant with a learning disability by the employer (D. Brown, 1984). Even though the Americans with Disabilities Act protects individuals with LD against discrimination in employment on the basis of their disability and gives them a right to reasonable accommodations at the job site, some still prefer to keep their disability hidden from employers for fear of rejection. Greenbaum, Graham, and Scales (1996) found this to be the case even in their study of college graduates with learning disabilities. Approximately 40% of the participants in their study

> who had been employed indicated that disclosure of their learning disability during the job application process would lead to not being hired. Similarly, after being hired, many of the participants were still unwilling to disclose their disability for fear of prejudice and stigmatization. (p. 172)

According to Cox (1977), failure in academic and social areas may make adults with LD more vulnerable to personality disorders. They may become socially withdrawn (Getzel & Gugerty, 2001) or emotionally dependent on others. Individuals with LD also find it extremely difficult to engage in small talk, enter a small circle of people, or introduce themselves to strangers. Some persons with LD may also manifest perceptional discrimination problems in interpersonal situations, such as an inability to discriminate between a happy and a sarcastic smile or "a stare and a thoughtful glance" (Getzel & Gugerty, 2001, p. 381). As a result of such behavioral limitations, they are often rejected by others (D. Brown, 1980).

A number of the observations mentioned above regarding the social adjustment of persons with learning disabilities have been supported via empirical research studies. Fafard and Haubrich (1981) conducted a follow-up study of 12 male and 9 female young adults with LD. All participants were White and from middle-class families. The participants reported a wide range of social activities that reflected a normal pattern. They also reported having had no problems in making friends. However, the participants tended to avoid answering questions regarding difficulty with social activities. Some of the participants' parents, however, expressed concerns about their child's independence beyond the family, their ability to make friends, and the quality of their social activities. There was also an indication that some participants depended on their family as the major source of social activities. D. Brown (1980) has also reported that many adults with LD remain at home well after their teenage years. This was also found to be the case in a survey of college graduates with LD by Greenbaum et al. (1996).

Meyers and Messer (1981) surveyed 12 youth with learning disabilities, 9 youth with behavior disorders, and 23 youth without disabilities. All participants had graduated from high school 2 or 3 years previously. The results showed that youth with LD have greater difficulty making and keeping friends, especially female friends, than the other two groups. Surprisingly, individuals with LD experienced more interpersonal conflict on the job than did those with behavior disorders.

Hinkebein, Koller, and Kunce (1992) reported the results of a personal interview survey of the problem behavior experienced by 46 adults with LD "who qualified for services in a midwestern state's Division of Vocational Rehabilitation" (p. 43). Sixty-five percent of these individuals reported psychosocial adjustment difficulties with frustration tolerance and anxiety, and approximately 40% reported difficulties with impulsivity, interpersonal communications, and social perception.

A study of social skill problems of adults with LD by Lehtinen-Rogan and Hartman revealed the following:

1. They feel responsible to form themselves into likeable and successful people but find it hard to do so.
2. They find social relationships trying. They want and need people but lack the confidence that people can like or respect them.
3. There is a "substantial tendency" to move between despondency and euphoria in social relationships because there is an underlying level of depression which is lifted by social contact.
4. They are very sensitive and easily hurt while being tense and anxious from their condition. (cited in Gerber & Kelley, 1984, p. 74)

Rehabilitation Potential

At the initiation of the rehabilitation process, many clients with specific learning disabilities will be unable to meet industrial performance standards on the job. Hence, the rehabilitation counselor must determine the person's current functioning level and the amount and type of practice needed if the person is to reach these competitive standards. For jobs in which the person with a specific learning disability expresses an interest, a basic question is how practical the job choice is based on the amounts of time and money that will be necessary to meet the expected functioning level criterion.

Previous academic assessment information can be very useful in determining practical versus impractical vocational choice directions in which to move with the client with LD. Simpson and Umbach (1989) elaborated on this point:

Obviously, if the client is weak in the area of reading, s/he should be directed away from vocations which require a great amount of reading. The same is true relative to mathematical skills, written language skills and oral language skills. Weak motor skills would negate placement in jobs requiring well developed motor skills. Counseling can assist the client in matching his/her skills to vocations in which his/her strengths are maximized and his/her weaknesses are minimized. (p. 53)

Vocational evaluation can provide useful information regarding functional limitations of people with LD and rehabilitation service prescriptions. Via vocational evaluation, it is important to determine how the individual learns to perform a job. For example, can the person perform the job function following standardized instruction communicated in a "traditional" format? If not, the optimal instruction format (e.g., written, oral, demonstration/modeling, or hands-on method) should be determined (N. M. Rubin & Ashley, 1983). Once determined, that optimal instruction format can be used in on-the-job training or vocational training with the client.

By participating in a learning assessment (identifying how an individual learns a job), the person with a specific learning disability "may find that there are other nonverbal ways to learn information, e.g., demonstrating/modeling, hands on, which allow him to succeed where he had previously failed" (McCray, 1979, p. 7). That insight can positively affect the self-concept of clients with verbal deficits who have probably not learned well in school because of the heavy verbal orientation of the instruction. Past failures in school may have led them to conclude that they cannot learn many new things (N. M. Rubin & Ashley, 1983).

By integrating results from the vocational evaluation report, psychological report, and intake interview summary, counselor and client can identify potential vocational choices and pertinent special services. Special services might include remediation of problems through special learning techniques (e.g., typing lessons, calculation techniques, audiotaped instructions), identification of job modifications, and identification of jobs that minimize relevance of the neurological deficit and/or, where possible, use the current skills of the individual. However, some clients may not be ready to move directly from vocational evaluation to making a vocational choice due to significant deficits in basic employability behaviors. Work adjustment training can address these problems, enabling many individuals with LD to become suitable candidates for competitive employment. Krishnaswami (1984) provided the following checklist of important employability behaviors needed if individuals with severe learning disabilities are to enter the labor market:

1. Hygiene, grooming, appropriate dress
2. Relating to supervisors and co-workers
3. Communication skills
4. Increasing frustration-tolerance
5. Appropriate responses to criticism
6. Appropriate social behavior on the job
7. Attendance and punctuality
8. Initiative in carrying out job tasks
9. Awareness of work rules and safety precautions

10. Increasing stamina/energy level (i.e., tolerance for a full work schedule)
11. Organization of job tasks
12. Establishing consistency of work
13. Increasing speed of task performance
14. Increasing independence of task performance
15. Attending to and following directions (p. 20)

Job adjustment problems manifested by persons with LD have been identified by others as well. These include slow work pace (D. Brown, 1979; Geib, Guzzardi, & Genova, 1981), arriving at work late (Bender, 1996), problems with supervisors and coworkers (Bender, 1996; Meyers & Messer, 1981), inefficiency, high error rate, accident-proneness, deficient academic skills (e.g., reading, computation), problems in learning a sequence of tasks, and social skill deficits (D. Brown, 1979). According to Getzel and Gugerty (2001),

> One of the primary reasons that individuals with LD lose their jobs is not the skill level required by the job but the individual's lack of organizational, self-monitoring, and self-correcting skills, all of which result from faulty executive functioning. (p. 396)

Executive functioning "includes attention, formulation of goals and plans to achieve those goals, monitoring and evaluating behavior and correcting behavior as needed to continue toward the goals" (Getzel & Gugerty, 2001, p. 396). It requires sufficient flexibility on the part of the individual to assess and modify behavior to achieve goals, something insuffiently present in many adults with LD (Getzel & Gugerty, 2001).

Many individuals with LD have difficulty making decisions. Therefore, it is very possible that the diagnostic information may indicate that a program to teach decision-making skills may have to be implemented at the initiation of the vocational choice-making, or goal-setting, process (Krishnaswami, 1984, p. 20).

Because many individuals with learning disabilities have either no or very limited work experience as well as poor self-concept, they may perceive few choices open to them. During the goal-setting process, persons with LD must examine what they can do in the world of work in spite of their disabilities. They must learn how their disability interacts with the work environment and what is "realistic." They must also be presented with occupational information that allows them to examine the pros and cons of several occupational choices. On-the-job training, as well as job tryouts and simulations, are excellent ways of expanding their horizon in regard to what they can do and thereby also positively affecting their vocational self-image (Krishnaswami, 1984, p. 21). With the aid of these experiences, clients can select an appropriate vocational rehabilitation goal as well as any necessary rehabilitation service subgoals that must be part of their rehabilitation plans.

As was alluded to earlier, the differential effect of a learning disability across work tasks should be taken into consideration in the job selection process. N. M. Rubin and Ashley (1983) provided the following example of a young woman with an auditory processing problem who acquired a job as a typist. She performed typing tasks well, completing work quickly with no errors. However, she took confused messages and called fellow workers by the wrong name, such as calling Mindy by the name of Cindy or Dan by the name of Stan. When asked to transcribe from an audiotape or dictaphone, she produced error-ridden work that made little sense.

Many times, job performance problems that might appear predictable for an individual with a learning disability for a particular job can be avoided via job modifications rather than by simply ruling out the job. D. Brown (1984) provided the following examples:

> John works as a sales manager in a plant which sells flour wholesale to bakeries. He is dyslexic and operates similarly to a blind person. He has a reader who comes in twice a week and a local group tapes his professional material. His boss tells him what to do, as well as putting it in writing. His secretary types work from dictation, fills out his sales forms, and tells him his phone messages. Sometimes she even reads to him. (p. 76)

While job opportunities can be created via job modifications, such placements might affect the opportunities of a person with a learning disability to move to other positions. A common problem with restructured positions is that they often become dead-end jobs with no career ladders (D. Dunn, 1974).

At times, the characteristics of the learning disability can indicate the types of jobs to avoid.

> For example, people with perceptual–motor problems would have difficulty laying bricks or building bookshelves. People with a tendency to reverse digits should not spend a lot of time operating a calculator where lines of numbers must be accurately copied. People with auditory perceptual problems should not work as a telephone switchboard operator where they spend the time taking messages. (D. Brown, 1984, p. 75)

It is important to realize that sometimes the learning disability can prove to be an advantage in carrying out a particular job function. D. Brown (1984) has provided a few brief examples:

> A person who is overly aware of background noise might become a sound engineer where the ability to hear this sound is important.... A technical writer had particular sensitivity to writing clear instructions in simple language due to a history of a reading problem. A hyperactive man covered more ground during his guard duty than any of his coworkers. (p. 75)

As the above discussion indicates, the successful job adjustment of an individual with a learning disability is greatly dependent on the job demands' being compatible with the client's strengths and not requiring skills where deficits exist (D. Brown, 1984). Rehabilitation professionals working with persons with LD should never forget that the key word in the term *specific learning disability* is *specific,* in that it indicates that while those with LD have deficits in some areas, they "frequently turn out to have surprising compensatory strengths in others" (Krishnaswami, 1984, p. 19). Rehabilitation professionals should also realize that the learning disability has probably had an impact on a number of areas in the individual's life, such as vocational skill development, social and interpersonal functioning, and leisure activities (Bender, 1996). Therefore, any existing psychosocial problems must also be addressed in the process of readying the individual with a learning disability for employment.

Post-school follow-up studies of adults with LD underscore the vocational potential of this group as well as the need to upgrade their educational and rehabilitation services. In a follow-up study of 90 adults with LD, Lehtinen and Dumas (1976) reported that 67% were employed. Of the employed individuals, 60% had full-time jobs, and 50% had been at the same job for 3 years or more. The jobs they held ranged from unskilled (23%) to professional (13%). Clerical jobs were held by 33% of those employed. A small number (6%) were marginally employed; these included some adults with emotional problems, seizures, and hearing losses who were in sheltered workshops. Of those employed, 52% were satisfied with their jobs, and 55% had earnings that allowed them to be financially independent. However, the group's median income was low given the fact that 78% were high school graduates and 38% had completed college.

In a study of the employment experiences of adolescents with LD, Sitlington and Frank (1990) surveyed, via face-to-face or telephone interviews, a sample of 911 individuals with LD. These individuals, who had graduated from or dropped out of high school, were contacted 1 year after leaving school. Seventy-seven percent of the sample were employed either full- or part-time 1 year after leaving high school. Ninety-nine percent of those employed were in competitive employment. The majority (about 66%) held "low status jobs as laborers or service workers" (p. 101). Seventy percent of those employed held full-time jobs. The mean hourly wage for those employed was about $1 above the minimum wage at that time. About half of the sample reported involvement "in some type of post secondary education or … training" (p. 110). Almost 90% of those employed indicated that they had not received assistance from their school or an adult agency in finding their current job. Sitlington and Frank (1990) felt that the overall results were disappointing. Only 54% of the sample met all of the authors' following criteria for reaching the goal of adult adjustment 1 year after high school: "(a) employed or 'otherwise meaningfully engaged'; (b) living independently or with a parent or relative; (c) paying at least a portion of their living expenses; and (d) involved in more than one leisure activity" (p. 108). One might hypothesize that if the individuals with LD in Sitlington and Frank's (1990) study had received more assistance from education and rehabilitation professionals in their transition from high school to adult (working) life, a high percentage would have made a better adjustment to post–high school adult life.

Consistent with the findings of Lehtinen and Dumas (1976) and Sitlington and Frank (1990), a number of other follow-up studies found that a greater percentage of adults with LD have lower paying jobs than adults without LD (Okolo & Sitlington, 1988). Overall, the postsecondary employment research for persons with LD suggests that underemployment rather than unemployment has been the bigger problem for this population (Bender, 1996).

Finucci, Gottfredson, and Childs (1986) surveyed 579 graduates of an independent school for boys with developmental dyslexia and 612 nondyslexic graduates (control group) from another independent school for boys 1 to 38 years after they left school. The members of both groups came from the middle to high socioeconomic classes and had average or better intelligence. About 50% of the graduates with LD had earned a bachelor's degree, compared to 95% of the control group. Graduates with LD also took more years to earn their degrees. About 50% of the graduates with LD were engaged in managerial work at the time of the survey. About 18% were in professional or technical positions. The adults with LD appeared to have benefited from the dyslexia school and from family support and encouragement. The types of jobs held by the adults with LD at the follow-up were clearly a function of both the severity of dyslexia at entry to the school and the extent of improvement in their reading skills while at the school.

Greenbaum et al. (1996) surveyed 49 former undergraduates with LD from the University of Maryland, 90% of whom had completed an undergraduate degree. They had attended the University of Maryland during the period 1980–1992. The average age of the participants was approximately 26. Only 7 of the participants were both unemployed and not in school at the time of their interview. Of the 35 participants who held jobs, 71% held professional, technical, or managerial positions, 6% had service jobs, and 23% were employed in clerical or sales positions. Their average salary was about $20,000 a year. The specific jobs in which they were employed "included customer service representative, bartender, medical researcher, reporter, camp director, bank teller, salesperson, mechanical engineer, artist, botanist, corporate vice president, teacher, embryologist, investment banker, paramedic, social worker, securities broker, line cook,… [and] office manager" (Greenbaum et al., 1996, p. 169). Although most of the employed participants liked their current jobs, the majority expressed a desire to change jobs, the primary reason being to perform more interesting work and to earn more money (Greenbaum et al., 1996).

The number of individuals with LD entering college has been increasing significantly in recent decades. They have become the single largest disability group on American campuses, with estimates of their number in institutions of higher education ranging from 160,000 to 300,000 (Raskind & Higgins, 1998). As a result, postsecondary vocational training has become an important vehicle for assisting in the vocational rehabilitation of persons with LD (Kavale & Forness, 1996).

Most individuals with learning disabilities who go on to postsecondary education tend to choose a 2-year as opposed to a 4-year college. This choice tends to be due to the greater availability of support services at the former and the less dramatic differences between a 2-year college and high school (Kavale & Forness, 1996).

Institutions of higher education are not legally (Section 504 of the Rehabilitation Act of 1973 and the Americans with Disabilities Act) expected to accommodate the needs of persons with disabilities by lowering academic standards or compromising "the integrity of the school or program" (S. S. Scott, 1994, p. 403). However, they are legally mandated (e.g., subpart E of Section 504 of the Rehabilitation Act of 1973) to provide students with disabilities with the environmental adjustments necessary for potential success in the educational environment (Raskind & Higgins, 1998; S. S. Scott, 1994). Those environmental adjustments or accommodations are more easily determined for people with a physical disability (e.g., curb cuts for those in wheelchairs) than for a person with a learning disability. Accommodating the latter student presents a much more complex problem. To do so, one must identify the thinking and learning processes associated with successfully negotiating an academic course or program of study affected by the learning disability and the reasonable accommodations necessary for allowing the student to succeed in that course or program (S. S. Scott, 1994). S. S. Scott (1994) has suggested that blanket accommodations stimulated by stereotypes for students with LD can do more harm than good. Such potential ineffectiveness of blanket accommodations can undermine the perceived value of providing resources for accommodations for persons with LD on college campuses (S. S. Scott, 1994). Raskind and Higgins (1998) pointed out that not only are all technological aids not beneficial to all adults with LD, but depending on the characteristics of the individual's learning disability, some may be detrimental. Consequently, they stressed that "it is imperative that technologies be chosen relative to the particular individual's strengths, weaknesses, interests, and experiences; the function to be performed; and the context of interaction" (p. 29).

Many types of assistive technology can help students in institutions of higher education succeed in spite of their specific learning disability. Raskind and Higgins (1998) pointed out that learning disabilities in the college student population can manifest themselves in one or more of the following problems that can be ameliorated through assistive technology: (a) written language disorder; (b) poor reading skills; (c) "difficulty remembering, organizing, and managing personal information" (p. 33); (d) listening difficulties; and (e) difficulties with math.

It has been estimated that "between 80% and 90% of adults with LD exhibit written language disorders" (Raskind & Higgins, 1998, p. 29). The use of personal computers with word processors containing proofreading capabilities and outlining programs can be useful to adolescents and adults with written language disorders (Raskind & Higgins, 1998, p. 29–30). Proofreading programs have been found to enable persons "with LD to write without having to be overly concerned with making errors, as text can be easily corrected on-screen prior to printing" (Raskind & Higgins, 1998, p. 29). Outlining programs can help students organize a paper "with regard to topic, categories, and sequence" by enabling them to feed information into the computer in an unstructured manner from which the program generates a list of categories and sequences them in an outline of the paper for the user (Raskind & Higgins, 1998, p. 30).

Individuals with reading difficulties can use speech synthesizers that can read aloud any text on a computer screen. For example, it is possible to insert a book recorded on a disk into a personal computer, and a person with LD could listen via the speech synthesis system. The text could be recorded on the disk by means of a full-page flatbed scanner (like a copy machine) or some other type of scanner (e.g., handheld). Raskind and Higgins (1998) advised that such "technology can be particularly helpful to individuals with LD who exhibit no difficulty comprehending spoken language … yet have problems understanding language in the written form" (p. 33).

A form of technology that can be helpful to those "with LD who have difficulty processing auditory information at standard playback rates" is the variable-speech-control tape recorder (Raskind & Higgins, 1998, p. 33). With the use of this device, the user can play back audiotaped text at a slower speed without loss of intelligibility (Raskind & Higgins, 1998).

Personal data managers in the form of software programs or handheld units are a form of assistive technology available to those individuals with LD who "have difficulty remembering, organizing, and managing personal information" such as daily calendars and to-do lists (Raskind & Higgins, 1998, p. 33). Several pocket-size data managers are available that "allow the user to enter and retrieve data by speaking into the device. Stored data are spoken back in the user's own voice" (Raskind & Higgins, 1998, p. 33).

The types of assistive technology for college students with LD discussed above can also be seen as potentially valuable aids for many individuals with LD in the competitive labor market. Depending on the characteristics of the person's learning disability and the specific demands of the job, any of the technological aids discussed above could make the difference between a successful and an unsuccessful job adjustment. In many cases, their appropriate utilization could result in an individual's being employed at a level consistent with his or her vocational potential, rather than being underemployed.

Visual Impairments and Blindness

Visual impairments and blindness can have an onset at any age beginning at birth. No group based on wealth, personality, gender, or physique has ever been exempt from the onset of visual limitations (Dickerson, Smith, & Moore, 1997). Onset of these conditions can be gradual or sudden, and the amount of vision loss can be slight or great. The loss of vision can take many forms, with the most handicapping forms related to reduced visual acuity at a distance or reduced visual field. Dickerson et al. (1997) pointed out that the most "significant functional problems resulting from impaired vision typically include diminished ability to read, recognize faces and facial expressions, perform visually guided motor tasks, be aware of important features of the immediate environment, and move freely within the environment" (p. 3).

A commonly accepted definition of *blindness* does not exist. It is estimated that only 25% of individuals with severe vision limitations have no vision; the remainder have some usable vision. All of the no-vision group and some of the latter group are defined as legally blind. However, there is more than one definition of legal blindness. The visual acuity criterion for distance vision for legal blindness seems to range from 20/200 or less to 20/500 or less (Ouellette & Leja, 1988). According to H. S. Schlesinger and Lee (1980), the most accepted definition of blindness in the United States is "visual acuity of less than 20/200 in the better eye with the use of a correcting lens, or with such limitation of the visual field that the widest diameter subtends an angle no greater than twenty degrees" (p. 368).

Visual acuity refers to how well an individual can make out the details of an object at particular distances (e.g., what the person can see clearly from 20 feet away) (Gearheart, Mullen, & Gearheart, 1993). "Normal visual acuity is considered 20/20 which specifies that a 20-foot target is discriminated at 20 feet" (K. E. Fraser, 1997, p. 88). For example, an individual with normal vision can read a ⅜-inch letter from 20 feet away (Heward, 2006).

The entire area that is visible to an individual while looking straight ahead is referred to as the visual field.

> Individuals with a normal field of vision are able to see 180 degrees. A restricted visual field means some smaller number of degrees or angle within which the individual is able to see…. Narrowed fields of vision are sometimes referred to as tunnel vision, tubular vision, or pinpoint vision, and may interfere with activities such as moving from place to place, playing some sports, and driving a car. (Gearheart et al., 1993, p. 272)

In further regard to the visual field, "some eye conditions make it impossible for people to see things clearly in the center of the visual field, but allow relatively good peripheral vision" (Heward, 2006, p. 384).

Blindness is not the only term encountered within the visual disability area. *Visual impairment* is a term that covers all individuals whose vision is less than optimal (e.g., 20/20) without correction. According to Ouellette and Leja (1988),

> visual impairment can be divided into categories of mild, moderate, or severe vision loss…. Mild impairment refers to visual problems that can be embellished by ordinary corrective lenses. Persons who are considered moderately vision impaired learn primarily through sight, but benefit from modifications to instructional materials. Finally, those with severe visual impairments must use senses other than vision in the educational process. (p. 155)

Those whose visual disability would classify them as at least legally blind would likely fall within the severe visual impairment category. In the United States, the estimated number of noninstitutionalized individuals whose visual disability falls within the severe visual impairment category is approximately 4.3 million. These would be individuals who reportedly are incapable of reading "ordinary newspaper print even when wearing glasses or contact lenses" (Dickerson et al., 1997, p. 7). Worldwide, the figure of those who would fall within the severe visual impairment category is approximately 42 million (Dickerson et al., 1997).

Rehabilitation Potential

Although work is an activity central to the life of the great majority of adults of working age, persons who have low vision or are blind are clearly "underrepresented in the competitive labor market" (Crudden & McBroom, 1999, p. 341). The unemployment rate for persons with severe visual impairment within the working age group has been estimated to range from 66% to 78% (Butler, Crudden, Sansing, & LeJeune, 2002). A number of reasons have been hypothesized for the high unemployment rate. One such reason is employment discrimination based on employer misconceptions about the capabilities of those with visual impairments (Dickerson et al., 1997; O'Day, 1999). Another reason involves disincentives to employment, such as Social Security payments that are readily available to those who are legally blind (O'Day, 1999). Many individuals with severe visual impairment "may find it more advantageous to remain non-workers and collect various available benefits than to accept low-paying, entry-level employment" (Ouellette & Leja, 1988, p. 164). Some students with visual disabilities who are enrolled in college feel that maintaining their Social Security benefits is an incentive for stretching out the completion of their academic program and thereby delaying the challenge of securing employment (Ouellette & Leja, 1988).

A high unemployment rate for those with severe visual impairments is not their only employment-related problem. They also experience underemployment and low pay. For example, Ouellette and Leja (1988) reported that the federal–state rehabilitation program closed the cases of 9,506 individuals who were blind and vocationally rehabilitated in 1981. Only 3,646 of those individuals acquired jobs in competitive employment; of the remainder, over 5,000 were closed as homemakers, 386 were placed in sheltered employment, and 110 were closed as unpaid family workers. Furthermore, the salaries of those who acquired jobs in the competitive employment market "were reported to be much lower than the national average for all households" (Ouellette & Leja, 1988, p. 165).

In an attempt to identify barriers to employment for people with visual impairments, O'Day (1999) interviewed 20 individuals whose ages ranged from 25 to 45 and who had been "diagnosed as legally blind at or near birth"

(p. 627). All 20 were unemployed, received Supplemental Security Income (SSI) or Social Security Disability Insurance (SSDI), and "expressed the desire to work" (p. 627). Seventy-five percent of those interviewed "had more than a high school education," with 7 having completed some college, 5 having gained a college degree, and 1 enrolled in graduate school at the time of this study (O'Day, 1999, p. 628). Barriers identified by O'Day (1999) through the revelations of the interviewees included the following:

1. Difficulty accessing information about job openings
2. Lack of assistance in filling out job applications
3. "Lack of career counseling and information about the methods that people who are blind use to perform job duties" (p. 631)
4. "Negative public attitudes toward blindness including limited expectations, stereotypes, and misunderstanding, as a major barrier to finding and keeping a job" (p. 632)
5. Unwillingness of employers to modify jobs or to purchase necessary adaptive equipment (assistive technology) for employees with visual impairments
6. Lack of sufficient public transportation to get from home to job site
7. Failure of SSI or SSDI service providers to sufficiently expect and emphasize the need for persons with visual impairment to prepare for and seek employment
8. Failure of SSI or SSDI service providers to effectively orient their benefit recipients to the work incentive provisions in Social Security Administration policies
9. Fear of losing Medicare or Medicaid coverage
10. Insufficient information about or understanding of the services provided by the Department of Rehabilitation Services

Crudden and McBroom (1999) addressed the issue of barriers to employment for persons with a visual impairment via a national mail survey of a random sample of 400 employed persons who were legally blind. Forty-four percent of the sample returned usable surveys. The average period of time that respondents had been employed in their current job was "11 years, with a total work history of approximately 23 years. They typically began to work after the onset of their visual impairments" (Crudden & McBroom, 1999, p. 343). Approximately one third of the respondents saw themselves as underemployed, about one fifth of whom considered themselves to be "overeducated for their current jobs" (Crudden & McBroom, 1999, p. 344).

Eighty-two percent of the respondents indicated that changing jobs was difficult due to their visual impairment. More specifically, a percentage of the respondents (noted in parentheses) cited the following reasons for their lack of job mobility: "employers' attitudes (27%), transportation problems (20%), difficulty in obtaining adaptive equipment and appropriate training (19%), and difficulty in gaining access to print materials (7%)" (Crudden & McBroom, 1999, p. 344).

In response to a list of potential employment barriers for persons who are visually impaired, the respondents in Crudden and McBroom's (1999) study most frequently identified the following:

> employers' attitudes toward visual impairments (69%), transportation problems (67%), discrimination in hiring (57%), inability to read print (53%), locating information about possible jobs (48%), the general public's attitudes toward visual impairments (43%), the skills or attitudes of rehabilitation counselors or placement staff (36%), the lack of available jobs in their communities (36%), the lack of money for equipment (27%), the lack of relevant work experience (27%), ... not knowing how to use Windows (25%) or a computer (18%), ... [and] fear of losing economic benefits (... 18%). (p 344)

Crudden and McBroom (1999) also pointed out that when the respondents in their study were asked to

> identify the most important thing that employers did to help them become or remain employed, 35% cited providing adaptive equipment or accommodations; 20%, encouragement; 16%, education and training; 14%, flexibility in the job; and 15%, clerical assistance, readers, and drivers. (p. 345)

Although the provision of adaptive equipment has been identified as a major facilitator for the acquisition and retention of employment by those with visual disabilities, lack of information about available adaptive equipment by consumers and rehabilitation service providers, as well as lack of funding for such devices, has greatly limited the number of persons with visual disabilities who have benefited from this technology in the employment arena (Butler et al., 2002; Monroe, 1978; O'Korn & Wheaton, 1995). Much of this useful technology is directed at providing access to printed text for individuals with a visual disability (O'Korn & Wheaton, 1995). Potential employers are often concerned about how job applicants with a significant visual impairment will access machine-produced or handwritten information (Wolfe, 1999). Wolfe (1999) elaborated on this concern:

> Employers worry that people who do not read ordinary print will be unable to keep up with written information shared internally between management personnel and their staffs, as well as among coworkers. They worry about how visually impaired employees will access employee manuals, training materials, posted bulletins, and other printed materials routinely shared in the work environment. In addition, they are concerned about how employees with visual impairments will retrieve written materials from customers and colleagues outside the company, such as letters, order forms, requests for information, and brochures. (p. 111)

Therefore, overcoming the lack of information and financial cost barriers to the utilization of available assistive technology for accessing and responding to written communication can be seen as imperative for expanding job opportunities for those with visual impairments.

Assistive technology for accessing and responding to written communication by a person with visual disabilities can be divided into four categories: speech synthesis, braille output, optical character recognition, and magnification (O'Korn & Wheaton, 1995). Speech synthesis is a category of assistive technology that converts text to speech. Often based on personal computers, text on the screen is communicated via speech to those who are incapable of reading the words on the screen. Such adaptive technology is often referred to as reading machines (A. M. Cook & Hussey, 2002).

Braille is a tactile reading substitute for those with visual impairments. Braille text is typically produced by embossing on heavy paper. Computer technology is available for converting text to braille, thereby allowing an individual with a visual disability to read a communication in braille (A. M. Cook & Hussey, 2002).

Optical character recognition (OCR) technology converts "printed text into electronic format which can then be stored in your computer for reviewing and editing" (O'Korn & Wheaton, 1995, p. 9). This is done with the aid of a scanner, a computer, and the necessary software. One main advantage of the combined technology of OCR and speech synthesis is that the person with a visual disability is much less dependent on human readers because written text can be scanned into the computer and then read orally by the computer to the individual (A. M. Cook & Hussey, 2002; O'Korn & Wheaton, 1995).

Because over 90 percent of those with visual disabilities have some usable vision, magnification aids can play a major role in facilitating utilization of printed text. In addition to obvious aids, such as handheld or mounted magnifiers and large-print books, newspapers, and menus, there are also electronic low-vision aids available. One such aid for magnifying text is a closed circuit television system, which consists of "a detachable video camera and a television type screen [that] can usually provide from 2X to about 60X magnification" (O'Korn & Wheaton, 1995, p. 9).

Difficulty in reading printed materials is obviously a major barrier to the acquisition or retention of employment. The four areas of adaptive equipment discussed above are excellent examples of reasonable workplace accommodations called for by the Americans with Disabilities Act. Utilizing such assistive technology more widely could result in a reduction in the unemployment rate for those with visual disabilities.

Concluding Statement

Individuals with disabilities possess certain limitations that handicap them in vocational functioning (as well as often in personal and/or social functioning).

The extent of this handicap depends in large part on the individual's situation, predisability history, current psychological adjustment, intellectual aptitudes and skills, and remaining physical capacities. Hence, it is more important to focus on the actual limitations resulting from a disability and the individual's psychological reaction to those limitations than on some diagnostic term such as *heart disease, psychosis, mental retardation,* or *diabetes.* Although useful in a general sense, labels often give only partial data as to what to expect regarding an individual's functional limitations. Of course, some disabilities such as spinal cord injury and end-stage renal disease have pronounced irreversible physical effects that have a more predictable impact on an individual's lifestyle.

Conclusions from clinical experience bear acknowledging. For example, some research indicates that individuals adopt a pattern of long-term adjustment to disability that can be broadly classified as successful or unsuccessful. Unsuccessful adjustment tends to be characterized by such defensive reactions as denial, withdrawal, overacceptance, or aggression. Successful adaptation tends to be characterized by responses such as compensation and behavioral coping, with a consequent focus on personal assets rather than limitations.

Many clinical interpretations regarding the effects of physical disability focus on a developmental sequence in which individuals move over time through denial, mourning, depression, and anger to positive coping. However, some studies (e.g., with people with spinal cord injuries) have found no support for the "stages" notion (i.e., some individuals who adjusted well to spinal cord injury never passed through a stage of depression).

Psychological factors are only part of the equation in determining how one responds to disability. The importance of sociological or social factors must not be underestimated. For example, individuals with disabilities must cope with a number of negative social attitudes fostered by the real or imagined differences attributed to them by others. Taking many forms, these attitudes often result in the stigmatization and segregation of people with disabilities. Compounding these attitudinal barriers are the many physical or architectural barriers that limit the mobility of individuals with disabilities.

Unfortunately, negative societal attitudes serve to mask the rehabilitation and vocational potential of individuals with disabilities. A number of studies have demonstrated the ability of persons with disabilities to perform successfully in a large variety of vocational roles.

Many of the comments regarding persons with physical disabilities can also be made for those having either an intellectual, an emotional, or a visual disability. Although a certain ceiling is imposed on them by their intellectual limitations, with proper training, many individuals with mental retardation can play a productive role in either competitive employment or sheltered workshops. Granted that the period of job induction is longer for persons with mental retardation, other factors such as greater persistence and less absenteeism on the job speak well for their employability.

Treatment of psychiatric disability has been slowed by the complexities of its causes, by the need for more reliable and valid diagnostic systems, and by the lack of proven treatment approaches. While it has been estimated that approximately 75% to 80% of the population of individuals with severe emotional disabilities are unemployed (J. Cook & Razzano, 2000), many of these individuals have substantial vocational potential and can benefit from vocational rehabilitation services and intensive case management strategies.

The mandate to serve people with specific learning disabilities clearly confronts rehabilitation professionals with the need to develop effective rehabilitation services and/or to modify existing services. Rehabilitation counselors must educate themselves regarding the problems created by specific learning disability and assimilate many types of information, including how the client learns, what coping techniques the client has used successfully in the past, and what services the client needs to function fully independently.

In regard to visual disabilities, the high unemployment and underemployment rates present a major challenge for rehabilitation counselors. Amelioration of this negative employment picture requires interventions by rehabilitation counselors that are directed at the removal of employer attitudinal barriers and the greater use of assistive technology consistent with the reasonable accommodations mandated by the ADA.

Chapter 8

The Role and Function of the Rehabilitation Counselor

One debate that can be expected to continue in the 21st century is the timeless argument about the proper role and function of the rehabilitation counselor. Although the specific issues may change, the debate will continue because of the multiple functions these professionals perform, the many institutions and disability groups they serve, and the types of training completed. Further insight into this debate requires an examination of both conceptual arguments and research-based conclusions regarding the role of the rehabilitation counselor.

The "Way It Should Be" Perspective

The Vocational Rehabilitation Act Amendments of 1954 stimulated efforts to clarify the role of the rehabilitation counselor. Since 1954, studies on the role of the rehabilitation counselor have focused on delineating both a unique professional identity and an appropriate educational curriculum for preparing persons for that role. In early writings on the professional role of the counselor, C. H. Patterson (1957, 1966, 1967, 1968, 1970) concentrated on whether the rehabilitation counselor should be trained as a *counselor* or a *coordinator.* Although both roles were considered necessary for serving people with disabilities, C. H. Patterson (1957) advocated a division of labor, with state rehabilitation agencies employing both rehabilitation counselors and rehabilitation coordinators. Viewing the training of counselors as the purpose of graduate education in rehabilitation, C. H. Patterson encouraged employment of graduate school–trained rehabilitation counselors to function as psychological counselors. Psychological counselors would work only with those clients who need to resolve personal adjustment problems.

On the other hand, the rehabilitation coordinator (counselor/coordinator) would work with all clients (C. H. Patterson, 1970). C. H. Patterson (1966, 1968) stressed that state rehabilitation agencies should employ rehabilitation coordinators to (a) find cases, (b) do intake interviews, (c) assemble reports, (d) determine eligibility, (e) manage cases, (f) arrange for services from other professions, (g) do public relations work, and (h) place clients on jobs. Hence, C. H. Patterson sought to resolve the role-and-function issue by distinguishing between two separate job roles. However, that separation of functions has never materialized because the great majority of rehabilitation counselors have always had to "wear both hats." Moreover, that division of labor is not likely to emerge because rehabilitation counselors must have both types of skills to be effective (Hershenson, 1990, 1998; Koch, Hennessey, Niese, Tabor, & Petro, 2004; Leahy, Chan, & Saunders, 2003).

Whereas C. H. Patterson advocated a "two hats theory," Whitehouse (1975) addressed the role-and-function issue through a "big hat theory." He described the rehabilitation counselor as a service provider who works with the whole person. That rehabilitation counselor must have multiple behavioral competencies coupled with a comprehensive knowledge base. Overall, Whitehouse viewed the rehabilitation counselor as a professional whose skills include those of therapist, guidance counselor, case manager, case coordinator, psychometrician, clinical life reviewer, vocational evaluator, educator, team member, social and family relator, placement counselor, community and client advocate, life engagement counselor, long-term conservator, and clinician. Whitehouse stressed that his global concept of the counselor warrants not the label "jack-of-all-trades," but rather the highly respected label of "rehabilitation clinician," a professional who can serve a person with a disability from a multifaceted but integrated service standpoint.

Other published positions are supportive of Whitehouse's position. For example, Chubon (1992) described rehabilitation counselors as mediators, that is, as professionals whose multiple roles are used to help individuals with disabilities maximize the quality of their lives within an environment of countervailing factors and forces. He stressed that counselors should seek to help people with disabilities achieve the "best fit" with their environments, which may require the environment, person, or both to change. Chubon's vision of the counselor as mediator is of a professional who advocates for the needs of the person with a disability within a milieu of "competing and conflicted" political, social, and economic factors (p. 29).

Stressing the primacy of the vocational outcome, Hershenson (1990) seemed to agree with many of the tenets of the "mediational" or "big hat" perspectives on the role of the counselor. To prevent certain disability-related functional limitations from becoming vocational handicaps, Hershenson (1998) stressed that rehabilitation counselors need counseling, coordinating, consulting, case managing, and critiquing expertise. Through their *counseling* function, rehabilitation counselors enable people with disabilities to reexamine and reconstitute their self-concepts and personal goals. *Coordinator* skills are needed by the rehabilitation counselor to select and monitor the wide variety of physical, psychosocial, and vocational services that clients require to achieve their rehabilitation goals. In their *consulting* function, rehabilitation counselors work with the client's family, friends, and employer to redesign the environment to maximize access and opportunity for people with disabilities. As *case managers,* counselors maintain individual case files, responding to agency reporting requirements in a timely and complete way. Finally, *by critiquing,* the counselor is expected to self-evaluate regarding his or her own needs for inservice training and professional development.

Although much of the research referred to in the remainder of this chapter supports the facets of the counselor's role described by Hershenson (1990, 1998), the question remains as to whether the debate is over. Goodwin (1992) projected that arguments regarding the rehabilitation counselor's role will continue into the future, although they will no longer focus on the counselor-versus-coordinator debate. He viewed employment in rehabilitation counseling as continuing to move further in the direction of specialization (e.g., in terms of work settings, types of clients, and even discrete functions). Noting that a large percentage of rehabilitation counselors worked in settings other than state rehabilitation agencies, he identified private-for-profit rehabilitation settings, mental hospitals, halfway houses, correctional programs, schools, and independent living centers as frequent employers of rehabilitation counselors.

Moreover, counselors in those settings may have single-disability case-loads, such as "substance abuse, mental retardation, hearing impairment, visual impairment, head injury, spinal cord injury, or mental illness" (Goodwin, 1992, p. 5). The fact that rehabilitation counselors work in multiple settings and often specialize in serving only one disability group results in a two-dimensional definitional job role grid (settings × specialties). That job role grid becomes more complex when a third dimension is added. Rehabilitation professionals often gravitate toward specific functions, such as job development and placement (e.g., placement specialist) or adjustment and affective counseling (e.g., clinical mental health counselor). Imagine a three-dimensional grid that leads to questions such as the following: How does the role of a rehabilitation counselor who provides placement services in a community reentry facility for people with developmental disabilities differ from the role of a private sector rehabilitation counselor who provides placement services to individuals with workplace injuries?

Goodwin's (1992) observations about the trend toward specialization in rehabilitation have considerable validity for the 21st century. Agreeing with Goodwin, the authors of a study addressing the training needs of rehabilitation counselors concluded that the growing complexity of rehabilitation may make it impossible to prepare counselors to work with all types of clients in all types of fields (Chan et al., 2003). Instead, prospective counselors may need to complete a set of core rehabilitation courses, followed by specialized coursework for practice in agency, community, or private sector settings. If such specialization occurs, the field of rehabilitation counseling must devote considerable time and effort to retaining a cohesive sense of professional identity and mission, given this diversity in regard to work settings, functions, and even membership in professional associations. Of course, empirical research will continue to provide one effective method for clarifying the impact of trends toward specialization on the practice of rehabilitation counseling and, thereby, the professional identity of the rehabilitation counselor.

The "Way It Is" Perspective

Over the years researchers have conducted empirical research to define the role and function of the rehabilitation counselor. Their efforts have focused either on reports of what counselors say they do or on observations of what they actually do. In an early study Muthard and Salomone (1969) found that most state rehabilitation agency field counselors estimated dividing their time roughly into thirds: one third solely devoted to counseling and guidance; one third divided among clerical work, planning, recording, and placement; and one third divided among professional growth, public relations, reporting, resource development, travel, and supervisory administrative duties.

Other pre–Rehabilitation Act of 1973 studies support Muthard and Salomone's (1969) finding that counseling and guidance is the single activity to which rehabilitation counselors report devoting their greatest amount of time. In a study of Iowa, Illinois, and Minnesota state rehabilitation agency counselors, L. A. Miller and Roberts (1971) found that counselors reported face-to-face contacts with clients as the job activity on which they spent the greatest amount of their time. In a study of 87 counselors drawn from 11 state rehabilitation agencies, S. E. Rubin, Richardson, and Bolton (1973) also found that rehabilitation counselors reported spending the greatest amount of their time in face-to-face contact with clients. Post–Rehabilitation Act of 1973 role and function research showed a small decline in the percentage of work time devoted to counseling and guidance (R. T. Fraser & Clowers, 1978; S. E. Rubin & Emener, 1979; Zadny & James, 1977). These studies indicated that rehabilitation counselors devote approximately one fourth of their work time to counseling and guidance activities.

Because rehabilitation counselors reported spending a substantial amount of their time in face-to-face contact with clients, the obvious question became, What do they actually do in these face-to-face contacts with clients? Having gathered tape recordings of the interview behavior of field office rehabilitation counselors from 11 state rehabilitation agencies, B. K. Richardson, Rubin, and Bolton (1973, pp. 34–35, 54) shed some light on the nature of the counselor–client interaction. Table 8.1 shows the mean percentage of interview responses accounted for by each of 12 subroles (clusters of counselors' interview behavior). As the data in Table 8.1 suggest, rehabilitation counselors devote the bulk of their interview time to information seeking (specific) and information giving (administrative). In other words, the face-to-face encounters seem to emphasize exchange of specific information more than "counseling."

Traditionally, rehabilitation counselors have placed a high value on their face-to-face counseling contacts with clients. For example, Neely (1974) sent a 25-item attitude survey to both general and special (serving only one disability type) caseload rehabilitation counselors employed by the Georgia Division of Vocational Rehabilitation. Although counselors in Neely's sample claimed that they did little counseling and were primarily service coordinators who performed a variety of functions, they felt that counseling should be their primary function. Compatible with Neely's finding, Emener and Rubin (1980) found that rehabilitation counselors wanted affective counseling to become a more substantial part of their job.

Research has indicated that due to large caseloads and agency pressure for large numbers of closures (i.e., clients rehabilitated into gainful occupation), many rehabilitation counselors have been unable to function primarily as counselors (Neely, 1974). Research has also demonstrated that excessive paperwork demands have required rehabilitation counselor time that could be spent in guidance and counseling activities. S. E. Rubin and Emener (1979) found that although rehabilitation counselors reported spending the greatest percentage of their time (mean = 38%) on recording (report writing and clerical work), they preferred to spend less of their time on that work activity and more of their time doing counseling and guidance.

TABLE 8.1

Description of Subrole Behavior Categories (N = 72 Rehabilitation Counselors)

Subrole	Behavior description	Average % of use
1. Information seeking– specific	Elicits specific factual information from clients regarding client background (e.g., work history, educational experiences).	23.2
2. Information giving– administrative	Informs the client about agency procedures and policies, the client's role in the rehabilitation process, appointments, etc.	22.6
3. Communication of values, opinions, and advice	Communicates (a) the subjective, personal, and judgmental opinions of the counselors; (b) the counselor's own personal past experiences, generalized to the client's situation; and (c) a specific, suggested course of action.	13.1
4. Listen/client expression	Describes the portion of the interview where the content of client expression regarding concerns was predominant.	9.1
5. Information giving– educational and occupational	Communicates information of an educational or vocational nature.	8.0
6. Information seeking– exploratory	Elicits information in an open-ended, exploratory manner; elicits client's feelings and attitudes toward self, others, and past, present, or future experiences.	6.0
7. Information giving– client based	Communicates information that pertains to the personal characteristics of the client (e.g., test scores, medical reports, etc.).	4.6
8. Clarification, reflection, and restatement	Clarifies for the client what he has experienced difficulty in expressing clearly through synthesizing in a more simplified form, and/or by communicating to the client an understanding of the client's feelings and attitudes, or restating the content of a previous response.	3.5
9. Friendly discussion– rapport building	Develops rapport with the client, permitting the client to experience being at ease in the interview.	3.1
10. Supportive	Conveys the counselor's acceptance, reassurance, and willingness to assist the client to discuss his problem; focuses on reducing the client's anxiety.	3.0
11. Information giving– structuring the relationship	Describes the structure of the client–counselor relationship.	2.6
12. Confrontation	Confronts the client with the reality aspects of the client's personality, discrepancies between the client's perception of himself and his actual behavior.	1.4

Note. From *Counseling Interview Behavior of Empirically Derived Subgroups of Rehabilitation Counselors* (Arkansas Studies in Vocational Rehabilitation, Series 1, Monograph 7), by B. K. Richardson, S. E. Rubin, and B. Bolton, 1973, Fayetteville: University of Arkansas, Rehabilitation Research and Training Center.

The preference to do more counseling expressed by rehabilitation counselors may stem more from idealizations of that function encountered in their graduate training than from a valid picture of the requirements of the jobs performed by many rehabilitation counselors. Indeed, research suggests that rehabilitation counselors do little "classical counseling" for at least two reasons. First, excessive paperwork has reduced the amount of possible face-to-face contact with clients in all human service professions. Second, and even more germane, the heterogeneous work role of the rehabilitation counselor—which includes central activities such as case management, job development, and placement—precludes the possibility that counseling will ever become *the* key descriptor of rehabilitation counseling (Roessler & Rubin, 2006). Because counseling is more accurately portrayed as *one* of the key descriptors, a multifaceted job role is the most accurate description of the professional identity of the rehabilitation counselor.

Rehabilitation Counselor: A Multifaceted Role

To fulfill the responsibilities of their job role, rehabilitation counselors must carry out (a) case finding, (b) intake, (c) diagnosis, (d) eligibility determination, (e) plan development and completion, (f) service provision, (g) placement and follow-up, and (h) postemployment services. That job role calls for broad-based knowledge and skills related to affective counseling, vocational assessment, vocational counseling, case management, job development, and placement counseling (Garner, 1985; Roessler & Rubin, 2006; S. E. Rubin et al., 1984).

In their study of job descriptions for entry-level counseling positions prepared by the 50 federal–state vocational rehabilitation agencies, Allen, Turpin, Garske, and Warren-Marlatt (1996) provided support for the importance of the aforementioned roles for the rehabilitation counselor. Based on expert ratings of content of the job descriptions, they reported that all 50 of the job descriptions stressed the following rehabilitation job components: vocational services, case management, medical/psychosocial issues, individual counseling, and assessment. To further clarify the role of the counselor as presented in job descriptions, the authors called for a universal definition of counselor duties for use in the federal–state system. Certainly, that universal description should include the six roles supported in research, specifically affective counseling, vocational assessment, vocational counseling, case management, job development, and placement counseling.

A review of the five-factor *Job Task Inventory* (JTI; S. E. Rubin et al., 1984), an instrument that measures the role and function of rehabilitation counselors, underscores the importance of affective counseling. The JTI contains an affective counseling factor, including items focusing primarily on the psychological counseling process aimed at changing the client's feelings and thoughts regarding self and others. Affective counseling tasks on the JTI that were rated by a national sample of rehabilitation counselors as a substantial part of their job include the following:

1. Reduces the client's anxiety by helping him or her face and realistically assess problems that seem insurmountable
2. Counsels with the client to help him or her achieve an emotional and intellectual acceptance of the limitations imposed by the disability
3. Counsels clients to help them understand or change their feelings about themselves and others
4. Discusses the client's interpersonal relationships in order to help him or her better understand their nature and quality

The results of the JTI study suggest that another basic rehabilitation counselor skill involves vocational assessment. The vocational assessment process demands that the rehabilitation counselor be aware of what information to collect for achieving vocational diagnostic accuracy. Therefore, the rehabilitation counselor must have an operational understanding of the components of a comprehensive diagnostic profile of the client's current and potential functioning in physical, educational/vocational, and psychosocial areas. The accuracy of this profile is critical for service planning. Vocational assessment tasks on the JTI that were rated by a national sample of rehabilitation counselors as a substantial part of their job include the following:

1. Uses test results as a diagnostic aid in gaining a thorough understanding of the whole client
2. Interprets results of work evaluation to clients
3. Consults with experts in a particular field prior to recommending a training/educational program to determine the potential for client placement in that field

The results of three national studies in the 1980s of the role and function of rehabilitation counselors indicate that vocational counseling is a major part of their job (Emener & Rubin, 1980; S. E. Rubin et al., 1984; G. N. Wright, Leahy, & Shapson, 1987). Items found in one or more of those studies (Roessler & Rubin, 2006, pp. 13–14) that can help define the vocational counseling part of the rehabilitation counselor's job include the following:

1. Counsels with clients regarding educational and vocational implications of test and interview information
2. Suggests to the client occupational areas compatible with the vocational, psychological, and social information gathered to improve the appropriateness of his or her rehabilitation choice
3. Examines with the client the consequence of his or her disability and its vocational significance

4. Explores with the client his or her vocational assets and liabilities in order to assure a realistic understanding and acceptance of them
5. Recommends occupational and/or educational materials for clients to explore vocational alternatives

Further illuminating both the complexity and the sophistication of the counselor's role is the fact that the position demands the ability to plan the rehabilitation program with the client as well as to deal with all community-based agencies whose services could augment the person's rehabilitation. These program development and resource utilization skills are necessary to carry out the case management functions related to service planning and coordination. Rehabilitation counselors must also have management and planning skills (i.e., the capability to utilize and coordinate multiple resources to resolve specific client problems). This significant case management aspect of the rehabilitation counselor's role is also clearly supported by research (Garner, 1985; S. E. Rubin et al., 1984). More specifically, case management tasks that were rated by a national sample of rehabilitation counselors as a substantial part of their job are as follows (S. E. Rubin et al., 1984):

1. Develops a rehabilitation plan with the client
2. Monitors client progress toward attaining the vocational goal specified in the written rehabilitation plan
3. Coordinates the activities of all agencies involved in a rehabilitation plan to assure optimal benefits to the client
4. Establishes timetables for performing assorted rehabilitation services
5. Refers clients for medical evaluation
6. Refers clients for psychological evaluation
7. Refers clients to training facilities for development of vocational skills
8. Explains available rehabilitation entitlement benefits to clients

A number of writers have stressed the importance of job development and placement activities in the rehabilitation counselor's job role. However, results of S. E. Rubin et al.'s (1984) study revealed a discrepancy in the profession regarding the importance of placement activities. Although the following placement-related functions were rated as important by rehabilitation counselors in state rehabilitation agencies, they were viewed as a minor part of the job role by rehabilitation counselors in private nonprofit rehabilitation facilities, mental health or mental retardation centers, and general or mental hospital settings:

1. Visits employers to solicit job openings for particular clients
2. Discusses the client's work with an employer and enumerates specific tasks the client can do
3. Secures information about the client's performance on and adjustment to his or her new job from the employer and the client
4. Arranges on-the-job training programs for the client

On the other hand, research suggests that, for the most part, the following placement counseling activities are a relatively important part of the rehabilitation counselor's job, regardless of work setting (S. E. Rubin et al., 1984):

1. Uses supportive counseling techniques to prepare clients emotionally for the stress of job hunting
2. Instructs clients about ways to locate jobs
3. Interviews an unmotivated client, perhaps over several meetings, to develop his or her motivation for remunerative employment
4. Discusses with the client alternative ways to respond to employer questions about his or her disability
5. Role-plays an employment interview, and reviews common employer questions to reduce the client's anxiety about job hunting

As is evident from the above discussion, the rehabilitation counselor is an important communication link between the client and the employer and between the client and other service providers. Therefore, counselors must have good written and verbal communication skills in order to summarize salient client considerations in their case files, as well as to present that same material verbally in staff meetings and to prospective employers (C. Tucker, Abrams, Brady, Parker, & Knopf, 1989). In this same vein, a competency of the rehabilitation counselor that is sometimes overlooked is salesmanship or persuasiveness. Implicit in several job development tasks on the JTI is the rehabilitation counselor's ability to encourage employers to hire people with disabilities.

Recent research on the "way it is" regarding the role of rehabilitation counselors reflects the need for an integrative perspective, given the many roles they play and the many settings in which they work. Encompassing more settings than the state rehabilitation agency, these studies were designed to clarify rehabilitation's "core." In an investigation of generic rehabilitation job tasks and knowledge, Beardsley and Rubin (1988) collected data on the *Rehabilitation Profession Job Task Inventory* and the *Rehabilitation Profession Knowledge Competency Inventory* from a large random sample (over 4,000) of rehabilitation counselors, vocational evaluators, work adjustment specialists, job development/placement specialists, rehabilitation nurses, and independent living service providers. Data clearly indicated that these rehabilitation professionals shared a number of job tasks that required a common knowledge base. Generic tasks to which all groups subscribed in the study included (a) formulating rehabilitation plans and service goals, (b) interviewing clients to obtain background information, (c) participating in case conferences, (d) identifying community agencies and resources, (e) ensuring continuity of services to clients, and (f) conducting affective counseling. The knowledge base required of all rehabilitation direct service providers included (a) medical technology and services, (b) the uses and effects of medication, (c) characteristics of specific disabling conditions, (d) theories of personality, (e) counseling theories and modalities, (f) behavior change techniques, (g) human service systems and community resources,

(h) legal and ethical issues related to rehabilitation practice, and (i) the effects of socioeconomic factors on the rehabilitation process.

Leahy, Shapson, and Wright (1987) extended the investigation of rehabilitation's "core" when they examined commonalities and differences not only among rehabilitation specialists but also among specialists working in different settings. Using the *Rehabilitation Skills Inventory,* they gathered data on the importance attached to 114 rehabilitation competencies by rehabilitation counselors, vocational evaluators, and job placement specialists in three work settings (public, private nonprofit, or private-for-profit). Regardless of setting or specialization, the respondents agreed that a common core of skills was important for direct service providers in rehabilitation. Encompassing 71 of the 114 items (62%), the five competency areas that the three specialty groups considered important were vocational counseling, assessment planning and interpretation, personal adjustment counseling, case management, and job analysis. Although the three groups agreed on the importance of the five areas, they also indicated that they devoted different amounts of time to them, depending on their specialty.

Leahy et al.'s (1987) findings are also consistent with the prediction that future debates about the core functions of the rehabilitation professional will focus on the trend toward specialization. For example, rehabilitation counselors rated vocational and personal adjustment counseling and case management higher in importance than did vocational evaluators. On the other hand, evaluators rated assessment competencies higher on importance than did counselor or placement specialists. Similarly, placement specialists viewed job analysis and placement as more important functions than did vocational evaluators. Overall, the rehabilitation counselors and job placement specialists were more alike in their importance ratings than were rehabilitation counselors and vocational evaluators or job placement specialists and vocational evaluators.

Research has continued to support the primacy of the counseling, coordinating, and consulting aspects of the rehabilitation counselor's role (Koch et al., 2004; Leahy et al., 2003). In research based on the responses of 631 certified rehabilitation counselors in a variety of settings, Leahy et al. (2003) identified seven generic dimensions of rehabilitation practice compatible with those three themes: providing vocational counseling and consultation, conducting counseling interventions, using community-based rehabilitation services, managing cases, applying research to practice, conducting assessment, and practicing professional advocacy. Although rating all of the areas as important, the counselors indicated that case management was their most important and most frequently performed function, followed by the areas of advocacy and vocational counseling and consultation.

At the same time, counselors working in various settings, such as proprietary rehabilitation settings, nonprofit rehabilitation programs, and public vocational rehabilitation (VR) programs, held different opinions about the importance of specific knowledge and job function domains (Leahy et al., 2003).

For example, in comparison with other groups, practitioners in the public VR program rated the following knowledge areas as more important: medical, functional, and environmental implications of disability and career counseling; assessment; and consultation services. Professionals in proprietary rehabilitation settings rated knowledge regarding health care and disability systems and career counseling, assessment, and consultation services (with the exception of comparisons with the public VR counselors) as more important than did other groups. In terms of job functions, rehabilitation counselors in public VR settings were more likely than other groups to view vocational counseling and consultation and use of community-based rehabilitation services as more important, whereas professionals in proprietary rehabilitation settings typically viewed "researching medical and labor market information for professional practice" as more important than did other groups (p. 77).

Still, the view of generic rehabilitation counseling skills emerging from Leahy et al.'s (2003) study is a helpful response to the concerns regarding the potential fragmentation of rehabilitation counseling resulting from overspecialization. Regardless of the setting under consideration, a contemporary description of the role of the rehabilitation counselor based on this research would include references to the counselor as case manager, counselor, advocate, and employment specialist. Duties involved in the counseling and case management functions were adequately covered in previous sections in the chapter, and duties involved in employment services were described previously, in part, as well. Duties involved in advocacy are detailed in the Leahy et al. (2003) study.

Advocacy involves the counselor in educating the public, including employers, regarding negative stereotypes of people with disabilities and the ways in which those stereotypes create attitudinal barriers toward full participation in society. Advocacy also requires that counselors apply the principles of rehabilitation legislation in their daily professional activities (Leahy et al., 2003). The importance of these advocacy services cannot be overemphasized. When asked what type of assistance they expected from their rehabilitation counselors, individuals with spinal cord injuries described their ideal counselor as someone who was dedicated to promoting their best interests (H. McCarthy & Leierer, 2001). Their depiction of the ideal counselor reaffirmed advocacy as one of the most critical services that clients expect.

Findings regarding the employment services part of the counselor's role are consistent with previous research as well, which spelled out the functions involved and the counselors' comfort performing them. Consistent with past findings, counselors expressed some hesitancy regarding the placement function. Specifically, this area was rated by the same 631 certified rehabilitation counselors (see Leahy et al., 2003) as the topic on which they felt they needed the most training (Chan et al., 2003). In the Chan et al. study, the topical area was labeled "career counseling, assessment, and consultation" (p. 85), and the training needs encompassed interventions (a) with people with disabilities (e.g., development of job retention skills), (b) with the job and job setting (e.g., job modification, restructuring and rehabilitation engineering), and (c) with the employer (e.g., consultation with employers regarding job development and return-to-work programs).

Results reported by Leahy et al. (2003) clarify the nature of job development and placement knowledge, which counselors rated as one of the most important knowledge domains in their practice. The job development and placement services factor contained the following knowledge items: "employer development and job placement, client job-seeking skills development, client job retention skills, job placement strategies, job and employer development, follow-up/postemployment services, occupational and labor market information, and vocational implications of functional limitations associated with disabilities" (p. 75).

The bottom-line implication of the years of role-and-function research is that rehabilitation counselors need many skills to ensure that people with disabilities are satisfied with the services that they receive (Kosciulek, 2004b). To be satisfied, individuals with disabilities expect to develop meaningful relationships with their counselors (H. McCarthy & Leierer, 2001), characterized by effective agency and counselor practices and by beliefs on the clients' part that they have exercised informed choice in their contacts with the counselors (Kosciulek, 2004b). Others have labeled relationships possessing all of these characteristics as "working alliances," and research clarifies why working alliances result in client satisfaction (Donnell, Lustig, & Strauser, 2004). Recipients of rehabilitation services who report more positive working alliances with their counselors are more likely to be employed as a result of services, to be satisfied with their jobs, and to be positive about their future employment prospects. All of the generic skills of the rehabilitation counselor discussed by previous researchers are necessary to achieve working alliances that result in positive employment outcomes.

Role and Function: Additional Thoughts

Although focusing on counselor skills needed to improve the placement success of people with disabilities, Ford and Sweet (1999) identified some generic functions that pertain to a wide variety of rehabilitation professionals. They based their observations on the changing needs of people with disabilities and the changing cultural context in which they live and work. These authors recommended that rehabilitation professionals possess such attributes as the ability to educate people with disabilities about the decision-making skills needed to make good choices about employment and career options. They stressed the advocacy role of the counselor in helping clients secure long-term services and support from rehabilitation (i.e., postemployment counseling and natural workplace supports) and other community agencies. Agreeing with Goodwin (1992) about the increasing specialization in the field of rehabilitation, they noted that rehabilitation professionals must communicate their areas of expertise clearly to clients, adding that state rehabilitation counselors must learn how to market their services in relation to those provided by private rehabilitation and facility counselors. Finally, consistent with other views of the counselor's role, Ford and Sweet called for increased knowledge on the counselor's part regarding alternative funding options (i.e., similar benefits), the impact of employment on a person's benefit program, and the cultural diversity in the communities they serve.

Jenkins and Strauser (1999) feared that unless rehabilitation counselors broaden their roles "horizontally," much of the preceding discussion about the role and function of the rehabilitation counselor will become of historical significance only. They predicted that the "niche" professional (i.e., the counselor serving only one customer group) would sooner or later pass from the scene. In their model, they recommended that rehabilitation counselors expand their roles to meet the demand-side job placement services required by employers as well as the needs of individual clients. These demand-side services include human resources issues, such as determining how work will be done, participating in hiring and staffing decisions, providing staff training on employment practices affected by programs such as workers' compensation and legislation such as the Americans with Disabilities Act, and consulting with employers and employees regarding prevention and retention issues. Their emphasis on the demand-side functions of the counselor is entirely consistent with Leahy et al.'s (2003) finding that vocational counseling and consultation is one of the seven major rehabilitation job dimensions. This dimension contains four subfactors: job development and placement, career counseling, employer consultation, and vocational planning (Leahy et al., 2003).

The Rehabilitation Counselor–Client Relationship

Regardless of setting, rehabilitation counselors must assist clients in navigating some or all of a complex rehabilitation process consisting of four phases: (a) evaluation, (b) planning, (c) treatment, and (d) termination. Each phase is comprehensively discussed in subsequent chapters. Although effective case management is dependent on the presence of multiple rehabilitation counselor skills, it is difficult to conceive of people with severe disabilities successfully completing their rehabilitation programs in the absence of a positive relationship with their rehabilitation counselor. As discussed in the following section, a number of factors affect the quality of the counseling relationship.

The Quality of the Counseling Relationship

Rehabilitation counselors must never lose sight of the importance of developing positive, facilitative relationships with their clients. In addition to having a genuine interest in their clients, rehabilitation counselors must help them influence or change the environments in which they function. Furthermore, the counselor must accept the individual and not reject him or her because of what the counselor deems unacceptable behavior.

Research indicates that clients expect counselors to be "experienced, genuine, expert, and accepting" (Tinsley & Harris, 1976, p. 173), themes echoed in the descriptions of the ideal counselor provided by people with spinal cord injuries who had participated in vocational rehabilitation (H. McCarthy & Leierer, 2001). Unfortunately, what is expected and what is found are not always the same. For example, negative attitudes toward people seeking services are a particular problem when those clients represent racial, ethnic, social, or economic backgrounds different from those of the counselor (Rosenthal & Bervin, 1999). Hence, a number of rehabilitation educators have called for increased multicultural training for rehabilitation professionals (Dodd, Nelson, Ostwald, & Fischer, 1991; Marshall, Leung, Johnson, & Busby, 2003; Stebnicki, Rubin, Rollins, & Turner, 1999; Watson, 1988; T. J. Wright, 1988), and research demonstrates that exposure to pertinent courses and training programs is related to higher levels of multicultural counseling skills (Bellini, 2002).

Defining cross-cultural or multicultural counseling as "relationships in which the counselor and client differ culturally, racially, or ethnically," Watson (1988) viewed rehabilitation education programs as playing an extremely important role in countering cultural "encapsulation" of counselors. More training is needed to sensitize prospective counselors to the values, beliefs, priorities, and characteristics of people from a variety of backgrounds—Asian Americans, African Americans, Hispanic Americans, and Native Americans. Fortunately, many rehabilitation education programs are aware of this need and are offering multicultural preparation as either a separate course or part of an existing course (Dodd et al., 1991).

At the same time, educators (Stebnicki et al., 1999) are also stressing that multicultural preparation requires a respect for the individual first and the way in which he or she has integrated the values, beliefs, and behaviors of his or her culture. Consistent with this position, Stebnicki et al. (1999) noted that one of the important outcomes of multicultural education for the student is the development of cultural awareness. As they noted, "developing cultural knowledge and understanding is a continuous process of engaging in self-examination, maintaining cognitive flexibility, and active attending" (p. 6).

Becoming culturally aware means that the counselor has gained important insights into many pertinent issues. For example, as they work with individuals from different cultural groups, counselors learn how individuals in that tradition define disability, its causes, decision-making roles of self and family, appropriate interventions, and expected social reactions to disability. With experience working with different groups, counselors can identify the language barriers that exist and develop either appropriate language skills or translation services. Counselors learn to avoid jargon or "agency-ese" in communicating the purpose and procedures of rehabilitation and in assuring clients of the confidentiality of the relationship. They also learn to avoid undue reliance on impersonal approaches in the meeting with the client, such as conducting the intake interview with a laptop rather than the person (Schaller, Parker, & Garcia, 1998).

Multicultural knowledge and awareness and cross-cultural counseling skills, as well as counselor qualities of empathy, respect, genuineness, and concreteness, represent core counseling skills (Faiver, Eisengart, & Colonna, 2004). These qualities are communicated not only in words but also through counselor "tone of voice, inflections, body movements, direction of gaze, frowns, and smiles" (Sulzer-Azaroff, 1974, p. 564). To create a situation in which a therapeutic relationship can develop, counselors need to maintain contact with their clients; respond to them in an empathic, respectful, and genuine manner; and encourage client participation (Kosciulek, 2004b; Schaller & De La Garza, 1999). Benjamin (1981) stressed that when such a relationship has been effectively achieved, clients will feel empowered to make their own decisions and free to express both positive and negative feelings.

As applied to rehabilitation counseling, the literature on the counseling relationship indicates that the rehabilitation counselor must establish a helpful relationship with the client from the beginning and be constantly aware of the need to maintain the relationship throughout the rehabilitation process. A quality relationship (i.e., one characterized by empathy, respect, genuineness, concreteness, and cultural sensitivity) facilitates client progress by providing a situation that the client will want to maintain, by helping the client to verbalize real concerns, and by making the counselor a potent reinforcer in the client's life. Although a necessary element, a good relationship is not sufficient for ensuring positive rehabilitation outcomes. As Kanfer and Goldstein (1991) pointed out, a client should expect a counselor to be both "technically proficient" and empathic, respectful, and genuine. Rehabilitation counselor skills must be sufficiently comprehensive so that it is unnecessary for clients to make a choice between the two.

The Rehabilitation Counselor as Counselor

The counseling that occurs between the rehabilitation counselor and the client is directed not at personality reconstruction but at reintegration of self-image and reformulation of personal goals to enhance the person's work adjustment and motivation (Hershenson, 1990, 1998). Personality reorganization is the goal of psychotherapy, a service that can be purchased by the rehabilitation counselor when necessary. Nevertheless, acute stress-related personal adjustment problems should be dealt with by the rehabilitation counselor to the extent that they interfere with achievement of the client's primary rehabilitation goals (e.g., employment, independent living).

In addition to not being trained to conduct long-term psychotherapy, rehabilitation counselors have very limited time to devote to that activity due to large caseloads and extensive case management responsibilities. Other resources, such as rehabilitation facilities, counseling psychologists, and clinical mental health specialists, are available to help the person overcome personal adjustment problems that hamper employability.

The rehabilitation counselor must, however, involve the client in problem solving relevant to independent living and vocational planning (Roessler & Rubin, 2006). That problem-solving activity focuses primarily on making vocational choices and determining avenues for realizing such goals. By necessity, then, rehabilitation counseling is action oriented and goal directed, with a strong vocational emphasis (Kosciulek, 2004b). Through only a brief series of contacts, its focus is on the (a) development of a specific vocational goal; (b) agreement on relevant physical, intellectual, and emotional subobjectives; (c) identification of barriers to reaching goals and subobjectives; (d) implementation of rehabilitation interventions; and (e) evaluation of client outcomes and satisfaction (Schultz & Ososkie, 1999).

Concluding Statement

For too long the field of rehabilitation has perpetuated a debate on whether the rehabilitation counselor is a counselor or a coordinator. The issue of counselor versus coordinator obscures the fact that rehabilitation counselors must have counseling, coordinating, and consulting skills, as well as a variety of other competencies in the areas of case management and personal professional development. Hence, a more inclusive perspective of the role is needed, such as the multifaceted viewpoint described in this chapter. Working from that model, the rehabilitation counselor is a skilled professional with counseling and case management skills located at the hub of a multispecialty-oriented program requiring the coordination of many disciplines to meet the needs of people with severe disabilities.

For rehabilitation clients coping with the effects of severe disability, the rehabilitation counselor represents the key person in the rehabilitation process. The rehabilitation counselor's responsibility is to secure and organize relevant information about the person and to involve him or her in the rehabilitation planning process. With the person's involvement, the counselor must develop a plan that integrates rehabilitation services and the services from other agencies and/or community-based private professionals. Although that is a difficult task in and of itself, it is not enough for rehabilitation counselors to simply develop such plans. They must also make sure that the plans are implemented and that clients are satisfied with the services received.

The emergence of rehabilitation counseling as a profession dates to the mid-1950s with the initiation of the first master's degree program in rehabilitation counseling. Today, approximately 90 such programs can be found throughout the United States. Most of the programs have been accredited by the Council on Rehabilitation Education, the national accreditation body for rehabilitation education programs. In April 1973 the Commission on Rehabilitation Counselor Certification was established as the national certifying body for rehabilitation counselors. With the establishment of solid accreditation and certification bodies, the rehabilitation counselor has reached the status of a respected professional in the community of health service providers.

Chapter 9

The Vocational Rehabilitation Process: Evaluation Phase

The end goals of the vocational rehabilitation process for people with disabilities are placement in competitive employment, personal satisfaction with the placement, and satisfactory performance on the job. To achieve those goals, the following rehabilitation process subobjectives must be reached:

1. The person with a disability should receive all information needed to understand the role and function of the rehabilitation agency and its service providers.
2. The individual should be properly informed of the purpose and expected outcomes of all services in which he or she is asked to participate.
3. A sound vocational counseling relationship—one that empowers the individual to express his or her own feelings, aspirations, and needs— must be developed early in and maintained throughout the rehabilitation process.
4. All information necessary for the development of a satisfactory placement should be acquired, including information on the person's ability to perform in actual job situations with the necessary support systems in place.
5. The counselor and the person with a disability should jointly develop an appropriate rehabilitation plan.
6. Each service called for by the rehabilitation plan should be thoroughly rendered and closely monitored.
7. Each case must be effectively terminated.

For many people with disabilities, the rehabilitation process is best described as a four-phase sequence, beginning with evaluation and moving through planning, treatment, and termination (placement). In fact, the chapters in the middle section of this text are organized in that same order—evaluation, planning, treatment, and termination. However, the rehabilitation process for some individuals may work more effectively if the traditional service sequence is altered. For example, the individual with a progressive or unpredictable condition such as multiple sclerosis may need additional evaluation of on-the-job needs following the termination or placement phase.

People with severe disabilities, such as mental retardation characterized by IQ scores of 55 or below, traumatic brain injury, certain emotional conditions, severe sensory disabilities, and autism, may also benefit from a more flexible approach to the traditional rehabilitation sequence of evaluation, planning, treatment, and termination (Parker, Szymanski, & Hanley-Maxwell, 1989). For example, an individual with a severe disability might first be placed on a job and then evaluated in terms of service and support needs. Subsequent service provision may be followed by another period of evaluation, planning, and service provision in order to enhance the individual's ability to perform in a competitive setting. Although the more flexible view of the rehabilitation process is compatible with serving the greatest number of people most effectively, it is difficult to describe a process without giving it a certain static character. Chapters 9 through 12 present the rehabilitation process as a traditional, four-phase sequence: evaluation, planning, treatment, and termination. The remainder of this chapter focuses on the evaluation phase, and the three subsequent chapters deal with the remaining phases.

The Evaluation Process

The objective of the evaluation phase of the vocational rehabilitation process is to help the person with a disability (a) better understand the range of his or her current and potential vocational functioning and interests, (b) become aware of potential job opportunities compatible with such functional capacities and interests, and (c) learn about rehabilitation services and supports necessary to optimize that functioning. To achieve that objective, counselors must have both comprehensive information about the person and a comprehensive knowledge of (a) functional demands of the jobs existing in the local job market; (b) available vocational training programs; (c) the variety of possible accommodations and supports, such as technological innovations and job coaches; (d) available restoration services; and (e) other necessary services, such as sources of temporary financial support, transportation assistance, or financial assistance to cover the costs of tools, uniforms, or licensure fees.

Evaluation data pertinent to understanding the vocational functioning of individuals with disabilities often accumulate across a sequential series of evaluation activities. Because of rehabilitation's vocational emphasis, that evaluation process focuses on uncovering the client's vocationally relevant existing and potential capabilities, skills, and interests. With such information, the counselor can help the individual identify and choose among occupations that potentially provide good client–job matches. However, these choices must not be made based on insufficient information. The rehabilitation counselor can consider diagnostic information to be adequate only if he or she is able to answer relevant planning questions (see Table 9.1). To answer those questions, the counselor must draw conclusions from information collected both from the client and from other sources during the evaluation process. The information-collection demands presented by those diagnostic questions provide some idea of the amount of information necessary for a thorough evaluation. Power (2006) has also stressed the comprehensive nature of the evaluation process, which encompasses the person's "unique skills, residual capacities, functional limitations, and resources,... with a particular emphasis on family and culture" (p. xiii).

The information-collection process begins with the *intake interview,* which generates a social–vocational history based on questions that the person can answer directly. Required by all public state rehabilitation agencies, the *general medical examination* (a) establishes the presence and extent of physical disability, (b) provides information on the physical functioning of the client, (c) determines the types of activities precluded by the disabling condition, and (d) identifies any additional medical evaluation necessary for achieving the first three purposes. For clients requiring additional evaluation, medical specialist

(text continues on p. 293)

TABLE 9.1

Information Processing Questions Related to Rehabilitation Plan Development

I. Physical factors

1. Is the client's disabling condition progressive or stable?
2. If the client is restricted in respect to activities of daily living:
   a. Can his or her capacity for carrying out such activities be increased?
   b. How much assistance will the client need from others to carry out activities of daily living?
3. If mobility is restricted by the client's physical disability, can mobility be increased?
4. Are there any available technological devices that can help the client overcome physical deficits?
5. In what ways is utilization of the client's vocational skills blocked by the presence of disability? Can the barrier be reduced?

II. Educational–vocational factors

1. Is the client's educational record an accurate reflection of intellectual capacity (i.e., Did the individual quit school because he or she had to or for financial reasons?)?
2. Has the client developed vocationally relevant skills that limit the functional impact of the disability?
3. Does the client's educational and work history suggest certain types of training and contraindicate others? Which does it suggest and which does it contraindicate?
4. Does the client have a good picture of personal skills and abilities?
5. Is there any evidence of undeveloped talents that have vocational relevance? Can and/or should such be developed?
6. Has the client had a positive work history (i.e., regular employment)?
7. What work skills does the client currently possess?
8. What information from the client's work history can be of value with respect to current vocational choice considerations? In what specific ways is that information useful?

III. Psychosocial factors

1. Has the client manifested psychological reactions toward his or her disability that would inhibit adequate vocational adjustment? If yes, how can they be ameliorated?
2. Is the client's disability being used as justification for failure to fulfill expectations for self or others? If yes, how can his or her motivation for rehabilitation be increased?
3. Is the client gaining dependency gratifications from being unemployed? If yes, how can motivation for rehabilitation be increased?
4. Is the client overly concerned about his or her general health?
5. Is there any reason to believe that the client's physical symptoms are psychologically based?
6. Is the client perceiving his or her functional limitations as being less than they actually are in spite of clear-cut evidence to the contrary?
7. How is the client likely to respond in a high production, high stress type of job?
8. Would the client work well on a job that demanded a large amount of collaborative effort with other workers?
9. Will the client respond appropriately to supervision on the job?
10. Is the client willing to sacrifice a substantial amount of free time for purposes of employment?

(continues)

TABLE 9.1 (Continued)

III. Psychosocial factors continued

11. Will the client's family facilitate his or her rehabilitation? Will any intervention be necessary to augment a positive effect?

12. Will it be necessary to attempt to improve the client's family adjustment? How can such a goal be achieved?

13. Will the client tend to obtain secondary gain-based reinforcement from his or her family that will reinforce dependency and act as a counter-incentive to achievement of vocational rehabilitation?

14. Is there any evidence of over-protectiveness by the client's family?

15. Are significant family members encouraging unrealistic client aspirations?

16. Is there any reason to believe that the way the client handles leisure time could pose problems in regard to job retention?

17. Are there cultural factors that should be taken into consideration in the formulation of the rehabilitation plan?

IV. Economic factors

1. Will maintenance need to be provided or obtained for the client?

2. If the client is receiving disability related financial support such as SSI, SSDI, Medicaid, Food Stamps, or Worker's Compensation, does it appear to be presenting a sufficient disincentive to create a significant barrier to rehabilitation? If yes, how can such a barrier be reduced?

3. If the client has significant outstanding debts, could they impede rehabilitation plan completion?

4. Is the client capable of independently managing personal finances?

V. Personal vocational choice considerations

1. Regarding current goals

   a. Does the client have an appropriate job goal (i.e., Are the client's vocational aptitudes, skills, and interests congruent with his or her vocational goals?)?

   b. Does the client have an understanding of the employment outlook in the field(s) that he or she is considering?

   c. Are there jobs available in the community for which the client is presently qualified?

   d. Does this client know what he or she wants to do vocationally? If the client does not have a "realistic" vocational goal, how can he or she be helped to make an appropriate vocational choice?

   e. Does this client have sufficient work experience on which to base a realistic vocational choice?

   f. Is the client aware of the general entry requirements and daily demand characteristics for the occupations in which he or she has expressed an interest?

   g. Does the client require any specific occupational information in order to make an appropriate vocational choice?

   h. Is the client people-oriented or thing-oriented?

   i. Are the conditions of work more important to the client than the actual type of work performed (job tasks)?

(continues)

TABLE 9.1 Continued

V. Personal vocational choice considerations continued

    2. Regarding potential goals

        a. Are there job redesign possibilities that can increase the client's employability?

        b. Is the client employable without work adjustment training?

        c. Is the client employable without vocational training?

        d. Are there any client leisure time activities that are suggestive of an appropriate vocational choice? How so?

    3. Regarding job acquisition

        a. Does the client's specific disability preclude consideration of certain work settings?

        b. If formerly employed, does the client have the physical and/or psychological capacity necessary for returning to that job?

        c. Can this client sell himself or herself to potential employers?

        d. Can the client satisfactorily fill out most job application blanks?

        e. How active will the counselor have to become in respect to client job acquisition?

Note. Adapted from *Intake Interview Skills for Rehabilitation Counselors,* by S. E. Rubin and R. C. Farley, 1980, Fayetteville: University of Arkansas, Rehabilitation Research and Training Center.

examinations or psychological evaluations are necessary. *Medical specialist examinations* answer questions not addressed in the general medical exam. Formal *psychological evaluations* can establish the presence of mental retardation, a learning disability, or a psychiatric disability, as well as yield insights into client aptitudes, interests, adjustment, and self-perceptions related to vocational functioning. Finally, the *vocational evaluation* component of the evaluation consists of different techniques, focusing specifically on assessing the relationship of the person's skills, mental abilities, personality characteristics, and physical tolerances to the performance demands of a variety of potential jobs.

The four-step evaluation process introduced above—intake interview, general medical examination, medical specialist examination/formal psychological evaluation, and vocational evaluation—indicates that the client's functional capacity is determined by information obtained directly from the client as well as from observations by others. The primary source of information from the individual with a disability is the rehabilitation counseling interview. Additional perspectives on the person's functioning are found in the interpretive aspects of reports from purchased services, such as medical, psychological, and vocational evaluation.

The steps of the evaluation phase, each of which yields a different type of information, occur sequentially for many individuals. As the process proceeds from one step to the next, knowledge of the person builds in a cumulative manner. When additional evaluation is necessary, information from earlier components should not be ignored but rather should be integrated with subsequently acquired information to more fully understand the person's situation.

The sufficiency of the information gained in early steps (intake interview and general medical exam) is greatly dependent on the severity or type of disability encountered. However, as one moves through the evaluation process, each subsequent step is much more costly than the previous one. Therefore, even though a logical relationship exists between the amount of information the counselor has about the person and his or her strengths, limitations, and needs, the value of an economical strategy should not be forgotten. Cost–benefit factors as they relate to the law of diminishing information returns should not be ignored when planning the evaluation process for any particular person. To keep evaluation costs as low as possible, a good rule of thumb would be to make the client evaluation process comprehensive within each step while using only those steps necessary for an optimal understanding of a client.

To gain maximum benefit from information collected, the counselor should process evaluation data immediately following the person's participation in each step of the evaluation process. Conclusions from periodic reviews of the available data enable the counselor to make wise determinations regarding the necessity for further evaluation. Generally speaking, sufficient information has been collected when the counselor can make reasonably accurate predictions for achieving specific rehabilitation goals given available rehabilitation services. At minimum, that would require a determination of the person's desires, the client's capacities to achieve those desires, and the rehabilitation services available to aid the person in the achievement of his or her goals.

The Evaluation-Based Intake Interview

The evaluation phase begins with the initial or intake interview. During the intake interview, several goals must be accomplished. First, the counselor should determine whether the individual has entered the correct office (when the counselor's office is the site of the first contact). If so, focus should then be placed on the following:

1. Determining the person's reasons for seeking rehabilitation services.
2. Providing the individual with necessary information about the role and function of the agency.
3. Developing adequate rapport, which has been achieved if the person feels he or she has freedom of expression, feels understood by the counselor, and has confidence in the counselor's ability to help. Power (2006) stated that one of the counselor's primary roles is "to be a communicator, namely someone who can establish a helping, interpersonal relationship with the client" (p. xxi).
4. Initiating the diagnostic process (information collection).
5. Informing the person of medical, vocational, or psychological evaluations that he or she must complete and the reasons for such evaluations.

During the intake interview, the counselor begins the most significant aspect of the evaluation phase, the social–vocational history. Information in the social–vocational history is useful in formulating the rehabilitation plan and in determining whether subsequent evaluations are needed. Most of the rehabilitation applicant's social–vocational history should be obtained during the intake interview. Ideally, all questions found in Table 9. 2 can be either fully or partially answered via the intake interview.

With so much potentially relevant information to collect, interview efficiency becomes crucial. Therefore, the counselor guides the person's focus during the intake interview. The counselor will be a more effective "navigator" if, prior to seeing the individual for purposes of collecting a social–vocational history, the counselor has a good idea of all the types of information that should be obtained during the interview. The counselor will be a better "pilot" if the interview is carried out in a systematic manner (Roessler & Rubin, 2006). Systematic interviewing occurs when the counselor concentrates on a single topic until optimally discussed or until the interviewee initiates the topical switch. Although they should be good listeners and avoid being "grand inquisitors," counselors should not hesitate to ask questions or to switch to new discussion topics when appropriate. It is naive to assume that all interviewees can (a) predetermine the significance of certain types of information, (b) discriminate between more or less significant topics of discussion, or (c) determine when a topic has already been optimally discussed (S. E. Rubin & Farley, 1980). In fact, if properly done, the counselor's use of information-collection questions will be perceived by the interviewee as an indication of both counselor competence and counselor respect for the interviewee as a reliable source of information (Benjamin, 1981; Roessler & Rubin, 2006).

Medical Evaluation

The Rehabilitation Act Amendments of 1998 continue to stress the need for medical documentation of a disabling condition in order to establish a person's eligibility for rehabilitation services from the public rehabilitation program. But it should be understood that the medical evaluation plays a far more important role than simply effecting eligibility determination. In addition to documenting the existence of an impairment that limits the person's range of activities, the medical examination provides information that clarifies the (a) functional implications of the impairment, (b) potential for possible recovery and services needed to achieve that goal, and (c) existing vocational capacities and limitations of the person (Hylbert & Hylbert, 1979).

The counselor should refer the client to an appropriate physician for the medical evaluation. An appropriate physician would be one who had treated the individual in the past or who is very knowledgeable in regard to the existing disabilities. Whether requesting a general medical or specialist examination, the counselor should also inform the physician of any tentative vocational

(*text continues on p. 298*)

TABLE 9.2
Information Collection Questions

I. Physical factors

1. What specific impairments are present?
2. What caused the disability?
3. How long has the client had a disability?
4. Has the client received any disability related treatment in the past (e.g., physical therapy)?
5. Has the client's disabling condition become worse over the last year?
6. Is the client receiving treatment for the disability?
7. Are there recent medical test results available on the client that are relevant to the question of extent of physical impairment?
8. In what manner and to what extent is the client's physical disability handicapping in regard to daily functioning?

II. Educational–vocational factors

1. Educational history
   a. How far did the client go in school?
   b. What did the client like or dislike about school?
   c. Why did the client leave school (graduate, other)?
   d. If the client did not complete high school, has he or she passed a high school equivalency exam?
   e. Has the client had any specific type of vocational training that prepared him or her to enter a particular occupation?
2. Work history
   a. What were the last three jobs held by the client?
   b. For each of those jobs:
      i. How much was earned weekly?
      ii. What was the length of employment (i.e., Was it long enough to acquire specific skills?)?
      iii. How much time has passed since the job was held (i.e., Has sufficient time passed for significant skill loss to take place?)?
      iv. What aspects of the job could the client do best?
      v. What aspects of the job did the client perform poorly?
      vi. What aspects of the job did the client like most? Why?
      vii. What aspects of the job did the client like least? Why?
      viii. What was the reason for termination of employment?
      ix. How well did the client get along with his or her supervisor?
   c. Prior to disability onset, were there any significant interruptions in work history? Why?
   d. Is the client presently unemployed? If yes, how long?
   e. Has the client been employed since onset of disability?

III. Psychosocial factors

1. Does the client have any fear of competitive situations?
2. Does the client have any fear of social exposure of his or her disability?

(continues)

TABLE 9.2 Continued

III. Psychosocial factors continued

   3. Does the client have any fear of overexertion?

   4. Are there any recent psychological test results available on the client that are relevant to the question of client psychological adjustment?

   5. Is there any agency or professional from whom the client is presently receiving psychological services?

   6. Has the client ever received professional treatment for a personal adjustment problem?

   7. Is the client taking any tranquilizers or sleeping pills?

   8. What is the client's marital status?

   9. Is the client living with his or her family?

   10. Does the client have any dependent age children?

   11. Will the most significant family members (e.g., spouse) be supportive of the client's rehabilitation plan?

   12. How does the client feel about his or her home environment?

   13. How does the client get along with other family members?

   14. Does the client have any close friends?

   15. Is the client satisfied with his or her social life?

   16. How does the client fill the hours of the day?

IV. Economic factors

   1. What is the client's primary source of support?

   2. In addition to this primary source of support, does the client have other sources of support?

   3. Does the client have any unpaid debts of significant size?

   4. Are there any current fixed living expenses, such as medication expenses, which cannot be reduced?

   5. Does the client have a worker's compensation case pending?

   6. Is the client receiving SSI or SSDI benefits?

   7. Does the client have any medical insurance?

   8. Is the client concerned about his/her economic situation?

V. Personal vocational choice considerations

   1. Is the client interested in vocational training?

   2. Is the client interested in any specific type of vocational training?

   3. Does the client have a specific vocational objective?

   4. Does the client have more than one potential vocational goal?

   5. How optimistic or pessimistic is the client about achieving each of the vocational goals?

   6. What does the client see himself or herself doing vocationally 5 years from now?

   7. What minimum salary would the client consider?

   8. Does the specific job task matter to the client?

   9. Does the client prefer to work collaboratively with other people or independently?

   10. Is the client willing to relocate geographically to acquire work?

Note. Adapted from *Intake Interview Skills for Rehabilitation Counselors,* by S. E. Rubin and R. C. Farley, 1980, Fayetteville: University of Arkansas, Rehabilitation Research and Training Center.

objectives that the person is considering. With knowledge of the individual's vocational goals, the physician is better prepared to assess the person's existing and potential physical functioning in light of the proposed objectives and make specific recommendations. In addition, the counselor should provide the examining physician with relevant social history information and medical records (e.g., records of hospitalizations in the last 6–8 months). Hospital records often supply useful information from routine "screening-type evaluations," such as physical examinations, urinalysis, blood count, chest X-ray, or blood chemistry. Older hospitalization records are relevant only to the extent that they provide information pertaining to conditions with a good possibility of recurrence, such as cancer (McCoy, 1972).

The examining physician should be informed of the type of medical feedback needed by the counselor. The following types of information should be requested: (a) a determination of the client's general health at present; (b) a description of the extent, stability, and prognosis of the present disability as well as any recommended treatment; (c) information on the present and future implications of the disability as it affects performance of essential job functions; and (d) a report of the presence of any residual medical conditions that, if untreated, could affect the individual during the rehabilitation process.

The rehabilitation counselor should provide the physician with a specific list of questions that need to be answered via medical evaluation. Using the case of Melinda as an example (see Melinda's case study for an example of the intake interview summary), the counselor would provide the following list of questions to the physician:

Pertaining to Diabetes

1. Can the client's diabetes be controlled at this time?
2. Is the client's current high blood sugar level related to failure to adhere to dietary regulations?
3. What work situations (e.g., varying number of hours worked from day to day, rotating shifts) should be avoided?
4. Can the client work 8-hour days and 40-hour weeks?
5. Is there any reason to delay placing the client on a job until her diabetes is controlled?

Pertaining to Rheumatoid Arthritis

1. Are there any current indications that the disease is in the active stage or beginning to move into the active stage?
2. If the disease is in a state of remission, is there much likelihood of the client's arthritis reentering the active phase in the near future? Distant future?
3. To what extent is the client's extension or flexing motion range restricted in her hands?
4. Can range of motion in the client's hands be increased by orthopedic surgery or physical therapy?

5. How far can the client walk at any time without getting excessively fatigued?
6. Should the client avoid certain work activities or daily living activities to reduce the possibility of additional joint damage?
7. Is the client likely to experience additional damage in the future that will further limit the function of the involved joints or involve additional joints?
8. Is the client physically capable of doing beautician's work? If not, why?

The preceding questions provide a model for rehabilitation counselors to follow when soliciting medical evaluation information. They demonstrate the counselor's need for relevant, comprehensive, and specific feedback from the physician. Again, using the case of Melinda for illustration, a model medical evaluation feedback report is presented from a physician. If medical reports fail to reach the standards demonstrated in Melinda's case study, the rehabilitation counselor is either providing insufficient guidelines to the physician or referring people to the wrong physician.

 ## Case Study: Melinda Bracken

Intake Interview Summary

Melinda Bracken is a 29-year-old married woman with two children, a 10-year-old daughter and a 3-year-old son. She lives in a metropolitan area with a population of 200,000. She came to the state rehabilitation agency seeking (a) medical services for rheumatoid arthritis and diabetes mellitus and (b) help in finding employment.

Melinda has had rheumatoid arthritis in her hands and feet since age 20. Five years ago her arthritis became so severe that she was having considerable difficulty walking and grasping. At that point she had surgery on both hands and both feet. Although the surgery improved her hands, it had little effect on her feet. Melinda reports that compared to 5 years ago, she is presently less restricted by her arthritic condition. Although her arthritis would be considered to be in the advanced stages, it appears to be currently inactive. Consequently, pain is not one of her major problems at present. However, her arthritis sometimes prevents her from standing and walking for extended periods. Melinda does not have total movement in her hands.

Melinda has had a moderate to severe diabetic condition since she was 24 years of age. She takes 50 units of insulin once a day and is supposed to limit consumption to 1,800 calories a day. However, her blood sugar level has been quite high lately. As a result, she must see a physician every 2 weeks until her blood sugar level stabilizes. Melinda's diabetic condition does not interfere with her ability to carry out her daily routine; however, overexertion can produce some type of diabetic reaction.

Melinda came to the interview well groomed with a neat and pleasant appearance, with the exception of her shoes. The arthritic disfigurement of her feet (large bumps) has caused her to wear canvas shoes with sections of the sides cut out. Because appearance is important to Melinda, she is bothered by the impression her shoes make on people.

(continues)

Melinda has been employed briefly three different times during the last year. Prior to that point, she never worked.

Melinda completed a cosmetology course a year ago in another state and obtained her hairdresser's license. Two of her jobs during the last year have been at beauty shops. Because of insufficient business, the first beauty shop job lasted only 4 days. The second job was a part-time job that lasted 6 weeks—from Thanksgiving to New Year's. That job terminated with the end of the increased holiday season business. Melinda never earned more than $250 per week as a hairdresser.

Melinda reported that she was able to set hair, but she was slower than the other beauticians. She figured out different ways to do things as a hairdresser because of the arthritis in her hands, and the outcome of her work was satisfactory. Standing on busy days in the beauty shop was rough on her. Washing hair was also difficult for her. However, she still felt she could do the job effectively, although at a slower pace.

In regard to vocational handicaps associated with her diabetic condition, Melinda has difficulty working certain hours. Her other job during the last year was at a fast-food restaurant. She worked there for about a month and earned minimum wage. Although she could handle the physical demands of the job, she found that night work disturbed her eating schedule.

Melinda likes to work with people. She works well with others and possesses the work personality needed to hold a job. Melinda has had no problems with supervisors or coworkers on any of her jobs. Her report of her experiences on her last three jobs suggests a brief but positive work history.

She was an average high school student, earning mostly B's and C's. Her favorite subjects were home economics, bookkeeping, and word processing. Melinda was married the summer following her high school graduation.

Melinda's primary motivation for seeking vocational rehabilitation services is economic. Although her husband is a construction worker with a net weekly income of approximately $500, he is rapidly becoming an alcoholic, and their marriage appears to be disintegrating just as rapidly. Melinda pointed out that during the last year his drinking has become progressively heavier, sometimes beginning on Friday evening and continuing throughout the weekend. It is not unusual for him to miss work on Monday as a result. He spends much of his money on alcohol and entertainment. Although he contributes some money for groceries and pays the rent and utility bills, many bills, including her medical bills, go unpaid. However, the majority of her medical bills are covered by her husband's hospitalization policy from work.

Overall, Melinda feels that her marriage is at a very low point. Concerned about the effects of her constant arguments with her husband on the children, she appears unwilling to tolerate the situation much longer and is seriously thinking of leaving her husband. He has told her that if she leaves he will not help support the children.

Although she currently expresses no psychological symptoms of stress or depression, her serious family problems get her down periodically. Fortunately, Melinda has two sisters living in the same city with whom she is very close. Although Melinda does not drive, adequate city bus service allows her to visit her sisters. They are both worried about her situation with her husband and support her desire to seek rehabilitation services and employment.

Melinda is confident that she can do hairdresser's work. Although Melinda has searched the newspapers for hairdresser openings for months, there have been none. She also has a second problem in this area: Melinda is not licensed for cosmetology in the state where she is currently residing. She is unable to cover the expenses of getting a license (travel, motel, fee, and model), which would be about $300.

If Melinda's marital situation continues to deteriorate, she may have three basic choices: (a) stay with her husband in an intolerable situation, (b) leave him and go on public assistance, or (c) get some kind of job so she can support herself and her two children. Melinda does not appear to be averse to vocational training, but she currently has little knowledge of feasible vocational alternatives to cosmetology.

Results of Medical Reports on Melinda Bracken

Although her rheumatoid arthritis appears to be in a state of remission, Melinda is experiencing some difficulty standing for extended periods and walking more than a quarter mile. Orthopedic surgery performed 5 years ago on her feet for removal of arthritic nodules (lime deposits) on the side of and below the first metatarsal phalangeal joint (big toe) and the fifth metatarsal phalangeal joint (little toe) has had little positive long-range benefit. Within 2 years following the surgery, the arthritic nodules returned.

Melinda currently has arthritic nodules on the side of her first metatarsal phalangeal joint on both feet protruding about ¾ inch (about the size of a half-dollar) and on the side of her fifth metatarsal phalangeal joint on both feet protruding about ½ inch (about the size of a quarter). Melinda has arthritic nodules on the bottom of the fifth metatarsal phalangeal joint on both feet protruding about ¼ inch (a little smaller than a quarter). Her toes on both feet are fixed in a hyperflexed position (hammer toes).

The condition of Melinda's feet coupled with the lack of proper footwear causes her difficulties with walking and standing. She wears canvas shoes with cutouts on the sides where necessary and has foam cushions stuffed between the nodules on the bottom of her feet. Although work requiring standing for long periods of time or much walking would not be recommended for Melinda, it is important that a referral be made to a podiatrist for proper footwear. Melinda needs molded shoes that would accommodate her arthritic nodules and remove the weight-bearing pressure from the nodules on the bottom of her toe joints for two reasons. First, proper footwear will prevent the development of corns on those nodules and, hence, the eventual development of ulcers, a very negative complication given her diabetic condition. Second, the molded shoes will help her stand longer and walk farther with less fatigue. Although shoes will cost between $250 and $350, they will last about 5 years. Additional surgery on her feet appears to be contraindicated because of the failure of the earlier surgery.

In the case of Melinda's hands, the previous orthopedic surgery was successful and resulted in restoring 90% of the movement to the first metacarpal phalangeal joints (where the fingers join the hand). However, the other two phalangeal joints (mid and upper finger) have subsequently become involved with arthritis. As a result Melinda has only a 40% extension of her fingers. Based on the earlier success of the hand surgery, orthopedic surgery on those joints followed by physical therapy for her fingers is recommended. Barring future recurrence of the arthritis, surgery and physical therapy could restore 60% of Melinda's hand movement.

Medical laboratory tests on Melinda suggest that the arthritis is near the "burn-out" stage. Proper medical care in the future, reduction of environmental stress, avoidance of physical exertion, and proper vocational placement will decrease the potential of reactivation of the arthritis.

(continues)

> If she follows suggestions for medical interventions and environmental modifications, Melinda should be capable of sedentary light work. Jobs requiring walking, standing, stooping, and kneeling should be avoided. Consequently, beautician's work would not be a very appropriate placement. Unnecessary physical stress on the legs and feet could reactivate the disease in the feet or activate it in the ankle or knee joints.
>
> Although the patient's diabetes is currently out of control, she should be able to stabilize her blood sugar level by monitoring her diet, keeping her activity level fairly consistent from day to day, and remaining under the supervision of a physician. The patient's difficult family situation, resulting in dietary and daily activity level violations, has exacerbated her diabetic condition. Regarding vocational placement, it would be wise to place Melinda in a daytime job in which the hours and activity level remain consistent from day to day.

Although state rehabilitation agency counselors are responsible for determining whether a person is eligible for services, they have access to medical consultants to help interpret the reports received from physicians. Medical consultation with regard to report interpretation can help counselors clarify issues such as the severity and progressive nature of the disability, the impact of the medical condition on vocational and daily living functioning, the potential for side effects of medication, and the availability of medical services for ongoing treatment.

Formal Psychological Evaluation

Although psychological evaluation is part of the rehabilitation process, it is not necessary to refer all clients to a psychologist for a battery of tests. Much relevant psychological information can be obtained during the intake interview or as part of the vocational evaluation process. Examples are observation of the person's verbal facility, general psychological state, and expressed feelings toward the disability and its effects. The counselor or the vocational evaluator could also independently administer certain standardized psychological and educational tests. With the exception of cases of mental retardation, learning disability, and emotional disturbance, which require formal psychological evaluation to determine client eligibility in the federal–state program, the responsibility for deciding on the extent of psychological evaluation lies with the counselor or vocational evaluator. Valid reasons for arranging for formal but nonrequired psychological evaluation include promoting greater client self-understanding or greater counselor understanding of the client and obtaining a better picture of the individual's functional capabilities and potential following onset of disabilities such as traumatic brain injury (Biller & White, 1989; Groth-Marnat, 1984; Power, 2006). Psychological test results also help to determine (a) the appropriateness of long-range vocational training and (b) the need for adjustment services. In addition, psychological test data may indicate that the counselor needs to confront the client regarding unrealistic vocational choices. When assessing clients with standardized paper-and-pencil instruments, such as interest or personality inventories, Power (2006) suggested two strategies for minimizing client apprehensiveness. First, the counselor could stress that completing such measures is a good way for clients to describe themselves to themselves. Second, the counselor could solicit and respond to any questions clients may have about the assessment measures.

When a formal referral is made to a psychologist, the counselor should provide the psychologist with a list of explicit questions to be addressed via the psychological evaluation. Failure to do so transfers the responsibility for determining the purpose of the psychological evaluation from the counselor to the psychologist. This inappropriate delegation of professional responsibility frequently leads to the administration of a "nonindividualized," standard battery of tests whose results are often of limited use to the rehabilitation counselor in the decision-making process (Maki, Pape, & Prout, 1979). Sample questions that could be sent to a psychologist are listed below:

1. Is a diagnosable emotional disorder present?
2. Should certain work stressors be avoided (e.g., frequent deadlines, multiple concurrent activities, working closely with others)?
3. What are the treatment recommendations and expected treatment outcomes?
4. What is the person's level of intellectual functioning?
5. Is a learning disability present?
6. What are the individual's aptitudes?

Vocational Evaluation

The purpose of vocational evaluation is to provide reliable and valid data regarding a person's (a) ability to work, (b) preferences for different types of jobs and work activities, (c) capacity to perform in a variety of vocational roles, and (d) need for training in specific and general skills required for success in employment (Caston & Watson, 1990). Roessler and Baker (1998) elaborated further:

> The rehabilitation counselor should expect vocational evaluation to (a) generate information on the client's current vocationally relevant levels of social, educational, psychological and physiological functioning; (b) estimate the individual's potential for behavior change and skill acquisition; (c) determine the client's most effective learning style; (d) identify jobs the client can do without additional vocational services; (e) identify educational or special training programs that might increase vocational potential; (f) identify potentially feasible jobs for the client with further vocational services; and (g) identify community support services that might augment job retention following successful client placement. Of course, a vocational evaluation does not supply all of the answers, and an evaluator does not have rehabilitation programming responsibility for

people referred by the rehabilitation counselor. Rather, similar to medical evaluation and psychological evaluation, vocational evaluation is yet another information resource that contributes to effective development of the rehabilitation program. (p. 83)

Not all people seeking rehabilitation services are referred for vocational evaluation. In fact, one study of a random sample of 185 individuals who were clients in a state vocational rehabilitation agency office indicated that only about 25% of the group were referred for a vocational evaluation (Caston & Watson, 1990). People involved in vocational evaluation have tended to be young, single, male, and not high school graduates. In addition, the majority of people in vocational evaluation have had more than one disability (Task Force #1, 1975). Many who participate in vocational evaluation can also be characterized as having little information on occupations and work demands and as learning by more direct means (i.e., by direct exposure to different work activities).

Preparing people for vocational evaluation involves two important steps. First, evaluators should communicate to clients the importance of their input throughout the evaluation process. In discussing empowerment, McAlees and Menz (1992) identified five building blocks of a productive evaluator–consumer partnership: (a) "recognized equality of all members," (b) "shared responsibility of both partners for planning and outcomes," (c) "acceptance of a goal or task orientation by both partners," (d) commitment to a "time limited relationship," and (e) maintenance of a "contractual relationship" (p. 216).

Research indicates that positive consumer changes are related to the empowerment philosophy in vocational evaluation. Farley, Bolton, and Parkerson (1992) demonstrated a self-directed evaluation approach titled "Know Thyself," which enables people with disabilities to interpret their own evaluation data and apply that knowledge in the selection of feasible vocational objectives. When coupled with a small-group occupation-exploration intervention, "Know Thyself" enabled participants to increase their self-confidence and career decidedness.

To promote consumer involvement, rehabilitation professionals should orient people with disabilities to the evaluation process itself. An effective orientation begins with a full explanation of the purpose and goals of the evaluation and a visit to the evaluation site before the person is actually scheduled for the evaluation. During the visit the person should meet the evaluator and discuss prospective evaluation tools and techniques (Grissom, Eldredge, & Nelson, 1990).

Although a wide range of disabilities are served by most vocational evaluation programs, the various programs "are not all equally equipped to assess the vocational potential of a diversified clientele" (Roessler & Baker, 1998, p. 84). To service a heterogeneous population, the vocational evaluation unit must have a large variety of verbal and nonverbal assessment instruments and approaches capable of providing meaningful information about intelligence level, vocational aptitudes, achievement, personality, and vocational interests on low-functioning as well as high-functioning individuals. These assessment instruments and approaches can be classified into standardized paper-and-pencil measures, work samples, situational assessment, and ecological assessment.

Paper-and-Pencil Measures

Psychological and educational tests designed to measure intelligence level, vocational aptitudes, achievement, personality, and vocational interests are widely used for diagnostic purposes with clients with disabilities (Cutler & Ramm, 1992; Power, 2006). Nadolsky (1994) pointed out that these types of tests

> have been used for vocational assessment purposes since the early 1900s—
> well before the discipline of vocational evaluation came into being.... Although not confined to [the discipline of vocational evaluation] ... such tests ... are extensively applied by vocational evaluators and remain an essential component of vocational evaluation's technology. (p. vii)

A number of tests in each category (intelligence, aptitudes, achievement, personality, and vocational interests) will be briefly described here. Some of the tests covered might be administered by the rehabilitation counselor or the vocational evaluator. At minimum, rehabilitation counselors need some familiarity with these tests (a few of which may not be totally paper-and-pencil instruments) because client results and interpretations based on any of them could appear in vocational evaluation reports used by rehabilitation counselors.

Intelligence Tests

Intelligence is a complex concept that appears to be easier to measure than to define. Many valid tests of general intelligence have been developed, but the construct they have been designed to measure has never been defined in a totally satisfactory manner (K. R. Murphy & Davidshofer, 1998). In fact, Neisser et al. (1996) pointed out that when two dozen prominent "intelligence" theorists were asked in the mid-1980s to independently define intelligence, two dozen somewhat different definitions resulted. Power (2006) pointed out that the "concept of intelligence common to all intelligence tests, however, is the ability to learn" (p. 162). Although they do not measure all aspects of intelligence, intelligence tests provide the most efficient means of assessing a person's general ability (Power, 2006). That index, which reflects the general learning ability of a person relative to his or her peers, can provide the rehabilitation practitioner with important information for rehabilitation planning purposes. This is because intelligence test scores tend to predict school achievement and indexes of postschool accomplishment, such as employment and wage-earning capability (Neisser et al., 1996). Although many instruments have been used to assess the IQ of clients in the evaluation phase, the following discussion will be limited to the *Wechsler Adult Intelligence Scale–Third Edition* (WAIS-III; Wechsler, 1997), the *Slosson Intelligence Test–Revised* (SIT-R; Slosson, 1998), and the *Revised Beta Examination–Third Edition* (Beta III; Kellogg & Morton, 1999).

"The WAIS-III contains 14 subtests grouped into a Verbal scale and a Performance Scale" (Sattler, 2001, p. 376). There are six standard Verbal subtests—Information, Digit Span, Vocabulary, Arithmetic, Comprehension, and Similarities—within the Verbal Scale. The overall Verbal IQ can be considered a measure of the individual's "ability to use verbal skills in reasoning and solving problems, and … capacity to learn verbal material" (Psychological Corporation, 1985, p. h).

The five standard Performance subtests—Picture Completion, Picture Arrangement, Block Design, Matrix Reasoning, and Digit Symbol–Coding—provide a measure of the individual's performance IQ. According to Groth-Marnat (1997), the performance subtests measure the individual's (a) "ability to integrate perceptual stimuli with relevant motor responses," (b) "capacity to work in concrete situations," (c) "ability to work quickly," and (d) "ability to evaluate visuospatial information" (p. 180).

According to Sattler (2001), two of the remaining three subtests—Symbol Search and Letter–Number Sequencing—"are designated as supplementary subtests because they contribute only to index scores which are essentially factor scores" (p. 376). The four index scores yielded by the WAIS-III are Verbal Comprehension, Working Memory, Perceptual Organization, and Processing Speed. The last remaining subtest, Object Assembly, "is designated as an optional subtest … [which can] provide useful clinical information about perceptual organization" (Sattler, 2001, p. 376).

Verbal, Performance, and Full Scale IQs are provided by the WAIS-III. The Full Scale IQ provides an index of the individual's overall performance on the test (Psychological Corporation, 1985). According to Wechsler (1997), the structure of the test allows for the use of the Performance subtests alone for individuals unable to comprehend or manage language and the use of the Verbal subtests alone for clients with severe visual or motor disabilities.

The *Slosson Intelligence Test–Revised* (Slosson, 1998) is an easily administered, individual, oral test of verbal intelligence. Designed as a quick screening test of intelligence, the SIT-R "taps skills in the following domains: vocabulary, general information, similarities and differences, comprehension, auditory, memory, and quantitative ability" (R. J. Cohen, Swerdlik, & Phillips, 1996, p. 321). The SIT-R can be administered in about 15 to 20 minutes. Correlations between the SIT-R and the *Wechsler Adult Intelligence Scale–Revised* Verbal IQ and Full Scale IQ have been found to be .88 and .81, respectively (Cohen et al., 1996). Power (2006) pointed out that because the SIT-R is an oral test,

> it can be used with individuals who are blind, have reading handicaps, have physical disabilities, cannot respond to paper-and-pencil tests, or cannot work effectively under the pressures of a timed test (e.g., those who are on heavy medication or are test anxious). (p. 173)

The *Revised Beta Examination–Third Edition* (Kellogg & Morton, 1999) is a nonverbal measure of general intellectual ability that is highly correlated with the Performance subtests of the WAIS-III. It is designed for use with adults (16 to 89 years old) suspected of having literacy problems or other language difficulties. The Beta III contains five subtests: Coding, Picture Completion, Clerical Checking, Picture Absurdities, and Matrix Reasoning. It is easy to administer and score and provides a quick assessment of adults' nonverbal intellectual abilities. Its uses include evaluating the employment readiness of potential new hires and determining appropriate placement of students in vocational schools (for more information on the Beta III, see the Harcourt Assessment Web site: http://harcourtassessment.com).

Aptitude and Achievement Tests

Much variability exists in the definition of the aptitude construct in the literature. Much of this variability appears to stem from lack of agreement as to whether a specific aptitude is in part innate or is totally developed through experiences of daily living (Parker, 1987). Most likely the scores an individual acquires on an aptitude test are the result of both nature and nurture factors. Droege (1987) provided the following purpose-oriented definition of aptitude tests that is very compatible with their function within the evaluation phase of the rehabilitation process:

> Aptitude tests measure occupational potentialities. They are useful in the selection of persons for referral to occupational training or to job openings for which neither training nor previous experience is required. They are also used in employment counseling for choice of vocational goals and planning for required training. (p. 170)

Achievement tests are directed at measuring what a person has learned in school or training. While achievement tests vary in their specific content focus, such as a test of reading comprehension or a test of punctuation skills, "they all serve a related function: to measure current skill level in a well defined domain" (Gregory, 1996). While aptitude tests attempt to assess the individual's potential for skill or knowledge acquisition (Power, 2006), achievement tests are directed at assessing how much an individual has learned already (R. M. Kaplan & Saccuzzo, 1993). In the achievement area, rehabilitation counselors would be very interested in the assessment of the verbal and numerical skills of the client. Reading and spelling skills are addressed under verbal achievement, while numerical achievement addresses factors such as "counting, reading number symbols, and performing written computations" (Power, 2006, p. 208).

One of the most frequently used aptitude tests in the vocational rehabilitation process is the *General Aptitude Test Battery* (GATB; U.S. Department of Labor, 1970). It has been "widely acknowledged [as] the premier test battery for predicting job performance" (Gregory, 1996). Developed by the U.S. Department of Labor in 1947, the GATB measures eight aptitudes via 12 timed tests (4 apparatus measures of finger and manual dexterity and 8 paper-and-pencil tests) (Droege, 1987; Gregory, 1996). The eight aptitudes, along with general intelligence, as defined by the U.S. Department of Labor (1979), are listed in Table 9.3, along with the GATB tests by which they are measured. Nine factor

TABLE 9.3
Aptitudes Measured by the *General Aptitude Test Battery*

Aptitude	GATB tests by which measured
Intelligence—General learning ability. The ability to "catch on" or understand instructions and underlying principles; the ability to reason and make judgments. Closely related to doing well in school.	Vocabulary, Arithmetic, Reasoning, Three-Dimensional Space
Verbal Aptitude—The ability to understand meaning of words and to use them effectively. The ability to comprehend language, to understand relationships between words, and to understand meanings of whole sentences and paragraphs.	Vocabulary
Numerical Aptitude—Ability to perform arithmetic operation quickly and accurately.	Arithmetic, Reasoning, Computation
Spatial Aptitude—Ability to think visually of geometric forms and to comprehend the two-dimensional representation of three-dimensional objects. The ability to recognize the relationships resulting from the movement of objects in space.	Three-Dimensional Space
Form Perception—Ability to perceive pertinent detail in objects or in pictorial or graphic material. Ability to make visual comparisons and discriminations and see slight differences in shapes and shadings of figures and widths and lengths of lines.	Tool Matching, Form Matching
Clerical Perception—Ability to perceive pertinent detail in verbal or tabular material. Ability to observe differences in copy, to proofread words and numbers, and to avoid perceptual errors in arithmetic computation. A measure of speed of perception, which is required in many industrial jobs even when the job does not have verbal or numerical content.	Name Comparison
Motor Coordination—Ability to coordinate eyes and hands or fingers rapidly and accurately in making precise movements with speed. Ability to make a movement response accurately and swiftly.	Mark Making
Finger Dexterity—Ability to move the fingers and manipulate small objects with the fingers rapidly or accurately.	Assembly, Disassembly
Manual Dexterity—Ability to move the hands easily and skillfully. Ability to work with the hands in placing and turning motions.	Place, Turn

scores (i.e., a score on each of the eight specific aptitudes and on general intelligence) are yielded by the 12 tests in the form of standard scores with a mean of 100 and a standard deviation of 20 (Gregory, 1996).

As on the WAIS-III, both verbal and performance tests are part of the GATB. Consequently, it is a long test to administer, typically consuming a 2-hour time period or longer (K. R. Murphy & Davidshofer, 1998). To identify occupations for which an individual has necessary aptitudes, a rehabilitation counselor can compare an individual's GATB factor scores to 66 Occupational Aptitude Patterns (OAPs) and approximately 500 Specific Aptitude Test Batteries (SATBs). "OAPs indicate the aptitude requirements for groups of ... [nonsupervisory] occupations [and SATBs] reflect aptitude requirements for specific occupations" (Droege, 1987, p. 173).

The *Woodcock-Johnson Psycho-Educational Battery–Third Edition* (WJ-III; Woodcock, McGrew, & Mather, 2001) was developed to measure cognitive abilities and academic achievement via a comprehensive set of individually administered tests. Consisting of two test batteries, the WJ-III can be used with both children and adults. The Cognitive Ability battery consists of 20 (10 standard and 10 supplemental) tests covering the following cognitive factors: Long-Term Retrieval, Short-Term Memory, Processing Speed, Auditory Processing, Visual Processing, Comprehension–Knowledge, and Fluid Reasoning. The Achievement Battery consists of 22 (12 standard and 10 supplemental) tests (Sattler, 2001). According to Sattler (2001), the achievement tests "are grouped into 19 different overlapping clusters, such as Broad Reading, Oral Language–Standard, Broad Math, Broad Written Language, and Academic Knowledge" (p. 586). It is rare to administer all of the WJ-III tests to an individual (Woodcock & Mather, 1989). In the rehabilitation process, the tests to be administered to a given person would be determined by the information needed for rehabilitation evaluation and planning purposes.

Woodcock and Mather (1989) described several uses of the *Woodcock-Johnson–Revised* (WJ-R), which directly preceded the WJ-III and would likely apply to the more recent version as well. Some uses that clearly relate to client evaluation and planning needs in the vocational rehabilitation process are as follows:

- The WJ-R can assist in making occupational choices, particularly when specific types of skills—such as reading or mathematics performance—are necessary for successful job performance.
- Information regarding the subject's strengths and weaknesses among the various abilities and skills measured in the WJ-R may be used to help develop an individualized, comprehensive service program in educational and vocational settings.
- WJ-R results can be helpful in determining the instructional needs for individuals working toward a General Equivalency Diploma (GED) or preparing to take a

minimum competency examination. In a rehabilitation setting, an appropriate service delivery program can be based
on data obtained from the WJ-R.

- Information obtained from administering the WJ-R may
be used to help an individual understand his or her present
status in cognitive abilities and academic skills and assist
in setting short- and long-term goals regarding education,
training, and vocational choices. (p. 8)

Other achievement tests frequently used by rehabilitation practitioners or
encountered in clients' vocational evaluation or psychological reports are the
Wide Range Achievement Test–Fourth Edition (WRAT-4) (see Power, 2006) and
the *Tests of Adult Basic Education,* Forms 5 and 6 (TABE 5 and 6) (see Cutler &
Ramm, 1992; Power, 2006).

The WRAT-4 (G. S. Wilkinson & Robertson, 2006) is the successor to
the WRAT-R (S. Jastak & Wilkinson, 1989) and the WRAT–3 (G. S. Wilkinson, 1993). Appropriate for persons ages 5 to 94, the WRAT-4 has a new
measure of reading achievement as well as measures of reading, spelling, and
math computation. As in previous versions of the WRAT, the Reading subtest
measures the individual's ability to recognize and name letters and pronounce
words out of context. The Spelling subtest measures the individual's ability to
write his or her own name and to write letters and words to dictation. The
Math Computation subtest measures the person's ability to count, read number symbols, solve oral problems, and perform written computations. Power
(2006) pointed out that the WRAT "is particularly helpful in assessing academic achievement when the client has not had recent educational experience
and the rehabilitation professional wants to determine basic reading and arithmetic capabilities for possible training" (p. 209).

The *Tests of Adult Basic Education,* Forms 5 and 6 (TABE 5 and 6; CTB/
McGraw-Hill, 1987), measure an individual's achievement in reading, mathematics, language, and spelling, the subject areas that adult basic education
programs address in order to prepare the person to function in society. The test
publisher (CTB/McGraw-Hill, 1987) indicates that the TABE

can be used to provide preinstructional information about an examinee's
level of achievement in basic skills, to identify areas of weakness in these
skills, to measure growth in skills after instructions, to involve the examinee in appraisal of his or her learning difficulties and to assist in preparing
an instructional program to meet the examinee's individual needs. (p. 1)

The TABE contains seven tests to measure the four content areas. Reading
grade level is measured through a vocabulary test and a comprehension test.
Mathematics grade level is measured through a mathematics computation test
and a mathematics concepts and applications test. Language is measured through
a language mechanics test and a language expression test. Spelling is measured
through a spelling test. Because the TABE has test forms at four levels of dif-

ficulty (i.e., Grades 2.6–4.9 to Grades 8.6–12.9) and a pretest to determine the level of test to administer, it is appropriate for use with a wide range of adults in regard to current level of academic achievement. With TABE results teachers can

> diagnose, evaluate, and successfully place examinees in adult education programs. In addition, correlations between TABE scores and scores on the Tests of General Educational Development (GED tests) provide a means of estimating scores on the GED tests based on scores obtained on TABE 5 or 6. (CTB/McGraw-Hill, 1987, p. 1)

Personality Tests

Personality tests are directed at assessing an individual's emotional, interpersonal, motivational, and attitudinal characteristics (Anastasi & Urbina, 1997). Power (2006) pointed out that personality assessment in the vocational rehabilitation process is directed at identifying those personality strengths or deficits that affect the individual's ability to adjust to particular work demands and environments. Although many paper-and-pencil self-report instruments have been used for assessing the personality of clients in the evaluation phase of the rehabilitation process, the following discussion is limited to the *Minnesota Multiphasic Personality Inventory–Second Edition* (MMPI-2; Butcher, Dahlstrom, Graham, Tellegen, & Kaemmer, 1989), the *California Psychological Inventory–Third Edition* (CPI-III; Gough & Bradley, 1996), the *16 Personality Factor Questionnaire–Fifth Edition* (16PF-5; Cattell, Cattell, & Cattell, 1993), and the *Emotional Problems Scales* (EPS; Prout & Strohmer, 1991).

Containing 567 affirmative statements to which the test taker responds true or false, the MMPI-2 includes 10 basic clinical scales—Hypochondriasis, Depression, Hysteria, Psychopathic Deviate, Masculinity-Femininity, Paranoia, Psychasthenia, Schizophrenia, Mania, and Social Introversion—plus seven validity scales, 12 supplemental scales (e.g., Ego Strength, Overcontrolled-Hostility, Social Responsibility), and 15 content scales (e.g., Social Discomfort, Family Problems, Work Interference) (Anastasi & Urbina, 1997; R. J. Cohen et al., 1996). The wide use of the original MMPI in rehabilitation settings (Kruz, 1987) is undoubtedly true of its successor, the MMPI-2. This personality inventory is useful for diagnosing an individual's social and personal maladjustment, including acute or chronic negative psychological states, such as depression, that can be associated with the onset of many physical disabilities (Power, 2006). Testing time ranges from 45 to 75 minutes (R. J. Cohen et al., 1996).

The *California Psychological Inventory–Third Edition* contains 434 items, almost half of which were taken from the MMPI. The test taker responds to each item as true or false. The inventory "was developed specifically for use with normal adult populations" (Anastasi & Urbina, 1997, p. 359). The CPI-III contains 20 scales that provide scores on personality dimensions associated with interpersonal behavior and social interaction (Anastasi & Urbina, 1997; Domino & Domino, 2006; K. R. Murphy & Davidshofer, 1998). "The basic goal of the

CPI is to assess those everyday variables that ordinary people use to understand and predict their own behavior and that of others" (Domino & Domino, 2006, p. 81). Scores on many of the scales can be useful for vocational assessment and planning purposes (Power, 2006). Examples include (a) the Sociability Scale, on which low scores are indicative of shyness and feelings of uneasiness in social situations, while high scores are indicative of being friendly and liking to be with people; (b) the Independence Scale, on which low scores are indicative of a lack of self-confidence and dependency on others, while high scores are indicative of self-sufficiency and resourcefulness; and (c) the Flexibility Scale, on which low scores are indicative of liking "a steady pace and well-organized life," while high scores are indicative of liking "change and variety" and being "easily bored by routine life and everyday experiences" (K. R. Murphy & Davidshofer, 1998, pp. 372–373). The CPI-III "can also be used to understand client maladjustments and to evaluate such specific problems as social immaturity and vulnerability to physical illness" (Power, 2006, p. 195). Testing time is approximately 1 hour (K. R. Murphy & Davidshofer, 1998). Groth-Marnat (1997) indicated that any of the following could be suggested if time to complete the CPI exceeds 1½ hours: (a) "major psychological disturbance such as severe depression or functional psychosis," (b) "low IQ combined with poor reading ability," or (c) "cerebral impairment" (p. 351).

The *16 Personality Factor Questionnaire–Fifth Edition* "contains 185 items responded to along a 3-point Likert Scale" (K. R. Murphy & Davidshofer, 1998, p. 378). It is suitable for use with persons 16 years of age or older with at least a fifth-grade reading level (Cohen et al., 1996). It yields scores on 16 bipolar primary personality factors and five global factors. Scores on many of the factors can be useful for vocational assessment and planning purposes (Power, 2006). Examples from the primary factors include (a) Factor A (Warmth), on which a low score indicates the individual is reserved, impersonal, and distant, while a high score indicates the person is warm, outgoing, and attentive to others; (b) Factor E (Dominance), on which a low score indicates the individual is deferential, cooperative, and avoids conflict, while a high score indicates one is dominant, forceful, and assertive; and (c) Factor H (Social Boldness), on which a low score indicates the individual is shy, threat sensitive, and timid, while a high score indicates the individual is socially bold, venturesome, and thick-skinned (K. R. Murphy & Davidshofer, 1998). Other primary bipolar factors include Reasoning, Emotional Stability, Liveliness, Rule-Consciousness, Sensitivity, Vigilance, Abstractness, Privateness, Apprehension, Openness to Change, Self-Reliance, Perfectionism, and Tension (Cohen et al., 1996; K. R. Murphy & Davidshofer, 1998). The five global factors that represent broader aspects of personality are Extroversion, Anxiety, Tough-Mindedness, Independence, and Self-Control (K. R. Murphy & Davidshofer, 1998).

The *Emotional Problems Scales* was designed to identify emotional problems and maladaptive behaviors among adolescents and adults with IQ scores between 55 and 83 (i.e., individuals with mild mental retardation and borderline intellectual abilities). It consists of two instruments, the Self-Report Inventory (SRI) and the Behavior Rating Scales (BRS), which are recommended to be used together as part of a comprehensive clinical evaluation. The SRI is a 147-item, paper-and-pencil test written at the fourth-grade reading level. The examinee responds to items with a "yes" (it generally describes me) or a "no" (it does not generally describe me). It contains items such as "I feel like a failure in life," "I lose my temper easily," "I have trouble falling asleep," and "I usually feel calm." If the test taker is incapable of reading the items, the examiner can read them to the examinee. It takes about 30 minutes to complete the SRI. Scores are yielded on five clinical scales: Thought/Behavior Disorder, Impulse Control, Anxiety, Depression, and Low Self-Esteem.

The BRS is a 135-item rating scale, which takes persons such as vocational evaluators, rehabilitation counselors, teachers, and work supervisors approximately 15 minutes to complete. Using a 4-point scale (*almost never, rarely, occasionally,* and *often*), raters indicate how often they have observed a client behave in ways such as the following within the last 30 days: "Pushes others," "Lies," "Avoids group activities," "Argues with those in charge," and "Says he or she is a bad person." Scores on the following 12 scales are yielded by the BRS: Thought/Behavior Disorder, Verbal Aggression, Physical Aggression, Sexual Maladjustment, Non-compliance, Distractibility, Hyperactivity, Somatic Concerns, Anxiety, Depression, Withdrawal, and Low Self-Esteem. Prout and Strohmer (1991) pointed out that several of the "scales are combined to form the Externalizing Behavior Problems scale and several other scales are combined to form the Internalizing Behavior Problems Scale" (p. 2).

Measures of Vocational Interests

Measuring the vocational interests of rehabilitation clients provides information that can be used to help identify jobs in which the client is likely to experience greater job satisfaction. Although knowledge of the match between the client's aptitudes and abilities and the skill demands of a job is important for predicting the likelihood of a client's satisfaction with a given job, that knowledge alone is often insufficient for vocational rehabilitation planning. It is also helpful to consider the match between the client's interests and the extrinsic and intrinsic rewards that can be acquired from the job.

A major function of interest inventories is to promote a client's vocational self-exploration. Many of the most recently developed interest measures provide the individual with opportunities to relate the detailed interest inventory results to occupational information, including data on job activities and environments that may be compatible or incompatible with those results. Although many measures of vocational interests are available, the following discussion is limited to the *Strong Interest Inventory,* Form T317 (Harmon, Hansen, Borgen, & Hammer, 1994); the *Self-Directed Search* (Holland, Powell, & Fritzche, 1994); the *McCarron-Dial Systems Vocational Exploration System* (McCarron & Spires, 1991); the *Wide Range Interest–Opinion Test* (Jastak & Jastak, 1979); and the *Reading-Free Vocational Interest Inventory* (Becker, 1981).

The *Strong Interest Inventory,* Form T317, is the latest edition of the *Strong Interest Inventory* (SII), which measures vocational interests. Published in 1985, the SII was a revised and expanded version of the *Strong Campbell Interest Inventory,* which was preceded by the *Strong Vocational Interest Blank* from 1928 (R. J. Cohen et al., 1996). The SII Form T317 contains "317 items measuring respondents' preferences for various occupations, school subjects, work–related activities, leisure activities, types of people, personal characteristics, and personal preferences" (K. R. Murphy & Davidshofer, 1998, p. 335). The items of the SII Form T317 are grouped into eight parts. Some parts require the respondent to indicate whether he or she likes, is indifferent to, or dislikes certain school subjects, "activities (e.g., making a speech, repairing a clock, raising money for charity), leisure activities, and day–to–day contact with various types of people (e.g., very old people, military officers, people who live dangerously)" (Anastasi & Urbina, 1997, p. 390). Other parts ask respondents "to express preferences between paired activities (e.g., dealing with things vs. dealing with people)" or "between all the possible pairings of four items from the world of work (i.e., ideas, data, things, and people)" (Anastasi & Urbina, 1997, p. 390). Finally, in part of the inventory, respondents are asked "to mark a set of self-descriptive statements 'Yes,' 'No,' or '?' " (Anastasi & Urbina, 1997, p. 390). The test taker's scores can be compared to the scores of employees who are satisfied with their jobs in each of 211 occupations (Anastasi & Urbina, 1997). The results of these comparisons indicate those occupations for which the greatest similarity exists between the interests of the test taker and the interests of people (e.g., bookkeepers, travel agents) "who are satisfied working in those occupations" (K. R. Murphy & Davidshofer, 1998, p. 343). The SII Form T317 results can be generalized to related occupations in the *Dictionary of Occupational Titles* (Anastasi & Urbina, 1997).

The *Self-Directed Search* provides a picture of an individual on six scales and yields an estimate of the person's resemblance to a particular personality type. The value of obtaining this picture rests on the theoretical assumption that work environments can be categorized according to the same personality types, and therefore information on the relationships between the personality of the individual and the personality of identified work environments can be helpful in the vocational choice process. The personality–job environment match generated by the SDS is based on the theoretical assumption that people are most satisfied in work roles that enable them to express personal preferences. In the SDS both personal orientation and work environments can be categorized as one of or a combination of the following six types: Realistic, Investigative, Artistic, Social, Enterprising, and Conventional (Holland, Powell, & Fritzche, 1994). Holland et al. (1994) defined the six personality types according to the jobs they like as follows:

- The *Realistic* type likes realistic jobs such as automobile mechanic, aircraft controller, surveyor, farmer, electrician. Has mechanical abilities, but may lack social skills ...

- The *Investigative* type likes investigative jobs such as biologist, chemist, physicist, anthropologist, geologist, medical technologist. Has mathematical and scientific ability but often lacks leadership ability ...
- The *Artistic* type likes artistic jobs such as composer, musician, stage director, writer, interior decorator, actor/actress. Has artistic abilities—writing, musical, or artistic—but often lacks clerical skills ...
- The *Social* type likes social jobs such as teacher, religious worker, counselor, clinical psychologist, psychiatric case worker, speech therapist. Has social skills and talents but often lacks mechanical and scientific ability ...
- The *Enterprising* type likes enterprising jobs such as salesperson, manager, business executive, television producer, sports promoter, buyer. Has leadership and speaking abilities but often lacks scientific ability ...
- The *Conventional* type likes conventional jobs such as bookkeeper, stenographer, financial analyst, banker, cost estimator, tax expert. Has clerical and arithmetic ability but often lacks artistic abilities ... (p. 6)

The Realistic type tends to be conforming, inflexible, practical, and uninsightful. The Investigative type tends to be analytical, intellectual, rational, and reserved. The Artistic type tends to be emotional, imaginative, nonconforming, and sensitive. The Social type tends to be cooperative, helpful, warm, sociable, and understanding. The Enterprising type tends to be adventurous, domineering, extroverted, energetic, and self-confident. The Conventional type tends to be careful, conscientious, inhibited, obedient, orderly, and practical. John Holland, the developer of the SDS, stated that "individuals seek environments that are congruent with their personality types; and such congruence enhances work satisfaction, job stability and achievement" (Anastasi & Urbina, 1997, p. 401).

The SDS was designed for self-administration, self-scoring, and self-interpretation by clients. The instrument contains two booklets. The client completes the assessment booklet to obtain a three-letter summary code (which shows the three personality types that most closely reflect the personality of the client), which "is then used to locate suitable occupations in the occupational classification booklet, *The Occupations Finder*" (Holland et al., 1994, p. 1). *The Occupations Finder* is used to find, among 1,335 occupations, those whose codes are similar to the respondent's summary code (Anastasi & Urbina, 1997).

Completing the SDS takes 40 to 50 minutes. Language used in the SDS is at an easy reading level (i.e., as low as fourth grade). The SDS was designed for use with persons ages 12 to 13 years or older and is inappropriate for use with individuals "who are grossly disturbed, uneducated, or illiterate" (Holland et al., 1994, p. 4).

There are four alternate forms of the SDS. Each was developed for use with a different population—one for high school students, college students, and adults (Form R); one for professionals and adults in transition from one occupation to another (Form CP); one for middle and junior high school students (Career Explorer version); and one for high school students and adults with limited reading skills (Form E). Form E requires only a fourth-grade reading level and uses *The Occupations Finder,* which focuses on jobs requiring lower levels of educational preparation (Holland et al., 1994).

The *McCarron-Dial Systems Vocational Interest Exploration System* is a computer-assisted, three-step process "designed to assist the individual in exploring the correspondence between his or her own preferences for working conditions and the requirements of specific entry level jobs" (McCarron & Spires, 1991, p. 1). In Step 1 the individual completes the 20-item VIE Work Preferences Questionnaire. For each item the individual chooses which of three working conditions he or she likes best. For example, for item 10 the individual would indicate whether he or she prefers work in which he or she is sitting, standing, or moving about most of the time. After the individual's responses on the 20 items are entered into a computer that "matches the individual's preferences with a sample of jobs involving those specified working conditions" (McCarron & Spires, 1991, p. 1), 6 to 10 possible jobs are identified. In Step 2 the individual examines information on each of these jobs (e.g., job duties, earnings, training needed) in Job Manuals contained in the VIE system. These manuals require about a fourth-grade reading level. In Step 3 the individual identifies the three jobs that he or she finds most attractive and proceeds to explore them further by comparing them in regard to "job duties, working conditions, abilities needed, related experience or training and personal limitations" (McCarron & Spires, 1991, p. 1). McCarron and Spires (1991) stated,

> The VIE System is designed to enhance the individual's capacity for occupational planning through the accomplishment of the objectives: (1) identifying personal preferences and individual orientation to work; (2) increasing knowledge of job requirements and opportunities; and (3) building decision-making processes based on a capacity to make comparisons between personal preferences and job requirements. The expected outcome of this vocational exploration process is the individual's improved ability to make realistic occupational decisions. (p. 2)

The *Wide Range Interest–Opinion Test* is a pictorial interest inventory that is suitable for use with many children and adults with low reading skills. It contains 450 pictures of individuals engaged in various job activities, sorted into groups of three (e.g., working as a hotel clerk, stopping fights, collecting carousel fares). For each set of three, respondents choose the activity they would most like to do and the one they would least like to do. The WRIOT yields scores on 18 occupational activity clusters (i.e., Art, Literature, Music,

Drama, Sales, Management, Office Work, Personal Service, Protective Service, Social Service, Social Science, Biological Science, Physical Science, Number, Mechanics, Machine Operation, Outdoor, and Athletics), which are also subdivided into areas of interest (i.e., liberal arts, business activities, services, the sciences, mechanical, outdoor, and sports) for ease of interpretation. For example, the mechanical area of interest consists of the Mechanics and Machine Operation occupational activity clusters (Jastak & Jastak, 1979). The WRIOT manual (Jastak & Jastak, 1979) provides a list of jobs associated with high scores on each of the occupational activity clusters. The WRIOT also yields scores on the following five attitudes-toward-work-conditions scales: Sedentariness, Risk, Ambition, Chosen Skill Level, and Sex Stereotype. According to Jastak and Jastak (1979, p. 72), high scores on each of the attitude dimensions indicate the following preferences in regard to working conditions:

Scale	Preference
Sedentariness	"sits mainly in one place on the job"
Risk	"takes on dangerous and risky jobs"
Ambition	"wants to improve self, income, status"
Chosen Skill Level	"works at shown level of difficulty"
Sex Stereotype	"prefers work formerly done by persons of own sex"

Scored either by hand or computer, the WRIOT can be administered to groups or individuals, with administration time ranging from 40 to 60 minutes. Jastak and Jastak (1979) pointed out the following advantages of the WRIOT over verbal-based interest inventories for use with persons with cognitive or psychiatric disabilities:

1. The WRIOT pictures are useful in the study of persons of good ability, but limited schooling and inferior reading ability.
2. The WRIOT may be used with young children and mentally retarded individuals who cannot read at all.
3. The WRIOT is applicable to emotionally disturbed persons who tend to misconstrue the meaning of printed directions or statements. (p. 2)

The *Reading-Free Vocational Interest Inventory* was designed for use with persons with learning disabilities or mental retardation ranging from age 13 to adult. It is a nonreading, 55–item vocational preference test. Each item contains three pictures showing individuals engaged in specific job tasks (e.g., "Servicing car with gas," "Delivering mail," "Constructing a wall") (Becker, 1981,

p. 6). For each item the examinee must choose the job task he or she would most like to perform. According to Becker (1981), the R–FVII items cover the types of occupational activities in which "persons with a learning disability or who are mentally retarded are proficient and productive" (p. 2). On average, it takes about 20 minutes for examinees to complete the inventory. Scores for male and female examinees are provided for the following 11 interest areas:

1. Automotive

2. Building Trades

3. Clerical

4. Animal Care

5. Food Service

6. Patient Care

7. Horticulture

8. Housekeeping

9. Personal Service

10. Laundry Service

11. Materials Handling

Each interest area is defined in the R–FVII manual. For example, automotive interest is defined as "preference for occupations dealing with parking, cleaning, polishing, lubricating, and refueling trucks, buses, and automobiles, and related servicing and maintenance activities" (Becker, 1981, p. 3). Becker provided the following as examples of jobs that would be suggested by a high score on the R–FVII Automotive interest occupational scale: "Service-station attendant, parking lot attendant, garage service man, car-wash worker, automobile body repairman helper, and tire recapper" (p. 3).

Work Samples

Work samples are designed so the individuals follow the procedures and use the tools and materials involved in actual jobs. According to experts in vocational evaluation, work samples may be used to assess a variety of constructs, such as vocational aptitudes, worker temperaments, vocational interests, hand dexterity, tolerance for standing or sitting, work habits and behaviors, learning styles, and understanding of written and oral instructions (Gice, 1985; B. Rosenberg, 1973). Botterbusch (1982) cited two explanations for the widespread use of work samples: (a) legislative mandates at a federal level to serve all people with severe disabilities and (b) the deceptive ease with which commercial work samples can be installed and implemented. He also noted the danger implicit in the second reason for using work samples.

The work sample movement originated in the late 1930s with the development of the TOWER System by the Institute for the Crippled and Disabled

(Pruitt, 1976, p. 10). Federal legislation was passed in the 1950s that appropriated funds for the development of work sample evaluation techniques (B. Rosenberg, 1973, p. 143). Between 1967 and 1980 several new work sample systems became available. They included the Valpar Component Work Sample Series; the JEVS Work Sample System, devised by the Philadelphia Jewish Employment and Vocational Service (JEVS); the Singer/Graflex Work Sample System; the Vocational Information and Evaluation Work Samples (VIEWS), also developed by Philadelphia JEVS; the Vocational Interest Temperament Aptitude System (VITAS), also developed by Philadelphia JEVS; and the Wide Range Employment Sample Test (WREST), developed by Guidance Association of Delaware (C. D. Brown, McDaniel, Couch, & McClanahan, 1994; Power, 2006; Pruitt, 1976). To provide at least a partial picture of the types of work samples included in these instruments, we describe Valpar and JEVS.

The Valpar Component Work Sample Series (Valpar) contains 16 self-contained work samples and three other activity units. An individual's performance on the work samples can help determine that individual's career potential "in jobs and job classifications described in the U.S. Labor Department's ... [latest] *Dictionary of Occupational Titles* and its related publications" (C. D. Brown et al., 1994, p. 49). Each work sample relates to one or more of the occupational requirement factors (worker traits needed to perform a job successfully) found in the U.S. Department of Labor's (1991b) *Revised Handbook for Analyzing Jobs* (C. D. Brown et al., 1994). These occupational requirements relate to factors such as aptitudes needed, physical demands one must be capable of meeting (e.g., standing, lifting, climbing, kneeling), and General Educational Development required (e.g., aspects of formal or informal education that "contribute to the worker's [a] reasoning development and ability to follow instructions, and [b] acquisition of 'tool' knowledge such as language and mathematical skills"; United States Department of Labor, 1991, p. 7-1).

Although not designed for use with any specific population, the Valpar work samples have been widely used in the vocational evaluation process with industrially injured workers. Because Valpar is a group of independent work examples rather than a vocational evaluation system, any number of its work samples can be administered in any order to a particular client (Botterbusch, 1987). The 16 work samples of the Valpar are as follows: Small Tools (Mechanical), Size Discrimination, Numerical Sorting, Upper Extremity Range of Motion, Clerical Comprehension and Aptitude, Independent Problem Solving, Multilevel Sorting, Simulated Assembly, Whole Body Range of Motion, Tri-Level Measurement, Eye-Hand-Foot Coordination, Soldering and Inspection–Electronic, Money Handling, Integrated Peer Performance, Electrical Circuitry and Print Reading, and Drafting. The time needed to complete each work sample varies from 15 minutes for Independent Problem Solving to 90 minutes for Small Tools (C. D. Brown et al., 1994).

The Philadelphia Jewish Employment and Vocational Service Work Sample System (JEVS) contains 28 work samples designed for use with special needs populations. The following work samples are found in the JEVS (not listed here in order of complexity):

Condensing Principle Drawing	Nut Packing
Blouse Making	Tile Sorting
Vest Making	Belt Assembly
Pipe Assembly	Sign Making
Resistor Reading	Budgette Assembly
Nail and Screw Sort	Washer Threading
Lock Assembly	Nut, Bolt, and Washer Assembly
Telephone Assembly	Payroll Computation
Computing Postage	Adding Machine
Grommet Assembly	Filing by Letters
Metal Square Fabrication	Proofreading
Ladder Assembly	Filing by Numbers
Union Assembly	Hardware Assembly
Collating Leather Samples	Rubber Stamping

Botterbusch (1987) pointed out that the "work samples are administered in order of complexity.... If a client is obviously not able to complete the work samples at one level, more complex work samples are usually not administered" (p. 93). Completion of the 28 work samples will usually take 6 or 7 days (Botterbusch, 1987). According to Botterbusch (1987), the "strongest points of the system are its stress upon careful observation and accurate recording of work behavior and performance factors" (p. 95).

The great increase in the number of commercial evaluation systems can be viewed both positively and negatively. On the negative side, purchasers can have difficulty determining which systems are appropriate for the people they serve. Indeed, very little reliability and validity data are available on some popular work sample systems (C. D. Brown et al., 1994). In fact, independent analyses of some commercial systems suggest that the validity of the measures may be far less than what is claimed in the promotional literature (Janikowski, Berven, & Bordieri, 1991). As Power (2006) stressed, the predictive validity of work samples is limited because they are only simulations and do not present the many other interpersonal and physical demands that are associated with a certain job. On the positive side, the existing competition among such systems for a large part of the market should logically lead to the refinement of systems in the direction of greater demonstrated predictive validity regarding appropriate vocational choices.

Smolkin (1973, p. 192) noted that not every work sample available in a particular facility should be administered to a person. Rather, work samples should be selected on the basis of (a) previously collected information regarding the individual's interests and (b) previously collected medical, psychological, educational, and work history information suggestive of the person's abilities and limitations. Crow (1973) demonstrated how previously collected data influence hypothesis formulation and evaluation via work samples:

> Early data may indicate interest in a particular area, such as welding, and psychological and medical data would not be contraindicative. A hypothesis would then be formulated that welding might be an appropriate vocation for the individual. This hypothesis could then be tested in a simulated or actual job tryout. (p. 33)

A number of advantages and disadvantages of work samples have been discussed in the vocational evaluation literature. Advantages include the following:

1. A work sample tends to look like work and therefore tends to hold the person's interest.
2. The individual gains increased self-understanding as a result of the opportunity to directly test the validity of preconceived skills and interests (Gelfand, 1966).
3. Actual work behavior can be observed by the evaluator.
4. A large number of areas can be evaluated—skills, interests, physical capabilities, and work behaviors (Gice, 1985).
5. Additional relevant medical information may be discovered, such as a client's difficulties using a prosthesis in a vocational task (B. Rosenberg, 1973).
6. Many prospective employers tend to prefer reports containing predictions based on work sample performance over other sources (Task Force #2, 1975).
7. Work samples provide an alternative to paper-and-pencil tests when such measures are inappropriate because a person has deficiencies in verbal or reading skills (Power, 2006).

The following are some disadvantages of work samples:

1. It is difficult to determine which work samples to construct because of the many possibilities.
2. The expense can be overwhelming if many different work samples are necessary, which is often the case because a variety of work samples

are needed to provide a well-rounded profile of the individual (Cutler & Ramm, 1992).

3. Work samples are time-consuming (evaluator must observe activity) and may require several days to complete (Cutler & Ramm, 1992).

4. Technical obsolescence is a problem in terms of accurately reflecting both the processes of jobs currently in the job market and advances in measurement technology pertinent to the work sample itself (Neff, 1985).

5. As basically a one-shot evaluation, work samples provide limited data for predicting performance in full-time (i.e., 8 hours a day, 5 days a week), competitive work positions (Meister, 1976).

6. Although work samples provide a picture of an individual's current performance level on a work task, they are limited in regard to predicting the person's potential level of performance on that task. Olshansky (1975) made the point clearly: "What a person can do as evidenced by work samples is not the same as what he can learn to do. Where a person is does not tell us where he can go!" (p. 48).

7. Work samples appear to yield better predictors of client performance in training than on posttraining jobs (Neff, 1985).

8. Significant differences may exist between the work sample setting and the industrial environment (Task Force #2, 1975, p. 57).

9. Because they are designed for easy use, work samples may be conducted by individuals with little background or training in vocational evaluation, which often leads to questionable results (Botterbusch, 1982).

10. Some work samples require intense effort over a period of several hours. Individuals with certain disabilities such as emotional problems are unable to concentrate on the same task for such a long time (Mulhern, 1981).

The purpose of work samples is to allow the comparison of a person's performance level on vocational tasks with relevant performance standards, usually referred to as *competitive norms* or *industrial standards*. Competitive norms can be developed by administering the work sample directly to workers on that particular job, by completing time and motion studies on the job, or by adopting preexisting industry standards. Because they are based on the performance of persons experienced at the task, industrial norms must be used cautiously. Both pure and applied research on motor learning and industrial performance indicates that people's effectiveness at motor skill tasks tends to improve rapidly during the first several trials and that progressive improvement continues to occur over several years of experience, although at a slower pace. Therefore, when using industrial norms, it would be wise to ask the question, "Can the client learn to perform the task at an acceptable rate?" (D. Dunn, 1976, p. 10).

People can also be allowed to practice a work sample as many times as necessary, until the person's potential to achieve a competitive employment performance level can be determined. In this situation, one must determine the amount of practice necessary for drawing valid comparisons (D. Dunn, 1976, p. 2). A protracted, built-in practice scheme would have to be approached cautiously, because it could unnecessarily increase frustration if care is not taken to determine by means of previous data the most appropriate work sample tasks to which a person should be assigned.

Situational Assessment

Situational assessment typically refers to the evaluation of an individual who is completing contract or simulated work on a job in a rehabilitation facility. When conducted in small, community-based programs, situational assessment is often limited to evaluating general employability factors (i.e., those worker behaviors needed for success, regardless of job held) because the work is largely of an unskilled nature, such as "unskilled assembly, packaging, and elementary clerical operations" (Neff, 1985, p. 180). Situational assessment can provide excellent insights regarding the person's general employability behaviors. Therefore, focus is placed on assessing the client's work potential in regard to factors such as ability to (a) accept supervision, (b) get along with coworkers, (c) stay on task, (d) sustain productivity for 8 hours, and (e) tolerate frustration. Specific questions such as the following can also be addressed: (a) How does the person respond to different types of supervision? and (b) Is the worker able to produce a sufficient quantity and quality of work?

Situational assessment has a variety of advantages and disadvantages. The following are advantages:

1. The person works regular working hours and is expected to relate to coworkers (Hoffman, 1972).
2. The person responds to realistic work quality and quantity expectations presented by a work supervisor.
3. A medium is provided in which styles of coping with people and tasks can be observed. Of course, as Power (2006) pointed out, the evaluator must have predetermined which work behaviors to observe and have a procedure for relating the observations to further assessment and rehabilitation planning.
4. During the process of situational assessment, the person is also learning how to play the role of worker, which enables the evaluator to assess a wide range of general and specific employability characteristics (Power, 2006).
5. Situational assessment does not provoke the type of test anxiety that is associated with more standardized evaluation methods (Brolin, 1982).

Several disadvantages of the situational approach have also been identified in the vocational evaluation literature:

1. Limited by available work contracts, the jobs available in community

facilities for assessment purposes typically consist of unskilled activities (Neff, 1985).

2. Sometimes facility personnel fail to establish and enforce rigorous quantity and quality standards consistent with industrial settings (Task Force #2, 1975).

3. Data collected during situational assessment may be impressionistic in nature and therefore difficult to quantify and interpret (Power, 2006).

4. People with higher level intellectual capabilities are unmotivated by the low-level work tasks associated with the situational approach (Brolin, 1982).

5. The simulated setting cannot provide the same variety of interpersonal and work demands as the actual job site.

Ecological Assessment

As the name clearly indicates, *ecological assessment* occurs in the natural setting in which the person is to function. In vocational evaluation, the natural setting would be the actual job site (or another similar actual job site) where the individual could potentially be a long-term employee. The goal is to evaluate the individual's capacity to meet the productivity demands of that setting at present (i.e., without any additional training or special on-the-job supports) or in the near future through the provision of training or on-the-job supports. These on-the-job supports can be artificial in nature (i.e., hiring a job coach to assist the evaluee/employee), natural (i.e., provided by the supervisor or coworkers in the setting without significantly changing their role), or some combination of both (e.g., transitioning from artificial to natural supports). Examples of ecological assessment can be seen in supported employment placements and in on-the-job evaluations.

Supported Employment

As a result of the supported employment movement, more people with severe disabilities are involved in ecological assessment. Ecological assessment is used to assess people who are unable to function at the worksite without support. Parker et al. (1989) stressed the need for on-site or ecological assessment for people with mental retardation (IQs of 55 or less), traumatic brain injury, chronic mental illness, or severe sensory disabilities.

Ecological assessment in a supported employment situation is qualitatively different from evaluation in a nonsupported employment situation in several respects. First, instead of occurring before placement and focusing solely on assessment of vocational readiness and feasible job–person matches, vocational evaluation in supported employment can occur after the person has assumed a particular job. Second, it is less of an evaluation to predict what a person cannot do than to predict what a person can do in a specific job setting with necessary social and vocational support systems in place. According to McAlees and Menz (1992), the trend toward supported employment models has required evaluators to concentrate on other issues such as (a) the need for worksite accommodations and supports, (b) the level of the person's independent living skills, and (c) the types of continuing services the person will need. In supported employment, the ecological assessment approach to evaluation involves the evaluator and the consumer in a closer working relationship at the job site to identify job modifications, supports, and training required to enhance the job–person match. Such ecologically based assessment can also greatly help rehabilitation professionals approach the "zero-exclusion" goal of placement—that is, finding places in community settings for all individuals with disabilities who want to work (Menchetti, 1991; Parker et al., 1989; Wesolek & McFarlane, 1992).

Costello and Corthell (1991) maintained that the rehabilitation facility setting has an important role in vocational evaluation for people entering supported employment. They recommended an initial staffing conducted at the rehabilitation facility involving the individual, family members, community support personnel, and agency workers. The staffing is dedicated to developing an assessment plan and securing the support of all key parties. Costello and Corthell also stressed that facility-based data collection provides valuable information regarding the person's learning style; social and vocational survival skills; quality of family support; and levels of specific job behaviors related to "proficiency, work rate, quality, preservation,... and physical endurance" (p. 81). Time spent in the rehabilitation facility completing evaluations preliminary to the ecological assessment of job–person interaction may also serve to allay the person's "potential fears and anxieties about working in the community" (p. 79).

On-the-Job Evaluation

On-the-job evaluation (OJE) provides an assessment of the functioning of individuals with disabilities in actual work settings where they are involved in activities presumed to be compatible with their vocational interests and skills. Focusing on a variety of variables, such as personality, attitudes, aptitudes, work traits, work skills, and physical capacities, on-the-job evaluations can occur within work stations in institutions, rehabilitation facilities, or business and industry. The person or employer may or may not receive remuneration for participating in on-the-job evaluation. Although such evaluations usually take between 1 and 2 weeks, the time period can "range from a day to a month or more" (Genskow, 1973, p. 22). Traditionally, it was recommended that OJE be used at the end of the evaluation process, with its selection based on the results of preceding evaluations (Genskow, 1973). However, emphasis on the place/train model in supported employment has underscored the importance of OJE early in the evaluation process. When supported employment placements and ongoing evaluation are possible, evaluations occurring in the actual worksite provide valuable insights into the person's coping skills and needs for further training (Wesolek & McFarlane, 1992).

Conducting an in-depth job analysis and a general job site inventory prior to placing a person in an on-the-job evaluation situation is recommended. For possible OJE placements in business and industry, the general job site inventory provides useful information about the size of the company, the types of work performed, and the nature of the work climate. The job analysis profiles job demands in regard to (a) vocational aptitudes such as manual dexterity, (b) physical demand characteristics of the job, and (c) interpersonal demand characteristics of the job. A person's ability to perform the particular job would suggest performance adequacy on many other jobs with similar job analysis profiles. On the other hand, if the individual is incapable of performing the job effectively, those specific job demands that appear to be problematic could be identified. This would provide a guide to (a) jobs with a more appropriate job analysis profile for the person, such as those that require a lower level of the specific vocational aptitudes in question, or (b) on-site supports or training required to enable the person to perform the job (Rogan & Hagner, 1990).

Several advantages and disadvantages of the on-the-job evaluation approach have been identified in the rehabilitation literature. Several of the indicated advantages are as follows:

1. The OJE site provides an opportunity to assess the person in the natural conditions of the worksite, thereby enabling the evaluator to observe how the person responds to the environment and the environment to the person (Parker et al., 1989). Evaluating the person in the actual work setting improves the accuracy of predictions regarding the types of job functions that the person performs well or poorly.
2. It gives the individual an opportunity for self-evaluation of performances, such as producing at specific rates of quantity and quality, reporting to work on time, and responding to supervision (Genskow, 1973).
3. On-site supervisors can supplement the evaluator's judgments with information from their perspectives regarding the person's suitability for a job or jobs (Genskow, 1973).
4. An OJE site comes equipped for the performance of a job task and thereby eliminates equipment costs to the evaluation program (Genskow, 1973, p. 23).
5. A positive recommendation from an actual work supervisor helps in later attempts to place the person with an employer who has a similar position open.

Disadvantages of on-the-job evaluation include the following:

1. Opportunities for on-the-job evaluation are often difficult to find or develop in the community (Cutler & Ramm, 1992).
2. Supervisors employed at the workplace may be reluctant to devote their time to the evaluation process or may be inclined to view the

person being evaluated simply as a source of inexpensive help (Hoffman, 1972).

3. Standardized procedures for evaluating the person's performance, including reference to normative scores, are often not available at OJE sites (Cutler & Ramm, 1992).

4. Premature placement in an OJE may exacerbate the person's fears and anxieties about working in the community (Costello & Corthell, 1991).

5. It is a very time-consuming evaluation technique (Nadolsky, 1973, p. 313).

The Vocational Evaluation Plan

A concrete vocational evaluation plan should be developed before beginning vocational evaluation activities. The quality of the vocational evaluation plan will greatly depend on the relevance and specificity of those questions provided to the work evaluator at referral. Examples of the type of feedback that the counselor should request are (a) how an individual responds under specific sets of circumstances, (b) what the individual can do best, (c) what the individual's greatest difficulty is, and (d) how the individual can be expected to perform following a specified treatment program. General questions such as, "Does the person have work potential?" invite general answers such as, "The client has potential for competitive employment." Provision of relevant and specific questions by the rehabilitation counselor to the vocational evaluator should facilitate the development of a vocational evaluation plan that is specific to the needs of the person being referred.

The Vocational Evaluation Report

The vocational evaluation process should culminate in an effective, comprehensive report that provides data relevant to the development of an appropriate rehabilitation plan. Therefore, such reports should not be characterized by vague or ambiguous recommendations. Instead, they should clearly specify feasible vocational objectives for the person to pursue. In a survey of 47 vocational evaluation plans written for people receiving rehabilitation services, Caston and Watson (1990) reported that only 13 reports (28%) included a specific job recommendation. Most of the reports concentrated on recommendations for service provision in areas such as counseling, work adjustment, and vocational training. Evaluators can avoid the lack of vocational specificity found in Caston and Watson's survey by following several recommended topical outlines for the comprehensive evaluation report (Cutler & Ramm, 1992; S. Thomas, 1986). Following a brief discussion of why the person was referred for evaluation, the report should contain (a) disability and other background information,

(b) transferable skills based on prior work history, (c) behavioral observations and their relevance to vocational functioning, (d) results of psychometric tests or work samples, (e) information relevant to daily living or social functioning skills, (f) a summary of the aforementioned data, and (g) recommendations for the individual's vocational rehabilitation program that include vocational options for the person to consider.

In a study of vocational evaluation reports, Crimando and Bordieri (1991) identified five factors that influence the perceived quality of a finished report: rehabilitation utility, report specificity, style and readability, jargon and grammar, and length. Reports with high utility provided (a) specific information regarding the person's readiness to work, (b) adequate documentation for job options considered appropriate for the person, and (c) responses to the initial referral questions.

The Pre–Rehabilitation Plan Evaluation Summary Report

After the person has completed all necessary components of the pre–rehabilitation plan evaluation phase, the rehabilitation counselor should be in a position to develop an evaluation report. That report provides the foundation for the counselor's "guided facilitation" of the individual's vocational self-exploration during the planning stage, which is the next phase of the rehabilitation process. To be of value, the report must truly integrate evaluation information necessary for understanding the person's current and potential strengths and weaknesses in regard to alternate vocational goals. One potential report format for summarizing the evaluation, the Information Processing Summary Form (see Figure 9.1), should facilitate the synthesis of information regarding the evaluation procedures used, the person's disability and resulting limitations, the person's strengths, the potential vocational goals, and the anticipated necessary services for achieving each goal. The summary provides information on pertinent vocational considerations in terms of physical, intellectual, and emotional categories. Research on vocational adjustment illustrates the importance of the vocational goals identified in these plans. Dawis and Lofquist (1984) cited one study showing a significant relationship between eventual job satisfaction and correspondence of the job held with the jobs in the counseling plan.

Trends in Vocational Evaluation

Evaluation personnel have demonstrated the effectiveness and efficiency of strategies such as the Rehabilitation Initial Diagnosis and Assessment of Clients (RIDAC) unit developed by Arkansas Rehabilitation Services. The RIDAC

(text continues on p. 332)

INFORMATION PROCESSING SUMMARY FORM

Name _____   Date _____

1. Potential vocational goals suggested by consideration of evaluation data:

   a. Most optimal vocational goal: _____

      Already suggested by client?   ☐ Yes   ☐ No

      i. Supporting evaluation data regarding physical functioning:

      _____

      _____

      _____

      ii. Supporting evaluation data regarding psychosocial functioning:

      _____

      _____

      _____

      iii. Supporting evaluation data regarding educational–vocational functioning:

      _____

      _____

      _____

      iv. Special considerations (e.g., economic, transportation, housing, childcare, placement needs):

      _____

      _____

      _____

(continues)

FIGURE 9.1. Information Processing Summary Form.

b. Next most optimal goal: _____

Already suggested by client?   ☐ Yes   ☐ No

  i. Supporting evaluation data regarding physical functioning:

_____

_____

_____

  ii. Supporting evaluation data regarding psychosocial functioning:

_____

_____

_____

  iii. Supporting evaluation data regarding educational–vocational functioning:

_____

_____

_____

  iv. Special considerations (e.g., economic, transportation, housing, childcare, placement needs):

_____

_____

_____

c. Third most optimal vocational goal: _____

Already suggested by client?   ☐ Yes   ☐ No

(continues)

FIGURE 9.1. *Continued.*

i. Supporting evaluation data regarding physical functioning:

_____

_____

_____

ii. Supporting evaluation data regarding psychosocial functioning:

_____

_____

_____

iii. Supporting evaluation data regarding educational–vocational functioning:

_____

_____

_____

iv. Special considerations (e.g., economic, transportation, housing, childcare, placement needs):

_____

_____

_____

2. Services needed for achieving each vocational goal:

   a. Most optimal vocational goal: _____

      i. Pertaining to physical functioning: _____

      ii. Pertaining to psychosocial functioning: _____

(continues)

FIGURE 9.1. *Continued.*

iii. Pertaining to educational–vocational functioning: _____

iv. Services for special considerations: _____

b. Next most optimal vocational goal: _____

   i. Pertaining to physical functioning: _____

   ii. Pertaining to psychosocial functioning: _____

   iii. Pertaining to educational–vocational functioning: _____

   iv. Services for special considerations: _____

c. Third most optimal vocational goal: _____

   i. Pertaining to physical functioning: _____

   ii. Pertaining to psychosocial functioning: _____

   iii. Pertaining to educational–vocational functioning: _____

   iv. Services for special considerations: _____

3. Vocational goals expressed by the client that appear to be inappropriate based on evaluation data. Discuss.

_____

_____

_____

_____

FIGURE 9.1. *Continued.*

unit produces an initial diagnostic evaluation of a client who has applied for rehabilitation services. Provided in a single location by a qualified team of evaluators, this initial diagnosis is adequate both for determination of eligibility and for program planning. Members of the RIDAC unit staff include a "coordinator, physician (part–time), psychiatric consultant (part–time), nurse (part–time), psychologist, two vocational evaluators, and a project counselor" (Bolton, 1982, p. 61). The RIDAC team travels to different locations throughout the state to provide this comprehensive evaluation service on a widespread basis.

Computers can speed the process of vocational evaluation by decreasing the amount of time required to record, analyze, interpret, and print evaluation results. Two examples of computer-based vocational evaluation systems include the Apticom and Computerized Assessment (COMPASS). Computer-based systems enable the person to complete a battery of aptitude and interest measures, with the resulting profile related to the requirements of different jobs (C. D. Brown et al., 1994).

The Apticom computer-based test battery contains an aptitude test covering 10 aptitudes closely related to those on the *General Aptitude Test Battery,* a vocational interest test covering 12 interest areas, and an education skills test covering language and math. The computer scores all the tests in the battery and, based on those scores, develops a list of jobs found in *The Enhanced Guide for Occupational Exploration–Second Edition* (Maze & Mayall, 1995) that are compatible with the individual's measured interests and occupational aptitudes. The entire test battery takes about 2 hours to complete (C. D. Brown et al., 1994).

COMPASS yields scores from 17 measures, 12 of which are computer-based subtests. The remaining five non–computer-based measures include three work samples and two surveys (C. D. Brown et al., 1994). C. D. Brown et al. (1994) stated that analysis of the examinee's results on the 17 measures of COMPASS will

> yield 17 factor scores which form a Worker Qualifications Profile reflecting client level of performance in the areas of Data–People–Things, GED reasoning, math and language, and the 11 Department of Labor aptitudes (General, Verbal, Numerical, etc.). Many of these factors are computed by combining the results of several of the subtests. (p. 13)

It takes approximately 70 minutes to administer the entire battery (C. D. Brown et al., 1994). Based on the examinee's 17 factor scores, optimal occupations can be identified for the examinee in the *Dictionary of Occupational Titles* (U.S. Department of Labor, 1991a).

Applications of vocational evaluation have also expanded to provide more in-depth assessment for specific groups, such as special needs students in high school special education programs. Vocational evaluation of students in special education should incorporate traditional academic assessment as well as commercial vocational evaluation systems, paper-and-pencil tests, work simulations, and ecological approaches. The results from these different methods can be combined in an individualized transition plan outlining the educational, vocational, and placement steps required to facilitate achievement of the student's vocational goal (National Information Center for Children and Youth with Disabilities, 1993).

Vocational evaluation is also a flexible process that is capable of accommodating the needs of individuals who are being served in greater numbers, such as people with head injuries. Weinberger (1984) pointed out that evaluation of individuals with head injuries is particularly complicated because of damage to "diffuse areas of the brain. As a result, each patient presents a unique set of symptoms and functional deficits" (p. 250). Rather than traditional standardized tests, flexible use of work samples and extended work tryouts are recommended (Weinberger, 1984). In elaborating on the flexible use of work samples, Kaiser and Modahl (1991) observed that it is possible to gather important information simply by watching the person complete the sample without relating the outcomes to normative scores. This more clinical use of the work sample clarifies what the person can do or can learn to do over time, which may allow the evaluator to "screen in" rather than "screen out."

Concluding Statement

The vocational rehabilitation process can be divided into four phases: (a) the evaluation phase, (b) the planning phase, (c) the treatment phase, and (d) the termination phase. This chapter comprehensively described the evaluation phase, which yields information needed for the determination of (a) appropriate vocational choice alternatives, (b) existing and potential client competencies related to such, and (c) necessary services for realizing vocational alternatives. Evaluation is a multistep process, with people participating only in those steps either required or deemed necessary by the rehabilitation counselor.

A comprehensive evaluation begins with an intake interview, the function of which is the gathering of a social history. The general or specialist medical examination is another evaluation component that is used to (a) establish the presence of a physical disability, (b) provide physical functioning information, and (c) determine the types of activities precluded by the disabling condition. For eligibility or service provision purposes in public rehabilitation programs, some applicants may also need to complete a formal psychological evaluation. The formal psychological evaluation can also yield insights into aptitudes, interests, and self-perceptions that relate to vocational functioning. Some people also participate in vocational evaluation, which is composed of a number of different techniques focusing specifically on the assessment of client vocational aptitudes, academic achievement, vocational interests, work attitudes, personality traits, behavior, and skills related to potential vocational roles.

Because the steps of the evaluation phase occur sequentially in many cases, they combine in a cumulative manner to provide a well-rounded picture of the person's assets, preferences, and needs. Each step is capable of providing a certain type of information. When additional evaluation is necessary, the information yielded by earlier steps should not be ignored but rather integrated with subsequently acquired information to more fully understand the person's situation.

Finally, the value of an economical evaluation strategy is stressed. This is necessary because as one moves through the evaluation process, each subsequent step can be more costly than the previous one. Therefore, the evaluation process should be comprehensive within each step while utilizing only those steps necessary for optimal understanding of a person.

Chapter 10

Planning the Rehabilitation Program

The vocational planning process begins after the counselor has collected all of the necessary client information during the evaluation phase. Based on appropriate combinations of intake, medical, psychological, and vocational evaluation data, the counselor initiates the first step of the planning process, a thorough vocational analysis of client work potential. During that process, the counselor integrates the available information on the individual's physical, psychosocial, and intellectual assets and liabilities in relation to potential vocational objectives. Upon completion of the vocational analysis, the counselor should be well prepared to facilitate a similar type of information processing on the client's part.

The sequential integration of the vocational analysis with client goal setting is depicted in Figure 10.1, the crux model. Vocational analysis and goal-setting activities suggest services needed if clients are to procure employment compatible with their physical capacities, aptitudes, interests, and personality (i.e., work in which personal characteristics are compatible with job demands and activities).

The purpose of Chapter 10 is twofold. First, a model counselor vocational analysis procedure is described. Second, the importance of involving the client in rehabilitation planning and procedures for involving the client in the planning process are discussed.

Developing Hypotheses: The Vocational Analysis

To develop insights regarding the client's current and potential functioning, the counselor must collect and process an extensive amount of information. If counselors can answer most of the questions listed in Table 9.1 in Chapter 9, they can generate preliminary predictions regarding both appropriate vocational objectives for their clients and the rehabilitation services necessary for attainment of those objectives.

To demonstrate the vocational analysis procedure, we continue with the case of Melinda, introduced in Chapter 9. A summary of the information known by the counselor at the completion of the intake interview is provided in Table 10.1. Having acquired that information from Melinda, her counselor can begin to think diagnostically and prognostically. Through such thinking, the counselor will generate hypotheses regarding potential vocational outcomes for Melinda.

The most significant unanswered question at this point in the counseling process is, Does the client have an appropriate vocational goal? The answer to that question depends greatly on the congruence of the person's vocational interests, aptitudes, physical capacities, personality characteristics, and existing and potential vocational skills with the vocational goal. If little such congruence exists, the next meaningful question becomes, Why has the client selected that goal?

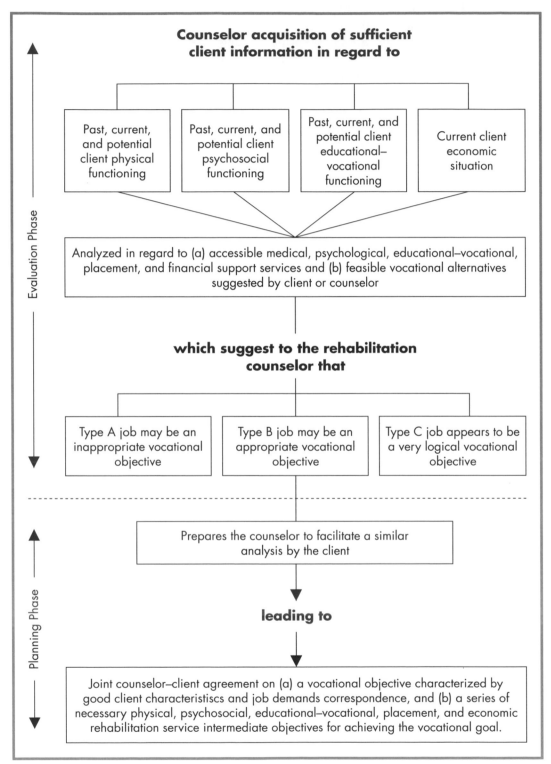

FIGURE 10.1. The crux model. From *Case Management and Rehabilitation Counseling: Procedures and Techniques* (4th ed., p. 45), by R. Roessler and S. E. Rubin, 2006, Austin, TX: PRO-ED. Copyright 2006 by PRO-ED, Inc. Reprinted with permission

TABLE 10.1
Summary of Melinda's Intake Interview

Area	Key points
Physical factors	Rheumatoid arthritis and diabetes mellitis; arthritis in hands (mild) and feet (severe). Problems standing and walking. Diet important.
Educational–vocational factors	High school graduate. Previously licensed as a cosmetologist. Brief but successful work history.
Psychosocial factors	Can meet social demands of work. Worried about effect of arthritis on appearance. Marital situation tense.
Economic factors	Facing financial difficulties.
Personal vocational choice considerations	Enjoyed work as a cosmetologist but may be open to other vocational alternatives.

There are many reasons for selecting an inappropriate vocational goal. Some clients may simply be unaware of the general entry requirements or daily demand characteristics of a particular occupation. Others may be demonstrating an insufficiently developed self-concept in their vocational choice. To the extent that the self-concept explanation pertains, readiness to choose a specific vocation would be questionable. Instead, services directed at helping the client clarify his or her vocational self-concept must be initiated (Savickas, 2005). Hence, the reason for an unrealistic vocational objective on the individual's part becomes an important early consideration.

In Melinda's case, information available on her physical functioning brings into question the appropriateness of her vocational goal of cosmetology (see Melinda's case study in Chapter 9). One could hypothesize that the poor fit is the result of Melinda's lack of awareness of more suitable vocational goals. Hence, the counselor's identification of more appropriate vocational alternatives for a person at Melinda's current as well as potential functional levels becomes highly significant. Fortunately, good references exist to help counselors and clients identify vocational alternatives. These include the O★NET (http://online.onetcenter.org), the *Dictionary of Occupational Titles* (U.S. Department of Labor, 1991, 2003), the *Enhanced Occupational Outlook Handbook* (Farr & Ludden, 2003), *The Guide for Occupational Exploration* (Farr, Ludden, & Shatkin, 2001), the annually published *Occupational Outlook Handbook* (e.g., U.S. Department of Labor, 2004), and *The Worker Traits Data Book* (Mayall, 1994). Counselors may also wish to administer Holland's *Self-Directed Search* (Form R; Holland, Powell, & Fritzche, 1994), which enables them to use accompanying reference material such as the *Dictionary of Holland Occupational Codes* (G. Gottfredson & Holland, 1996).

Use of the O*NET

The online O*NET (http://online.onetcenter.org) enables counselors and clients to generate valuable information from vocational interest assessments, self-report skill inventories, data-driven job–person matches, job descriptions (i.e., summary reports), and linkages to websites such as the Job Accommodation Network (JAN). After completing a self-report skill analysis and reviewing job titles related to their skill profiles, clients can link to the JAN website (http://www.jan.wvu.edu) and identify job accommodations and recommended vendors using the SOAR (Searchable Online Accommodation Resource) connection. Clients can print information from the O*NET self-assessments and job descriptions and from the Searchable Online Accommodation Resource to add to their vocational portfolio. Job descriptions in the O*NET are organized in terms of the Standard Occupational Classification (SOC) system, which the federal government uses to classify job titles into 23 categories such as "installation, maintenance, and repair occupations" (49) and "production occupations" (51) (Farr & Shatkin, 2004).

With assistance from her counselor, Melinda could access the O*NET website and begin a process of vocational self-exploration. This self-directed approach to investigating the feasibility of other jobs would enable Melinda to expand her range of options, thus encouraging her to consider employment in areas other than cosmetology. O*NET would list these job options as a result of Melinda's completing the self-report skill search. If she was not satisfied with the information available in the O*NET on job duties, Melinda and her counselor could turn to the *Dictionary of Occupational Titles* (online or in printed form) for further information.

Use of the *Dictionary of Occupational Titles*

The client and counselor can use the *Dictionary of Occupational Titles* (DOT) (http://www.occupationalinfo.org) to become familiar with the task demands of over 12,000 jobs. Each job in the DOT is described in detail and is assigned a nine-digit code for identification purposes. The first three digits code each job in regard to occupational category, division, and group. The jobs in the DOT are divided among the following nine occupational categories (the first digit of the code):

0/1 Professional, technical, and managerial occupations

2   Clerical and sales occupations

3   Service occupations

4   Agricultural, fishery, forestry, and related occupations

5   Processing occupations

6   Machine trades occupations

7   Benchwork occupations

8   Structural work occupations

9   Miscellaneous occupations

For each occupational category, the DOT provides a list of subcategories (occupational divisions, as indicated by the second digit of the three-digit code), such as the following found under Service Occupations:

30 Domestic service occupations

31 Food and beverage preparation and service occupations

32 Lodging and related service occupations

33 Barbering, cosmetology, and related service occupations

34 Amusement and recreation service occupations

35 Miscellaneous personal service occupations

36 Apparel and furnishings service occupations

37 Protective service occupations

38 Building and related service occupations

Each occupational division is further divided into homogeneous occupational groups (the third digit of the code). For example, barbering, cosmetology, and related occupations are subdivided among the following:

330 Barbers

331 Manicurists

332 Hairdressers and cosmetologists

333 Make-up occupations

334 Masseurs and related occupations

335 Bath attendants

338 Embalmers and related occupations

339 Barbering, cosmetology, and related service occupations

The second three digits report the functional demands of each job in regard to worker relationships with data, people, and things. "Every job requires a worker functioning to some degree in relation to data, to people, and to things" (Mayall, 1994, p. 7). A rating for every job on each of the three areas is provided through use of the following scales:

Data (4th digit)	People (5th digit)	Things (6th digit)
0 Synthesizing	0 Mentoring	0 Setting Up
1 Coordinating	1 Negotiating	1 Precision Working
2 Analyzing	2 Instructing	2 Operating–Controlling
3 Compiling	3 Supervising	3 Driving–Operating
4 Computing	4 Diverting	4 Manipulating
5 Copying	5 Persuading	5 Tending
6 Comparing	6 Speaking–Signaling	6 Feeding–Offbearing
	7 Serving	7 Handling
	8 Taking Instructions–Helping	

As can be observed in each list, the lower the number (rating), the more complex the functional demand. Finally, the third three-digit set merely aids in discriminating among closely related jobs within the same occupational group. For example, the codes for Cosmetologist, 332.271-010, and Cosmetologist Apprentice, 332.271-014, differ only on the last digit.

From the DOT, the counselor can learn about the job function of a beautician to assess the appropriateness of Melinda's vocational goal. For example, the counselor can select the job title "cosmetologist" online or find the job in the DOT and read the following definition:

332.271-010 Cosmetologist (personal ser.) alternate titles: beautician; beauty culturist; beauty operator; cosmetician

Provides beauty services for customer: Analyzes hair to ascertain condition of hair. Applies bleach, dye, or tint, using applicator or brush, to color customer's hair, first applying solution to portion of customer's skin to determine if customer is allergic to solution. Shampoos hair and scalp with water, liquid soap, dry powder, or egg, and rinses hair with vinegar, water, lemon, or prepared rinses. Massages scalp and gives other hair and scalp-conditioning treatments for hygienic or remedial purposes [Scalp-Treatment Operator (personal ser.) 339.371-014]. Styles hair by blowing, curling, trimming, and tapering, using clippers, scissors, razors, or blow-wave gun. Suggests coiffure according to physical features of patron and current styles, or determines coiffure from instructions of patron. Applies water or waving solutions to hair and winds hair around rollers, pin curls and finger-waves hair. Sets hair by blow-dryer or natural-set, or presses hair with straightening comb. Suggests cosmetics for conditions, such as dry or oily skin. Applies lotions and creams to customer's face and neck to soften skin and lubricate tissues. Performs other beauty services, such as massaging face or neck, shaping and coloring eyebrows or eyelashes, removing unwanted hair, applying solutions that straighten hair or retain curls or waves in hair, and waving or curling hair. Cleans, shapes, and polishes fingernails and toenails [Manicurist (personal ser.) 331.674-010]. May be designated according to beauty service provided as Facial Operator (personal ser.); Finger Waver (personal ser.); Hair Colorist (personal ser.); Hair Tinter (personal ser.); Marceller (personal ser.); Permanent Waver (personal ser.); Shampooer (personal ser.).

Given Melinda's physical limitations, the counselor should be concerned with a beautician's involvement in tasks requiring finger dexterity and eye–hand coordination, such as cutting and trimming hair, shampooing hair and scalp, winding hair around rollers and fingers, and scalp massaging. In addition, many of these activities are done while standing. Because of the standing and finger dexterity demands of cosmetology, the counselor must identify more appropriate vocational alternatives for Melinda.

Concerns about the physical demands of cosmetology are reinforced in information presented in the second three-digit set in the code number. The first two digits, which indicate the data and people demands of cosmetology, should not present problems for Melinda. The data functioning level is rated at 2, which indicates that a beautician must be able to analyze data for purposes of decision making. The second digit, 7, refers to the demands of cosmetology in terms of working with people. The people rating of 7 indicates that a beautician's work emphasizes serving people rather than leading or supervising. However, the third digit, 1, suggests hand and finger dexterity demands that exceed Melinda's capacities in a full-time employment situation.

Because Melinda has already qualified for the job by passing a beautician's license examination, one could hypothesize that she could handle many other jobs that do not call for higher ratings than 2 on data and 7 on people. In fact, she might be able to handle more complex people functions. Because of her arthritis, however, she would have difficulty sustaining good performance on jobs requiring a 1 level on things. Hence, a counselor who knows what work the client has performed successfully in the past and the data, people, and things demands of those jobs, as well as what work the client wants to do in the future, is in a good position to use the DOT to generate vocational alternatives.

To identify additional occupational possibilities for Melinda, the counselor can review the broad occupational category of service occupations under which cosmetology is subsumed. The counselor may also wish to survey other DOT occupational categories holding some promise for the client. In Melinda's case it appears that clerical and sales occupations (2) might be appropriate given her aptitudes in bookkeeping and business (identified in the intake interview; see Chapter 9) and her interests in working with people in a service capacity. However, clerical and sales positions should be selected carefully to avoid jobs with manual and finger dexterity demands that exceed Melinda's capacities. A long, detailed list of clerical, sales, and service occupations is provided in the DOT. By reviewing these jobs, the counselor can identify several additional job possibilities for Melinda, such as Companion (309.677-010), Ticket Taker (344.667-010), Cashier (drugstores, theaters, restaurants, small shops, etc.) (211 .462-010), Receptionist (237.367-038), Motel/Hotel Desk Clerk (238.367-038), and Teacher Aide II (249.367-074). Again, any of the job possibilities must provide working conditions for Melinda that do not exacerbate her arthritic condition. Melinda could also guide her search for job possibilities based on her interests as well as her ability to perform job tasks. Two good resources for such a search are the *Guide for Occupational Exploration* (Farr et al., 2001) and Holland's *Self-Directed Search* (Holland et al., 1994).

Use of *The Guide for Occupational Exploration*

In the third edition of *The Guide for Occupational Exploration,* Farr et al. (2001) present job descriptions of 1,000 jobs that represent most of the employment opportunities in the U.S. economy. Grouped into 14 occupational areas (artistic, entertainment, and media; science, math, and engineering; plants and animals; law, law enforcement, and public safety; mechanics, installers, and repairers; construction, mining, and drilling; transportation; industrial production; business detail; sales and marketing; recreation, travel, and other personal services; education and social service; general management and support; and medical and health services), these job descriptions offer a wealth of information for Melinda. For example, she could select the area that includes cosmetology—specifically, recreation, travel, and other personal services—and examine related jobs. Because Melinda enjoyed cosmetology, she could expect to enjoy other jobs in the same occupational area. Again, with the counselor's help, she could review and select vocational alternatives to allay her fears that she might have no other vocational goals than cosmetology to pursue in her rehabilitation plan. Melinda can use two approaches to using the *Guide* to find additional job possibilities. As noted previously, she can locate cosmetology in an occupational area of interest or she can use the alphabetic index at the back of the *Guide*.

Using *The Self-Directed Search*

Another avenue open to Melinda for exploring vocational options, which will require some additional assistance from her counselor, is to complete *The Self-Directed Search* (SDS; Holland et al., 1994). The purpose of the SDS is to help individuals clarify their vocational personalities in terms of preferences for realistic, investigative, artistic, social, enterprising, or conventional occupations. People with a realistic inclination like to use machines, tools, and things, whereas investigative types prefer exploring and understanding things or events. Artistic people like to read, write, and participate in musical or artistic activities, and people with a social preference enjoy teaching and therapeutic activities. The enterprising person enjoys persuading or directing others, and the conventional type prefers to follow orderly routines and have clear standards.

An efficient and cost-effective vocational interest assessment, the SDS produces a profile of the person's vocational preferences in terms of a three-letter code corresponding to the six types, specifically, R (realistic), I (investigative), A (artistic), S (social), E (enterprising), and C (conventional). Holland's system is based on the premise that all jobs are comprised of some combination of these six types (RIASEC) and that the goal of vocational counseling is to help people find a match between personality and job types. For example, the code for an accountant is CRI; thus, individuals with a CRI high point or Holland code would enjoy the work of an accountant. Of course, their success as an accountant would depend on their ability and training level.

In Melinda's case, her Holland high point code is social–enterprising–artistic (SEA), which is consistent with the code for cosmetologist. The S reflects Melinda's interest in working with people, and the E reflects her inclination to guide or direct people, as in helping them select appropriate hair colors and styles. A scan of the Dictionary of Holland Codes reveals approximately 50 other job options with the SEA code; Melinda may wish to consider whether any of those possibilities suggest new vocational hypotheses for her. For example, Melinda may wish to consider jobs involving teaching, counseling, advising, case management, social work, or other functions in the field of personal service.

The Occupational Outlook Handbook

Following the development of a list of vocational hypotheses based on reviews of the O*NET, DOT, *Guide for Occupational Exploration,* and SDS, rehabilitation clients and counselors may need additional information about employment projections, educational preparation, typical functions, and wage or salary levels in order to compare different jobs. Information pertaining to specific jobs is available in *The Occupational Outlook Handbook* (U.S. Department of Labor, 2003; see also http://www.bls.gov/OCO) and the *Enhanced Occupational Outlook Handbook* (Farr & Ludden, 2003). Details about jobs in printed resources apply only in general, of course, and are no substitute for the knowledge that counselors possess about specific positions in their local communities (Hein, Lustig, & Uruk, 2005).

The Worker Traits Data Book

Comparisons of occupational options are also possible using *The Worker Traits Data Book* (Mayall, 1994). This book provides ratings (information beyond that found in the DOT) on every job found in the DOT in regard to minimal aptitude levels needed, physical demands of the job, environmental conditions, and worker temperaments associated with performing the job well (e.g., temperament for adapting to a variety of work situations).

Each job is rated regarding the extent to which it requires the person to possess each of the following aptitudes: General Learning Ability (G), Verbal Aptitude (V), Numerical Aptitude (N), Spatial Aptitude (S), Form Perception (P) ("The ability to perceive pertinent detail in objects or in pictorial or graphic material"), Clerical Perception (Q) (e.g., "The ability to perceive detail in verbal or tabular material"), Motor Coordination (K), Finger Dexterity (F), Manual Dexterity (M), Eye–Hand–Foot Coordination (E), and Color Discrimination (C).

Knowing that Melinda was capable of performing successfully as a cosmetologist suggests that, at minimum, she would have the aptitudes to perform other jobs requiring the same or lower aptitude levels, with the exception of those reduced by her disability (e.g., Motor Coordination, Finger Dexterity, Manual Dexterity, and Eye–Hand–Foot Coordination). Table 10.2 provides the reader with an opportunity to compare the necessary minimal aptitude levels (rated on a 5-point scale with 1 highest and 5 lowest) for each of the six alternative jobs identified in the previous discussion of the DOT with those required for Cosmetologist. The motor and dexterity aptitudes are omitted from Table 10.2 because, to accommodate Melinda's arthritis, all of the jobs were selected for the list based on their low functional demands on things (of data, people, and things). The comparative data in Table 10.2 suggest that a person who has the aptitude levels of a cosmetologist would also have the aptitude levels necessary for performing any of the six occupational alternatives with the possible exception of Cashier, which requires a higher numerical aptitude. In regard to the physical demands rating, Cosmetologist was rated as *light work* (on the following 5-point scale: sedentary work, light work, medium work, heavy work, and very heavy work). All six of the identified alternative job possibilities were rated as either *sedentary* or *light work* in regard to physical demands and appear to be within Melinda's physical capabilities in terms of level of strength and endurance needed. With respect to environmental conditions, none of the six alternative occupations contains any environmental conditions (e.g., "Contact with water or other liquids or exposure to non-weather-related humid conditions") (Mayall, 1994, p. 18) that could be seen as incompatible with Melinda's disabilities. Therefore, in regard to environmental conditions, they are all more desirable for Melinda than Cosmetologist, which requires frequent contact with water (e.g., washing hair), an environmental condition that is not compatible with the arthritis in Melinda's hands.

As indicated earlier, each job in *The Worker Traits Data Book* (Mayall, 1994) is also rated for significant temperaments needed (i.e., work situations associated with the job to which the worker must be capable of adapting). The possible temperaments (and their letter codes) involved in any particular job include Directing, Controlling, or Planning Activities of Others (D); Performing Repetitive or Short-Cycle Work (R); Influencing People in Their Opinions, Attitudes, and Judgments (I); Performing a Variety of Duties (V); Expressing Personal Feelings (E); Working Alone or Apart in Physical Isolation from Oth-

TABLE 10.2

Aptitudes and Temperaments Associated with Potential Occupations for Melinda

Occupation	Aptitudes						
	G	**V**	**N**	**S**	**P**	**Q**	**C**
Cosmetologist (V, P, J)	3	3	4	3	2	4	2
Companion (V, P)	3	3	4	4	4	4	5
Ticket Taker (R, P)	4	4	4	4	4	4	4
Cashier (V, P, T)	3	3	3	4	3	2	5
Receptionist (R, P)	3	3	4	4	4	3	5
Motel/Hotel Clerk (V, P)	3	3	3	4	4	3	5
Teacher Aide II (V, P, J)	3	3	3	4	4	3	5

Note. Temperaments required for each job are in parentheses. (See text for explanation of letter codes.) From *The Worker Traits Data Book* (p. 29), by D. Mayall, 1994, Indianapolis, IN: JIST. Copyright 1994 by JIST Works. Reprinted with permission.

ers (A); Performing Effectively Under Stress (S); Attaining Precise Set Limits, Tolerances, and Standards (T); Working Under Specific Instructions (U); Dealing with People (P); and Making Judgments (J) (Mayall, 1994). Table 10.2 also shows the temperaments (in parentheses) required for each job. As can be observed in Table 10.2, none of the temperaments needed by any of the jobs appears to be incompatible with Melinda's personality traits. However, given that there are some differences among the jobs in regard to temperaments required, it is likely that Melinda will prefer some jobs over others.

Balancing Job Aptitudes and Job Satisfaction

As is readily apparent, the information collected during the evaluation phase enables the counselor and client to use occupational information resources to assess the appropriateness of the client's expressed vocational objectives. Through this analysis, by focusing on aptitudes and functional demands, the counselor and client can find other possible jobs. However, level of work adjustment depends on more than the individual's ability to perform the job. As was previously alluded to in the analysis of temperaments associated with different occupations, adjustment also depends on whether the job contains the types of activities and experiences the individual likes. To restrict one's focus solely to aptitudes is to attempt to predict work adjustment with only half of the data. The other half of the data pertains to what the individual likes and wants to gain from work (Roessler & Rubin, 2006).

Research on the theory of work adjustment (Dawis, 2005; Dawis & Lofquist, 1984) clearly indicates that, depending on the specific job, work provides individuals with more or less access to sources of satisfaction in six areas: achievement, comfort, status, altruism, safety, and autonomy. Each of these areas of satisfaction covers specific human needs. Of course, each person is different in terms of his or her preferences for different types of need satisfaction present in work. For example, two human needs addressed within the achievement area are the need to utilize one's abilities and the need for achievement. Human needs addressed within the comfort area are the needs for activity, independence, variety, compensation, security, advancement, and good working conditions. Three status needs are recognition, authority, and social status. The human needs addressed within the altruism area include the need to do work without feeling it is morally wrong and to do work that benefits other people. Human needs addressed within the safety area include working for a company that administers policies fairly, hires bosses who back up their workers, and makes sure that bosses train their workers well. The needs for creativity and responsibility are two needs emphasized within the autonomy area (Dawis, 2005; Dawis & Lofquist, 1984; S. Rosen, Weiss, Hendel, Dawis, & Lofquist, 1972).

Patterns of these various needs have been generated for 148 different occupations. The value of occupational information pertinent to types of personal satisfaction possible in different jobs can be demonstrated with the case of Melinda. Knowing that Melinda enjoyed the occupation of cosmetologist directs the counselor to the beautician profile (S. Rosen et al., 1972) as an optimal one for Melinda. The beautician profile indicates that individuals in the job are able to (highly descriptive characteristics appear in capital letters):

- MAKE USE OF THEIR INDIVIDUAL ABILITIES (ability utilization)
- TRY OUT THEIR OWN IDEAS (creativity)
- HAVE WORK WHERE THEY DO THINGS FOR OTHER PEOPLE (social service)
- Get a feeling of accomplishment (achievement)
- Have good working conditions (working conditions)
- Have steady employment (security)
- Make decisions on their own (responsibility)
- Receive recognition for the work they do (recognition)
- Do *not* tell other workers what to do (authority)

Although information from the O★NET and the DOT would suggest that Melinda may not have the physical capacities to be a beautician, it is obvious that any vocational alternatives should provide access to the aspects of that work that she enjoyed. Hence, the counselor must identify other occupations characterized by ability utilization, creativity, and social service. Any suggested alternative must be considered tentative, however, with confirmation requiring the presentation of all possibilities to Melinda during the goal-setting interview.

Client Involvement in Rehabilitation Planning

An effective rehabilitation goal-setting interview increases the probability that people with disabilities will select occupations compatible with their needs and abilities. Setting rehabilitation goals follows the same problem-solving logic that pervaded the vocational analysis. However, goal setting requires active client involvement in the consideration of potential vocational choices. Only through involvement in a counseling relationship can the vocational planning process become a psychologically relevant experience for the rehabilitation client. This involvement must possess certain qualities if it is to result in greater client satisfaction with and improved outcomes from rehabilitation services. For example, based on a qualitative analysis of responses of 1,346 rehabilitation clients to a question about ways to improve their vocational rehabilitation services, Hein et al. (2005) concluded that counselor characteristics such as respect, attention, and expertise were critical to the establishment of a good working alliance (Donnell, Strauser, & Lustig, 2004; Lustig, Strauser, Rice, & Rucker, 2002). From the clients' perspectives, expertise in the job placement area included counselor knowledge of (a) job options in the community and (b) client interests and abilities so that a proper job–person match resulted.

Instead of discussing counselor factors, Goldberg (1992) elaborated on client characteristics that affect motivation to participate in the development of a vocational rehabilitation plan. His research indicated that client involvement in vocational planning depends greatly on whether the client has a positive "rehabilitation outlook," which includes a desire to "return to work, a realistic assessment of capacities and physical limitations, and optimism about future recovery" (Goldberg, 1992, p. 170). Therefore, to create a firm foundation for potential vocational plans, the rehabilitation counselor must involve the individual in exploration of both the world of work and the person's expectations regarding rehabilitation services. The counselor should use occupational information to help the person acquire a clearer picture of the work environment in terms of day-to-day demands, possible rewards, and potential frustrations. The resulting identification and understanding of possible work roles for the client should better enable that individual to determine the best match between his or her characteristics, marketable skills, and personal preferences, and available jobs with or without specific job modifications (Jome & Phillips, 2005; Kosciulek, 2003a; Waterman, 1991).

Meaningful participation in the rehabilitation planning process enables individuals to make informed vocational choices (Kosciulek, 2004b). Informed vocational choices result when clients can do the following:

1. Identify potential vocational objectives
2. Evaluate these objectives for personal relevance, desirability, and practicality
3. Select a vocational objective to pursue in rehabilitation

4. Understand which counseling, restoration, and training steps need to be taken to reach the goal
5. Follow through on the plan to successful placement and long-term tenure on the job

As a context in which to conduct rehabilitation planning with people with disabilities, the counselor is reminded of important conclusions regarding the shortcomings of current theories of vocational development:

1. Due to lack of opportunity resulting from economic deprivation and discrimination, many people with disabilities have been "excluded from exercising options that most nondisabled persons take for granted" (Conte, 1983, p. 325).
2. Previous life experiences, as they affect skill and self-concept development, require special consideration in counseling with people with disabilities (Savickas, 2005).
3. Vocational development theories focusing on personal traits and characteristics present only a partial picture of the factors influencing vocational behavior; environmental factors are often far more significant in determining the degree of handicap, particularly if proper job accommodations are not provided (Szymanski, Enright, Hershenson, & Ettinger, 2003).
4. Counselors must broaden their perspective regarding the vocational development of people with disabilities beyond a traditional focus on a job to a comprehensive one involving career and needed social changes (i.e., client advocacy) (H. McCarthy & Leierer, 2001).

Based on his research on vocational development of people with disabilities, Goldberg (1992) offered some additional insights relevant to rehabilitation planning. He first distinguished between the differential experiences of people with acquired disabilities and those of people with congenital disabilities. According to Goldberg's findings, people with acquired disabilities (spinal cord injury, heart disease, cancer, or kidney disease) tend to choose postdisability vocational objectives that are consistent with their previous occupations. The person's predisability identity, as manifested in vocational plans, interests, and values, has a greater impact on selection of a vocational goal than does severity of the disability.

Continuity is in evidence when people with congenital disabilities make a vocational choice but, in this case, their choices fall into occupational groups that are consistent with parental aspirations, social class, and gender (L. Gottfredson, 2005). Influences such as social discrimination or cognitive disorders can, however, impair the person's ability to make realistic choices. As Goldberg (1992) noted, social stigma experienced by young people with visible disabilities is a force that continuously impinges on their career development.

Promoting Client Self-Understanding

Rehabilitation counselor effectiveness in planning can be enhanced through use of concrete procedures designed to facilitate client self-understanding. These procedures should be directed at helping people clarify both potential vocational goals and the relationship of personal strengths and limitations to those vocational alternatives.

Reviewing Available Client Information

Rehabilitation planning begins with the person's exploration of two significant areas: (a) evaluation results pertinent to the vocational plan and (b) vocational areas of potential interest. Through the use of relevant forms, such as the Information Processing Summary Form (see Figure 9.1 in Chapter 9), the counselor can guide client consideration of evaluation data and occupational alternatives. Presenting a summary of client data (physical, psychosocial, educational–vocational, and special considerations) in relation to vocational alternatives, the Information Processing Summary Form provides a basis for client goal setting. Counselor–client discussion of the form's contents in light of expressed and potential client vocational interests should stimulate establishment of realistic directions and objectives for the rehabilitation plan. For demonstration purposes, Melinda's Information Processing Summary Form is presented in Figure 10.2.

Identifying and Comparing Vocational Choice Alternatives

Research in the area of career development has demonstrated that a sound vocational choice process includes self-assessment, including assessment of the impact of factors that interrupt career development, such as a disability (Kosciulek, 2003a); exploration of job/career possibilities; development of a job seeking plan; and self-evaluation of outcomes of the job seeking plan (Jaffe & Scott, 1991; Saks, 2005). Therefore, the client and counselor should discuss the client's (a) vocational goals, (b) perception of self as a worker, (c) perceptions of the impact of disability, and (d) perceptions of barriers to employment.

The self-exploration process can be facilitated through the use of a balance sheet (Janis & Mann, 1977). The first balance sheet step involves the person in ranking vocations in order of desirability. The pros and cons for each of the top alternatives are then processed through the balance sheet in terms of four categories: gains and losses for self, gains and losses for others, approval or disapproval by others (social approval), and self-approval or self-disapproval.

(text continues on p. 358)

INFORMATION PROCESSING SUMMARY FORM

Name ___Melinda Bracken_____ Date _____

1. Potential vocational goals suggested by consideration of evaluation data:

   a. Most optimal vocational goal: ___Receptionist_____

   Already suggested by client? ☐ Yes ☑ No

      i. Supporting evaluation data regarding physical functioning:

      ___Work demands would not overtax manual dexterity and standing capacities. Sed-___

      ___entary job with minimal manual function. Regular hours a plus.___

      ii. Supporting evaluation data regarding psychosocial functioning:

      ___Client has basic skills for job but is willing to complete short courses or on-___

      ___the-job training. Client has a history of good work adjustment regarding re-___

      ___sponding to supervision, working cooperatively, and working independently.___

      iii. Supporting evaluation data regarding educational–vocational functioning:

      ___Client has high school education, organizational skills, and ability to deal with the___

      ___public. Job has low demands on manipulation of things. Client has average or___

      ___above average intelligence and is good with data and people. Provides a "good"___

      ___match with previously demonstrated vocational interest patterns.___

      iv. Special considerations (e.g., economic, transportation, housing, childcare, placement needs):

      ___Investigate minor job modifications. Client needs financial support during train-___

      ___ing and childcare.___

      _____

                                                                      (continues)

FIGURE 10.2. Completed Information Processing Summary Form for Melinda Bracken.

b. Next most optimal goal: <u>Motel/hotel desk clerk</u>

  Already suggested by client?   ☐ Yes ☑ No

  i. Supporting evaluation data regarding physical functioning:

  <u>Regular hours; day shift mandatory. Light work requiring a moderate activity</u>

  <u>level.</u>

  ii. Supporting evaluation data regarding psychosocial functioning:

  <u>Client enjoys working with people. Client is willing to engage in short-term voca-</u>

  <u>tional training.</u>

  iii. Supporting evaluation data regarding educational–vocational functioning:

  <u>Client is able to work with people and data at a sufficiently high level. She has</u>

  <u>general intelligence appropriate for the position. Position enables one to be of</u>

  <u>assistance to others. Lower levels of creativity, achievement, and ability utilization</u>

  <u>on this job may pose some problems.</u>

  iv. Special considerations (e.g., economic, transportation, housing, childcare, placement needs):

  <u>Financial support and childcare needed.</u>

c. Third most optimal vocational goal: <u>Bookkeeper</u>

  Already suggested by client?   ☐ Yes ☑ No

  (continues)

FIGURE 10.2. *Continued.*

i. Supporting evaluation data regarding physical functioning:

Client is able to use office equipment at a slow but steady pace. The job must not involve high-speed performance demands and standing. The job's activity demands are the key concerns.

ii. Supporting evaluation data regarding psychosocial functioning:

Client is willing to complete on-the-job training. Concerned somewhat about high-demand work setting involving use of cash register or other business machines. Client also wishes to work more closely with people.

iii. Supporting evaluation data regarding educational–vocational functioning:

Client has bookkeeping and office skills from high school. Her general intelligence level is adequate for job. Client is able to work with both data and people at adequate level. Bookkeeping may not provide opportunities for creativity, ability utilization, and achievement. Still, the job will provide the money the client needs to support self and family.

iv. Special considerations (e.g., economic, transportation, housing, childcare, placement needs):

See second most optimal vocational goal.

2. Services needed for achieving each vocational goal:
   a. Most optimal vocational goal: Receptionist
      i. Pertaining to physical functioning: Postoperative physical therapy as needed. Continued medical supervision of diabetic condition until blood sugar normalizes.
      ii. Pertaining to psychosocial functioning: Resolve family conflict.

(continues)

FIGURE 10.2. *Continued.*

iii. Pertaining to educational–vocational functioning: _Business college short-_
course. On-the-job training.

iv. Services for special considerations: _Maintenance, food stamps, and other_
supplementary financial aid while in training. Childcare.

b. Next most optimal vocational goal: _Motel/hotel desk clerk_

   i. Pertaining to physical functioning: _See most optimal vocational goal._

   ii. Pertaining to psychosocial functioning: _See most optimal vocational goal._

   iii. Pertaining to educational–vocational functioning: _On-the-job training._

   iv. Services for special considerations: _Maintenance, food stamps, and other_
   supplementary financial aid while in training. Childcare.

c. Third most optimal vocational goal: _Bookkeeper_

   i. Pertaining to physical functioning: _See most optimal vocational goal._

   ii. Pertaining to psychosocial functioning: _See most optimal vocational goal._

   iii. Pertaining to educational–vocational functioning: _On-the-job training._

   iv. Services for special considerations: _See second most optimal vocational goal._

3. Vocational goals expressed by the client that appear to be inappropriate based on evaluation data. Discuss.

   Beautician: Main problem pertains to physical demands. Too much standing; too much
   use of the hands and fingers in massaging and waving activities.

FIGURE 10.2. *Continued.*

With the counselor's assistance, the client writes the pros and cons for self and others for several of the more desirable vocational alternatives. After writing balance sheet entries for the top few alternatives, the client rates each pro (+) and con (−) factor on a 5-point importance scale (5 = *very important,* 1 = *little or no importance*). Melinda's balance sheet (Table 10.3) indicates that she and her counselor had already eliminated the bookkeeping possibility and now wish to further explore cosmetology, motel/hotel desk clerk, and reception-ist work.

Upon completion of the balance sheet analysis and discussion of the rated pros and cons, client and counselor consider the implications of the exercise for selecting a vocational objective that will provide a nucleus for the rehabilitation plan. Of course, some clients will lack the intellectual capacity to complete all aspects of the balance sheet. In such cases, the counselor may simply discuss the positive and negative factors related to various job alternatives with the client.

Generating a Rehabilitation Plan

Another essential activity in the formulation of the rehabilitation plan is the intermediate objective analysis. Using Melinda again as an example, Table 10.4 shows her responses to the question, "What do you need to do to reach your vocational rehabilitation goal?" The intermediate objective analysis helps the individual identify basic physical, educational–vocational, and emotional needs, as well as any social considerations that might affect the outcome of the pro-gram. With the counselor's help, the client then explores the difference between needs in a given area and the steps that must be taken to meet those needs. For example, Melinda stated, "I need to get my medical problems under control," a statement that must be broken down into concrete steps, such as (a) check with doctor about insulin intake, diet, condition of hands and feet, and an-other operation on hands; (b) make appointment with podiatrist for molded shoes; and (c) make preparations for possible operation on hands. Melinda also mentioned objectives in the personal problems, educational–vocational, and special considerations areas that must be broken down into specific steps. The intermediate objective analysis, therefore, helps people identify their needs, the steps that must be taken to resolve those needs, and the order in which the steps must be taken.

After completing the Information Processing Summary Form, the bal-ance sheet, and the intermediate objective analysis, client and counselor should be in a good position to finalize the rehabilitation plan. The process of drawing up a rehabilitation plan covers several basic tasks: (a) Select a feasible vocational goal, (b) describe the steps needed to achieve the vocational goal, (c) identify critical intermediate objectives, (d) describe the steps needed to accomplish each intermediate objective, (e) set deadlines for accomplishing all goals and objectives, (f) clarify responsibilities of each party—client and counselor—for the plan, and (g) specify expected outcomes of goal attainment efforts (see
(text continues on p. 361)

TABLE 10.3
Melinda's Balance Sheet

Consideration	Alternative 1: Beautician	Importance rating	Alternative 2: Motel/hotel desk clerk	Importance rating	Alternative 3: Receptionist	Importance rating
Gains for self	Not dependent on husband.	4	Not dependent on husband.	4	Better for health.	5
	Get to work sooner.	3	Not too physically demanding.	4	Not dependent on husband.	4
	Work I really like to do.	4			Adequate pay.	3
Losses for self	Arthritis might get worse.	-5	Childcare costs.	-2	Childcare costs.	-2
	Childcare costs.	-2	Not as interesting as cosmetology.	-4	Not as interesting as cosmetology.	-3
	Earn less because slow worker.	-4				
Gains for others	Regular money for family.	5	Regular money for family.	5	Regular money for family.	5
Losses for others	Be away from children all day.	-3	Be away from children all day.	-3	Be away from children all day.	-3
Social approval	Sisters glad I have a job.	4	Sisters glad I have a job.	4	Sisters glad I have a job.	4
Social disapproval	Customers wanting me to work faster.	-3				
Self-approval	Proud that I have a job.	5	Proud that I have a job.	5	Proud that I have a job.	5

(continues)

TABLE 10.3 Continued

Consideration	Alternative 1: Beautician	Importance rating	Alternative 2: Motel/hotel desk clerk	Importance rating	Alternative 3: Receptionist	Importance rating
Self-disapproval			May not like being behind registration desk all day.	–4	Don't want to do same thing all day.	–4
Sum rated positive anticipation:		25		22		26
Sum rated negative anticipation:		–17		–13		–12
Balance		8		9		14

TABLE 10.4
Melinda's Intermediate Objective Analysis for Employment Goal as Receptionist

Client needs regarding			
Medical condition	**Personal problems**	**Educational–vocational**	**Special considerations**
Get blood sugar under control.	Settle problems with husband.	Develop vocational skills for a receptionist job.	Get some support to cover living expenses while in training.
Increase ability to stand and walk.			
Increase ability to use hands.			

TABLE 10.5
Expected Outcomes of Melinda Bracken's Rehabilitation Plan

Objectives	Expected outcomes
Vocational goal	To get a receptionist job paying $2,700 a month by December 15
Physical objectives (medical)	To work an 8-hour day by December 15
	To increase hand functioning beyond preoperative and pretherapy levels by January 18
	To reduce blood sugar and maintain an A1C level lower than 7% by September 20
Psychosocial objectives (personal)	To have three discussions with spouse in the 2-week period from September 1 to September 15 that do not end in arguments
Educational–vocational goals	To complete receptionist short-course at a vocational school with a "C" grade or better by November 15
	To complete receptionist on-the-job training by December 15
Special consideration objectives	To obtain financial support during training totaling $500 a month (food stamps, maintenance, rent, subsidy, etc.) by September 1

Table 10.5). In the process of program development, the counselor and client must integrate previously discussed and developed material into a physical, psychosocial, educational–vocational, and special consideration goal program that is consistent with the individual's vocational objective.

In completing the rehabilitation program, client and counselor should also establish a procedure for monitoring plan progress. Goal attainment follow-up is based on data provided by the client and others in relation to the vocational goal and physical, psychosocial, educational–vocational, and special consideration intermediate objectives. The purpose of the follow-up is to determine whether program steps are being followed and whether progress is as expected. Modifications in the plan may result from monitoring sessions.

People with disabilities are the primary developers of their vocational plans. Thus, counselor involvement is to plan "with the client and not for the client" (Riggar & Patrick, 1984). Because they have exerted a leadership role in developing precise, concrete vocational plans, clients not only identify with but understand the features of their plans. The plan has not been imposed upon the person but rather has evolved gradually through joint discussion of relevant factors. Before closing the planning phase, to be sure that the client still values the vocational objective of the plan, the counselor and client should discuss the following questions:

1. Does the vocational goal still fit your image of the kind of work that you want to do?
2. Do you know what you need to do to achieve your vocational goal?
3. Are you ready to start taking action that will help you achieve your goal?
4. Are you committed to your goal? (adapted from Glasser, 1981)

Adopting a Career Perspective

Before leaving the planning phase of the rehabilitation process, we wish to stress the importance of a "career perspective" on the part of the rehabilitation counselor. That perspective is the basis for the following question that should go through the counselor's mind: Is the client aware of how his or her immediate vocational goal fits into his or her long-term career aspirations? As Hershenson and Szymanski (1992) stressed, occupational choice, as reflected in a vocational objective in a rehabilitation plan, is the outcome of choosing one job at one specific point in time. A career, on the other hand, often constitutes multiple vocational choices and experiences over one's entire working lifetime. To have a career perspective and to implement effective career counseling, therefore, the counselor must acquire a clear picture of the client's short- and long-term vocational aspirations and the bases for those aspirations.

Research indicates that career counseling, assessment, and consultation are critical job functions of rehabilitation counselors (Leahy, Chan, & Saunders, 2003). Moreover, other research indicates the need to improve such services in vocational rehabilitation settings. In an intensive interview with a small sample of rehabilitation clients ($N = 14$), S. Murphy (1988) found that the majority of respondents felt that they were closed (i.e., placed) in jobs below their levels of aspiration and training. They were not satisfied with their vocational goals, their vocational plans, or the extent to which those plans increased their probability of beginning a career.

At the same time, other research suggests that many clients are receiving services from vocational rehabilitation counselors that are consistent with quality career counseling. In a study of 100 rehabilitation clients in West Virginia, Walls and Dowler (1987) found that 75 participants reported that the vocational objective in their rehabilitation plan was either their own choice or their choice based on advice from the counselor. The vast majority of participants stated that their vocational objective was consistent with a lifelong aspiration.

The importance of adopting a career perspective with many clients cannot be stressed enough. People with disabilities are often seeking not only services to begin or resume a career but also services to maintain a career. Therefore, during the rehabilitation planning process, the counselor must consider the client's need for postemployment services, such as (a) help with the costs of assistive devices; (b) assistance in changing jobs in the same company due to disability-related problems; (c) access to fringe benefits, treatment, and pay equal to other workers'; and (d) provision of long-term follow-up services needed to maintain employment (Roessler & Schriner, 1992; Rumrill & Roessler, 1999). Scherer (1990) corroborated the finding that people with disabilities attach great importance to services needed to retain employment. Based on in-depth interviews with people with severe disabilities, Scherer noted that many rehabilitants needed ongoing assistance in the selection, use, and financing of accommodation devices. Participants in her study desired to stay in rehabilitation longer and to resume services at a later date when necessary.

Other research has demonstrated that employment of people with severe physical disabilities decreases as the disease progresses, unless follow-up services are provided (Kornblith, LaRocca, & Baum, 1986; LaRocca, Kalb, Scheinberg, & Kendall, 1985). These researchers concluded that more people with severe disabilities could remain employed if they received follow-up services designed to help them identify needed accommodations and communicate those accommodations to their employers. Further evidence for such an assertion may be found in Gibbs's (1990) research, which demonstrated that 25% of approximately 2,500 successful rehabilitants in Virginia were no longer employed 3 months following closure. Even more startling, the majority of successful rehabilitants in the sample were unemployed 1 year after closure.

Concluding Statement

Vocational planning in rehabilitation counseling represents a confluence of many processes. For example, effective planning with a client requires a relationship characterized by rapport and trust. In addition, the counselor must have collected sufficient information during the evaluation phase of the rehabilitation process to determine the appropriateness of the potential vocational objectives. Evaluating the appropriateness of vocational objectives involves a complete vocational analysis based on data collected through interviews with the client and through all necessary medical, psychological, and vocational evaluation techniques. The vocational analysis process initially done by the counselor must subsequently be manifested in the client's thoughts regarding vocational choice.

We discussed in this chapter facilitative activities, including the use of occupational information resources, that enable the client to explore self, job, and environmental factors related to vocational planning. A clearer understanding of these personal and environmental factors increases the probability that individuals will select appropriate vocational objectives for their rehabilitation plans. The vocational objective becomes the nucleus around which the rehabilitation plan is developed; however, the vocational objective is a choice made at only one point in time. Counselors must be sensitive to the career development needs of people with disabilities and enable them to begin and maintain employment that is consistent with their long-term career aspirations.

This chapter is important for two reasons: (a) It describes the processes of vocational and career counseling in rehabilitation and (b) it demonstrates procedures for counselor information processing and client involvement in vocational planning. The model in Figure 10.1 operationalizes a series of activities for counselor and client to undertake in developing a realistic and pragmatic vocational rehabilitation plan.

Chapter 11

Utilizing Rehabilitation Facilities and Support Services

Services for rehabilitation clients range from medical restoration to vocational training and placement. The rehabilitation counselor often must secure medical and adjustment services from independent specialists in the community. In other cases the counselor can secure these services from a number of different public and private facilities. The purpose of this chapter is to describe rehabilitation facilities and many of the medical and vocational support services that rehabilitation counselors can use to enhance the vocational rehabilitation of people with disabilities. Integration of many of these same services in school-to-work transition programs for youth with disabilities is also discussed.

Rehabilitation Facilities

Rehabilitation facilities include comprehensive residential centers, such as the Hot Springs Rehabilitation Center (Hot Springs, Arkansas) and the Woodrow Wilson Rehabilitation Center (Fishersville, Virginia), and smaller not-for-profit community-based rehabilitation facilities. Many facilities are certified by the Commission on Accreditation of Rehabilitation Facilities (CARF), which exists to identify programs offering comprehensive and quality services. Established in 1966, the commission has published standards that facilities must meet to obtain accreditation. CARF accredits programs providing adult day services, behavioral health services, employment and community services, and medical rehabilitation services.

Growing out of the rehabilitation medical model, large comprehensive rehabilitation centers have as their primary objective the meeting of medical needs of persons through such services as occupational therapy, physical therapy, and related medical services. Community facilities originated in response to the need for community-based vocational evaluation services, sheltered work experiences, and work adjustment training. These facilities provide transitional vocational evaluation and adjustment experiences for some persons and long-term employment for other individuals. More and more, community facilities have increased their efforts to place individuals with severe disabilities in competitive employment in the community, making wider use of the techniques of supported employment. Through the use of job coaches and coworker support, many facilities have increased their supported employment placements in integrated work settings (Degeneffe, 2000). They have expanded their efforts to help individuals move from depending on the program for support to living independently in their own homes and communities (McCuller, Moore, & Salzberg, 1990). In the sections that follow, rehabilitation center and community facility programs are described in detail.

Historical Overview

Although slow to develop during the early part of the 20th century, comprehensive rehabilitation centers gradually emerged as a more viable concept for people with severe physical disabilities. To counteract fragmentation of rehabilitation services, these centers offered a coordinated medical and vocational preparation program in a single institution. Allan (1958) observed that "crippled children's clinics, the orthopedic hospitals and, finally, the program of the Cleveland Rehabilitation Center which dates back to 1889, were early milestones in the search for a better way to serve the needs" of persons with disabilities (p. 46). Comprehensive programs were later established by the Red Cross at the Institute for Crippled and Disabled in New York in 1917 and at the League for the Handicapped of Detroit, founded in 1920 as a voluntary vocational rehabilitation center (Nelson, 1971).

As with the entire field of rehabilitation, it was during World War II and the years directly thereafter that center and community programs came into their own. Prior to that time their widespread development had been restricted by the limited "training around the disability" focus of state rehabilitation agencies. Before World War II, state rehabilitation agencies were not interested in maintaining institutions, particularly programs that involved the agencies in providing medical services (Redkey, 1971). By 1946, however, state rehabilitation agencies were directly involved in the development of comprehensive rehabilitation centers and, in 1954, they received some federal support under the Hill-Burton Act to develop rehabilitation centers (Redkey, 1971). A decade later, in 1965, the federal government was providing considerable support for the development of rehabilitation centers and staff.

The workshop or community facility movement also began developing at a rapid rate following World War II. Nelson (1971) estimated that the number of new workshops established between 1950 and 1965 equaled twice the number of workshops that existed before that time. Much of that development was attributed to an attempt to meet the needs of people with developmental disabilities, such as mental retardation or cerebral palsy, as well as the needs of the growing number of older individuals and people with severe emotional illness (B. Black, 1965).

Workshops

Historically, workshops have been viewed as either transitional or long-term (sheltered) in nature (G. Wright, 1980). Although the first workshops were long term—that is, programs in which there was no expectation that the client would move on to competitive employment—the historical trend has been toward transitional programs. In fact, even in respect to long-term workshops, Olshansky (1971) pointed out some years ago that the meaning of *long term* is "for as long as necessary." In other words, clients are to remain in these workshops only as long as it takes to ready them for competitive employment. Today, this viewpoint regarding segregated settings for people with disabilities is more strongly held than ever as advocates for people with disabilities call either for the elimination of workshops (Degeneffe, 2000) or for true transitional programming as described by Olshansky (1971).

Transitional Workshops

Transitional workshops provide a work environment that facilitates an individual's development to a higher level of functioning, with the emphasis on moving the person into the labor market within a specific period of time. This is accomplished through a variety of services that assess work potential, prepare individuals for the work world, counsel with individuals regarding appropriate vocational goals and job matches, and refer individuals to programs offering employment services such as supported employment. McCuller et al. (1990) stressed that community programs must focus on developing the vocational competence of their clientele. Vocational competence consists of three types of skills: job responsibility (e.g., arriving on time), task production (e.g., meeting competitive production standards), and social–vocational competence (e.g., cooperating with coworkers). Individuals unable to develop such competencies at a competitive level in transitional programs or to function successfully on the job within the supported employment model (see Chapter 12) require a long-term facility placement. Again, Olshansky's (1971) reminder is pertinent: The placement is only for as long as necessary, with continual efforts made to provide the person with a work role in an integrated setting.

Long-Term or Extended Workshops

The long-term or sheltered workshop program has come under considerable scrutiny. Criticized for segregating people with disabilities, many workshops have not demonstrated a commitment to periodic reevaluation of people coupled with efforts to place them in competitive settings. Parent, Hill, and Wehman (1989) cited outcome statistics to support this point. On an annual basis only about 12% of workshop clients moved into competitive employment, and only 3% were able to maintain such placements for 2 years.

Parent et al. (1989) argued for converting sheltered employment programs in workshops and activity centers into supported employment programs. Their seven-step management plan clarifies how such a conversion may be accomplished: (a) Define goals and objectives, (b) reorganize management structure, (c) train staff competencies, (d) redirect funding sources, (e) implement supported employment services, (f) develop interagency agreements, and (g) evaluate outcomes. The employment specialist is the service provider with the primary responsibility for implementing the supported employment program. As such, the employment specialist is involved in the following activities:

> Identifying and analyzing jobs in the community; completing functional consumer assessments; writing task analyses; matching job requirements with consumer skills; utilizing behavioral training strategies; implementing systematic fading techniques; communicating with parents, employers, and other agency representatives; developing environmental modifications; and negotiating for additional community support when needed. (Parent et al., 1989, p. 55)

Hagner and Murphy (1989) described how three programs increased their emphasis on supported employment but also noted that "closing the workshop" was not an accurate description of what happened. What actually occurred was a reduction of the size of the sheltered program or a modification of it into a small business operation coupled with additional supported employment programming. As Hagner and Murphy (1989) noted, not every client was successful in a supported employment placement. Hence, even when placing their highest priority on nonsegregated placements, workshops must continue to offer stable, structured work opportunities for some individuals with severe disabilities. These long-term work roles can be offered, however, within facilities with characteristics of more "normalized" environments. M. Rosen, Bussone, Dakunchak, and Cramp (1993) described one workshop or "production facility" that employed workers with and without disabilities and used "high-tech" equipment (also used by people with disabilities) to meet the requirements of a Defense Department contract.

Rehabilitation Centers

Nelson (1971) traced the origins of the rehabilitation center to the latter part of the 19th century and the early part of the 20th century. With the experience gained in serving soldiers injured during World War II, the concept of a rehabilitation center offering coordinated medical, vocational, educational, and psychological services for people with disabilities gained considerable recognition. Comprehensive services were clearly needed to rehabilitate veterans with disabilities, a lesson that was soon applied to civilian rehabilitation.

Noted for comprehensive programs, rehabilitation centers provide most, and in some cases all, of the following services (Allan, 1958; G. Wright, 1980):

1. Medical, vocational, educational, and psychological evaluation
2. Occupational therapy, physical therapy, speech pathology and audiology, and other medical services, such as nursing care and prosthetic fitting and training
3. Work adjustment training and vocational counseling
4. Social services, such as social work, personal counseling, and recreation therapy
5. Liaison services with other community health and human service agencies
6. Both temporary and long-term sheltered employment
7. Job placement services

Centralization of rehabilitation services is the primary rationale for the comprehensive center. For example, the rehabilitation center can bring the physician into direct contact with the rehabilitation team. Hence, the team has the benefit of direct and constant medical supervision. At the same time the team itself is composed of a wide range of professional rehabilitation specialists. Based on their different perspectives, team members can devise an inclusive, individualized treatment program for each client. The treatment program emphasizes functional approaches to therapy and training (i.e., skill building that enables the person to return to a maximal degree of independent living). As clients near the end of their rehabilitation programs, they will also have the benefits of follow-up from center staff who assist clients in their reentry into home, job, and other social settings.

Comprehensive rehabilitation centers have experimented with a family-oriented approach to service delivery as well. For example, the Arizona Job Colleges Family Rehabilitation Project (Casa Grande, Arizona) worked with low-income families on a full-time, in-house basis. On the average a family spent approximately 1 year in attendance at the program. Program services for family members included vocational assessment and counseling, family health and physical restoration services, and domestic and home maintenance skills training (Nau, 1973). To be eligible for the program, families were required to meet certain income guidelines and to have a primary wage earner with a physical or mental disability that was a significant handicap to employment. Evaluation research indicated that family rehabilitation participants secured a wide range of job placements and maintained rehabilitation gains. Family income levels increased, and notable improvements occurred in project members' contributions to family and community living. Nau (1973) commented that the children of families in the program also demonstrated improved health practices, academic achievement, and motivation and independence in school.

Strengths of Rehabilitation Centers and Facilities

One strength of facility and center programs lies in the client evaluation area. For example, facilities can provide extensive information on the person regarding (a) physical strengths and limitations, (b) psychological strengths and limitations, (c) educational strengths and limitations, and (d) vocational areas of strengths and weaknesses. In fact, through observation of the individual in program experiences, facility and center personnel can answer many questions important to the client's overall rehabilitation, such as these:

1. Does the person have the skills and abilities required to perform preferred work activities?
2. Are there medical limitations not previously noted by the rehabilitation counselor?
3. How well does the person deal with supervisors and coworkers?
4. Can the person transfer learning from one task to another?
5. On which vocational task does the individual demonstrate the greatest potential?

6. How does the person's family support or fail to support rehabilitation goals?

Finally, individualization and integration of service programs is one of the great advantages of a facility or center program. For example, programs can be individualized in terms of the type of services, work, supervision, pressure, interpersonal relationships, and performance-based feedback.

Limitations of Facilities

As previously stated the workshop has been criticized for its tendency to impede the integration or reintegration into society of individuals with severe disabilities. Olshansky's (1966) rendering of the problem is as appropriate today as it was some years ago:

> Too many shops still confirm rather than challenge a client's sense of worthlessness by having him come to a slum-located shop, poorly decorated, and inadequately furnished, and by confronting him with work tasks which can only underline his limitations and test his capacity for boredom. (p. 29)

Other aspects of sheltered workshops that impede integration into society or competitive employment include pay far below minimum wage (Fleischer & Zames, 2001), "few or no employment benefits" (Hagner & Dileo, 1993, p. 5), "tolerance of behavior that will not be acceptable in competitive employment, and a tendency to keep good workers (due to their contribution to production goals) rather than making efforts to move them to higher levels of employment" (Gearheart, Mullen, & Gearheart, 1993, p. 116). Unless characterized by frequent reevaluation of clients and by efforts to secure external (community) placements, workshop services present another denormalizing experience for persons with disabilities and their families. The commitment to continual client evaluation and integrated placement is as important as ever given that data indicate that trends toward workshop placements did not slow in the 1990s (Degeneffe, 2000).

In a survey of administrators of rehabilitation and developmental disabilities agency personnel, Whitehead, Davis, and Fisher (1989) found that the majority of respondents recognized the need for workshops to broaden their programs from a sole emphasis on sheltered work placements. Although few of the administrators advocated discontinuing long-term sheltered work placements, they did endorse the need for facilities to operate a broad range of external employment programs commonly used in supported employment. These external employment programs encompassed individual placements in competitive (integrated) settings, mobile work crews working on a contractual basis with the private and public sectors, and enclaves or groups of workers with disabilities who were employed by business and industry.

The majority of facility administrators responding in the survey (83%) were of the opinion that their programs should offer both external placement and extended sheltered work roles, because sheltered work roles continue to meet a need for some people with severe disabilities. For those individuals working in sheltered settings, many steps can be taken to minimize the potential stigmatizing effects of such placements (Gardner, 1981; Olshansky, 1971). The workshop should provide a quality program utilizing well-trained staff and modern buildings and equipment. The atmosphere of the workshop should reflect an optimistic attitude and stress the importance of client behavior change. Work tasks should be varied and as similar as possible to the tasks the client might do in competitive employment. Four important sources exist for generating this type of work for the shop: (a) industrial subcontract work, (b) service contracts, (c) renovating and processing of used materials, and (d) manufacturing of new goods (Goldenson, 1978a).

To normalize the workshop setting further, the client should work regular hours, receive fair compensation, and have supervision consistent with that of competitive employment. The workshop itself should be integrated into a business setting in which clients can interact with nondisabled workers in a regular work routine. Workshop clientele should reflect a wide range of age, racial and ethnic, gender, and disability groups. Finally, workshop clients should have the opportunity to use high-tech equipment so that they are learning skills transferable to jobs in the local economy (M. Rosen et al., 1993).

Workshops must also deal with the conflict of being both a rehabilitation facility and a business enterprise, two goals that are essentially incompatible. Too much emphasis on the business aspect of the workshop results in production becoming the dominant focus rather than the ancillary one (Power & Marinelli, 1974). The program's priorities shift, and it begins to concentrate more on marketing and competing than on evaluation and work preparation services. Money crises follow, causing client wages to decrease and program improvements to be postponed. According to Gardner (1981), workshops must define their identities as human service providers "utilizing work and business management principles" (p. 188).

To resolve the strain between being both a rehabilitation facility and a business enterprise, workshops must find ways to overcome financial pressures that cause an overemphasis on production. Loans, federal and state grants, and low-cost consultation from engineering and management specialists could provide the additional financial and technical support that workshops need (Gardner, 1981; Power & Marinelli, 1974). Client motivation might be increased by supplementing fair wages with additional pay based on a piece rate. It might also be possible to press for the development of tax credits for industries using workshop settings in their own production processes (Power & Marinelli, 1974) for both satellite and on-site production activities.

With an increased emphasis on external placement, workshops must improve their support programs for exiting clients. Many people will need clothes, money, transportation, childcare, paid time to seek work, and housing or help with finding housing (Shaw, 1995; Whitehead et al., 1989). Overlooking any of these areas of assistance for the exiting client can have detrimental effects on the person's outcome. In addition, some individuals, rather than moving directly to independent employment, desire further education or on-the-job training. For example, enrollment in vocationally oriented school programs would provide some people with an opportunity to build additional social skills and work abilities. Similarly, on-the-job training can provide the client with needed continuity between the workshop setting and the competitive work setting.

Limitations of Centers

Because of their semiprotected nature, rehabilitation centers suffer from many of the same limitations as community facilities. For example, practices resulting in denormalization may start as early as the person's evaluation, a time when individuals are often labeled with diagnostic terms. If not careful, evaluation personnel may forget the person and relate only to the label. The same label then gets passed from the evaluator to the counselor and, finally, to other center personnel, such as vocational instructors (Baker, Baker, & McDaniel, 1975).

The role of the client in a rehabilitation center can be counter to life role expectations. For example, some center personnel may expect clients to be compliant and passive, yet independent living requires self-care, initiative, and ingenuity. Although many clients participate in recreational activities, if not integrated with community activities, the recreational program can also be denormalizing. Baker et al. (1975) stressed that clients need to use public recreational facilities when they are available to the general public. Recreational programs within a center further isolate clients into their own subculture and deemphasize the skills needed for the use of public recreation facilities.

A key concern for many observers of center practices is the physical facility itself. For example, medically oriented areas in rehabilitation centers have characteristics of a hospital environment (e.g., institutionalized interior decorating, white uniforms worn by staff, hospital-labeled linen, patient gowns). Hence, these medical specialty areas, rather than communicating that the person is someone who will reenter society, treat the individual as a person who is ill. Being treated as a "patient" may decrease motivation to overcome the limitations of the disability and encourage adoption of the "sick role."

Selecting and Using a Rehabilitation Facility

Before referring a person to a center or facility program, the counselor must involve the individual in a discussion of the pros and cons of the placement. If the person decides to enroll, then the counselor must decide which centers or facilities meet necessary quality standards for client rehabilitation as evidenced by certification by CARF or by previous positive experiences with their programs. Determining which programs to consider for client referral requires answers to many questions (Brolin, 1973; Whitehead et al., 1989), for example,

1. Is the staff well qualified?
2. Are the facilities adequate and accessible?
3. Does a comprehensive program exist, including evaluation, counseling, work adjustment, social and vocational training, recreation, research, and placement?
4. Does the facility work with the family?
5. Are adequate reports provided to the counselor regarding the client's vocational and social progress?
6. Does the facility emphasize upgrading its own staff through orientation and in-service training?
7. Is the facility committed to enabling individuals to work in a least restrictive environment, which requires availability of both internal and external placements?

Ideally, the client and counselor should have a choice among high-quality facilities that they could visit prior to choosing the one that best meets the person's needs. These visits could be made in person, or the client and counselor could review audiovisual and written materials descriptive of facility settings and their services (Esser & Scheinkmann, 1975; Power & Marinelli, 1974). Both predecision visits and the use of audiovisual orientation presentations can help to reduce client anticipatory anxiety regarding program entrance and thereby facilitate initial adjustment to the facility. Once a facility has been selected, the rehabilitation counselor should provide staff members with relevant information on the person's medical status, interests, aptitudes, values, and needs. It is also important for the rehabilitation counselor to maintain contact with the individual while he or she is at the facility.

Rehabilitation Services

Many services that people need to complete their rehabilitation programs are provided within rehabilitation facilities, but many services are found outside rehabilitation facilities as well. Therefore, the rehabilitation counselor has multiple resources for meeting client needs.

Professional Services

Many highly trained professionals can play a vital role in the rehabilitation process. Services offered include physical medicine, rehabilitation nursing, prosthetics–orthotics, physical therapy, occupational therapy, speech–language pathology and audiology, rehabilitation psychology, rehabilitation engineering/assistive technology, therapeutic recreation, and advocacy.

Physical Medicine

Physical or rehabilitation medicine is a recognized medical specialty dealing with the treatment and rehabilitation of individuals with disabilities. The physician specializing in physical medicine is referred to as a physiatrist. The physiatrist must establish realistic goals for maximum recovery of the individual and use a team of rehabilitation specialists, such as nurses, physical therapists, occupational therapists, psychologists, prosthetists, orthotists, speech pathologists, and audiologists, to accomplish the goals of the rehabilitation plan (Goldfine, 1977; Rehabilitation Services Administration, 1997). Through drug therapy, corrective surgery, and patient training, physical medicine brings the individual up to maximal functioning, given his or her limitations (Goldenson, 1978b). Physiatrists work in public and private medically oriented rehabilitation hospitals and facilities. They may have completed specialty training in areas such as traumatic brain injury, spinal cord injury, or neuromuscular diseases (Rehabilitation Services Administration, 1997).

Rehabilitation Nursing

The rehabilitation nurse assists the physiatrist and other ancillary medical specialists, such as the physical or occupational therapist, who treat the rehabilitation client. The rehabilitation nurse plays a central role in working with both the client and the rehabilitation team. The nurse provides basic medical care for clients—for example, observation and charting, maintenance of antiseptic surroundings, patient safety and comfort, and patient hygiene (Ince, 1974). Rehabilitation nurses instruct people with disabilities and their families in appropriate medical care procedures, such as skin care and bowel and bladder training for individuals with spinal cord injury (Coulter, 1974; Felts, 1976). The nurse is actively involved with the person during both the acute and long-term care phases of the rehabilitation program, offering educational and motivational services to individuals with disabilities and their families (Rehabilitation Services Administration, 1997).

Rehabilitation nurses are also active in disability management roles with people receiving workers' compensation. Performing as case managers, nurses serve as liaisons with the employer, insurance agencies, medical teams, and family to enable the injured worker to resume employment as quickly as possible (S. Scott, 1990).

Prosthetics–Orthotics

The specialties devoted to the design, modification, and maintenance of artificial devices that increase a person's functional capacities play an important part in rehabilitation medical services. The orthotist fits patients with orthoses (braces) that compensate for a variety of disabling conditions of the spine and extremities. The prosthetist cares for clients by fitting them with prostheses to replace missing limbs and limb segments (Rehabilitation Services Administration, 1997). The prosthetist–orthotist works in research facilities, hospitals, university teaching and research programs, rehabilitation centers, and government agencies such as the Veterans Administration (J. Kennedy, 1976; Rehabilitation Services Administration, 1997). These professionals typically work in close collaboration with a clinical team composed of medical, rehabilitation, and social work specialists (Dankmeyer, 1977).

Although orthotists perform a variety of functions, their chief concern involves designing and fitting external devices to support an upper limb or limbs, a lower limb or limbs, or the spine. Sometimes referred to as splints, supports, or devices, orthoses may support the body, correct for bodily conditions, protect injured areas, prevent further structural damage, and/or control involuntary body movements (Ince, 1974). Besides designing, fitting, and maintaining orthoses, the orthotist instructs the patient on the use of the devices and modifies mobility aids, such as wheelchairs (Dankmeyer, 1977; Rehabilitation Services Administration, 1997).

The prosthetist is concerned primarily with assessment of the person's prosthetic needs (e.g., for functional and/or cosmetic purposes), prescription and fitting of a suitable prosthesis, and evaluation of the adequacy of the prosthesis. Prostheses or artificial limbs are designed for upper and lower extremities and can be fit for amputations at any level. Although they cannot replace the functioning of the hand, upper limb prostheses are capable of lifting, grasping, and punching. Generally, the more cosmetics are stressed, the less functional the prosthesis. Myoelectrical prostheses are available that are responsive to electrical impulses in the muscles (Falvo, 2005).

Dankmeyer (1977, p. 247) noted that approximately 90% of amputations involve lower limbs adversely affected by vascular diseases such as diabetes. Lower limb prostheses are designed to aid ambulation as much as possible. Above-the-knee amputations require prostheses that replace knee and ankle–foot functioning. Lower extremity prostheses replace lost ankle and foot functioning (Falvo, 2005).

Physical Therapy

Physical therapy has the following goals: "restore function, improve mobility, relieve pain, and prevent or limit permanent physical disabilities of patients suffering from injuries or disease" (U.S. Department of Labor, 2004, p. 291). Based on the results of a careful evaluation (neuromuscular, sensorimotor, and range-of-motion tests) (Latimer, 1977; Litton, Veron, & Griffin, 1982), the physical therapist selects among a variety of treatment modes, including passive exercise (therapist moves the body part), active exercise (person moves the body part), use of heat or cold, massage, manipulations, electrotherapy, and ultrasound (Falvo, 2005). Patients receiving physical therapy services generally fall into categories such as "orthopedic, pediatric, geriatric, and neuralgic"

(Rehabilitation Services Administration, 1997, p. 10). Their problems typically are of a neuromuscular or musculoskeletal nature, often accompanied by pain, and affect their "strength, endurance, balance, coordination, sensation, and joint range of motion" (Latimer, 1977, p. 280). Typical conditions causing such problems include "amputation, arthritis, bursitis, cerebral palsy, cerebral vascular accidents, chest and heart conditions, circulatory diseases, fractures, multiple sclerosis, muscular dystrophy, peripheral nerve injuries, poliomyelitis, spinal cord injuries, and sprains and strains" (Hickey, 1957, p. 481).

Occupational Therapy

Occupational therapy services include sensorimotor activities, daily living and leisure skills training, recommendations regarding necessary modifications of the physical environment, development and application of orthotic and prosthetic devices, work-hardening services, and driver evaluations for persons with disabilities (Litton et al., 1982; Mirch, 1999; Veron & Poulton, 1980). Mirch (1999) pointed out that driver evaluations by occupational therapists are often necessary for clients with "a medical condition that impairs brain functioning and upper and lower extremity movement ... [as in the cases of] persons who have epileptic seizures, brain injuries, and/or spinal cord injuries" (p. 300). The goals of occupational therapy services include rehabilitation of functional deficits, development of new functional abilities, and maintenance of both over time (Lansing & Carlsen, 1977; Lindberg, 1976). Burk (1975b) noted that the distinguishing feature of occupational therapy is the way in which purposeful activities are used to accomplish both physical and emotional gains on the part of rehabilitation clients. These gains come about through the "development and maintenance of functions and skills" needed to "engage in play, work, and the various self-maintenance activities" (Lansing & Carlsen, 1977, p. 212).

Occupational therapy is prescribed to meet a wide variety of needs, including improving the client's muscle strength, range of motion, coordination, endurance, sensory function, working capacity, cognitive functions, social relatedness, personal habits, time management, and role functioning (Ad Hoc Committee of the Commission on Practice, 1980). The hallmark of occupational therapy is its ability to help people perform more effectively in both their daily living and work environments, including through instruction in use of the computer to help people improve skills such as memory, decision making, and problem solving (U.S. Department of Labor, 2004).

Litton et al. (1982) pointed out that the traditional concern of the physical therapist has been postural modifications and gross motor development and that of the occupational therapist has been perceptual–motor and fine motor development. "However,... these traditional roles have blurred so that both types of professionals are concerned with both types of motor development" (p. 66). Occupational therapists work with persons with mental illness as well as with those with physical disabilities. When working with people with mental illness, occupational therapists "may be responsible for group or individual treatment activities designed to help individuals learn personal or social behavior skills" (Rehabilitation Services Administration, 1997, p. 14).

Speech–Language Pathology and Audiology Services

Speech–language pathology services are provided by speech pathologists. Their primary functions include assessment, diagnosis, treatment, and therapy to prevent disorders in speech, language, cognition, communication, and swallowing (U.S. Department of Labor, 2004). Individuals with a variety of diagnoses—stroke, brain injury, degenerative diseases, learning disabilities, cerebral palsy, mental retardation, hearing impairments, and autism—can profit from the services of a speech–language pathologist (Brostrand, 2005; Rehabilitation Services Administration, 1997).

Audiology services are provided by audiologists. Using audiometers, computers, and other testing devices, audiologists determine the type of hearing impairment present and ways that the person with the hearing impairment can most fully utilize residual hearing (U.S. Department of Labor, 2004). The audiologist can assist individuals in need of a hearing aid or other listening device by helping them select and fit the proper hearing device as well as learn to use the device effectively (American Speech-Language-Hearing Association, n.d.). Speech–language pathologists and audiologists work in hospitals, private and public clinics, rehabilitation centers, home health agencies, schools, and universities. They may also have their own private practice (Rehabilitation Services Administration, 1997).

Rehabilitation Psychology

Rehabilitation psychologists typically complete a doctoral degree approved by the American Psychological Association that includes emphases in such areas as neuropsychology, behavioral psychology, or rehabilitation psychology. Addressing such issues as adaptation to disability and vocational adjustment, rehabilitation psychologists perform functions such as disability determination, psychological and vocational evaluation, treatment planning, and counseling and psychotherapy. They work in rehabilitation hospitals and centers and a variety of state and community facilities such as community mental health centers (Rehabilitation Services Administration, 1997).

Rehabilitation Engineering/Assistive Technology

From its beginning during World War II, rehabilitation engineering has assumed a more and more prominent role in alleviating handicapping conditions (Sixth Institute on Rehabilitation Issues, 1979). Reswick (1980) defined *rehabilitation engineering* as a combination of engineering and scientific technology with medicine to improve the lives of people with disabilities. These improvements may require restructuring of the environment or equipping the person with needed prosthetics, orthotics, or assistive technology (M. Parsons & Rappaport, 1981). Rehabilitation engineers must be competent professionals in their own fields as well as capable of working as part of a multidisciplinary professional health team. Dedicated to developing the most effective devices, therapy modes, and environmental modifications possible, they also need a working understanding of marketing, manufacturing, and distributing.

A service of the Office of Disability Employment Policy (ODEP) of the U.S. Department of Labor, the Job Accommodation Network (JAN; http://janweb.icdi.wvu.edu) is a valuable mechanism for disseminating rehabilitation engineering technology. JAN serves both as a repository of information on successful job accommodations and as a job accommodation consultation service. In operation since July 1984 and located at West Virginia University, JAN provides job accommodation consultation to consumers, employers, and rehabilitation professionals at no charge. JAN consultants are available to help people with disabilities with accommodation issues related to job acquisition, retention, and advancement. In one year's time (fiscal year 1997), JAN responded to more than 40,000 telephone calls or e-mail inquiries for information. About three fourths of the requests were "case-specific," that is, situations in which a person wanted information about a particular job accommodation. As a further indication of interest in JAN, its website had recorded over 2 million "hits" by 1999 (President's Committee on Employment of People with Disabilities, 1999a). Two sample job accommodations recommended by JAN consultants are displayed in Table 11.1 (D. Alexander & Greenwood, 1985).

Many job accommodations can be achieved at low cost while yielding high client benefits. For example, a U.S. Department of Labor (DOL) study (Berkeley Planning Associates, 1982) reported that 51% of the industrial accommodations identified cost nothing, 30% cost less than $500, and only 8% cost more than $2,000. The executive summary of the DOL study stated,

> The accommodations that have been done are not the expensive purchases of equipment or difficult removals of architectural barriers which are often the types of accommodations discussed in the news media and which are the fear of many firms. Rather, firms and disabled workers find ways to make the disabled worker productive through minor adjustment of the job and workplace, transferring the worker to a job or physical site where the impairment or disability does not give rise to a handicap, transferring some tasks to other workers, moving furniture, raising a desk or lowering a phone, and so on. (Berkeley Planning Associates, 1982, p. 85)

Approximately 10 years later, information obtained via a survey of 108 users of JAN revealed that approximately one third of the accommodations (31%) cost the business nothing. The majority of the accommodations (57%) cost under $1,000 (Hendricks & Hirsh, 1991). Data on job accommodations gathered in 1997 support these same cost trends. In a review of accommodation costs experienced by 665 companies that contacted JAN in fiscal year 1997, data indicated that 21% of the accommodations cost nothing; 49% cost $1 to $500; and

TABLE 11.1
Job Accommodation Network Examples

Job Accommodation Example 1

Nature of disability:

Above-the-wrist amputation of left hand (employee was left-hand dominant)

Job title and description:

Furnace charger: operate buttons on charge box with two hands to raise and lower charge buckets. Climb steps to top of furnace. Use rod to release wishbone.

Functional limitations accommodated:

Lifting

Carrying

Reaching

Grasping

Handling/fingering

Pushing/pulling

Solution/modification:

Employee wanted to return to preinjury job. An orthopedic appliance manufacturer was contacted to develop an appliance that would be sturdy enough to withstand the heat and dust as well as functional enough to operate the panel box. A duplicate of the panel box was provided for dimensions and operation. Eventually, an appliance was designed and the employee was able to perform his preinjury job.

Accommodation method:

Purchase of commercially developed device for $1,800.

Job Accommodation Example 2

Nature of disability:

Deafness, retinitis pigmentosa (visual impairment)

Type of job:

Data entry operator/backup computer operator—input data for all functions of payroll, accounts payable, general ledger, job cost, equipment, and critical path, and aids and fills in for computer operator.

Functional limitations accommodated:

Hearing

Talking

Reading

Solution/modification:

Taught coworkers sign language as method of communication. Designed and printed input forms with sharp color contrasts to add to reading ease. Installed special switch outside of computer room which, when pushed, turns off light in computer room as a means of notifying the employee that a person seeks help or entry into the room.

Accommodation method:

Adaptation to existing equipment at a cost of $300.

Note. Adapted from "Designing Jobs for Handicapped Workers," by D. Alexander and R. Greenwood, 1985, *Conference Proceedings.* Chicago: Institute of Industrial Engineers.

11% cost $501 to $1,000. Thus, 70% of the accommodations made by employers cost no more than $500 (President's Committee on Employment of People with Disabilities, 1999b).

Therapeutic Recreation

Therapeutic recreation activities, such as hobbies, sports, and other leisure-time pursuits, can contribute to the recovery and well-being of individuals with disabilities. According to Brostrand (2005), a certified therapeutic recreation specialist (CTRS) uses such activities to promote positive gains in the social, cognitive, emotional, and physical functioning of persons with disabilities. For example, a CTRS might design and implement an exercise/recreation treatment plan for an individual who has had a heart attack.

Through leisure counseling and leisure education, a CTRS can help people with disabilities clarify their leisure interests and learn to use their leisure time productively. The CTRS and the client with a disability can approach the selection of leisure activities in a problem-solving format. Using a variety of assessment techniques, the recreation therapist first helps the person identify interests; aptitudes; and physical, cognitive, or emotional limitations. The person then selects areas of interest that can be translated into leisure pursuits (Overs, 1970). Leisure counseling can promote the participation of people with disabilities in leisure activities and in positive leisure-based social relationships through which they can also develop greater self-esteem and build functional skills contributing to both independent living and vocational potential (Rehabilitation Services Administration, 1992).

Advocacy

Advocates for people with disabilities and legal and paralegal professionals are available in each state as a result of funding of Client Assistance Programs (CAPs) by the Rehabilitation Services Administration (Blankenship, 2005). CAP personnel and other advocates assist people with disabilities by providing

> information/referral, counseling and advice regarding rights and responsibilities relative to the projects and programs funded under the Rehabilitation Act; mediation and negotiation to resolve problems/concerns; assistance with (administrative) appeals to resolve grievances, including representation of impartial hearings; and access to legal services as needed. (Rehabilitation Services Administration, 1997, p. 18)

According to Blankenship (2005), half of the 56 CAPs in the United States and U.S. territories exist in protection and advocacy organizations. "Sixteen are housed in a variety of state and private entities, including a governor's office, legal aid, and a private law firm. The remaining 12 are located internally in state vocational rehabilitation agencies" (p. 219).

Personal Skill Development Services

Because adequate psychological and interpersonal functioning can be considered a prerequisite to the maintenance of employment (Bissonnette, 1999; Neff, 1985), personal skill development services play an important role in the overall rehabilitation of many people. Instructional programs of value address such areas as physical fitness, relaxation, medication management, assertiveness, stress management, pain management, rational thinking, self-advocacy, self-control, interpersonal communications, assertiveness, value clarification, goal setting, problem solving, and time management (Akridge & Means, 1982; Glueckauf & Quittner, 1992; Sievert, Cuvo, & Davis, 1988).

These programs can be delivered in a variety of settings—hospitals, rehabilitation facilities, and rehabilitation field offices. Bradshaw and Straker (1974) discussed a hospital-based approach (Intermediate Rehabilitation Unit) to developing independent living skills in Veterans Administration clients, many of whom had psychological disabilities. In addition to helping clients develop employability skills, the Intermediate Rehabilitation Unit served as a place where individuals could receive group counseling and social skills training to help them cope with problems encountered during the day when they were involved in extrahospital activities.

Rehabilitation facilities offer a variety of personal skill training programs. For example, a comprehensive training program based on a model of physical, intellectual, and emotional (PIE) growth was implemented in a rehabilitation center (Roessler, Bolton, Means, & Milligan, 1975). Components of the PIE program included instruction in physical fitness, goal setting, and interpersonal communication skills. Examination of the effects of implementing the PIE program showed that personal functioning in the three skill areas could be improved through systematic training. Psychological gains for program participants were also observed.

Roessler, Cook, and Lillard (1977) evaluated the effects of a systematic group counseling program, Personal Achievement Skills (PAS; Means & Roessler, 1976), in a work adjustment program in a comprehensive rehabilitation center. The program provided instruction in communication and problem-solving skills in a group counseling format. Clients included in the PAS training were general rehabilitation clients who had been referred to work adjustment for a variety of reasons (e.g., deficiencies in basic vocational skills, the need to establish work tolerances, and behavioral problems interfering with vocational training). When compared with the control group, individuals in the PAS program had higher self-reported gains in life optimism and vocational maturity. They reported greater attainment of self-selected personal adjustment goals and development of more realistic expectations regarding work. Similar gains in psychological adjustment resulted from the use of PAS with individuals with visual impairments (Roessler, 1978).

Given the importance of computer skills in today's economy and the positive correlation between literacy and numerical abilities and employment outcomes, many observers are calling on rehabilitation professionals to arrange for basic educational skill training for people with disabilities (Kosciulek, 2004a;

Shaw, 1995; Strauser, Waldrop, & Katz, 1999). C. Ryan (1995) included literacy, numeracy, basic academic skills, computer literacy, problem solving, communication, and personal flexibility among the skills needed for success in the 21st century. Stressing the importance of basic academic skills, Shaw (1995) called for career preparation services as a central feature of the "employment, education, and training services delivery model" that rehabilitation facilities must adopt. He also emphasized the need for a comprehensive approach to worker preparation including not only the aforementioned social and educational skills but also essential employment skills. Traditionally, work adjustment training is one approach for developing basic employment skills.

Work Adjustment Training

The basics of work adjustment training that deal with deficiencies in crucial work behaviors are presented in the form of answers to the following questions:

1. What is work adjustment training?
2. Where is work adjustment training conducted?
3. What do individuals need from work adjustment training?
4. How is work adjustment training conducted?
5. What other factors affect work adjustment?

What Is Work Adjustment Training?

Work adjustment training involves a series of activities designed to teach people the behaviors needed to fulfill the work role in society. Therefore, work adjustment training is a behavior modification approach that emphasizes eliminating undesirable behavior and reinforcing desirable behavior in three domains: job responsibility, task production, and social–vocational competence (McCuller et al., 1990). Gregory, Whitlow, Levine, and Wasmuth (1982) listed 40 different work adjustment techniques. These strategies may be used to enhance "physical capacities, psychomotor skills, appropriate dress and grooming capacities, interpersonal and communicative skills, job seeking skills, productive skills, orientation to work practices, work habits, and other work related skills" (Gardner, 1981, p. 186).

Where Is Work Adjustment Training Conducted?

Work adjustment training may occur in a variety of settings ranging from comprehensive rehabilitation centers to professionally supervised school and community facilities to on-the-job training in integrated settings via supported employment or community-based educational strategies (see Chapter 12). When work adjustment training is conducted in facility or school settings, it must not be limited solely to the classroom. It must occur in settings in which the environmental and work activity demands are comparable to those found in an industrial setting (McCuller et al., 1990). Unfortunately, it is often difficult to secure the type of work contracts necessary for the creation of such an authentic environment within the facility setting.

What Do Clients Need from Work Adjustment Training?

Work adjustment services are designed to increase the probability that an individual can make the transition into competitive employment. Hence, the services are targeted at diagnosing and ameliorating such problems as fluctuating production output, social skills deficits, disruptive behavior, lack of persistence, and poor responses to coworkers or supervisors (Marr & Roessler, 1994). Diagnosis of work adjustment training needs is followed by development of a treatment plan. Marr (1982, pp. 127–128) stressed the need for this planning to take into consideration both the person's behavioral assets that will enhance employability and the behavioral surpluses and deficits constituting employability problems. He further described how the process of behavioral assessment could be applied in the development of a work adjustment plan. Use of behavioral techniques in work adjustment planning involves such steps as

1. specifying problems and objectives in terms of observable behaviors or the products of those behaviors;
2. measuring behaviors prior to intervention;
3. selecting intervention procedures (e.g., the 40 techniques described in Gregory et al., 1982) based on research evidence;
4. measuring the target behavior continually during the intervention to assess success; and
5. attributing any failure of the intervention to the technique employed, not to the person.

How Is Work Adjustment Training Conducted?

Work adjustment training evolved from a behavior management approach focusing mainly on the decrease of inappropriate behavior to one stressing acquisition of positive behavior. Commonly used techniques include "programmed instruction, audiovisual demonstration, and videotape modeling feedback and simulation training ... to assist individuals in learning work, social, and job readiness behaviors" (Sawyer & Morgan, 1981). A variety of training interventions use these didactic, modeling, and role-play strategies to teach skills involved in maintaining personal hygiene; grooming; being assertive; using transportation; budgeting; job interviewing; filling out application forms; and understanding employer expectations, fringe benefits, and safety regulations (Brolin & Roessler, 1992; Roessler, Lewis, & Hinman, 1986). Some approaches, referred to as microtraining (Sawyer & Morgan, 1981), help people develop functional behaviors such as the following:

1. Dealing with problem topics in the employment interview (e.g., disability-related questions, production concerns)
2. Interacting with coworkers (e.g., social conversation situations)
3. Controlling one's behavior in the work setting
4. Maintaining a proper role relationship with the supervisor
5. Expressing anger or disapproval related to job situations in a constructive manner
6. Scheduling, monitoring, and evaluating one's job performance
7. Maintaining appropriate work habits
8. Adhering to basic work setting rules

Behavioral approaches based on the principles of operant conditioning described by Skinner (1953) can play a major role in work adjustment. In these approaches, desired behavior is followed as soon as possible by positive reinforcement. The reinforcement must be seen as powerful for the particular individual and is therefore part of an individualized behavioral approach (Gearheart et al., 1993). Gearheart et al. (1993) stressed that operant conditioning–based behavioral approaches typically follow five steps:

1. Identifying problem behaviors
2. Observing and recording baseline data
3. Identifying appropriate, powerful reinforcers
4. Implementing the intervention, observing and recording data related to it
5. Evaluating the effects of the intervention and making modifications if the desired change is not taking place (p. 174)

Marr and Roessler (1985, 1994) described how to apply a variety of operant techniques to help people develop productive work behaviors. They used a behavior rating approach, the Work Personality Profile (WPP; Neath & Bolton, 2006; Roessler & Bolton, 1985b), in simulated work settings to identify behavioral strengths and liabilities. Results from the WPP directed the rehabilitation professional in the use of 18 different behavior modification strategies to improve client behavioral responses to the following work tasks: accepting the work role, responding satisfactorily to change, being a productive worker, monitoring own work and work needs, accepting supervision, and working with coworkers.

The use of operant conditioning–based behavior modification has many precedents in the literature. For example, N. Campbell (1971) documented the positive outcomes associated with the use of automated equipment, token economies, work reinforcement systems, and isolation and avoidance techniques.

Using automated equipment to provide the client with constant feedback regarding production, N. Campbell conducted a research study in a Goodwill Workshop. The data on the automated equipment approach indicated that the equipment was less effective in increasing production than in enabling clients to maintain a steady work rate. On the other hand, an experimental token economy reinforcement system was found to be extremely effective in increasing the frequency of desirable behaviors and the rate of production in the workshop. The token reinforcement system provided points for certain desirable behaviors that clients demonstrated in the work setting. Clients could exchange their points for a number of different reinforcers. Hill, Wehman, and Combs (1979) described the effects of self-administered reinforcement on the production rates of two individuals with mental retardation. Besides the supervisor-delivered reinforcers, clients were trained to pay themselves a token for assembling a prescribed number of "photo envelopes containing seven order coupons" (p. 7). The self-reinforcing strategies were positively related to both maintaining and accelerating work production.

N. Campbell (1971) also evaluated a work reinforcement system. In the work reinforcement program, he used one task that the client liked to perform as a reinforcement for doing a task the client did not like. Experimentation with the work reinforcement system indicated that production tended to increase on both the desirable and undesirable tasks. He also employed the technique of time-out from reinforcement, or isolation-avoidance, as a consequence of certain undesirable behaviors. In other words, clients who were not maintaining a previously agreed upon production rate were removed from the group setting and placed in an isolated or individual situation. To return to the group, the client had to demonstrate a previously agreed upon production rate. Before it was instituted, the isolation-avoidance approach was discussed with the clients in the workshop. Overall, the procedure effectively controlled certain target behaviors without otherwise negatively affecting the person's performance.

What Other Factors Affect Work Adjustment?

A number of factors affect the progress that the individual makes in programs offering work adjustment services (Bolton, 1982; J. Campbell & O'Toole, 1971). For example, does the setting present realistic work requirements; that is, does it make demands on clients that are consistent with those made by an industrial setting? Are the contracts or the work tasks meaningful or "make-work" type activities? Naturally, the more the setting approximates an industrial one and the more meaningful the work within that setting, the greater the progress that can be expected from individuals receiving work adjustment services.

The attitude of the facility staff toward the clients is also an extremely important factor. For example, staff should feel that their principal function is one of enhancing clients' skills rather than one of ensuring certain levels of production. In other words, the training setting should provide ample support for counselor–client interaction revolving around the counseling and skill objectives of the client's individual program. The client should be treated as an integral part of the program and as an individual whose point of view matters. Appropriate client reactions and recommendations should be worked into service delivery over time (J. Campbell & O'Toole, 1971).

Finally, the counselor needs to help clients appreciate the variety of factors on the job that will affect client work performance. Some of these factors cannot be simulated in the facility setting and can only be described as those things that clients might encounter after leaving the facility. For example, the demands of the new job may differ somewhat from the demands of the job or jobs the client learned in the facility. These new work demands may interact in a unique way with the disabling condition of the client. Because adjustment needs will occur beyond the workshop or center setting, it is important that rehabilitation services extend to include follow-up services after the person is on the job.

Gains made in the rehabilitation center or facility setting must be reinforced as clients make the transition into their other living and working situations. Awareness of the importance of this transition has long existed in rehabilitation (e.g., follow-up and follow-along services are part of the rehabilitation counselor's responsibilities to the client). Indeed, these follow-up services are further emphasized in the postemployment service sections of the Rehabilitation Act and its subsequent amendments and in public school transition programs that work in concert with vocational rehabilitation.

Effective School-to-Work Transition Services

The approach required to help youth with disabilities develop the skills and aspirations needed to make a successful transition from public school settings to the world of work is no different from that involved in any transition. Hence, popular literature about setting and achieving life goals, such as the work of Stephen Covey (1989, 2004), is relevant. Three of Covey's eight well-known habits of effective people clarify the attributes that youth and rehabilitation professionals need to succeed in the school-to-work transition process. In his first book, *The 7 Habits of Highly Effective People,* Covey (1989) stressed that the probability of achieving desired results increases considerably if individuals take the initiative (i.e., are proactive) and if they "begin with the end in mind." Covey's (2004) eighth principle underscores the need for each person to seek his or her own greatness—that is, the need for each person to find his or her own voice, which is consistent with the emphasis in rehabilitation on the concept of "informed choice." Covey's eighth principle reminds rehabilitation professionals of the importance of helping youth with disabilities achieve their own individuality and voice.

For Covey (1989), being proactive simply means taking action, which, when applied to school-to-work transition services, means that parents, youth, rehabilitation professionals, and teachers are responsible for developing, implementing, evaluating, and modifying the transition services that are needed in schools, vocational and rehabilitation settings, work sites, and communities. According to Covey, being proactive means that all parties must base their actions on self-chosen values rather than on personal moods, feelings, and circumstances. Thus, transition initiatives must reflect the goals of key constituents that are based on the ends that they wish to achieve—hence, the importance of Covey's second principle, "begin with the end in mind."

In the case of transition services, one of the most important ends to have in mind is that of improving the quality of life of young people with disabilities. Researchers (e.g., Salkever, 2000) have stressed the importance of a variety of psychological indicators that are central to the quality of life of young people with disabilities, including self-esteem, self-efficacy, acceptance, independence, and employment. Transition services represent one means by which students with disabilities achieve or enhance these aspects of their lives—that is, the ends that students, parents, rehabilitation professionals, and teachers have in mind. Importantly, these goals or "ends" that are central to transition programs are totally consistent with the federal legislation guiding educational and school-to-work services for youth with disabilities. In recent legislative activity,

> IDEA has been amended to clarify that one of the primary purposes of the law is to ensure a free appropriate public education designed to meet each student's unique needs and to prepare them [*sic*] for further education, employment, and independent living. (National Collaborative on Workforce and Disability for Youth, 2004, p. 3)

Youth with disabilities have no difficulty communicating their unique needs in their own voices (R. Roessler, 2005, personal communication). In a classroom discussion regarding their hopes, high school students with disabilities mentioned outcomes such as good jobs, steady work, and good pay. They wanted to earn money so that they could purchase automobiles, high-definition televisions, clothes, and makeup. When they described their fears about the future, they did not want to be unemployed or underemployed; be in poor health, hurt, or sick; be mad, upset, or angry; or have too little money to live a comfortable life. The students had vocational goals in mind that ranged from the somewhat fantastic to the very practical. One wanted to be a race car driver, another wanted to be an actress, another planned on becoming a nurse, and two expected to work for major retailers. Clearly, the students had their voices and their ideas of individuality. They had ends in mind—good jobs, good health, material possessions, and personal happiness—and they wanted transition programs to help them achieve their own versions of greatness.

The Irony of Transition

Widespread commitment to school-to-work transition services and outcomes for youth with disabilities is not a recent phenomenon. In fact, the irony of school-to-work transition services is that some ground has been lost in terms of collaboration between the public schools and vocational rehabilitation. In the 1960s, school-to-work transition services represented a national cooperative effort supported jointly by the public schools and the Rehabilitation Services Administration. However, as new legislation evolved in the 1970s (e.g., the Education for All Handicapped Children Act of 1975), the legal responsibility for preparing youth with disabilities shifted directly to the schools. Coupled with changes in funding patterns and funding cutbacks typical of the late 1970s, this shift in responsibility resulted in a gradual withdrawal of vocational rehabilitation from involvement in transition programs (Szymanski & Danek, 1985). Fortunately, the pendulum has swung back in the other direction. Today, the responsibility for school-to-work transition is once again shared jointly by the schools and the federal–state vocational rehabilitation system (Wittenburg, Golden, & Fishman, 2002), as evidenced in mandates in special education (the Individuals with Disabilities Education Act [IDEA] of 1997) and rehabilitation (the Rehabilitation Act Amendments of 1998) legislation. These mandates call for delivery of transition services "within a results oriented process" that is "focused on improving the academic and functional achievement of the student" (National Collaborative on Workforce and Disability for Youth, 2004, p. 1).

The Definition of Transition

In the mid-1980s one of the foremost pioneers and supporters of transition services, Madeleine Will (1985), then assistant secretary of the Office of Special Education and Rehabilitation Services, called for a results orientation in transition. She defined *transition from school to work* as an "outcome oriented process encompassing a broad array of services and experiences leading to employment" (p. 1). Her definition of *transition* continues to be important, as evidenced by emphases in IDEA that require inclusion of transition services in the first Individualized Education Program (IEP) following the student's 16th birthday (National Collaborative on Workforce and Disability for Youth, 2004). These services must be a coordinated set of activities, designed within an outcome-oriented process, which promotes movement from school to post-school activities, including postsecondary education, vocational training, integrated employment (including supported employment), continuing and adult education, adult services, independent living, and community participation. Based on individual need and consistent with the student's preferences and interests, transition services include instruction, community-based experiences, and the use of adult living objectives. Legislative requirements for transition can be met only through a concerted, coordinated, community-based effort drawing on employers, local school districts, and a number of state and federal programs (Texas Education Agency, 1999; Wittenburg et al., 2002). Kohler (1993) identified the following "best practices" related to positive transition outcomes for youth with disabilities: vocational training, parent involvement, interagency collaboration and service delivery, social skills training, paid work experience, individualized transition planning, employability skills training, and placement in integrated, least restrictive environments.

Koch (2000) applied a similar "best practices" analysis specifically to the services that students with disabilities require if they are to achieve improved vocational outcomes, a critical issue given that students with disabilities are less likely to secure employment following graduation (Nagle, 2001). Koch arrayed these best practices in a four-phase career counseling process that includes specific activities pertinent to (a) career exploration and decision making (e.g., participating in job shadowing, volunteer work, and work experiences), (b) career planning (e.g., preparing a career planner and career portfolio), (c) job development and placement (e.g., joining a job club and learning job seeking and job-search-organizing skills), and (d) career maintenance (e.g., receiving supported employment and accommodations planning services). In addition to providing career-oriented services, best practices in transition must be implemented with four key terms in mind: *accountability, process, array of services,* and *outcome.* These terms are discussed in the following sections.

Accountability

Though an extremely important accountability criterion to assess, achievement of academic outcomes alone is insufficient to ensure successful employment of youth with disabilities (McDonnell, Mathot-Buckner, & Ferguson, 1996). Progress toward other objectives that fall into the broad area of career education must also be ensured. For example, Wehman (1992) included the following among transition outcomes: employment and financial independence, community and home living arrangements, independent mobility, peer relationships, and sexuality and self-esteem. Reference is made in IDEA to other important goal areas, such as postsecondary education, community participation, and recreation and leisure activities (Texas Education Agency, 1999).

Career education materials such as the Life Centered Career Education (LCCE) curriculum are available to help students develop the skills needed to achieve transition outcomes. Life Centered Career Education consists of lesson plans in three areas: (a) daily living skills, (b) personal/social skills, and (c) occupational guidance and preparation skills. Designed to enhance students' life and employability skills, the Life Centered Career Education curriculum integrates special and vocational education instruction, assistance from rehabilitation and other community programs, and experiential learning in community living and work sites (Brolin, 2005a, 2005b; Roessler & Brolin, 2004). The curriculum helps students overcome deficiencies such as (a) unrealistic impressions of their strengths and weaknesses, (b) little idea of what they want to do after high school, and (c) inadequate information about the variety of jobs and careers available to them (Vatour, Stocks, & Kolek, 1983). Because of lack of exposure to work, students with disabilities are often not familiar with the vocabulary of the working world. Equally important, they have deficiencies in desirable work behaviors, such as punctuality, following directions, task completion, and responsibility for one's actions.

To meet their accountability obligations, public school transition programs, therefore, must address not only academic goals but also independent living and work-related goals of students with disabilities. Only by addressing multiple outcome goals can school-based programs reduce the current high unemployment and underemployment rate of youth with disabilities (McDonnell et al., 1996). For example, when compared with students without disabilities, students with mild mental retardation were much more likely to be unemployed 6 months or 30 months after leaving high school (73% vs. 41% and 67% vs. 47%, respectively; Affleck, Edgar, Levine, & Kortering, 1990). Even when employed, students with mild disabilities are too frequently hired for low-skill, low-pay, part-time positions that they are frequently unable to maintain (D'Amico & Marder, 1991; Neubert, Tilson, & Ianacone, 1989; S. Siegel, Avoke, Paul, Robert, & Gaylord-Ross, 1991). Moreover, a great many students with multiple or severe disabilities are unemployed, ranging from 90% in one study (D'Amico & Marder, 1991) to 60% in other studies (Anderson & Asselin, 1996; P. Levine & Nourse, 1998; Louis Harris & Associates, 1989). In the late 1980s the W. T. Grant Foundation (1988) clarified the scope of the problem when it referred to youth with disabilities as "one of the most economically disadvantaged subgroups in American society" (p. 106). Years later, data continue to indicate that students with disabilities are not connecting with postsecondary educational and employment options in an effective manner (Anderson & Asselin, 1996; P. Levine & Nourse, 1998; Nagle, 2001). Thus, to improve employment and other life outcomes of youth with disabilities, a sound planning process involving input from many disciplines is needed (Cronin, Patton, & Lock, 2004).

Process

The transition process for a student requires both a multidisciplinary team and a comprehensive planning methodology, and evidence exists to support the positive impact that such coordination has on transition outcomes (Eisenman, 2003). This planning methodology includes such procedural steps as assessment of the student's preferences, strengths, and needs; development of feasible options; matching of the student with educational and vocational options; training and preparation to succeed in selected options; and placement and follow-along (Condon, Enein-Donovan, Gilmore, & Jordan, 2004). Professionals from special education, vocational education, vocational rehabilitation, vocational evaluation, school counseling, school psychology, school social work, physical therapy, and occupational therapy, as well as parents or significant caregivers, have critical roles in the planning process (Cronin et al., 2004; Szymanski & Danek, 1985). Drawing on their expertise and personal knowledge of the student, these team members contribute to the student's development of academic, independent living, and work-related goals and plans.

Transition goals for the student relate to one another in a sequential fashion so that accomplishments in basic academic and career education areas complement work-related placements in the community, such as work shadowing, work center placements, volunteer work, and part- or full-time competitive employment (S. Davis, Anderson, Linkowski, Berger, & Feinstein, 1985). These goals as well as the procedures for accomplishing them are recorded on the student's IEP, which is a joint product of student, family, and professional input. Updated on an annual basis, the IEP should culminate in placement of the student at the end of secondary schooling in an adequate residential situation, supportive social relationships, and appropriate employment or postsecondary educational training (Cronin et al., 2004; Lichtenstein & Michaelides, 1993; Wittenburg et al., 2002).

Array of Services

The multiple services that are the hallmark of effective transition programs have already been described in part. Coordinated by the special education teacher, evaluation of and instruction in reading, self-expression, and computational skills are essential. For many years employers have encouraged the schools to revitalize their approach to teaching the three R's (Wilms, 1984), and recent evidence clearly supports the positive relationship between consumer reading and mathematics levels and outcomes in vocational rehabilitation such as competitive employment and wage/salary level (Kosciulek, 2004a). Looking to the needs of a "post-industrial economy," C. Ryan (1995) renewed this call for better academic preparation of people with disabilities, with special emphasis on computer literacy and problem-solving skills. Vatour et al. (1983) stressed the need to train students in generalizable skills appropriate to many jobs rather than in skills of a narrow task or occupation. In other words, employers support instruction in such areas as "positive work habits, sound basic interpersonal and work skills, problem-solving skills, and adaptability to the work environment" (Eleventh Institute on Rehabilitation Issues, 1984; Wilms, 1984), although they recognize that the importance of technical skill training increases when more complex jobs are considered (C. Ryan, 1995).

Many service providers contribute to the transition of youth with disabilities. Vocational educators involve students in appropriate vocational training and work exposure experiences (Roessler, Brown, Reed, & Getch, 1999). Representatives from school counseling, school psychology, and social work contribute evaluation and case management assistance. Representatives outside the school setting have valuable services to provide. In fact, IDEA specifies that the IEP indicate how different agencies will contribute to the student's postschool support system. For example, the plan may indicate how the rehabilitation counselor will assist. Duties of the rehabilitation counselor include "assessment of vocational potential, vocational planning, consultation with team members on the vocational and educational implications of disability, vocational and work adjustment counseling, coordination of planning and service delivery, job placement, and follow-up services" (Szymanski & Danek, 1985, p. 84). Mental health and mental retardation agencies, independent living centers, and Social Security offer a wide range of employment, postsecondary education, benefits planning, and adult and independent living services essential for effective transition planning as well (Roessler, 2002).

Often, special efforts referred to as job creation are required to help students with disabilities find suitable employment (Condon et al., 2004). For example, rehabilitation professionals may develop a job that never existed "such as a mail delivery clerk at a business where personnel used to pick up their own mail at a central location" or they may create a new job by restructuring existing functions such as hiring a worker "in an office to support only copying and filing needs" (p. 1).

The process of job creation, however, is only one step in a more complex five-step process (Condon et al., 2004). Job creation begins with the development of a student or job seeker profile, including not only what the student likes to do and can do but also the types of work environments the student prefers and the types of accommodations he or she needs to succeed in those environments. Job creation requires that a group of individuals participate in developing this profile, establishing support networks, and gathering information regarding employment opportunities. Ideas about real possibilities for employment open the door to direct contacts with employers to learn more about the duties required in those jobs, the resources the student needs to carry out those duties, and the value that the student represents to the employer (e.g., reducing costly overtime or contract work). When school and rehabilitation professionals have taken these preliminary steps, the probability of the student's finding and retaining satisfying work is increased considerably. Condon et al. (2004) described some of the possible outcomes that students can achieve as a result of job creation—for example, operator of a snack bar within a large company, a data entry clerk or mail deliverer, a greeter in a health club or Y, a vacuum cleaner operator for a home or office cleaning team, a copier or shredder of information at a university or hospital, or a pricer or stocker in a retail business during rush seasons.

Outcome

The final element in the transition model is outcome, which directly relates to Covey's (1989) recommendation to begin with the end in mind and to determine whether that end has been achieved. Historically, transition services have placed a strong emphasis on employment, which is indeed "the most desirable objective of transition programs" (Salkever, 2000, p. 9). Special strategies such as job creation (Condon et al., 2004) are often needed to achieve employment outcomes. At the same time, research supports the notion that activity of many sorts is strongly related to perceived quality of life. Students who report involvement in multiple pursuits, such as postsecondary schooling, volunteer work, housework, and paid employment, are more likely to be satisfied with the quality of their lives (Salkever, 2000). Based on findings from a national consumer survey with people with developmental disabilities and their families, Salkever reported that "overall life satisfaction was clearly lowest for persons who were idle or who only reported housework as an activity" (p. 9).

Salkever's (2000) research findings are consistent with admonitions (Cronin et al., 2004; Halpern, 1985) that employment as an outcome is only part of the overall social integration of a young person with a disability. If individuals with disabilities are to live full and satisfying lives, they must also have access to quality residential environments and social networks. Each of these areas—employment, residential situation, and social networks—represents a "pillar" of community adjustment. Halpern (1985) cited evidence for the independence of these areas, stressing that success in one area does not ensure success in the other two. "Each must support the other or the whole structure will fall" (Halpern, 1985, p. 481).

Some Recommendations

Successful transition services rest on basic commitments of everybody involved to Covey's (1989, 2004) principles to be proactive, to begin with the end in mind, and to help students find their voices. This commitment also extends to the recognition by special educators, vocational educators, and vocational rehabilitation counselors of the need to collaborate in helping students identify and access both educational and adult services (Wittenburg et al., 2002). The emphasis in the IEP on the three pillars of community adjustment must be increased, and improved career education assessment and intervention devices are needed (Cronin et al., 2004; Eisenman, 2003; Halpern, 1985; Hursh, Shrey, Lasky, & D'Amico, 1982; Koch, 2000). Community barriers to employment, such as negative social attitudes toward people with disabilities, must be countered (Vatour et al., 1983). IEP goals and services should be expanded in scope to include the skills and support the student needs to achieve an appropriate level of independence in the community (Cronin et al., 2004). Education of the student in independent living and vocational skills needs to take place in the community and on the job. Transition programs must "move their base of operations from schools to work fronts, agencies, and work environments" (Pawelski & Groveman, 1982, p. 24). They must extend their programs beyond school hours as well to teach recreation, social, independent living, and vocational skills in the community. Schools must increase parental involvement in the development of school-to-work transition programs and in support of career education goals through activities in the home (Mpofu & Wilson, 2004; Roessler & Brolin, 2005).

Concluding Statement

To enable people with disabilities to attain their vocational objectives, state rehabilitation agency field counselors secure and coordinate a variety of rehabilitation services. This chapter focused on many of the available services, which fall into the medical, personal–social, or work adjustment categories. Special attention was given to the role and function of the rehabilitation facility in the rehabilitation process (e.g., to provide an in-depth evaluation of client needs and the required services and training programs in vocational and nonvocational areas).

To meet the multiple needs of armed services personnel with war injuries, the number of rehabilitation centers increased tremendously in the years during and directly after World War II. Initially stressing rehabilitation medicine, some centers expanded to incorporate vocational training and placement. Professional services often available in rehabilitation centers include physiatry (physical medicine), rehabilitation nursing, orthotics–prosthetics, physical therapy, occupational therapy, speech–language pathology and audiology, rehabilitation psychology, rehabilitation engineering, and therapeutic recreation. These services are complemented by skill-oriented training in the personal, social, and work adjustment areas.

Between 1950 and 1965 the workshop or community facility movement in the United States experienced tremendous growth. Community facilities provide comprehensive services in psychosocial, recreational, educational, and vocational areas. Reflecting a more inclusive philosophy, such facilities have broadened their employment programs to include both internal and external placements. External placements result from both the traditional individual placement model and the supported employment model, with its use of job coaches, work teams, and enclaves.

Many factors hinder the effectiveness of facilities and centers. For example, community facilities must deal with the conflict between being both a rehabilitation program and a business enterprise. Community programs must guard against decreasing the clients' feelings of worth by having them work in inadequate surroundings (e.g., where equipment is nonexistent or antiquated, and the facility itself is located in a run-down section of the community). Rehabilitation centers suffer from many of the same limitations. In addition, rehabilitation centers may overemphasize the medical aspects of their program, making the individual feel more like a patient than someone who is capable of greater independence. As a result, some clients fall into a docile, dependent role.

Because rehabilitation facilities vary in both purpose and effectiveness, the counselor should assess the competency of the program to meet desired rehabilitation objectives. Once a suitable facility has been selected, the counselor should maintain sufficient contact with the client while he or she is at the rehabilitation facility.

Establishing and maintaining contact with students with disabilities in school-to-work transition programs is another important rehabilitation service. As part of a multidisciplinary team, the rehabilitation counselor helps youth with disabilities and their families develop academic, independent living, and work-related educational plans during the secondary school years. These Individualized Education Programs present goals and strategies that result in quality residential, social support, and employment outcomes.

Chapter 12

Job Placement

After completing vocational preparation services, clients are ready for appropriate job placement assistance. To achieve their placement objectives, some people will require job seeking skills training to acquire employment independently, some clients will require direct placement intervention and job coaching services (supported employment), and others may benefit from both types of services. Making the wrong choice among job seeking skills, direct intervention, or both can have a detrimental effect. The choice of job seeking skills training only when direct intervention is necessary could result in the person's failing to obtain a job. Direct placement intervention where job seeking skills training is sufficient could result in unnecessary questioning of the individual's competence by the employer as well as by the job seeker.

In reviewing placement techniques, this chapter discusses job seeking skills training programs, direct placement intervention, supported employment, job development, and employer concerns. Although the chapter concentrates on describing different placement strategies, the reader is reminded that placement efforts on the part of the counselor are influenced by a host of factors. For example, counselors have seen increased attention given to issues such as "federal emphasis on serving people with more significant disabilities, societal pressures for cost-effective social services, and changing consumer expectations about choice and control" (Ford & Sweet, 1999, p. 355).

Job Seeking Skills Training

Research (Roessler, Hinman, & Lewis, 1987; G. Wright, 1980) documents the job seeking skills deficiencies of rehabilitation clients. These individuals often experience difficulty explaining the employment significance of their educational background, job history, or skills. In addition to not looking for work frequently enough, some individuals fail to dress appropriately for the job interview. Other research indicates that many rehabilitation clients are unaware of the techniques for securing and following up on job leads and for completing applications neatly and accurately (Mathews & Fawcett, 1984). With little history of job procurement success, they may also be pessimistic about their chances of obtaining a job and convey that attitude in employment interviews (Goodwin, 1972; Roessler & Bolton, 1985a).

Poor job seeking skills, therefore, are one reason why many rehabilitation clients secure only entry-level, secondary labor market positions. Unfortunately, being in entry-level jobs, many clients find themselves in expendable positions during massive shifts in the economy—the last hired, first fired (D. Ryan, 2004). Without job seeking skills, they are unable to reenter the workforce on their own initiative. Fortunately, both self-help and group techniques exist that enable individuals to improve their job seeking skills.

Early efforts in the development of job seeking skills programs, such as Keith's (1976, 1977) *Employment Seeking Preparation and Activity* (ESPA), contain the essential elements required to teach job seeking behaviors on an individual, self-help basis. Materials included in the package teach participants how to (a) determine job suitability, (b) assess occupational assets and liabilities, (c) prepare a resume, (d) perform in a job interview, and (e) secure job leads. Keith, Engelkes, and Winborn (1977) assessed the effectiveness of ESPA with clients (people with physical, emotional, or sensory disabilities) who were judged ready for employment and who were served within four district offices of the Michigan Vocational Rehabilitation Services Agency. During the 2-month period following initiation of the study, "42% of the ESPA group, but only 10% and 14% of the two control groups, obtained jobs" (Keith et al., 1977).

The Minneapolis Rehabilitation Center (MRC) developed a 2-day job seeking skills training program. Using a group training approach, the package includes instruction on finding job leads, completing job application blanks, and interviewing for jobs. McClure (1972) compared the effectiveness of the MRC program and normal agency placement services with job-ready state rehabilitation agency and state employment service clients. The MRC program was found to be significantly superior in regard to (a) acquisition of client employment and (b) counselor time required to obtain a placement. McClure (1972) stated that the "consensus of the counselors was that the course increased the motivation, confidence, and enthusiasm for job procurement activities of participating clients" (p. 193).

The MRC program did, however, overlook one important facet of job seeking skills training, namely an opportunity for clients to have supervised practice in seeking jobs during the course of the training. The results of one study (Kemp & Vash, 1971) suggested that such an addition is essential for guaranteeing program effectiveness. Pumo, Sehl, and Cogan (1966) developed one of the earliest job seeking skills training programs containing actual client job seeking activity. They reported the results of three job-readiness clinics held in Toledo, Ohio, in 1965 and 1966 for clients from Goodwill Industries and the Ohio Bureau of Vocational Rehabilitation. Although they either had just completed training and entered a ready-for-employment status or had been in a ready-for-employment status 6 months or longer, most participants were considered to have poor employment potential. People involved in the training had such disabilities as mental retardation, emotional disturbance, cerebral palsy, orthopedic impairment, and partial blindness.

The job-readiness clinic contained the following activities, among others:

1. Instruction on where to find job leads and on preparation of personal resumes.
2. An exercise on filling out employment applications.
3. A presentation on working by an employed person with a disability.
4. Information from a personnel director on hiring practices and employer needs.
5. Role-played employment interviews by a rehabilitation and placement counselor, followed by a critique by the clients as to errors and proper mannerisms.
6. Encouragement, after the third session, to apply for several jobs over a 3-day period. Group discussion of the job seeking experiences took

place during the next session. This was followed by the clients' applying for several other jobs and then by a second group discussion on
their experiences.

7. Practice in the fifth session with role-playing employment interviews
with each other. The group analyzed the role-play performance. The
sixth session was devoted to review and discussion of the program's effectiveness.

Seventy-three percent of the participants successfully obtained employment.
Other job seeking skills training programs with many similarities to the Pumo
et al. (1966) program have been successfully conducted with a group of men
who had been unemployed from 3 to 10 years (Kemp & Vash, 1971); a group
of state vocational rehabilitation agency clients reporting psychiatric, physical,
sensory, and social disabilities (Stude & Pauls, 1977); and individuals with arthritis or rheumatic disease (Allaire, Anderson, & Meenan, 1997).

The Job Club is another successful approach to job seeking skills training (Azrin & Besalel, 1980; Azrin, Flores, & Kaplan, 1977; Azrin & Phillip,
1979; Corrigan, Reedy, Thadani, & Ganet, 1995; Gray & Braddy, 1988; Jacobs,
Kardashian, Kreinbring, Ponder, & Simpson, 1984). Consistent with the other
programs previously described, the Job Club uses multiple proven techniques to
increase client job seeking capabilities, such as a buddy system, family support,
role models, intense role-play practice of job interviews, and practice in completing job applications (Matthias, 1981). Several studies have demonstrated the
positive impact that the Job Club has on employment of participants. For example, Azrin and Phillip (1979) reported that after a 6-month period, 95% of a
Job Club's clients were employed, compared with 28% of individuals in a comparison group. Retention of participants in the Job Club is an issue, however,
particularly for people with psychiatric disabilities. Jacobs et al. (1984) found
that 66% of a group of clients with psychiatric disabilities who started a Job
Club finished the program and were engaged in productive activity (e.g., were
employed or enrolled in vocational training). Corrigan et al. (1995), on the
other hand, reported that 70% of the participants with severe mental illness
dropped out in another study.

Recommended Components
for a Job Seeking Skills Curriculum

A comprehensive job seeking skills curriculum would cover the following
topics with clients (Allaire et al., 1997; Frank & Bellini, 2005; Mathews,
Whang, & Fawcett, 1980, 1984; Potts, 2005; Roessler & Brolin, 2004; Roessler
& Rumrill, 1994; D. Ryan, 2004; Tesolowski, 1979; Volkli, Eichman, &
Shervey, 1982):

1. Why people work and what you want from a job

2. What you like and do not like about work
3. What kind of worker you are: abilities, skills, interests, and goals
4. Your vocational prospects: jobs desired, how to learn more about them, vocational projections for the next 10 years, selecting a job goal, résumé writing, and scheduling informational interviews
5. Your employment rights
6. How to build your social and job contact network
7. How to find a job: seeking a job lead from a friend, telephoning a potential employer regarding a job lead, and writing a letter in response to a help-wanted advertisement
8. How to get a job: writing an application letter, completing the job application, performing in the job interview, writing a letter to follow up on a job interview, and soliciting letters of recommendation
9. How to keep and advance on a job: acceptable and unacceptable job maintenance behaviors, requesting reasonable accommodations, and advancing on the job

The following sections serve to elaborate on several areas mentioned in this list: (a) sources of good job leads, (b) employment rights, (c) employer expectations for prospective employees, (d) organization of the job search, (e) completion of job application blanks, (f) job interview training, (g) supervised practice in job seeking, and (h) the accommodation request process.

Sources of Job Leads

In the past, rehabilitation clients have relied on direct application and newspaper classified ads as sources of job leads (Zadny & James, 1978). Direct application is beneficial because many companies review unsolicited job applications before consulting with employment services. Newspaper ads and other sources of leads, such as unions, state employment services, and private employment agencies, are worthwhile but not as valuable as informal sources, such as private communication channels, friends, and relatives (Gilbride, Thomas, & Stensrud, 1998; Potts, 2005). In recent years the Internet has been an expanding source of job leads. A list of job openings can be found on many websites, such as those of specific employers (Gilbride & Stensrud, 2003), trade magazines, and professional organizations. Individuals with disabilities should also inquire about job leads from other people with disabilities who are currently working (Finch, 1981). However, as D. Dunn (1981) advised, the best overall strategy for finding job leads involves extensive use of every possible source.

Employment Rights

The current employment era for people with disabilities is significantly influenced by the civil rights protections available in Title I of the Americans with Disabilities Act of 1990 (ADA), the priority on addressing diversity in the workplace, and the projected decrease in available workers at a time when large numbers of baby boomers are retiring (Gilbride & Stensrud, 1992; Schramm & Burke, 2004; Sheffield, 2005; see Chapter 3 for a full discussion of the ADA). The ADA clearly mandates that employers not discriminate against people in the hiring process because they have disabilities. The critical issue on which employers may discriminate is, instead, whether the person can perform the essential functions of the position with or without reasonable accommodation. The employer should describe these essential job functions in a job description available to the applicant for review, and the applicant should have a basic understanding of the definition of *essential function*. For example, the applicant needs to understand that the function is so critical, such as driving in the case of a taxi driver, that the position would not exist without its performance, or the function "is so highly specialized that the person in the position is hired for his or her expertise or ability to perform the particular function" (Sheffield, 2005, p. 4).

The applicant is not required to disclose the presence of a disability during the interview, and the employer may not ask if the person has a disabling condition. However, at some point immediately following the offer of employment, prospective employees with disabilities are required to inform employers if they will need accommodations. Employers are not held responsible for providing accommodations if they are not notified of such needs by the applicant. In fact, lack of knowledge regarding the existence of an applicant's disability on the part of the responsible hiring agent is an excellent way for an employer "to win or avoid ADA lawsuits" (Sheffield, 2005, p. 7).

Satcher (1992, p. 39) described a variety of examples of clear-cut discrimination that are prohibited by the ADA, such as the following:

1. Classifying a job applicant with a disability, on the basis of the disability, in a way that limits or denies the person's job opportunities
2. Using employment standards or criteria that limit or deny equal employment opportunity for a person with a disability
3. Failing to provide reasonable accommodation during the application process
4. Administering employment tests that tend to screen out people with disabilities
5. Failing to provide accommodation on employment tests that measure skills necessary to perform the essential functions of the job

Because many people with disabilities may be unfamiliar with the ADA (e.g., 71% in a random sample polled by Louis Harris & Associates in 1993), it is important to include information on employment rights in a comprehensive job seeking skills training program (Governmental Activities Office, 1993).

Employer Expectations

Because some employers may hold negative attitudes toward employing them (Goodwin, 1972; Nordstrom, Huffaker, & Williams, 1998; Roessler & Bolton,

1984), people with disabilities need opportunities for personal contact and communication with employers. Through contact with employers, such as in job interviews, the job seeker with a disability can learn more about what employers look for in prospective employees, and the employer can learn more about the potential of individuals with disabilities. People with disabilities need to know how to manage the effects of often subtly expressed negative attitudes during these contacts (Schneider & Anderson, 1980). For example, rather than "bristling at condescending attitudes," persons with disabilities need to learn how to refocus employers on the capabilities that they bring to the job (Bissonnette, 1994; Finch, 1981).

Organization of the Job Search

Another important facet of job seeking skills programs is training on organizing and managing the job search process. Wesolowski (1981) discussed a number of useful job seeking aids, such as developing lists of companies in a given locale, marking the companies' locations on a street map, identifying public transportation routes, planning an itinerary for each day's calls, and maintaining a record of the results of employer contacts. D. Ryan (2004) described how to organize the job search using a set of time management forms that enable the job seeker to log appointments and their outcomes, to schedule a variety of job hunting activities, to note time usage in different job seeking activities, and to record correspondence, telephone calls, and follow-up commitments. Taking a similar but less comprehensive approach, Azrin and Besalel (1980, pp. 180–181) presented a "places to go/things to do" schedule that the job seeker should keep. This schedule includes names of companies to contact, names of the contact people, the companies' locations, the results of the visits, and the dates of all activities involved in the job search.

Completion of Job Application Forms

At a minimum, people with disabilities should be instructed on completing the types of items found on most job application forms. Realistic practice of this skill can be acquired by having clients complete job applications of local employers. As stressed in the literature available from state employment agencies, individuals should complete every item neatly, accurately, and within the space provided. In the case of education and work history, the person should prepare the information on a small file card in advance so that he or she can quickly transfer it to the application form. In completing the application, the individual should stress his or her capabilities to do the job while avoiding reference to problems irrelevant to the job. Research indicates that individuals can improve their ability to complete job applications through behavioral instruction (Mathews & Fawcett, 1984). If possible, the job seeker should request that the employer mail a copy of the application to his or her home or make a personal visit to the employer to request an application to complete at home.

The Internet is increasingly used as a way to solicit potential employees, and applicants may need to learn how to complete employers' applications online through a company website or through a job bank (D. Ryan, 2004).

Roessler and Brolin (2004) developed a detailed approach for improving an individual's skills for completing job applications. Their program begins with a brief review of various forms with which most people are familiar, such as motor vehicle registrations, school enrollment forms, voter registration forms, and doctors' office registration forms. These forms require not only some of the same information as do job applications but also many of the same skills. Hence, guidelines such as the following for completing most types of forms are equally appropriate for filling out job applications: (a) Carry a personal information card listing your address, telephone number, previous educational and work experience, and personal references; (b) read the directions on the form carefully; (c) read the entire form before beginning to complete it; (d) work slowly and carefully; and (e) respond to every item (draw a line in the blank if the question does not apply).

The personal information card or data sheet is a useful aid for the job seeker during the application process. Job seekers can transfer information directly from the data sheet to the job application. In addition to name, address, telephone number, and Social Security number, the data sheet should contain specifics regarding the person's educational background, work experience, and personal references. Because many applications require that work experience be listed with most recent employment first, the person is advised to list his or her employment history on the personal data sheet in this way.

Job Interview Training

A review of the job interview training literature reveals the following clusters of critical interview skills: starting the interview; describing work-related skills; describing education and work history; discussing accommodation needs; discussing salary, fringe benefits, and advancement; and closing the interview (Roessler, Lewis, & Hinman, 1986; D. Ryan, 2004). People should also be taught to "respond completely to the interviewer's questions" and to "initiate questions regarding work tasks, company policies, and promotional possibilities" during job interviews (Keil & Barbee, 1973, p. 51). Instruction should also be provided on appropriate appearance, attitude, and behavior for the job interview. Some examples provided by Gilbride and Stensrud (2003) related to this point follow:

- "Consumers need to recognize that their clothes and grooming must meet the expectations and culture of the employer" (p. 417).
- "Consumers need to demonstrate confidence in their ability to perform the essential functions of the job without appearing cocky or condescending toward the employer or the type of work they would be expected to perform" (p. 417).

- The consumer should "be on time for the interview," not chew gum or smoke in the interview, not discuss "salary or benefits early in an interview," and not make "derogatory statements about previous employers" (p. 418).

Job seekers should also understand that while employers are interested in determining if applicants have the specific skills required to perform job tasks, they may be equally or even more interested in traits of applicants "such as dependability, punctuality, and ... ability to relate to both co-workers and supervisors" (Kiernan & Rowland, 1989, p. 258).

Hall, Sheldon-Wildgen, and Sherman (1980) found that job interviewing skills could be effectively taught via modeling and role-playing strategies. Farley and Hinman (1987) demonstrated the value of relaxation training as an effective means for improving job interview skills. Their findings supported the thesis that many people could perform more effectively in interviews when not inhibited by high levels of anxiety. In other words, people may know how to respond in the interview but be too nervous to do so effectively.

Supervised Practice in Job Seeking

Experience with job seeking skills training programs indicates that many employer contacts may be necessary before a client secures employment. Hence, ongoing support and practice for the job seeking process are necessary components of any training program. Not only can trainees learn from each other as they discuss their experiences in looking for work, but they also can provide encouragement for continuing the search. Social support during the follow-along sessions helps clients cope with any discouragement stemming from lack of success in their initial job seeking efforts. The use of taped commentaries or face-to-face talks by former job seekers who experienced some early failures, but were eventually successful, can also temper trainee discouragement. Moreover, follow-up sessions should be available to those who lose a job secured through a systematic job seeking program. They should be allowed to reenter the program at any time they are actively looking for work (Azrin & Besalel, 1980).

The Accommodation Request Process

Title I of the ADA explicitly bars discrimination in the hiring and employment process against qualified individuals with disabilities who can perform the essential functions of a position, with or without accommodations. It also requires that the applicant inform the interviewer of the need for an accommodation during the hiring process. However, if an applicant only needs accommodations to perform essential functions of the position, he or she is not required to disclose such needs until after a job offer has been made. Thus, individuals should understand how to approach the accommodation request process both in terms of timing (after the offer) and in terms of recommended strategies.

In their discussion of the "win-win approach to reasonable accommodation," Roessler and Rumrill (2002) recommended that job seekers with disabilities plan their approach and even rehearse their presentation with a friend. They should have suggestions for reasonable accommodations that have worked in the past, understanding that employers make the final decisions about types of accommodations to implement (Sheffield, 2005). Introducing the need for an accommodation using language such as "I would like to explore with you ..." is preferable to such phrases as "You have to ..." or "I am entitled to ..." (Roessler & Rumrill, 2002, p. 15). Applicants can anticipate encountering some resistance regarding provision of accommodations from employers, although they should begin the process with the "win-win" attitude (Frank & Bellini, 2005).

Trainer Familiarity with Job Market

Even though job seeking skills training programs are designed to facilitate the client's procurement of employment without direct counselor intervention with the employer, the job seeking skills trainer (who may or may not be the client's rehabilitation counselor) must be familiar with the local job market (e.g., types of jobs; skill demands of those jobs; types of accommodations, pay scales, fringe benefits, and supervisory practices; locations of jobs; accessibility of work sites). Familiarity with the local job market can best be gained through direct contacts with employers and work site visitations. Job seeking skills trainers with such knowledge will be more effective, because of their ability to direct clients with vocational goals toward the most logical potential employers in the local community. Such direction should reduce the likelihood that clients will experience nonproductive job searches and the resulting personal discouragement and diminished motivation (Roessler & Rubin, 2006). There is no reason why the rehabilitation counselor could not act as a personal reference, even to the extent of paving the way with the employer for the job seeking skills client. "Paving the way" for clients may also involve counselors in some important job development communications with employers. In these contacts counselors may need to defuse the unspoken but powerful fears that some employers have regarding hiring people with disabilities, such as concerns about the presumed high cost of accommodations, about firing a person with a disability, about lack of follow-up support from the counselor, and about poor attendance or productivity records of employees with disabilities (Peck & Kirkbride, 2001).

Vandergoot (1996) also discussed extending the role of the job seeking skills trainer or counselor beyond simply being a source of job leads. Consistent with "paving the way," he referred to the rehabilitation counselor as a labor market intermediary who serves both the client and the employer. In their client services, counselors conduct transferable skills analyses and job seeking skills training. They involve clients in vocational goal setting, but not in the narrow sense of identifying one or two job titles to pursue in the community. Instead, they help clients see how employment benefits them in larger ways, such as providing access to adequate income, fringe benefits, and preferred geographic locales, as well as enabling them to implement their interests, talents, and skills. With this greater diversity of goals in mind, people with disabilities can see the relevance of a wider range of vocational roles, which improves their chances of finding suitable employment in the local labor market.

For the placement process to have the highest probability of success, counselors must respond to the needs of employers as well. For example, at no cost to employers, rehabilitation counselors can provide a pool of prescreened applicants who possess the skills employers need. They can offer employers valuable follow-up services to help workers adjust well to the job both in the initial stages and in the long run. Through these services counselors develop close working relationships with employers and increase the counselors' credibility as a source of both job leads and job applicants (Gilbride & Stensrud, 2003; Millington, Miller, Asner-Self, & Linkowski, 2003; Vandergoot, 1996).

Direct Placement Intervention

Some rehabilitation clients require more direct placement intervention and support to secure and maintain employment. Clients in this group can include (a) persons with schizophrenia with a history of institutionalization, (b) young adults with moderate retardation without a job history, and (c) persons with severe physical disabilities without work experience or with a poor predisability work history. Acquisition of jobs by these individuals often requires the help of an aggressive rehabilitation counselor or placement specialist who can both sell employers on hiring people with disabilities and supply the necessary on-the-job supports (Salomone, 1996). As demonstrated in employment interventions with people with schizophrenia (Lysaker & Bell, 1995), on-the-job support, which is exemplified in the supported employment model, increases the probability of job retention. G. Rose (1963, p. 13) presented an early version of transitional or supported employment when he used the term "rigorous postemployment services," which he described as having "someone on the staff … work the first hour, the first day, or the first week" with the newly placed worker.

Direct placement intervention can also enable people with severe physical disabilities, such as spinal cord injuries, to identify the types of accessibility and job modifications needed to gain access to the work site and perform essential functions of the job. Consideration of client skills, abilities, and limitations, as well as functional demands of potential jobs, is required for purposes of identifying accommodations needed to enhance the match between the worker and the job. Improving the match provides the person with a disability a better chance to perform capably during the early phases of the job and, thus, to demonstrate his or her feasibility for employment and potential for career advancement (Brodwin, Parker, & DeLaGarza, 2003). In the past, efforts to modify the work environment to meet the needs and capabilities of the individual were referred to as selective placement, which can be defined as the "precise and detailed matching" of an individual's abilities with the requirements of the job (Pati & Adkins, 1981, pp. 114–115).

Determining the requirements of the job necessitates visits to the job site and observation of actual working conditions. Reading job descriptions in occupational information resources is no substitute for firsthand knowledge. For example, production quotas could vary across job sites, reflecting differences in psychological and/or physical stress factors. In one work unit the job may be performed standing and in another sitting down. At one job site workers may have to retrieve the work from another part of the plant, while at another job site the work may be brought to them (Pinner & Altman, 1966).

Selective Placement and Job Analysis: A Proper Marriage

Enhancing the fit between worker capabilities and job demands via reasonable accommodations, as called for by Title I of the ADA, is quite compatible with the selective placement philosophy. The selective placement approach has its roots in the job analysis movement, which—although developed for other reasons (e.g., increasing industrial efficiency)—shifts the focus from individual limitations to characteristics of the physical environment and the demands of the job. Job analysis techniques, therefore, benefit people with disabilities by clearly demonstrating two important facts: (a) "No job requires all of the physical and mental capacities of human beings" (Kessler, 1953, p. 145) and (b) alternative strategies and technological aids can facilitate the performance of any given job function.

Through job analysis a specific job is divided into tasks and subtasks (essential functions) that are related to specific skills that the worker must possess. Job analysis provides information on (a) physical demands of the job, (b) mental demands of the job, (c) job-related stress factors, (d) characteristics of the work environment (e.g., noise, dust, ventilation), (e) type and amount of supervision, (f) customer service skills required, and (g) existing and potential hazards (HR Zone, 1998; Pati & Adkins, 1981; J. B. Patterson, 2003). Results of the analysis can be used to determine the fit between person and job and the modifications required to enhance that fit.

Bissonnette's (1994) approach to employer-focused job creation represents a slightly different slant on job analysis. Bissonnette advocated that job developers cultivate relationships with employers in order to develop an in-depth knowledge of the employers' needs. In other words, job developers study production processes and business practices to identify new ways that employers could operate more effectively and efficiently. Some of these "new ways" may necessitate hiring additional workers with a special blend of skills. Thus, the job developer actually creates new positions based on the information from job analyses. But the developer goes beyond describing duties of the new position and how it will save the employer money or increase operating efficiency. The developer also has a particular person with a disability in mind who could fill that job successfully. Using Bissonnette's approach to job analyses, job developers produce job orders for which they just happen to have an appropriate applicant—a qualified person with a disability. Because she also specifies the employment conditions sought by the candidate (e.g., preferred wage rate, work hours, and/or benefits), Bissonnette argues convincingly that her "employer-focused" approach represents a "win–win" situation for people with disabilities, placement professionals, and employers.

One final perspective on job analysis focuses directly on barriers to productivity experienced by current employees with disabilities. Using *The Work Experience Survey* (WES), a 30- to 60-minute structured interview (Allaire, Li, & LaValley, 2003; Roessler, 1995; Roessler & Rumrill, 1998), the placement professional can help the employee identify accommodation needs in terms of barriers to job performance in four areas: accessibility, performance of essential functions, job mastery, and job satisfaction. With the help of the rehabilitation professional, the individual prepares a job accommodation plan that includes a priority ranking of barriers, possible solutions to those barriers, and resources for barrier removal (Roessler, Reed, & Brown, 1998). Analysis of on-the-job accommodation needs is an essential service to help new employees with disabilities successfully adjust to a new job. At the same time, meeting accommodation needs is not a one-time event that occurs early in the employment process. Particularly in the case of progressive conditions, accommodation planning is an ongoing process to ensure long-term job retention of employees with disabilities.

Rehabilitation counselors have a direct role in helping people with disabilities address accommodation needs and other employment-related issues beyond the first few days of placement. In his model of career counseling and job placement, Salomone (1996) included long-term postemployment services as the final phase in his five-stage sequence. Through such services the counselor helps employees with disabilities clarify and achieve goals related to retention, long-term adjustment, and advancement on the job. Others have made similar arguments, noting particularly how the progressive and unpredictable nature of chronic illnesses such as multiple sclerosis and arthritis continually affects the job–person relationship (Allaire et al., 2003; Rumrill & Roessler, 1999; Vandergoot, 1996). For example, in a series of case studies, Roessler et al. (1998) described the on-the-job barriers to productivity faced by employed individuals with chronic illnesses. These case studies also illustrated the counselor's role in both barrier identification and barrier removal. With the help of their counselors, employees with disabilities identified and implemented job accommodations such as installation or modification of equipment, job restructuring, or changes in the physical environment. Thus, one important type of postemployment intervention concentrates primarily on remediation of productivity-reducing factors in the work environment. The importance of the continuous availability of such interventions as part of the job placement process is compatible with a point made by Gilbride and Stensrud (2003), that employers "will be more open to placement-related contacts, if they know long-term follow-up will be provided" (p. 430).

Salomone (1996) also mentioned other elements of postemployment services. He described how rehabilitation counselors can help people with disabilities arrange for adequate childcare and transportation. He also wrote of the importance of contingency planning in which counselors help individuals establish support networks and health care systems needed for long-term maintenance of health and employment. Counselors should assist individuals with disabilities in looking beyond their first jobs to a variety of future roles, if they continue their training and education. Through continued involvement in industry-based training or further formal education, employees with disabilities improve their potential to achieve career maintenance and advancement goals.

The Supported Employment Model

The supported employment or supported work model is another comprehensive selective placement approach (Salomone, 1996). Supported employment advocates emphasize that job preparation for many people with severe disabilities, particularly people with severe developmental disabilities (e.g., mental retardation), should take place in a competitive employment setting rather than in a sheltered workshop and that intensive follow-along services should be provided to the client in either individual or group models (Hanley-Maxwell, Owen-Johnson, & Fabian, 2003; Wehman & Kregel, 1985). Its priorities on job-site training, advocacy procedures, and long-term job retention and follow-up services differentiate the supported work model from other job placement approaches. According to Wehman and Kregel (1985), the supported work approach to job placement

> allows clients to be placed who do not possess all the necessary work or social skills required for immediate job success. This represents a significant departure from traditional placement approaches that require the client to be "job ready" before placement can occur.... In sharp contrast to rehabilitation programs that typically provide follow-up services for several months, clients within the supported work model may receive systematically planned job retention and follow-up services for many years after initial placement. Finally, the supported work model is perhaps unique in its identification of a single "job coordinator" who is responsible for all facets of the placement, training, advocacy, assessment, and follow-up process. (p. 27)

The development of the supported work model stems in part from the realization that only a small minority of the individuals with mental retardation placed in sheltered workshops moved on to competitive jobs (Wehman, 1986,

p. 24). According to Wehman and Kregel (1985), the supported work model is an excellent job placement approach for groups of people with moderate to severe disabilities.

> Within public school settings, [the model may be applicable to] students labeled moderately ... or ... mildly mentally retarded.... Within community service programs, the model may be applicable to persons who are usually labeled by rehabilitation facilities as possessing severe disabilities and who are most frequently served in sheltered workshops or activity centers. (p. 26)

Supported employment may occur in both individual and group models. The individual model stresses the importance of immediate placement of the individual in a competitive work setting with the support of a job coach. According to Hanley-Maxwell et al. (2003), the individual model is the most prevalent and the most preferred. Individual placements in integrated settings are consistent with the underlying philosophy of supporting people with severe disabilities in their desires to live and work in "least restrictive environments." Support for the worker in this model is possible through both an on-site direct services provider, such as a job coach, and an employment facilitator, such as a coworker, who organizes existing or natural supports in the workplace on behalf of the employee with a disability. Use of natural supports is considered far less intrusive and therefore an improvement over more visible forms of external support, such as a job coach.

Although they run the danger of isolating workers with disabilities even in integrated settings, group models of supported employment are sometimes required for individuals considered too severely disabled to benefit from the individual model (Hanley-Maxwell et al., 2003). The mobile work crew and the enclave are examples of group models of supported employment. Mobile work crews travel from job site to job site, performing specific functions such as landscape or building maintenance. This approach may subvert the notion of placement in an integrated setting if the cleaning crew completes its assignments in office buildings at night. Potentially allowing for more efficient use of job coaches (i.e., one coach for a group of individuals with disabilities), enclaves consist of groups of workers with disabilities who perform clearly defined tasks in a particular employment setting. If they work as a group in a separate section of the plant away from the general workforce, enclaves also are contrary to the goal of integration. An example of such a situation occurred in a plant that produced fiberglass bathtubs in which part of the production of the tubs was completed by an enclave working in a separate area of the plant. For this reason, Hanley-Maxwell et al. (2003) recommended the "dispersed" approach to enclaves in which the workers are integrated throughout the production site.

The two classic approaches to supported employment are frequently referred to as train–place–train–follow-up (Lagomarcino, 1986) and place–train–follow-up (Wehman, 1986).

Train–Place–Train–Follow-up

The train–place–train–follow-up (TPTF) approach has been described as having four major components: "(1) surveying potential employers to determine important vocational and social survival skills that need to be trained, (2) training individuals to perform such skills, (3) placing training clients into competitive employment, and (4) providing long-term follow-up training" (Lagomarcino, 1986, p. 66). Component 1 places a heavy emphasis on identifying potential job placements in the community, as well as conducting a job analysis for each of those potential positions. Component 2 utilizes "time-limited preemployment training programs in which individuals are placed into community-based training stations [located in an ongoing industry] and taught the skills needed for competitive employment for a period of time not exceeding 6 months" (Lagomarcino, 1986, p. 68). For example, a food service vocational training program would draw upon a variety of local training sites of that industry, such as a restaurant, a hospital kitchen, and a college dormitory kitchen (Lagomarcino, 1986, p. 69). Component 3 of the TPTF approach, placement, provides necessary services to move the client from training to competitive employment. Any of the services described in both the "Job Seeking Skills Training" and "Direct Placement Intervention" parts of this chapter can be provided under Component 3 of the TPTF approach by an employment specialist to whom the client is referred for "preplacement programs (i.e., Job Club) as well as job placement" (Lagomarcino, 1986, p. 69). Training as a follow-up service (Component 4) following placement in the new job in the TPTF approach "is less intensive and shorter in duration than training at the community-based training sites" (Lagomarcino, 1986, pp. 69–70). Follow-up services can also be provided to help the new employee overcome any job induction problems (e.g., problems interacting with new supervisors or coworkers).

In the late 1970s the TPTF supported work approach was developed and field tested by the University of Illinois (Champaign) in collaboration with a local adult service agency, the Developmental Services Center. Two training programs were used in the field test, a Janitorial Vocational Training Program and a Food Service Vocational Training Program. Of the 134 persons who participated in the training, 108 "(most of whom had a primary diagnosis of mild or moderate mental retardation)... completed training and were placed on jobs in the community" (Lagomarcino, 1986, p. 66).

Place–Train–Follow-up

The place–train–follow-up (PTF) supported work approach contains the following four major components: "(1) job placement, (2) job-site training [and advocacy], (3) ongoing assessment, and (4) job retention" (Wehman, 1986, p. 23). Staff activity under this approach is directed at assisting the client to acquire employment, "learn the skills required at the job site, adjust to the work environment, and, ultimately, retain the job" (Wehman, 1986, p. 23).

Wehman (1986, p. 24) listed staff activities for each component of the PTF approach. For example, in Component 1 (job placement), staff activities include (a) structuring job finding efforts for the client and matching the client's strengths to job needs, (b) interacting with employers on the client's behalf, (c) planning transportation and/or travel training, and (d) promoting family involvement as necessary in identifying appropriate jobs for the client. Under Component 2 (job site training), staff activities include (a) providing behavioral skill training and any necessary social skills training for the client at the job site, (b) working with the employer and coworkers in helping the client, and (c) helping the client and coworkers adjust to each other. In Component 3 (ongoing assessment), staff activities include (a) obtaining feedback from the employer on the client's progress; (b) monitoring the client's progress in learning the job via observation of "behavioral data on the student's work speed, proficiency, need for staff assistance, etc." (p. 24); and (c) periodically checking with the client and the client's family regarding their satisfaction with the program. Finally, Component 4 (job retention) staff activities include (a) fading the amount of staff intervention at the job site, (b) following up with the employer, and (c) assisting the client to find a new job if necessary.

As was the case with the TPTF supported work approach, as well as for all other selective placement–oriented approaches, job analysis is a crucial aspect of the PTF approach. As opposed to the TPTF approach, which emphasizes job training preceding placement in a "permanent" competitive job, the PTF approach emphasizes placement at a specific job site where the client will receive on-the-job training and can also expect long-term competitive employment. It should also be noted that the PTF on-the-job training approach does not place the responsibility for training on the employer. Job site training is conducted by a professional rehabilitation team staff person, such as a job coach, who is responsible for the client's job training.

Questions about the use of job coaches at the work site have, however, arisen. Some observers are concerned that the high cost of providing a job coach may weaken support for supported employment (Rusch, Conley, & McCaughrin, 1993). Other rehabilitation professionals have expressed concern about the intrusiveness of the job coach and failure to gradually withdraw (i.e., fade) the job coach from the work setting, which may increase workplace stigma and decrease workplace integration for the employee with a disability (Fabian & Luecking, 1991; Salomone, 1996).

To lessen the intrusiveness and cost of the job coach, Fabian and others (Fabian & Luecking, 1991; Fabian, Luecking, & Tilson, 1995) emphasized the importance of identifying and implementing natural workplace supports. These supports include (a) using coworkers as job trainers, (b) creating mentoring relationships between more experienced workers and supported employees, and (c) using environmental cues (e.g., seeing coworkers begin work) to stimulate appropriate on-the-job behavior. However, none of these alternatives provides the long-term training required to enhance the person's job maintenance and advancement potential. Therefore, Fabian and Luecking (1991) recommended that the employer become more involved in assuming training responsibilities for supported employees. They felt that this suggestion was feasible for a variety of reasons. Employers are taking more responsibility for basic literacy and job training. Industry-based training programs are effective outreach mechanisms to people with disabilities and people from different cultural and ethnic groups. The authors also noted how state rehabilitation agency funding of such on-the-job training for supported employees could increase employer receptivity. However, support to employers in this process must extend beyond financial support. Employers need follow-up services from rehabilitation counselors that include "disability awareness training, technical assistance in job analysis, and job task training" (Fabian et al., 1995, p. 48).

In conclusion, both the TPTF and PTF supported work approaches are clearly selective placement approaches that are more comprehensive and intensive than most of the selective placement approaches previously noted in this chapter. They also contain several characteristics that would qualify them as a job development activity.

Job Development

Developing job opportunities, like many other placement activities for people with disabilities, requires a comprehensive knowledge of the local labor market. The rehabilitation counselor must know

> the types of industries and business in the community; the work tasks within these places of employment; the physio-chemical environment in which work tasks are situated; the physical and mental demands of the work tasks; aptitudes required to perform the tasks; intellectual and academic requirements of the work; and employment practices of the industries and businesses. (R. D. Newman, 1973, p. 21)

Although a number of books provide information on the world of work, such as *The O*Net Dictionary of Occupational Titles* (Farr & Shatkin, 2004) and the *Occupational Outlook Handbook* (U.S. Department of Labor, 2004), the best way to obtain comprehensive and accurate information on the local labor market is to tour business establishments and talk with employers. During such visits rehabilitation counselors could identify jobs that are difficult to fill or that have high turnover rates. With this knowledge the counselor can assist with the recruitment and accommodations of employees with disabilities (Gilbride & Stensrud, 1992).

Once job openings and reasonable accommodations have been identified, it is important to place clients with a very high probability of success at the beginning of a relationship with each firm. Success tends to reduce the employers' reluctance to hire additional people with disabilities in the future. However, rehabilitation counselors cannot afford to rest on their laurels with any employer. Subsequent contacts are necessary both for determining additional current openings and for checking on the satisfactoriness of previously placed clients. Counselors cannot assume that employers will automatically call when additional openings appear or, for that matter, even when problems arise with a previously placed client (Peck & Kirkbride, 2001).

Job Development Activities

Bissonnette (1994) and others (Roessler, 1982; Zadny & James, 1979) have stressed the importance of contact with employers in as many ways as possible without exhausting the employers' patience. For example, Zadny and James (1979) reported that the number of contacts with employers is positively correlated with the number of people with disabilities hired. Roessler (1982) found a general trend for approaches that included personal contacts with owners and personnel managers through visits, letters, and phone calls to result in more job leads than a control condition involving a letter stressing the capabilities of people with disabilities and a survey form requesting the employer to identify high-turnover and hard-to-fill positions.

In an evaluation of the business approach to job development, I. Williams, Petty, and Verstegen (1998) underscored the importance of how contact is made. Specifically, they recommended "warming up" the cold call. They determined that the number of placements increased and the number of rejections decreased when job developers used the "referral" method of job development as opposed to the cold call approach. The referral method of job development requires that job developers first identify advocates who are both credible sources in the eyes of employers and proponents of the agencies seeking employment for people with disabilities. Advocates make the first contact with the businesses to pave the way for the job developers. In their contacts, advocates stress not only the reliability of the agency and its clients but also the benefits of hiring people with disabilities. Because they often know decision makers in large firms, these advocates begin a process of top-down communication that creates greater readiness on the part of hiring personnel to discuss placement opportunities. In the referral model, job developers must prospect for advocates in the same way that they prospect for potential employers.

Once advocates have made their initial contacts, job developers are ready to approach employers, following through on the agreements made by the advocates with the employers. At this point, job developers are in an excellent position to initiate the traditional steps of learning about the business, scheduling and making the initial contact, surveying the employer's needs, conducting a site survey to identify job opportunities, and presenting a hiring proposal. I. Williams et al. (1998) provided some very compelling evidence regarding the value of the referral method: "49 business contacts are necessary in the Cold Call Method to yield an average of seven placements in comparison to only needing to contact nine advocates to achieve the same seven placements" (p. 28).

No matter how job development contacts with employers are made, they should emphasize certain factors:

1. The capability of the agency to prepare job-ready individuals (Peck & Kirkbride, 2001; I. Williams et al., 1998)
2. The willingness of agency representatives to learn about the company and to screen and follow up on referrals (Bissonnette, 1994; Peck & Kirkbride, 2001)
3. The employer's obligation to maintain nondiscriminatory hiring practices (Sheffield, 2005)
4. The economic benefits of employing persons with disabilities with respect to a wide range of issues, such as "efficiency, turnover, cost savings, training and support, community image, reliability, and increased sales/customer service" (I. Williams et al., 1998, p. 24)

A number of programs expanding the nature of the rehabilitation–industry contacts beyond that of job development specialists' visits to businesses have shown promise. Zuger (1971) described a placement program at the Institute for Physical Medicine that resulted in the placement of 139 clients with severe physical disabilities. A group of 25 business leaders met monthly. Their goal was to increase job opportunities for people with severe disabilities in either their own companies or the companies of their colleagues. The group reviewed background information on ready-to-work clients and met with small groups of candidates at the meetings.

The development of cooperative state rehabilitation agency and employer on-the-job training programs has also served as an avenue to employment for certain clients. Although the format of these programs has varied, the state rehabilitation agency generally supplies a percentage of the employee's salary, with the employer responsible for the remainder. The size of the state rehabilitation agency's percentage diminishes over time (Sinick, 1976). Such programs have been found to facilitate placement even when the amount of subsidy was limited to the client's initial 2 weeks of salary. Knape (1972) compared the effectiveness of such a minimum-cost on-the-job placement program with the effectiveness of routine placement procedures. Both experimental and control groups contained the same disability distribution: 25 individuals with neuropsychiatric disabilities, 4 persons with orthopedic disabilities, and 2 persons with sensory disabilities. Experimental group clients were placed with willing employers whose only responsibility for the first 2 weeks was job orientation. One selling point of the program was that all the experimental group clients were legally considered employees of Baylor University for the initial 2-week period, even though they were working for private companies. Therefore, employers had a trial work period with the employee in which employers were not involved in tax accounting and insurance provision until they decided to hire the person on a permanent basis. The subsidized placement procedure proved superior to traditional placement procedures in regard to speed and ease of placement, while demonstrating equal effectiveness in regard to "immediate satisfaction of the employer and employees as reflected by quit and discharge rates" and in regard to "stability of the placement gauged by long-term follow-ups" (Knape, 1972, p. 31).

R. J. Jones and Azrin (1973) studied the effect of publicly advertising a substantial monetary reward ($100) for information on job openings that resulted in employment of a member of a job-seeking pool. The reward technique was compared with the typical "positions desired" advertising technique "commonly used by private and public employment bureaus." Both advertisements were placed in the only local newspaper serving the county where the study was conducted. The results showed that the reward approach produced significantly more calls (14 vs. 2), more reports of job openings (20 vs. 2), more applicants sent for interviews (19 vs. 1), more applicants hired (8 vs. 1), and more applicants employed for at least a month (8 vs. 1). Seventeen of the 20 job leads were from people who had hiring responsibility or were occupationally or socially related to the employer. All eight placements came from that subsample of leads. R. J. Jones and Azrin (1973) pointed out that the cost–benefit ratio for the advertisement procedure of $130 per placement was superior to "the average cost of $490 that private agencies would have charged for these placements, based on the standard fees authorized by the State of Illinois Department of Labor" (p. 352).

The job fair is another proven technique for placing people with disabilities (Poor & Delaney, 1974). Roessler, Brown, and Rumrill (1993) reported on the effectiveness of the All Aboard Job Fair for encouraging employment of people with disabilities. Originating as a pilot project with Days Inn of America (Better Days Job Fairs), All Aboard Job Fairs were held in eight communities in Arkansas and Kansas. Each job fair was sponsored by a local business, such as Wal-Mart, or by the community's Chamber of Commerce. Open to people with disabilities and senior citizens, the eight All Aboard Job Fairs attracted 313 people with disabilities, 163 senior citizens, and 126 employers. Seventy-three people with disabilities acquired employment through the program in a wide variety of positions, such as housekeeper, janitor, cashier, construction worker, machine operator, library aide, research clerk, bookkeeper, and assembler.

One of the more interesting anecdotes regarding the All Aboard Job Fairs pertained to outcomes at a state park that participated as an employer in one of the job fairs. Subsequent to the job fair, a state park employee interviewed 10 job fair participants and hired 4 for positions in the park. In addition, resulting from contacts made at the job fair, state park personnel learned of a local resource agency that placed young people with developmental disabilities in work in the community. The park hired five people from this program for maintenance positions. Additionally, information gained from the fair encouraged park employees to complete their plans for a barrier-free camping area. They also renovated a playground to make it accessible.

Developers of All Aboard described two ways to improve future job fairs: (a) preplan with employers to encourage them to recruit more actively for management positions at the job fair and (b) register job seekers and job openings in advance so that participants could receive a list of feasible openings to pursue during the fair. All in all, the job fair is a cost-effective means of linking qualified applicants with disabilities with interested employers.

The success of the job development activities described by Zuger (1971), Knape (1972), R. J. Jones and Azrin (1973), and Roessler et al. (1993) underscores the importance of rehabilitation–business working relationships as the foundation for all successful job development activities. The importance of such partnerships was discussed previously in stressing the need for the job seeking skills trainer and rehabilitation counselor to serve the employer as well as the client. Others have elaborated on partnership development as an important goal of the rehabilitation professional. For example, Van Lieshout (2001) described the operation of the Business Leadership Network, in which rehabilitation providers encourage local employers to take the leadership in and the ownership of a plan to increase the employment of people with disabilities. In these networks, employers establish goals and the procedures for improving employment outcomes, drawing on rehabilitation providers as partners or consultants. Developed through the initiative of the employers, the resulting plans may include outreach strategies such as connecting with high schools and colleges, placement techniques such as job fairs, and informational campaigns addressing the ADA or types of reasonable accommodations.

In the Twenty-Third Institute on Rehabilitation Issues, a study group of rehabilitation professionals offered guidelines for establishing formal working partnerships with employers (Fry, 1997). They began with principles for contacting employers simply to discuss the idea of such a partnership. Among their recommendations in this regard, they cautioned agencies to recognize the importance of first contacts by sending high-level administrators to begin exploratory talks with employers. They also stressed that agencies coordinate these efforts so that employers are not confused by contacts from multiple agencies. The study group offered other practical suggestions as well, such as helping companies hire for positions that are open now and avoiding spending too much time discussing how the agency can help with future employment needs. Rehabilitation counselors should tour the company to learn the culture and the hiring mechanisms. The study group recommended that counselors seek to minimize the need for accommodation in their initial referrals. Given this initial positive experience, company recruiters become more responsive later to investing both time and money in planning more extensive accommodations for some workers. Above all, the study group stressed the importance of maintaining the relationship over time by refining the referral process so that unsuccessful applicants are kept to a minimum and by following up on placements to help resolve problems encountered after the hiring process. Clearly, collaborative rehabilitation–business partnerships could do a great deal to overcome the concerns that many employers express regarding hiring individuals with disabilities.

Employer Concerns and Attitudes

In the job development process, rehabilitation counselors are confronted with a number of employer concerns regarding the employment of people with disabilities (Bissonnette, 1994; Greenwood & Johnson, 1985; Peck & Kirkbride, 2001). One concern is the possible elevation of workers' compensation insurance rates (Pati & Adkins, 1981, p. 17), an issue that rehabilitation counselors can defuse by providing prospective employers with accurate information. Such insurance costs are based on two factors: (a) the hazardous nature of the work itself and (b) the previous accident rate of the firm and the amount of resulting compensation and medical costs charged to the insurance carrier (Greenwood & Johnson, 1985).

Research evidence shows that employees with disabilities do not have higher accident rates than nondisabled workers. In a random sample of their workers with significant work disabilities, the DuPont Corporation (1990) reported that 97% of them were rated average or better in safety on the job. In addition, most states have second-injury laws, which provide funds to cover the additional costs resulting from a second injury. Where these laws are in effect, employers are liable for fair compensation only for the injury occurring while the worker was in their employ, rather than for the extent of handicap resulting from the combined effect of present and past injuries.

Research findings on employer attitudes toward hiring persons with disabilities suggest that employers expect to experience more problems with employees with disabilities than with able-bodied employees in regard to absenteeism, productivity, and ability to perform the job (Ellner & Bender, 1980; Honey, Meager, & Williams, 1998; Peck & Kirkbride, 2001). These concerns are incompatible not only with results in the DuPont (1990) survey but also with a long history of research findings. In 1948 the Bureau of Labor Statistics conducted a study of the performance of workers with physical impairments in manufacturing industries. Their comparison of 11,000 workers with physical impairments and 18,000 workers without such impairments showed the two groups to be similar with respect to the "quantity of work produced and the quality of work performance" (Allan, 1958, pp. 107–108). Goodyear and Stude (1975) compared the performance of employees with severe disabilities (cerebral palsy, blindness, deafness, and spinal cord injury) with the performance of nondisabled employees at the Internal Revenue Service Center in Fresno, California. The supervisory ratings of the two groups did not differ significantly regarding "the quality and quantity of their work, learning and adapting to new tasks, undertaking increased work loads, and relationships with co-workers and supervisors" (Goodyear & Stude, 1975, p. 215). In regard to employees with mental retardation, the W. T. Grant Company reported performance ratings of "3% as poor, of 24% as fair, and of 73% as good or excellent" (Sinick, 1968, p. 26). Honey et al. (1998), in a mail survey of over 1,800 employers, found that

75% of the employers who had employees with disabilities experienced no additional problems with this segment of their workforce in terms of productivity levels. Finally, Bromoge (1999) reported that people with disabilities were less likely to be absent from work and much less likely to voluntarily leave their place of employment.

Reviews of studies with employers (Hernandez, Keys, & Balcazar, 2000; Rimmerman, 1998) indicate that employers' attitudes toward hiring individuals with disabilities are moderated by a variety of factors. Specifically, positive hiring attitudes toward people with intellectual and other types of disabilities are often associated with the company's size, previous contact with people with such disabilities, and prior history of hiring applicants with intellectual disabilities. Larger companies that have had greater contact with and exposure to employees with disabilities report more positive attitudes toward individuals with disabilities. In one survey of experienced employers, J. Levy, Jessop, Rimmerman, Francis, and Levy (1993) demonstrated not only that the group held favorable attitudes toward hiring people with disabilities but also that favorable perceptions were more often held by (a) employers in the government sector, (b) companies with more employees and lower annual sales, (c) female employers, and (d) employers with college or graduate school degrees. Most important, they reported that respondents who had hired employees with severe disabilities during the previous 3-year period were more positive on three measures of employer perceptions than were employers from companies that had not hired people with severe disabilities. Experience with employees with disabilities and positive employer perceptions of their employability went hand-in-hand.

The type of disability under consideration also influences the nature of employer attitudes. Byrd, Byrd, and Emener (1977) conducted a telephone survey of 25 employers in Tallahassee, Florida, regarding their attitudes toward hiring people with 20 different types of severe disabilities. Of the 20 disabilities, employers indicated the greatest reluctance (in the order listed here) to hire people with the following types of disabilities: alcoholism, blindness, cerebral palsy, muscular dystrophy, multiple sclerosis, paraplegia, mental illness, mental retardation, social disorder, deafness, and epilepsy.

In another study, C. Williams (1972) surveyed by mail 108 employers located in Minnesota whose firms ranged in size from 45 to over 10,000. For each of 10 different disability groups, employers were asked to indicate whether they would always, usually but not always, sometimes but not usually, or never hire them for each of four types of jobs: (a) production, (b) management other than first-line production supervisor, (c) clerical, and (d) sales. The majority of sampled employers had little reluctance to hire an individual with diabetes, or peptic ulcers, or loss of one leg, for all four job areas. On the other hand, regardless of the type of job being considered, the great majority of employers were very reluctant to hire persons with visual impairment or mental retardation. Although much less the case than for blindness or mental retardation, employers were also reluctant to hire persons with epilepsy, deafness, or coronary disabilities. However, employers expressed little reluctance to hire individuals with any of those three disabilities for clerical positions. The majority of employers appeared to resist hiring persons with one arm or with back ailments only for the production job category.

In a study of hiring preferences of 334 industrial technology students, L. T. Thomas and Thomas (1985) reported findings that corroborated the conclusion from an American Management Survey of employers (Ellner & Bender, 1980). When it comes to hiring decisions, nondisabled individuals are somewhat more inclined to consider a person's job competence rather than unrelated factors such as gender and disability. Consistent with other research (Schneider & Anderson, 1980), the only disability-related factor influencing the hiring decisions of the industrial technology students was the unpredictability of the job seeker's behavior. In this study, individuals with multiple sclerosis received lower "would hire" ratings than did individuals with paraplegia or epilepsy. Acknowledging the weaknesses of investigations that use hypothetical case studies, the authors speculated that public opinion may be becoming more compatible with equal employment and nondiscriminatory hiring mandates.

If an employer seems to have less than optimal attitudes toward hiring persons with a disability, it is important for the job developer not to strengthen such negative predispositions through his or her communications with the employer regarding potential job applicants with a disability. Although the ADA prohibits covered employers from asking about an applicant's disability, job developers from rehabilitation agencies often cannot avoid such discussion if for no other reason than their employment affiliation suggests that their agency exists to serve persons with disabilities (Hagner & Dileo, 1993). Hagner and Dileo have provided some examples about how to talk about disability with potential employers to diminish any preconceived apprehensions about hiring people with disabilities. For example, rather than saying,

> "*John is autistic with stereotypical movements, a below average production rate and a tendency toward perseveration,*" one might try to describe the disability functionally avoiding labels or clinical descriptions as follows: "*John is very attentive to detail and careful in his work and enjoys predictable tasks.*" (p. 111)

Hagner and Dileo presented the following example of how a negative characteristic might be described in a positive or semipositive manner: "*He can become upset if things aren't always in the same place, and I think you'll find he'll keep the shelves organized just the way you want them*" (p. 112). Consequently, job developers must be well prepared to advocate for their clients with employers in as *realistic* and positive a manner as possible, while also stressing their availability to the employer whenever help is needed during the job induction period and beyond if necessary.

Rehabilitation professionals can take advantage of any growing receptivity to hiring and accommodating people with disabilities stimulated by the ADA by providing high-quality consultation services to employers. For example, rehabilitation counselors working with employers can provide consultation on how to rehabilitate the work environment—that is, to alter how work is done using job analysis, accommodation, and work flow strategies. An altered work environment provides greater employment opportunities for people with disabilities. Head and Baker (2005), for example, recommended focusing on five areas for possible workplace modifications: process (modification of policies, such as allowing more frequent breaks), technology (addition of assistive technology to increase employee productivity), location (enabling the worker to work from home), structural (removal of physical barriers to the workplace), and education (training to increase the employee's knowledge of the job).

Placement professionals continue to recommend more traditional employer services such as Projects with Industry (PWI). PWI involves the public and private sectors in collaborative ventures to train and place people with disabilities. Rehabilitation professionals working in PWIs ranked their services to employers, in order of importance, as follows: (1) referrals of job-ready people with disabilities, (2) disability awareness training for employers, (3) assistance in acquiring tax incentive and wage subsidies, (4) consultation on job modifications, (5) assistance with employees who are disabled on the job, and (6) consultation on work site accessibility and architectural barrier removal (Greenwood, Schriner, & Johnson, 1991).

In the future, placement personnel must act on the lessons of the past. Certainly, the findings of C. Williams (1972), Byrd et al. (1977), and L. T. Thomas and Thomas (1985) underscore the need to provide more job development effort for individuals from certain disability groups. Also, the range of placement services is broadening to encompass both "supply" and "demand" issues (Gilbride & Stensrud, 1992; Millington et al., 2003; Vandergoot, 1996). Linking employers and qualified applicants with disabilities and providing the necessary on-the-job supports address supply concerns. However, rehabilitation professionals must also help employers satisfy their pressing demands, namely increasing productivity and retaining workers in hard-to-fill positions. Success in achieving these goals often involves rehabilitation of the work environment by means of job modification, restructuring, and other accommodations such as those described in the ADA as examples of reasonable accommodations.

Concluding Statement

The appropriateness of a particular placement activity depends on the individual's needs. To acquire a job some people with disabilities require the direct intervention of the rehabilitation counselor with potential employers. Moreover, these same individuals may need extensive support on the job if they are to retain their positions. This support can be provided by a job coach who provides long-term follow-up services after the placement is made. Over time, however, the rehabilitation professional should shift the responsibility for follow-up and training to natural workplace supports.

Direct intervention activities by the counselor with employers can have negative effects when the client really does not require such assistance. For example, because the job was obtained for the client, he or she is more likely to leave it after a short period. Second, loss of jobs obtained through direct counselor interventions is more likely to result in the need for further counselor assistance to find employment, because the client has not yet developed any job seeking skills. Hence, job seeking skills training appears to be a sufficient placement approach with some clients. The effectiveness of job seeking skills training is maximized when it is designed as a comprehensive service with the following emphases: (a) identification of multiple sources of job leads, (b) information on employment rights and responsibilities, (c) instruction on what employers look for in prospective employees, (d) instruction on organizing and managing the job search, (e) practice in completing job application blanks, (f) job interview training, (g) supervised practice in job seeking skills, (h) support during the job seeking process, (i) orientation to the accommodation request process and examples of reasonable accommodations, and (j) reentry into the job seeking group should the person be laid off or terminated.

Research evidence suggests that the worst counselor placement approach would be to leave clients totally on their own. Zadny and James (1976) reported the results of a study by Mooney (1966) comparing the effectiveness of three approaches to placement—(a) employer contact on behalf of the client, (b) a client job seeking skills development approach, and (c) a no-assistance approach—on the basis of percentage of clients closed successfully (i.e., after 30 days of continuous employment). The two intervention approaches were found to be superior to no additional assistance. No additional assistance resulted in a 24% success rate, whereas direct employer contact and client preparation resulted in 50% and 49% success rates, respectively. Continued support of the value of appropriate employment interventions is also found in recent research (Rogers, Bishop, & Crystal, 2005) indicating that people with severe disabilities were three times more likely to secure employment if their rehabilitation plans included job placement services.

When it comes to promoting the hiring of individuals with disabilities, one cannot overlook employer concerns and attitudes. Employer misperceptions regarding the effects of integrating workers with disabilities into their business must be dealt with in an effective and ethical way by the counselor. One method for addressing these concerns is through the strong rehabilitation–business partnerships advocated in this chapter. These partnerships build the mutual knowledge and trust that ensures employer receptivity to hiring people with disabilities.

Chapter 13

Assistive Technology: Prospects and Problems

For people with disabilities, assistive technology paves the way to greater productivity and self-sufficiency by replacing or extending the capacities needed to cope with many different types of social, educational, vocational, and daily living demands. The importance of technology in the lives of people with disabilities is underscored by mandates in important pieces of legislation at both the federal and state levels. Section 504 of the Rehabilitation Act of 1973 laid the groundwork for greater participation by people with disabilities in any programs receiving federal funding, particularly postsecondary educational institutions. Two years later the Education for All Handicapped Children Act of 1975, now referred to as the Individuals with Disabilities Education Act (IDEA), guaranteed access to technology for children in the public schools. Included in the 1998 Amendments to the Rehabilitation Act of 1973, Section 508 opened the "electronic era" to people with disabilities in terms of access to electronic equipment and databases purchased or maintained by the federal government. In 1990 provisions in the Americans with Disabilities Act, such as those in Title I, referred to the obligation of employers to provide reasonable accommodations in the workplace (Lindsey, 1999).

Amended in 2004, the Assistive Technology Act of 1998 (P.L. 108-364, often referred to as the Tech Act) replaced the Technology Related Assistance for Individuals with Disabilities Act, passed in 1988, which expired in 1998 (University of Washington Center for Technology and Disability Studies, 2003). The Tech Act is the centerpiece of all technology legislation. Calling for improved coordination of and access to technology assistance, this act established, on a state-by-state basis, the Assistive Technology Projects (ATPs). Features of these projects include device loan, demonstration, reutilization, and financing activities. ATPs also have the obligation to work at the systems level to influence policies and laws that result in greater use of assistive technology by people with disabilities (J. Wallace, 2003). The National Assistive Technology Technical Assistance Partnership (NATTAP; http://www.resna.org/taproject/index.html) provides technical support to the 56 state and territory ATP programs.

The Tech Act defines an "assistive technology device as any item, piece of equipment, or product system, whether acquired commercially, off the shelf, modified, or customized, that is used to increase, maintain, or improve functional capabilities of individuals with disabilities" (University of Washington Center for Technology and Disability Studies, 2003). "The device may be purchased commercially or modified to meet the individual's needs" (Resources for Rehabilitation, 1993, p. 57). Table 13.1 lists major categories of assistive technology (Seventeenth Institute on Rehabilitation Issues, 1990); many of the listed devices and aids are described in greater detail in this and other chapters.

Because it serves to "increase, maintain, or improve functional capabilities," technology is extremely important in the lives of people with disabilities. For the most part, this chapter examines how assistive technology restores functioning of the person. At the same time, one must understand that the "enabling" process (Brandt & Pope, 1997) encompasses both person and environment. Indeed, it is frequently reasonable to consider the increased functional capacity of the person as an outcome of the interaction of changes in the individual and modification of the environment.

TABLE 13.1
Categories of Assistive Technology

Aids for Daily Living: self-help aids for use in activities such as eating, bathing, cooking, dressing, toileting, and home maintenance.

Augmentative Communication: electronic and nonelectronic devices that provide a means for expressive and receptive communication for persons without speech.

Computer Applications: input and output devices (voice, Braille), alternate access aids (headsticks, light pointers), modified or alternate keyboards, switches, special software, and so on, that enable persons with disabilities to use a computer.

Environmental Control Systems: primarily electronic systems that enable someone without mobility to control various appliances, electronic aids, security systems, and so on, in their room, home, or other surroundings.

Home/Worksite Modifications: structural adaptations or fabrications in the home, worksite, or other area (ramps, lifts, bathroom changes) that remove or reduce physical barriers for an individual with a disability.

Prosthetics and Orthotics: replacement, substitution, or augmentation of missing or malfunctioning body parts with artificial limbs or other orthotic aids (splints, braces, etc.).

Seating and Positioning: accommodations to a wheelchair or other seating system to provide greater body stability, trunk/head support and an upright posture, and reduction of pressure on the skin surface (cushions, contour seats, lumbar).

Aids for Vision/Hearing Impaired: aids for specific populations including magnifiers, Braille or speech-output devices, large-print screens, hearing aids, TDDs, visual alerting systems, and so on.

Wheelchairs/Mobility Aids: manual and electric wheelchairs, mobile bases for custom chairs, walkers, three-wheel scooters, and other utility vehicles for increasing personal mobility.

Vehicle Modifications: adaptive driving aids, hand controls, wheelchair and other lifts, modified vans, or other motor vehicles used for personal transportation.

Note. From *The Provision of Assistive Technology in Rehabilitation* (p. 109), by the Seventeenth Institute on Rehabilitation Issues, 1990, Fayetteville: Arkansas Research and Training Center in Vocational Rehabilitation. Reprinted with permission.

Many authors have presented classification schemes of human functioning (A. Cook, Leins, & Woodall, 1985; Crewe & Athelstan, 1984; DeWitt, 1991; Georgia Institute of Technology, 1999; Halpern, 1984; Indices, Inc., 1979; Sigelman, Vengroff, & Spanhel, 1979). A synthesis of these models results in categories such as mobility, communication, health maintenance, cognitive–intellectual, visual, social and recreational, and daily living. The underlying implication is that restoration of functioning leads to enhanced social integration of an individual with a disability, which lessens the extent to which one is perceived as "handicapped." In the remainder of this chapter, prospects for restoring functioning in these areas through technology are discussed. Following that presentation, a number of information resources on technological devices and modifications and rehabilitation applications are described. The chapter then turns to a discussion of the marketing problems associated with the development and distribution of adaptive technology. To close, trends in the development of high technology are reviewed, culminating in policy and practice recommendations that must be implemented if technology is to play a greater part in the lives of people with disabilities.

Mobility and Manipulation

Technology can contribute to social integration of individuals with disabilities through enhanced mobility and manipulative capabilities. Mobility aids include such common devices as wheelchairs, as well as more complex solutions such as driving aids, robotics, and acoustic cue systems (Institute of Medicine, 1997).

Wheelchairs

Although there are a number of wheeled mobility devices (e.g., power-operated scooter, manual and power wheelchairs), for persons with functional limitations in the lower extremities, the wheelchair is the most widely used mobility aid. There are at least three basic types of manual wheelchairs: (a) the standard manual wheelchair; (b) the lightweight, high-strength wheelchair; and (c) the adjustable, ultralight wheelchair. The standard manual wheelchair is the least expensive but also the least functional of the three manual wheelchairs. These wheelchairs are usually heavy and provide little possibility for adjusting for increased comfort and cannot be adjusted for enhanced performance. Difficult to propel, they are most functional when pushed by another person (Gibson & Huss, 1995).

As the name suggests, the lightweight, high-strength wheelchair is constructed with materials that are lighter than those used to construct the standard chair. Gibson and Huss (1995) pointed out that the position of its wheels "can be changed to create a tilt in the chair that will improve its user's posture. Also, the seat can be lowered to allow the user to use his or her lower extremities to help propel the wheelchair" (p. 97).

The adjustable, ultralight wheelchair has a number of desirable characteristics. For example, the back and arms can be repositioned to provide optimal postural support and freer arm movement. Also, the wheels can be repositioned to "change the tilt and better approximate the user's center of gravity" (Gibson & Huss, 1995, p. 96). Both adjustments make it easier to propel the wheelchair "and allow for increased speed" (Gibson & Huss, 1995, p. 96). Depending on the selected options (e.g., type of upholstery, rear wheel sizes), the cost for ultralight manual wheelchairs can range from $3,500 to $7,500 (Sources for Independent Living Services, personal communication, March 30, 2007).

Battery-powered wheelchairs (power wheelchairs) are a viable option for those individuals who "have difficulty propelling a manual wheelchair" (A. M. Cook & Hussey, 2002, p. 335). The most common control system for a powered wheelchair is the four-direction joystick. Joysticks can be positioned for use with the hand, chin, foot, or head. "When a chin joystick is used, an additional switch (often activated by a shoulder shrug) can be used to control the powered arm that moves the joystick into position for use," as well as out of the way when necessary so it will not interfere with activities such as talking or eating (A. M. Cook & Hussey, 2002, p. 348). However, control devices other than a joystick, such as "noncontact switches that respond proportionately to changes in the user's head positions" (Gibson & Huss, 1995, p. 99), greatly expand the number of persons with severe physical disabilities who can use power wheelchairs. The cost for a power wheelchair may range from $6,000 to $24,000, depending on the types of specialized adaptations (Sources for Independent Living Services, personal communication, March 30, 2007). Some high-quality power wheelchairs, which are designed to last at least 10 years and contain special features that reduce physiological complications such as dysreflexia and skin sores that could require hospitalization, can cost as much as $24,000 (Cooper, 1998).

Wheelchair technology continues to advance as evidenced by the INDEPENDENCE iBOT Mobility System developed by Johnson & Johnson. Approved by the U.S. Food and Drug Administration in 2003, the iBOT can operate as a standard battery-powered chair with all four wheels on the ground. It also has the capacity to become an elevated chair with two wheels maintaining contact with the ground, allowing the person to reach objects above chair level or to conduct conversations at eye level. Most impressive of all, the system has the capability of climbing stairs, one stair at a time. A person needs certain cognitive and physical skills to use the iBOT, such as judgment to determine the feasibility of crossing rough terrain or climbing steep steps, and the use of one arm to manipulate chair controls. Results from clinical trials indicated that people properly matched to system requirements could safely and efficiently manage the iBOT (U.S. Food and Drug Administration, 2003).

Driving Aids

With over 50 types of driving aids available, vehicle modification is one feasible approach to enhancing a person's mobility. Prevalent examples are hand controls and low-energy steering systems that allow individuals with limitations in lower and upper body strength to operate an automobile. Several types of hand control systems exist: push–pull, twist–push, right-angle push, and floor-mounted push–pull. Hand controls can be coupled with a low-energy steering system, with appropriate backups, to produce an automobile or van that can be driven by many persons with disabilities involving lower and/or upper body limitations.

As with many other applications of technology, modifying a vehicle is an expensive process. An adapted van for a person with a severe spinal cord injury may cost in excess of $50,000. This price includes the cost of the van ($25,000 to $35,000) and both driving aids and a wheelchair lift ($20,000). Wheelchair lifts alone range from $5,500 to $7,000 for vans. Price ranges for other important adaptations are as follows: (a) automatic door opener, $2,000; (b) power seat, $2,000 to $3,000; (c) wheelchair tie-down system, $650 for a manual chair and $1,700 for an electric chair; (d) reduced- or zero-effort steering, $4,000 to $5,000; (e) reduced- or zero-effort braking, $3,500 to $3,800; (f) power seat, $2,250; and (g) parking brake, $800 for a hand control and $1,300 for a power control (Presidential Conversions, personal communication, June 20, 2006). "Adapted vans can be built to specifics at the factory or retrofitted after being purchased" (Gibson & Huss, 1995, p. 100). Of course, equipping a car for someone with upper body strength would be considerably less expensive (i.e., at least 30% to 50% cheaper), because less costly alternatives to wheelchair lifts exist, such as cartop carriers and van ramps. Although factory-installed options are considered to be reliable, quality control is an issue for many of the driving "add-ons." The Veterans Administration (VA) is one source of accurate information on the quality of drivers' aids. Purchasers of adapted vans may have access to mobility grants up to $1,000 that are available from the manufacturer. Owners must apply for reimbursement no later than 6 months after initial purchase of the vehicle and 60 days after installation of the driving aids (Flandez, 2005).

Robotics

Replacement of manipulative capabilities is also possible through robotics. Progress in this area is exemplified in some of the lower body movement devices that enable individuals with paraplegia to walk. It is also exemplified in the myoelectric hand and the myoelectric hand orthosis. The myoelectric hand has been described as follows:

> Natural in appearance, its shell contains electrodes and amplifiers that pick up surface electrical signals from underlying muscles. These signals are usually picked up from extensors and flexors in below-the-elbow amputees and from biceps and triceps in above-the-elbow amputees.... The myoelectric hand opens and closes as electric signals are transmitted to a battery-powered motor. An amputee learns through practice and with visual or biofeedback to activate muscles that would lie dormant with a hook-and-cable prosthesis. This electric hand makes possible many simple

two-handed operations by allowing the prosthesis to grasp a tool or a jar, assisting the work of the normal hand. ("Prosthesis Innovations," 1984, p. 43)

Benjuya and Kenney (1990) described a myoelectric hand orthosis developed for people with spinal cord injuries at the C5–6 level. Responding to "bioelectric potentials picked up by surface electrodes," the orthosis restores the person's capacity to "pinch, grip, and release objects during daily living activities" (p. 149). When fitted with both a hand and a forearm piece, people with spinal cord injuries can learn to control the devices with about 10 minutes of training.

Advances in Enhancing Mobility

Lancioni, Oliva, and Bracalente (1998) described two individuals with multiple severe disabilities, including blindness, who improved their ability to independently move about and conduct activities using a portable control device and an acoustic cue system. Initially, the individuals were oriented to using acoustic cues, emanating from sources placed in different locations, to help them travel in an indoor area. Using radio signals, researchers linked the sound sources in the various destinations to a portable control device. The developers of the system programmed the control device to respond to simple commands, enabling individuals with severe disabilities to indicate the destination to which they wanted to travel. The next phase of the training involved teaching the two people to enter desired destination commands so that they could receive guidance for moving from one activity area to another. These commands triggered acoustic cues, which the individuals successfully followed to reach different locations in three rooms and a connecting hall. By restoring independent mobility skills to these individuals, this system not only enhanced their ability to make choices but also reduced significantly the amount of external assistance needed by the clients. Each sound source cost approximately $140, and the portable control device cost about $500. Lancioni et al. stressed benefits of the system, such as portability and 24-hour access. They also noted that the system promotes rapid learning of mobility skills in new settings.

Other advances in enhancing mobility are in the offing. Ray Kurzweil, inventor of numerous devices that improve the communication abilities of people with blindness, commented on the potential for developing artificial muscles for people with neurological and muscular impairments, as well as the possibility of transferring nerve impulses from the brain to muscles wirelessly to bypass obstructed or destroyed pathways resulting from spinal cord injury or multiple sclerosis. He described experimental work on a "robotic exoskeleton" that would enable individuals who use wheelchairs to walk and climb stairs (Ira, 2003).

Communication

Applications of technology can extend the communication capabilities of people with disabilities in many ways. Most enhanced communication capabilities are due to the sophistication of the computer and the Internet, which can reduce communication and daily living limitations of individuals with various types of disabling conditions. In a survey of people with disabilities (Voorde, 2005), 40% of the respondents reported that they used the Internet for their business and social affairs approximately 20 hours a week, and 48% believed that access to the Internet had significantly improved the quality of their lives. The market significance of this fact is evident in that people with disabilities are estimated to have approximately $220 billion in discretionary spending.

Many examples exist as to how the Internet improves the communication abilities of people with disabilities. For example, individuals with mobility impairments can do their shopping, banking, research, and personal communication using the Internet. Individuals with total vision loss can listen to the latest stock quotations or content of the daily newspaper (Institute of Medicine, 1997). People with disabilities can also share information through the growing network of "listservs" and mail service programs accessible through computers and telephone lines. Described later in the chapter, computer technology can enable individuals with mobility impairments to conduct a wide range of household tasks, such as turning on and off appliances and lights, setting a thermostat, and controlling security systems (Lazzaro, 1993). Voice- or control panel–activated environmental control systems managed by computers can give individuals greater control over the world around them.

The widespread use of the Internet has not come without problems, however. First and foremost, web pages and online educational programs typically operate in a visual environment. Therefore, people with visual impairment or blindness are unable to access them without workstations that are both physically and electronically accessible (e.g., workstations with JAWS and Dragon Dictate software for screen reading and voice input). This visual environment has implications for other users as well. For example, Whitney and Upton (2004) pointed out that flashing icons in Powerpoint presentations or on web pages may cause seizures in individuals with seizure disorders. A. M. Cook and Hussey (2002) indicated that those with "learning disabilities and dyslexia ... find it increasingly difficult to access complicated Web sites that may include flashing pictures, complicated charts, and large amounts of audio and video data" (p. 276). Consequently, a pressing need exists to screen electronic media for use by people with disabilities. Fortunately, systems exist to do so, such as the "Bobby Checker, A-prompt, WAVE, the HTML Validation Service, and the CSS Validation Service" (Whitney & Upton, 2004, p. 26), although the use of any one of the systems may not be enough to ensure that electronic media conforms with Section 508 regulations (in the 1998 Amendments to the Rehabilitation Act of 1973). Frequently overlooked in the screening process, the user review is another excellent strategy for gauging the accessibility of electronic media for people with disabilities (Voorde, 2005). According to Paciello (2005), the "best solution to ensuring accessible user experience involves a combination of automated testing tools, expert usability inspections, and controlled task testing" (p. 6). Stressing the importance of the type of standards used in such inspections, Voorde (2005) recommended that web site designers use the "World Wide Web Consortium's (W3C) Web Content Accessibility Guidelines (WCAG) rather than Section 508 as the standard to evaluate against" (p. 3). Characteristics of accessible web sites include text-based descriptions of graphic images, the availability of a map or table of contents, and high color contrast against the background. Accessible sites do not use frames that divide the screen into separate compartments, and they have no "flashing items, pop-up windows, or scrolling text" (Ritchie & Blanck, 2003, p. 13).

Information Input and the Computer

Individuals typically input information into the computer using a standard keyboard, which is an example of a user interface. For individuals with hearing impairments, the functional demands of a keyboard pose no problem. People with coordination, dexterity, strength, and/or visual limitations, however, do encounter difficulty with the keyboard. Hence, software and hardware designers have generated highly creative solutions to bring together computers and people with disabilities. Alternatives to the standard keyboard interface are usually achieved through modifications that enable standard software to respond to the commands as if they were coming from a keyboard. These modifications range from "low-tech" examples, such as a weight on a hinge to depress a shift key, to "high-tech" solutions, such as braille input and voice recognition (i.e., a computer capable of responding to voice commands).

The best means for inputting information depends on the limitations and residual abilities of the prospective user. For example, people with minor coordination difficulties may be able to use enlarged keyboards (available in QWERTY or alphabetic styles) and keyguards (a template placed over the keys, providing holes through which the individual can stick a finger or mouthpiece to depress the key; Jasch, 1998). Preventing unintended keystrokes, keyguards may provide "key latches" or levers that hold down the Control or Shift keys (Lazzaro, 1993). Other people may prefer miniature keyboards suitable for operation with a finger, handheld pointer, or mouthstick (Jasch, 1998). For those with severe physical limitations, Morse code data entry is possible through switches operated by the big toe of each foot, wherein one toe communicates dots, the other, dashes. Similar commands are possible through sip-and-puff (inhaling or exhaling through a straw) or head switch mechanisms (rocking head left or right for dots or dashes) (McWilliams, 1984). According to Lazzaro (1991), "if a person has at least one functional, voluntary movement, for example, a finger, foot, eye blink, or such, an adaptive system can be configured to suit that individual" (p. 249).

Various user interfaces exist, such as an optical head point or light beam switch, manual pointer, magnet pointer, mouse, touch screen and on-screen keyboard, joystick, rocker lever, track ball, touch pads, tongue switch, air cushion switch, arm slot control, video camera, and voice input (Brodwin, Star, & Cardoso, 2004; Infinitec, n.d.; Jasch, 1998; LC Technologies, 1999; Prentke Romich Co., n.d.; Resources for Rehabilitation, 1993). Adaptations of any of these interfaces through custom design are also possible. Custom designing, however, is not always needed. For example, versions of standard mass-produced interfaces, such as the mouse or track ball, are readily used by individuals with disabilities such as arthritis. Through gross hand movements, rather than through finger depression of keys, an individual with arthritis can communicate with the computer. Because they are mass produced and widely available, both the mouse and track ball are excellent solutions to the user interface issue.

Voice recognition devices serve as a "set of ears" for the computer. They enable people to control the computer through voice input. Typically, the systems are speaker-dependent voice recognition approaches, which require the user to have significant voice volume and clarity and to spend about an hour training the system (i.e., storing voice patterns on the hard disk) (Infinitec, n.d.; Lazzaro, 1993). Some speech recognition systems convert dictation at between 40 and 70 words per minute into written text. This technology is especially useful for individuals whose oral language is superior to their written language, such as people with severe learning disabilities (Raskind, 1993). The Dragon Systems computer software programs allow individuals with disabilities to control Windows-based software through voice input. More advanced versions (e.g., Dragon NaturallySpeaking 9 by Nuance Communications) enable the user to speak continuously into a microphone, using a natural tone of voice, and the words are translated into text (Jasch, 1998).

Other innovative interfaces utilize residual functions such as head movement or eye gaze to control the computer. For example, the Headmaster Plus, developed by Prentke Romich, combines head movement and a sip-and-puff tube to move the cursor and make selections. Although more expensive, eye gaze systems are available that use a video camera to control the computer (Infinitec, n.d.). According to C. Brown (1989), the greatest benefit of this technology is its reliance on one of the most reliably controlled body movements—eye gaze—which produces rapid commands that are not fatiguing for the person. LC Technologies (1999) described how this eye gaze/video camera method of controlling the computer enables individuals with severe physical disabilities to use word processing programs as well as to control a variety of daily functions such as using the telephone and turning appliances and lights on and off. By looking at a key on the computer screen for a specified amount of time, the user is able to depress the key and "navigate around the Eyegaze programs independently" (p. 1). The eyegaze technology works better in fluorescent lighting than in incandescent lighting. With available supplementary programs, the basic system costs approximately $17,000.

Great progress has been made in bringing together computers and people with disabilities. However, problems are continually being discovered in this application process. For example, the flexibility of computers for people with disabilities needs to be increased so that computers can attend to multiple tasks simultaneously (e.g., environmental control, note taking, and program access). Techniques are also needed to speed the information transfer process. Single- or dual-command modes ("this one," "yes/no") are extremely time-consuming ways to enter data. Responses to this problem exist, such as storage of frequently used phrases in memory that can be activated by using a mouse command on a symbol or a minimal number of keystrokes. Another solution is the use of abbreviation expansion routines, which allow the user to enter preprogrammed commands such as I-W-D to result in a message of "I want a drink of water" at a savings of 20 keystrokes (Burkhead, 1992; Lazzaro, 1993). Word completion software to expand abbreviated or incomplete words is also included as a standard feature of popular word processing programs.

All of the previously discussed interfaces with the computer are available in today's market, but one breakthrough is still far into the future. Developers of assistive technology are in the beginning stages of translating thought patterns into responses from electronic devices. These control systems are based on translating muscle contractions and changes in air pressure in the ear canal that occur as the result of "action-related thoughts" (Infinitec, n.d., p. 7). It appears that these contractions and changes in air pressure are both replicable and unique so that thought patterns could, at some point in the future, be translated into commands for the computer.

Communication Devices for Persons with Visual or Hearing Impairments

Any discussion of communication devices is incomplete without mentioning some of the applications of technology for individuals with visual or hearing disabilities. People with limited hearing may use amplified telephones, fax machines, and closed-loop microphone systems. For people who are deaf, one of the most common devices is the TDD, telecommunication device for deaf persons, which enables them to use the telephone service (Resources for Rehabilitation, 1993). The TDD or Text Telephone (TT or TTY) looks like a small typewriter that visually displays all messages sent or received. Some have printers to record the messages on paper as well. Designed for use with the telephone system, the TDD uses an acoustic coupler for the headset of a conventional telephone or a computer modem to "convert outgoing TDD impulses into acoustic tones and incoming acoustic tones into TDD impulses" (Strauss, 1991, p. 239). Both the sender and the receiver must have a TDD to communicate. Other communication alternatives for deaf people are available due to advances in cellular communication devices such as the Blackberry. Using a Blackberry, individuals who are deaf have e-mail communication abilities at their fingertips.

With the passage of Title IV of the Americans with Disabilities Act of 1990, people who are deaf are assured far greater access to universal telephone service through techniques such as the dual-party relay. In a dual-party relay, the person using a TDD is connected with a person using a standard telephone through a relay operator. Regardless of whether the call is initiated by the party with the TDD or the conventional telephone, the operator translates all TDD impulses into voice messages and all voice communications into TDD messages. All relay service providers must meet certain statutory requirements, such as confidentiality of the message, availability of continuous service, and no restrictions on the length or content of the calls (A. M. Cook & Hussey, 2002; Resources for Rehabilitation, 1993; Strauss, 1991). The toll-free number for telecommunication relay services is listed in the local telephone directory.

Recent innovations in office technology facilitate communications for people who are deaf both within and outside of the office with customers or other business associates. Fax machines and e-mail are two examples of useful technology. In addition to the use of professional interpreters, businesses can also use real-time captioning technology and video training materials with captions to communicate with employees who are deaf.

Hearing aids are a common technological device used to amplify sound. They are available in different configurations, including behind-the-ear, in-the-ear, in-the-canal, and completely-in-the-canal types (A. M. Cook & Hussey, 2002). Hearing aids have a significant shortcoming: They amplify both desired and undesired sound. Undesired sound or background noise (noise interference) is a common barrier to functioning effectively in group settings for people with hearing loss. For this reason, assistive listening devices (ALDs) are effective alternatives. They provide a technological solution to problems such as sounds fading at a distance, troublesome background noise, and poor room acoustics.

Composed of a transmitter and a receiver, ALDs are typically one of three types: (a) induction loop, (b) FM (frequency modulated), and (c) infrared. The person with hearing loss wears the receiver, and the speaker wears the transmitter, which includes a microphone. The induction loop system requires a wire loop spanning the entire listening area. The ALD signal is then available to anyone wearing the proper receiver who is within the looped area. Because FM transmitters use radio frequencies to transmit signals to FM receivers, no wire loop is required. FM receivers may have a built-in hearing aid or transmit directly to a person's hearing aid. Infrared systems transmit sound via infrared light emitters to headset receivers, but "receivers must be positioned in line-of-sight to an emitter" (National Institute on Disability and Rehabilitation Research, 1990, p. 2).

The cochlear implant or electronic ear can improve hearing capabilities directly rather than through the use of electronic systems, voice synthesizers, or visual displays. Through multichannel implants that stimulate inner ear nerve endings, an electronic processor converts mechanical vibrations from sound into electronic impulses. These impulses are then sent, via implanted electrodes, as signals along the auditory nerve (cochlea) to the brain (Berke, 1999).

If the person's eighth cranial nerve is intact, stimulation can be provided via implanted electrodes (A. M. Cook & Hussey, 2002).

Consisting of both internal or surgically implanted parts (internal coil and electrodes) and external parts (microphone, speech processor, and external coil), the cochlear implant makes it possible for some deaf individuals to hear conversations and warning signals (National Institute on Deafness and Other Communication Disorders, 2006). Controversy exists regarding use of cochlear implants in the deaf community, some members of which strongly support the concept of a deaf community and the notion that deafness is not necessarily a condition to be cured. However, this controversy does not always extend to use of the implant in individuals who became deaf in adulthood (Rawlinson, 2000).

At the present time visual functioning cannot be replaced. As a result the use of other modalities is expanding to compensate for visual loss. For people with partial sight, closed-circuit Viewscan systems (CCTVs) are extremely useful devices (Uslan, Shen, & Shragai, 1996) that increase a person's reading ability and reading time. These systems utilize electronic equipment to magnify items on a printed page. This enlargement is produced by using a stand-mounted camera for in-line viewing or by moving a small handheld camera across and down the page, creating a bright magnified image on the monitor screen. Software-based magnification is also available in many word processing programs, enabling people with minimal vision loss to select and expand text they are having difficulty reading. Written communication is possible for individuals who are blind via the Perkins Brailler (manual) or by braille input devices connected to the computer via translator software. Moreover, it is possible for the computer to print in braille as well as translate braille output into standard manuscript text (Resources for Rehabilitation, 1993).

For individuals with total vision loss, optical character recognition technology (OCR) and reading machines are extremely useful. OCR technology converts printed material into an electronic format for storage in the computer. Software, a scanner, and the recognition processor are needed to accomplish this task. The Kurzweil Reading Machine scans printed material and speaks it via a voice synthesizer. Extensive computer technology is required for the reading machine to translate the written word into spoken English with proper grammar and syntax. Fortunately, scanning technology has advanced significantly, resulting in more powerful and less expensive access to the printed word (Lazzaro, 1993). Upgrades of the reading machine allow users to select a preferred voice type. For individuals with visual capabilities, the Kurzweil Reading Machine also displays graphic materials that accompany the text. Given its ability to produce text to voice output and display graphics, the Kurzweil Reading Machine is a useful device for individuals with learning disabilities as well (Kurzweil Products, 1999).

Important developments contributing to the functioning of individuals with visual impairments are voice recognition and speech synthesizer technologies. Compatible with various types of computers, these systems allow voice input and output (Lazzaro, 1993). Through speech synthesizer modifications, individuals who are blind have also gained access to word processors, which is a great advantage to people who do not use braille (O'Korn & Wheaton, 1995).

Another means for expanding the capacities of people with visual impairments involves braille and computer linkages. Devices are available that enable the computer not only to process braille input but also to print in braille or standard text. Because it is electronic, the Brailler requires minimal pressure to depress the keys, a positive feature for individuals with visual and upper extremity limitations. Connected with a computer and telephone modem, this braille input/output system can access a vast array of information sources, such as computerized databases, books, magazines, newspapers, and stock reports (Brodwin, Star, & Cardoso, 2004; J. Williams, 1984).

In conclusion, many functional communication limitations can be eliminated or significantly reduced through technology. The promise is for greater integration of people with disabilities in society as a result of these technical advances.

Health Maintenance

Technology has also made promising contributions to people's abilities to maintain their personal health. Described in the NASA Center for AeroSpace Information (NASA, 1999), examples of significant developments along these lines include the Trilogy cardiac pacemaker, the Biotran, the CAD/CAM system, and space-age telemedicine service delivery. The Trilogy cardiac pacemaker, manufactured by Pacesetter, Inc., is a fourth-generation pacemaker with improved diagnostic and programmable features. It combines innovations in space communications, smaller implantable pulse generators from space microminiaturization, and longer life batteries from spacecraft electrical systems. Using a powerful microprocessor that allows more functions to operate automatically, the Trilogy pacemaker provides detailed information on the performance of the pacing system and on the person's health.

Developed by Cybex to help physicians diagnose and treat people with movement limitations resulting from chronic illnesses or injuries, the Biotran is an apparatus to test an individual's weight-bearing capabilities. Computer-developed and -directed exercises guide the person through tests that provide data on strength, balance, and reaction time. Data from these tests are used to determine both the individual's initial level of functioning and the person's progress as a result of completing the exercises over time.

The CAD/CAM system is a practical solution to a growing problem with respect to the production of orthopedic footwear, specifically the shortage of skilled shoemakers. Given the mechanization of shoe manufacture and the exporting of such jobs overseas, few skilled shoemakers are available in the United States to fit and produce orthopedic shoes. With the support of the Veterans Administration and the National Institute on Disability and Rehabilitation Research, North Carolina State University and the University of Missouri–Columbia applied NASA space-age technology to this problem. They created a CAD/CAM approach to the design of orthopedic footwear linking a camera (CAM) and computer-aided design (CAD) software. Based on analyses of photographs, the computer can produce design specifications for the manufacture of the shoes.

NASA has made "earth-bound" applications of its space communications systems as well. Using NASA technology, expertise, funding, and off-the-shelf computer and networking systems, NASA has helped hospitals develop telemedicine services. These services enable smaller hospitals in rural areas to improve the quality of their services for people with disabilities. Using two-way audio–video relay programs, specialists at the University of Texas Health Science Center in San Antonio linked with the South Texas Hospital in Harlingen. In this way, specialists are easily accessed by small hospitals in rural settings for expert advice on the diagnosis and treatment of conditions such as cancer and tuberculosis.

Cognitive–Intellectual Functioning

Another area in which additional advances can be expected is the augmentation of cognitive–intellectual functioning through computer technology. These systems of technology rely on progress in the development of software to enhance written language skills and in the highly experimental field of artificial intelligence as applied to computer processing. For example, people with learning disabilities can benefit from many new types of software that enhance their capabilities to produce written communications. Some of these software systems are very familiar, such as word processing, which enables people to express themselves without concentrating on the mechanics of writing, and spell-check programs, which enable the writer to correct misspelled words. Proofreading programs are available that extend the person's capability to check the text for grammatical and punctuation errors. Software technology has not stopped with the review of written material. Through brainstorming programs for personal computers, the individual is able to generate an outline with major and minor headings to guide the writer in creating material (Raskind, 1993).

Social and Recreational Activities

Technology has many social and recreational applications. Although this section concentrates on recreational opportunities involving the microcomputer and innovative data entry devices, noncomputer types of recreational accommodations also are possible. For example, a controlling mechanism held in the mouth (bite switch) allows an individual with lower extremity limitations to control the sustaining pedal on a piano (Ellis & Sewell, 1984); portable handrails enable people with visual impairments to bowl; and specially designed equipment permits people who use wheelchairs to water ski or snow ski (ICAN, 1992).

Moon, Hart, Komisar, and Friedlander (1995) pointed out the utility of velcro for "persons having difficulty holding recreational equipment. A piece of velcro attached to a golf glove and a club help a person play golf. The same principle would apply to holding paddles, bats, or gardening tools" (p. 193).

A large number of games can be played on a computer using either the mouse or joystick. Some games, however, require use of the keyboard, which becomes a problem for people with disabilities affecting use of their upper extremities. Therefore, keyboard adaptations are required (Dumper & Connine, 1985), such as keyguards, expanded keyboards, scanning, Morse code, and voice input. Keyguards are placed directly over the existing keyboard and have holes through which the individual can stick a finger or a mouthstick to depress a key. For individuals with coordination limitations, the guard ensures contact with the desired key. Made of plastic or metal, a keyguard can support the weight of a person's hands without causing any key to be depressed. This protective feature is particularly helpful for children with muscular dystrophy who need to rest their hands on the keyboard while they input a response.

Enlarged keyboards have been developed to help people with gross motor, but not fine motor, coordination to use the keyboard. Spaced well apart, keys up to 2 inches in diameter are located on a keyboard 14 inches wide and 26 inches long. This spacing eliminates striking keys accidentally and even makes the keyboard accessible for individuals who only have use of their toes.

Scanning eliminates the keyboard altogether. A game can be controlled by a switch device such as sip and puff, very light touch, or voice input. The individual activates the switch whenever he or she sees either an alphanumeric character or a response on the display screen that he or she wishes to select. Use of the switch directly operates a sensor, which then stops at the desired character or response. To speed this data processing procedure, Morse code can be used to enter commands into the computer. Microswitches of a wide variety are available to enter the dots and dashes, which are equivalent to other types of computer commands.

The most efficient mode of response for many people with disabilities is vocal input. If the computer has been programmed for voice recognition, vocal commands can be used to control the game. All of these modifications, from keyguards to voice input, increase the accessibility of everything from high-tech computer games to old standby parlor games played on a computer, such as chess, checkers, and Othello (Church & Glennen, 1992; Dumper & Connine, 1985).

Daily Living

Applications of technology to daily living tasks have been referred to either directly or indirectly in previous sections of this chapter. The following discussion specifically addresses the use of technology for expanding the functional capacity of individuals with disabilities for carrying out activities of living. The most sweeping development in this area has been referred to as the "house of the future." Through computer technology, the house is programmed to respond to voice or other commands registered on a control panel linked to receiver stations. Such tasks as dimming the lights, starting or stopping appliances, raising or lowering the temperature, and locking or unlocking doors and windows are possible via the spoken word. The technology can be expanded to include a vocally controlled home security and informational system as well (Lazzaro, 1993).

Remote environmental control has been available through computer technology for some time. However, its utilization potential has been increased by recent advances in vocal control systems, as in the house of the future, as well as through the development of wireless communication aids that can be attached to a wheelchair, thus giving the wheelchair user contact with stationary equipment regardless of where he or she is in the house (Prentke Romich Company, n.d.).

Still in the developmental stages, household robots are another promising boon to people with disabilities. Industrial robotics provides the basic technology for home use of robots. Indeed, it is projected that robots could serve as personal care attendants in the future for individuals with disabilities. At a minimum these robots could perform repetitive, simple tasks, allowing human attendants to devote their time to other needs of the person with a disability (F. Bowe & Little, 1984; McLaughlin, 1984). Research on robotics has concentrated on "increasing visual acuity in robots, increasing their tactile control abilities, developing multi-arm and multi-finger coordination, developing the ability to manipulate soft materials, and motion planning (devising collision-free paths through obstacle-filled environments)" (Bilheimer, 1985).

Not all methods for improving the daily living of people with disabilities involve electronic technology. Some improvements result simply from sound design. For example, the Center for Rehabilitation Technology at Georgia Institute of Technology designed an accessible kitchen based on the principles of universal design. Universal design considers a broad range of limitations (mobility, sight, perception, hearing, strength, stamina, and balance) and seeks to eliminate all barriers to the person's "wayfinding, safety, and communication" (Carter & Patry, 1990).

Focusing on function rather than fashion, the application of universal design principles results in living environments and instruments that are usable by everyone (i.e., "ergonomically friendly" built materials; Institute of Medicine, 1997). For example, the universal kitchen consists of a series of components (work surfaces, cabinets, and appliances) that can be arranged at different heights and in different sequences to fit the needs of the person regardless of the disability-related limitations. Using these products, builders and remodelers can construct kitchens as they wish without eliminating the flexibility of the materials. Materials can be easily rearranged should a person with a disability purchase the home or should someone in the family acquire a disability (Ellis & Sewell, 1984). Without a doubt, this universal design concept is a positive response to the pervasive problems of environmental inaccessibility in the traditional "built" environment.

Unfortunately, universal design concepts are not yet widely implemented. If they were, people with disabilities would face far fewer barriers. Experts stress that wider application of universal design principles would not only make the environment more accessible but also increase the market appeal of facilities and products. According to Adelson (2004, p. 31), universal design principles include the following:

1. Equitable use—curb cuts make it easier for everyone to cross the street
2. Flexibility in use—sensor-activated faucets have hands-free operation
3. Simple and intuitive use—high contrast "on–off" levers require no training
4. Perceptible information—remote controls and telephones with bigger numbers are easier to see and use
5. Tolerance for error—low sheen hard floors reduce glare and are less slippery
6. Low physical effort—sensor-activated doors are easier for everyone to operate
7. Size and space for approach and use—standard width for doorways results in easy use for everyone

Adelson (2004) described how universal design of kitchen utensils, specifically using wider, cushioned grips on knives, can openers, and peelers, increased sales of the products to baby boomers, who appreciated the "ease, comfort, and safety" features of the tools (p. 33).

Resources

Because technology is changing so rapidly, the person with a disability, rehabilitation service provider, or interested family member may have difficulty staying informed. Hence, up-to-date resources for acquiring information on technology-related issues, products, software, and accommodations are extremely important. A number of these resources exist, some on a national level and others on a local level.

Based on Smith's (1987) research, Galvin and Langton (1998) presented a list of the types of organizations that provide technology-related services. Public programs and agencies such as special education, vocational rehabilitation, and independent living centers provide information and equipment to support people with disabilities in living, learning, and working settings. Other public programs such as the Veterans Administration are active in conducting research on technology and providing such services and aids through their hospitals.

Not-for-profit local affiliates of national organizations such as the Easter Seals Society, United Cerebral Palsy Association, and Muscular Dystrophy Association are sources of assistive technology information and services.

Technology services are also available from private sector sources, including technology consultants and suppliers. Finally, volunteer programs exist that help link people with disabilities with technology (e.g., Telephone Pioneers of America, Volunteers for Medical Engineering).

Valuable technology services are available from statewide consultation projects funded through the Assistive Technology Act of 1998. Web sites for these statewide consultation projects are easily found on the Internet using available search engines or ABLEDATA (http://www.abledata.com). In addition, the RESNA Technical Assistance Project (http://www.resna.org/taproject/index .html) is an excellent source of information regarding services available through the state assistive technology projects. The purpose of these projects is to provide consumers with information on assistive technology, funding sources, and technology-related policies. These programs may also provide low-cost loans for the purchase of assistive technology and technology assessments and training (Armstrong & Wilkinson, 1998; J. Wallace, 2003). Focus group research involving consumers with disabilities resulted in a number of conclusions regarding ways to improve the operation of these technology projects (Hayward, Tashjian, & Wehman, 1995). For example, participants in the groups called for (a) more help from case managers to identify and secure assistive technology, (b) greater access to funding specialists for information on financing assistive technology, and (c) more practical methods for trying out technology and sharing information with other interested users.

The Internet provides easy access to a vast array of resources on assistive technology. The following are selected examples:

> http://www.microsoft.com/enable
>
> http://www.apple.com/education/k12/disability
>
> http://trace.wisc.edu
>
> http://www.familyvillage.wisc.edu

Three other valuable sources of information on assistive technology include ABLEDATA (http://www.abledata.com), the Job Accommodation Network (JAN; http://www.jan.wvu.edu), and Ability Hub (http://www.ability hub.com). Located in Silver Springs, Maryland (800/227-0216), ABLEDATA can provide information on a wide variety of technological devices, such as the functions they perform, their costs, and sources for the devices. Established at West Virginia University in Morgantown, JAN provides consultation services on job accommodations and technology (800/526-7234) and on the Americans with Disabilities Act (800/232-9675). JAN also maintains a computer bulletin board (800/342-5526) that contains valuable current information on technology resources. Specializing in helping individuals identify adaptive equipment to increase computer access, Ability Hub is maintained by a RESNA certified technology specialist.

Resources for information on microcomputer technology for persons with severe disabilities include the Trace Research and Development Center at the University of Wisconsin–Madison (1550 Engineering Dr., Madison, WI 53706-1609; 608/262-6966; http://www.trace.wisc.edu) and the Georgia Institute of Technology Center for Assistive Technology and Environmental Access (490 Tenth St. NW, Atlanta, GA 30332-0156; 404/894-4960; http:// www.catea.org). The Trace Center provides industrial consultation as well as an international registry of software programs and hardware modifications for individuals with disabilities. The Center for Assistive Technology and Environmental Access provides individual consultation and information packets related to disability and computer access (National Rehabilitation Information Center, 2006). Other useful information on assistive technology, computer accommodations, and universal design is available from resources listed in Table 13.2 (Adelson, 2004; Center for Assistive Technology, n.d.). The list of technological resources in Table 13.2 does not include the information resources or electronic bulletin boards that exist in many communities.

All of the resources cited in this section serve to bring together people with disabilities and technology. Unfortunately, they do not address many of the complex questions related to producing and marketing technological advances for persons with disabilities. Production incentives and marketing strategies to bring new technological developments into the marketplace are critical needs.

Technology and the Marketplace

Many potential applications of technology on behalf of people with disabilities have never made it beyond the idea stage. Reasons for this sad state of affairs often relate to marketing, financing, or governmental red tape. In regard to marketing, the Office of Technology Assessment (1983) reported that it is often difficult to estimate the number of consumers with disabilities. Market statistics simply do not exist for many different types of products. Because some investors view the market as fragmented and hard to reach, their interest in investing in products for people with disabilities is dampened. Investors are also concerned about the strength of the demand—the length of time that consumer desire for a device or service will persist. These market concerns stifle many initiatives to develop new technological adaptations.

Financiers are also concerned about the return rate on their investments in devices for individuals with disabilities. New technological aids for people with disabilities are expensive to produce, and many require special modifications to meet the needs of the individual consumer. Moreover, these products and their individual adaptations must meet rigorous "functional, technical, reliability, and safety" standards (Office of Technology Assessment, 1983, p. 96). Expenses do not end with the development and production of the device; the manufacturer must also train individuals in use of the new technology and maintain the equipment in service.

Entry of technological devices into the market is also slowed by red tape. It is difficult to secure protection for new ideas through the patent process.

TABLE 13.2
Selected Resources for Technological Information

Organization/address	Topics/services
Adult Loss of Hearing Association 4001 East Ft. Lowell Tucson, AZ 85712 520/795-9887 (voice) 520/795-9585 (TTY) http://www.alohaaz.org	Information and consultation for adults with hearing impairments
Alexander Graham Bell Association for the Deaf and Hard of Hearing 3417 Volta Place, NW Washington, DC 20007-2778 202/337-5220 (voice) 202/337-5221 (TTY) http://www.agbell.org	Information on signaling/assistive devices
American Foundation for the Blind 11 Penn Plaza, Suite 300 New York, NY 10011 212/502-7600 (voice)	Information on consumer products for people with visual impairments; information and referral database on assistive devices
American Speech-Language-Hearing Association 10801 Rockville Pike Rockville, MD 20852 800/638-8255 (voice) 301/897-5700 ext. 4157 (TTY) http://www.asha.org	Information and assistance to individuals and families with communication disorders
Association for Children and Adults with Learning Disabilities 4900 Girard Road Pittsburgh, PA 15227 412/881-2253 http://www.acldonline.org	Information, referral, and advocacy assistance for people with learning disabilities
Center for Assistive Technology and Environmental Access 490 Tenth St. Atlanta, GA 30332-0156 404/894-4960 (voice, TTY) http://www.catea.org	Information regarding computer applications and assistive devices and design and development of accessible environments
Center for Computer Assistance for the Disabled 1950 Stemmons Freeway, Suite 4041 Dallas, TX 75207 214/746-4217 http://www.necfoundation.org	Responses to inquiries regarding use of assistive technology to reduce barriers to self-sufficiency

(continues)

TABLE 13.2 *Continued*

Organization/address	Topics/services
Center for Universal Design College of Design North Carolina State University Campus Box 8613 Raleigh, NC 27695-8613 919/515-3082 (voice, TTY) Info line: 800/647-6777 http://www.design.ncsu.edu/cud	Information on application of universal design principles in housing, public and commercial facilities, and related products
Heath Resource Center George Washington University 2134 G St., NW Washington, DC 20052-0001 800/544-3284 (voice, TTY) http://www.heath.gwu.edu	Information on computer technology, assistive technology, and funding sources specific to postsecondary education for students with disabilities.
Post-Polio Health International 4207 Lindell Blvd., #110 St. Louis, MO 63108-2915 314/534-0475 http://www.post-polio.org	*Post-Polio Health,* publication on independent living and technology for polio survivors and their families

Liability concerns, such as lawsuits resulting from "malfunctioning devices" (Office of Technology Assessment, 1983, p. 96), deter others. Finally, approving devices for third–party payments by governmental or private insurance agencies is time–consuming.

D. Brown (1984) recounted two real–life examples of difficulties that must be overcome if technological devices are to reach the marketplace. Initially, there was very little interest among investors in the Eyetyper. They considered the device too expensive to develop and the market too small to support it. Backers worked for over a year and half to overcome this perception and to acquire the necessary capital to produce the Eyetyper.

The Personal Communicator took even longer to reach the production stage. After seeking funding from government agencies for several years, the developer finally started his own company in 1980. He interviewed deaf people to determine what they wanted in a communication device, designed the Personal Communicator to fit the market, and approached 10 investors. Soon $2 million was raised to hire a staff and begin production of the Personal Communicator for the 3 million people who have lost their hearing in midlife.

Reaching the marketplace is not the only significant issue that must be addressed through governmental policy and financial support. Other problems interfere with the use of technology. In the remainder of this chapter, these problems are reviewed and some possible solutions proposed.

Problems and Solutions in the Use of Technology

If technology's potential to improve the lives of individuals with disabilities is to be reached, a number of problems must be addressed. For example, rehabilitation providers must develop technical problem-solving skills. Other problems include lack of sufficient financial resources, information, consumer involvement, and support services, as well as barriers to microcomputer use.

Technical Problem Solving

Before discussing specific barriers to the development of assistive technology, one should describe the process of "technical problem solving" (Long, Huang, Woodbridge, Woolverton, & Minkel, 2003; Seventeenth Institute on Rehabilitation Issues, 1990; Strobel & McDonough, 2003). Use of technical problem-solving skills by people with disabilities and rehabilitation professionals increases the probability that the aids or devices chosen are appropriate for the person and the task demands to which the person must respond. Ten steps are involved: (a) problem identification, (b) evaluation of needs, (c) assessment of barriers to implementation of new technology, (d) development of alternative solutions, (e) selection of an alternative, (f) identification of reputable suppliers, (g) acquisition of funding for technology and required support services, (h) solution trial, (i) reevaluation, and (j) follow-up.

Kutsch (1990) provided an interesting example of technical problem solving in his description of an accommodation provided for a deaf person who was employed as a darkroom technician. Both the employer and the employee were concerned about the best way to notify the employee of an emergency evacuation situation that might occur while the employee was working in the darkroom. Although a light that would flash in the case of an emergency was installed in the person's office, such a solution to the problem would obviously not work in the darkroom.

The employee and employer discussed other possible solutions to the problem, such as a "buddy system" for warning the employee of emergencies. After some consideration the employee and employer decided that the buddy system was not entirely reliable because the buddy might be sick or might forget to warn the employee. They also discussed the feasibility of a vibrating pad on the floor that would alert the person to fire alarms or other emergencies. Unfortunately, the employee did not always work in one spot in the darkroom. After some deliberation, the employee and employer decided to use a vibrating pocket pager coupled with the buddy system as a backup. They implemented and evaluated the strategy over a period of time, and both concluded that it was an effective coupling of high- and no-tech techniques to solve the problem of how to signal a deaf employee in the darkroom.

Kutsch (1990, p. 8) indicated that the success of any technical problem-solving effort depends on affirmative answers to the following questions:

1. Was the employee actively part of the accommodation process through all phases?
2. Does special equipment take advantage of the employee's unique abilities?
3. Was a simple, minimal-cost solution found?
4. Was the "right" problem solved?
5. Is the solution portable and appropriate for other assignments within the company?
6. Has an accessible career path been provided for the employee?
7. Were all accommodations that the employee requested truly "reasonable"?

Arriving at affirmative responses to Kutsch's (1990) seven questions does not happen by chance. As Galvin and Langton (1998) stressed, "assistive technology is a diverse and often complex resource that requires expertise beyond what some organizations are prepared to offer" (p. 19). Thus, they recommend a team approach to solving technology problems that includes the person with a disability, a rehabilitation engineer, an assistive technology specialist, and representatives of other health professions (e.g., occupational, physical, and speech therapy). Assistive technology specialists may include professionals with training in rehabilitation, rehabilitation engineering, or occupational therapy who have extensive experience in restoring individual functioning through the application of technology.

Research on factors affecting the adoption of assistive technology by people with disabilities has underscored the importance of the cultural perspective of the user as well (Parette & Brotherson, 2004). For example, the Eurocentric emphasis on independence is at the heart of assumptions regarding the need for assistive technology solutions for people with disabilities. Some cultures emphasize collaborative or family-based solutions to problems, whereas others prize the notion of "fitting in" (i.e., not looking different from anyone else). Consequently, discussions of the use of assistive technology must begin with an examination of the value positions of all involved parties. After reaching an understanding of any differences in opinions, the parties can negotiate whether to seek an assistive technology solution, the type of technology needed, and the settings in which the person wishes to use the technology.

Financial Resources

One problem slowing the adoption of technological devices and aids by people with disabilities is the lack of financial resources. This problem manifests itself in several ways. For example, one survey indicated that technological research and development for people with disabilities received only a small amount of federal funding, particularly when compared with the amount of money devoted to income support programs. Without more research and development, much of the potential and most of the adaptations of technology for individuals with disabilities will never be discovered (Office of Technology Assessment, 1983).

Lack of financial resources is also a serious problem for the individual with a disability. Due to underemployment or unemployment, and therefore limited buying power, many people cannot afford to purchase technological devices and aids, such as adapted computers, drivers' aids, reading machines, and automated home environment systems. It has been estimated that over 2.5 million people in the United States are "in need of assistive technology devices that they do not have, mostly because they cannot afford them" (J. F. Wallace, 1995, p. 245). On the positive side, mass production of disability-related products such as TDDs and computers has resulted in price decreases. In addition, several sources of financial support exist to help people purchase technological devices (Dillingham, 1996; Schlachter & Weber, 2006; J. F. Wallace, 1995). These resources are described in Table 13.3.

Availability of Information on Technology

Given the rapid increase in the number of assistive devices, lack of information on available technological devices and aids is an ever-present problem for people with disabilities. In fact, two large-scale national surveys of providers and consumers (Justesen & Menlove, 1994) documented that both groups felt uninformed about recent advances in assistive technology. As a result most people with disabilities must fall back on informal sources to learn about technology. Mann (1991) recounted the problems implicit in the typical technology delivery model, the "consumer purchase model." After the person with a disability, a family member, or a friend hears about a device, the person with a disability purchases the device, often based solely on a description in a catalog. According to Mann (1991), "purchases are made that do not work, are not appropriate, are not compatible with other equipment, or that require additional installation, service, or training that is not available" (p. 18). New approaches to distribution of technology information and advice must occur if people with disabilities are to avoid wasting their time and money.

Several solutions to the information problem exist. Dixon and Enders (1984) suggested the rehabilitation extension agent concept. Representing a technology resource on the local level, the extension agent would possess "specialized knowledge and skills regarding inexpensive ways of providing technological aids and designing low cost accommodations" (p. 7). Although making a good point, Dixon and Enders should have recommended instead that rehabilitation counselors become more knowledgeable regarding the applications of technology to problems related to disability (Justesen & Menlove, 1994;

TABLE 13.3
Funding Sources for Assistive Technology

Funding source	Qualifications
Credit financing	Good credit history and/or collateral
Medicaid (Title XIX)	Medical need and poverty-level income
Medicare, Part B (Title XVIII)	Age of 65 or older or presence of severe disability and eligibility for Social Security Disability Insurance (SSDI)
Private Insurance	Insurance policy with coverage limited to terms of the policy
Vocational Rehabilitation	Severe disability and technological needs related to goal of competitive employment
Special Education	School age, presence of a disability, and technology needs related to educational goals
Veterans Administration	Military service, income limitations, and medical or rehabilitation needs
Workers' Compensation	Work-related injury and technological needs related to the rehabilitation process
Plan to Achieve Self-Support (PASS)	Severe disability, income limitations and Supplemental Security Insurance (SSI) eligibility
Tax Equity and Fiscal Responsibility Act	Age of 6 years or younger and extreme medical complications

Note. Adapted from *Use of Technology to Aid Clients in Employment* (Unpublished manuscript, pp. 28–29), by J. Dillingham, 1996, Hot Springs: Arkansas Research and Training Center, and *Funding Manual,* by University of Washington Center for Technology and Disability Studies, 2003, Seattle, WA: Author.

Noll, 1991). The extension agent concept is consistent with the services that the rehabilitation counselor should provide on the local scene to individuals with disabilities. In their efforts to assist individuals in the selection of assistive technology, rehabilitation counselors should have accurate answers to a series of questions (see Chandler, Czerlinsky, & Wehman, 1993):

1. How expensive or complicated is the device?
2. Is another solution simpler?
3. Is another, less expensive device available that gives the same results?
4. Does the system increase the individual's dependence on a technical device without a backup in case of equipment failure?
5. Does the system work in both the home and the work environments?
6. Can an off-the-shelf, or commercially available, piece of equipment be used instead of a custom design?
7. Will the device last long enough to justify its cost?

Unfortunately, as Justesen and Menlove (1994) noted, too many rehabilitation counselors have not received adequate training in assistive technology services in either preservice or in-service settings. They went on to describe the topics that counselors should cover regarding assistive technology (AT), such as AT devices; AT funding; AT legislation; AT services and service providers; strategies using high, low, and no-tech; and AT for the future.

Provisions in the Rehabilitation Act Amendments of 1992 and 1998 underscore the need for rehabilitation counselors to be knowledgeable about assistive technology. The amendments require state vocational rehabilitation agencies to describe how (a) technology services would be provided throughout the rehabilitation process and the state; (b) rehabilitation counselors, client assistance personnel, and other related professionals would be trained to provide consultation on technology; and (c) assessments of technology needs would be conducted to determine an individual's eligibility and vocational rehabilitation needs (RESNA Technical Assistance Project, 1993). Each client's individualized plan for employment must specify how services will meet the person's current needs for assistive technology.

A community technology capability team is another local resource that could be developed (Dixon & Enders, 1984). Composed of volunteers, rehabilitation counselors who have received specialized training (Noll, 1991), and/or individuals with disabilities, this team could advise people with disabilities regarding available devices, low-cost modifications, and product comparability. Local agencies such as the public library could also collect and organize information on technological aids and devices.

Valuable information on assistive technology is available through personal web pages and through national information clearinghouses accessible on the Internet. These databases include information on do-it-yourself solutions, inexpensive modifications of mass-marketed products, and adaptations of new technology, all of which would supplement information available from ABLEDATA, which mainly describes commercially available products. By accessing both ABLEDATA and these grassroots databases, rehabilitation professionals and consumers with disabilities have a vast information resource at their fingertips.

Mann (1991) mentioned other ways to disseminate information on technology, such as through the services of rehabilitation facilities or independent living centers. Although these organizations can play a vital role, they possess certain drawbacks. For example, Mann (1991) expressed concerns about (a) the low compliance rate that has typically existed for devices and aids prescribed by rehabilitation facilities, (b) solutions developed outside of the person's home and community, and (c) the difficulty the person would experience in maintaining contact with the facility. Acknowledging that centers for independent living have valuable technology services to offer, such as evaluation, prescription, and peer counseling, Mann (1991) observed that, historically, inadequate funding of independent living programs has severely limited their capabilities to provide technological consultation.

Mann (1991) believed that the solution to the technology information and consultation gap lies with the development of statewide planning and technology services that are supported by the Tech Act. For example, New York implemented statewide planning, which led to the development of an updated database, an 800 number for technology consultation, and a computer bulletin board service. Many other states have initiated such local-level services designed to enable people with disabilities to obtain answers to their questions about assistive technology.

Consumer Involvement and Support

Lack of consumer involvement has impeded the adaptation of technology to the needs of people with disabilities in many ways. Without consumer input, ill-conceived and unreliable products can result (Gray, Quatrano, & Lieberman, 1998). One such example was the voice-activated wheelchair ("New Project," 1984), which worked well in the confines of a quiet laboratory but responded erratically in the noisier environment of the real world. Device developers would, therefore, do well to change their "we know what is best for you" attitude (Schrader, 1984).

Although consumers are sometimes consulted, those who are consulted are only a small segment of the market, such as people in hospitals, rather than those leading active, independent lives in spite of the problems of disability. The independent living uses of a device often require greater flexibility, versatility, strength, endurance, and portability than the more limited applications of the device in a hospital setting ("New Project," 1984). In response to this problem, Pfrommer (1984) recommended that a greater number of "qualified consumers" be consulted. According to Pfrommer (1984), qualified consumers are those who

> (1) have a disability, (2) possess social maturity, (3) use technical products and services, (4) participate in consumer organizations or demonstrate good contact with the community of persons with disabilities, (5) represent the point of view of a sizable number of persons with varying disabilities, and (6) possess a working knowledge of the area in which they are participating. (p. 242)

Lack of consumer involvement in the process of selecting assistive technology can also result in lack of acceptability. As was the case for many prosthetic devices in the past, future technological devices will be no more likely to leave the closet if they are basically unacceptable to the consumer. Consequently, Brodwin, Star, and Cardoso (2003) emphasized the importance of consumers' identifying their personal goals for technology prior to the selection of any type of assistive technology. They must be convinced that the solution meets criteria of effectiveness, reliability, ease of use, and comfort, and that it is consistent with expectations of significant others such as family, peers, and employers. Examples of potential problems in these areas include the development of robots or training of animals to meet attendant care needs. Negative aspects of these applications include decreasing the amount of human contact the person with a disability has and increasing the individual's feeling of depersonalization. Kenneth Zola, while executive director of the Boston Self-help Center, felt that having one's personal care needs met by an animal or a robot is "invalidating to the person" (D. Brown, 1984, p. 74). The way in which technology replaces human assistance is, therefore, very important and must be developed based on input from individuals with disabilities.

Consumer Training and Product Service

Many support services that commonly exist for mass-marketed products are simply nonexistent for technological devices designed for people with disabilities. Raskind (1993) stressed the need for clear, easy-to-read documentation on how to set up and use products, and for an 800 number for assistance from the manufacturer. Service and repair of a purchased device are also important. Indeed, F. Bowe and Little (1984) noted that the consumer is fortunate if the company that produced the device still exists when repairs are needed. Even when still operating, many companies have made little or no provisions for repair services. For all of the above reasons, the Alliance for Technology Access (1994, p. 101) recommended that users of assistive technology ask vendors the following questions:

1. What kind of technical assistance is available?...
2. Do you offer telephone support?...
3. Is there a charge for technical assistance?
4. Do you have a product newsletter?
5. What are your policies on refunds, exchanges, repairs, and replacements?
6. How do you handle upgrades of your product for users of earlier versions?

People with disabilities have addressed the need to improve the warranties on assistive technology devices they purchase. Some assistive technology devices costing consumers a considerable amount of money may come with only a 90-day or 6-month warranty. To correct this problem, consumers have initiated action in many states to develop and pass "lemon laws" that apply to assistive technology. Most of these laws require a 12-month warranty that begins on the date of delivery, not on the date of order. Coverage is typically limited to motorized wheelchairs or to devices costing in excess of an established figure. Louisiana has one of the more stringent laws, which includes desirable provisions such as broad coverage (all assistive devices) and clear criteria to qualify as a "lemon" (e.g., out of service for the same reason twice in a year or out of service for any reason for 30 days during the first year of ownership) (Area Education Agency 13, 1999).

Concluding Statement

The promise of technology for enhancing the lifestyles of individuals with disabilities has not gone unnoticed. Indeed, technology is one of the keys to greater personal independence and social integration for people with disabilities. At the same time, these claims for technology may be exaggerated if designers become so involved with the intricate features of various technologies that they forget to study the human functions that technology is to replace. Without a better understanding of human functioning and dysfunctioning, technological designers will be unable to recreate the versatility and complexity of many human capabilities. As a result, the great promise of technology will be only partially realized.

Throughout this chapter the importance of accessibility and acceptability of technology has been continually stressed. If accessibility is not addressed when new technology is designed, the "high-tech/electronic" era may provide no more opportunities for people with disabilities than did previous eras. People will not use aids that do not meet their needs, both physical and psychological. For example, robots and animals that provide some of the functions of an attendant also diminish the possibility of human contact. Products that function poorly, usually due to lack of consumer involvement, will also be rejected.

With accessibility and acceptability, technology can play a vital role in restoring or replacing limited human functioning. Technological aids exist to augment human capabilities such as mobility, communication, health maintenance, cognitive–intellectual functioning, hearing, vision, social and recreational activities, and daily living. To incorporate these technological advances into their lives, people with disabilities must first know about them. Before the advent of the World Wide Web and national resources such as ABLEDATA and JAN, information was available on a spotty basis at best. Local resources, such as electronic bulletin boards, state assistive technology projects, and state chapters of disability advocacy organizations, also exist to help people with disabilities access and share information on innovations in assistive technology.

The prospects for technology to improve the lives of people with disabilities can be improved if certain specific problems are addressed. For example, many potential applications of technology never reach the production and marketing stage. Investors are unsure of the market. They are concerned about protection of their "new ideas" and about their personal liability in case of device malfunctions. Solutions that encourage investment in and production of technological devices are therefore needed.

One important step involves greater commitment of federal dollars to research and development activities undertaken by government agencies and private industry. Consumers also need additional financial resources to purchase technological aids and devices through health insurance benefits and low-interest guaranteed loans. Device developers and investors need assurance of protection through revised patent laws. Finally, employers need incentives such as tax breaks for using "high-tech" aids and devices in job modifications. In addition to the "carrot," private industry must see the government wielding a stick by enforcing Title I of the Americans with Disabilities Act.

Resources at the local level are also needed. For example, rehabilitation counselors should become better informed about the variety and availability of technological aids and devices. They should know how to access the many national data repositories on technological products and adaptations. They could also start community programs related to use of technology, such as technology assistance teams, databases at public libraries, and local electronic bulletin boards.

Finally, rehabilitation professionals should promote the principle of designing for accessibility (i.e., universal design). For example, if computer hardware and software are designed from inception with the needs of people with disabilities in mind, then everyone will have an equal footing in the information age. Moreover, if individuals with disabilities can learn of the many technological advances available to them, they will be able to gain new independence in both social and vocational roles. These outcomes are not automatic. Without advocacy for people with disabilities on the part of consumers and rehabilitation professionals, the promise of technology will remain a promise, not a reality. Individuals with disabilities will look back on the first half of the 21st century as a time of opportunities that might have been, rather than opportunities realized.

Chapter 14

Women with Disabilities: Special Issues in Rehabilitation

Walter Chung
and
Stanford E. Rubin

The total population of women with a disability ages 5 years and over is approximately 25 million (U.S. Census Bureau, 2000). Therefore, almost one in five women in this country is living with disabilities. The disability rate for women older than 65 is even higher, with 42% reporting a disability (U.S. Census Bureau, 2005). A majority of women with disabilities (65%) have severe functional limitations and about 20% need personal assistance service (W. Jones, 2004).

Before 1980, literature about women with disabilities was limited generally to medical articles (Smith, 2002). In the past two decades, articles addressing women with disabilities from sociopolitical perspectives have become more abundant (e.g., Garland-Thomson, 2002; Hanna & Rogovsky, 1991). Many of the authors have been female scholars with personal experience with a disability (Traustadottir, 1990). One pervading theme in this literature is that women with disabilities are significantly disadvantaged and have, historically, been marginalized in society (Garland-Thomson, 2002). Women with disabilities have less education, fewer employment opportunities, and a higher poverty rate than either people without disabilities or men with disabilities (Blanchard & Hosek, 2003; Traustadottir, n.d.). Compared to men with disabilities, women with disabilities are twice as likely not to receive Society Security disability payments (Grady & Lemkau, 1998). Many unique problems experienced by women with disabilities in areas such as feminine health needs and health care access, sexuality, and motherhood have also traditionally been neglected. The terms *double handicap* and *double discrimination* therefore have commonly been used by scholars to describe the conditions of women with disabilities (e.g., Deegan & Brooks, 1985; Schur, 2004; Traustadottir, 1990).

As a result of an expanding focus on respect for diversity in the United States during the last few decades, adequate cultural sensitivity and cultural competence have become important practice standards for all counseling professions (e.g., American Counseling Association, 2005; American Psychological Association, 2002; American School Counseling Association, 2004). Although many current counseling textbooks address gender and disabilities under the umbrella of diversity issues (e.g., T. L. Robinson, 2005; Sue & Sue, 2003), few specifically address the unique challenges and experience of women with disabilities. This chapter discusses some of the previously insufficiently addressed major issues, such as employment inequality, health needs, sexuality and intimacy, motherhood, and abuse, of which rehabilitation counselors should be aware when serving women with disabilities. The theoretical premise of this chapter is that vocational rehabilitation operates not in a vacuum, but in a combined personal, social, political, and cultural context that requires rehabilitation counselors to perceive a female consumer from a holistic or ecological perspective. In the process of providing vocational services for a woman with a disability, other than the traditional vocational assessment, the rehabilitation counselor must also assess and understand the unique challenges that a woman can encounter in her personal life (e.g., health needs, abuse, motherhood) and in her social and cultural environment (e.g., attitudinal and physical barriers). Successful vocational rehabilitation for the female client depends not only on optimal vocational services, but also on the provision of any interventions needed for her to handle challenges in her personal life as well as in her social and cultural environment.

The above theoretical premise is consistent with perspectives on disability that have developed during the past few decades. According to DePoy, Gilson, and Cramer (2003), there are four models regarding the meaning of disability, and all of them have significant implications for understanding the marginal status of women with disabilities. Traditionally, the *medical model* explains disability as a result of biological impediment, with rehabilitation services and supports focusing on medical intervention, exclusive of such issues as the abuse and discrimination experienced by women with disabilities. The *social model* attributes much of the negative condition of women with disabilities to a socially constructed, disability-hostile environment that includes negative societal attitudes. Rehabilitation services and supports, therefore, must address the need to remove social and environmental barriers. The *political model* perceives disability as "a value-based, changing determination shaped by the opinions of human worth held by dominant social groups" (DePoy et al., 2003, p. 179). The political model shifts the construct of disability into the realm of power and resources and calls for political action. Finally, DePoy et al. (2003) explained the *cultural model* of disability as follows:

> Cultural views of disability suggest that all individuals who define themselves as disabled belong to a unique group which shares experiences, tacit rules, language, and discourse. In this view, the notion of disability is about group belongingness and distinction from other groups who do not share the disability identity. (p. 179)

In other words, the cultural model defines women with disabilities as a unique group because the common experiences and similar social and political circumstances that these women share bind them together. They have a unique group identity that is not shared with other groups, including men with disabilities.

In view of these four models of disability, it is imperative that rehabilitation counselors perceive the conditions and needs of women with disabilities from an *ecological paradigm,* as detailed in this chapter. Holding an ecological paradigm means that one recognizes the personal, social, political, and cultural contexts in assessing, planning, and implementing rehabilitation services for women with disabilities. Counselors who comprehensively understand the unique challenges encountered by women with disabilities will then become sensitive to "how gender and disability interact to create attitudinal and environmental barriers for women" (Kahn & Harrison, 2004, p. 3). A culturally sensitive rehabilitation counselor also tends to operate beyond the "conventional counselor/therapist mode" (Sue & Sue, 2003, p. 23). Specifically, the rehabilitation counselor will assume the roles of being a resource person (i.e., consultant), going to the client's community (i.e., outreach), and protecting the client against a discriminatory social and political system (i.e., ombudsman).

Employment Inequalities

Approximately 62% of women with disabilities ages 16 to 64 (i.e., 9.9 million women) are reported to have an employment disability (U.S. Census Bureau, 2000). Researchers consistently comment that the "double handicap" or "dual disadvantage" of being a woman and having a disability results in serious employment and economic inequalities for women with disabilities in the United States (e.g., M. Fine & Asch, 1985; Fulton & Sabornie, 1994; O'Hara, 2004; Schur, 2004). This observation has been supported by empirical data. Analyzing the data collected in the Survey of Income and Program Participation (SIPP) between 1994 and 1995, McNeil (1997) found that women with disabilities ages 21 to 64 had not only a lower employment rate but also lower median monthly earnings than women without disabilities and men with disabilities. According to Schur (2004), data collected from the SIPP in 1999 and two national household surveys administered after the November elections in 1998 and 2000 demonstrate a continuing discrepancy in employment and income levels between women with disabilities and women without disabilities and men with disabilities. For example, the 1999 SIPP data indicated that the employment rate for women with disabilities was 44.2%, compared to an employment rate for women without a disability of 75.5%, and that there was an approximate $7,000 difference in the median annual income of the two groups in favor of the women without a disability. The difference in median annual income between women and men with a disability was even greater in favor of the men (Schur, 2004).

The high unemployment rate for women with disabilities is a great concern among social policy and health care professionals because work not only is essential to economic independence but also is positively related to women's self-concept and social and psychological well-being. As Zeitzer and Duncan (2004) stated,

> In Western societies, a woman's employment or profession often defines her social status. In any case, whether out of financial necessity or merely social interaction, the truth is that work is an integral part of life in all communities. The corollary is that an individual's inability to participate in the workplace frequently results in her being marginalized and often consigned to the fringes of the society. (p. 10)

Magnus (2001) conducted in-depth interviews among women with disabilities to examine how disability may influence career and identity. An interesting finding was that engaging in meaningful occupations after disability allows women to redefine the meaning of disability; to form a new identity; and to "tie together their past, present, and future life" (p. 122).

Many factors contribute to the low employment rate and low income level of women with disabilities. Beyond the factors that affect both men and women with disabilities (e.g., lack of transportation, inaccessible buildings), women with disabilities often face other forms of barriers that are unique to them. These barriers are usually categorized into external and internal (Fulton & Sabornie, 1994). Table 14.1 summarizes some of the unique barriers that have been addressed in the literature (e.g., Feist–Price & Khanna, 2003; Fulton & Sabornie, 1994; Noonan & Gallor, 2004; Russo & Jansen, 1988; Traustadottir, 1990).

Focused on the career success of women with disabilities, some studies have been conducted to examine the facilitators of better employment outcomes for women with disabilities. Doren and Benz (1998) analyzed the data of 147 young women with disabilities. They concluded that the optimal employment outcome of these young women was positively predicted by having two or more jobs in high school and using the family support network during the job search. Negative predictors of the employment outcomes of young women with disabilities were low family income level (i.e., less than $25,000) and low self-esteem. Individuals who had both negative predictors were found to be six times less likely to obtain competitive employment than those young women who had high self-esteem and family income. In another study Slappo and Katz (1989) surveyed 120 women with disabilities in nontraditional careers (i.e., professional careers such as engineer and skilled/semiskilled careers such as forklift operator) and reported that major factors related to their career success were previous work experience, personal motivation, and support from mentors. Results from these studies demonstrated the need for rehabilitation counselors working with women with disabilities to be sensitive to both internal and external factors of employment.

TABLE 14.1

Unique Barriers for Women with Disabilities in Career Development and Employment

External	Internal
Workplace: sexual harassment, lack of mentors and role models, gender division in the labor market	*Personal attitude:* low motivation for leadership, poor self-esteem and self-efficacy expectations, fear of competition
Training: tend to be trained in low-paying occupations	*Skills:* deficit of working skills due to social norm that women's major role is at home
Social stereotypes: tend to be seen as passive, dependent, and incompetent to work	*Family:* unable to work because of need to take care of children, role conflicts
Vocational rehabilitation services: less likely to be involved in vocational rehabilitation services than men, tend to be "successfully rehabilitated" into part-time jobs or to be "homemakers"	

Implications

Rehabilitation counselors first need to self-examine their values, attitudes, and beliefs about providing vocational services to women with disabilities. They should be aware of how gender bias and sex-role stereotyping may affect their vocational planning and placement services for women with disabilities (Lesh & Marshall, 1984). As Russo and Jansen (1988) stated,

> Rehabilitation counseling is deeply rooted in traditional theories and approaches to counseling and psychology, approaches that themselves have viewed women as inferior and as less capable than men.... Thus, women who attempt to secure rehabilitation services are frequently confronted by rehabilitation counselors who believe that women are more suited for careers as caretakers (nurses, teachers, childcare workers) or as service providers (sales clerks, secretaries, social workers), and that disabled women are those that need to be taken care of and to receive those services. (pp. 240–241)

Women with disabilities, therefore, should be given access to gender-blind training and preparation and work experiences similar to those of men with respect to wages, hours, and type of work (Fulton & Sabornie, 1994). It is important for rehabilitation counselors to encourage women with disabilities to pursue nontraditional careers by organizing support networks and role models for them. The role models can be females with or without disabilities who work in nontraditional occupations (Slappo & Katz, 1989). Role models may enable women with disabilities to make social comparisons by providing a basis for them to evaluate their capabilities and accomplishments, leading to a sense of self-worth (M. Fine & Asch, 1985).

Based on the fact that having had two or more jobs in high school is positively correlated with postschool employment, rehabilitation counselors should develop and strengthen school-to-work transition programs at the high school level (Fulton & Sabornie, 1994). These programs can target young women with disabilities and actively "engage them in relevant learning opportunities that prepare them for the kind of higher skill, higher wages careers being targeted in current educational reform efforts" (Doren & Benz, 1998, p. 440).

In addition to focusing on vocational skill training, rehabilitation counselors are urged to address the cognitive and affective needs of their female clients with disabilities. Career aspirations can be enhanced by completing such homework assignments as field trips and self-examination of dysfunctional career thoughts (Keim, Strauser, & Ketz, 2002). To inspire career motivation, the successful stories of women with disabilities in employment can be highlighted (Feist-Price & Khanna, 2003). Rehabilitation counselors also can play a significant role in the community to promote the employment of women with disabilities. For instance, employers and their workers can be educated in advance to minimize negative stereotypes and promote workplace support before new female employees with disabilities begin their employment (Feist-Price

& Khanna, 2003). Women with disabilities can be encouraged to participate in proactive political and advocacy activities (Noonan & Gallor, 2004; Schur, 2004). Some of these activities include joining professional organizations that have strong political interest groups and supporting candidates for public office who understand and sympathize with the needs of women with disabilities. In sum, a culturally competent rehabilitation counselor seeks to increase the employability of a woman with disabilities by addressing both internal and external barriers. The counselor should conduct a comprehensive evaluation of the woman's life and should address any health, emotional, social, and family challenges that will hinder her success in acquiring and maintaining competitive employment.

Health Concerns and Health Care Access

Disability has often been defined as a major functional limitation in one or more life activities caused by any impairment (Blanchard & Hosek, 2003). The U.S. Census Bureau (2000) further classified the types of disability experienced by females ages 5 to 65 years and over into physical, mental, sensory, self-care, going outside the home, and employment categories. Over 12 million females with disabilities who are age 5 or older report a physical impairment and 6.2 million report a mental impairment. For those age 16 and older, 10 million report difficulty leaving the home (see Table 14.2). Compared to men with disabilities, women with disabilities are more likely to claim difficulty in going outside by themselves (30% vs. 21%), leading to greater social alienation (Schur, 2004).

TABLE 14.2

Census 2000: Types of Disability Among Women with Disability in Different Age Groups

Disability type	Age 5–15	Age 16–64	Age 65+	Total
Physical	203,609	5,870,634	5,955,541	12,029,784
Mental	691,109	3,329,808	2,212,852	6,233,769
Sensory	200,188	1,735,781	2,561,263	4,497,232
Self-care	174,194	1,686,691	2,138,930	3,999,815
Going outside the home	NA	5,845,146	4,456,389	10,301,535
Employment disability	NA	9,913,784	NA	9,913,784

NA = not available. *Note.* From *Disability Status 2000—Census 2000 Brief,* by U.S. Census Bureau, 2000. Retrieved October 23, 2005, from http://www.census.gov/hhes/www/disability/disabstat2k/table1.html

Health Concerns
for Women with Disabilities

In a national survey of 475 women with physical disabilities, Nosek, Howland, Rintala, Young, and Chanpong (1997) found that the primary disabilities were spinal cord injury (26%), polio (18%), neuromuscular disorders (12%), cerebral palsy (10%), multiple sclerosis (10%), joint and connective tissue disease (8%), and skeletal abnormalies (5%). Regardless of the types of primary disability, women with disabilities often had more complicated health needs resulting from their disabling conditions (Blanchard & Hosek, 2003; Centers for Disease Control and Prevention, n.d.-c). Many of these complications are known as secondary conditions of disability. Hough (1999) defined secondary conditions as "those physical, medical, cognitive, emotional, or psychosocial consequences to which the persons with disabilities are more susceptible by virtue of an underlying condition, including adverse outcomes in health, wellness, participation, and quality of life" (p. 186).

One common secondary condition experienced by women with disabilities is osteoporosis. Recent research concluded that women with physical and cognitive disabilities are highly vulnerable to osteoporosis and osteoporosis-related fractures (Schrager, 2004). Possible factors that contribute to this secondary condition are lack of mobility; insufficient sunlight exposure, leading to vitamin D deficiency; and the long-term use of medications such as anticonvulsants, steroids, and immunosuppressants (Schrager, 2004; Shabas & Weinreb, 2000). Uusi-Rasi, Sievanen, Rinne, Oja, and Vuori (2001) also found that their visually impaired female subjects had lower bone mineral density (BMD) in the weight-bearing proximal femur than normal-sighted women, possibly because of insufficient load-bearing physical activities.

Other prominent secondary conditions found in women with disabilities are obesity, cardiovascular diseases, fatigue, chronic pain, and depression (Blanchard & Hosek, 2003; Centers for Disease Control and Prevention, n.d.-c). Analyzing the data of 30,526 working-age women with and without disabilities collected from the 1997 and 1998 National Health Interview Survey, G. C. Jones and Bell (2004) reported that women with disabilities were more likely than women without disabilities to be overweight and to be both current and heavy smokers. Women with disabilities also reported higher prevalence rates of hypertension, bone/joint/fracture problems, chronic pain, diabetes, and depression than women without disabilities (G. C. Jones & Bell, 2004). Depression, which reputedly is disproportionately experienced by women, was reported as the most common secondary condition (44% lifetime; 40.7% within the past 12 months) in a study of health behaviors of 386 women with disabilities (Nosek & Hughes, 2003). J. A. Cook (2003) further found that depression experienced by women is associated with disproportionately higher levels of disability in the areas of social, physical, and work-related functioning. In sum, women with depression are more likely than men to report impairment in areas of family and marriage roles (e.g., parenting), in activities of daily living (e.g., eating, bathing) or instrumental activities of daily living (e.g., preparing meals, handling finances), and in the ability to secure gainful employment and income.

The health problems of women with psychiatric disabilities can be complicated by the use of psychotropic medications. Each year over 4 million women are treated for a psychiatric illness such as depression, bipolar disorder, schizophrenia, panic disorder, or obsessive–compulsive disorder (National Women's Health Information Center, n.d.). In their literature review using a MEDLINE search, Perese and Perese (2003) concluded that women with serious mental illness are highly vulnerable to disorders associated with the use of psychotropic medications. Some of these psychotropic medication–related health problems are excessive weight gain, hyperprolactinemia (a condition of elevated serum prolactin), amenorrhea (absence of menstrual bleeding), galactorrhea (inappropriate lactation), sexual dysfunction, breast cancer, immune disorders, and cardiac complications.

Health Care Access

In spite of having many complicated health needs, women with disabilities are found to have trouble accessing health care services. For example, research has indicated that women with disabilities are less likely than women without disabilities to receive preventive screening for breast and cervical cancer (Jans & Stoddard, 1999). The difficulty women with disabilities have accessing health care services may be due to various factors such as limited finances and ignorance of the importance of preventive health checkups and screenings (Blanchard & Hosek, 2003; Thierry, 1998; Welner, 1998). However, the two major contributors to the problem are believed to be physical and attitudinal barriers (Centers for Disease Control and Prevention, n.d.-a; Steinberg, Wiggins, Baramada, & Sullivan, 2002; Thierry, 2000).

Many forms of physical barriers can prevent women with disabilities from receiving preventive and routine health care services such as mammograms and gynecologic examinations. These barriers include lack of accessible transportation, lack of adjustable-height examination tables or chairs, difficulty entering the physician's office, and trouble adjusting the wheelchairs for mammograms (Blanchard & Hosek, 2003; Centers for Disease Control and Prevention, n.d.-b; Thierry, 2000).

Negative attitudes of health care professionals further deter women with disabilities from accessing health care services. According to the U.S. Department of Health and Human Services (2001), some health care providers tend to provide a lower quality of services to women than to men. For example, health care professionals tend to "give women less thorough evaluations for similar complaints, minimize their symptoms, provide fewer interventions for the same diagnosis, prescribe some types of medications more often, or provide less explanations in response to questions" (U.S. Department of Health and

Human Services, 2001, p. 2). In a national survey of women with physical disabilities, participants with disabilities reported having difficulty finding health care providers who understood all of their health care needs, and 31% of them reported even being denied services because of their disabilities (Nosek et al., 1997). Steinberg et al. (2002) found that lack of common language between the health care providers and female deaf clients could create miscommunications and insensitive practices that cause anxiety and embarrassment in clients. For instance, one female participant who was deaf in Steinberg et al.'s study described her unique personal health care experience as follows:

> A man came up to me and said, "Do you read lips?" and I said, "Yes." And he said, "Fine, c'mon." So I follow him to a dressing room. He was speaking to me, and I was looking very closely at his lips, and he said, "From the waist down." I had to take my clothes off and leave my clothes on, on top. And that's fine, so I repeated that. And I repeated to him, "Take my clothes off from the waist down and leave my top on, clothes on top." "Well, yeah, from the waist down, leave the top part on." So I got changed, and I went in and the man went in, and he looked at me and said, "No, no, no, no, no! It's from the waist up you take your clothes off and leave your bottom clothes on." And I was so embarrassed. I misunderstood him. I felt rotten, and I had to go change and went back in and I was still wondering why I had misunderstood him. (p. 735)

This woman's embarrassing experience could have been prevented if the health care provider had used an interpreter to facilitate communication or had taken the time and effort to communicate with her by clearly articulating the words and meaning of his instructions.

Implications

Because women with disabilities have a high incidence of osteoporosis, obesity, and cardiovascular diseases, rehabilitation counselors should motivate their female clients with ambulatory or partial ambulatory ability to actively participate in weight-bearing activities at home or work to maintain bone density. There is also a need to advocate for osteoporosis screening for women with disabilities and encourage them to follow the physician's recommended diet in regard to calcium and vitamin D supplements (Schrager, 2004).

According to the Centers for Disease Control and Prevention (n.d.-d), many of the secondary conditions found in women with disabilities could be prevented or delayed by helping them to engage in a higher level of physical activity. A low rate of physical activity has been a common life pattern of people with disabilities. Heath, Chang, and Barker (cited in U.S. Department of Health and Human Services, 1999) found that people with disabilities were more likely to be physically inactive than people without disabilities (32.0% vs. 27.0%). People with disabilities also were less likely than those without disabilities to engage in regular moderate physical exercise (27.2% vs. 37.4%) and in regular vigorous physical exercise (9.6% vs. 14.2%).

Many personal factors may contribute to the lack of physical exercise in women with disabilities. These include fear of aggravating the disability by exercising and lack of time to engage in exercise because of extra effort required to complete other routine living tasks (Nosek et al., 1997). Rehabilitation counselors will need to help female clients develop an efficient time and task management plan and acquire appropriate exercise information from their physicians and physical and occupational therapists. Peer-facilitated and psychoeducational support groups have been found to be effective in increasing the level of self-efficacy for health-promoting behaviors. In a study conducted by Hughes, Nosek, Howland, Groff, and Mullen (2003), women with physical disabilities were assigned to a seven-session weekly support group. Results indicated that group participation significantly improved various measures of health behavior, including diet, medical decision making, positive social interaction, vitality, physical functioning, and role limitations caused by physical problems.

Environmental factors can also limit the participation of women with disabilities in physical exercise. Other than the inaccessibility of facilities and exercise equipment, ignorance of the public also restricts the physical activity of women with disabilities. For example, women with disabilities tend to be considered as incapable of participating in physical exercise and are therefore "frequently excluded from gym and health education classes during school years" (Welner, 1998, p. 281). Rehabilitation counselors, therefore, should play an active role in educating the community about the physical activity needs of women with disabilities and of possible accommodations for meeting their physical activity participation needs.

To help women with disabilities to use health care services, rehabilitation counselors can arrange necessary transportation and provide them information on health care providers in the community who are friendly and capable of serving women with disabilities. Rehabilitation counselors may also communicate with health insurance companies and health care professionals regarding specific health needs of female clients with disabilities. Due to the complications of disability-related diagnoses and treatment, women with disabilities may sometimes need specialists to be their primary care providers (Nosek et al., 1997). Rehabilitation counselors, therefore, can assume the role of ombudsman in negotiating with insurance companies regarding coverage for female clients. Rehabilitation counselors can also play a consultant role with health care professionals by updating their information on assistive technology so that certain physical barriers to accessing health care can be minimized.

Sexuality and Intimacy

Due to the relationship between a woman's sexual or body image and her confidence (Basson, 1998; Bonwich, 1985; Center for Research on Women with Disabilities [CROWD], n.d.-b), the positive sexual self-image and sexual fulfillment of a woman with a disability may facilitate her potential success in competitive employment by enhancing her self-esteem and self-confidence. Nevertheless, health care providers and rehabilitation professionals tend to offer less assistance for women with disabilities to develop a positive sexual self-image and fulfilling sexual life. For example, women with disabilities are less likely to receive information and counseling on contraception, birth control, pregnancy, and safe-sex practices than women without disabilities (A. Asch & Fine, 1988; Drey & Darney, 2004). According to Nosek et al. (1997), 41% of the 439 women with physical disabilities surveyed reported that their physicians had not provided sufficient information about the impact of their disability on their sexual functioning.

Even though women with disabilities tend to have a normal desire for courtship, intimacy, and sex, their caregivers may attempt to restrict their sexual activity (CROWD, n.d.-c). Anxious parents who overprotect their daughters with disabilities may ultimately hinder them from developing the social and emotional skills necessary for friendship and romantic relationships. Parents may also discourage a daughter with a disability from marriage because they fear that their daughter may not be able to take care of her spouse after marriage (Limaye, 2003). Not surprisingly, some women with disabilities, frustrated with the societal oppression on their sexual fulfillment, have proclaimed more concern "with being loved and finding sexual fulfillment than getting on a bus" (Traustadottir, 1990, p. 11).

Two basic stereotypes may contribute to the societal oppression of sexuality and intimacy of women with disabilities. First, many people believe that physical and mental deviations from statistical normality impair a person's sexual capability (DeLoach, 1994). They assume women with physical disabilities have no sexual desire or are incapable of experiencing sexual fulfillment (Limaye, 2003; Traustadottir, 1990). Also, some perceive women with disabilities as "eternal children" rather than as capable, independent adults with a need for intimacy and sexual fulfillment (Traustadottir, 1990). According to Garland-Thomson (2002), women with disabilities are stereotyped as "asexual, unfit to reproduce, overly dependent, unattractive—as generally removed from the sphere of true womanhood and feminine beauty" (p. 17). Basson (1998) provided the following list of common myths and negative stereotypes regarding the sexuality of women with disabilities:

1. Disabled women are asexual.
2. Only independently functioning women can handle sexual relationships.
3. Disabled women who are single are celibate.
4. Disabled women cannot be mothers.
5. All disabled women are heterosexual.
6. Disabled women should be grateful for sexual relationships.
7. Disabled women are different.
8. Youth and beauty are essential to sexuality (p. 359).

Such myths have likely produced attitudinal barriers that have resulted in reports of very negative sexual experiences by some women with disabilities who are capable of developing romantic relationships (M. McCarthy, 1999). Compared to women without disabilities, the women with physical disabilities surveyed by Nosek et al. (1997) indicated less sexual activity, poorer sexual responses, and less satisfaction with their sex lives. McCarthy (1999) proposed that at least the following factors may contribute to the negative sexual experience of women with disabilities: (a) Their sexual experience is predominantly at the physical level, rather than at the emotional and psychological level; (b) some may have experienced sexual abuse in the past; and (c) they often lack much choice in their sexual relationships, in terms of "what they want to do, with whom, when, and how" (p. 203).

Research has found that women with disabilities are less likely to get married (Frankin, 1977, cited in A. Asch & Fine, 1988, p. 13). In fact, results from the 1992 National Health Interview Survey indicated that only 50% of women with disabilities were currently married, whereas, the marriage rates for women without disabilities, men with disabilities, and men without disabilities were 64%, 68%, and 69%, respectively (LaPlante & Carlson, 1996). Even when women with disabilities get married, their marriage is more likely to end in divorce (Traustadottir, 1990). Women with disabilities tend to see themselves as burdensome to their partners (Nosek et al., 1997). In a study of women with spinal cord injury, over 50% of the participants indicated that their relationship with a husband or a lover was terminated, by either the man or the woman with spinal cord injury, after the sustaining disability (Bonwich, 1985). Respondents offered various reasons for why their relationships were dissolved, but one prominent reason was the fear of being rejected and hurt by the partner. One woman in Bonwich's study disclosed her feelings about breaking up with her partner as follows:

> He was afraid of hurting me sexually. His passion was so strong that he was not sure he could be faithful. I was afraid I would be jealous and insecure as the years went by. If I put all my eggs in one basket—marriage—I would be overly vulnerable to someone else taking him away. (p. 60)

Disability may produce negative changes to the marital or loving relationship, causing feelings of insecurity and jealousy within a woman with a disability. Based on the survey responses of 475 women with physical disabilities, Nosek et al. (1997) concluded that some of the negative changes included less emotional intactness, less compatibility in the relationship, less respect by the partner, less sexual desire by the partner, and a sense of being overly protected (see Table 14.3).

Under the combined pressures of disability, failure of relationship, social alienation, and devaluation, it is not surprising that women with disabilities tend to have a negative body image. Women with spinal cord injuries reported that they perceived themselves as 50% less attractive postinjury than before their injury (Basson, 1998). In an interview of 17 women with learning dis-

TABLE 14.3
Negative Changes in Marital Relationship Due to Disabilities

Types of negative changes	Percentage of respondents
Becoming emotionally distant	42%
Becoming less compatible	35%
Partner no longer shows respect	31%
Partner no longer asks for sex	30%
Partner is overly protective	18%

Note. Changes reported by women with physical disabilities.

abilities, M. McCarthy (1999) found that most had difficulty identifying positive aspects of their bodies.

Research also indicated that women with disabilities tend to have lower self-esteem than either women without disabilities (Nosek & Hughes, 2003) or men with disabilities (M. Fine & Asch, 1985). After examining literature on self-esteem, Darling (cited in A. Asch & Fine, 1988) concluded that girls with disabilities have lower self-esteem than three other groups—girls without disabilities and boys with or without disabilities. One possible reason that men with disabilities possess higher self-esteem than women with disabilities is that men have the choice of identifying themselves with the role of the advantaged "male" instead of only the disadvantaged "disabled." Women with disabilities, however, have no choice but to identify themselves with two disadvantaged roles—"disabled" and "female"—which are both perceived as weak and dependent in U.S. society (M. Fine & Asch, 1985; Hanna & Rogovsky, 1991).

Implications

Rehabilitation counselors need to recognize the interconnection between positive sexual self-image and positive self-esteem and their effects on the employment motivation of women with disabilities. Therefore, assessing the sexual concerns of women with disabilities and helping them to develop a positive sexual self-image can be a necessary component of some vocational rehabilitation plans. Vocational rehabilitation counselors may not have sufficient knowledge to address certain sexual issues of female clients, but these concerns can be addressed through referral to appropriate counselors and physicians (Bonwich, 1985).

Environmental barriers hinder women with disabilities from participating in social activities and developing meaningful relationships. Rehabilitation counselors, therefore, can provide women with disabilities information on accessible recreational facilities and transportation (Nosek et al., 1997). Rehabilitation counselors sometimes may need to address the negative stereotypes and attitudinal barriers in the community by campaigning to promote the public awareness and recognition of the sexuality and rights of women with disabilities (Limaye, 2003).

There is a strong need to provide sex education to women with disabilities (M. McCarthy, 1999). Sex education programs can be offered in both school and community settings so that women with disabilities will realize that a fulfilling sexual life is possible for them (Nosek et al., 1997). Characteristics of the sex education program recommended by Limaye (2003) include (a) using an interdisciplinary approach; (b) covering topics of cultivating meaningful relationships, enhancing self-esteem, and developing an awareness of sexuality; (c) developing a mature sexual personality by integrating the areas of social responsibilities and physical experience; and (d) providing both sexual and social skills training that will enhance the social–sexual development of women with disabilities. Parents of women with disabilities should also be assisted in learning how to facilitate the sexual development of their daughters with disabilities. Some possible training foci for these parents are learning how to handle their own unnecessary anxiety and tendency to overprotect their daughters, learning how to provide accurate sexuality information to their daughters, and learning how to facilitate the social skills development of their daughters (Limaye, 2003; Nosek et al., 1997).

Motherhood

Research has indicated that when a woman with a disability is pregnant, her body tends to be perceived by her coworkers as more "normal" and therefore she is more accepted in the workplace (Buzzanell, 2003). However, women with disabilities historically have been discouraged from becoming pregnant because of the fear that they would have defective children (Carty, 1998). Women with disabilities of child-bearing age were once the victims of forced sterilization or separated from mainstream society in institutions (Traustadottir, 1990). Some state laws prohibited women with mental retardation, epilepsy, or psychiatric disability from marrying in an effort to prevent their bearing and raising of children (A. Asch & Fine, 1988). Because women with disabilities have been perceived as unfit for motherhood (Carty, 1998; DeLoach, 1994), they also have had less chance of winning custody of their children after divorce and have experienced greater discrimination when seeking to become foster or adoptive parents than women without disabilities (A. Asch & Fine, 1988; Traustadottir, 1990).

Frequently, families are concerned about potential harmful effects of pregnancy on the physical health and functioning of the woman with a disability (Lipson & Rogers, 2000). Consequently, a pregnancy can create enormous emotional turmoil for the woman with a disability and her family members. As a woman with polio stated, "Each time I announced I was pregnant, everyone in the family looked shocked, dropped their forks at the dinner table—not exactly a celebration" (A. Asch & Fine, 1988, p. 12). In a qualitative study conducted by Lipson and Rogers (2000), a respondent described her heated argument with her family members over whether she could raise a child:

> Your whole family is in the room and they are talking about it, and I'm sitting there saying, "I am sorry if you feel this way; I'm sorry if I'm damaging somebody's feelings of how I am supposed to be." I would just wheel out of the room and say, "You guys just deal with your feelings—when you feel comfortable and confident enough to talk to me about this, I'll talk to you." (p. 15)

Nevertheless, increasing numbers of women with disabilities are choosing to have children because of medical advances and the gradually increasing affirmation of a woman's rights in reproductive decision making (Blackford, Richardson, & Grieve, 2000). In a survey of women with disabilities conducted by Berkeley Planning Associates (1997), almost 40% of the respondents reported having children. Analyzing the data from the 1993 Survey of Income and Program Participation (SIPP), Toms-Barker and Maralani (cited in Jans & Stoddard, 1999) reported that the number of adult parents with a disability was about 6.9 million. About one third of women with disabilities had children under the age of 18, and women with disabilities were more likely to parent children than were men with disabilities. Besides, the percentage of women with disabilities (31% to 33%) parenting children under the age of 18 was similar to that of men without disabilities and only slightly less than that of women without disabilities (see Table 14.4).

TABLE 14.4

Percentage of Adult Parents with Children Under the Age of 18 in Home, by Status of Disability and Gender

Status	Percentage
Women	
Without disabilities	45%
With disabilities	33%
With severe disabilities	31%
Men	
Without disabilities	35%
With disabilities	26%
With severe disabilities	18%

The large population of mothers with disabilities parenting children under the age of 18 suggests that their parenting needs must be understood and necessary supportive services provided. Several studies have addressed the pregnancy and child-rearing experiences, challenges, and needs of women with disabilities (e.g., Blackford et al., 2000; Carty, 1998; Lipson & Rogers, 2000; Shaul, Dowling, & Laden, 1985). Carty (1998) stated that two major concerns of pregnant women with disabilities are (a) keeping themselves and their babies healthy during the periods of pregnancy, labor, birth, and postpartum, and (b) the physical ability to take care of their babies. However, their concerns are often ignored because many health care providers lack the necessary knowledge to work with pregnant women with disabilities. In a qualitative study of the pregnancy, birth, and postpartum experience of 12 women with physical disabilities, Lipson and Rogers (2000) found that few physicians realize the importance of referring pregnant women with disabilities to physical or occupational therapy. In fact, physical therapy may improve the range of motion of the hips and reduce the need for a Cesarean section. Occupational therapy could help women with disabilities after childbirth because of difficulty in carrying and moving the baby (Lipson & Rogers, 2000). After interviewing eight mothers with chronic illnesses, Blackford et al. (2000) reported that most of them reported stress and anxiety during their pregnancy. As one diabetic woman worrying about the possibility of a fetal defect stated, "I [had] been worried about my blood sugars.... You're always under that kind of tension because ... they do say they can't tell everything from an ultra-sound" (p. 901).

In the first few years after childbirth, a mother with a disability may need more energy to manage her child than a mother without a disability, which could lead to burnout (Shaul et al., 1985). Insensitive health care providers can increase tension and anxiety for mothers with disabilities (Lipson & Rogers, 2000). Even though most mothers receive some instruction on baby care before they leave the hospital, the information is mostly geared for women without disabilities. Too few nurse educators have the knowledge needed to provide alternative baby care information and adaptive equipment solutions for mothers with disabilities (Lipson & Rogers, 2000).

The greatest complaint from women with disabilities regarding motherhood is that limited information and learning resources are available for them on self-care and baby care (Blackford et al., 2000; Lipson & Rogers, 2000; Shaul et al., 1985). Mothers with disabilities often feel that they have to figure out on their own how to deal with their problems and concerns about pregnancy and parenting. As a mother with multiple sclerosis (MS) recalled,

> I am really upset with MS Society. They acted like, "YOU had a baby?" The peer counselor evidently was new. I asked if there was any literature I could read about, you know, parents with disabilities and any referrals they could give me and he says, "No, we don't have anything, there is just nothing." I said, "So you're just saying I'm on my own?" (Lipson & Rogers, 2000, p. 16)

Even though resources like Through the Looking Glass—an agency that specializes in providing assistance and information to parents with disabilities—are available, the extent to which mothers with disabilities are aware of these resources remains unknown (CROWD, n.d.-d).

Implications

Rehabilitation counselors need to respect the rights of women with disabilities to assume the role of motherhood. Counselors have the responsibility to provide support for women with disabilities to become successful mothers and, thereby, help reduce the negative societal stereotypes of women with disabilities. In their interview with women with chronic illnesses, Blackford et al. (2000) found that women with disabilities need the following types of assistance in pregnancy and childcare: (a) obtaining information on self-care such as appropriate types of exercise and diet related to their disability conditions, (b) sharing their anxiety with others, (c) receiving support from peers, (d) enhancing communication with family members, and (e) learning how to take care of their children. Therefore, it is important for rehabilitation counselors to arrange regular peer support groups for their female clients. Rehabilitation counselors should also actively collaborate with health care professionals from other disciplines to assure that their female clients receive up-to-date information on disability and pregnancy and parenting (Lipson & Rogers, 2000; Shaul et al., 1985). Carty (1998) recommended the following specific supportive services for pregnant women with disabilities:

1. Based on comprehensive physical and psychological assessments, develop a written plan of care to address the needs of women with disabilities during the periods of pregnancy, labor, birth, and postpartum.
2. Provide necessary information on pregnancy and child rearing for specific disabilities, including the potential impact of medication.
3. Ensure that a caring facility is physically accessible during the pregnancy and after the birth.
4. Collaborate with other agencies in the community for motherhood training, such as in child behavior management.
5. Prepare women with disabilities for family adjustment, and explore adaptive equipment to facilitate childcare.

In addition to providing support services to women with disabilities, rehabilitation counselors can also advocate for their female clients by promoting training on disability and pregnancy in health care education programs and medical school curricula (Shaul et al., 1985). Reducing environmental barriers for women with disabilities will enable them to assume the role of motherhood and become part of mainstream society.

Abuse and Violence

Research on women with disabilities has also focused on the issue of abuse and violence (Fearday & Cape, 2004; Li, Ford, & Moore, 2000; Powers, Curry, Oschwald, & Maley, 2002). Abuse of women is traditionally understood as a conscious and deliberate act that causes physical, sexual, and emotional harm (D. B. Berry, 2000). Physical abuse refers to violent acts against the body of a woman, such as kicking, beating, and restraining. Physical abuse can be short term (i.e., 6 months to 1 year) or long term (i.e., 1 year or longer), and it poses great danger to women with disabilities (Lissette & Kraus, 2000). Sexual abuse refers to forced engagement in various forms of sexual activities such as looking, touching, or intercourse in which the woman is an involuntary participant (D. B. Berry, 2000). Emotional abuse refers to behavior that verbally demoralizes another person's feelings and can occur with or without physical and sexual abuse (Lissette & Kraus, 2000). Some examples of emotional abuse are calling a person names, threatening to take children away, and refusing to give affection or attention (D. B. Berry, 2000).

Some consider the traditional descriptions of abuse and violence as insufficient for women with disabilities because some types of abuse are unique to the population (Hassouneh-Phillips & Curry, 2002). Therefore, Nosek, Hughes, Taylor, and Howland (2004) suggested that abuses should be defined in the context of disability:

> Disability-related emotional abuse often includes emotional abandonment and rejection or denial of disability. Disability-related physical abuse includes physical restraint or confinement; withholding needed orthotic equipment, medications, or transportation; or refusing to provide assistance with essential daily living needs, such as dressing or getting out of bed. Disability-related sexual abuse includes demeaning or expecting sexual activity in return for help or taking advantage of physical weakness and an inaccessible environment to force sexual activity. (p. 334)

Based on this disability-specific definition of abuse, research has consistently found a high prevalence rate of abuse and violence against women with disabilities (e.g., Nosek et al., 1997; Powers et al., 2002). Abusers can include family members, friends, personal care assistants, other individuals with disabilities, and staff members of public or private agencies (Hassouneh-Phillips & Curry, 2002).

In Nosek et al.'s (1997) survey study, 62% of the 439 women with physical disabilities reported having experienced some form of lifetime abuse. Compared to women without disabilities, women with physical disabilities have also been found to endure longer durations of abuse and have experienced more abuse from health care providers. They can also be the victims of abuse from personal assistants. Analyzing the survey results of 1,876 persons with disabilities in the areas of violence and substance use, Li et al. (2000) reported that women with disabilities were more likely to become victims of substance abuse–related violence than men with disabilities. In another survey, Powers et al. (2002) examined 200 women with disabilities and found that 67% of the subjects had been physically abused and 53% of the subjects had been sexually abused by a perpetrator. In addition, the prevalence rates of women who reported being physically abused and being inappropriately touched by their personal assistants were 14% and 11%, respectively.

Many existing personal, environmental, and social barriers hinder the abilities of women with disabilities to seek and obtain help from abuse intervention programs. In regard to personal barriers, a woman with a disability may be unable to escape the abuse due to her physical immobility. When a family member is the abuser, the woman with a disability may deny the existence of abuse for fear of losing custody of her children or losing caregiving and financial assistance from the perpetrator (Hassouneh-Phillips & Curry, 2002; Nosek et al., 1997; Nosek et al., 2004). If the abuser is a personal assistant, the woman may be concerned about losing the essential service or fear possible retaliation from the service provider (Powers et al., 2002).

Environmental barriers render some domestic violence shelter and abuse intervention program offices inaccessible. Surveying 67 community-based domestic violence programs providing services to women with disabilities in North Carolina, Chang et al. (2000) found that one major hindrance to effective services was structural limitations in program facilities. Due to insufficient funding, these programs were unable to provide adequate staffing and training, purchase necessary equipment, and renovate the facilities to meet the special needs of women with disabilities. In another study, Swedlund and Nosek (2000) interviewed staff members of 36 independent living centers. One of the most frequent problems discussed by the respondents was inaccessibility of the shelters and abuse intervention program offices for women with disabilities. The following are some specific examples provided by the respondents: (a) inadequate physical accessibility of facilities, (b) lack of interpretation assistance for women with hearing impairment, (c) lack of personal care service in the shelter, and (d) inadequate transportation assistance to the shelter or abuse program office. Similarly, DePoy et al. (2003) made the following comment:

> Looking at the domestic violence services in social agencies, many shelter and non-shelter community services are characterized by physically inaccessible settings, lack of material that women with visual and/or cognitive impairments can read, shortage of staff proficient in the use of American Sign Language to communicate with women with hearing impairments, and lack of training to provide services on multiple cognitive, receptive and expressive levels…. Thus the locus of the "problem," as seen through the social lens of disability, is limitations in environmental support and accessibility. (pp. 181–182)

Beyond personal and environmental barriers, social barriers also discourage women with disabilities from seeking help for preventing or stopping abuse. Social alienation can result in a woman with a disability being unaware of available abuse prevention resources (Powers et al., 2002). Stereotypes of the asexuality of women with disabilities may limit the response of health care professionals when women with disabilities disclose sexual abuse (A. Asch & Fine, 1988; DePoy et al., 2003). Unless the barriers to accessing shelters and abuse program intervention offices are removed, women with disabilities will continue to suffer various adverse health consequences resulting from abuse. Some of these health problems are depression, phobias, substance abuse, eating disorders, and increased severity of disability (DePoy et al., 2003; Nosek et al., 2004), all of which will inevitably impede the employability of women with disabilities. In a survey of 535 rehabilitation service providers, 95% recognized that abuse can hinder the achievement of vocational and independent living goals of a woman with disabilities. However, only 19% of them practiced routine screening of abuse at work (CROWD, n.d.-a).

Implications

As one of the primary service providers for women with disabilities, a rehabilitation counselor has an obligation to conduct routine screening of abuse for female clients (CROWD, n.d.-e). Some abuse screening instruments for women with disabilities include the *Abuse Assessment Screen–Disability* developed by CROWD (McFarlane et al., 2001) and the eight-item abuse screening questionnaire developed by the Center for Self-Determination in Portland, Oregon (Hassouneh-Phillips & Curry, 2002). Rehabilitation counselors may need to teach some women with disabilities to identify abusive acts, such as inappropriate touching, so instruments can be completed accurately (Nosek et al., 1997).

Rehabilitation counselors also need to initiate appropriate interventions for their female clients who experience abuse and violence. To do so, the counselors should (a) have sufficient knowledge in the areas of abuse and domestic violence, (b) be aware of the accessible shelter and community resources for women with disabilities, (c) be efficient in arranging necessary services such as interpretation for women with hearing impairments and transportation for those with mobility problems, and (d) be able to cooperate with law enforcement and other professionals to provide support and emergency services for their female clients (CROWD, n.d.-e; Hassouneh-Phillips & Curry, 2002; Swedlund & Nosek, 2000).

Rehabilitation counselors need to develop safety plans for women with disabilities who are victims of violence and abuse (Nosek et al., 2004). The safety plan should include the following important components (Oakland County Coordinating Council Against Domestic Violence, n.d.):

1. Important contact numbers (e.g., police, hotlines, friends, the local shelter)

2. Safe places to go in case of emergency (e.g., a friend's house or a shelter)

3. Ways to leave home safely and get to the safe location (e.g., by taxi, being picked up by a friend)

4. A list of important items that need to be brought (e.g., cash, legal documents, items for children, medications)

Female victims can be involved in recovery group therapy, which has been found to promote sharing, bonding, and empowerment of group participants (Fearday & Cape, 2004). Since networking is considered a good strategy to overcome challenges of insufficient funding, lack of training, and structural limitations among community-based domestic violence programs (Chang et al., 2003), rehabilitation counselors can actively provide networking support for these community agencies. Rehabilitation counselors may coordinate resources such as interpretation and transportation, organize cross-training activities, provide current information on funding sources, and serve on the boards of some agencies.

Concluding Statement

This chapter has provided an overview of the unique challenges and inequalities experienced by women with disabilities in U.S. society. A pervading theme in the literature on women with disabilities is their significant disadvantagement and marginalization in society (Garland-Thomson, 2002). They tend to have less education, fewer employment opportunities, and a higher poverty rate than either people without disabilities or men with disabilities (Blanchard & Hosek, 2003; Hanna & Rogovsky, 1991; Traustadottir, n.d.). Due to the social stigma of being female and disabled, women with disabilities face many barriers to their efforts to gain access to employment, to health care, and to sexual and intimacy fulfillment.

The theoretical premise of this chapter is that vocational rehabilitation does not operate in a vacuum, but operates in a combined personal, social, political, and cultural context that requires rehabilitation counselors to perceive a female consumer from a holistic or ecological perspective. Rehabilitation counselors must also self-examine their values, attitudes, and beliefs in regard to the role of women with disabilities in society. They should be aware of how gender bias and sex-role stereotyping may affect their vocational planning and placement activities for women with disabilities (Lesh & Marshall, 1984). In the process of providing vocational services for a woman with a disability, the rehabilitation counselor must, in addition to administering the traditional vocational assessment, assess and understand the unique challenges that a woman can encounter in her personal life (e.g., health needs, abuse, motherhood) and in her social and cultural environment (e.g., attitudinal and physical barriers). Successful vocational rehabilitation for the female client depends not only on optimal vocational services, but also on the provision of any interventions needed for her to handle challenges in her personal life as well as in her social, political, and cultural environment. Rehabilitation counselors who are sensitive to the attitudinal and environmental barriers produced by the double handicap of having a disability and being a woman will be better positioned to comprehensively understand the unique challenges encountered by women with disabilities and therefore be more capable of serving them effectively.

Chapter 15

Independent Living

ndependent living is not a new concept. Its roots date back to the first civilian rehabilitation act, the Smith-Fess Act of 1920, in which homemaking was considered a legitimate training program and occupational objective. Although attempts were made to add a specific independent living (IL) rehabilitation provision to the rehabilitation legislation in the early 1960s, it was not until the 1970s that the goal began to be realized. Success at that point was greatly the result of actions taken by persons with severe disabilities themselves. In testimony before congressional committees, persons with disabilities made their real needs known. They also developed "consumer initiated IL programs around the nation" (DeLoach, Wilkins, & Walker, 1983, p. 17).

Defining *independent living* requires an examination of many basic rehabilitation concepts. Roberts (1977) began a discussion of independent living by presenting definitions for two common rehabilitation terms, *disability* and *handicap*. *Disability* was defined as a medical condition that the person can learn to cope with and, thus, assimilate into his or her self-concept. *Handicap,* on the other hand, was seen as determined by the extent of environmental barriers and the availability of human services. Therefore, to live independently, persons with severe disabilities are greatly dependent on the availability of both person-change and environment-change services. This two-dimensional position contrasts with the traditional unidimensional focus of the medical model, which primarily addresses changing the person according to prescriptions by physicians and rehabilitation professionals.

The Independent Living Movement

Countless observers of society's reaction to disability have described how socially imposed roles of dependency limit the freedom of choice of individuals with disabilities. Such social practices deny individuals with disabilities control over their lives, especially in regard to participation in the community consistent with their personal desires and capabilities. The independent living movement, which dates back to the late 1960s, emerged as a reaction to those social practices. It found its core constituency at that time in groups with mobility impairments such as those stemming from "spinal cord injury, muscular dystrophy, cerebral palsy, multiple sclerosis, and post-polio disablement" (DeJong, 1979a, p. 436). Because most of these conditions either are developmental disabilities or occur during the late teens or early adulthood, IL's charter constituency was relatively young; therefore, the movement focused primarily on the needs of older adolescents and younger working-age adults. The most active members of the IL movement during its first decade generally resided in large academic communities. The IL movement stressed that persons with disabilities expect to have the opportunity to participate in the making of all decisions that affect them both directly and indirectly (Fleischer & Zames, 2001; Kilbury, Stotlar, & Eckert, 2005). The participants in this movement questioned the validity of cultural expectations, which kept them in a state of relative dependency, as well as the appropriateness of many of the conventional societal practices that stemmed from those expectations. As advances in medical science have increased the life span of persons with severe physical disabilities, and as other segments of the disability population—such as people with sensory impairments, mental illness, or mental retardation—were exposed to the IL philosophy, the core constituency of the IL movement became much more heterogeneous in respect to disability type, age, and geography. The challenge of broadening that core constituency to more people from racial and ethnic minorities has only been partially met, although IL programs are devoting more of their efforts to active outreach campaigns (Flowers, Crimando, Forbes, & Riggar, 2005).

The IL movement can be characterized as a political or civil rights movement involving individuals with severe disabilities who have been denied access to those rights. Indeed, Gliedman and Roth (1980) underscored the fact that persons with disabilities in this country constitute a hidden minority. In testimony before the Vermont Advisory Committee of the Civil Rights Commission on November 5, 1983, Jean Mankowsky, executive director of the Vermont Center for Independent Living and an individual with a severe disability, attempted to clarify that minority status by drawing upon personal examples. In regard to segregation, she stated,

> They don't have to put a sign on the building that says "no cripples allowed" to let me know that I'm not welcome. When you see stairs at 90% of the places you want to go into during your life, you feel shut out. You don't feel like you are a part of society. ("We Are a Minority," 1983, p. 2)

In regard to attitudinal barriers, she stated,

> When I go out with my husband, Dennis, people address him and not me. They make the assumption that I am not able to talk ... or that I don't know my own name, or that I am not capable of making decisions. ("We Are a Minority," 1983, p. 2)

In regard to discrimination, she stated,

> I went to get an application for my driver's license (having already gotten one in another state).... I said "I'd like to get a Vermont license" and they said "You have to take a road test" ... I said, "Well my husband's going to get one too, does he have to take a road test?" "No." Is it because I have had a bad driving record? "No." Is it because there are proven statistics that people with disabilities are bad drivers? "No." It's because I look like I might have an accident. But that's the way it is. ("We Are a Minority," 1983, p. 2)

In regard to economic disadvantagement, she stated,

> Most of us are poor. If you are not poor and you become disabled, you'll become poor quickly, because you're going to have to spend your life's

earnings before you can be eligible for Medicaid. If you're on Social Security, SSI, you're not allowed to amass any money. There are disincentives built into the system. Once you're down there it's pretty hard to get back up. ("We Are a Minority," 1983, pp. 2–3)

As is evident in Jean Mankowsky's testimony, people with disabilities are aware of their minority status and are asserting their rights to share fully in the responsibilities and joys of society.

The civil rights movement, with its emphasis on entitlement (right to vote and hold office) and benefit (income assistance and medical care) rights, has provided an effective action-oriented model for the IL movement. For example, the IL movement actively fought for the right to equal access to employment as well as to medical care, education, social services, transportation, and housing by lobbying for the inclusion of Title V in the Rehabilitation Act of 1973 and the Americans with Disabilities Act of 1990. When regulations were still not present in the *Federal Register* for implementing the antidiscrimination section (Section 504) of Title V, sit-in demonstrations were held on April 5, 1977, by persons with disabilities at U.S. Department of Health, Education and Welfare (HEW) offices in 10 cities across the country. Although the demonstration lasted only 1 day in most cities, in San Francisco a group of over 150 demonstrators found sympathetic local government officials and manifested an ability to persevere (C. W. Levy, 1988). Among those who participated in the San Francisco sit-in until the Secretary of HEW signed the Section 504 regulations on April 28th was Mary Jane Owen. Owen (1987) described the experience at the San Francisco sit-in as follows:

> After sleeping the first night on the hard floors, mattresses were delivered from the supplies of the State Health Department. Food arrived from McDonald's, Delancy House's drug programs, the Black Panthers and Safeway. The Mayor himself scolded the federal officials for ignoring the needs of the uninvited guests and brought in shower attachments to be used in the tiled restrooms.
>
> Some of us decided to call a hunger strike to confirm to ourselves and others our commitment to stay at any cost. There were so many [heroes]—Steve, who lay day after day and night upon night, [recording] events—because he knew what was happening was important enough to risk his health; Jeff, who … wrote new words for old civil rights songs with which we loudly greeted federal employees [each] morning; the deaf woman who entered the building to teach a class in sign language and stayed; the mentally retarded woman who always injected a note of realism into our too-abstract deliberations. (cited in C. W. Levy, 1988, p. 17)

By fighting for the rights of virtually every disability, the demonstrators saw their actions as uniting the members of the diverse disability population (C. W. Levy, 1988).

Once implemented, Section 504, which prohibits discrimination against persons with disabilities in any program or activity receiving federal funds, stimulated many reasonable accommodations. In so doing, it positively affected the independent living movement by helping to "open up the environment" to persons with disabilities. Curb cuts, handicapped parking spaces, ramps at entrances to public buildings, special services for persons with disabilities at universities, and equal employment practices are examples of the many changes that can be attributed either partially or wholly to Section 504 (DeLoach et al., 1983, p. 21).

It is one thing for a person with a severe disability to secure work; it is another to be able to afford to work. Therefore, like African Americans, the members of the IL movement fought for benefit rights, such as "income assistance benefits or attendant care benefits," as well as civil rights (DeJong, 1979a, p. 439). One example of a benefit right acquired can be found in the Social Security Disability Amendments of 1980 (P.L. 96-265). That legislation helped remove "certain disincentives to work by allowing disabled people to deduct independent-living expenses in computing income benefits" (DeJong & Lifchez, 1983, p. 42), a trend that was continued in the work incentives and benefits planning provisions of the Ticket to Work and Work Incentives Improvement Act of 1999 (Roessler, 2002).

The IL movement has dovetailed with several other social movements, such as consumerism, self-help, demedicalization, and deinstitutionalization (DeJong, 1979a). *Consumerism* in independent living manifests itself in the demands of persons with disabilities for control over the services provided to them. Service provision and planning are no longer the sole province of the rehabilitation and medical professions; the consumer has a vital role to play as well. A good example can be found in state rehabilitation agencies, where the rehabilitation counselor and client with a disability jointly develop a rehabilitation plan. This is consistent with the doctrine of consumer sovereignty, consumer involvement, or informed choice (Kosciulek, 2004b), which asserts that because persons with disabilities "are the best judges of their own interests, they should have a larger voice in determining what services are provided in the disability services market" (DeJong, 1979a, p. 439).

The *self-help movement* in the United States has been stimulated by consumer dissatisfaction with professional service providers (Nosek, Zhu, & Howland, 1992). Through cooperative efforts, people with disabilities have helped each other meet needs not met by social agencies. In fact, the many centers for independent living (CILs) around the country epitomize a self-help model. Planned and staffed by persons with disabilities, centers for independent living are characterized by "substantial consumer involvement in the direction and delivery of services" (DeJong, 1979a; Kilbury et al., 2005; Nosek et al., 1992, p. 175).

One of the earliest indigenous group efforts dates back to the early 1970s. In 1972 the nonresidential Berkeley CIL was established. Primarily managed and staffed by persons with disabilities, the Berkeley CIL provided a wide range of related services, such as peer counseling, health maintenance counseling, advocacy services, attendant care referral, training in independent living skills, health maintenance, housing referral, wheelchair repair, and van transportation (CIL Berkeley, n.d.; DeJong, 1979a; Nosek, 1992). That pioneering effort, which has served as a model of the many IL programs in existence today, "was designed to help others with disabilities to live independently and promote a more accessible society" (Nosek et al., 1992, p. 174).

Another factor associated with the self-help movement is the desire among persons with medically stabilized disabilities to take control of their own health and self-care needs rather than be dependent on the medical profession. Referred to as *demedicalization* (DeJong, 1979a), this self-help orientation to daily care enables many individuals to escape the constraints of the sick role, in which the individual with a permanent disability would be relieved of all responsibilities except to work toward a recovery that could not be achieved. The self-help orientation also helps avoid the debilitating aspects of the impaired role, where the person is expected to accept the condition as permanent and to become a permanently dependent second-class citizen. Both roles rob the individual of the necessary sense of personal control over one's life that research has shown to be an important element in adapting successfully to the demands of independent living (Currie-Gross & Heimbach, 1980; Devins & Shnek, 2000).

Demedicalization is compatible with the IL rehabilitation movement's desire to move from the current dominance of the rehabilitation paradigm in public policy to a point of dominance for the IL paradigm. DeJong (1979a) contrasted the two paradigms:

> In the rehabilitation paradigm, problems are generally defined in terms of inadequate performance in activities of daily living (ADL) or in terms of inadequate preparation for gainful employment. In both instances, the problem is assumed to reside in the individual. It is the individual who needs to be changed. To overcome his/her problem, the disabled individual is expected to yield to the advice and instruction of a physician, a physical therapist, an occupational therapist, or a vocational rehabilitation counselor. The disabled individual is expected to assume the role of "patient" or "client." While the goal of the rehabilitation process is maximum physical functioning or gainful employment, success in rehabilitation is to a large degree determined by whether the patient or client complied with the prescribed therapeutic regime....
>
> According to the IL paradigm, the problem does not reside in the individual but often in the solution offered by the rehabilitation paradigm—the dependency-inducing features of the physician–patient or professional–client relationship. Rehabilitation is seen as part of the problem, not the solution. The locus of the problem is not the individual but the environment that includes not only the rehabilitation process but also the

physical environment and the social control mechanisms in society-at-large. To cope with these environmental barriers, the disabled person must shed the patient or client role for the consumer role. Advocacy, peer counseling, self-help, consumer control, and barrier removal are the trademarks of the IL paradigm. (pp. 443–444)

Driven by both economic and normalization considerations, another societal movement embraced by the IL movement is *deinstitutionalization*. The deinstitutionalization movement stresses the importance of community-based services aimed at enabling the individual to resume a normal life with family, friends, and coworkers. It assumes that, provided the proper support service and an accessible environment, many individuals with severe disabilities can lead fulfilling lives outside total care institutions such as nursing homes. Although some deinstitutionalized persons with severe disabilities may fail in their efforts to live independently, the right to take risks is a significant component of the philosophy of the IL movement. "Without the possibility of failure," the person with a disability lacks true independence (DeJong, 1979a, p. 441).

Independent Living Programs as an Emerging Social Innovation

In the process of being implemented, social innovations proceed through two sequential phases, *adoption in theory* and *adoption in practice*. Applied to social innovations such as IL services for persons with disabilities, the idea of independent living rehabilitation would be conceptualized in clearly designed models, publicized, and implemented on a small-scale experimental basis during the adoption-in-theory phase. During this phase, legislative support is usually minimal. However, if efforts during this phase attract the interest and support of societal leaders, appropriate legislation follows, "regulations are issued, and judicial enforcement begins to occur" (Flynn & Nitsch, 1980, p. 365). In the case of independent living, the adoption-in-theory phase began around 1970 and culminated in the independent living provisions (Title VII) of the Rehabilitation Act Amendments of 1978 (DeLoach et al., 1983, p. 13). That 1978 legislation officially established independent living as a standardized service entitlement, thereby initiating its move into the adoption-in-practice phase.

Independent living programs have had an inherent instinct for survival that suggests their superiority over other alternative service models for persons with severe disabilities. As evidence of their "survivability," the number of CILs operating in the United States in 2005 was 430 (Kilbury et al., 2005), a number that does not include the large number of residential IL programs in existence. Considering that only a handful of IL programs existed in 1973 (Cole, 1979), the growth has been dramatic. Most of the growth has occurred since 1978, when only 35 programs were operating that met the definition of an IL rehabilitation program (Frieden, 1983, p. 65).

Independent Living and Vocational Rehabilitation: A Continuum of Services

Independent living services should be viewed as complementary to, rather than competitive with, vocational rehabilitation services. Indeed, IL services may very well mark the beginning of a process that will enable many individuals to resume a vocational role. This is especially true today. Due to advances in medical and rehabilitation technologies, many persons with severe disabilities capable of achieving independent living but not employment in the 1960s would be routinely prepared through vocational rehabilitation services for gainful employment today.

Historically, a conflict has existed between vocational rehabilitation professionals and their consumer counterparts in the IL movement as to whether independent living and vocational rehabilitation should be viewed as separate programs, with each having its own distinct set of goals. Some vocational rehabilitation professionals see IL programs as being for those incapable of achieving vocational rehabilitation. To those "in the independent living movement, whose involvement does not originate in the vocational rehabilitation tradition," the distinction "is potentially sinister in that it implicitly places an undesirable arbitrary limit to the goals" that a person with a disability might set for him- or herself (DeJong, 1979a, p. 440).

How widespread this dichotomous perception is among rehabilitation professionals is difficult to determine. One hopes that its prevalence is small. It is both more realistic and socially responsible to consider IL rehabilitation and vocational rehabilitation as continuous elements of a larger process. For example, Trieschmann (1974) discussed a sliding scale of rehabilitation goals in which an individual might receive rehabilitation services to develop capabilities of medical self-care, to become more active in family and community life, and/or to seek a vocational goal. The first two phases of Trieschmann's sliding scale of goals incorporate the chief interests of independent living programs; the last stage deals with the principal objective of vocational rehabilitation. The important point is that independent living and vocational goals are found on the same sliding scale; they are complementary, not competing, goals.

Independent Living Rehabilitation Services

Independent living programs provide services that enable individuals with severe disabilities to exercise more freedom of choice and control over their lives. Independent living services are directed at remediating personal and environmental difficulties. Studies of IL programs emphasize the importance of flexibility. No one concern or set of concerns clearly emerges when reviewing the presenting problems of individuals seeking IL rehabilitation services (Muzzio et al., n.d.). However, research (Putnam et al., 2003; Stoddard, 1980a, p. 13) has identified several central problem areas for IL services to address, such as the client's negative self-image, emotional well-being, functional limitations, interpersonal skills, and personal health behaviors, as well as external or environmental barriers existing at both the community level (e.g., social supports, medical providers) and systems level (e.g., physical access, financing, regulations). These problem areas reflect the many personal and environment factors that affect the social and vocational adjustment of individuals with disabilities.

The appropriateness of IL services should be judged against the criteria implicit in increased access of individuals with disabilities to dignity, freedom, and control of their own destinies. Overall, the IL service model places much greater emphasis on changing the environment than on changing the person (Kilbury et al., 2005). Therefore, the major focus is on adapting the environment to the person rather than on adapting the person to the environment.

A comprehensive empirical picture of the types of services provided by IL rehabilitation programs can be found in a 1988 survey that requested information on the types of services the programs provided (Nosek et al., 1992). Of the 189 programs that responded, approximately 90% reported providing information and referral, housing and attendant referral, consumer advocacy services, community advocacy, peer counseling, and independent living skills training. The majority of the programs offered activities to promote barrier reduction (85%), financial benefits counseling (81%), recreational activities (69%), transportation (62%), family counseling (60%), and attendant management training (56%). "More than three quarters of the programs promoted consumer involvement in civic activities and community affairs" (Nosek et al., 1992, p. 184). Permanent residential facilities or transitional living programs were offered by almost 20% of the IL programs (Nosek et al., 1992).

Service Delivery Models

A number of different kinds of independent living programs currently exist. Nosek (1988, p. 49) noted that they tend to vary among themselves in six basic ways:

1. *the service setting* may range from residential to non-residential;
2. *the service delivery method* may range from direct to indirect, or a combination of both;
3. *the service delivery style* may range from professional to consumer;
4. *the vocational emphasis* may range from primary to incidental;
5. *the goal orientation* may range from transitional to ongoing; and
6. *the disability type* served may range from single to many.

Three major IL program models are (a) centers for independent living, (b) independent living residential programs, and (c) independent living transitional programs (Cole, 1979; Frieden, 1983). The latter two can be more meaningfully discussed as residential programs. These models emerged in response to a need for support services that allow persons with severe disabilities to live in the community (Stoddard, 1980b). Kilbury et al. (2005) pointed out that although residential programs "are generally viewed as being inconsistent with the intent of the IL movement due to their segregatory nature, transitional and residential programs have nevertheless proven their worth throughout the history of rehabilitation" (p. 305).

Centers for Independent Living

Centers for independent living (CILs) are nonresidential, community-based, nonprofit programs that are controlled by consumers with disabilities. National data on those served by CILs in 1994 revealed that 45% had physical disabilities, 18% had sensory disabilities, 8% had mental disabilities, 9% had cognitive disabilities, and 19% had multiple disabilities (ILRU Insights, 1995).

According to Title VII of the 1998 Amendments to the Rehabilitation Act, many IL services are to be provided through centers for independent living. To provide the necessary services, these programs must be comprehensive and multipurpose. Moreover, individuals with disabilities must play a substantial part in the policy direction and service provision of these programs (Potter, 1996). Frieden (1983) pointed out that CILs "depend on the people who receive their services to provide leadership and assistance by serving on boards of directors or advisory committees, and by working as paid or volunteer staff" (p. 63). At least 51% of the policymaking boards for these centers must consist of persons with disabilities (Kilbury et al., 2005). Consumer involvement in the running of these programs is seen as necessary to ensure that they remain responsive to their clients' needs (Bartels, 1985; Frieden, 1983; Potter, 1996). In 1994, of the 845 staff members who were serving in decision-making positions at CILs, 66% had disabilities (ILRU Insights, 1995); by 2003, that figure increased to 72% in CILs in the midwest (Flowers et al., 2005).

Every CIL that receives funds through the Rehabilitation Act must provide certain core services. These core services are information and referral services, independent living skills training, peer counseling, and advocacy (Kilbury et al., 2005). Although these categories of services must be provided by each CIL, the specific services provided under each category can differ among the many CILs located throughout the United States. For example, the menu of services provided by the Berkeley CIL includes personal assistance services, blind services, the client assistance project, deaf and deaf/blind services, employment services, financial benefits counseling, and housing and independent living skills services (CIL Berkeley, n.d.).

Information and referral services can include any of the following: housing information or referral; referral of attendants, readers, and/or interpreters;

information on or referral for adaptive equipment (e.g., walkers, Braillers, TDDs, shower chairs, adapted toys); information on civil and benefit rights; transportation information and referral; and information on or referral to community support groups.

Independent living skills training services can include any skills training services directed at helping individuals with disabilities reach higher levels of proficiency in self-care, in living independently, and in participating in community activities. Examples include training in cooking, cleaning, household finances, and shopping; training in attendant management; education and training in social interaction skills, including building friendships from informal, spontaneous interpersonal contacts in public meeting places (e.g., laundromats, church socials, health clubs, supermarkets, public libraries, coffeehouses, malls, cruise ships, casinos, bars); training in applying for benefits from social service and rehabilitation agencies (e.g., self-advocacy skills); orientation to community training (including the use of public transportation systems); job seeking skills training; training to deal with discriminatory and insensitive behavior by the general public; and training in making human service professionals aware of the needs of a person with a disability.

Peer counseling is a process in which counseling is provided by a person with a disability "who has attained disability-related experiences, knowledge, and coping skills" to other individuals with disabilities and their significant others to help them "cope with disability related experiences" (Rehab Brief, 1984, p. 1). Peer counseling in a CIL can be provided by a staff person or a peer volunteer (e.g., a former recipient of services from the CIL). Some peer counseling takes the form of education (e.g., training in how to manage one's personal assistant) rather than that of therapeutic counseling. However, regardless of the form it takes, peer counseling is provided by an individual who can serve as a role model for the consumer, views the consumer as an equal, is willing to share personal experiences with the consumer to encourage a sense of autonomy, and serves as a link to community resources (Kilbury & Stotlar, 1996; Kilbury et al., 2005).

Advocacy as an independent living rehabilitation service can focus on the right of persons with disabilities to (a) make contracts; (b) hold professional, occupational, or vehicle driver's licenses; (c) make a will; (d) marry; (e) adopt or bear children; (f) hold and convey property; (g) access publicly owned or financed buildings, publicly used but privately owned buildings, public streets, sidewalks, and transportation facilities and rolling stock; (h) have equal educational opportunities in the least restrictive and least denormalizing environment possible; (i) have equal employment opportunities; (j) receive just payment for labor; (k) have equal access to medical services (Rigdon, 1977); and (l) vote and participate actively in political affairs.

Because of their need for comprehensive services, individuals with severe disabilities may also need advocacy assistance with multiple social agencies.

Cull and Levinson (1977) identified numerous rights of individuals involved in transactions with human service agencies. For example, clients of human service agencies have the right to (a) an explanation of the goals, functions, procedures, and operations of the agency; (b) referral and advocacy in instances where the agency contacted cannot help; (c) an explanation of the appeal process; (d) full partnership in the selection of service providers and placements; (e) periodic review of the plan and, if needed, modification of the intermediate and long-range program objectives; (f) access to agency records related to the client; (g) prompt evaluation, eligibility decisions, and services; (h) advocacy services on their behalf; (i) free expression of views regarding the quality of their program; and (j) high-quality professional attention throughout the service process.

Kilbury and Stotlar (1996) and Kilbury et al. (2005) described two categories of advocacy services—consumer advocacy and community or systemic advocacy—both of which CILs are required to provide by law. Consumer advocacy services are directed primarily at helping consumers served by CILs to develop those self-advocacy skills needed to achieve their IL goals, including access to any community activities to which they have been previously denied because of their disability. When providing community or systemic advocacy, CILs are expressing the disability community's insistence on the removal of environmental barriers and disincentives in public policy that have a disabling effect on the population served by CILs.

In addition to the services mentioned above, CILs can also provide assistive technology services, interpreter and reader services, and individual and group social and recreational services. Overall, the above list is not meant to be all-inclusive in regard to services offered by CILs. The services that a CIL can provide to promote the greater independence of persons with disabilities are primarily limited by the CIL's resources and the imagination of its personnel.

During the 1970s little emphasis was placed on vocational services in CILs. However, the situation began to change in the 1980s, with some "centers, such as the Center for Independent Living in Memphis,… developing cooperative plans with other facilities to obtain evaluation, training, and employment services for their clients" (DeLoach et al., 1983, p. 219). Today, it is not unusual to find CILs—such as the ones in Carbondale, Illinois, and Berkeley, California—also providing vocational counseling and job placement services.

Residential Programs

DeLoach et al. (1983) classified residential programs into three groups: (a) transitional independent living centers, (b) long-term residential centers, and (c) group homes. A fourth type could be referred to as a combination residential center.

Transitional Independent Living Centers

Transitional IL centers are designed to facilitate the movement of people with severe disabilities from comparatively dependent living situations to comparatively independent living situations (Seventh Institute on Rehabilitation Issues, 1980). Their service program focuses heavily on IL skills training directed at enabling a person with a disability "to reach new levels of proficiency in self-care.… The transitional IL center is usually goal- or time-oriented, having predetermined criteria regarding the desirable level of proficiency or length of residence expected of the client" (DeLoach et al., 1983, p. 224).

Although no longer in operation, the New Options program in Houston, Texas, represented an excellent example of the transitional IL center. Operating as a Rehabilitation Services Administration research and demonstration project serving persons with severe disabilities, the New Options project provided a 6-week training program with shared attendant and transportation services. Training "in skills needed to live and work with a minimum of assistance" was emphasized (Cole, 1979, p. 459). One of the strengths of the New Options project was the use of positive role models (i.e., active people with severe disabilities who taught the clients independent living skills) (Cole, Sperry, Board, & Frieden, 1979).

Long-Term Residential Centers

It is not easy to differentiate between transitional IL centers and long-term residential centers. They differ primarily on two criteria: "the expected length of client participation and the goal of the services provided" (DeLoach et al., 1983, p. 227). Transitional programs tend to be short-term and focus on "basic skills for social reentry." Long-term "residential programs usually have more severely disabled clients and seek to provide more complete training in a broader range of service areas" (DeLoach et al., 1983, p. 227). In addition to providing many of the services found in transitional IL centers, the long-term centers frequently provide medical rehabilitation services, occupational therapy, personal adjustment counseling, supervised recreational activities, instruction in independent living skills such as locating and obtaining appropriate housing, and household management. Vocational services, including vocational evaluation and training for employment, can also be found in some long-term residential programs (DeLoach et al., 1983).

Group Homes

Group homes are basically single buildings (small-group homes) or cluster housing arrangements (large-group homes) for a group of persons with severe disabilities who would have difficulty living in a totally independent living situation. The residents typically share central services, such as an attendant pool, limited transportation, houseparent-type assistance, and recreational facilities. The large-group homes are differentiated from the long-term residential centers in that "the large group homes are often places of permanent residence" for people with disabilities (DeLoach et al., 1983, p. 231). DeLoach et al. (1983) stated,

> Group homes ... generally serve people who have reached almost maximum recovery and cannot, or do not wish to, live alone in the community.... The typical group home allows the resident less privacy than a private residence or apartment, but it provides many important benefits. In addition to the group home's facilities, there is the communal atmosphere and emotional support of staff and peers and the security of prompt medical support when an emergency arises. (pp. 234–235)

Combination Residential Centers

In a combination program, two or three of the previous models may be combined. For example, the Boston Center for Independent Living (BCIL) initially combined transitional living, cluster housing, and independent living components in its program (Corcoran, Fay, Bartelo, & McHaugh, 1977). In their transitional living program, persons with severe disabilities lived in an apartment complex where they received training in social and physical skills. In the cluster housing program, individuals lived in modified apartments with an attendant pool and night attendants. This particular cluster housing system provided more independence than the transitional living approach. The final component of the BCIL program included accessible apartments in which individuals lived more independently, usually with the help of an attendant.

Vocational Rehabilitation Agency and IL Program Relationships

Although some CILs have begun to offer vocational counseling and placement services, a close working relationship between CILs and state vocational rehabilitation (VR) agency programs is still critical. Freedom of movement between state VR agency services and CILs, and vice versa, is essential. It is also not rare for VR and CIL services to overlap. During the rehabilitation service process, some individuals may need independent living services from a CIL. Conversely, many CIL clients will develop vocational feasibility with time and may need the VR services offered by a state VR agency to enter or reenter gainful employment.

Important considerations for enhancing the CIL–VR linkage include (a) development of methods of monitoring client status and service outcomes so that program referrals can be made between CILs and VR agencies,

(b) promoting collaboration between the case management personnel in both programs, and (c) measuring client outcomes from such collaborative initiatives for purposes of program evaluation.

Concluding Statement

Independent living is a concept that reflects the recognition by individuals with severe disabilities of their capability to gain greater control over their lives given certain support services and the removal of environmental barriers. The IL movement stresses the need for public policies and human service initiatives for persons with disabilities that promote active participation in valued social roles, such as working, owning a home, raising a family, and being free from segregation and isolation. The movement itself has its roots in other social currents, such as civil rights, consumerism, self-help, demedicalization, and deinstitutionalization. By combining the implications for social and political practice of all these movements, individuals involved in independent living have created an emphasis that calls for the provision of services without a vocational goal test.

By definition, independent living rehabilitation services emphasize areas other than vocational training and placement (although these services may be appropriately provided to some individuals in independent living). Currently, independent living programs are required by federal law to place great emphasis on services such as information and referral, independent living skills training, peer counseling, and advocacy (Kilbury et al., 2005). Because none of these core services is incompatible with vocational rehabilitation objectives, collaboration between the CILs and VR programs should be the expected norm.

One can view the purpose of available interrelated IL and VR services as promoting the quality of life of persons with disabilities. A person's quality of life is greatly determined by the individual's ability to meet certain basic needs. Abraham Maslow placed these needs on a hierarchy in terms of their motivating primacy, if not sufficiently met in the life of an individual (cited in Hall, Lindzey, Loehlin, & Manosevitz, 1985). The most basic needs in Maslow's hierarchy, from lower order to higher order, are physiological needs, safety needs, belongingness and love needs, esteem needs, and the need for self-actualization. When "physiological needs are satisfied, the safety needs become salient and can be attended to; when the physiological and safety needs are both satisfied, the needs for belongingness and love become salient and can be attended to; and so forth" (Maddi, 1980, p. 109). However, lower order needs do not have to be completely satisfied before an individual is motivated to meet a higher order need (Hall et al., 1985). Therefore, cooperation between IL rehabilitation services and VR services is often required to address the unmet needs of a client that fall at multiple levels of Maslow's hierarchy. Achieving the ideal goal—that is, facilitating the development of a fully functioning individual in society—requires that rehabilitation service providers utilize IL and VR services to help their clients approximate Maslow's self-actualized state. Maslow (1971) described this state of being as follows:

> By definition, self-actualizing people are gratified in all their basic needs (of belongingness, affection, respect, and self-esteem). This is to say that they have a feeling of belongingness and rootedness, they are satisfied in their love needs, have friends and feel loved and loveworthy, they have status and place in life and respect from other people, and they have a reasonable feeling of worth and self-respect. If we phrase this negatively—in terms of the frustration of these basic needs and in terms of pathology—then this is to say that self-actualizing people do not (for any length of time) feel anxiety-ridden, insecure, unsafe, do not feel alone, ostracized, rootless, or isolated, do not feel unlovable, rejected, or unwanted, do not feel despised and looked down upon, and do not feel deeply unworthy, nor do they have crippling feelings of inferiority or worthlessness. (p. 299)

For people with severe disabilities to achieve this state of self-actualization, two events must occur. First, they must receive both IL and VR services in the complementary manner stressed in this chapter. Second, they must benefit fully from promising public policy initiatives such as the Americans with Disabilities Act (ADA). Such benefits can occur only if the mandates of the ADA are aggressively enforced in the battle against attitudinal barriers to the full participation of persons with disability in our society. Although, as discussed in Chapter 3, the full intent of the ADA in facilitating the full participation of persons with disabilities in American society has yet to be realized, the ADA has stimulated much progress in regard to equality of opportunity for members of that subpopulation. That progress is clearly reflected in the following statement made by Lex Frieden (2001), an individual with a severe physical disability and one of the true leaders of the IL movement:

> I can now ride on virtually any public conveyance in the United States, I can enter virtually any public or private building, and I can compete on a fair basis for virtually any job that I am qualified to perform. Furthermore, if I am frustrated by what I regard as unreasonable or unjustified barriers to entry into facilities, participation in programs, access to services, or employment, I have the right to lodge a formal complaint or to have my complaint heard in court by a jury of my peers. (p. 422)

Chapter 16

Rehabilitation in
the Private-for-Profit Sector:
Opportunities and Challenges

Martin G. Brodwin

There are three sectors of rehabilitation counseling: the public sector, the private-nonprofit sector, and the private-for-profit sector. The goal of this chapter is to familiarize rehabilitation counselors with the various areas of private-for-profit rehabilitation and to suggest possibilities of potential employment and future opportunities in the profession. Private-for-profit rehabilitation involves the provision of rehabilitation counseling services on a fee-for-service basis. Rehabilitation professionals produce fees from private sources on a fee-for-service basis with public agencies, private-nonprofit organizations, insurance carriers, and in the area of forensics. Many rehabilitation counselors currently practice in the private-for-profit sector, which has been a viable part of the rehabilitation counseling profession since the 1970s.

There has been significant growth in the field of private sector rehabilitation during the past four decades. The factors that have promoted this growth include (a) the realization by business and industry of the high and steadily increasing costs of disability and lost time from work in the workforce; (b) legislation mandating vocational rehabilitation under state workers' compensation; (c) legislation protecting and promoting the rights of persons with disabilities, such as the Rehabilitation Act of 1973 (P.L. 93-112) and its subsequent amendments, and the Americans with Disabilities Act of 1990 (ADA; P.L. 101-336); (d) the ability of private sector rehabilitation counselors to provide timely and cost-effective services; (e) the entry of rehabilitation professionals into the forensic arena; (f) the increasing role of rehabilitationists in case management practice; and (g) the development of a cadre of rehabilitationists with entrepreneurial skills necessary for owning and managing companies.

Several professional roles have evolved to meet these emerging factors. Private sector rehabilitation counselors have become case managers, disability management specialists and consultants to business and industry, specialists in the area of workers' compensation vocational rehabilitation, and vocational experts in the legal arena.

Rehabilitation counselors working within the private-for-profit sector of rehabilitation provide disability insurance rehabilitation, including workers' compensation, federal employees' compensation, longshore and harbor workers' rehabilitation, and long-term disability. Counselors in the private sector provide consultation services in disability management and medical case management to industry, business, and government. These counselors emphasize early intervention, minimizing functional limitations associated with disability, using workers' transferable skills, decreasing disability-related costs to employers, prevention of industrial accidents, and wellness in the workplace. Private sector rehabilitation counselors also provide services within employee assistance programs, specializing in substance abuse problems. Some of the newest fields in the private sector involve life-care planning and consultation under the ADA. Rehabilitationists practicing within the forensic arena offer expert testimony in Social Security Disability Insurance, personal injury litigation, marriage dissolution, employment discrimination, and medical malpractice.

Vocational evaluation and assessment, career development, and job placement are integral components of the role and function of rehabilitation counselors employed in the private-for-profit sector. To provide comprehensive services, these professionals need expertise in such activities as job analysis, vocational assessment, labor market surveys, job placement, career development, application of transferable skills, assessment of functional limitations, and determination of rehabilitation potential.

This chapter reviews professional practice within private sector rehabilitation. It details the recent and continuing expansion of rehabilitation practice in this area and discusses emerging opportunities available for professionals. The section on disability insurance rehabilitation outlines the following areas of rehabilitation practice: workers' compensation, the Federal Employees' Compensation Act, the Longshore and Harbor Workers' Compensation Act, and long-term disability insurance. An area of increasing interest, forensic rehabilitation (expert witness testimony), takes the rehabilitation counselor into the legal arena. Additional areas discussed in this chapter include life care planning, disability management, substance abuse counseling, and ADA consultation. The chapter concludes with a discussion of the specialized skills of rehabilitation counselors who work within the private-for-profit sector.

Expanding Opportunities

Rehabilitation counseling is experiencing a continuing dramatic growth and expansion. This profession offers diverse opportunities for employment in a variety of helping and human service settings. Additional rehabilitation counselors are needed and will continue to be in demand in the future because of the increasing need for services in all areas of rehabilitation (National Council on Rehabilitation Education, n.d.).

There is a continuing and increasing number of employment opportunities for rehabilitation professionals within the private-for-profit sector, with more positions available than graduates to fill them. Rehabilitation education programs have responded to this need. Undergraduate programs, typically in rehabilitation services, have expanded course content to include private sector areas. These undergraduate programs prepare professionals to work in such jobs as job placement specialists, rehabilitation technicians, employment and placement counselors, personnel specialists, social service caseworkers, public health workers, client advocates, probation and parole officers, job coaches, workshop and supported employment specialists, vocational evaluators, employment specialists, chemical dependency counselors, human resource specialists, independent living specialists, and rehabilitation technologists.

Master's degree programs in rehabilitation counseling have steadily increased content in areas involving work within the private-for-profit sector. Content includes vocational assessment and evaluation, job analysis, job development and placement, job retention, disability management, managed care, life care planning, forensic rehabilitation, and labor market exploration. According to the *Accreditation Manual for Rehabilitation Counselor Education Programs* (Council on Rehabilitation Education, 2004), master's degree programs need to include content on private-for-profit rehabilitation to meet current accreditation standards. Rehabilitation counselor education programs have responded to this requirement by infusing their programs with information pertinent to practicing in the private-for-profit sector. Since 1989 the International Association of Rehabilitation Professionals (IARP), an organization representing rehabilitation professionals in the private sector, has had a representative on the Council on Rehabilitation Education's Commission on Standards and Accreditation. This commission establishes standards for and provides accreditation of rehabilitation counselor education programs at the master's-degree level.

Two major forces will continue to increase the demand for private-for-profit rehabilitation in the near future. The first is the continually increasing costs for health care and work-related injuries and the efforts of employers to reduce their costs for employees who acquire disability or are seriously injured at work. Second, the ADA, passed in 1990, continues to increase and expand employment and career opportunities for rehabilitation counselors. These two forces are affecting the role and function of rehabilitation counselors in the private-for-profit sector who will need knowledge and expertise in these areas to provide effective and cost-saving services. The knowledge and expertise that counselors need in the first area include information on business and industry, identification of characteristics of employees at risk, transitional work programs, early and prompt intervention, job modification, reasonable accommodation, employee assistance programs, case management, union and management practices, human resources, medical aspects of disability, work hardening, insurance, wellness, and stress management/reduction (Hanley-Maxwell, Owens-Johnson, & Fabian, 2003; Roessler & Rubin, 2006). In the area of ADA consultation, counselors need expertise in determining whether a person with a disability is qualified for a job, undue hardship, essential job functions, reasonable accommodations, job modification/restructuring, transferable work skills, nondiscrimination in employment, and environmental barriers to employment, as well as knowledge of employer and employee policies and procedures (Akabas, Gates, & Galvin, 1992; Gilbride & Hagner, 2005).

Disability Insurance Rehabilitation

Workers' Compensation

Vocational rehabilitation of industrially injured workers currently provides a large segment of work for counselors practicing in the private-for-profit sector. Counselors need specific information on workplace injuries, medical aspects of injuries and disabilities that frequently occur in employment, state workers' compensation policies and procedures, job analysis, labor market surveys, labor laws, workers' compensation eligibility, and transferable skills analysis.

History

The first workers' compensation laws in the United States were passed in 1911. Over the next 25 to 30 years, various states passed legislation to cover workers injured on the job. Systems to enforce these laws had three major objectives: (a) to reduce the previously existing tort-based system's inequities and uncertainties in compensating disabled and injured workers; (b) to create appropriate employer incentives for safety by internalizing the costs of accidents to the firm; and (c) to introduce a no-fault, prefunded insurance mechanism to guarantee certain benefits to workers injured on the job (Durbin, 1997). According to Matkin (1997), workers' compensation laws involved a new economic and legal principle—liability without fault. The laws protected both employee and employer in different ways. Employees benefited by receiving medical services for their work-related injuries and illnesses and financial compensation (income) for time off work, regardless of fault. Employers were protected from lengthy and costly lawsuits. Each state currently has its own workers' compensation laws, which vary in scope and coverage from state to state. The original workers' compensation legislation did not include vocational rehabilitation as a mandatory benefit.

In the 1970s many states passed workers' compensation laws that included vocational rehabilitation benefits. In general, these included payment for (a) vocational rehabilitation services provided by counselors, (b) testing and evaluation, (c) training or education, (d) tools and equipment necessary for a new occupation, and (e) transportation during the rehabilitation program. The nature and extent of these services covered by workers' compensation laws vary across states (Bruyére & Brown, 2003; Keane, 1985). However, legislation has changed over the years, and most states no longer mandate vocational rehabilitation benefits under workers' compensation. In fact, some states that previously allowed for more comprehensive rehabilitation services have substantially curtailed or eliminated vocational rehabilitation benefits available under workers' compensation.

Goals and Priorities

The goal of rehabilitation within workers' compensation systems is different from that of public sector rehabilitation programs. Whereas the primary goal of public sector rehabilitation is to maximize an individual's human potential and quality of life, the goal of workers' compensation rehabilitation is to return the injured employee to gainful employment in the most expedient way possible. In concentrating on returning injured employees to work in an effective and timely manner, several authors developed a hierarchy of most-to-least-viable return-to-work options (R. K. Lynch & Lynch, 1998; Matkin, 1997):

1. Return to work at the same (preinjury) job with the same employer.
2. Return to work at the same job with the same employer, with modified duties to accommodate the worker's functional limitations.

3. Return to work at a different job with the same employer.
4. Return to work at the same job (with or without modification) with a different employer.
5. Return to work at a different job (with or without on-the-job training) with the same or a different employer.
6. Return to work after a training or educational program. Shorter training programs are preferred over longer educational programs.
7. Self-employment (rarely considered unless there are good reasons to substantiate that the employee can be successful).

The priority of rehabilitation in workers' compensation is to return injured workers to gainful employment in the most expedient way possible, taking into consideration the person's level of vocational functioning, preinjury salary level, capabilities, and functional limitations. Caseloads in workers' compensation are usually smaller than in the public sector, but intensity of services is much greater. A typical caseload for a counselor is 25 to 40 clients; caseloads within the public sector are often well over 100. There is also greater involvement with job analysis, labor market surveys, job placement, and court testimony in the private sector, while personal–social counseling and quality of life issues are emphasized less. Despite having a diverse caseload, the workers' compensation counselor sees many workers with back injuries and with disabilities of less severity than those seen by public sector rehabilitation counselors.

Characteristics
The emphasis in the public sector is on serving clients with severe disabilities; however, severe disabling conditions are rarely seen in workers' compensation caseloads. Insurance companies and third-party administrators provide workers' compensation funding. Vocational rehabilitation services are to be provided quickly and efficiently because (a) the goal of vocational rehabilitation is to return the injured employee to work as quickly as possible and (b) insurance companies provide monthly maintenance allowance benefits while the worker is involved in rehabilitation. Services do not usually extend beyond a year, whereas in public rehabilitation consumers may participate for several years.

Ethics
Workers' compensation counselors are confronted with various ethical dilemmas when providing services. Insurance companies are paying for services and may attempt to control the direction of rehabilitation. Central to the issue of conflicting interests is the question, Who is the client? Potential conflicts of interest may arise, as the counselor must work closely not only with the employee with a disability, but also with the referral and funding source, and often with the worker's employer. Above all, the injured worker should be considered the client. Counselors need to be keenly aware of the ethical standards of

professional organizations. The International Association of Rehabilitation Professionals (2004) and other organizations have specific codes of ethical standards for professionals employed within the private-for-profit sector.

The Federal Employees' Compensation Act and the Longshore and Harbor Workers' Compensation Act

The U.S. Department of Labor's Office of Workers' Compensation Programs (OWCP) administers major disability compensation programs that provide wage replacement benefits, medical treatment, vocational rehabilitation, and other benefits to federal workers or their dependents who are injured at work or acquire an occupational disease. The Federal Employees' Compensation Program and the Longshore and Harbor Workers' Compensation Program serve the specific employee groups that are covered under the relevant statutes and regulations by mitigating the financial burden resulting from workplace injury.

The Federal Employees' Compensation Act (FECA) provides compensation benefits to civilian employees who are working for federal agencies and are injured at work or have an employment-related illness or disease. FECA protects 3 million federal workers from economic hardship due to work injury and illness. Included among the executive, legislative, and judicial branch employees covered by FECA are civilian defense workers, medical workers in veterans hospitals, and the 800,000 workers of the U.S. Postal Service, the country's largest civilian employer. To be eligible for services, an individual must have sustained a permanent, job-related injury and be unable to perform the customary job duties because of that injury or illness. This system of compensation is based on the concept of wage loss. The employee can receive financial compensation as long as "medical evidence indicates total or partial disability and the employee is suffering lost wages due to the injury" (Deneen & Hessellund, 1986, p. 147). Vocational rehabilitation services under this system include vocational assessment and evaluation, vocational testing, labor market research, job placement, and follow-up services. Vocational plans may include college training, vocational technical training, on-the-job training, immediate job placement without training, and self-employment.

The Department of Labor's Office of Workers' Compensation Programs administers FECA. To become certified and provide services as a vocational rehabilitation counselor under OWCP, one must meet the following minimum requirements: (a) a bachelor's degree from an accredited 4-year college or university, (b) 2 years of workers' compensation vocational rehabilitation counseling experience, and (c) evidence of licensure in states requiring a license in vocational rehabilitation counseling. Counselors are evaluated on timeliness of services, quality of rehabilitation services, successful closures, and adherence to OWCP procedures and instructions. The Federal Employees Health Benefits Program's (2003) guidelines specify expected services, including

(a) the vocational rehabilitation process, (b) management of OWCP forms, (c) reports and requirements for reporting, and (d) bills and procedures for billing of vocational rehabilitation services. The benefits offered under this system are significantly more comprehensive than those benefits provided under workers' compensation.

The Longshore and Harbor Workers' Compensation Act covers U.S. Maritime employees and some employees in closely related employment situations, and is administered by the Department of Labor's Employment Standards Administration. The act defines *disability* as incapacity due to an injury to earn the wages at the time of injury, in the same or any other employment. Therefore, disability is an economic concept instead of a physical concept (White, 1986). The law covers injuries and diseases arising out of employment; benefits are comparable to the federal workers' benefits and exceed workers' compensation benefits. The goal of the Longshore and Harbor Workers' Compensation Act is to facilitate the return to employment of injured workers who are receiving compensation, have permanent impairment, and cannot return to their former occupation. Counselors are instructed to attempt this avenue of rehabilitation before considering other options, such as training, on-the-job training, or educational programs. Rehabilitation services may include vocational assessment and evaluation, rehabilitation counseling, training, job modification, job placement, and follow-up services. The intent of this voluntary program in the act is to provide prompt and timely services that will help injured workers return to work at an income as close as possible to their preinjury income.

Long-Term Disability

Long-term disability (LTD) is a disability insurance income system that may be referred to as LTD insurance or accident and health insurance. Administered by LTD insurance carriers, LTD insurance policies can be provided by employers or taken out by individual employees. Most professional organizations offer group policies to their members. Each policy defines disability specifically within the particular policy; there is great variability in benefits offered by these policies.

LTD policies vary in terms of the waiting period (the time the policyholder must be considered disabled before benefits are initiated) and the length of time benefits will be paid. Although the waiting period might be as short as 1 month and the benefit period as long as the person's 65th birthday, the majority of policies have a 90-day waiting period before benefits begin and provide benefits for a limited time. The definition of successful return to gainful employment varies. A policy may state that the insured must return to work at a salary level comparable to that earned at the time of injury before benefits will be terminated. Comparable-level salary is a percentage of the prior salary, such as two thirds of the gross salary at the time the insured acquired the disability and stopped working. If the individual takes a salary lower than this amount, he or she may be entitled to continuing benefits. Other policies involve the concept of residual disability. If the insured returns to work at a lower paying job, the insurance carrier may be responsible for paying a percentage of the difference between the prior salary and the current salary. Many policies provide insurance coverage for up to 2 years if the individual is unable to perform the prior occupation; coverage may continue beyond this time if the person is considered unable to perform any occupation because of disability.

Many LTD policies have an offset for Social Security disability income. If the insured is eligible for and obtains Social Security Disability Insurance (SSDI) benefits because of a disability, the insurance company may be able to reduce the monthly insurance disability benefits according to a structured formula. Insurance companies may insist that the insured individual apply for SSDI benefits. Some companies assign an attorney to help with the paperwork and represent the individual in court. It is illegal for an insured individual not to report Social Security benefits to the insurance company if there is a financial offset specified within the insurance policy (Deneen & Hessellund, 1986; Patterson, Bruyére, Szymanski, & Jenkins, 2005).

There are advantages to providing rehabilitation counseling services within the LTD insurance income system. The nature of the policies allows the counselor greater latitude in establishing return-to-work rehabilitation plans. In establishing these plans, the counselor has the opportunity to use the insured's educational achievement, employment history, and career goals to a greater extent. As with the Federal Employees' Compensation Program and Longshore and Harbor Workers' Compensation Program, the LTD system may allow a rehabilitation counselor to establish a plan that involves additional college education. The majority of insured individuals within the LTD system are skilled workers and professionals with advanced education. A counselor will need to offer sufficient rehabilitation services to enable the insured to return to work at a comparable-level salary; otherwise, disability payments may continue.

Services that may be offered to this population include vocational assessment, transferable skills analysis, labor market research, job development, detailed job analysis of both the job at the time of disability and the proposed return-to-work goal, and career development based on the results of information provided by assessment and ongoing interviews with the insured. Specialized vocational training or additional college education may be appropriate. Within this system, rehabilitation counselors rely heavily on using clients' transferable skills in attempting to locate comparable-level work.

Forensic Rehabilitation: Expert Witness Testimony

With increasing frequency rehabilitation counselors are appearing in court to testify as expert witnesses. Many counselors choose to testify as part of their professional practices. The rehabilitationist can testify as a vocational expert witness in Social Security Disability Insurance, personal injury litigation, life care planning, marriage dissolution (rehabilitation, alimony), employment discrimination, and medical malpractice. A vocational expert must have certain qualifications, including possession of a master's degree or a doctorate in rehabilitation counseling or one of the behavioral sciences, and several years' experience in rehabilitation practice (Donnell, Reyes, Cogdal, & Porter, 2004; Havranek, 1997). The counselor needs knowledge and experience in the areas of medical aspects of disability, functional limitations, rehabilitation potential, transferable skills analysis, marketability, and employability. Beyond this, one needs self-confidence to withstand direct examination and cross-examination; cross-examination from the opposing attorney can be particularly demanding. Emotional stability and confidence are necessary to endure the hours of cross-examination that may occur in certain personal injury, life care planning, discrimination, or marriage dissolution cases. Although either the plaintiff or defendant has hired the expert witness, it is necessary to be ethical and as unbiased as possible. If a counselor fails to maintain objectivity, he or she may be seen more as a "paid witness" than as a professional counselor. As succinctly noted by Woodrich and Patterson (2003), "objectivity, or client neutrality, rather than beneficence, must be the guiding principle for ethical practice in forensic rehabilitation. When rehabilitation professionals confuse their roles (advocate versus objective evaluator), unethical behavior can occur" (p. 46).

The Social Security Administration's Office of Hearings and Appeals hires rehabilitation counselors as vocational experts to testify as nonbiased professionals regarding a claimant's capacities to engage in substantial gainful activity. The expert is not hired to represent either the administration or the claimant; hearings are relatively short and several are scheduled in one day. Scheduling occurs well in advance, and cases take place as scheduled. Intense cross-examination is not part of these hearings. Counselors who are uncomfortable with lengthy, intense cross-examination, questioning of their expertise and credentials, uncertainty as to the date and time of testimony, and lengthy hearings may enjoy this type of court testimony. The remuneration, however, is considerably less than in other areas of forensic testimony.

Thorough preparation in forensic rehabilitation is necessary if a counselor is considering expert witness testimony. A counselor should not attempt to testify in a court of law until he or she has had the opportunity to speak with other counselors as to what will occur in court, what is expected, and how to conduct comprehensive preparation. It is advised that before testifying, the counselor observe several cases where other counselors are providing expert witness testimony. Most experienced counselors will not object to another counselor observing their testimony; many rehabilitation counselors remember the first time they testified as expert witnesses in court. Vocational experts should testify in their area of expertise, the vocational area, and not on psychological or medical factors or other nonvocational areas.

Life Care Planning

Life care planning is a branch of medical and catastrophic case management services; rehabilitation counselors working in the private sector may provide life care planning services to clients who have had catastrophic injuries or chronic, debilitating illnesses. Counselors who are accustomed to working with catastrophic injuries often see their job not only as involving vocational rehabilitation, but also as providing a long range of services that enhance a person's quality of life and long-term care. Life care planning addresses both the challenges and costs that persons who have experienced catastrophic injury face following medical rehabilitation.

Life care planning for individuals with catastrophic injuries is a part of case management. The life care planner designs a plan of comprehensive rehabilitation to assist individuals and their families. P. M. Deutsch (1994) postulated that rehabilitation counselors, as coordinators of interdisciplinary services in the care of permanently injured patients, are uniquely qualified to help develop future life care plans. "Rehabilitation counselors who have experience with catastrophic injuries, combined with formal rehabilitation training in assessment, independent living, medical, psychosocial, and occupational aspects of disability, have ideal preparation for preparing life care plans" (R. K. Lynch & Lynch, 1998, p. 92).

The life care plan is designed with two primary objectives: (a) to communicate in a systematic manner all the intricate details involved in a catastrophic injury case from the day of evaluation through the projected end of the client's life and (b) to provide a format for the client's family. Several authors (Braun, 2003; Brodwin & Mas, 1999; P. M. Deutsch, 1994) have overviewed the topic areas covered in the life care plan: projected evaluations and therapeutic modalities, diagnostic testing/educational assessment, aids for independent functioning, orthopedic equipment needs, drug/supply needs, home/facility care, future medical care, transportation, health and strength maintenance, architectural renovations, vocational/educational planning, and leisure and/or recreational equipment and services. The rehabilitation professional analyzes each of these areas as a way to estimate the extent of an individual's disability. "A comprehensive life care plan is an approach that encompasses financial, legal, social, medical, and religious aspects of an individual's life and can play a significant role in bringing peace of mind to the family" (Braun, 2003, p. 37). The life care plan helps assure the family that a comfortable and meaningful lifestyle is possible for the individual with a disability.

Life care planning is a specialization within the profession of rehabilitation counseling that is expanding in scope and will continue to do so in the future. Given the projected growth of life care planning, the field will continue to offer future opportunities for rehabilitation counselors.

Disability Management

Disability management was defined by Schwartz, Watson, Galvin, and Lipoff (1989) as follows: "Disability management means using services, people, and materials to (a) minimize the impact and cost of disability to employers and employees; and (b) encourage return to work for employees with disabilities" (p. 1). Another definition was proposed by Akabas et al. (1992):

> Disability management is a workplace prevention and remediation strategy that seeks to prevent disability from occurring or, lacking that, to intervene early following the onset of disability, using coordinated, cost-conscious, and quality rehabilitation service that reflects an organizational commitment to continued employment for those experiencing functional work limitations. (p. 2)

These authors cited the remediation goal of disability management to be successful job maintenance or optimum timing for return to work for employees with disabilities.

Disability management in business and industry was developed because of steadily increasing costs for injuries on the job and workers' compensation claims, and the effects of these claims on business. Counselors working in disability management are involved with human resource management, early intervention, coordination of services, cost-effective services, and returning the injured employee to work. Employment legislation is the fastest changing area of human resources today. For a variety of reasons, employers have been slow to recognize the value of including rehabilitation counselors in the disability management process. One factor may be that disability management practices among employers vary in terms of quality, philosophical orientation, scope, support services, and return-to-work methods (Habeck, Kress, Scully, & Kirchner, 1994). Due to the diversity of disability management programs in the employer community, it is difficult to find consensus regarding the essential job functions of the disability management professional (Olsheski & Rosenthal, 1999).

Currently, there appear to be four prevailing models of disability management and prevention: the medical model, the physical rehabilitation model, the job-match model, and the managed care model. The *medical model* emphasizes the physician's role in defining a person's functional limitations and job restrictions. In the *physical rehabilitation model,* rehabilitation professionals communicate the importance of exercise and muscle reconditioning to help an individual resume normal work activities. The *job-match model* relies on the ability of employers to accurately communicate physical job requirements. The *managed care model* focuses on dissemination of acceptable standards for medical treatment and duration of work absence, and interventions by case managers when these standards are exceeded (Pransky, Shaw, Franche, & Clarke, 2004).

Disability management involves a broad array of integrated services, including early and proactive services with the goal of reducing the risk of injury, attending to employees with chronic medical conditions, and addressing the effects of disability once it occurs. The following elements can maximize success in a disability management program for companies, organizations, and agencies (Akabas et al., 1992; Havranek, Field, & Grimes, 2005; Millington, Miller, Asner-Self, & Linkowski, 2003; Scully & Habeck, 1999):

1. The most important single factor: a human resource management policy committed to managing disability, including attitude enhancement and a thorough understanding of disability
2. Education, involvement, and cooperation at all company levels, including administrative, management, supervisory, and all employees
3. Understanding of the Americans with Disabilities Act and how to apply this law and other disability legislation in practice
4. A team approach to case management and medical management, including treating physicians, social service providers, and rehabilitation services
5. An ongoing advocacy philosophy for people with disabilities, including employees and potentially qualified employees who have disabilities
6. An injury prevention plan and a health/wellness promotion program
7. An organized return-to-work program, including modified work and light-duty and sedentary jobs, and a method for employees to transition back to their customary positions when feasible
8. An early intervention program, including supervisor identification of potentially disabling situations at the work site
9. Expanded "reasonable accommodation" to minimize the impact of disability
10. A coordinated "place and train" model, rather than "train and place"
11. Vocational flexibility—a developmental process, rather than a static, singular event
12. Development and utilization of an employee assistance program
13. An HIV/AIDS policy and education component to help workers with this disability maintain employment in a positive work environment

All parties benefit when disability management is provided in a comprehensive, effective, and non–stress-producing manner. Rehabilitation counseling is becoming instrumental in helping industry, business, and government maintain an effective and productive multicultural workforce, which includes individuals with disabilities.

Within the practice of disability management, rehabilitation counselors are involved with different work settings. The counselor may become (a) an employee of a larger company that is providing disability management services for its employees; (b) part of an insurance company offering disability management services; (c) a counselor hired by a private-for-profit rehabilitation company offering disability management services; or (d) an owner of a rehabilitation company providing disability management. Counselors will vary their roles and functions depending on the needs and requests of the particular referral source. Case management is the essential element to provide effective disability management services within business and industry (Roessler & Rubin, 2006). To be an effective disability manager, the counselor needs to be an effective and efficient case manager.

Substance Abuse Rehabilitation in the Private-for-Profit Sector

Substance abuse continues to be a significant problem within the modern workforce. It is estimated that the incidence of drug and alcohol abuse in the general population is as high as one out of every three individuals. Estimated cost of substance abuse to employers is approximately $80 billion, including health care costs, lost job productivity, absenteeism, and job–related accidents (Akabas & Gates, 2002; Stude, 2002).

Rehabilitation counselors often provide substance abuse counseling in business and industry through employee assistance programs (EAPs). There has been a recent growth and expansion of drug and alcohol counseling programs to assist employees who may be losing work productivity due to substance abuse. EAPs deal not only with substance abuse concerns but also with a variety of mental and physical health issues that affect job performance. EAP-related treatment programs are located outside the employing organization so workers can seek assistance without the knowledge or intervention of the employer or other employees. As stated by Akabas and Gates (2002), many EAPs have expanded their services to include disability management, stress management, work and family issues, training, reasonable accommodation, organizational consultation, team building, and change efforts.

Rehabilitationists employed in workers' compensation, long-term disability, and other rehabilitation systems need to address the issues of substance abuse with many of their clients. As stated by Stude (2002), substance abuse "is a disability that is prevalent in vocational rehabilitation caseloads, either as a primary or a secondary disability" (p. 27). Counselors' attitudes toward substance abusers are typically negative. It has been shown that the most important factor in successful intervention is not a practitioner's techniques, but his or her attitude. To be effective, rehabilitation counselors need to adopt positive attitudes toward the treatment of persons who abuse substances. They need to (a) be aware of substance abuse as a problem that requires intervention; (b) acknowledge that relapses may occur during vocational rehabilitation intervention and recovery; and (c) recognize substance abuse as a legitimate concern in all private sector rehabilitation systems (Stude, 1990). If the counselor ignores the problem of substance abuse with a client, the possibility of a successful vocational rehabilitation intervention is greatly diminished.

Successful intervention involves a combination of factors, including strengthening the person's ego, increasing self-esteem, and developing a constructive and effective support system. Return to work in an atmosphere that encourages psychological well-being and within an environment that supports drug abstinence helps the individual remain drug free. A return to paid employment itself correlates with successful recovery; work is a crucial component in maintaining long-term abstinence.

Consultation on the Americans with Disabilities Act

According to the Rehabilitation Act of 1973 and the Americans with Disabilities Act of 1990, a qualified individual with a disability is "a person with a disability who, with or without reasonable accommodation, can perform the essential functions of the employment position that such a person holds or desires" (West, 1991, p. 35). Private sector rehabilitationists, therefore, through knowledge and practical application of reasonable accommodation, can assist employers in hiring people with disabilities and in accommodating employees currently working who acquire disabilities either through injury or chronic illness. As the workforce ages, there is an increasing number of employees with disabilities and chronic medical conditions who will continue to work.

The ADA provided landmark legislation protecting the rights of persons with disabilities. *Reasonable accommodation* (job accommodation), a pivotal and integral part of this legislation, is defined by the U.S. Office of Personnel Management (Berkeley Planning Associates, 1982) as a logical adjustment made to a job and/or the work environment enabling a qualified person with a disability to perform the duties of that position. The ADA requires reasonable accommodation in three aspects of employment: the application process, the performance of the essential functions of the job, and the benefits and privileges of employment. There are various ways to provide reasonable accommodation. They include job restructuring, modified work schedules, part-time work, reassignment to vacant positions within the company, adaptations of equipment or tools used on the job, modifications of employee examinations or training materials, changes in employee policies, and the provision of readers or interpreters (Brodwin, Parker, & DeLaGarza, 2003).

With implementation of the ADA, rehabilitation service providers in the private-for-profit sector have discovered opportunities for employment as consultants to industry, business, and government on disability discrimination law. The ADA covers all entities in both public and private sectors with 15 or more employees. Rehabilitation counselors need strategies and techniques appropriate to meet the needs of consumers with disabilities, as well as skills to consult with employers who can no longer legally discriminate against employees with disabilities.

Specialized Skills of Practitioners in the Private-for-Profit Sector

Before addressing the specialized skills needed by rehabilitation counselors employed within the private-for-profit sector, generic skills should also be noted. Generic skills include counseling techniques, assessment and appraisal, case management, client advocacy, career (vocational) counseling, community agency liaison and referral, and follow-up services. More specialized skills are discussed in this section.

Job Analysis

Rehabilitation counselors practicing within the private-for-profit sector need the ability to achieve a detailed and complete job analysis (Brodwin, Brodwin, & Liebman, 1992; Weed & Field, 2004). The Bureau of Law and Business (1982) defined *job analysis* as "the process of obtaining information about a particular job in order to establish a basis of accurately describing it and for determining its specifications and requirements" (p. 1). Rehabilitation counselors use the information from job analysis to assist injured workers and those with chronic medical conditions to continue with or return to work, to identify and analyze occupationally significant characteristics of jobs (worker traits), and to determine transferable work skills. Other uses of job analysis include recruitment and orientation of employees, job development and placement using identified skills and abilities, exploration of training and educational programs to increase chances for successful rehabilitation, stress and wellness management in industry, career counseling, retirement planning, providing necessary information for job modification and reasonable accommodation, and consulting on the ADA.

Vocational Evaluation

Work is an essential part of life that affects one's self-image, lifestyle, and even the nature and quality of interpersonal relationships. Vocational evaluation and assessment are major dimensions of the work functions of rehabilitation counselors in the private-for-profit sector. Proper and appropriate vocational evaluation and assessment increases the probability that the client's rehabilitation program or plan will lead to successful procurement of gainful and meaningful employment. Appropriate testing needs to be conducted in areas such as intelligence, aptitude, achievement, personality, and vocational interests. For some clients, physical capability and emotional tolerances also need evaluation. Meaningful assessment of a person's functioning will help alleviate future problems in vocational adjustment and job satisfaction, and enable a person to attain maximum functioning and independence. Improper evaluation, however, may result in development of a rehabilitation program that is inappropriate and results in failure.

Labor Market Surveys

A rehabilitation counselor working in the private-for-profit sector needs to be skilled in conducting labor market surveys. The purpose of these surveys is to determine what jobs, and approximately how many, exist and are available in a particular local economy. Two major reasons for labor market surveys are (a) to learn if there is a viable job market to justify a rehabilitation plan or program and (b) to obtain information that will be used when a counselor testifies in a court of law. To justify a rehabilitation plan, a labor market survey must identify the likelihood that a particular plan will result in employability. The labor market survey thus establishes groundwork for the job development and placement phase of rehabilitation.

Job Placement/Career Development

A major goal of rehabilitation is to maximize the employability, independence, and participation of people with disabilities in the workplace (Patterson et al., 2005). Success in many rehabilitation systems is dependent on effective and realistic job development and placement. Counselors need to develop skills in placing clients who have a wide range of disabilities and also in placing clients with multiple disabilities.

Rehabilitation counselors need skills in evaluating the functional limitations of clients and their rehabilitation potential, as well as a working knowledge of how to provide reasonable accommodations to effectively serve clients on the job and in job placement and career development. People searching for employment often lack the job seeking skills that are needed for becoming successful in job placement. Such individuals often (a) have difficulty explaining their disabilities and accompanying functional limitations to prospective employers, (b) cannot fill out job applications correctly, (c) lack résumé preparation skills, (d) have problems with appropriate personal appearance for interviewing, (e) do not have effective interviewing skills, and (f) are unable to develop systematic methods for job search activities. Elaboration on specific areas crucial to an effective job search can be found in Chapter 12.

As emphasized by Kosciulek (1998), rehabilitation counselors should help individuals with disabilities in the area of career counseling, rather than simply placing them on jobs. This is necessary to help clients secure meaningful employment and develop more control over their lives. Counselors employed in both private and public sectors are feeling an increased demand to investigate careers and career paths for their clients with disabilities.

Private-for-profit sector rehabilitation counselors spend at least one fourth of their time engaged in job development and placement (Matkin, 1997). It is essential to persons with disabilities that counselors receive appropriate training in job seeking skills, résumé and job application form preparation, employment interviewing techniques, networking, job referral services, and follow-up. Whether the counselor does the actual job development or refers this activity to a job placement specialist, he or she will need the knowledge to successfully prepare clients for the often-challenging task of seeking and successfully obtaining employment.

When vocationally placing individuals, counselors need to take into account potential for job satisfaction, career development, career advancement opportunities, and self-esteem issues. The new job or career should provide meaningful life activity, whenever possible. To lead a satisfying life through work, the person needs to be able to develop his or her maximum potential. These factors, along with salary level, job stability, and opportunities for advancement, need to be taken into account. The individual should have a satisfying job, and the employer should be satisfied with the worker's job performance.

Transferable Skills

The use of an extensive and thoroughly detailed job analysis is one of the best methods of providing reasonable accommodation and identifying potential transferable skills. A job analysis can help the counselor identify both the essential and nonessential aspects of the job. At times, essential aspects may be modified, and nonessential aspects can be changed, reassigned, or eliminated. Job analysis also will provide information on the client's skills that may be transferable to similar work activities. As stated by Mueller (1990), "job accommodation for people with disabilities is a creative process requiring unique solutions to unique situations" (p. 1).

To determine transferability of work skills, the rehabilitation counselor needs to identify jobs and occupations consistent with a worker's capabilities, considering that the individual's capacity to perform work may be reduced due to injury or disease. It is important to consider the person's work experience, skills, and knowledge acquisition specific to job functions, including the ability to use personal judgment, work with specific equipment and devices, operate tools and complex machinery, or work with people or ideas at high levels of involvement (Brodwin & Brodwin, 2002; Weed & Field, 2004).

Rehabilitation professionals must be capable of analyzing a worker's capabilities and functional limitations, and then considering alternative work the person may be capable of performing. Skilled and professional workers who possess advanced knowledge, skills, and abilities are likely to have highly marketable skills that have a wide application. Through careful analysis of these skills, the rehabilitation counselor and client may find alternatives at a salary comparable to the prior job's without the necessity of additional training or education.

The rehabilitation counselor uses expertise in analyzing transferable skills when a client's past employment history is at a skilled or semiskilled level. Use of transferable skills facilitates job accommodation, modification of a job, or job restructuring that is necessary because of a worker's newly acquired functional limitations due to disability. The following strategies should be considered (Brodwin & Brodwin, 2002; West, 1991):

1. Modifying the physical layout of a job facility to make it accessible to individuals who use wheelchairs or who have other limitations that make access difficult
2. Restructuring a job to enable the person with a disability to perform the essential functions of the job
3. Establishing a part-time or modified work schedule (e.g., accommodating people with disabilities who have medical treatment appointments or fatigue problems)
4. Reassigning a person with a disability to a vacant job
5. Acquiring or modifying equipment or devices (e.g., buying a hearing telephone amplifier for a person with a hearing impairment)
6. Adjusting or modifying exams, training materials, or policies (e.g., giving an application examination orally to a person with dyslexia, or modifying a policy against dogs in the workplace for a person with a service dog)
7. Providing qualified readers or interpreters for people with vision or hearing impairments

Transferable skills can be used when attempting to place an individual who has a professional, skilled, or semiskilled work history into exertionally or emotionally less demanding work. The person's skills may be readily transferable within the current labor market. Factors to consider are how much time has elapsed since the work was last performed, whether the skills are outdated or forgotten, and whether the skills are marketable. The counselor must investigate if the client's skills are transferable to lighter work that is within the client's new functional limitations and make sure the individual has interest in this line of work. Using transferable skills helps the client maintain his or her prior salary level, a factor that is crucial to many workers who have lengthy work histories, high earnings, and high financial obligations. The more skilled the person, the easier it is for the rehabilitation counselor to find comparable work. Use of transferable skills in job placement is one of the most effective means to help minimize the impact of functional limitations, maximize the individual's rehabilitation potential, and maintain a salary at or close to the prior level.

Transition

Under the Individuals with Disabilities Education Act (IDEA), the U.S. Congress assigned ultimate legal responsibility for the development and implementation of transition plans to state education agencies. However, rehabilitation counselors are in an ideal position to provide leadership in the planning and delivery of these services. They can take leadership roles with school districts, other social service agencies, and families of persons involved in transition. To be successful leaders, rehabilitation counselors must be knowledgeable of the content and application of relevant federal, state, and local laws, all of which have significant influence on the service delivery system. Rehabilitation professionals need to understand disability law and be able to apply the law in the context of transition.

Currently, most transition teams include only school district personnel. These teams often lack a practical understanding of the adult service delivery system and transition options with respect to community activities. Federal law, specifically the Workforce Investment Act (Title IV), mandates collaboration between vocational rehabilitation and the public education system. Congress has stated that there must be an improvement in transition outcomes. Legislation does not dictate the conditions under which this improvement will occur. In addition to school personnel, family members, and the client, transition teams should include representatives from vocational rehabilitation, developmental disabilities, and others who can suggest strategies for service delivery (S. E. Brown & Johnson, 1994).

Assistive Technology

Assistive technology (AT) is defined as any item, piece of equipment, or product, whether acquired commercially, off the shelf, modified, or customized, that is used to increase, maintain, or improve the functional capabilities of individuals who have disabilities. Counselors in the private sector can assist clients with disabilities through the use and application of AT, which can enhance clients' potential for rehabilitation, diminish functional limitations, improve independence, ease integration or reintegration into society, and improve employment possibilities. Through greater understanding of the benefits of AT, counselors are able to offer more meaningful counseling and rehabilitation services (Star, Brodwin, & Cordoso, 2004). As noted by Scherer (2002), technology is radically changing the lives of people with disabilities. It has helped enhance the quality of life and extended the lifespans of individuals who have congenital and developmental disorders, as well as those with acquired disorders and chronic medical conditions.

Upward social mobility and a greater sense of personal well-being for people with disabilities become more realistic and practical due to enhanced educational and employment opportunities. AT has allowed many people who have disabilities to exert greater control over their own lives; participate in, and contribute more fully to, activities in their homes, school, work, and community; interact to a greater extent with nondisabled individuals; and benefit from opportunities that are taken for granted by people who do not have disabilities (Kelley, 2003). Technology helps remove limitations and barriers by enabling individuals to function strictly on their capabilities, training, education, and experience. Through exploration of the client's abilities, functional limitations, and feelings about technology, rehabilitation counselors can best provide effective rehabilitation services.

Concluding Statement

Career opportunities for rehabilitation counselors have expanded dramatically over the last four decades in all sectors of rehabilitation, including the private-for-profit sector. To adequately train new counselors, rehabilitation counselor education programs need to respond to the many developments and challenges within the private-for-profit sector that have already occurred and will continue in the future. Many rehabilitation counseling programs have been responding to these changes by implementing new coursework in the various areas of the private-for-profit sector; other programs have been slower to respond.

For the past 15 years, the Council on Rehabilitation Education (CORE) has required that accredited rehabilitation counselor education programs include educational content in the area of private sector rehabilitation. This has provided an impetus for all programs accredited by CORE to add information and material to their master's level programs in this area.

To educate students in the knowledge and work roles of rehabilitation within the private-for-profit sector, all rehabilitation counselor education programs should include the following content areas (Havranek & Brodwin, 1994; Wilson, Livneh, & Duchesneau, 2002):

1. Workers' compensation issues, such as history, philosophy, policies and procedures, insurance rehabilitation, and insurance claims handling
2. Program planning and evaluation procedures and methodologies in the private sector
3. Case management, disability management, employee assistance programs, life care planning, transition, assistive technology, and service coordination
4. Vocational assessment/evaluation, job placement, career development, and use of transferable skills as applicable within the private-for-profit sector of rehabilitation
5. Gathering, synthesizing, and reporting to different audiences, including injured workers, physicians, attorneys, insurance carriers, and employers
6. Identifying and utilizing short-term vocational training programs

7. Skills in assessment of labor markets, job analyses, and job modification and restructuring
8. Referrals, marketing, and case finding methods and techniques for private sector rehabilitation
9. Legal and ethical issues, including vocational expert testimony, malpractice, privacy, confidentiality, credentialing, and licensure
10. Entrepreneurial skills to set up and manage a rehabilitation business
11. Knowledge of assistive technology that can improve employment opportunities for people with disabilities

The labor market for private-for-profit sector rehabilitation counselors, like many other emerging and expanding professions in the new millennium, is rich in opportunities for appealing and challenging employment. The opportunities are diverse and meaningful and offer many ways for counselors to apply their knowledge, skills, and abilities to help people who have disabilities. Rehabilitation counselors can enter the field seeking full-time employment or doing part-time work to supplement other income. Counselors in the private-for-profit sector also may do work for more than one entity, such as providing consultation to business and industry on reasonable accommodation and the ADA, giving vocational expert testimony in the area of Social Security disability, and teaching part-time in an educational institution. Many possibilities exist in the arena of private-for-profit rehabilitation. It is up to each individual to choose the best options to suit his or her specific needs and career interests.

References

Aaron, H. J. (1967). Social Security: International comparisons. In O. Eckstein (Ed.), *Studies in the economics of income maintenance.* Washington, DC: Brookings Institution.

Abram, M., & Wolf, S. (1984). Public involvement in medical ethics: A model for government action. *New England Journal of Medicine, 310,* 627–632.

Achenbach, T. M. (1982). *Developmental psychopathology* (2nd ed.). New York: Wiley.

Ackerman, G., & McReynolds, C. (2005). Strategies to promote successful employment of people with psychiatric disabilities. *Journal of Applied Rehabilitation Counseling, 36*(4), 35–40.

Acton, N. (1982). The world's response to disability: Evolution of a philosophy. *Archives of Physical Medicine and Rehabilitation, 63,* 145–149.

Ad Hoc Committee of the Commission on Practice. (1980). *American Occupational Therapy Association representative assembly.* Rockville, MD: Occupational Therapy Association.

Adams, J. E. (1991). Judicial and regulatory interpretation of the employment rights of persons with disabilities. *Journal of Applied Rehabilitation Counseling, 22*(3), 28–46.

Adams-Shollenberger, G. E., & Mitchell, T. E. (1996). A comparison of janitorial workers with mental retardation and their non-disabled peers on retention and absenteeism. *Journal of Rehabilitation, 62*(3), 56–60.

Adelson, R. (2004). Universal design: Opening every door. *Inside MS, 22*(4), 30–34.

Administration on Developmental Disabilities. (1994, June 8). *The Developmental Disabilities Assistance and Bill of Rights Act.* Retrieved April 9, 1999, from http://www.acf.dhhs.gov/programs/add/dd-a.htm

Affleck, J. Q., Edgar, E., Levine, P., & Kortering, L. (1990). Postschool status of students classified as mentally retarded, learning disabled, or nonhandicapped: Does it get better with time? *Education and Training in Mental Retardation, 25,* 315–324.

Agich, G. (1982). Disease and values: A rejection of the value neutrality thesis. *Theoretical Medicine, 4,* 27–41.

AIDS fears emerge in Iowa newspaper poll. (1986, November). *Daily Egyptian,* p. 2.

Akabas, S. H., & Gates, L. B. (2002). *The role of employee assistance programs in supporting workers with health conditions.* New York: New York Work Exchange.

Akabas, S. H., Gates, L. B., & Galvin, D. E. (1992). *Disability management: A complete system to reduce costs, increase productivity, meet employee needs, and ensure legal compliance.* New York: AMACOM.

Akridge, R., & Means, B. (1982). Psychosocial adjustment skills training. In B. Bolton (Ed.), *Vocational adjustment of disabled persons* (pp. 149–166). Baltimore: University Park Press.

Albertsons Inc. v. Kirkingburg, 119 S.CT. 2162 (1999).

Albrecht, G. L. (Ed.). (1981). *Cross national rehabilitation policies.* Beverly Hills, CA: Sage.

Alexander, D., & Greenwood, R. (1985). Designing jobs for handicapped workers. *Conference Proceedings.* Chicago: Institute of Industrial Engineers.

Alexander, L. (1949). Medical science under dictatorship. *New England Journal of Medicine, 241,* 39–47.

Allaire, S., Anderson, J., & Meenan, R. (1997). Outcomes from the Job-Raising Program, a self-improvement model of vocational rehabilitation among persons with arthritis. *Journal of Applied Rehabilitation Counseling, 28*(2), 26–31.

Allaire, S., Li, W., & LaValley, M. (2003). Work barriers experienced and job accommodations used by persons with arthritis and other rheumatic diseases. *Rehabilitation Counseling Bulletin, 46,* 147–156.

Allan, W. S. (1958). *Rehabilitation: A community challenge.* New York: Wiley.

Allen, D., Turpin, J., Garske, G., & Warren-Marlatt, R. (1996). Rehabilitation counseling in the state sector: Do job descriptions accurately reflect expected duties? *Journal of Applied Rehabilitation Counseling, 27*(2), 14–18.

Alliance for Technology Access. (1994). *Computer resources for people with disabilities.* Alameda, CA: Hunter House.

Alston, R. J. (1996). Multiculturalism in rehabilitation education: Editor's introduction and overview. *Rehabilitation Education, 10,* 69–71.

Alston, R. J., & Bell, T. J. (1996). Ideological synthesis of multiculturalism and rehabilitation education. *Rehabilitation Education, 10,* 73–82.

Alston, R. J., & Mngadi, S. (1992). The interaction between disability status and the African-American experience: Implications for rehabilitation counseling. *Journal of Applied Rehabilitation Counseling, 23*(2), 12–15.

Altman, B. M. (1981). Studies of attitudes toward the handicapped: The need for a new direction. *Social Problems, 28,* 321–337.

American Association on Mental Retardation. (1992). *Mental retardation: Definition, classification, and systems of supports* (9th ed.). Washington, DC: Author.

American Bankers Association. (1992). *Americans with Disabilities Act: Alert for CEOs.* Washington, DC: Author.

American Counseling Association. (2005). *ACA code of ethics.* Retrieved December 23, 2006, from http://www.counseling.org/Resources/CodeoOfEthics/TP/Home/CT2.aspx

American Psychiatric Association. (1994). *Diagnostic and statistical manual of mental disorders* (4th ed.). Washington, DC: Author.

American Psychological Association. (2002). *Guidelines on multicultural education, training, research, practice, and organizational change for psychologists.* Retrieved December 23, 2006, from http://www.apa.org/pi/multiculturalguidelines/guideline3.html

American Public Transit Association v. Lewis, 556 F2d 1271 (DC Cir 1981).

American School Counseling Association. (2004). *Ethical standards for school counselors.* Retrieved December 23, 2006, from http://www.schoolcounselor.org/files/ethical%20standards.pdf

American Speech-Language-Hearing Association. (n.d.). *Recognizing communication disorders* [Brochure]. Rockville, MD: Author.

Americans with Disabilities Act of 1990, 42 U.S.C. § 12101 *et seq.*

Ames, T., & Boyle, P. (1980). The rehabilitation counselor's role in the sexual adjustment of the handicapped client. *Journal of Applied Rehabilitation Counseling, 11*(4), 173–178.

Anastasi, A., & Urbina, S. (1997). *Psychological testing* (7th ed.). Upper Saddle River, NJ: Prentice Hall.

Anderson, J., & Asselin, S. (1996). Factors affecting the school-to-community transition of students with disabilities. *Journal of Vocational Special Needs Education, 18,* 63–68.

Angell, M. (1983). Handicapped children: Baby Doe and Uncle Sam. *New England Journal of Medicine, 309,* 659–661.

Annino, P. (2005). The revised IDEA: Will it help children with disabilities? *Mental and Physical Disability Law Reporter, 29*(1), 11–14.

Anthony, W. (1980). A rehabilitation model for rehabilitating the psychiatrically disabled. *Rehabilitation Counseling Bulletin, 24,* 6–21.

Anthony, W., Cohen, M., & Nemec, P. (1987). Assessment in psychiatric rehabilitation. In B. Bolton (Ed.), *Handbook of measurement and evaluation in rehabilitation* (2nd ed., pp. 299–312). Baltimore: Brookes.

Anthony, W. A., & Blanch, A. (1987). Supported employment for persons who are psychiatrically disabled: An historical and conceptual perspective. *Psychosocial Rehabilitation Journal, 11*(2), 5–23.

Arc, The. (1999, September 1). *Workforce Investment Act signed into law.* Arlington, TX: Author. Retrieved April 1, 1999, from http://www.thearc.org

Area Education Agency 13. (1999, September). Assistive technologies home page. Retrieved September 3, 1999, from http://www.netins.net

Armstrong, A., & Wilkinson, M. (1998). Assistive technology from a user's perspective. In P. Wehman & J. Kregel (Eds.), *More than a job* (pp. 225–246). Baltimore: Brookes.

Arokiasamy, C. V. (1993a). Further directions for rehabilitation theory: Reactions to Hershenson and McAlee. *Rehabilitation Education, 7,* 105–108.

Arokiasamy, C. V. (1993b). Multiculturalism: Its implications for head injury rehabilitation. *Journal of Head Injury, 3*(2), 14–19.

Arokiasamy, C. V. (1993c). A theory for rehabilitation? *Rehabilitation Education, 7,* 77–98.

Arokiasamy, C. V. (1996). Reactions to the portrayal of disability in the film "The Hunchback of Notre Dame." *Rehabilitation Education, 10,* 331–336.

Arokiasamy, C. V., Strohmer, D. C., Guice, S., Angelocci, R., & Hoppe, M. S. (1994). The effects of politically correct language and counselor skill level on perceptions of counselor credibility. *Rehabilitation Counseling Bulletin, 37,* 304–314.

Arras, J. (1984). Toward an ethic of ambiguity. *The Hastings Center Report, 14*(2), 25–33.

Asch, A. (1984). The experience of disability: A challenge for psychology. *American Psychologist, 39,* 529–536.

Asch, A., & Fine, M. (1988). Beyond pedestals. In M. Fine & A. Asch (Eds.), *Women with disabilities: Essays in psychology, culture, and politics* (pp. 1–37). Philadelphia: Temple University Press.

Asch, S. E. (1952). *Social psychology.* Englewood Cliffs, NJ: Prentice Hall.

Ashby, H. (Director). (1978). *Coming home* [Motion picture]. United States: United Artists.

Assistive Technology Act of 1998, U.S.C. § 2201 *et seq.*

Atkins, B. (1988). An asset-oriented approach to cross cultural issues: Blacks in rehabilitation. *Journal of Applied Rehabilitation Counseling, 19*(4), 45–49.

Atkins v. Virginia, 536 U.S. 304 (2002).

Atkins, B., & Wright, G. (1980). Three views of vocational rehabilitation of blacks: The statement. *Journal of Rehabilitation, 46*(2), 40–46.

Aubert, V., & Messinger, S. S. (1965). The criminal and the sick. In V. Aubert (Ed.), *The hidden society* (pp. 25–54). Totawa, NJ: Bedminister Press.

Azrin, N., & Besalel, V. (1980). *Job Club counselor's manual.* Baltimore: University Park Press.

Azrin, N., Flores, T., & Kaplan, S. J. (1977). Job finding club: A group assisted program for obtaining employment. *Rehabilitation Counseling Bulletin, 21,* 130–140.

Azrin, N., & Phillip, R. (1979). The Job Club method for the job handicapped: A comparative outcome study. *Rehabilitation Counseling Bulletin, 23,* 144–155.

Baker, E., Baker, R., & McDaniel, R. (1975). Denormalizing practices in rehabilitation facilities. *Rehabilitation Literature, 36,* 112–115.

Bartels, E. C. (1985). A contemporary framework for independent living rehabilitation. *Rehabilitation Literature, 46,* 325–327.

Barth v. Gelb, 2F. 3d 1180 (D.C. Cir. 1993).

Basson, R. (1998). Sexual health of women with disabilities. *Canadian Medical Association Journal, 159,* 359–362.

Batavia, A., & Schriner, K. (2001). The Americans with Disabilities Act as engine of social change: Models of disability and the potential of a civil rights approach. *Policy Studies Journal, 29,* 690–702.

Bayh, B. (1979). Employment rights of the handicapped. *Journal of Rehabilitation Administration, 3,* 57–61.

Beale, A. (1985). Employment for clients who are mentally retarded: Misconceptions and realities. *Journal of Applied Rehabilitation Counseling, 16*(4), 41–43.

Beale, J. (2002). Affirmative action and violation of union contracts: The EEOC's new requirements under the Americans with Disabilities Act. *Capital University Law Review, 29,* 811–834.

Beardsley, M., & Rubin, S. E. (1988). Rehabilitation service providers: An investigation of generic job tasks and knowledge. *Rehabilitation Counseling Bulletin, 32,* 122–139.

Beauchamp, T., & Childress, J. (1989). *Principles of biomedical ethics* (3rd ed.). New York: Oxford University Press.

Beauchamp, T., & Childress, J. (2001). *Principles of biomedical ethics* (5th ed.). New York: Oxford University Press.

Becker, R. L. (1981). *Reading-free vocational interest inventory* (manual). Columbus, OH: Elbern.

Befort, S. F. (2002). The most difficult ADA reasonable accommodations issues: Reassignment and leave of absence. *Wake Forest Law Review, 37,* 440–472.

Bell v. Maryland, 37 U.S. 226 (1964).

Bellini, J. (2002). Correlates of multicultural competencies of vocational rehabilitation counselors. *Rehabilitation Counseling Bulletin, 45,* 66–75.

Bender, W. N. (1996). Learning disabilities. In P. J. McLaughlin & P. Wehman (Eds.), *Mental retardation and developmental disabilities* (2nd ed., pp. 259–279). Austin, TX: PRO-ED.

Benjamin, A. (1981). *The helping interview* (2nd ed.). Boston: Houghton Mifflin.

Benjuya, N., & Kenney, S. (1990). Myoelectric hand orthosis. *Journal of Prosthetics and Orthotics, 2,* 149–154.

Berke, J. (1999, July). *Cochlear implants.* New York: Author. Retrieved July 8, 1999, from http://www.deafnessminingco.com

Berkeley Planning Associates. (1982). *A study of accommodations provided to handicapped employees by federal contractors.* Washington, DC: United States Department of Labor, Employment Standards Administration.

Berkeley Planning Associates. (1997). *Serving mothers with disabilities in your child care program.* Oakland, CA: Author.

Berkman, A. H. (1975). Sexuality: A human condition. *Journal of Rehabilitation, 41*(1), 13–15, 37.

Berkowitz, E. D. (1992). Disabled policy: A personal postscript. *Journal of Disability Policy Studies, 3*(1), 2–16.

Berkowitz, M. (1984). The economist and rehabilitation. *Rehabilitation Literature, 45,* 354–357.

Berkowitz, M., & Berkowitz, E. (1985). Widening the field: Economics and history in the study of disability. *American Behavioral Scientist, 28,* 405–417.

Berliner, L. (1996). A survey of significant ADA Title II and Title III decisions within the Second Circuit. *Quarterly Law Review, 15,* 537–553.

Bernstein, J. (1966). Mental retardation: New prospects for employment. *Journal of Rehabilitation, 32*(3), 16–17, 35–37.

Berry, D. B. (2000). *The domestic violence sourcebook* (3rd ed.). Los Angeles: Lowell House.

Berven, N., & Driscoll, J. (1981). The effects of past psychiatric disability on employer evaluation of a job applicant. *Journal of Applied Rehabilitation Counseling, 12,* 50–55.

Bhatt, U. (1963). *The physically handicapped in India.* Bombay, India: Popular Book Depot.

Bikenbach, J. E. (1993). *Physical disability and social policy.* Toronto, ON: University of Toronto.

Bilheimer, E. (Ed.). (1985, Winter). High technology in rehabilitation. *Arkansas Rehabilitation Services, 2*(1), 1–2.

Biller, E., & White, W. (1989). Comparing special education and vocational rehabilitation in serving persons with specific learning disabilities. *Rehabilitation Counseling Bulletin, 33*(1), 4–17.

Bissonnette, D. (1994). *Beyond traditional job development.* Chatsworth, CA: Milt Wright.

Bissonnette, D. (1999). *30 ways to shine as a new employee: A guide to success in the workplace.* Chatsworth, CA: Milt Wright.

Black, B. (1965). The workshop in a changing world—The three faces of the sheltered workshop. *Rehabilitation Literature, 37,* 168–171.

Black, T. J. (1976). Where do I go from here? The involvement of vocational rehabilitation and occupational education with the learning disabled in North Carolina. *Rehabilitation Literature, 37,* 168–171.

Blackford, K. A., Richardson, H., & Grieve, S. (2000). Prenatal education for mothers with disabilities. *Journal of Advanced Nursing, 32,* 898–904.

Blanchard, J., & Hosek, S. (2003). *Financing health care for women with disabilities.* Santa Monica, CA: RAND.

Blanck, P. D. (2000). The economics of the employment provisions of the Americans with Disabilities Act: Workplace accommodations. In P. D. Blanck (Ed.), *Employment, disability, and the Americans with Disabilities Act* (pp. 201–227). Evanston, IL: Northwestern University Press.

Blanck, P. (2004). Stories about Americans with disabilities and their civil rights. *The Journal of Gender, Race, and Justice, 8,* 1–30.

Blanck, P., Schur, L., Kruse, D., Schwochau, S., & Song, C. (2003). Calibrating the impact of the ADA's employment provisions. *Stanford Law and Policy Review, 14,* 267–290.

Blankenship, C. (2005). Client assistance programs and protection and advocacy services. In W. Crimando & T. F. Riggar (Eds.), *Community resources: A guide for human service workers* (2nd ed., pp. 218–224). Long Grove, IL: Waveland Press.

Bleyer, K. (1992). The Americans with Disabilities Act: Enforcement mechanisms. *Mental & Physical Disability Law Reporter, 16,* 347–350.

Board of Trustees of University of Alabama v. Garrett, 531 U.S. 356, 369 (2001).

Bockhoven, J. S. (1963). *Moral treatment in American psychiatry.* New York: Springer.

Bockhoven, J. S. (1971). The legacy of moral treatment. *American Journal of Occupational Therapy, 25,* 223–224.

Bogden, R., Biklen, D., Shapiro, A., & Spelkoman, D. (1982). The disabled: Media's monster. *Social Policy, 13*(2), 32–35.

Bolton, B. (1982). Assessment of employment potential. In B. Bolton (Ed.), *Vocational adjustment of disabled persons* (pp. 53–70). Baltimore: University Park Press.

Bond, G. R. (1992). Vocational rehabilitation. In R. P. Liberman (Ed.), *Handbook of psychiatric rehabilitation* (pp. 244–275). New York: Macmillan.

Bond, G. R., Dietzen, L. L., McGrew, J. H., & Miller, L. D. (1995). Accelerating entry into supported employment for persons with severe psychiatric disabilities. *Rehabilitation Psychology, 40,* 75–94.

Bonwich, E. (1985). Sex role attitudes and role organization in spinal cord injured women. In M. J. Deegan & N. Brooks (Eds.), *Women with disability: The double handicap* (pp. 56–67). New Brunswick, NJ: Transaction.

Botterbusch, K. (1982). Commercial vocational evaluation systems. In B. Bolton (Ed.), *Vocational adjustment of disabled persons* (pp. 93–126). Baltimore: University Park Press.

Botterbusch, K. F. (1987). *Vocational assessment and evaluation systems: A comparison.* Menomonie: University of Wisconsin–Stout, Stout Vocational Rehabilitation Institute, Materials Development Center.

Bowe, F. (1978). *Handicapping America: Barriers to disabled people.* New York: Harper & Row.

Bowe, F. (1980). *Rehabilitating America: Toward independence for disabled and elderly people.* New York: Harper & Row.

Bowe, F. (1985). *Jobs for disabled people* [Pamphlet]. New York: Public Affairs Committee.

Bowe, F. F. (2000). *Physical, sensory, and health disabilities: An introduction.* Upper Saddle River, NJ: Merrill/Prentice Hall.

Bowe, F., Fay, F., & Minch, J. (1980). Consumer involvement in rehabilitation. In E. L. Pan, T. E. Backer, & C. L. Vash (Eds.), *Annual review of rehabilitation.* New York: Springer.

Bowe, F., & Little, N. (1984). Accommodations circa 2000. *American Rehabilitation, 10*(3), 3–4.

Bowers, E. (1930). *Is it safe to work?* New York: Houghton Mifflin.

Braddock, D. L., & Parish, S. (2001). An institutional history of disability. In G. Albrecht, K. D. Seelman, & M. Bury (Eds.), *Handbook of disability studies* (pp. 11–68). Thousand Oaks, CA: Sage.

Bradshaw, B., & Straker, M. (1974). A special unit to encourage giving up patienthood. *Hospital and Community Psychiatry, 25,* 164–165.

Brainard, B. (1954). Increasing job potentials for the mentally retarded. *Journal of Rehabilitation, 20*(2), 4–6, 23.

Brammell, H., McDaniel, J., Roberson, D., Darnell, R., & Niccoli, S. (1979). *Cardiac rehabilitation.* Denver, CO: Webb-Waring Lung Institute.

Brandt, E., & Pope, A. (1997). *Enabling America: Assessing the role of rehabilitation science and engineering.* Washington, DC: National Academy Press.

Branson, R. (1973). The secularization of American medicine. *Hastings Center Studies, 1*(2), 17–18.

Branson, W. G. (1979). *Macroeconomic theory and policy* (2nd ed.). New York: Harper & Row.

Braun, B. M. (2003). A comprehensive life care planning approach for families of individuals with disabilities. *International Association of Rehabilitation Professionals Journal (The Rehabilitation Professional), 11,* 37–39.

Brennan, J. (1968). Standard pay to token pay for rehabilitation of mental patients. *Journal of Rehabilitation, 34*(2), 26–28.

Brickley, M., & Campbell, D. (1981). Fast food employment for moderately and mildly retarded adults: The McDonald's project. *Mental Retardation, 19,* 113–116.

Brislin, R. W. (1990). *Applied cross-cultural psychology*. Newbury Park, CA: Sage.

Brodwin, M. G., & Brodwin, S. K. (2002). Rehabilitation: A case study approach. In M. G. Brodwin, F. A. Tellez, & S. K. Brodwin (Eds.), *Medical, psychosocial, and vocational aspects of disability* (2nd ed., pp. 1–13). Athens, GA: Elliott & Fitzpatrick.

Brodwin, M. G., Brodwin, S. K., & Liebman, R. (1992). Job analysis procedures in rehabilitation counseling. In L. Vandecreek, S. Knapp, & T. L. Jackson (Eds.), *Innovations in clinical practice: A source book* (Vol. 11, pp. 363–386). Sarasota, FL: Professional Resource Press.

Brodwin, M. G., & Mas, L. O. (1999). The rehabilitation counselor as life care planner. *Journal of Forensic Vocational Assessment, 2,* 16–21.

Brodwin, M. G., Parker, R. M., & DeLaGarza, D. (2003). Disability and accommodation. In E. M. Szymanski & R. M. Parker (Eds.), *Work and disability: Issues and strategies in career development and job placement* (2nd ed., pp. 201–246). Austin, TX: PRO-ED.

Brodwin, M. G., Star, T., & Cardoso, E. (2003). Users of assistive technology: The human component. *Journal of Applied Rehabilitation Counseling, 34*(4), 23–29.

Brodwin, M. G., Star, T., & Cardoso, E. (2004). Computer assistive technology for people who have disabilities: Computer adaptations and modifications. *Journal of Rehabilitation, 70*(3), 28–33.

Brolin, D. (1973). The facility you choose. *Journal of Rehabilitation, 39*(1), 25–26.

Brolin, D. (1982). *Vocational preparation of persons with handicaps*. Columbus, OH: Merrill.

Brolin, D. (2005a). *Competency units for daily living skills*. Reston, VA: Council for Exceptional Children.

Brolin, D. (2005b). *Competency units for personal/social skills*. Reston, VA: Council for Exceptional Children.

Brolin, D., Durand, R., Kromer, K., & Muller, P. (1975). Post-school adjustment of educable retarded students. *Education and Training of the Mentally Retarded, 10,* 144–148.

Brolin, D., & Roessler, R. (1992). *Life centered career education*. Reston, VA: Council for Exceptional Children.

Bromoge, N. (1999). Employing the disabled: It could be you. *Management Accounting: Magazine for Chartered Management Accountants, 77*(8), 69.

Brostrand, H. (2005). Home based rehabilitation. In W. Crimando & T. F. Riggar (Eds.), *Community resources: A guide for human service workers* (2nd ed., pp. 29–39). Long Grove, IL: Waveland Press.

Brown v. Board of Education, 347 U.S. 483 (1954).

Brown, C. (1989). Research focusing on freedom of choice, communication, and independence using eyegaze and speech recognition assistive tech. In A. Vanviervliet & P. Perette (Eds.), *Proceedings of the first South Central Technical Access Conference* (pp. 27–34). Little Rock: University of Arkansas–University Affiliated Program.

Brown, C. D., McDaniel, R. S., Couch, R. H., & McClanahan, M. (1994). *Vocational evaluation systems and software: A consumer's guide*. Menomonie: University of Wisconsin–Stout, Stout Vocational Rehabilitation Institute, Materials Development Center.

Brown, D. (1979). *Learning disabled adults face the world of work*. Proceedings from the President's Committee on Employment of the Handicapped. Washington, DC: National Institute of Education. (ERIC Document Reproduction Service No. ED185744)

Brown, D. (1980). *Steps to independence for people with learning disabilities*. Washington, DC: Parents' Campaign for Children and Youth.

Brown, D. (1984). Employment considerations for learning disabled adults. *Journal of Rehabilitation, 50*(2), 74–77.

Brown, J. (1970). Mental patients work back into society. *Manpower, 2*(2), 20–25.

Brown, S. E., & Johnson, K. L. (1994). Recent federal legislation and the role of vocational rehabilitation in the transition from school to community. *Rehabilitation Education, 8,* 67–78.

Browning, P., & Irvin, L. (1981). Vocational evaluation, training, and placement of mentally retarded persons. *Rehabilitation Counseling Bulletin, 24,* 374–409.

Brubaker, D., & Wright, T. (Eds.). (1979). *News report of the National Rehabilitation Counselor Association and the American Rehabilitation Counselor Association, 20*(8), 1–6.

Bruyére, S. M. (2000). Civil rights and employment issues of disability policy. *Journal of Disability Studies, 11*(1), 18–28.

Bruyére, S. M., & Brown, J. A. (2003). Legislation affecting employment for persons with disabilities. In E. M. Szymanski & R. M. Parker (Eds.), *Work and disability: Issues and strategies in career development and job placement* (2nd ed., pp. 39–78). Austin, TX: PRO-ED.

Buchanan, A. (1990). Justice as reciprocity versus subject-centered justice. *Philosophy & Public Affairs, 19,* 227–252.

Bulmash, K. J. (1982). The irony of the insanity defense: A theory of relativity. *The Journal of Psychiatry and Law, 10,* 285–308.

Bureau of Law and Business. (1982). *How to analyze jobs: A step-by-step approach.* Stamford, CT: Author.

Burgdorf, R. L. (1991). Equal access to public accommodations. In J. West (Ed.), *The Americans with Disabilities Act: From policy to practice* (pp. 183–213). New York: Milbank Memorial Fund.

Burk, R. (1975a) Medical characteristics of importance in determining severe disability. In K. Mallik, S. Yuspeh, & J. Mueller (Eds.), *Comprehensive vocational rehabilitation for severely disabled persons* (pp. 19–25). Washington, DC: George Washington University Medical Center Job Development Laboratory.

Burk, R. (1975b). Occupational therapy. In R. Hardy & J. Cull (Eds.), *Services of the rehabilitation facility* (pp. 107–125). Springfield, IL: Thomas.

Burkhead, J. (1992). Computer applications in rehabilitation. In R. Parker & E. Szymanski (Eds.), *Rehabilitation counseling: Basics and beyond* (2nd ed., pp. 365–400). Austin, TX: PRO-ED.

Burling, K., Tarvydis, V., & Maki, D. (1994). Human sexuality and disability: A holistic interpretation for rehabilitation counseling. *Journal of Applied Rehabilitation Counseling, 25*(1), 10–17.

Burns, B. J., & Santos, A. B. (1995). Assertive community treatment: An update of randomized trials. *Journal of Psychiatric Services, 46,* 669–675.

Burns, E., & Ralph, P. (1958). *World civilization* (2nd ed.). New York: Norton.

Bury, M. R. (1979). Disablement in society: Towards an integrated perspective. *International Journal of Rehabilitation Research, 2*(1), 33–40.

Busse, D. (1973). Vocational rehabilitation: Success or failure. *Journal of Rehabilitation, 39*(4), 11–13.

Butcher, J. N., Dahlstrom, W. G., Graham, J. R., Tellegen, A., & Kaemmer, B. (1989). *Manual for administration and scoring: Minnesota Multiphasic Personality Inventory–Second Edition (MMPI–2).* Minneapolis: University of Minnesota Press.

Butler, S. E., Crudden, A., Sansing, W. K., & LeJeune, B. J. (2002). Employment barriers: Access to assistive technology and research needs. *Journal of Visual Impairment & Blindness, 96,* 663–667.

Buzzanell, P. M. (2003). A feminist standpoint analysis of maternity and maternity leave for women with disabilities. *Women & Language, 26,* 53–65.

Byrd, E. K., Byrd, P. D., & Emener, W. G. (1977). Student counselor and employer preparations of employability of severely retarded. *Rehabilitation Literature, 38,* 42–44.

Campbell, J. (1994). Unintended consequences in public policy: Persons with psychiatric disabilities and the Americans with Disabilities Act. *Policy Studies Journal, 22*(1), 133–145.

Campbell, J., & O'Toole, R. (1971). A situational approach. *Journal of Rehabilitation, 37*(4), 11–13.

Campbell, N. (1971). Techniques of behavior modification. *Journal of Rehabilitation, 37*(4), 28–31.

Camus, A. (1960). *Resistance, rebellion, and death.* New York: Vintage.

Canon v. Clark. (1995). *Americans with disability cases: Vol. 4.* Washington, DC: The Bureau of National Affairs.

Capella, M. E. (2002). Inequalities in the VR system: Do they still exist? *Rehabilitation Counseling Bulletin, 45,* 143–153.

Caplan, N., & Nelson, S. (1973). On being useful: The nature and consequences of psychological research on social problems. *American Psychologist, 28,* 199–211.

Carson, G. (1973). The income tax and how it grew. *American Heritage, 25*(1), 4–9, 79–88.

Carter, S., & Patry, D. (1990). Universal design and office accommodations. In R. Greenwood (Ed.), *Applying technology in the work environment* (pp. 18–25). Fayetteville: Arkansas Research and Training Center in Vocational Research.

Cartwright, B. Y. (2001). Multicultural counseling training: A survey of CORE-accredited programs. *Rehabilitation Education, 15,* 233–242.

Carty, E. M. (1998). Disability and childbirth: Meeting the challenges. *Canadian Medical Association Journal, 159,* 363–369.

Caston, H., & Watson, A. (1990). Vocational assessment and rehabilitation outcomes. *Rehabilitation Counseling Bulletin, 34*(1), 61–66.

Castorena v. Runyon, WL 240762 (D. Kan. 1994).

Cattell, R. B., Cattell, A. K., & Cattell, H. E. (1993). *16 personality factor questionnaire* (5th ed.). Champaign, IL: Institute for Personality and Ability Testing.

Center for Assistive Technology. (n.d.). *Cornucopia of disability information.* Retrieved June 18, 2006, from http:codi.buffalo.edu

Center for Research on Women with Disabilities. (2006a). *Fact sheet #1: Violence against women with disabilities.* Retrieved December 23, 2006, from http://www.bcm.edu/crowd/?pmid=1409

Center for Research on Women with Disabilities. (2006b). *Psychosocial health—Body image.* Retrieved December 23, 2006, from http://www.bcm.edu/crowd/?pmid=1421

Center for Research on Women with Disabilities. (2006c). *Sexuality and reproductive health—Information.* Retrieved December 23, 2006, from http://www.bcm.edu/crowd/?pmid=1628

Center for Research on Women with Disabilities. (2006d). *Sexuality and reproductive health—Parenting.* Retrieved December 23, 2006, from http://www.bcm.edu/crowd/?pmid=1447

Center for Research on Women with Disabilities. (2006e). *Violence against women with disabilities—Guidelines for professionals, service providers.* Retrieved December 23, 2006, from http://www.bcm.edu/crowd/?pmid=1465

Centers for Disease Control and Prevention. (n.d.-a). *Women with disabilities: Access to health.* Retrieved December 23, 2006, from http://www.cdc.gov/ncbddd/women/access.htm

Centers for Disease Control and Prevention. (n.d.-b). *Women with disabilities: Breast cancer screening.* Retrieved December 23, 2006, from http://www.cdc.gov/ncbddd/women/cancer.htm

Centers for Disease Control and Prevention. (n.d.-c). *Women with disabilities: Health and wellness for women with disabilities.* Retrieved December 23, 2006, from http://www.cdc.gov/ncbddd/women/default.htm

Centers for Disease Control and Prevention. (n.d.-d). *Women with disabilities: Physical activity for women with disabilities.* Retrieved December 23, 2006, from http://www.cdc.gov/ncbddd/women/physical.htm

Chan, F., Leahy, M., Saunders, J., Tarvydas,V., Ferrin, J., & Lee, G. (2003). Training needs of certified rehabilitation counselors for contemporary practice. *Rehabilitation Counseling Bulletin, 46,* 82–91.

Chan, F., McMahon, B. T., Cheing, G., Rosenthal, D. A., & Bezyak, J. (2005). Drivers of workplace discrimination against people with disabilities: Physical vs. mental behavioral genesis. *Work: A Journal of Prevention, Disability and Rehabilitation, 25,* 14–22.

Chandler, S., Czerlinsky, T., & Wehman, P. (1963). Provisions of assistive technology. In P. Wehman (Ed.), *The ADA mandate for social change* (pp. 117–133). Baltimore: Brookes.

Chang, J. C., Martin, S. L., Moracco, K. E., Dulli, L., Scandlin, D., Loucks-Sorrel, M. B., et al. (2003). Helping women with disabilities and domestic violence: Strategies, limitations, and challenges of domestic violence programs and services. *Journal of Women's Health, 12,* 699–708.

Chemerinsky, E. (1999). Unfulfilled promise: The Americans with Disabilities Act. *Trial, 35*(9), 88–90.

Chubon, R. (1992). Defining rehabilitation from a systems perspective: Critical implications. *Journal of Applied Rehabilitation Counseling, 23*(1), 27–32.

Church, G., & Glennen, S. (1992). *The handbook of assistive technology.* San Diego, CA: Singular.

Ciardiello, J., & Bingham, W. (1982). The career maturity of schizophrenic clients. *Rehabilitation Counseling Bulletin, 26,* 3–9.

CIL Berkeley. (n.d.). Home page. Retrieved June 17, 2005, from http://www.cilberkeley.org

Civil Rights Act of 1964, 42 U.S.C. § 2000 *et seq.*

Cohen, C. (1983). "Quality of life" and analogy with the Nazis. *The Journal of Medicine and Philosophy, 8,* 113–135.

Cohen, D., & Shields, D. (2005, March 14–19). *Presidential initiatives: Using technology to increase employment of people with disabilities.* Paper presented at the Technology and Persons with Disabilities Conference, California State University, Northridge, CA.

Cohen, R. J., Swerdlik, M. E., & Phillips, S. M. (1996). *Psychological testing and assessment* (3rd ed.). Mountain View, CA: Mayfield.

Coil, J. H., & Shapiro, L. J. (1996). The ADA at three years: A statute in flux. *Employee Relations Law Journal, 21*(4), 5–38.

Cole, J. (1979). What's new about independent living. *Archives of Physical Medicine and Rehabilitation, 60,* 458–462.

Cole, J., Sperry, J., Board, M., & Frieden, L. (1979). *New options.* Houston, TX: The Institute for Rehabilitation and Research.

Coleman, J. C. (1964). *Abnormal psychology and modern life* (3rd ed.). Chicago: Scott Foresman.

Colker, R. (2005). *The disability pendulum.* New York: New York University Press.

Collings v. Longview Fibre Co., 63F3d 828 (9th Cir. 1995).

Commager, H. S. (1950). *The American mind.* New Haven, CT: Yale University Press.

Condon, C., Enein-Donovan, L., Gilmore, M., & Jordan, M. (2004). When existing jobs don't fit: A guide to job creation. *The Institute Brief, 17*(2), 1–6.

Conley, R. (1969). Benefit–cost analysis of the Vocational Rehabilitation Program. *Journal of Human Resources, 4,* 226–252.

Connine, T. (1984). Sexual rehabilitation: The roles of allied health professionals. In D. Krueger (Ed.), *Rehabilitation psychology* (pp. 81–87). Rockville, MD: Aspen.

Conte, L. (1983). Vocational development theories and the disabled person: Oversight or deliberate omission? *Rehabilitation Counseling Bulletin, 26,* 316–328.

Cook, A., Leins, D., & Woodall, H. (1985). Use of microcomputers by disabled persons: A rehabilitation engineering perspective. *Rehabilitation Counseling Bulletin, 28,* 283–292.

Cook, A. M., & Hussey, S. M. (2002). *Assistive technologies: Principles and practice* (2nd ed.). St. Louis, MO: Mosby.

Cook, D. (1998). Psychosocial impact of disability. In R. Parker & E. Szymanski (Eds.), *Rehabilitation counseling: Basics and beyond* (3rd ed., pp. 303–326). Austin, TX: PRO-ED.

Cook, J., & Razzano, L. (2000). Vocational rehabilitation for persons with schizophrenia: Recent research and implications for practice. *Schizophrenia Bulletin, 26*(1), 87–103.

Cook, J. A. (2003). Depression, disability, and rehabilitation services for women. *Psychology of Women Quarterly, 27,* 121–129.

Cook, T. M. (1991). The Americans with Disabilities Act: The move to integration. *Temple Law Review, 64,* 393–469.

Cooper, R. (1998). Incorporating human needs into assistive technology design. In D. Gray, L. Quatrano, & M. Lieberman (Eds.), *Designing and using assistive technology* (pp. 151–170). Baltimore: Brookes.

Corcoran, P., Fay, F., Bartelo, E., & McHaugh, R. (1977). *The BCIL report.* Boston: Boston Center for Independent Living.

Corrigan, P., Reedy, P., Thadani, D., & Ganet, M. (1995). Correlates of participation and completion in a Job Club for clients with psychiatric disability. *Rehabilitation Counseling Bulletin, 39,* 42–53.

Costello, J., & Corthell, D. (1991). Assessment for community-based employment. In Vocational Evaluation and Work Adjustment Association (Ed.), *Fifth national forum on issues in vocational assessment* (pp. 79–84). Menomonie: University of Wisconsin–Stout, Materials Development Center.

Coudrouglou, A. (1990). Professional ideology: A response to a critique. *Rehabilitation Psychology, 29,* 205–210.

Coulter, P. (1974). The role of the nurse in the prevention of illness and in health teaching. In V. Christopherson, P. Coulter, & M. Wolaninn (Eds.), *Rehabilitation nursing: Perspectives and applications* (pp. 99–113). New York: McGraw-Hill.

Council on Rehabilitation Education. (2004). *Accreditation manual for rehabilitation counselor education programs.* Rolling Meadows, IL: Author.

Covey, S. (1989). *The 7 habits of highly effective people.* New York: Simon & Schuster.

Covey, S. (2004). *The eighth habit: From effectiveness to greatness.* New York: Free Press.

Cox, S. (1977). The learning disabled adult. *Academic Therapy, 13,* 79–86.

Crewe, N., & Athelstan, G. (1984). *Functional assessment inventory manual.* Menomonie: University of Wisconsin–Stout, Materials Development Center.

Crimando, W., & Bordieri, J. (1991). Do computers make it better? Effects of sources on students' perceptions of vocational evaluation report quality. *Rehabilitation Counseling Bulletin, 34,* 332–343.

Crimando, W., & Riggar, T. (1996). *Utilizing community resources.* Delray Beach, FL: St. Lucie Press.

Cronbach, L. J. (1982). *Designing evaluations of educational and social programs.* San Francisco: Jossey-Bass.

Cronin, M., Patton, J., & Lock, R. (1997). Transition planning. In T. Harrington (Ed.), *Handbook of career planning for students with special needs* (pp. 319–353). Austin, TX: PRO-ED.

Cronin, M., Patton, J., & Lock, R. (2004). Transition planning. In T. Harrington (Ed.), *Handbook of career planning for students with special needs* (3rd ed., pp. 373–416). Austin, TX: PRO-ED.

Crow, S. H. (1973). The role of evaluation in the rehabilitation process. In R. E. Hardy & J. G. Cull (Eds.), *Vocational evaluation for rehabilitation services* (pp. 29–39). Springfield, IL: Thomas.

Crowther, R. E., Marshall, M., Bond, G. R., & Huxley, P. (2001). Helping people with severe mental illness to obtain work: A systematic review. *British Medical Journal, 332*(7280), 204–208.

Crudden, A., & McBroom, L. W. (1999). Barriers to employment: A survey of employed persons who are visually impaired. *Journal of Visual Impairment & Blindness, 93,* 341–350.

Crystal, R. M., Witten, B. J., & Wingate, J. A. (1982). A diagnostic and rehabilitation model for learning disabled clients. *Journal of Applied Rehabilitation Counseling, 13,* 34–67.

CTB/McGraw-Hill. (1987). *Tests of adult basic education—Examiner's manual.* Monterey, CA: Author.

Cull, J. (1972). Adjustment to disability. In J. Cull & R. Hardy (Eds.), *Vocational rehabilitation: Profession and process.* Springfield, IL: Thomas.

Cull, J., & Levinson, K. (1977). The rights of consumers of rehabilitation services. *Journal of Rehabilitation, 43*(3), 29–32.

Culturally sensitive rehabilitation. (1993). *Rehab Brief, 15*(9).

Currie-Gross, V., & Heimbach, J. (1980). The relationship between independent living skills attainment and client control orientation. *Journal of Rehabilitation, 46,* 20–22.

Cushman, L., & Dijkers, M. (1991). Depressed mood during rehabilitation of persons with spinal cord injury. *Journal of Rehabilitation, 57*(2), 35–38.

Cutler, F., & Ramm, A. (1992). Introduction to the basics of vocational evaluation. In A. Choppa, F. Cutler, J. Siefker, et al. (Eds.), *Vocational evaluation in private sector rehabilitation* (pp. 31–66). Menomonie: University of Wisconsin–Stout, Materials Development Center.

Cutright, P. (1965). Political structure, economic development, and national social security programs. *American Journal of Sociology, 70,* 537–550.

Dain, N. (1964). *Concepts of insanity in the United States, 1789–1865.* New Brunswick, NJ: Rutgers University Press.

Dalgin, R. S. (2001). Impact of Title I of the Americans with Disabilities Act on people with psychiatric disabilities. *Journal of Applied Rehabilitation Counseling, 32*(1), 45–50.

D'Amico, R., & Marder, C. (1991). *The early work experiences of youth with disabilities: Trends in employment rates and job characteristics.* Menlo Park, CA: SRI International.

Danek, M. (1992). The status of women with disabilities revisited. *Journal of Applied Rehabilitation Counseling, 23*(4), 7–13.

Daniels, N. (1981). Health care needs and distributive justice. *Philosophy & Public Affairs, 10,* 146–179.

Dankmeyer, C. (1977). Orthotics and prosthetics. In P. Valletutti & F. Christoplos (Eds.), *Interdisciplinary approaches to human services* (pp. 237–252). Baltimore: University Park Press.

Davies, L. J. (1995). *Enforcing normalcy: Disability, deafness, and the body.* New York: Verso.

Davis, E. L., & Rubin, S. E. (1996). Multicultural instructional goals and strategies for rehabilitation counselor education. *Rehabilitation Education, 10,* 104–114.

Davis, L. (1994). Get your buildings ADA OK: Implementing a compliance plan. *School Business Affairs, 60*(1), 21–25.

Davis, S., Anderson, C., Linkowski, D., Berger, K., & Feinstein, C. (1985). Developmental tasks and transitions of adolescents with chronic illnesses and disabilities. *Rehabilitation Counseling Bulletin, 29*(2), 69–80.

Dawis, R. (2005). The Minnesota theory of work adjustment. In S. Brown & R. Lent (Eds.), *Career development and counseling: Putting theory and research to work* (pp. 3–23). New York: Wiley.

Dawis, R., & Lofquist, L. (1984). *A psychological theory of work adjustment.* Minneapolis: University of Minnesota Press.

Deegan, M. J., & Brooks, N. A. (1985). Introduction. In M. J. Deegan & N. Brooks (Eds.), *Women with disability: The double handicap* (pp. 1–5). New Brunswick, NJ: Transaction.

Degeneffe, C. (2000). Supported employment services for persons with developmental disabilities: Unmet promises and future challenges for rehabilitation counselors. *Journal of Rehabilitation, 51*(2), 41–47.

DeJong, G. (1979a). Independent living: From social movement to analytic paradigm. *Archives of Physical Medicine and Rehabilitation, 60,* 435–446.

DeJong, G. (1979b). *The movement for independent living: Origins, ideology, and implications for disability research.* East Lansing: Michigan State University, University Center for International Rehabilitation.

DeJong, G., & Batavia, A. (1990). The Americans with Disabilities Act and the current state of U.S. disability policy. *Journal of Disability Studies, 1*(3), 65–82.

DeJong, G., & Lifchez, R. (1983). Physical disability and public policy. *Scientific American, 248*(6), 41–49.

DeLoach, C. (1992). Career outcomes for college graduates with severe physical and sensory disabilities. *Journal of Rehabilitation, 58*(1), 57–63.

DeLoach, C. P. (1994). Attitudes toward disability: Impact on sexual development and forging of intimate relationships. *Journal of Applied Rehabilitation Counseling, 25*(1), 18–25.

DeLoach, C., Wilkins, R., & Walker, G. (1983). *Independent living: Philosophy, process, and services.* Baltimore: University Park Press.

Dembo, T. (1968). The prophetic mission of rehabilitation: Curse or blessing? *Journal of Rehabilitation, 34*(1), 34.

Deneen, L. J., & Hessellund, T. A. (1986). *Counseling the able disabled: Rehabilitation consulting in disability compensation systems.* San Francisco: Rehabilitation Publications.

Dennin v. Connecticut Interscholastic Athletic Conference, 913 F. Supp. 633 (D. Conn. 1995).

DeOre, J. (1983, October 14). Reagan handicaps the handicapped. *Chicago Tribune,* Section 1, p. 13.

DePoy, E., & Gilson, S. F. (2004). *Rethinking disability: Principles for professional and social change*. Belmont, CA: Thomson Brooks/Cole.

DePoy, E., Gilson, S. F., & Cramer, E. P. (2003). Understanding the experiences of and advocating for the service and resource needs of abused, disabled women. In A. Hans & A. Patri (Eds.), *Women, disability and identity* (pp. 177–187). Thousand Oaks, CA: Sage.

Deutsch, A. (1948). *The shame of the states*. New York: Harcourt Brace.

Deutsch, A. (1949). *The mentally ill in America* (2nd ed.). New York: Columbia University Press.

Deutsch, P. M. (1994). Life care planning: Into the future. *National Association of Rehabilitation Professionals in the Private Sector Journal, 9,* 79–84.

Devience, A., & Convery, J. (1992). The primer on the new workforce law: The Americans with Disabilities Act. *Journal of Rehabilitation Administration, 16*(2), 40–45.

Devins, G. (1989). Enhancing personal control and minimizing illness intrusiveness. In N. Kutner, D. Cardenas, & J. Bower (Eds.), *Maximizing rehabilitation in chronic renal disease* (pp. 101–135). New York: PMA.

Devins, G., & Shnek, Z. (2000). Multiple sclerosis. In R. Frank & T. Elliot (Eds.), *Handbook of rehabilitation psychology* (pp. 163–184). Washington, DC: American Psychological Association.

DeWitt, J. (1991). Removing barriers through technology. In J. West (Ed.), *The Americans with Disabilities Act: From policy to practice* (pp. 313–332). New York: Milbank Memorial Fund.

Dexter, L. (1964). *The tyranny of schooling*. New York: Basic Books.

Diamond, M. (1974). Sexuality and the handicapped. *Rehabilitation Literature, 35,* 34–40.

Dickerson, L. R., Smith, P. B., & Moore, J. E. (1997). An overview of blindness and visual impairment. In J. E. Moore, W. H. Graves, & J. B. Patterson (Eds.), *Foundations of rehabilitation counseling with persons who are blind or visually impaired* (pp. 3–23). New York: American Foundation for the Blind.

Dickinson, G. L. (1961). *Greek view of life*. New York: Collier Books.

Dillingham, J. (Ed.). (1996). *Use of technology to aid clients in employment*. Unpublished manuscript, Arkansas Research and Training Center, Hot Springs.

Dispenza, M. L. (2002). Overcoming a new digital divide: Technology accommodations and the undue hardship defense under the Americans with Disabilities Act. *Syracuse Law Review, 52,* 159–181.

Dixon, G. L., & Enders, A. (1984). *Low cost approaches to technology and disability*. Washington, DC: National Rehabilitation Information Center, National Council on Rehabilitation Education DATA Institute, Catholic University of America.

Dodd, J., Nelson, J., Ostwald, S., & Fischer, J. (1991). Rehabilitation counselor education programs' response to cultural pluralism. *Journal of Applied Rehabilitation Counseling, 22*(1), 46–48.

Dole, R. (2004, April 9). The benefits of vocational rehabilitation. *Washington Times,* p. 16.

Domino, G., & Domino, M. L. (2006). *Psychological testing: An introduction*. New York: Cambridge University Press.

Donnell, C., Lustig, D., & Strauser, D. (2004). The working alliance: Rehabilitation outcomes for people with severe mental illness. *Journal of Rehabilitation, 70*(2), 12–18.

Donnell, C. M., Reyes, S. S., Cogdal, P., & Porter, D. F. (2004). Examining rehabilitation counselor preparedness as vocational experts. *Journal of Forensic Vocational Analyses, 7,* 35–44.

Doren, B., & Benz, M. R. (1998). Employment inequality revisited: Predictors of better employment outcomes for young women with disabilities in transition. *The Journal of Special Education, 31,* 425–442.

Drehmer, D. E., & Bordieri, J. E. (1985). Hiring decisions for disabled workers: The hidden bias. *Rehabilitation Psychology, 30,* 157–164.

Drew, C., Logan, D., & Hardman, M. (1992). *Mental retardation: A life cycle approach* (5th ed.). New York: Macmillan.

Drey, E. A., & Darney, P. D. (2004). Contraceptive choices for women with disabilities. In S. L. Welner & F. Haseltine (Eds.), *Welner's guide to the care of women with disabilities* (pp. 109–130). Philadelphia: Lippincott Williams & Wilkins.

Droege, R. C. (1987). The USES testing program. In B. Bolton (Ed.), *Handbook on measurement and evaluation in rehabilitation* (2nd ed., pp. 169–182). Baltimore: Brookes.

Dugger, R. (1983). *On Reagan: The man and his presidency.* New York: McGraw-Hill.

Dumper, C., & Connine, T. (1985). High technology games for disabled children and adults. *Journal of Rehabilitation, 51,* 72–73.

Dunn, D. (1974). *Placement services in the vocational rehabilitation program.* Menomonie: University of Wisconsin–Stout.

Dunn, D. (1976). *Using competitive norms and industrial standards with work samples* (Interface No. 9). Menomonie: University of Wisconsin–Stout, Vocational Rehabilitation Institute.

Dunn, D. (1981). Current placement trends. In E. Pan, T. Backer, & C. Vash (Eds.), *Annual review of rehabilitation* (pp. 113–146). New York: Springer.

Dunn, L. M. (1961). A historical review of the treatment of the retarded. In J. Rothstein (Ed.), *Mental retardation* (pp. 13–17). New York: Holt, Rinehart & Winston.

DuPont Corp. (1990). *Equal to the task II.* Wilmington, DE: Author.

Durbin, D. (1997). Workplace injuries and the role of insurance: Claims costs, outcomes, and incentives. *Clinical Orthopaedics & Related Research, 336,* 18–32.

Dye, T. R. (1978). *Understanding public policy* (3rd ed.). Englewood Cliffs, NJ: Prentice Hall.

Dziekan, K., & Okocha, A. (1993). Accessibility of rehabilitation services: Comparison by racial–ethnic status. *Rehabilitation Counseling Bulletin, 36,* 183–189.

Eazell, D. E., & Johnston, M. V. (1981). *The cost benefits of stroke rehabilitation.* Washington, DC: National Association of Rehabilitation Facilities.

Echazabal v. Chevron USA. Inc., 226 F.3d 1063, 1066–67 (9th Cir. 2000), cert. granted, 70 U.S.L.W. 3314 (U.S. 2001) (No. 00-1406).

Edgar, C. (1975). *Creation of a barrier-free society.* Unpublished manuscript, University of Arkansas at Fayetteville.

Edmonds, C. D. (2002). Snakes and ladders: Expanding the definition of "major life activity" in the Americans with Disabilities Act. *Texas Tech Law Review, 33,* 321–376.

Education for All Handicapped Children Act of 1975, 20 U.S.C. § 1400 *et seq.*

Eisenman, L. (2003). Theories in practice: School-to-work transitions for youth with mild disabilities. *Exceptionality, 11*(2), 89–102.

Eleventh Institute on Rehabilitation Issues. (1984). *Continuum of services: School to work.* Menomonie: University of Wisconsin–Stout, Research and Training Center.

Ellis, R., & Sewell, J. (1984). Sensible products. *Disabled USA, 2,* 32–35.

Ellner, J. R., & Bender, H. E. (1980). *Hiring the handicapped: An AMA research study.* New York: AMACOM.

Emener, W. G., & Rubin, S. E. (1980). Rehabilitation counselor roles and functions and sources of role strain. *Journal of Applied Rehabilitation Counseling, 11,* 57–69.

Erlanger, H. S., & Roth, W. (1985). Disability policy: The parts and the whole. *American Behavioral Scientist, 28,* 319–346.

Esser, T., & Scheinkmann, N. (1975). Improving client participation in vocational rehabilitation planning through audio-visual orientation. *Journal of Applied Rehabilitation Counseling, 6,* 88–95.

Fabian, E., & Coppola, J. (2001). Vocational rehabilitation competencies in psychiatric rehabilitation education. *Rehabilitation Education, 15,* 133–142.

Fabian, E., & Luecking, R. (1991). Doing it the company way: Using internal company supports in the workplace. *Journal of Applied Rehabilitation Counseling, 22,* 32–35.

Fabian, E., Luecking, R., & Tilson, G. (1995). Employer and rehabilitation personnel perspectives on hiring persons with disabilities: Implications for job development. *Journal of Rehabilitation, 61*(1), 42–49.

Fabian, E., Waterworth, A., & Ripke, B. (1993). Reasonable accommodations for workers with serious mental illness: Type, frequency, and associated outcomes. *Psychosocial Rehabilitation Journal, 14,* 164–172.

Fafard, M. B., & Haubrich, P. A. (1981). Vocational and social adjustment of learning disabled young adults: A follow-up survey. *Learning Disability Quarterly, 4,* 122–130.

Fagen, T., & Wallace, A. (1979). Who are the handicapped? *Personnel and Guidance Journal, 58,* 215–220.

Faiver, C., Eisengart, S., & Colonna, R. (2004). *The counselor intern's handbook.* Belmont, CA: Brooks Cole.

Falvo, D. (2005). *Medical and psychosocial aspects of chronic illness and disability* (3rd ed.). Sudberry, MA: Jones & Bartlett.

Falvo, D. R., Allen, H., & Maki, D. R. (1982). Psychosocial aspects of invisible disability. *Rehabilitation Literature, 43,* 2–6.

Farley, R., Bolton, B., & Parkerson, S. (1992). Effects of client involvement in assessment on vocational development. *Rehabilitation Counseling Bulletin, 35,* 146–153.

Farley, R., & Hinman, S. (1987). Enhancing the potential for employment of persons with disabilities: A comparison of two interventions. *Rehabilitation Counseling Bulletin, 31*(1), 4–16.

Farr, J. M., & Ludden, L. (2003). *Enhanced occupational outlook handbook.* Indianapolis, IN: JIST.

Farr, J. M., Ludden, L., & Shatkin, L. (2001). *The guide for occupational exploration* (3rd ed.). Indianapolis, IN: JIST.

Farr, J. M., & Shatkin, L. (2004). *The O*Net dictionary of occupational titles.* Indianapolis, IN: JIST.

Farrow, J. (1990). Sexuality counseling with clients who have spinal cord injuries. *Rehabilitation Counseling Bulletin, 33,* 251–258.

Faulkner, H. U. (1931). The quest for social justice, 1898–1914. In A. M. Schlesinger & D. Fox (Eds.), *A history of American life* (Vol. 11). New York: Macmillan.

Fearday, F. L., & Cape, A. L. (2004). A voice for traumatized women: Inclusion and mutual support. *Psychiatric Rehabilitation Journal, 27,* 258–265.

Federal Employees Health Benefits Program. (2003). *FEHB Guide: Individuals receiving compensation from the Office of Workers' Compensation* (OWCP). Washington, DC: U.S. Office of Personnel Management, Retirement, and Insurance Service.

Federal Register, Vol. 39, No. 128 (1974).

Federal Register, Vol. 40, No. 245 (1975).

Federal Register, Vol. 41, p. 18234 (1976).

Federal Register, Vol. 46, p. 37492 (1981).

Federal Register, Vol. 48, p. 40684 (1983).

Federal Register, Vol. 51, p. 18994 (1986).

Feist-Price, S., & Khanna, N. (2003). Employment inequality for women with disabilities. *Women and Disability, 33,* 10–12.

Fekete, D. M., Bond, G. R. McDonel. E. C., Salyers, M., Chen, A., & Miller, L. (1998). Rural assertive community treatment: A field experiment. *Psychiatric Rehabilitation Journal, 21,* 371–379.

Feldblum, C. (1991). Employment protections. In J. West (Ed.), *The Americans with Disabilities Act: From policy to practice* (pp. 81–110). New York: Milbank Memorial Fund.

Felts, J. (1976). Nursing aspects of the program. In W. Jenkins, R. Anderson, & W. Dietrich (Eds.), *Rehabilitation of the severely disabled* (pp. 187–190). Dubuque, IA: Kendall/Hunt.

Fenderson, D. A. (1984). Opportunities for psychologists in disability research. *American Psychologist, 39,* 524–528.

Fielder, J. F. (1994). *Mental disabilities and the Americans with Disabilities Act.* Westport, CT: Quorum Books.

Fielding, G. J. (1982). Transportation for the handicapped: The politics of full accessibility. *Transportation Quarterly, 36,* 269–282.

Fields, C. (1977). Califano signs guidelines on handicapped: Cost of compliance worries college. *The Chronicle of Higher Education, 11*(11), 12–13.

Filkins, L. D., Clark, C. D., Rosenblatt, C. A., Carlson, W. L., Kerlan, M. W., & Manson, H. (1970). *Alcohol abuse and traffic safety: A study of fatalities, DWI offenders, alcoholics, and court-related treatment approaches* (Tech. Reps. FH-11-6555 and FH-11-7129). Washington, DC: U.S. Department of Transportation, National Highway Safety Bureau.

Finch, E. (1981). Job hunting. *Disabled USA, 4*(9–10), 7.

Fine, M., & Asch, A. (1985). Disabled women: Sexism without the pedestal. In M. J. Deegan & N. Brooks (Eds.), *Women with disability: The double handicap* (pp. 6–22). New Brunswick, NJ: Transaction.

Fine, M., & Asch, A. (1988). Disability beyond stigma: Social interaction, discrimination, and activism. *Journal of Social Issues, 44*(1), 3–21.

Fine, S. (1956). *Laissez faire and the general-welfare state.* Ann Arbor: University of Michigan Press.

Finucci, J. M., Gottfredson, L. S., & Childs, B. (1986). A follow-up study of dyslexic boys. *Annals of Dyslexia, 35,* 117–136.

Fitting, M. D. (1986). Ethical dilemmas in counseling elderly adults. *Journal of Counseling Development, 64,* 325–327.

Flandez, R. (2005, October 6). Reinventing the wheel: The latest in car technology. *Wall Street Journal,* p. D6.

Flannery, W. (1993, April 11). ADA experts vary on business impact of 1st court test. *Chicago Tribune,* pp. 1E, 5E.

Flannigan, J. (1982). Measurement of quality of life: Current state of the art. *Archives of Physical Medicine and Rehabilitation, 63,* 56–59.

Fleischer, D. Z., & Zames, F. (2001). *The disability rights movement: From charity to confrontation.* Philadelphia: Temple University Press.

Flemmings v. Howard University, 198 F.3d 857, 861 (D.C. Cir. 1995).

Flexer, R. W., Bihm, E., Shaw, J., Sigelman, C. K., Raney, B., & Janeson, D. (1982). Training and maintaining work productivity in severely and moderately retarded persons. *Rehabilitation Counseling Bulletin, 26,* 10–17.

Flowers, C., Crimando, W., Forbes, W., & Riggar, T. (2005). A regional survey of rehabilitation cultural diversity within the CILs: A ten-year follow-up. *Journal of Rehabilitation, 71*(2), 14–21.

Flynn, R. J., & Nitsch, K. E. (1980). Normalization: Accomplishments to date and future priorities. In R. J. Flynn & K. E. Nitsch (Eds.), *Normalization, social integration, and community services.* Baltimore: University Park Press.

Fonosch, G. G. (1980). Three years later: The impact of Section 504 regulations on higher education. *Rehabilitation Literature, 41,* 162–168.

Ford, L., & Sweet, E. (1999). Job placement and rehabilitation counselors in the state–federal system. *Rehabilitation Counseling Bulletin, 42,* 354–366.

Foss, G., & Bostwick, D. (1981). Problems of mentally retarded adults: A study of rehabilitation service consumers and providers. *Rehabilitation Counseling Bulletin, 25,* 66–73.

Foss, G., & Peterson, S. L. (1981). Social–interpersonal skills relevant to job tenure for mentally retarded adults. *Mental Retardation, 19,* 103–106.

Foucault, M. (1965). *Madness and civilization: A history of insanity in the age of reason.* London: Tavistock.

Fowler, C., & Wadsworth, J. (1991). Individualism and equality: Critical values in North American culture and the impact on disability. *Journal of Applied Rehabilitation Counseling, 22*(4), 19–23.

Frank, J., & Bellini, J. (2005). Barriers to the accommodation request process of the Americans with Disabilities Act. *Journal of Rehabilitation, 71*(2), 28–39.

Fraser, K. E. (1997). Low vision and low vision devices. In J. E. Moore, W. H. Graves, & J. B. Patterson (Eds.), *Foundations of rehabilitation counseling with persons who are blind or visually impaired* (pp. 80–104). New York: American Foundation for the Blind.

Fraser, R. T., & Clowers, M. R. (1978). Rehabilitation counselor functions: Perceptions of time spent and complexity. *Journal of Applied Rehabilitation Counseling, 9,* 31–35.

Freed, E. (1964). Opinions of psychiatric hospital personnel and college students toward alcoholism, mental illness and physical disability. *Psychological Bulletin, 15,* 168–170.

Fried, C. (1983). An analysis of "equality" and "rights" in medical care. In J. Arras & R. Hunt, (Eds.), *Issues in modern medicine* (pp. 1–31). Palo Alto, CA: Mayfield.

Frieden, L. (1983). Understanding alternative program models. In N. Crewe & I. Zola (Eds.), *Independent living for physically disabled people.* San Francisco: Jossey-Bass.

Frieden, L. (2001). International perspectives on the status of people with disabilities. *Rehabilitation Education, 15,* 421–428.

Friedson, E. (1966). Disability as social deviance. In M. B. Sussman (Ed.), *Sociology and rehabilitation* (pp. 71–89). Washington, DC: American Sociological Association.

Friedson, E. (1970). *Profession of medicine.* New York: Dodd, Mead.

Frierson, J. G. (1997). Heads you lose, tails you lose: A disturbing judicial trend in defining disability. *Labor Law Journal, 48,* 419–430.

Fry, R. (1997). *Developing effective partnerships with employers as a service delivery mechanism.* Menomonie: University of Wisconsin–Stout, Institute on Rehabilitation Issues.

Fukuyama, M. A. (1990). Taking a universal approach to multicultural counseling. *Counselor Education and Supervision, 30,* 6–17.

Fulton, S. A., & Sabornie, E. J. (1994). Evidence of employment inequality among females with disabilities. *The Journal of Special Education, 26,* 149–165.

Furnas, J. C. (1969). *The Americans.* New York: Putnam.

Furnham, A., & Pendred, J. (1983). Attitudes toward the mentally and physically disabled. *British Journal of Medical Psychiatry, 56,* 179–187.

Galvin, J., & Langton, A. (1998). *Designing and delivering quality assistive technology services.* Tucson, AZ: CARF, The Rehabilitation Accreditation Commission.

Gardner, K. (1981). The private nonprofit work-oriented rehabilitation facility. In E. Pan, T. Backer, & C. Vash (Eds.), *Annual review of rehabilitation* (Vol. 2, pp. 173–191). New York: Springer.

Garland-Thomson, R. (2002). Integrating disability, transforming feminist theory. *NWSA Journal, 14*(3), 1–32.

Garner, W. E. (1985). *An identification of competencies critical to practicing rehabilitation counselors: Implications of validating the rehabilitation counselor certification examination.* Unpublished doctoral dissertation, Southern Illinois University, Carbondale.

Garrett, J. F. (1969). Historical background. In D. Malikin & H. Rusalem (Eds.), *Vocational rehabilitation of the disabled* (pp. 29–38). New York: New York University Press.

Garske, G., & McReynolds, C. (2005). Psychiatric rehabilitation: A means of destigmatizing severe mental illness. *Journal of Applied Rehabilitation Counseling, 36*(4), 28–34.

Gartner, A. (1982). Images of the disabled and disabling images. *Social Policy, 13(2),* 15.

Gatens-Robinson, E. (1992). Beneficence and the habilitation of people with disabilities. *Contemporary Philosophy, 14*(2), 8–11.

Gearheart, B., Mullen, R. C., & Gearheart, C. (1993). *Exceptional individuals: An introduction.* Belmont, CA: Brooks/Cole.

Geib, B. B., Guzzardi, L. R., & Genova, P. M. (1981). Intervention for adults with learning disabilities. *Academic Therapy, 16,* 317–325.

Geis, H. J. (1972). The problem of personal worth in the physically disabled patient. *Rehabilitation Literature, 33,* 34–39.

Gelfand, B. (1966). The concept of reality as used in work evaluation and work adjustment. *Journal of Rehabilitation, 32*(6), 26–28.

Gellman, W. (1959). Roots of prejudice against the handicapped. *Journal of Rehabilitation, 25,* 4–6.

Genskow, J. K. (1973). Evaluation: A multi-purpose proposition. *Journal of Rehabilitation, 39*(3), 22–25.

Georgia Institute of Technology. (1999, July). *Information on disabilities.* Atlanta, GA: Author. Retrieved July 8, 1999, from http://www.gatech.edu

Gerber, P. J., & Kelley, R. H. (1984). Learning disabilities and social skill development: Research-based implications for the developmental life span. In W. Cruickshank & J. Kliebhan (Eds.), *Early adolescence to early adulthood* (pp. 69–77). Syracuse, NY: Syracuse University Press.

Getzel, E. E., & Gugerty, J. J. (2001). Applications for youth with learning disabilities. In P. Wehman (Ed.), *Life beyond the classroom* (pp. 371–398). Baltimore: Brookes.

Gibbs, W. (1990). Alternative measures to evaluate the impact of vocational rehabilitation services. *Rehabilitation Counseling Bulletin, 34*(1), 33–43.

Gibson, B. B., & Huss, D. S. (1995). Mobility: Getting to where you want to go. In K. Flipper, K. Inge, & J. M. Barcus (Eds.), *Assistive technology* (pp. 87–103). Baltimore: Brookes.

Gice, J. (1985). In search of ... "The perfect vocational evaluation." *Vocational Evaluation and Work Adjustment Bulletin, 18*(1), 4–7.

Gilbert, J. S. (2001). Prior history, present discrimination, and the ADA's "Record of" disability. *The University of Memphis Law Review, 31,* 659–676.

Gilbride, D., & Hagner, D. (2005). People with disabilities in the workplace. In R. M. Parker, E. M. Szymanski, & J. B. Patterson (Eds.), *Rehabilitation counseling: Basics and beyond* (4th ed., pp. 363–393). Austin, TX: PRO-ED.

Gilbride, D., & Stensrud, R. (1992). Demand-side job development: A model for the 1990s. *Journal of Rehabilitation, 58,* 34–39.

Gilbride, D., & Stensrud, R. (2003). Job placement and employer consulting: Services and strategies. In E. Szymanski & R. Parker (Eds.), *Work and disability* (2nd ed., pp. 407–440). Austin, TX: PRO-ED.

Gilbride, D., Thomas, J. R., & Stensrud, R. (1998). Beyond status 26: Development of an instrument to measure quality of placements in the state–federal program. *Journal of Applied Rehabilitation Counseling, 29*(1), 3–7.

Glasser, W. (1981). *Stations of the mind.* New York: Harper & Row.

Gliedman, J., & Roth, W. (1980). *The unexpected minority.* New York: Harcourt, Brace, Jovanovich.

Glueckauf, R., & Quittner, A. (1992). Assertiveness training for disabled adults in wheelchairs: Self-report, role-play, and activity pattern outcomes. *Journal of Consulting and Clinical Psychology, 60,* 419–425.

Goffman, E. (1961). *Asylums: Essays on the social situation of mental patients and other inmates.* Chicago: Aldine.

Goldberg, R. (1992). Toward a model of vocational development of people with disabilities. *Rehabilitation Counseling Bulletin, 35,* 161–173.

Golden, M., Kilb, L., & Mayerson, A. (1994). *Explanation of the contents of the Americans with Disabilities Act of 1990.* Berkeley, CA: Disability Rights Education and Defense Fund.

Goldenson, R. (1978a). Rehabilitation professions. In R. Goldenson, J. Dunham, & C. Dunham (Eds.), *Disability and rehabilitation handbook.* New York: McGraw-Hill.

Goldenson, R. (1978b). The sheltered workshop. In R. Goldenson, J. Dunham, & C. Dunham (Eds.), *Disability and rehabilitation handbook.* New York: McGraw-Hill.

Goldfine, L. (1977). Physical medicine. In P. Valletutti & F. Christoplos (Eds.), *Interdisciplinary approaches to human services* (pp. 267–278). Baltimore: University Park Press.

Goldston, R. (1968). *The great depression.* New York: Fawcett Premier Books.

Goldstone, D., & Collins, R. (1970). Concepts of vocational rehabilitation. In A. McLean (Ed.), *Mental health and work organizations* (pp. 251–265). Chicago: Rand McNally.

Goodwin, L. (1972). *Do the poor want to work?* Washington, DC: Brookings Institution.

Goodwin, L. (1992). Rehabilitation counselor specialization: The promise and the challenge. *Journal of Applied Rehabilitation Counseling, 23*(2), 5–11.

Goodyear, D. L., & Stude, D. W. (1975). Work performance: A comparison of severely disabled and non-disabled employees. *Journal of Applied Rehabilitation Counseling, 6,* 210–216.

Gordon, G. (1966). *Role theory and illness: A sociological perspective.* New Haven, CT: New Haven College and University Press.

Gordon, W., Bellile, S., Harasymiw, S., Lehman, L., & Sherman, B. (1982). The relationship between pressure sores and psychosocial adjustment in persons with spinal cord injury. *Rehabilitation Psychology, 27,* 185–191.

Gostin, L. O. (1991). Public health powers: The imminence of radical change. In J. West (Ed.), *The Americans with Disabilities Act: From policy to practice* (pp. 268–290). New York: Milbank Memorial Fund.

Gottfredson, G., & Holland, J. (1996). *Dictionary of Holland occupational codes* (3rd ed.). Lutz, FL: Psychological Assessment Resources.

Gottfredson, L. (2005). Applying Gottfredson's theory of circumscription and compromise in career guidance and counseling. In S. Brown & R. Lent (Eds.), *Career development and counseling: Putting theory and research to work* (pp. 71–100). New York: Wiley.

Gough, H. G., & Bradley, P. (1996). *California psychological inventory* (3rd ed.). Palo Alto, CA: CPP.

Gove, W. R. (1970). Societal reaction as an explanation of mental illness: An evaluation. *The American Sociological Review, 35,* 873–884.

Governmental Activities Office. (1993, August–September). Harris poll: Only 29% of people with disabilities know about ADA. *Word from Washington* (United Cerebral Palsy Association), p. 20.

Grady, K. E., & Lemkau, J. P. (1998). Introduction. *Psychology of Women Quarterly, 2,* 379–380.

Graham, L. R. (1981). *Between science and values.* New York: Columbia University Press.

Granger, B. (2000). The role of psychiatric practitioners in assisting people in understanding how best to assert their ADA rights and arrange job accommodations. *Psychiatric Rehabilitation Journal, 23,* 215–223.

Gray, D., & Braddy, B. (1988). Experimental social innovation and client centered job-seeking progress. *American Journal of Community Psychology, 16,* 325–343.

Gray, D., Quatrano, L., & Lieberman, M. (1998). Conclusions: Moving to the next stage of assistive technology development. In D. Gray, L. Quatrano, & M. Lieberman (Eds.), *Designing and using assistive technology* (pp. 299–309). Baltimore: Brookes.

Greenbaum, B., Graham, S., & Scales, W. (1996). Adults with learning disabilities: Occupational and social status after college. *Journal of Learning Disabilities, 29,* 167–173.

Greenburg, J. C. (2002, June 11). High court limits protection of ADA. *Chicago Tribune,* Section 1, p. 4.

Greenhouse, L. (1999, June 23). High court limits disability law. *The News Journal* (Daytona Beach, FL), pp. 1A, 11A.

Greenwood, R., & Johnson, V. (1985). *Employer concerns regarding workers with disabilities.* Fayetteville: University of Arkansas, Rehabilitation Research and Training Center.

Greenwood, R., & Johnson, V. (1987). Employer perspective on workers with disabilities. *Journal of Rehabilitation, 53*(1), 37–44.

Greenwood, R., Schriner, K., & Johnson, V. (1991). Employer concerns regarding workers with disabilities and the business–rehabilitation partnership: The PWI practitioners' perspective. *Journal of Rehabilitation, 57*(1), 21–25.

Greer, D. (1996, July/August). The Hunchback of Notre Dame. *The Independent,* pp. 1, 4, 6. Fresno, CA: Center for Independent Living.

Gregg, C. (1980). Rehabilitation implications of sexual and reproductive problems in diabetes. *Journal of Applied Rehabilitation Counseling, 11,* 76–79.

Gregory, R. J. (1996). *Psychological testing* (2nd ed.). Boston: Allyn & Bacon.

Gregory, R. J., Whitlow, C. B., Levine, M., & Wasmuth, W. (1982). The techniques of work adjustment. *Vocational Evaluation and Work Adjustment Bulletin, 15*(1), 5–10.

Grissom, J., Eldredge, G., & Nelson, R. (1990). Adapting the vocational evaluation process for clients with a substance abuse history. *Journal of Applied Rehabilitation Counseling, 21*(3), 30–32.

Grob, G. N. (1966). *The state and the mentally ill: A history of Worcester State Hospital in Massachusetts, 1830–1920.* Chapel Hill: University of North Carolina Press.

Grob, G. N. (1973). *Mental institutions in America: Social Policy to 1875.* New York: Free Press.

Groce, N. (1992). *The U.S. role in international disability activities: A history and a look towards the future.* Durham, NH: International Exchange of Experts and Information in Rehabilitation.

Groth-Marnat, G. (1984). *Handbook of psychological assessment.* New York: Van Nostrand Reinhold.

Groth-Marnat, G. (1997). *Handbook of psychological assessment* (3rd ed.). New York: Wiley.

Growick, B. (2004). *Reforming the Social Security disability system: A clarion call for action and change*. Presentation to the Social Security Advisory Board Forum on the Social Security Definition of Disability, Washington, DC.

Gulick, E. (1992). Model for predicting work performance among persons with multiple sclerosis. *Nursing Research, 41,* 266–272.

Gwee, A. L. (1969). A study of Chinese medical practice in Singapore. *Singapore Medical Journal, 10,* 2–7.

Gwee, A. L. (1971). Traditional Chinese methods of mental treatment. In N. N. Wagner & E. S. Tan (Eds.), *Psychological problems and treatment in Malaysia*. Kuala Lumpur, Malaysia: University of Malaya Press.

Habeck, R. V., Kress, M., Scully, S., & Kirchner, K. (1994). Determining the significance of the disability management movement for rehabilitation counselor education. *Rehabilitation Education, 8,* 195–240.

Hagner, D., & Dileo, D. (1993). *Working together: Workplace culture, supported employment, and persons with disabilities*. Cambridge, MA: Brookline Books.

Hagner, D., & Murphy, S. (1989). Closing the shop on sheltered work: Case studies of organizational change. *Journal of Rehabilitation, 55*(3), 68–74.

Hahn, H. (1982). Disability and rehabilitation policy: Is paternalistic neglect really benign? *Public Administration Review, 42,* 385–389.

Hahn, H. (1983). Paternalism and public policy. *Society, 20*(3), 36–46.

Hahn, H. (1985a). Changing perception of disability and the future of rehabilitation. In L. G. Perlman & G. F. Austin (Eds.), *Social influences in rehabilitation planning: Blueprint for the 21st century*. A report of the Ninth Mary E. Switzer Memorial Seminar, National Rehabilitation Association, Alexandria, VA.

Hahn, H. (1985b). Disability policy and the problem of discrimination. *American Behavioral Scientist, 28,* 293–318.

Hahn, H. (1987). Civil rights for disabled Americans: The foundation of a political agenda. In A. Gartner & T. Joe (Eds.), *Images of the disabled, disabling images* (pp. 181–203). New York: Praeger.

Hahn, H. (1988a). Can disability be beautiful? *Social Policy, 18*(3), 26–32.

Hahn, H. (1988b). The politics of physical differences: Disability and discrimination. *Journal of Social Issues, 44*(1), 39–47.

Haliker, D. (1983). Allowing the debilitated to die: Facing our ethical choices. *New England Journal of Medicine, 308,* 716–719.

Hall, C., Lindzey, G., Loehlin, J., & Manosevitz, M. (1985). *Introduction to theories of personality*. New York: Wiley.

Hall, C., Sheldon-Wildgen, J., & Sherman, J. (1980). Teaching job interview skills to retarded clients. *Journal of Applied Behavior Analysis, 13,* 433–442.

Haller, M. H. (1963). *Eugenics: Hereditarian attitudes in American thought*. New Brunswick, NJ: Rutgers University Press.

Halpern, A. (1984). Functional assessment and mental retardation. In A. Halpern & M. Fulner (Eds.), *Functional assessment in rehabilitation* (pp. 61–78). Baltimore: Brookes.

Halpern, A. (1985). Transition: A look at the foundations. *Exceptional Children, 51,* 479–486.

Halpern, A., Browning, P., & Brummer, E. (1975). Vocational adjustment of the mentally retarded. In M. J. Begab & S. A. Richardson (Eds.), *The mentally retarded and society* (pp. 365–376). Baltimore: University Park Press.

Hamburger, M., & Hess, H. (1970). Work performance and emotional disorders. In A. McLean (Ed.), *Mental health and work organizations* (pp. 170–195). Chicago: Rand McNally.

Hamilton, K. (1950). *Counseling the handicapped in the rehabilitation process.* New York: Ronald Press.

Hammerman, S., & Maikowski, S. (Eds.). (1981). *The economics of disability: International perspectives.* New York: Rehabilitation International.

Hanley-Maxwell, C., Owens-Johnson, L., & Fabian, E. (2003). Supported employment. In E. M. Szymanski & R. M. Parker (Eds.), *Work and disability: Issues and strategies in career development and job placement* (2nd ed., pp. 373–406). Austin, TX: PRO-ED.

Hanna, W., & Rogovsky, B. (1991). Women with disabilities: Two handicaps plus. *Disability, Handicap, and Society, 6*(1), 49–63.

Harmon, L. W., Hansen, J. C., Borgen, F. H., & Hammer, A. L. (1994). *Strong interest inventory—Applications and technical guide.* Palo Alto, CA: CPP.

Harris, J. (1981). Ethical problems in the management of some severely handicapped children. *Journal of Medical Ethics, 7,* 117–120.

Harris v. H & W Contracting Co., 6 AD Cases 460 (11th Cir. 1996).

Hartlage, L. (1965). Expanding comprehensiveness of psychiatric rehabilitation. *Mental Hygiene, 49,* 238–243.

Hasazi, S., Gordon, L., & Roe, C. (1985). Factors associated with the employment status of handicapped youth exiting high school from 1979–1983. *Exceptional Children, 51,* 455–469.

Hassouneh-Phillips, D., & Curry, M. A. (2002). Abuse of women with disabilities: State of the science. *Rehabilitation Counseling Bulletin, 45,* 96–104.

Havranek, J. E. (1997). *Forensic rehabilitation: A resource for vocational experts.* Athens, GA: Elliott & Fitzpatrick.

Havranek, J. E., & Brodwin, M. G. (1994). Rehabilitation counselor curricula: Time for a change. *Rehabilitation Education, 8,* 369–379.

Havranek, J. E., Field, T., & Grimes, J. W. (2005). *Vocational assessment: Evaluating employment potential* (4th ed.). Athens, GA: Elliott & Fitzpatrick.

Hay, J. R. (1978). *The development of the British welfare state, 1880–1975.* London: Edward Arnold.

Hayward, B., Tashjian, M., & Wehman, P. (1995). Development of assistive technology systems. In K. Flippo, K. Inge, & J. M. Barcus (Eds.), *Assistive technology: A resource for school, work, and community* (pp. 23–40). Baltimore: Brookes.

Head, L., & Baker, P. (2005, March 14–19). *Workplace accommodations and ADA Title I: Policy and the metrics of "reasonable."* Paper presented at the Technology and Persons with Disabilities Conference, California State University, Northridge.

Hearne, P. G. (1990). The Americans with Disabilities Act: A new era. In L. G. Perlman & C. E. Hansen (Eds.), *Employment and disability trends and issues for the 1900s* [Switzer Monograph No. 14]. Alexandria, VA: National Rehabilitation Association.

Heider, F. (1958). *The psychology of interpersonal relations.* New York: Wiley.

Hein, S., Lustig, D., & Uruk, A. (2005). Consumers' recommendations to improve satisfaction with rehabilitation services: A qualitative study. *Rehabilitation Counseling Bulletin, 49,* 29–39.

Hendricks, D. J., & Hirsh, A. (1991). The job accommodations network: A vital resource for the 90's. *Rehabilitation Education, 5,* 261–264.

Herbert, J. T., & Cheatham, H. E. (1988). Afrocentricity and the Black disability experience: A theoretical orientation for rehabilitation counselors. *Journal of Applied Rehabilitation Counseling, 19*(4), 50–54.

Hernandez, B., Keys, C., & Balcazar, F. (2000). Employer attitudes toward workers with disabilities and their ADA employment rights: A literature review. *Journal of Rehabilitation, 66*(4), 4–16.

Hersen, M. (1976). Historical perspectives in behavioral assessment. In M. Hersen & A. Bellack (Eds.), *Behavioral assessment: A practical handbook* (pp. 3–22). New York: Pergamon Press.

Hershenson, D. B. (1974). Vocational guidance and the handicapped. In E. Herr (Ed.), *Vocational guidance and human development* (pp. 478–501). Boston: Houghton Mifflin.

Hershenson, D. (1990). A theoretical model for rehabilitation counseling. *Rehabilitation Counseling Bulletin, 33,* 268–278.

Hershenson, D. (1998). Systemic, ecological model for rehabilitation counseling. *Rehabilitation Counseling Bulletin, 42,* 40–50.

Hershenson, D., & Szymanski, E. (1992). Career development of people with disabilities. In R. Parker & E. Szymanski (Eds.), *Rehabilitation counseling* (2nd ed., pp. 273–304). Austin, TX: PRO-ED.

Heward, W. (2006). *Exceptional children: An introduction to special education* (8th ed.). Upper Saddle River, NJ: Pearson/Merrill/Prentice Hall.

Heward, W., & Orlansky, M. (1992). *Exceptional children: An introductory survey of special education* (4th ed.). New York: Macmillan.

Hickey, H. (1957). The physical therapist. In H. Patterson (Ed.), *The handicapped and their rehabilitation* (pp. 481–504). Springfield, IL: Thomas.

Hill, J., Wehman, P., & Combs, J. (1979). Use of self-administered reinforcement to increase work production behavior. *Vocational Evaluation and Work Adjustment Bulletin, 12*(2), 7–10.

Himler, L. (1958). Motivation of the patient in rehabilitation. *Industrial Medicine and Surgery, 27,* 439–442.

Hindman, D. (1985, August 23). Letter to the editor. *Southern Illinoisan Newspaper,* p. 8.

Hinkebein, J., Koller, J., & Kunce, J. (1992). Normal personality and adults with learning disabilities: Rehabilitation counseling implications. *Journal of Rehabilitation, 58*(4), 40–46.

Hochstedler, E. (1982). The compelled psychiatric examination: Search, seizure, and interrogation. *Journal of Psychiatry and Law, 10,* 265–284.

Hoffman, P. R. (1972). Work evaluation: An overview. In J. G. Cull & R. E. Hardy (Eds.), *Vocational rehabilitation: Profession and process* (pp. 188–211). Springfield, IL: Thomas.

Hofstadter, R. (1948). *American political tradition.* New York: Vintage Books.

Hofstadter, R., Miller, W., & Aaron, D. (1959). *The American republic since 1865: Volume 2.* Englewood Cliffs, NJ: Prentice Hall.

Hohmann, G. (1981). Foreword. In C. Vash (Ed.), *The psychology of disability* (pp. vii–ix). New York: Springer.

Holbrook, S. H. (1957). *Dreamers of the American dream.* Garden City, NY: Doubleday.

Holcomb, R. L. (1938). Alcohol in relation to traffic accidents. *Journal of the American Medical Association, 111,* 1076–1085.

Holden, J., & Klein, H. (1967). Problems in the rehabilitation of chronic schizophrenics. *Rehabilitation Literature, 28,* 345–347.

Holland, J., Powell, A., & Fritzche, B. (1994). *The self-directed search* (Professional user's guide). Odessa, FL: Psychological Assessment Resources.

Honey, S., Meager, N., & Williams, M. (1998). *Employers' attitudes towards people with disabilities.* Grantham, England: Institute for Employment Studies.

Hough J. (1999). Disability and health: A national public health agenda. In R. J. Simeonsson & L. N. McDevitt (Eds.), *Issues in disability and health: The role of secondary conditions and quality of life* (pp. 161–203). Chapel Hill: University of North Carolina Press.

Howie, J., Gatens-Robinson, E., & Rubin, S. E. (1992). Applying ethical principles in rehabilitation counseling. *Rehabilitation Education, 6,* 41–55.

HR Zone. (1998). *Simple job analysis.* Retrieved June 23, 2003, from www.hrzone.com

Hughes, R. B., Nosek, M. A., Howland, C. A., Groff, J. Y., & Mullen, P. D. (2003). Health promotion for women with physical disabilities: A pilot study. *Rehabilitation Psychology, 48,* 182–188.

Hull, K. (1979). *The rights of physically handicapped people.* New York: Avon Books.

Hume, K., & Marshall, C. (1980). Implementing the rehabilitation approach in mental health settings. *Rehabilitation Counseling Bulletin, 24,* 61–71.

Humphrey v. Memorial Hospitals Association, 239 F.3d 1128, 1136 (9th Cir. 2001).

Hursh, N., Shrey, D., Laskey, R., & D'Amico, M. (1982). A career education model for students with special needs. *Teaching Exceptional Children, 15,* 52–56.

Hylbert, K., Sr., & Hylbert, K., Jr. (1979). *Medical information for human service workers* (2nd ed.). State College, PA: Counselor Education Press.

ICAN. (1992). *Funding guide for Arkansas.* Little Rock, AR: Increasing Capabilities Access Network.

Illich, I. (1973). *Tools for conviviality.* New York: Harper & Row.

Illich, I. (1976). *Medical nemesis: The expropriation of health.* New York: Pantheon Books.

ILRU Insights. (1995). Key findings from the 704 Reports of 1995. *The National Newsletter for Independent Living, 13*(4), 3–5.

Ince, L. (1974). *The rehabilitation medicine services.* Springfield, IL: Thomas.

Indices, Inc. (1979). *Functional limitations: A state of the art review* (Final project report, 13-P-5922013-01, RSA). Falls Church, VA: Department of Health, Education, and Welfare.

Individuals with Disabilities Education Act of 1990, 20 U.S.C. § 1400 *et seq.*

Infinitec. (n.d.). *Alternative mice: More than one way to use a computer.* Retrieved December 26, 2006, from http:www.infinitec.org/learn/learningaboutat/altmice.htm

Ingelfinger, F. J. (1972). Rights of authors and of patients. *New England Journal of Medicine, 286,* 486–487.

Institute of Medicine. (1997). *Enabling America: Assessing the role of rehabilitation science and engineering.* Washington, DC: National Academy Press.

International Association of Rehabilitation Professionals. (2004). *Standards and ethics.* Santa Cruz, CA: Author.

Ira, V. (2003). Ray Kurzweil: Q & A on technology and education. *The Exceptional Parent, 33*(6), 30–31.

Jackman, M. (1983). Enabling the disabled: Paternalism is enemy number one. *Civil Rights Quarterly Perspective, 15*(1/2), 23–26.

Jacobs, H., Kardashian, S., Kreinbring, R., Ponder, R., & Simpson, A. (1984). A skills-oriented model for facilitating employment among psychiatrically disabled persons. *Rehabilitation Counseling Bulletin, 28,* 87–96.

Jaffe, D., & Scott, C. (1991). Career development for empowerment in a changing work world. In J. Kummerow (Ed.), *New directions in career planning and the workplace.* Palo Alto, CA: CPP.

Janikowski, T., Berven, N., & Bordieri, J. (1991). Validity of the Microcomputer Evaluation Screening and Assessment aptitude scores. *Rehabilitation Counseling Bulletin, 35*(1), 38–51.

Janis, I., & Mann, L. (1977). *Decision making.* New York: Free Press.

Jans, L., & Stoddard, S. (1999). *Chartbook on women and disability in the United States: An InfoUse report.* Washington, DC: U.S. National Institute on Disability and Rehabilitation Research.

Jastak, J., & Jastak, S. (1979). *Wide range interest–opinion test* (manual). Wilmington, DE: Jastak Associates.

Jastak, S., & Wilkinson, G. S. (1989). *Wide range achievement test–Revised*. Austin, TX: PRO-ED.

Jenkins, W., Patterson, J. B., & Szymanski, E. M. (1992). Philosophical, historical, and legislative aspects of the rehabilitation counseling profession. In R. M. Parker & E. M. Szymanski (Eds.), *Rehabilitation counseling: Basics and beyond* (2nd ed., pp. 1–41). Austin, TX: PRO-ED.

Jenkins, W., & Strauser, D. (1999). Horizontal expansion of the role of the rehabilitation counselor. *Journal of Rehabilitation, 65*(1), 4–9.

Jome, L., & Phillips, S. (2005). Counseling for choice implementation. In S. Brown & R. Lent (Eds.), *Career development and counseling: Putting theory and research to work* (pp. 466–482). New York: Wiley.

Jones, A. (1988). *A synopsis of the Rehabilitation Act of 1973 as amended by the Rehabilitation Amendments of 1986 and the Civil Rights Restoration Act of 1987*. Dunbar: West Virginia Research & Training Center.

Jones, E. E., Farina, A., Hastof, A. H., Markus, H., Miller, D. T., & Scott, R. A. (1984). *Social stigma: The psychology of marked relationships*. New York: Freeman.

Jones, G. C., & Bell, K. (2004). Adverse health behaviors and chronic conditions in working-age women with disabilities. *Family & Community Health, 27*, 22–36.

Jones, N. L. (1991). Essential requirements of the act: A short history and overview. In J. West (Ed.), *The Americans with Disabilities Act: From policy to practice* (pp. 25–54). New York: Milbank Memorial Fund.

Jones, R. J., & Azrin, N. H. (1973). An experimental application of a social reinforcement approach to the problem of job-finding. *Journal of Applied Behavior Analysis, 6*, 345–353.

Jones, W. (2004). Introduction. In S. L. Welner & F. Haseltine (Eds.), *Welner's guide to the care of women with disabilities* (pp. 1–16). Philadelphia: Lippincott Williams & Wilkins.

Jordan, T. (1972). *The mentally retarded* (3rd ed.). Columbus, OH: Merrill.

Judge, M. (1976). A brief history of social services: Part I. *Social and Rehabilitation Record, 3*(5), 2–8.

Justesen, T., & Menlove, M. (1994). Assistive technology education in rehabilitation counselor programs. *Rehabilitation Education, 7*, 253–260.

Kahn, D. L., & Harrison, T. C. (2004). Foreword. *Family & Community Health, 27*(1), 3.

Kailes, J. I. (1985). Watch your language please! *Journal of Rehabilitation, 51*, 68–69.

Kaiser, J., & Modahl, T. (1991). Work sample usage: A different perspective. In Vocational/Evaluation and Work Adjustment Association (Eds.), *Fifth national forum on issues in vocational assessment* (pp. 69–71). Menomonie: University of Wisconsin–Stout, Materials Development Center.

Kamieniecki, S. (1985). The dimensions underlying public attitudes toward Black and disabled people in America. *American Behavioral Scientist, 28*, 367–385.

Kanfer, F., & Goldstein, A. (1991). *Helping people change* (2nd ed.). New York: Pergamon Press.

Kanner, L. (1964). *A history of the care and study of the mentally retarded*. Springfield, IL: Thomas.

Kaplan, A. B. (2001). Father doesn't always know best: Rejecting paternalistic expansion of the "direct threat" defense to claims under the Americans with Disabilities Act. *Dickinson Law Review, 124*, 389–413.

Kaplan, D. (2000). The definition of disability: Perspective of the disability community. *Journal of Health Care Law and Policy, 3*, 352–364.

Kaplan, H. S. (1974). *The new sex therapy*. New York: Brunner/Mazel.

Kaplan, R. M., & Saccuzzo, D. P. (1993). *Psychological testing.* Pacific Grove, CA: Brooks/ Cole.

Karlan, P. S., & Rutherglen, G. (1996). Disabilities, discrimination, and reasonable accommodation. *Duke Law Journal, 46*(1), 1–41.

Kates, N., Nikolaou, L., Baillie, B., & Hess, J. (1997) On in-home employment programs for people with mental illness. *Psychiatric Rehabilitation Journal, 20,* 56–60.

Katzmann, R. (1991). Essential requirements of the act: A short history and overview. In J. West (Ed.), *The Americans with Disabilities Act: From policy to practice* (pp. 214–237). New York: Milbank Memorial Fund.

Kavale, K. A., & Forness, S. R. (1996). Learning disability grows up: Rehabilitation issues for individuals with learning disabilities. *Journal of Rehabilitation, 62*(1), 34–41.

Keane, R. M. (1985). Providing rehabilitation services to the insurance industry. In L. J. Taylor, M. Golter, G. Golter, & T. E. Backer (Eds.), *Handbook of private sector rehabilitation* (pp. 27–54). New York: Springer.

Keen, L. (1999, June 25). Rulings cut into ADA. *The Washington Blade,* pp. 1, 23.

Keil, E. C., & Barbee, J. R. (1973). Behavior modification and training the disadvantaged job interviewee. *Vocational Guidance Quarterly, 22,* 50–55.

Keim, J., Strauser, D. R., & Ketz, K. (2002). Examining the differences in career thoughts of women in three low socioeconomic status groups. *Journal of Employment Counseling, 39,* 31–42.

Keith, R. D. (1976). *Employment seeking preparation and activity.* East Lansing, MI: Preval.

Keith, R. D. (1977). *Job placement trainer's guide: Employment seeking preparation and activity.* East Lansing, MI: Preval.

Keith, R. D., Engelkes, J. R., & Winborn, B. B. (1977). Employment-seeking preparation and activity: An experimental job-placement training model for rehabilitation clients. *Rehabilitation Counseling Bulletin, 21,* 159–165.

Keller, S., & Buchannan, D. (1984). Sexuality and disability: An overview. *Rehabilitation Digest, 15*(1), 3–7.

Kelley, B. (2003). Putting assistive technology to work. *International Association of Rehabilitation Professionals Journal (The Rehabilitation Professional), 11,* 36.

Kellogg, C. E., & Morton, N. W. (1999). *Beta III.* Odessa, FL: Psychological Corp.

Kelly, J., & Simon, A. (1969). The mentally handicapped as workers: A survey of company experience. *Personnel, 46,* 58–64.

Kemp, B. J., & Vash, C. L. (1971). A comparison between two placement programs for hard-core unemployed persons. *Journal of Employment Counseling, 8,* 108–115.

Kennedy, J. (1976, September 19). Prosthetics–orthotics holds opportunity. *The Commercial Appeal,* p. C6.

Kennedy, T. (1986, November). Our right to independence. *Southern Illinois Parade,* pp. 4–5, 7.

Kenny, D. (1998). Returning to work after workplace injury: Impact of worker and workplace factors. *Journal of Applied Rehabilitation Counseling, 29*(1), 13–19.

Kerr, N. (1961). Understanding the process of adjustment to disability. *Journal of Rehabilitation, 27,* 16–18.

Kerr, N. (1977). Understanding the process of adjustment to disability. In J. Stubbins (Ed.), *Social and psychological aspects of disability* (pp. 317–324). Baltimore: University Park Press.

Kessler, H. (1953). *Rehabilitation of the physically handicapped.* New York: Columbia University Press.

Kessler, H. (1968). *The knife is not enough.* New York: Norton.

Keynes, J. M. (1964). *The general theory of employment, interest and money.* New York: Harcourt Brace Jovanovich.

Kiernan, W. E., & Rowland, S. (1989). Factors contributing to success and failure in the work environment: An industry perspective. In W. E. Kiernan & R. L. Schalock (Eds.), *Economics, industry, and disability: A look ahead* (pp. 253–263). Baltimore: Brookes.

Kilbury, R., & Stotlar, B. (1996). Centers for independent living. In W. Crimando & T. F. Riggar (Eds.), *Utilizing community resources: An overview of human services.* Orlando, FL: FMD.

Kilbury, R. F., Stotlar, B. J., & Eckert, J. M. (2005). Centers for independent living. In W. Crimando & T. F. Riggar (Eds.), *Community resources* (2nd ed., pp. 304–314). Long Grove, IL: Waveland Press.

Kilpatrick, J. J. (2004, February 22). Diabetes and disabled act. *The Southern Illinoisan,* p. 2E.

Kimbro v. Atlantic Richfield Co., 889 F.2d 869, 879 (9th Cir. 1989).

Kirk, F. (1999). Notes from Washington. *The Alliance for Rehabilitation Counseling, 3*(1), 1–3.

Kirk, S., & Gallagher, J. (1983). *Educating exceptional children* (4th ed.). Boston: Houghton Mifflin.

Kirszner, M., Baron, R., & Rutman, I. (1992). *Employer participation in supported and transitional employment for persons with long-term mental illness* (Final report to National Institute of Rehabilitation and Disability Research). Philadelphia: Matrix Research Institute.

Kitchener, K. (1984). Intuition, critical evaluation, and ethical principles: The foundation for ethical decisions in counseling psychology. *Counseling Psychologist, 12*(3), 43–55.

Kittrie, N. (1973). *The right to be different: Deviance and enforced therapy.* Baltimore: Penguin Books.

Kleinfield, S. (1977). The handicapped: Hidden no longer. *The Atlantic Monthly, 240*(6), 86–96.

Kline, M., & Hoisington, V. (1981). Placing the psychiatrically disabled: A look at work values. *Rehabilitation Counseling Bulletin, 24,* 366–369.

Knape, C. S. (1972). Placement: A try-out experiment. *Journal of Rehabilitation, 38*(6), 29–32.

Koch, L. (2000). Career development interventions for transition-age youth with disabilities. *Work, 14,* 3–11.

Koch, L., Hennessey, M., Niese, N., Tabor, T., & Petro, C. (2004). Preparing for a career in rehabilitation counseling: The perspectives of practicing rehabilitation counselors. *Rehabilitation Education, 18*(2), 93–105.

Kohler, P. (1993). Best practices in transition: Substantiated or implied. *Career Development for Exceptional Individuals, 16,* 107–121.

Kokaska, C. J. (1984). Disabled superheroes in comic books. *Rehabilitation Literature, 45*(9–10), 286–288.

Kokaska, C. J., Woodward, S., & Tyler, L. (1984). Disabled people in the Bible. *Rehabilitation Literature, 45*(1–2), 20–21.

Kolata, G. (1993, January 4). A losing battle. *Chicago Tribune,* Tempo Section, pp. 1, 3.

Kopelman, L. M. (1996). Ethical assumptions and ambiguities in the Americans with Disabilities Act. *The Journal of Medicine and Philosophy, 21,* 187–208.

Kornblith, A., LaRocca, N., & Baum, H. (1986). Employment in individuals with multiple sclerosis. *International Journal of Rehabilitation Research, 9,* 155–165.

Kosciulek, J. (1998). Empowering the life choices of people with disabilities through career counseling. In N. C. Gysbers, M. J. Heppner, & J. A. Johnston (Eds.), *Career counseling: Process, issues, and techniques* (pp. 109–122). Boston: Allyn & Bacon.

Kosciulek, J. (2003a). An empowerment approach to career counseling with people with disabilities. In N. Gysbers, M. Heppner, & J. Johnston (Eds.), *Career counseling: Process, issues, and techniques* (2nd ed., pp. 139–153). Boston: Allyn & Bacon.

Kosciulek, J. (2003b). A multidimensional approach to the structure of consumer satisfaction. *Rehabilitation Counseling Bulletin, 46,* 92–97.

Kosciulek, J. (2004a). Research applications of the longitudinal study of the Vocational Rehabilitation Services Program. *Rehabilitation Counseling Bulletin, 47,* 173–180.

Kosciulek, J. (2004b). Theory of informed consumer choice in vocational rehabilitation. *Rehabilitation Education, 18*(2), 3–11.

Kraepelin, E. (1962). *One hundred years of psychiatry.* New York: Citadel Press.

Kriegal, J., O'Mara, S., & West, M. (2003). *Consumer advocacy in the implementation of the Ticket to Work Act.* Richmond: Virginia Commonwealth University, Research and Training Center on Workplace Supports.

Kriegel, L. (1982). The wolf in the pit in the zoo. *Social Policy, 13*(2), 16–23.

Krishnaswami, U. (1984). Learning to achieve: Rehabilitation counseling and the learning disabled adult. *Journal of Applied Rehabilitation Counseling, 15,* 18–22.

Krueger, D. (1984). Psychological rehabilitation of physical trauma and disability. In D. Krueger (Ed.), *Rehabilitation psychology* (pp. 3–14). Rockville, MD: Aspen.

Kruz, S. E. (1987). Self-report measures of personality. In B. Bolton (Ed.), *Handbook of measurement and evaluation in rehabilitation* (2nd ed.). Baltimore: Brookes.

Kuehl v. Wal-Mart Stores Inc. 909 F. Supp. 794 (D. Colo. 1995).

Kuehn, M. D. (1991). An agenda for professional practice in the 1990s. *Journal of Applied Rehabilitation Counseling, 22*(3), 6–15.

Kunce, J. (1970). Is work therapy really therapeutic? *Rehabilitation Literature, 31,* 297–299.

Kurzweil Products. (1999, October). *Kurzweil Reading Machine product description.* Burlington, MA: Author. Retrieved October 5, 1999, from http://www.ihsl.com

Kutsch, J. (1990). The consumer's role in job accommodation. In R. Greenwood (Ed.), *Applying technology in the work environment* (pp. 2–9). Fayetteville: Arkansas Research and Training Center.

La Forge, J. (1991). Preferred language practice in professional rehabilitation journals. *Journal of Rehabilitation, 57,* 49–51.

LaChance v. Duffy's Draft House Inc., 146 F.3d 832 (11th Cir. 1998).

Lagomarcino, T. (1986). Community services. In F. Rusch (Ed.), *Competitive employment issues and strategies* (pp. 65–75). Baltimore: Brookes.

Laing, R. D., & Esterson, A. (1970). *Sanity, madness and the family.* Harmondsworth, England: Penguin Books.

Lamborn, E. (1970). The state–federal partnership. *Journal of Rehabilitation, 36*(5), 10–15.

Lancioni, G., Oliva, S., & Bracalente, S. (1998). A portable control device for promoting independent indoor travel by persons with severe multiple disabilities. *Journal of Visual Impairment and Blindness, 92*(1), 63–70.

Lanhann, J., Graham, M., & Schaberg, D. (n.d.). *Employment of the handicapped: An eighteen year experience.* Unpublished manuscript, Dow Chemical Company, Midland, MI.

Lansing, S., & Carlsen, P. (1977). Occupational therapy. In P. Valletutti & F. Christoplos (Eds.), *Interdisciplinary approaches to human services* (pp. 211–236). Baltimore: University Park Press.

LaPlante, M. P., & Carlson, D. (1996). *Disability in the United Stated: Prevalence and causes, 1992* (Disability Statistics Report 7). Washington, DC: National Institute on Disability and Rehabilitation Research.

LaRocca, N., Kalb, R., Scheinberg, L., & Kendall, P. (1985). Factors associated with unemployment of patients with multiple sclerosis. *Journal of Chronic Diseases, 38,* 203–210.

LaRue, C. (1972). *The development of vocational rehabilitation programs, 1880–1940: A case study in the evolution of the provision of public services in the United States* (Working Paper No. 188/R5014). Berkeley: University of California, Institute of Urban and Regional Development.

Lassiter, R. S. (1972). History of the rehabilitation movement in America. In J. G. Cull & R. E. Hardy (Eds.), *Vocational rehabilitation: Profession and process* (pp. 5–58). Springfield, IL: Thomas.

Latimer, R. (1977). Physical therapy. In P. Valletutti & F. Christoplos (Eds.), *Interdisciplinary approaches to human services* (pp. 279–305). Baltimore: University Park Press.

LaVor, M., & Duncan, J. (1976). Vocational rehabilitation—The new law and its implications for the future. *Journal of Rehabilitation, 42,* 20–28, 39.

Lazzaro, J. (1991). Opening doors for people with disabilities: Adaptive technology lets personal computer users lead more productive lives. *Rehabilitation Education, 5,* 245–252.

Lazzaro, J. (1993). *Adaptive technologies for learning and work environments.* Chicago: American Library Association.

LC Technologies. (1999). *The eyegaze system.* Fairfax, VA: Author.

Lea, H. C. (1957). *Materials towards a history of witchcraft.* New York: Yoseloff.

Leaf, A. (1984). The doctor's dilemma—and society's too. *New England Journal of Medicine, 310,* 718–721.

Leahy, M., Chan, F., & Saunders, J. (2003). Job functions and knowledge requirements of certified rehabilitation counselors in the 21st century. *Rehabilitation Counseling Bulletin, 46,* 66–81.

Leahy, M., Shapson, P., & Wright, G. (1987). Rehabilitation practitioner competencies by role and setting. *Rehabilitation Counseling Bulletin, 31,* 119–130.

Lee, C. C. (1991). Promise and pitfalls of multicultural counseling. In C. C. Lee & B. L. Richardson (Eds.), *Multicultural issues in counseling: New approaches to diversity.* Alexandria, VA: American Association for Counseling and Development.

Lee, C. C., & Richardson, B. L. (Eds.). (1991). *Multicultural issues in counseling: New approaches to diversity.* Alexandria, VA: American Association for Counseling and Development.

Lee, G., Chronister, J., Tsang, H., Ingraham, K., & Oulvey, E. (2005). Psychiatric rehabilitation training needs of state vocational rehabilitation counselors: A preliminary study. *Journal of Rehabilitation, 71*(3), 11–19.

Lee, M. (1997). Searching for patterns and anomalies in the ADA employment constellation: Who is a qualified individual with a disability and what accommodations are courts really demanding? *The Labor Lawyer, 13*(1), 149–196.

Lehtinen, L., & Dumas, L. (1976). *A follow-up study of learning disabled children as adults: A final report.* Evanston, IL: Cove School Research Office. (ERIC Document Reproduction Service No. ED 164-728)

Lehtinen-Rogan, L. L., & Hartman, L. A. (1976). *A follow-up study of learning disabled children as adults* (Final Rep. Project No. 443CH60010, Grant No. OEG-0-7453). Washington, DC: U.S. Department of Health, Education and Welfare, Bureau of Education for the Handicapped.

Lemert, E. (1951). *Social pathology.* New York: McGraw-Hill.

Lenihan, J. (1977). Disabled Americans: A history [Bicentennial issue]. *Performance, 27*(5,6,7). Washington, DC: The President's Committee on Employment of the Handicapped.

Lesh, K., & Marshall, C. (1984). Rehabilitation: Focus on disabled women as a special population. *Journal of Applied Rehabilitation Counseling, 15,* 18–21.

Levine, L. (1959). The impact of disability. *Journal of Rehabilitation, 25*(6), 10–12.

Levine, P., & Nourse, S. (1998). What follow-up studies say about postschool life for young men and women with learning disabilities: A critical look at the literature. *Journal of Learning Disabilities, 31,* 212–233.

Levitan, S. A., Mangum, G. L., & Marshall, R. (1976). *Human resources and labor markets.* New York: Harper & Row.

Levitan, S., & Taggert, R. (1982). Rehabilitation employment and the disabled. In J. Rubin & V. La Porte (Eds.), *Alternatives in rehabilitating the handicapped: A policy analysis* (pp. 89–149). New York: Human Sciences Press.

Levitas, A. S., & Reid, C. S. (2003). An angel with Down syndrome in a sixteenth century Flemish Nativity painting. *American Journal of Medical Genetics, 116A*(4), 399–405.

Leviticus. (1966). In A. Jones (Gen. ed.), *The Jerusalem Bible* (pp. 131–168). London: Darton, Longman, & Todd.

Levy, C. W. (1988). *A people's history of the independent living movement.* Lawrence: University of Kansas Research and Training Center on Independent Living.

Levy, J., Jessop, D., Rimmerman, A., Francis, F., & Levy, P. (1993). Determinants of attitudes of New York State employers towards the employment of persons with severe handicaps. *Journal of Rehabilitation, 59*(1), 49–54.

Li, L., Ford, J. A., & Moore, D. (2000). An exploratory study of violence, substance abuse, disability, and gender. *Social Behavior and Personality, 28,* 61–72.

Lichtenstein, S., & Michaelides, N. (1993). Transition from school to young adulthood: Four case studies of young adults labeled mentally retarded. *Career Development for Exceptional Individuals, 16,* 183–195.

Limaye, S. (2003). Sexuality and women with sensory disabilities. In A. Hans & A. Patri (Eds.), *Women, disability and identity* (pp. 89–100). Thousand Oaks, CA: Sage.

Lindberg, A. (1976). Occupational therapy. In W. Jenkins, R. Anderson, & W. Dieterich (Eds.), *Rehabilitation of the severely disabled* (pp. 191–194). Dubuque, IA: Kendall/ Hunt.

Lindsey, J. (1999). *Technology and exceptional individuals* (3rd ed.). Austin, TX: PRO-ED.

Lipson, J. G., & Rogers, J. G. (2000). Pregnancy, birth, and disability: Women's healthcare experiences. *Health Care for Women International, 21,* 11–26.

Lissette, A., & Kraus, R. (2000). *Seven steps to taking back your life: Free yourself from an abusive relationship.* Alameda, CA: Hunter House.

Litton, F., Veron, L., & Griffin, H. (1982). Occupational therapists and physical therapists: Vital members in the rehabilitation and educational process of disabled students. *Journal of Rehabilitation, 48*(1), 65–67.

Locke, D. C. (1990). A not so provincial view of multicultural counseling. *Counselor Education and Supervision, 30,* 18–25.

Long, T., Huang, L., Woodbridge, M., Woolverton, M., & Minkel, J. (2003). Integrating assistive technology into an outcome-driven model of service delivery. *Infants and Young Children, 16,* 272–283.

Longmore, P. K., & Umansky, L. (Eds.). (2001). *The new disability history: American perspectives.* New York: New York University Press.

Lorber, J. (1981). Commentary I and reply. *Journal of Medical Ethics, 7,* 120–122.

Louis Harris & Associates. (1989). *The ICD Survey III: A report card on special education.* New York: International Center for the Disabled.

Lowenfeld, B. (1973). 100 years ago: The Vienna Congress of teachers of the blind. *New Outlook for the Blind, 67,* 337–345.

Lubove, R. (1965). *The professional altruist.* Cambridge, MA: Harvard University Press.

Luckasson, R., Coulter, D., Polloway, E., Reiss, S., Schalock, R., Snell, M., et al. (2002). *Mental retardation: Definition, classification, and systems of supports* (10th ed.). Washington, DC: American Association on Mental Retardation.

Luke. (1966). The Gospel according to Saint Luke. In M. A. Jones (Gen. ed.), *The Jerusalem Bible* (pp. 90–136). London: Darton, Longman, & Todd.

Lustig, D., Strauser, D., Rice, N., & Rucker, T. (2002). The relationship between working alliance and rehabilitation outcomes. *Rehabilitation Counseling Bulletin, 46,* 25–33.

Lynch, E., & Lewis, R. (1988). *Exceptional children and adults.* Glenview, IL: Scott.

Lynch, R. K., & Lynch, R. T. (1998). Rehabilitation counseling in the private sector. In R. M. Parker & E. M. Szymanski (Eds.), *Rehabilitation counseling: Basics and beyond* (3rd ed., pp. 71–105). Austin, TX: PRO-ED.

Lysaker, P., & Bell, M. (1995). Work performance over time for people with schizophrenia. *Psychosocial Rehabilitation Journal, 18*(3), 141–146.

MacDonald, M. E. (1944). *Federal grants for vocational rehabilitation.* Chicago: University of Chicago Press.

Mackelprang, R. W., & Salsgiver, R. O. (1999). *Disability: A diversity model approach in human service practice.* Pacific Grove, CA: Brooks Cole.

Mackie v. Runyon, 804 F. Supp. 1508 (M.D. Fla. 1992).

Maddi, S. (1980). *Personality theories: A comparative analysis* (4th ed.). Homewood, IL: Dorsey Press.

Maddox, S. (2003). *Paralysis resource guide.* Springfield, NJ: Christopher and Dana Reeve Paralysis Resource Center.

Magnus, E. (2001). Everyday occupations and the process of redefinition: A study of how meaning in occupation influences redefinition of identity in women with a disability. *Scandinavian Journal of Occupational Therapy, 8,* 115–124.

Mainstream, Inc. (1998). ABA study shows employers win overwhelming majority of Title I ADA cases. *Employment in the Mainstream, 23*(4), 10–11.

Maki, D. R., Pape, D. A., & Prout, H. T. (1979). Personality evaluation: A tool of the rehabilitation counselor. *Journal of Applied Rehabilitation Counseling, 10,* 119–128.

Malikin, D., & Rusalem, H. (1976). Counseling the mentally retarded. In H. Rusalem & D. Malikin (Eds.), *Contemporary vocational rehabilitation* (pp. 161–174). New York: New York University Press.

Mancuso, L. (1990). Reasonable accommodation for workers with psychiatric disabilities. *Psychosocial Rehabilitation Journal, 14*(2), 3–20.

Mann, W. (1991). State-wide planning for access to technology applications for individuals with disabilities. *Journal of Rehabilitation, 57*(1), 17–20.

Mansouri, L., & Dowell, D. A. (1989). Perceptions of stigma among the long-term mentally ill. *Psychosocial Rehabilitation Journal, 13*(1), 79–91.

Manus, G. I. (1975). Is your language disabling? *Journal of Rehabilitation, 41,* 35.

Marini, I., & Reid, C. (2001). A survey of rehabilitation professionals or alternate provider contractors with social security: Problems and solutions. *Journal of Rehabilitation, 67*(2), 36–41.

Mark. (1966). The Gospel according to St. Mark. In A. Jones (Gen. ed.), *The Jerusalem Bible* (pp. 65–89). London: Darton, Longman, & Todd.

Marr, J. (1982). Behavioral analysis of work problems. In B. Bolton (Ed.), *Vocational adjustment of disabled persons* (pp. 127–148). Baltimore: University Park Press.

Marr, J., & Roessler, R. (1985). Behavior management in work settings [Richard J. Baker Memorial Monograph]. *Vocational Evaluation and Work Adjustment Association, 2.*

Marr, J., & Roessler, R. (1994). *Supervision and management: A guide to modifying work behavior.* Fayetteville: University of Arkansas Press.

Marshall, C., Leung, P., Johnson, S., & Busby, H. (2003). Ethical practice and cultural factors in rehabilitation. *Rehabilitation Education, 17*(1), 55–65.

Martin, J. E., Rusch, F. R., Tines, J. J., Brulle, A. R., & White, D. M. (1985). Work attendance in competitive employment. Comparison between employees who are non-handicapped and those who are mentally retarded. *Mental Retardation, 23*(3), 142–147.

Maslow, A. H. (1971). *The farther reaches of human nature.* New York: Viking Press.

Mathews, M., & Fawcett, S. (1984). Building the capacity of job candidates through behavioral instruction. *Journal of Community Psychology, 12,* 123–129.

Mathews, M., Whang, P., & Fawcett, S. (1980). Development and validation of an occupational skills assessment instrument. *Behavioral Assessment, 2,* 71–85.

Mathews, M., Whang, P., & Fawcett, S. (1984). *Getting along on the job.* Lawrence: University of Kansas, Research and Training Center on Independent Living.

Matkin, R. E. (1997). Public and private rehabilitation counseling practices. In D. R. Maki & T. F. Riggar (Eds.), *Rehabilitation counseling: Profession and practice* (pp. 139–150). New York: Springer.

Matthew. (1966). The Gospel according to Saint Matthew. In A. Jones (Gen. ed.), *The Jerusalem Bible* (pp. 15–64). London: Darton, Longman, & Todd.

Matthias, V. (1981). Baltimore's job squad for the handicapped. *Rehabilitation Counseling Bulletin, 24,* 304–307.

Mayall, D. (1994). *The worker traits data book.* Indianapolis, IN: JIST.

Mayer, T., & Andrews, H. (1981). Changes in self-concept following a spinal cord injury. *Journal of Applied Rehabilitation Counseling, 12,* 135–137.

Maze, M., & Mayall, D. (1995). *The enhanced guide for occupational exploration* (2nd ed.). Indianapolis, IN: JIST.

McAlees, D., & Menz, F. (1992). Consumerism and vocational evaluation. *Rehabilitation Education, 6,* 213–220.

McAllan, L., & Ditillo, D. (1994). Addressing the needs of lesbian and gay clients with disabilities. *Journal of Applied Rehabilitation Counseling, 25*(1), 26–35.

McCarron, L. T., & Spires, H. P. (1991). *McCarron-Dial system vocational interest exploration instructor's manual.* Dallas, TX: McCarron–Dial Systems.

McCarthy, H., & Leierer, S. (2001). Consumer concepts of ideal characteristics and minimum qualifications for rehabilitation counselors. *Rehabilitation Counseling Bulletin, 45,* 13–21.

McCarthy, M. (1999). *Sexuality and women with learning disabilities.* London: Jessica Kingsley.

McClure, D. P. (1972). Placement through improvement of clients' job-seeking skills. *Journal of Applied Rehabilitation Counseling, 3,* 188–196.

McCoy, L. F. (1972). Working with the physician. In J. G. Cull & R. E. Hardy (Eds.), *Vocational rehabilitation: Profession and process* (pp. 449–469). Springfield, IL: Thomas.

McCray, P. (1979). *Learning assessment in vocational evaluation.* Menomonie: University of Wisconsin–Stout, Materials Development Center.

McCuller, G., Moore, S., & Salzberg, C. (1990). Programming for vocational competence in sheltered workshops. *Journal of Rehabilitation, 56*(3), 41–44.

McDonald, J., & Rosman, J. (1997). EEOC guidance on psychiatric disabilities: Many problems, few workable solutions. *Employee Relations Law Journal, 23*(2), 5–29.

McDonnell, J., Mathot-Buckner, C., & Ferguson, B. (1996). *Transition programs for students with moderate/severe disabilities.* Pacific Grove, CA: Brookes/Cole.

McFarlane, J., Hughes, R. B., Nosek, M. A., Groff, J. Y., Swedlend, N., & Mullen, P. D. (2001). Abuse assessment screen–Disability (AAS-D): Measuring frequency, type, and perpetrator of abuse toward women with physical disabilities. *Journal of Women's Health & Gender-based Medicine, 10,* 861–866.

McGowan, J. F., & Porter, T. L. (1967). *An introduction to the vocational rehabilitation process.* Washington, DC: United States Department of Health, Education, and Welfare; Vocational Rehabilitation Administration.

McKay v. Toyota Motor Manufacturing, 878 F. Supp. 1012 (E.D. Ky. 1995).

McManus, L. (2001, July). *TWWIAA: Return to work under the Social Security Administration.* Paper presented at the TWWIIA and Ethics in Rehabilitation meeting, Southern University, Baton Rouge, LA.

McNeil, J. (1997, August). *Current population reports. Americans with disabilities: 1994–95.* Washington, DC: U.S. Department of Commerce.

McWilliams, P. (1984). *Personal computers and the disabled.* Garden City, NY: Quantium Press.

Mead, P. (2004). The SSA tries a new deal for disability. *The Insider, 83*(3), 73–75.

Means, B., & Roessler, R. (1976). *Personal achievement skills leader's manual and participant's workbook.* Fayetteville: University of Arkansas, Rehabilitation Research and Training Center.

Meisler, N., & Williams, O. (1998). Replicating effective supported employment models for adults with psychiatric disabilities. *Psychiatric Services, 49,* 1419–1421.

Meister, R. K. (1976). Diagnostic assessment in rehabilitation. In B. Bolton (Ed.), *Handbook of measurement and evaluation in rehabilitation* (pp. 161–171). Baltimore: University Park Press.

Menchetti, B. (1991). Should vocational assessment and supported employment be partners or competitors: A research perspective. In Vocational Evaluation and Work Adjustment Association (Eds.), *Fifth national forum on issues in vocational assessment* (pp. 49–52). Menomonie: University of Wisconsin–Stout, Materials Development Center.

Meyers, G. S., & Messer, J. (1981). The social and vocational adjustment of learning disabled/behavior disordered adolescents after H.S.: A pilot survey. *Proceedings from the International Conference on the Career Development of Handicapped Individuals* (pp. 70–83). Washington, DC: National Institute of Education. (ERIC Document Reproduction Service No. Ed 213 245)

Michaels, C., & Risucci, D. (1993). Employer and counselor perceptions of workplace accommodations for persons with traumatic brain injury. *Journal of Applied Rehabilitation Counseling, 24*(1), 38–45.

Mikochik, S. L. (1991). The constitution and the Americans with Disabilities Act: Some first impressions. *Temple Law Review, 64,* 619–628.

Miller, J. C. (1966). *The first frontier: Life in colonial America.* New York: Dell. (Original work published 1952)

Miller, L. A., & Roberts, R. R. (1971). *Understanding the work milieu and personnel in developing continuing education for rehabilitation counselors.* Studies in Continuing Education for Rehabilitation Counselors (Rep. No. 2). Iowa City: University of Iowa, College of Education.

Miller, R. D. (1982). The involvement of judicial officials other than judges in decision making in involuntary commitment. *The Journal of Psychiatry and Law, 10,* 491–502.

Millington, M., Miller, D., Asner-Self, K., & Linkowski, D. (2003). The business perspective on employers, disability, and vocational rehabilitation. In E. Szymanski & R. Parker (Eds.), *Work and disability* (2nd ed., pp. 317–342). Austin, TX: PRO-ED.

Milton v. Scrivner Inc., 53 F. 3d 1118 (10th Cir. 1995).

Mirch, M. (1999). Community resources and services. In F. Chan & M. Leahy (Eds.), *Health care and disability case management* (pp. 293–316). Lake Zurich, IL: Vocational Consultants Press.

Mithaug, D., Horiuchi, C., & Fanning, P. (1985). A report on the Colorado-state follow-up survey of special education students. *Exceptional Children, 51,* 397–404.

Mohamed v. Marriott International Inc., 905 F. Supp. 141 (S.D.N.Y. 1995).

Monroe, C. H. (1978). Adjustment services for the blind. *Journal of Rehabilitation, 44*(1), 30–34.

Moon, M. S., Hart, D., Komisar, C., & Friedlander, R. (1995). Making sports and recreation activities accessible. In K. Flipper, K. Inge, & J. M. Barcus (Eds.), *Assistive technology* (pp. 187–208). Baltimore: Brookes.

Mooney, W. L. (1966). *An experiment in the use of two vocational techniques with a population of hard-to-place rehabilitation clients* (Final report, Grant No. RD907P-63). (NTIS No. PB197525)

Moore, C. L., Feist-Price, S., & Alston, R. J. (2002). VR services for persons with severe/profound mental retardation. *Rehabilitation Counseling Bulletin, 45*(3), 162–167.

Moore, J. (1979). Impact of the 504 regulations. *Journal of Rehabilitation, 45*(2), 81–84.

Morison, S. L. (1965). *The Oxford history of the American people* (Vol. 3). New York: Mentor Books.

Morris, P., & Lloyd, C. (2004). Vocational rehabilitation in psychiatry: A re-evaluation. *Australian Journal of Psychiatry, 38,* 490–494.

Moses v. American Nonwovens Inc., 97 F.3d 446 (11th Cir. 1996), *cert denied,* 519 U.S. 1118 (1997).

Mpofu, E., & Wilson, K. (2004). Opportunity structure and transition practices of students with disabilities: The role of family, culture, and community. *Journal of Applied Rehabilitation Counseling, 35*(2), 9–16.

Mueller, J. (1990). *The workplace workbook: An illustrated guide to job accommodation and assistive technology.* Washington, DC: Dole Foundation.

Mueser, K., & McGurk, S. (2004). Schizophrenia. *The Lancet, 363,* 2063–2071.

Mulhern, J. (1981). Marketing work sampling systems: An evaluator's perspective. *Vocational Evaluation and Work Adjustment Bulletin, 14,* 4–5.

Mullins, J. B. (1979). Making language work to eliminate handicapism. *Education Unlimited, 1,* 20–24.

Murphy v. United Parcel Service, Inc., 119 S.CT. 2133 (1999).

Murphy, G., & Athanasou, J. (1994). Vocational potential and spinal cord injuries: A review and evaluation. *Journal of Applied Rehabilitation Counseling, 25*(3), 47–52.

Murphy, J. M. (1976). Psychiatric labeling in cross-cultural perspective. *Science, 191,* 1019–1028.

Murphy, K. R., & Davidshofer, C. O. (1998). *Psychological testing* (4th ed.). Upper Saddle River, NJ: Prentice Hall.

Murphy, P. A., & Williams, J. M. (1999). *Assessment of rehabilitative and quality of life issues in legislation.* Boca Raton, FL: CRC Press.

Murphy, S. (1988). Counselor and client views of vocational rehabilitation success and failure: A qualitative study. *Rehabilitation Counseling Bulletin, 31,* 185–197.

Muthard, J. E., & Salomone, P. R. (1969). Roles and functions of the rehabilitation counselor [Special issue]. *Rehabilitation Counseling Bulletin, 13.*

Muther, T. J. (1996). "Qualified" and "reasonable accommodations" under Title I of the ADA: Employer compliance. *Preventive Law Reporter, 15*(1), 18–20.

Muzzio, T., La Rocca, J., Koskel, J., Durke, E., Chapmen, B., & Gutoriski, M. (n.d.). *Planning for independent living rehabilitation: Lessons from the section 130 demonstration.* Washington, DC: The Urban Institute.

Nadolsky, J. M. (1973). A model for vocational evaluation of the disadvantaged. In R. E. Hardy & J. E. Cull (Eds.). *Vocational evaluation for rehabilitation services.* Springfield, IL: Thomas.

Nadolsky, J. (1994). Foreword. In C. Brown, R. McDaniel, R. Couch, & M. McClanahan (Eds.), *Vocational evaluation systems and software: A consumer's guide.* Menomonie: University of Wisconsin–Stout, Materials Development Center.

Nagle, K. (2001). Transition to employment and community life for youths with visual impairments: Current status and future directions. *Journal of Visual Impairment and Blindness, 95,* 725-738.

National Aeronautics and Space Administration. (September, 1999). *Spinoff Database: Technology transfer office.* Houston, TX: Author. Retrieved September 12, 1999, from http://www.sti.nasa.gov/tto/spinselect.html

National Association for Retarded Citizens. (1986). Mentally retarded citizens in the open job market. *Personnel Journal, 56,* 238–239, 252–253.

National Collaborative on Workforce and Disability for Youth. (2004). Navigating the road to work. *Intersection, 1*(10), 1–6.

National Council on Disability. (1986). *Toward independence.* Washington, DC: Author.

National Council on Disability. (1988). *On the threshold of independence.* Washington, DC: Author.

National Council on Rehabilitation Education. (n.d.). *The growing profession of rehabilitation education.* Emporia, KS: Author.

National Information Center for Children and Youth with Disabilities. (1993). Transition services in the IEP. *NICHCY Transition Summary, 3*(1), 1–20.

National Institute on Deafness and Other Communication Disorders. (2006, May 1). Cochlear implants. Retrieved December 26, 2006, from http://www.nidcd.nih.gov/health/hearing/coch.htm

National Institute on Disability and Rehabilitation Research. (1990). Assistive listening devices in education and vocational rehabilitation. *Rehab Brief, 12*(10), 1–4.

National Institute on Disability and Rehabilitation Research. (1991, December). People with activity limitations in the U.S. *Disability Statistics Abstract,* DS1–2.

National Organization on Disability. (1998). *Closing the gap: 1998.* Washington, DC: Author.

National Organization on Disability. (2002). *Closing the gap.* Washington, DC: Author.

National Organization on Disability. (2004). *The 2004 N.O.D./Harris Survey of Americans with disabilities.* Washington, DC: Author.

National Rehabilitation Information Center. (2006). *Information resources for assistive technology.* Lanham, MD: Heitech Services.

National Women's Health Information Center. (n.d.). *Psychiatric disabilities.* Retrieved January 13, 2002, from http://www.4woman.gov

Nau, L. (1973). Why not family rehabilitation. *Journal of Rehabilitation, 39*(3), 14–17.

Navarro, V. (1982). Where is the popular mandate? *New England Journal of Medicine, 307,* 1516–1518.

Neath, J., & Bolton, B. (2006). *Work personality profile: Manual and software.* Austin, TX: PRO-ED.

Neely, C. R. (1974). Rehabilitation counselor attitudes: A study to compare the attitudes of general and special counselors. *Journal of Applied Rehabilitation Counseling, 5,* 153-158.

Neff, W. S. (1985). *Work and human behavior.* New York: Aldine.

Neilson, R. A. (1967, April). *A survey of post-mortem blood-alcohols from 41 California counties in 1966.* San Francisco: California Traffic Safety Foundation.

Neilson, R. A. (1969, September). *Alcohol involvement in fatal motor vehicle accidents, California, 1962–1968.* San Francisco: California Traffic Safety Foundation.

Neisser, U., Boodoo, G., Bouchard, T., Boykin, A. W., Brody, N., Ceci, S., et al. (1996). Intelligence: Knowns and unknowns. *American Psychologist, 51,* 77–101.

Nelson, N. (1971). *Workshops for the handicapped in the United States.* Springfield, IL: Thomas.

Nemec, P., & Gagne, C. (2005). Recovery from psychiatric disabilities. *Journal of Applied Rehabilitation Counseling, 36*(4), 4–10.

Neubert, D., Tilson, G., & Ianacone, R. (1989). Postsecondary transition needs and employment patterns of individuals with mild disabilities. *Exceptional Children, 55,* 494-500.

New project explores disability research. (1984). *AAASNEWS, 13,* 157.

Newill, B., Goyette, C., & Fogarty, T. (1984). Diagnosis and assessment of the adult with specific learning disabilities. *Journal of Rehabilitation, 50*(2), 34–39.

Newman, L. (1970). Instant placement: A new model for providing rehabilitation services within a community mental health program. *Community Mental Health Journal, 6,* 401–410.

Newman, R. D. (1973). Personal polarity and placement problems. *Journal of Rehabilitation, 39*(6), 20–25.

Nichtern, S. (1974). *Helping the retarded child.* New York: Grosset & Dunlap.

Ninth Institute on Rehabilitation Issues. (1982). *Rehabilitation of clients with specific learning disabilities.* Hot Springs: Arkansas Rehabilitation Research and Training Center.

Noble, J. H. (1984). *Ethical considerations facing society in rehabilitating severely disabled persons* (Action Paper No. 5). Washington, DC: National Rehabilitation Association, Ninth Mary Switzer Memorial Seminar.

Noll, A. (1991). Training models for the utilization of assistive technology in vocational rehabilitation. *Rehabilitation Education, 5,* 279–282.

Noonan, B. M., & Gallor, S. M. (2004). Challenge and success: A qualitative study of the career development of highly achieving women with physical and sensory disabilities. *Journal of Counseling Psychology, 51,* 68–80.

Nordstrom, C., Huffaker, B., & Williams, K. (1998). When physical disabilities are not liabilities: The role of applicant and interviewer characteristics on employment interview outcomes. *Journal of Applied Social Psychology, 28,* 283–306.

Nosek, M. (1988). Independent living and rehabilitation counseling. In S. E. Rubin & N. Rubin (Eds.), *Contemporary challenges to the rehabilitation counseling profession* (pp. 45–60). Baltimore: Brookes.

Nosek, M. (1990). Personal assistance: Key to employability of persons with physical disabilities. *Journal of Applied Rehabilitation Counseling, 21,* 3–8.

Nosek, M. (1992). Independent living. In R. Parker & E. Szymanski (Eds.), *Rehabilitation counseling* (2nd ed., pp. 103–133). Austin, TX: PRO-ED.

Nosek, M. (1993). A response to Kenneth R. Thomas' commentary: Some observations on the use of the word "consumer." *Journal of Rehabilitation, 59*(2), 9–10.

Nosek, M., & Fuhrer, M. (1992). Independence among people with disabilities: I. A heuristic model. *Rehabilitation Counseling Bulletin, 36*(1), 6–20.

Nosek, M. A., Howland, C. A., Rintala, D. H., Young, M. E., & Chanpong, G. F. (1997). *National study of women with physical disabilities: Final report.* Retrieved December 26, 2006, from http://www.bcm.edu/crowd/?pmid=1408

Nosek, M. A., & Hughes, R. B. (2003). Psychosocial issues of women with physical disabilities: The continuing gender debate. *Rehabilitation Counseling Bulletin, 46,* 224–233.

Nosek, M. A., Hughes, R. B., Taylor, H. B., & Howland, C. A. (2004). Violence against women with disabilities. In S. L. Welner & F. Haseltine (Eds.), *Welner's guide to the care of women with disabilities* (pp. 333–345). Philadelphia: Lippincott Williams & Wilkins.

Nosek, M., Zhu, Y., & Howland, C. (1992). The evolution of independent living programs. *Rehabilitation Counseling Bulletin, 35,* 174–189.

Nowak, L. (1983). A cost effectiveness evaluation of the federal/state vocational rehabilitation program using a comparison group. *American Economist, 27,* 23–29.

Nugent, T. (1976). Architectural accessibility. In *State White House conference workbook (Social concerns)* (pp. 63–73). Washington, DC: Department of Health, Education, and Welfare.

Nunnally, J. C. (1961). *Popular conceptions of mental health: Their development and change.* New York: Holt, Rinehart & Winston.

Oakland County Coordinating Council Against Domestic Violence. (n.d.). *Personalized safety plan.* Retrieved December 26, 2006, from http://www.domesticviolence.org/plan.html

Obermann, C. E. (1965). *A history of vocational rehabilitation in America.* Minneapolis, MN: Dennison Co.

Obermann, C. E. (1967). The limitations of "history." In G. N. Wright (Ed.), *Madison lectures on vocational rehabilitation.* Madison: The University of Wisconsin, Rehabilitation Counselor Education Program.

Occupational outlook handbook. (n.d.). Retrieved December 26, 2006, from http://www.bls.gov/oco/home.htm

O'Day, B. (1999). Employment barriers for people with visual impairments. *Journal of Visual Impairment & Blindness, 93,* 627–642.

Office of Technology Assessment. (1983). *Technology and handicapped people.* New York: Springer.

O'Hara, B. (2004). Twice penalized: Employment discrimination against women with disabilities. *Journal of Disability Policy Studies, 15,* 27–34.

Okolo, C., & Sitlington, P. (1988). The role of special education in LD adolescents' transition from school to work. *Learning Disability Quarterly, 11,* 292–306.

O'Korn, D. W. D., & Wheaton, J. E. (1995). Assistive technology for people with visual impairments. *Journal of Applied Rehabilitation Counseling, 26*(4), 8–10.

Olick, R. S. (2000). Genes in the workplace. In P. D. Blanck (Ed.), *Employment, disability, and the Americans with Disabilities Act* (pp. 285–314). Evanston, IL: Northwestern University Press.

Olney, M. F., & Kennedy, J. (2002). Racial disparities in VR use and job placement rates for adults with disabilities. *Rehabilitation Counseling Bulletin, 45,* 177–185.

Olshansky, S. (1966). A look at professionals in workshops. *Rehabilitation Record, 7*(5), 27–31.

Olshansky, S. (1968). The vocational rehabilitation of ex-psychiatric patients. *Mental Hygiene, 52,* 556–561.

Olshansky, S. (1971). Breaking workshop exit barriers. *Rehabilitation Record, 12*(6), 27–30.

Olshansky, S. (1975). Work samples: Another view. *Rehabilitation Literature, 36,* 48–49.

Olshansky, S., & Unterberger, H. (1965). Prejudice against the mentally restored: Fact or fancy? *Journal of Rehabilitation, 31*(5), 23–24.

Ondusko, D. (1991). Comparision of employees with disabilities and able-bodied workers in janitorial maintenance. *Journal of Applied Rehabilitation Counseling, 22*(2), 19–24.

O★NET OnLine. (n.d.). Retrieved December 26, 2006, from http://online.onetcenter.org

Orcutt, J. D., & Cairl, R. E. (1979). Social definitions of the alcoholic: Reassessing the importance of imputed responsibility. *Journal of Health and Social Behavior, 20,* 290–295.

Ouellette, S. E., & Leja, J. A. (1988). Rehabilitation counseling considerations with sensory impaired persons. In S. E. Rubin & N. M. Rubin (Eds.), *Contemporary challenges to the rehabilitation counseling profession* (pp. 153–182). Baltimore: Brookes.

Overs, R. (1970). A model for avocational counseling. *Journal of Health, Physical Education and Recreation, 1*(27), 36–38.

PACER Center. (1999). Ambitious new disability initiatives for 1999. *Point of Departure, 4*(2), 1.

Paciello, M. (2005). Testing usability for all. *Accessible Content Magazine, 1*(1), 6–7.

Parent, W., Hill, M., & Wehman, P. (1989). From sheltered to supported employment outcomes: Challenges for rehabilitation facilities. *Journal of Rehabilitation, 55*(4), 51–57.

Parette, H., & Brotherson, M. (2004). Family-centered and culturally responsive assistive technology decision making. *Infants and Young Children, 17,* 355–367.

Parker, R. M., Szymanski, E., & Hanley-Maxwell, C. (1989). Ecological assessment in supported employment. *Journal of Applied Rehabilitation Counseling, 20*(3), 26–33.

Parker, R. M., Thoreson, R., Haugen, J., & Pfeifer, E. (1970). Vocational rehabilitation service needs of mental patients: Perceptions of psychiatric hospital staff. *Rehabilitation Counseling Bulletin, 13,* 271–279.

Parry-Jones, W. L. (1972). *The trade on lunacy.* London: Routledge & Kegan Paul.

Parsons, M., & Rappaport, M. (1981). Rehabilitation engineering. In A. Speigel, S. Podair, & E. Fiorito (Eds.), *Rehabilitating people with disabilities into the mainstream of society* (pp. 71–88). Park Ridge, NJ: Noyes.

Parsons, T. (1951). *The social system.* Glencoe, IL: Free Press.

Pati, G. (1985). Economics of rehabilitation in the workplace. *Journal of Rehabilitation, 5*(4), 22–30.

Pati, G., & Adkins, J. (1981). *Managing and employing the handicapped: The untapped potential.* Lake Forest, IL: Human Resource Press.

Patterson, C. H. (1957). Counselor or coordinator. *Journal of Rehabilitation, 23*(3), 13–15.

Patterson, C. H. (1966). The rehabilitation counselor: A projection. *Journal of Rehabilitation, 32*(1), 31, 49.

Patterson, C. H. (1967). Specialization in rehabilitation counseling. *Rehabilitation Counseling Bulletin, 10,* 147–154.

Patterson C. H. (1968). Rehabilitation counseling: A profession or a trade? *Personnel and Guidance Journal, 46,* 567–571.

Patterson, C. H. (1970). Power, prestige and the rehabilitation counselor. *Rehabilitation Research and Practice Review, 1*(3), 1–7.

Patterson, J. B. (2003). Occupational and labor market information: Resources and applications. In E. Szymanski & R. Parker (Eds.), *Work and disability* (2nd ed., pp. 247–279). Austin, TX: PRO-ED.

Patterson, J. B., Bruyére, S., Szymanski, E. M., & Jenkins, W. (2005). Philosophical, historical, and legislative aspects of the rehabilitation counseling profession. In R. M. Parker, E. M. Szymanski, & J. B. Patterson (Eds.), *Rehabilitation counseling: Basics and beyond* (4th ed., pp. 27–53). Austin, TX: PRO-ED.

Patterson, J. B., & Witten, B. J. (1987). Disabling language and attitudes toward persons with disabilities. *Rehabilitation Psychology, 32,* 245–248.

Patterson, J. B., & Woodrich, F. (1986). The client assistance projects: 1974–1984. *Journal of Rehabilitation, 52*(4), 49–52.

Patton, M. Q. (1997). *Utilization focused evaluation* (3rd ed.). Thousand Oaks, CA: Sage.

Pawelski, C., & Groveman, A. (1982). The community based model for life skills training. *The Pointer, 26*(4), 21–24.

Peck, B., & Kirkbride, T. (2001). Why businesses don't employ people with disabilities. *Journal of Vocational Rehabilitation, 16,* 71–75.

Peckham, R. (1951). Problems in job adjustment of the mentally retarded. *American Journal of Mental Deficiency, 56,* 448–453.

Pedersen, P. B. (1991). Foreword. In C. C. Lee & B. L. Richardson (Eds.), *Multicultural issues in counseling: New approaches to diversity.* Alexandria, VA: American Association for Counseling and Development.

Peerce, L. (Director). (1975). *The other side of the mountain* [Motion picture]. United States: Universal Pictures.

Pegg, C. H. (1947). *American society and the changing world* (2nd ed.). New York: Crofts.

Perese, E. F., & Perese, K. (2003). Health problems of women with severe mental illness. *Journal of the American Academy of Nurse Practitioners, 15,* 212–219.

Perrin, B., & Nirje, B. (1985). Setting the record straight: A critique of some frequent misconceptions of the normalization principle. *Australia and New Zealand Journal of Developmental Disabilities, 11*(2), 69–74.

Perrucci, R. (1974). *Circle of madness.* Englewood Cliffs, NJ: Prentice Hall.

Peterson, W. (1998). Public policy affecting universal design. *Assistive Technology, 10*(1), 13–20.

Pfeiffer, D. (1994). Eugenics and disability discrimination. *Disability and Society, 9,* 481–499.

Pfeiffer, D., & Finn, J. (1997). The Americans with Disabilities Act: An examination of compliance by state, territorial and local governments in the USA. *Disability and Society, 12,* 753–773.

Pfrommer, M. (1984). Utilization of technology: Consumer perspective. In C. Smith (Ed.), *Technology for disabled persons* (pp. 237–242). Menomonie: University of Wisconsin–Stout, Materials Development Center.

Phillips, S. D., Burns, B. J., Edgar, E. R., Mueser, K. T., Linkins, K. W., Rosenheck, R. A., et al. (2001). Moving assertive community treatment into standard practice. *Psychiatric Service, 52*(6), 771–779.

Pimentel, R. (1995). *The return to work process: A case management approach.* Chatsworth, CA: Milt Wright.

Piner, K. E., & Kahle, L. R. (1984). Adapting to the stigmatizing label of mental illness: Foregone but not forgotten. *Journal of Personality and Social Psychology, 47,* 805–811.

Pinner, J. I., & Altman, A. H. (1966). Selective placement in industry. *Journal of Rehabilitation, 32*(2), 71–73.

Poister, T. H. (1982). Federal transportation policy for the elderly and handicapped: Responsive to real need? *Public Administrative Review, 42*(1), 6–14.

Pollett, S. L. (1995). Mental illness in the workplace: The tension between productivity and reasonable accommodation. *The Journal of Psychiatry & Law, 23,* 155–184.

Poor, C., & Delaney, J. (1974). Houston job fair for the handicapped. *Journal of Rehabilitation, 40*(2), 26–30.

Popick, B. (1967). Social security and rehabilitation: On the move. *Journal of Rehabilitation, 33*(3), 10–12.

Posner, B. (1974). Employment. In J. Wortis (Ed.), *Mental retardation and developmental disabilities* (pp. 230–248). New York: Bruner/Mazel.

Potter, C. G. (1996). After independent living, what next? A primer on independence for people with disabilities, their families, and service providers. *Journal of Applied Rehabilitation Counseling, 27*(2), 36–39.

Potts, B. (2005). Disability and employment: Considering the importance of social capital. *Journal of Rehabilitation, 71*(3), 20–25.

Power, P. (2006). *A guide to vocational assessment* (4th ed.). Austin, TX: PRO-ED.

Power, P., & Marinelli, R. (1974). Normalization of the sheltered workshop: A review and proposal for change. *Rehabilitation Literature, 35,* 66–72.

Powers, L. E., Curry, M. A., Oschwald, M., & Maley, S. (2002). Barriers and strategies in addressing abuse: A survey of disabled women's experiences. *Journal of Rehabilitation, 68,* 4–13.

Pransky, G. S., Shaw, W. S., Franche, R., & Clarke, A. (2004). Disability prevention and communication among workers, physicians, employers, and insurers—Current models and opportunities for improvement. *Disability and Rehabilitation, 26,* 625–634.

Preen, B. (1976). *Schooling for the mentally retarded: A historical perspective.* New York: St. Martin's Press.

Prentke Romich Co. (n.d.). *Access to computers for the physically handicapped.* Shreve, OH: Author.

President's Committee on Employment of People with Disabilities. (1999a, November). *Employment programs for the current workforce.* Washington, DC: Author.

President's Committee on Employment of People with Disabilities. (1999b, January). *President announces disability-related initiatives.* Washington, DC: Author.

President's Committee on Mental Health. (1978). *Report.* Washington, DC: U.S. Government Printing Office.

Preston, T., & Jansen, M. A. (1982). National rehabilitation policy and rehabilitation psychology. *Rehabilitation Psychology, 27*(4), 203-215.

Prince, P., & Gerber, G. (2005). Subjective well-being and community integration among clients of assertive community treatment. *Quality of Life Research, 14,* 161–169.

Prosthesis innovations promise amputees a more versatile future. (January, 1984). *Medical World News, 25*(1), 43–44.

Prout, H. T., & Strohmer, D. C. (1991). *Emotional problems scales.* Odessa, FL: Psychological Assessment Resources.

Pruitt, W. A. (1976). Vocational evaluation: Yesterday, today, and tomorrow. *Vocational Evaluation and Work Adjustment Bulletin, 9*(4), 8–16.

Pryor, R. L. (1968). *Public expenditures in communist and capitalist nations.* Homewood, IL: Irwin.

Psychological Corporation. (1985). *WAIS-R analysis worksheet: Description of the WAIS-R scales and subtests.* San Antonio, TX: Author.

Public called callous toward AIDS victims. (1986, September). *Daily Egyptian,* p. 1.

Pumo, B., Sehl, R., & Cogan, F. (1966). Job readiness: Key to placement. *Journal of Rehabilitation, 32*(5), 18–19.

Pumpian, I., Fisher, D., Certo, N., & Smalley, K. (1997). Changing jobs: An essential path of career development. *Mental Retardation, 35*(1), 39–48.

Putnam, M., Greenan, S., Powers, L., Saxton, M., Finney, S., & Dautel, P. (2003). Health and wellness: People with disabilities discuss barriers and facilitators to well-being. *Journal of Rehabilitation, 69*(1), 37–45.

Rabkin, J. G. (1972). Opinions about mental illness: A review of the literature. *Psychological Bulletin, 77,* 153–171.

Randolph, A. H. (1975). The Rehabilitation Act of 1973: Implementation and implications. *Rehabilitation Counseling Bulletin, 18,* 200–204.

Raskind, M. (1993). Assistive technology and adults with learning disabilities: A blueprint for exploration and advancement. *Learning Disability Quarterly, 16,* 185–196.

Raskind, M. H., & Higgins, E. L. (1998). Assistive technology for postsecondary students with learning disabilities: An overview. *Journal of Learning Disabilities, 31,* 27–40.

Rawlinson, S. (2000). *NETAC teacher tipsheet: Serving deaf students who have cochlear implants.* St. Paul, MN: Midwest Center for Postsecondary Outreach.

Ray, J. M., & Gosling, F. G. (1982). Historical perspectives on the treatment of mental illness in the United States. *The Journal of Psychiatry and Law, 10,* 135–161.

Reagles, S. (1981). Economic incentives and employment of the handicapped. *Rehabilitation Counseling Bulletin, 25*(1), 13–19.

Redkey, H. (1971). Development and utilization of rehabilitation centers and facilities in the United States. In R. Pacinelli (Ed.), *Research utilization in rehabilitation facilities* (Grant No. 22-P-55091/3-01, pp. 75–82). Washington, DC: Department of Health, Education, and Welfare.

Region V News. (Summer, 1997). *Newsletter of the Great Lakes ADA Center* (Vol. 19). Chicago: University of Illinois.

Rehab Action. (1993). Important points to emphasize. *In the Public Interest, 2*(3), 2.

Rehab Brief. (1979). *Independent living rehabilitation: Results of five demonstration projects.* Gainesville, FL: University of Florida Rehabilitation Research Institute.

Rehab Brief. (1984). *Peer counseling: As a movement, as a rehabilitation service* (Vol. 7, No. 2, pp. 1–4). Washington, DC: National Institute of Handicapped Research.

Rehab Brief. (1987). Rehabilitation of nonwhite disabled people. *Rehab Brief, 9.*

Rehabilitation Act of 1973, 29 U.S.C. § 701 *et seq.*

Rehabilitation Act Amendments of 1992, 29 U.S.C. § 701 *et seq.*

Rehabilitation Act Amendments of 1998, 29 U.S.C. § 701 *et seq.*

Rehabilitation Services Administration. (1992). *Rehabilitation-related professions.* Washington, DC: Office of Special Education and Rehabilitative Services.

Rehabilitation Services Administration. (1993). *A synopsis of the Rehabilitation Act Amendments of 1992.* Washington, DC: Author.

Rehabilitation Services Administration. (1997). *Careers in rehabilitation.* Washington, DC: Author.

Reno, V. (2004). *Social security as part of our integrated national disability policy.* Washington, DC: National Academy of Social Insurance.

RESNA Technical Assistance Project. (1993). Reauthorized Rehabilitation Act increases access to assistive technology. *A.T. Quarterly, 41*(1), 1–7.

Resources for Rehabilitation. (1993). *Meeting the needs of employees with disabilities* (2nd ed.). Lexington, MA: Author.

Reswick, J. (1980). Rehabilitation engineering. In E. Pan, T. Backer, & C. Bash (Eds.), *Annual review of rehabilitation* (Vol. 1, pp. 55–79). New York: Springer.

Richardson, B. K., Rubin, S. E., & Bolton, B. (1973). *Counseling interview behavior of empirically derived subgroups of rehabilitation counselors* (Arkansas Studies in Vocational Rehabilitation, Series 1, Monograph 7). Fayetteville: University of Arkansas, Rehabilitation Research and Training Center.

Richter, N. S. (2002). The Americans with Disabilities Act after University of Alabama v. Garrett: Should the states be immune from suit? *Chicago-Kent Law Review, 77,* 879–898.

Rigdon, L. (1977). *Civil rights of the handicapped.* Washington, DC: White House Conference on Handicapped Individuals.

Riggar, T., & Patrick, D. (1984). Case management and administration. *Journal of Applied Rehabilitation Counseling, 15*(3), 29–33.

Rimmerman, A. (1998). Factors relating to attitudes of Israeli corporate executives toward the employment of persons with intellectual disability. *Journal of Intellectual & Developmental Disability, 23,* 245–254.

Risley, B., & Hoehne, C. (1970). The Vocational Rehabilitation Act related to the blind. *Journal of Rehabilitation, 36*(5), 26–31.

Ritchie, H., & Blanck, P. (2003). The promise of the Internet for disability: A study of online services and Web site accessibility at Centers for Independent Living. *Behavioral Sciences and the Law, 21,* 5–26.

Robbins, K. (1985). Traumatic spinal cord injury and its impact upon sexuality. *Journal of Applied Rehabilitation Counseling, 16*(1), 24–27, 31.

Roberts, L. (1977). Foreword. In S. Stoddard-Pflueger (Ed.), *Emerging issues in rehabilitation.* Washington, DC: Institute for Research Utilization.

Robinson, N., & Robinson, H. (1976). *The mentally retarded child* (2nd ed.). New York: McGraw-Hill.

Robinson, T. L. (2005). *The convergence of race, ethnicity, and gender* (2nd ed.). Upper Saddle River, NJ: Prentice Hall.

Robinson v. Global Marine Drilling Co. 3 ADD Sec. 3-126, 6 AD Cases 97 (5th Cir. 1996).

Rodgers, B. (1968). *The battle against poverty: Volume I—From pauperism to human rights.* London: Routledge & Kegan Paul.

Rodgers, B. (1969). *The battle against poverty: Volume II—Towards a welfare state.* London: Routledge & Kegan Paul.

Roessler, R. (1978). An evaluation of personal achievement skills training with the visually handicapped. *Rehabilitation Counseling Bulletin, 21,* 300–305.

Roessler, R. (1982). *A comparison of job development procedures for employment of individuals with disabilities.* Fayetteville: University of Arkansas, Rehabilitation Research and Training Center.

Roessler, R. (1995). *The work experience survey.* Fayetteville: University of Arkansas, Research and Training Center.

Roessler, R. (2002). TWWIIA initiatives and work incentives: Return-to-work implications. *Journal of Rehabilitation, 68*(3), 11–15.

Roessler, R., & Baker, R. J. (1998). Vocational evaluation. In R. T. Roessler & S. E. Rubin (Eds.), *Case management and rehabilitation counseling* (3rd ed., pp. 83–98). Austin, TX: PRO-ED.

Roessler, R., & Bolton, B. (1984). Vocational rehabilitation of individuals with employability deficits: Problems and recommendations. *Research Monograph.* Fayetteville: University of Arkansas, Rehabilitation Research and Training Center.

Roessler, R., & Bolton, B. (1985a). Employment patterns of former rehabilitation clients and implications for VR practice. *Rehabilitation Counseling Bulletin, 28,* 179–187.

Roessler, R., & Bolton, B. (1985b). The work personality Profile: An experimental rating instrument for assessing job maintenance. *Vocational Evaluation and Work Adjustment Bulletin, 18*(1), 8–11.

Roessler, R., Bolton, B., Means, B., & Milligan, T. (1975). The effects of physical, intellectual and emotional training on rehabilitation clients. *Journal of Applied Rehabilitation Counseling, 6*(2), 106–112.

Roessler, R., & Brolin, D. (2004). *Competency units for occupational guidance and preparation* (Vol. 2). Reston, VA: Council for Exceptional Children.

Roessler, R., Brown, P., Reed, C., & Getch, Y. (1999). *Improving special education–vocational education linkages and outcomes for special education students.* Fayetteville: University of Arkansas, Rehabilitation Research and Training Center.

Roessler, R., Brown, P., & Rumrill, P. (1993). All Aboard job fairs: A joint endeavor of the public and private sectors. *Journal of Rehabilitation, 59,* 24–28.

Roessler, R., Cook, D., & Lillard, B. (1977). Effects of systematic group counseling on work adjustment clients. *Journal of Counseling Psychology, 24,* 313–317.

Roessler, R., Hinman, S., & Lewis, F. (1987). Job interview deficiencies of "job ready" rehabilitation clients. *Journal of Rehabilitation, 53*(1), 33–36.

Roessler, R., Lewis, F., & Hinman, S. (1986). *Getting employment through interview training (GET-IT!).* Fayetteville: University of Arkansas, Rehabilitation Research and Training Center.

Roessler, R., Reed, C., & Brown, P. (1998). Coping with chronic illness at work: Case studies of five successful employees. *Journal of Vocational Rehabilitation, 10,* 261–269.

Roessler, R., & Rubin, S. E. (2006). *Case management and rehabilitation counseling: Procedures and techniques* (4th ed.). Austin, TX: PRO-ED.

Roessler, R., & Rumrill, P. (1994). *Enhancing productivity on your job: The "win–win" approach to reasonable accommodations.* New York: National Multiple Sclerosis Society.

Roessler, R., & Rumrill, P. (1998). Reducing workplace barriers to enhance job satisfaction: An important post-employment service for employees with chronic illnesses. *Journal of Vocational Rehabilitation, 10,* 219–229.

Roessler, R., & Rumrill, P. (2002). *The win–win approach to reasonable accommodations.* New York: National Multiple Sclerosis Society.

Roessler, R., Rumrill, P., Hennessey, M., Vierstra, C., Pugsley, E., & Pittman, A. (2003). Perceived strengths and weaknesses in employment policies and services among people with multiple sclerosis: Results of a national survey. *Work, 21,* 25–36.

Roessler, R., & Schriner, K. (1992). *Employment priorities for the '90s for people with disabilities.* Washington, DC, & Fayetteville, AR: President's Committee for Employment of People with Disabilities and Arkansas R&T Center in Vocational Rehabilitation.

Rogan, P., & Hagner, D. (1990). Vocational evaluation in supported employment. *Journal of Rehabilitation, 56*(1), 45–51.

Rogers, J. B., Bishop, M., & Crystal, R. M. (2005). Predicting rehabilitation outcome for Supplemental Security Income and Social Security Disability Income recipients: Implications for consideration with the Ticket to Work program. *Journal of Rehabilitation, 71*(3), 5–10.

Rose, G. (1963). Placing the marginal worker: A lesson in salesmanship. *Journal of Rehabilitation, 29*(2), 11–13.

Rose, M. E. (1981). *The relief of poverty, 1834–1914*. London: Macmillan.

Rosen, M., Bussone, A., Dakunchak, P., & Cramp, J. (1993). Sheltered employment and the second generation workshop. *Journal of Rehabilitation, 59*(1), 30–34.

Rosen, M., Clark, G. R., & Kivitz, M. S. (1977). *Habilitation of the handicapped*. Baltimore: University Park Press.

Rosen, S., Weiss, D., Hendel, D., Dawis, R., & Lofquist, L. (1972). *Occupational reinforcer patterns: Vol. 2* (Minnesota Studies in Vocational Rehabilitation Monograph 29). Minneapolis: University of Minnesota, Industrial Relations Center.

Rosenbaum, C., & Katz, S. (1980). Attitudes toward the physically disabled: Beliefs and their evaluation. *International Journal of Rehabilitation Research, 3*(1), 15–20.

Rosenberg, B. (1973). The work sample approach to vocational evaluation. In R. E. Hardy & J. G. Cull (Eds.), *Vocational evaluation for rehabilitation services* (pp. 139–166). Springfield, IL: Thomas.

Rosenberg, C. (1968). *The trial of the assassin Guiteau: Psychiatry and law in the guilded age*. Chicago: University of Chicago Press.

Rosenbloom, A. L. (1972). Medical traditions in Malaysia. *Journal of Florida Medical Association, 59*(4), 37–43.

Rosenhan, D. L. (1973). On being sane in insane places. *Science, 179,* 250–258.

Rosenhan, D. L. (1975). The contextual nature of psychiatric diagnosis. *Journal of Abnormal Psychology, 84,* 462–474.

Rosenthal, D., & Bervin, N. (1999). Effects of client race on clinical judgment. *Rehabilitation Counseling Bulletin, 42,* 243–264.

Rosenthal, D. A., & Olsheski, J. A. (1999). Disability management and rehabilitation counseling: Present status and future opportunities. *The Journal of Rehabilitation, 65,* 31–38.

Rossi, P. H., & Freeman, H. E. (1982). *Evaluation: A systematic approach* (2nd ed.). Beverly Hills, CA: Sage.

Rothman, D. J. (1971). *The discovery of the asylum: Social order and disorder in the new republic*. Boston: Little, Brown.

Rothman, D. J. (1972). Our brothers' keepers. *American Heritage Magazine, 24*(1), 38–42, 100–105.

Rothstein, L. J. (1984). *Rights of physically handicapped persons*. New York: McGraw-Hill.

Roybal, E. R. (1984). Federal involvement in mental health care for the aged: Past and future directions. *American Psychologists, 39,* 163–166.

Rubin, N. M., & Ashley, J. (1983). Rehabilitation considerations with adult learning-disabled individuals. In S. E. Rubin & R. Roessler (Eds.), *Foundations of the vocational rehabilitation process*. Austin, TX: PRO-ED.

Rubin, S. E. (1977). A national rehabilitation program evaluation research and training effort: Some results and implications. *Journal of Rehabilitation, 43*(2), 28–31.

Rubin, S. E., & Emener, W. G. (1979). Recent rehabilitation counselor role changes and role strain: A pilot investigation. *Journal of Applied Rehabilitation Counseling, 10*(3), 142–147.

Rubin, S. E., & Farley, R. C. (1980). *Intake interview skills for rehabilitation counselors*. Fayetteville: University of Arkansas, Rehabilitation Research and Training Center.

Rubin, S. E., Matkin, R. E., Ashley, J., Beardsley, M. M., May, V. R., Onstott, K., et al. (1984). Roles and functions of certified rehabilitation counselors [Special issue]. *Rehabilitation Counseling Bulletin, 27.*

Rubin, S. E., Richardson, B. K., & Bolton, B. (1973). *Empirically derived rehabilitation counselor sub-groups and their biographical correlates* (Arkansas Studies in Vocational Rehabilitation, Series I, Monograph VI). Fayetteville: University of Arkansas, Rehabilitation Research and Training Center.

Rumrill, P., & Roessler R. (1999). New directions in vocational rehabilitation: A "career development" perspective on closure. *Journal of Rehabilitation, 65*(1), 26–30.

Rumrill, P., Roessler, R., McMahon, B., & Fitzgerald, S. (2005). Multiple sclerosis and workplace discrimination: The national EEOC ADA research project. *Journal of Vocational Rehabilitation, 23,* 179–187.

Rusalem, H. (1976). A personalized recent history of vocational rehabilitation in America. In H. Rusalem & D. Malikin (Eds.), *Contemporary vocational rehabilitation* (pp. 29–45). New York: New York University Press.

Rusalem, H., & Malikin, D. (Eds.). (1976). *Contemporary vocational rehabilitation.* New York: New York University Press.

Rusch, F., Conley, R., & McCaughrin, W. (1993). Benefit–cost analysis of supported employment in Illinois. *Journal of Rehabilitation, 59,* 31–36.

Rusch, F., & Hughes, C. (1990). Historical overview of supported employment. In F. Rusch (Ed.), *Supported employment: Models, methods, and issues* (pp. 5–14). Sycamore, IL: Sycamore.

Rusk, H. A. (1972). *A world to care for.* Pleasantville, NY: Reader's Digest Condensed Books.

Russo, N. F., & Jansen, M. A. (1988). Women, work, and disability: Opportunities and challenges. In M. Fine & A. Asch (Eds.), *Women with disabilities: Essays in psychology, culture, and politics* (pp. 229–244). Philadelphia: Temple University Press.

Rutman, I. (1994). How psychiatric disability expresses itself as a barrier to employment. *Psychosocial Rehabilitation Journal, 17*(3), 17–35.

Ryan, C. (1995). Work isn't what it used to be: Implications, recommendations, and strategies for vocational rehabilitation. *Journal of Rehabilitation 61*(4), 8–15.

Ryan, D. (2004). *Job search handbook for people with disabilities.* Indianapolis, IN: JIST.

Sade, R. (1971). Medical care as a right: A refutation. *New England Journal of Medicine, 285,* 1288–1292.

Safilios-Rothschild, C. (1970). *The sociology and social psychology of disability and rehabilitation.* New York: Random House.

Safilios-Rothschild, C. (1976). Disabled persons' self-definitions and their implications for rehabilitation. In G. Albrecht (Ed.), *The sociology of physical disability and rehabilitation* (pp. 39–56). Pittsburgh, PA: University of Pittsburgh Press.

Safilios-Rothschild, C. (1981). Disability and rehabilitation: Research and social policy in developing nations. In G. L. Albrecht (Ed.), *Cross-national rehabilitation policies* (pp. 111–122). Beverly Hills, CA: Sage.

Saks, A. (2005). Job search success: A review and integration of the predictors, behaviors, and outcomes. In S. Brown & R. Lent (Eds.), *Career development and counseling: Putting theory and research to work* (pp. 155–179). New York: Wiley.

Salkever, D. (2000). Activity status, life satisfaction, and perceived productivity for young adults with developmental disabilities. *Journal of Rehabilitation, 66*(3), 4–13.

Salomone, P. (1996). Career counseling and job placement: Theory and practice. In E. Szymanski & R. Parker (Eds.), *Work and disability: Issues and strategies in career development and job placement* (pp. 365–420). Austin, TX: PRO-ED.

Samuelson, R. (1999, July 5). Dilemmas of disability. *The Washington Post Weekly Edition,* p. 27.

Sand, R. (1952). *The advance of social medicine.* London: Staples Press.

Sandowski, C. (1976). Sexuality and the paraplegic. *Rehabilitation Literature, 37,* 322–327.

Sarason, S. B., & Doris, J. (1979). *Educational handicap, public policy, and social history.* New York: Free Press.

Satcher, J. (1992). Responding to employer concerns about the ADA and job applicants with disabilities. *Journal of Applied Rehabilitation Counseling, 23,* 37–40.

Sattler, J. M. (2001). *Assessment of children: Cognitive application* (4th ed.). San Diego, CA: Jerome Sattler.

Savickas, M. (2005). The theory and practice of career construction. In S. Brown & R. Lent (Eds.), *Career development and counseling: Putting theory and research to work* (pp. 42–71). New York: Wiley.

Sawyer, H., & Allen, H. A. (1983). Sexuality and spinal cord injured individuals: A challenge for counselors and trainers. *Journal of Applied Rehabilitation Counselors, 14*(3), 14–19.

Sawyer, H., & Morgan, B. (1981). Adjustment techniques in transition. *Vocational Evaluation and Work Adjustment Bulletin, 14*(1), 20–27.

Schall, C. M. (1998). The Americans with Disabilities Act—Are we keeping our promise? An analysis of the effect of the ADA on the employment of persons with disabilities. *Journal of Vocational Rehabilitation, 10,* 191–203.

Schaller, J., & De La Garza, D. (1999). "It's about relationships": Perspectives on people with cerebral palsy on belonging in their families, schools, and rehabilitation counseling. *Journal of Applied Rehabilitation Counseling, 30*(2), 7–18.

Schaller, J., Parker, R., & Garcia, S. (1998). Moving toward culturally competent rehabilitation counseling services: Issues and practices. *Journal of Applied Rehabilitation Counseling, 29*(2), 40–48.

Scheff, T. (1966). *Being mentally ill: A sociological theory.* Chicago: Aldine.

Scherer, M. (1990). Assistive device utilization and quality of life in adults with spinal cord injuries or cerebral palsy two years later. *Journal of Applied Rehabilitation Counseling, 21*(4), 36–44.

Scherer, M. (2002). *Assistive technology: Matching device and consumer for successful rehabilitation.* Washington, DC: American Psychological Association.

Schlachter, G., & Weber, D. (2006). *Financial aid for the disabled and their families: 2006–2008.* El Dorado Hills, CA: Reference Service Press.

Schlesinger, A. M. (1957). *The crisis of the old order.* Boston: Houghton Mifflin.

Schlesinger, A. M. (1962). *The politics of hope.* Boston: Houghton Mifflin.

Schlesinger, H. S., & Lee, M. (1980) Sensory disabilities. In E. L. Pan, T. E. Backer, & C. L. Vash (Eds.), *Annual review or rehabilitation* (pp. 356–381). New York: Springer.

Schneider, C., & Anderson, W. (1980). Attitudes toward the stigmatized: Some insights from recent research. *Rehabilitation Counseling Bulletin, 23,* 299–314.

Schrader, B. (1984). Reading but not grasping. *Disabled USA, 4,* 24–28.

Schrager, S. (2004). Osteoporosis in women with disabilities. *Journal of Women's Health, 13,* 431–437.

Schramm, J., & Burke, M. (2004). *2004–2005 workplace forecast: A strategic outlook.* Alexandria, VA: Society for Human Resources.

Schultz, J., & Ososkie, J. (1999). Utilizing brief therapy principles in rehabilitation counseling. *Journal of Rehabilitation Counseling, 30*(1), 4–8.

Schur, L. (2004). Is there still a "double handicap"? In B. G. Smith & B. Hutchison (Eds.), *Gendering disability* (pp. 253–271). New Brunswick, NJ: Rutgers University Press.

Schur, L., Kruse, D., & Blanck, P. (2005). Corporate culture and the employment of persons with disabilities. *Behavioral Sciences and the Law, 23,* 3–20.

Schwartz, G. E., Watson, S. D., Galvin, D. E., & Lipoff, E. (1989). *The disability management source book.* Washington, DC: Washington Business Group on Health/Institute for Rehabilitation and Disability Management.

Scotch, R. K. (1984). *From good will to civil rights*. Philadelphia: Temple University Press.

Scott, R. (1969). *The making of blind men*. New York: Russel Sage Foundation.

Scott, S. (1990). The white cap faces a new challenge. *Journal of Rehabilitation, 56*(1), 15–16.

Scott, S. S. (1994). Determining reasonable academic adjustments for college students with learning disabilities. *Journal of Learning Disabilities, 27*, 403–412.

Scull, A. T. (1977). Madness and segregative control: The rise of the insane asylum. *Social Problems, 24*, 337–351.

Scully, S. M., & Habeck, R. V. (1999). Knowledge and skills areas associated with disability management practice for rehabilitation counselors. *Rehabilitation Counseling Bulletin, 43*, 20–30.

Seventeenth Institute on Rehabilitation Issues. (1990). *The provision of assistive technology in rehabilitation*. Fayetteville: Arkansas Research and Training Center in Vocational Rehabilitation.

Seventh Institute on Rehabilitation Issues. (1980). *Implementation of independent living programs in rehabilitation*. Fayetteville: University of Arkansas, Rehabilitation Research and Training Center.

Shabas, D., & Weinreb, H. (2000). Preventive healthcare in women with multiple sclerosis. *Journal of Women's Health, 9*, 389–395.

Sharp, W., & West, M. (1996). Severe mental retardation. In P. McLaughlin & P. Wehman (Eds.), *Mental retardation and developmental disabilities* (2nd ed., pp. 131–145). Austin, TX: PRO-ED.

Shaul, S., Dowling, P. J., & Laden, B. F. (1985). Like other women: Perspectives of mothers with physical disabilities. In M. J. Deegan & N. Brooks (Eds.), *Women with disability: The double handicap* (pp. 133–142). New Brunswick, NJ: Transaction.

Shaw, K. (1995). The role of the rehabilitation facility in the 21st century. In L. Perlman & C. Hansen (Eds.), *Vocational rehabilitation: Preparing for the 21st century* (pp. 62–70). Washington, DC: National Rehabilitation Association.

Sheffield, J. (2005). Navigating current trends under the ADA. *Employee Relations Law Journal, 31*(1), 3–20.

Sheldon, J. R. (2002). *Work incentives for persons with disabilities under the Social Security and SSI programs* (2nd ed.). Buffalo, NY: National Assistive Technology Project, Neighborhood Legal Services.

Sheldon, J., & Trach, J. (1998). Social Security Disability Insurance and Supplemental Security Income Work Incentives with recommendations for policy change. *Journal of Applied Rehabilitation Counseling, 29(4)*, 8–17.

Shelton, R. (1978). Human rights and distributive justice in health care delivery. *Journal of Medical Ethics, 4*, 165–171.

Sherman, P., & Porter, R. (1991). Mental health consumers as case management aides. *Hospital and Community Psychiatry, 42*, 494–498.

Shontz, F. (1977). Six principles relating disability and psychological adjustment. *Rehabilitation Psychology, 24*, 207–210.

Shrey, D., Bangs, S., Mark, L., Hursh, N., & Kues, J. (1991). Returning social security beneficiaries to the work force: A practice disability management model. *Rehabilitation Counseling Bulletin, 34*, 257–273.

Shurka, E., Siller, J., & Dvonch, P. (1982). Coping behavior and personal responsibility as factors in the perception of disabled persons by the nondisabled. *Rehabilitation Psychology, 27*, 225–233.

Siegel, M. (1969). The vocational potential of the quadriplegic. *Medical Clinics of North America, 53*, 713–718.

Siegel, S., Avoke, S., Paul, P., Robert, M., & Gaylord-Ross, R. (1991). A second look at the lives of participants in the Career Ladder Project. *Journal of Vocational Rehabilitation, 1,* 9–24.

Siegler, M. (1980). A physician's perspective on right to health care. *Journal of the American Medical Association, 244,* 1591–1596.

Siegler, M., & Osmond, H. (1973). The sick role revisited. *Hastings Center Studies, 1*(3), 41–58.

Sievert, A., Cuvo, A., & Davis, P. (1988). Training self-advocacy skills in adults with mild handicaps. *Journal of Applied Behavior Analysis, 21,* 299–309.

Sigelman, C., Vengroff, L., & Spanhel, C. (1979). Disability and the concept of life functions. *Rehabilitation Counseling Bulletin, 23,* 103–111.

Siller, J. (1969). The psychological situation of the disabled with spinal cord injuries. *Rehabilitation Literature, 30,* 290–296.

Silverstein, R. (2001). Proposed regulations implementing the ticket to work and self-sufficiency program: The ticket to work program. *Center for the Study and Advancement of Disability Policy Brief, 3*(1), 1–21.

Simpson, R., & Umbach, B. (1989). Identifying and providing vocational services for adults with specific learning disabilities. *Journal of Rehabilitation, 55*(3), 40–55.

Singh, S., & Magnes, T. (1975). Sex and self: The spinal cord injured. *Rehabilitation Literature, 36,* 2–10.

Sinick, D. (1968). Educating the community. *Journal of Rehabilitation, 34*(3), 25–27, 40.

Sinick, D. (1976). The job placement process. In H. Rusalem & D. Malikin (Eds.), *Contemporary vocational rehabilitation* (pp. 195–208). New York: New York University Press.

Sink, J., Field, T., & Gannaway, T. (1978). History and scope of adjustment services in rehabilitation. *Journal of Rehabilitation, 44*(1), 16–19.

Sitlington, P. L., & Frank, A. R. (1990). Are adolescents with learning disabilities successfully crossing the bridge into adult life? *Learning Disability Quarterly, 13,* 97–111.

Sixth Institute on Rehabilitation Issues. (1979). *Rehabilitation engineering: A counselor's guide.* Menomonie: University of Wisconsin–Stout, Materials Development Center.

Skelley, T. (1980). National developments in rehabilitation: A Rehabilitation Services Administration perspective. *Rehabilitation Counseling Bulletin, 24,* 24–33.

Skinner, B. F. (1953). *Science and human behavior.* New York: Macmillan Free Press.

Slappo, J., & Katz, L. J. (1989). A survey of women with disabilities in nontraditional careers. *Journal of Rehabilitation, 55,* 23–30.

Slosson, R. L. (1998). *Slosson intelligence test–Revised.* East Aurora, NY: Slosson Educational Publications.

Smart, J. (2001). *Disability, society and the individual.* Gaithersburg, MD: Aspen.

Smart, L. (1990). Excerpts of reviews and comments. In L. G. Perlman & C. E. Hansen (Eds.), *Employment and disability: Trends and issues for the 1990s* (pp. 20–21). Alexandria, VA: National Rehabilitation Association.

Smith, R. (1987). Models of service delivery in rehabilitation technology. In *Rehabilitation technology service delivery: A practical guide.* Washington, DC: RESNA Press.

Smith, R. (2002). Female forms: Experiencing and understanding disabilities. *Disability, Culture and Education, 1,* 63–68.

Smith v. Kitterman Inc., 897 F. Supp. 423 (D. Mo. 1995).

Smolkin, D. (1973). The work evaluation report. In R. E. Hardy & J. G. Cull (Eds.), *Vocational evaluation and rehabilitation services* (pp. 177–194). Springfield, IL: Thomas.

Social Security Administration. (1991). *Red book on work incentives—A summary guide to Social Security and Supplemental Security Income work incentives for people with disabilities.* Washington, DC: Author.

Social Security Administration. (1995). *Red book on work incentives.* Washington, DC: Author.

Social Security Administration. (1999, April). *Social Security and Supplemental Security Income disability programs: Managing for today, planning for tomorrow.* Washington, DC: Author.

Social Security Administration. (2006a). *Social security disability insurance beneficiaries.* Retrieved from http://www.ssa.gov/OACT/STATS

Social Security Administration. (2006b). *Ticket to work ticket tracker, the work site.* Available online from http://www.ssa.gov/work

Spaniol, L. (2001). Recovery from psychiatric disability: Implications for rehabilitation counseling education. *Rehabilitation Education, 15,* 167–175.

Spellane, B. (1978). Look who's enforcing Section 503: Simple modification can make the difference. *Disabled USA, 1*(7), 4–6.

St. Louis Developmental Disabilities Treatment Center v. Mallory, 591 F. Supp. 1416 (W. D. Mo. 1984).

Star, T., Brodwin, M. G., & Cordoso, E. (2004). Understanding the benefits of human engineering: Matching assistive technology to individual needs. *International Association of Rehabilitation Professionals Journal (The Rehabilitation Professional), 12,* 55–61.

Stebnicki, M., Rubin, S., Rollins, C., & Turner, T. (1999). A holistic approach to multicultural rehabilitation counseling. *Journal of Applied Rehabilitation Counseling, 30*(2), 3–6.

Steinberg, A. G., Wiggins, E. A., Baramada, C. H., & Sullivan, V. J. (2002). Deaf women: Experiences and perceptions of healthcare system access. *Journal of Women's Health, 11,* 729–741.

Steinbock, R., & Lo, B. (1986). The case of Elizabeth Bouvia: Starvation, suicide, or problem patient? *Archives of Internal Medicine, 146,* 161.

Stevens, H. A., & Conn, R. A. (1976). Right to live/involuntary pediatric euthanasia. *Mental Retardation, 14*(3), 3–6.

Stewart, T. (1981). Sex, spinal cord injury, and staff rapport. *Rehabilitation Literature, 42,* 347–350.

Stiker, H. J. (2000). *A history of disability (Corporealities).* Ann Arbor: University of Michigan Press.

Stoddard, S. (1980a). *Evaluation report on the state's independent living centers.* Berkeley, CA: Berkeley Planning Associates.

Stoddard, S. (1980b). Independent living. *Annual Review of Rehabilitation,* pp. 231–278.

Stoll, C. S. (1968). Images of man and social control. *Social Forces, 47,* 119–127.

Stone, C. I., & Sawatzki, B. (1980). Hiring bias and the disabled interviewee: Effects of manipulating work history and disability information on the disabled job applicant. *Journal of Vocational Behavior, 16,* 96–104.

Stone, D. A. (1979). Physicians as gatekeepers: Illness certification as a rationing device. *Public Policy, 27,* 227–254.

Stone, J. B., & Gregg, C. H. (1981). Juvenile diabetes and rehabilitation counseling. *Rehabilitation Counseling Bulletin, 24,* 283–291.

Strange, H. (1973). Illness and treatments in a Malay village. *Asian Journal of Medicine, 9,* 362–366.

Straus, R. (1965). Social change and the rehabilitation concept. In M. B. Sussman (Ed.), *Sociology and rehabilitation* (pp. 1–34). Washington, DC: American Sociological Association.

Strauser, D. R., Waldrop, D. G., & Katz, K. (1999). Reconceptualizing the work personality. *Rehabilitation Counseling Bulletin, 42,* 290–301.

Strauss, K. P. (1991). Implementing the telecommunications provisions. In J. West (Ed.), *The Americans with Disabilities Act: From policy to practice* (pp. 238–267). New York: Milbank Memorial Fund.

Strickland, C., & Arrell, C. (1967). Employment of the mentally retarded. *Exceptional Children, 34,* 21–24.

Strobel, W., & McDonough, T. (2003). Workplace personal assistance service and assistive technology. *Journal of Vocational Rehabilitation, 18,* 107–112.

Stubbins, J. (1988). The politics of disability. In H. E. Yuker (Ed.), *Attitudes toward persons with disabilities* (pp. 22–32). New York: Springer.

Stude, E. W. (1990). Professionalization of substance abuse counseling. *Journal of Applied Rehabilitation Counseling, 21*(3), 11–15.

Stude, E. W. (2002). Drug abuse. In M. G. Brodwin, F. Tellez, & S. K. Brodwin (Eds.), *Medical, psychosocial, and vocational aspects of disability* (2nd ed., pp. 27–39). Athens, GA: Elliott & Fitzpatrick.

Stude, E. W., & Pauls, T. (1977). The use of a job seeking skills group in developing placement readiness. *Journal of Applied Rehabilitation Counseling, 8,* 115–120.

Sue, D. W., Arredondo, P., & McDavis, R. (1992). Multicultural counseling competencies and standards: A call to the profession. *Journal of Counseling and Development, 70,* 477–486.

Sue, D. W., & Sue, D. (1990). *Counseling the culturally different: Theory and practice* (2nd ed.). New York: Wiley.

Sue, D. W., & Sue, D. (2003). *Counseling the culturally diverse: Theory & practice* (4th ed.). New York: Wiley.

Sulzer-Azaroff, B. (1974). Book review: Action counseling for behavior change. *Personal and Guidance Journal, 52,* 564–565.

Sutton v. United Airlines, Inc., 119 S.CT. 2139 (1999).

Swedlund, N. P., & Nosek, M. A. (2000). An exploratory study on the work of independent living centers to address abuse of women with disabilities. *Journal of Rehabilitation, 66,* 57–64.

Switzer, M. E. (1969). Legislative contributions. In D. Malikin & H. Rusalem (Eds.), *Vocational rehabilitation of the disabled: An overview* (pp. 39–55). New York: New York University Press.

Szasz, T. (1961). *The myth of mental illness.* New York: Dell.

Szasz, T. (1963). *Law, liberty, and psychiatry: An inquiry into the social uses of mental health practices.* New York: Macmillan.

Szasz, T. (1965). *Psychiatric justice.* New York: Macmillan.

Szasz, T. (1966). *The manufacture of madness.* New York: Harper & Row.

Szasz, T. (1973). *The age of madness.* New York: Anchor Books.

Szasz, T. (1977). *Psychiatric slavery.* New York: The Free Press.

Szymanski, E., & Danek, M. (1985). School-to-work transition for students with disabilities: Historical, current, and conceptual issues. *Rehabilitation Counseling Bulletin, 29*(2), 81–89.

Szymanski, E., Enright, M., Hershenson, D., & Ettinger, J. (2003). Career development theories, constructs, and research: Implications for people with disabilities. In E. Szymanski & R. Parker (Eds.), *Work and disability* (2nd ed., pp. 91–154). Austin, TX: PRO-ED.

Talbot, H. (1961). A concept of rehabilitation. *Rehabilitation Literature, 22,* 358–364.

Tan, E. S., & Wagner, N. N. (1971). Psychiatry in Malaysia. In N. N. Wagner & E. S. Tan (Eds.), *Psychological problems and treatment in Malaysia* (pp. 1–13). Kuala Lumpur: University of Malaya Press.

Task Force #1. (1975). Vocational evaluation services in the human services delivery system [Special ed.]. *Vocational Evaluation and Work Adjustment Bulletin, 8,* 7–48.

Task Force #2. (1975). The tools of vocational evaluation [Special ed.]. *Vocational Evaluation and Work Adjustment Bulletin, 8,* 49–64.

Taylor, H., Kagay, M., & Leichenko, S. (1986). *The ICD Survey of Disabled Americans: Bringing disabled Americans into the mainstream.* New York: Louis Harris.

Taylor-Gooby, P., & Dale, J. (1981). *Social theory and social welfare.* London: Edward Arnold.

Technology Related Assistance for Individuals with Disabilities Act of 1988, 29 U.S.C. § 2201 *et seq.*

Ten Hoor, W. (1980). National developments in rehabilitation: A National Institute of Mental Health perspective. *Rehabilitation Counseling Bulletin, 24,* 34–47.

Tesolowski, D. (1979). *Job readiness training curriculum.* Menomonie: University of Wisconsin–Stout, Materials Development Center.

Texas Education Agency. (1999). *IDEA: Final regulations.* Austin, TX: Division of Special Education.

Thierry, J. M. (1998). Promoting the health and wellness of women with disabilities. *Journal of Women's Health, 7,* 505–507.

Thierry, J. M. (2000). Increasing breast and cervical center screening among women with disabilities. *Journal of Women's Health, 9,* 9–12.

Thomas, L. T., & Thomas, J. E. (1985). The effects of handicap, sex and competence on expected performance, hiring and salary recommendations. *Journal of Applied Rehabilitation Counseling, 16*(1), 19–23.

Thomas, R. (1970). The expanding scope of services. *Journal of Rehabilitation, 36*(5), 37–40.

Thomas, S. (1986). *Report writing in assessment and evaluation.* Menomonie: University of Wisconsin–Stout, Materials Development Center.

Thomas, S., & Wolfensberger, W. (1982). The importance of social imagery in interpreting socially devalued people to the public. *Rehabilitation Literature, 43,* 356–358.

Thompson, J. (1992). New directions for consumers and professionals. *Regional Perspectives, 1*(1).

Thoreson, R., & Kerr, N. (1978). The stigmatizing aspects of severe disability. *Journal of Applied Rehabilitation Counseling, 9*(2), 21–26.

Ticket to Work and Work Incentives Advisory Panel. (2003). *Annual report to the President and Congress.* Washington, DC: Social Security Administration.

Ticket to Work and Work Incentives Advisory Panel. (2004). *Annual report to the President and Congress.* Washington, DC: Social Security Administration.

Tinsley, H., & Harris, D. (1976). Client expectations for counseling. *Journal of Counseling Psychology, 23,* 173–177.

Tishler, H. S. (1971). *Self-reliance and social security, 1870–1917.* Port Washington, NY: Kennikat Press.

Traustadottir, R. (1990, July). Obstacles to equality: The double discrimination of women with disabilities. Retrieved November 1, 2005, from http://www.independentliving.org/doc3/chp1997.html

Traustadottir, R. (n.d.). *Women with disabilities: The double discrimination.* Retrieved November 1, 2005, from http://thechp.syr.edu/womdis2.htm

Travis, M. A. (2002). Perceived disabilities, social cognition, and "innocent mistakes." *Vanderbilt Law Review, 55,* 481–579.

Triandis, H. C. (1972). *The analysis of subjective culture.* New York: Wiley.

Triandis, H. C., Bontempo, R., Leung, K., & Hui, C. H. (1990). A method for determining cultural, demographic and person constructs. *Journal of Cross-Cultural Psychology, 21,* 302–318.

Trieschmann, R. (1974). Coping with the disability: A sliding scale of goals. *Archives of Physical Medicine and Rehabilitation, 55,* 556–560.

Trieschmann, R. (1975). Sex, sex acts, and sexuality. *Archives of Physical Medicine and Rehabilitation, 56,* 8–13.

Trieschmann, R. (1984). The psychological aspects of spinal cord injury. In C. Golden (Ed.), *Current topics in rehabilitation psychology* (pp. 125–137). Orlando, FL: Grune & Stratton.

Trieschmann, R. (1988). *Spinal cord injuries: Psychological, social, and vocational rehabilitation* (2nd ed.). New York: Demos.

Trotter, S., Minkoff, K., Harrison, K., & Hoops, H. (1988). Supported work: An innovative approach to the vocational rehabilitation of persons who are psychiatrically disabled. *Rehabilitation Psychology, 33*(1), 27–35.

Tucker, B. P. (1990). Section 504 of the Rehabilitation Act after ten years of enforcement: The past and the future. *University of Illinois Law Review, 4,* 845–921.

Tucker, B. P. (1998). *Federal disability law in a nutshell.* St. Paul, MN: West.

Tucker, C., Abrams, J., Brady, B., Parker, J., & Knopf, L. (1989). Perceived importance of counselor characteristics among vocational rehabilitation counselors and supervisors. *Rehabilitation Counseling Bulletin, 32,* 333–341.

Turnbull, A. P., Turnbull, H. R., Shank, M., & Leal, D. (1995). *Exceptional lives.* Englewood Cliffs, NJ: Prentice Hall.

Tyler, A. F. (1962). *Freedom's ferment.* New York: Harper & Brothers.

Unger, D. D., Campbell, L. R., & McMahon, B. T. (2005). Workplace discrimination and mental retardation. *Journal of Vocational Rehabilitation, 23,* 145–154.

United Cerebral Palsy Association. (1999, April 9). *Title IV—Rehabilitation Act Amendment.* Washington, DC: Author.

United States v. Ellerbe Beckett Inc., 976 F. Supp. 1262 (D. Minn. 1997).

University of Washington Center for Technology and Disability Studies. (2003). *Funding manual.* Seattle, WA: Author.

Urban Institute. (1975). *Report of the comprehensive service needs study* (HEW Contract No. 100-74-0309). Washington, DC: Author.

U.S. Catholic Bishops Conference. (1978). *Pastoral statement of U.S. Catholic bishops on handicapped people.* Washington, DC: National Catholic Office for Persons with Disabilities.

U.S. Census Bureau. (2000). *Disability status 2000—Census 2000 brief.* Retrieved October 23, 2005, from http://www.census.gov/hhes/www/disability/disabstat2k/table1.html

U.S. Census Bureau. (2005, July 19). *Facts for features: 15th Anniversary of Americans with Disabilities Act: July 26, 2005* (CB05-FF.10-2). Washington, DC: Author.

U.S. Commission on Civil Rights. (1983). *Accommodating the spectrum of individual abilities.* Washington, DC: Author.

U.S. Department of Education. (2002). *Twenty-fourth annual report to Congress on the implementation of the Individuals with Disabilities Education Act.* Washington, DC: Author.

U.S. Department of Health & Human Services. (1999). *Physical activity and health: A report of the surgeon general.* Retrieved November 23, 2005, from http://www.cdc.gov/nccd php/sgr/sgr.htm

U.S. Department of Health and Human Services. (2000). *Healthy people 2010: Understanding and improving health* (2nd ed.). Washington, DC: U.S. Government Printing Office.

U.S. Department of Health and Human Services. (2001). *Women's health issues: Overview.* Retrieved October 23, 2005, from http://www.ahrq.gov/research/womenix .htm#overview

U.S. Department of Justice. (1992). *The Americans with Disabilities Act: Title III technical assistance manual.* Washington, DC: Author.

U.S. Department of Justice. (1997). *Enforcing the ADA: A status report from the Department of Justice (October–December 1997).* Washington, DC: Civil Rights Division Disability Rights Section.

U.S. Department of Labor. (1970). *Manual for the USES General Aptitude Test Battery: Section III. Development.* Washington, DC: U.S. Government Printing Office.

U.S. Department of Labor. (1979*). Manual for the USES General Aptitude Test Battery: Section II. Occupational aptitude pattern structure.* Washington, DC: U.S. Government Printing Office.

U.S. Department of Labor. (1991a). *Dictionary of occupational titles* (Vol. 1, 4th ed. rev.). Washington, DC: U.S. Government Printing Office.

U.S. Department of Labor. (1991b). *Revised handbook for analyzing jobs.* Indianapolis, IN: JIST.

U.S. Department of Labor. (2003). *Dictionary of occupational titles.* Retrieved January 3, 2006, from http://www.occupationalinfo.org

U.S. Department of Labor. (2004). *Occupational outlook handbook, 2004-2005.* Indianapolis, IN: JIST.

U.S. Equal Employment Opportunity Commission. (1991). *Americans with Disabilities Act handbook.* Washington, DC: Author.

U.S. Equal Employment Opportunity Commission. (1992). *A technical assistance manual on the employment provisions (Title 1) of the Americans with Disabilities Act.* Washington, DC: Author.

U.S. Equal Employment Opportunity Commission. (1996). *Disability discrimination.* Washington, DC: Author.

U.S. Equal Employment Opportunity Commission. (1998). *Disability discrimination.* Washington, DC: Author.

U.S. Equal Employment Opportunity Commission. (1999). *Enforcement guidance: Reasonable accommodations and undue hardships under the Americans with Disabilities Act.* Washington, DC: Author.

U.S. Food and Drug Administration. (2003, August 13). FDA approves stair-climbing wheelchair. *FDA News,* pp. 1–2.

U.S. General Accounting Office. (1997). *Social Security disability programs promoting return to work: Report to congressional committees.* Washington, DC: Health, Education and Human Services Division.

U.S. Workforce. (1999, April). *The "plain English" version of the act.* Washington, DC: Author.

Uslan, M., Shen, R., & Shragai, Y. (1996). The evolution of video magnification technology. *Journal of Visual Impairment and Blindness, 90,* 465–478.

Uusi-Rasi, K., Sievanen, H., Rinne, M., Oja, P., & Vuori, I. (2001). Bone mineral density of visually handicapped women. *Clinical Physiology, 21,* 498–503.

Vandergoot, D. (1996). Refashioning vocational rehabilitation services to focus on placement. *Journal of Job Placement, 12*(1), 1216.

Van Lieshout, R. (2001). Increasing the employment of people with disabilities through the Business Leadership Network. *Journal of Vocational Rehabilitation, 16,* 77–81.

Vash, C. (1981). *Psychology of disability.* New York: Springer.

Vash, C. (1982). Employment issues for women with disabilities. *Rehabilitation Literature, 43,* 198–207.

Vatour, J., Stocks, C., & Kolek, M. (1983). Preparing mildly handicapped students for employment. *Teaching Exceptional Children, 16*(1), 54–58.

Veatch, R. M. (1980). Voluntary risks to health: Ethical issues. *Journal of the American Medical Association, 243,* 50–55.

Veron, L., & Poulton, S. (1980). *Guidelines: Occupational therapy and physical therapy in the schools.* Baton Rouge: Louisiana State Department of Education.

Verville, R. (1979). The disabled and current public policy. *Journal of Rehabilitation, 45*(2), 48–51, 89.

Volkli, J., Eichman, L., & Shervey, J. (1982). *Employment orientation workshop.* Menomonie: University of Wisconsin–Stout, Materials Development Center.

Vontress, C. E. (1971). Racial differences. *Journal of Counseling Psychology, 18,* 7–13.

Voorde, M. (2005). Community news. *Accessible Content Magazine, 1*(1), 3.

W. T. Grant Foundation. (1988). *The forgotten half: Non-college youth in America.* Washington, DC: Author.

Waldrop, J., & Stern, S. (2003). *Disability status: 2000.* Washington, DC: U.S. Census Bureau.

Walker, S., Akpati, E., Roberts, V., Palmer, R., & Newsome, M. (1986). Frequency and distribution of disabilities among Blacks: Preliminary findings. In S. Walker, F. Z. Belgrave, A. M. Banner, & S. Nicholls (Eds.), *Equal to the challenge: Perspectives, problems and strategies in the rehabilitation of nonwhite disabled* (pp. 27–38). Washington, DC: The Bureau of Educational Research, School of Education, Howard University. (ERIC Document Reproduction Service No. ED 276 196)

Wallace, J. (2003). A policy analysis of the assistive technology alternative funding program in the United States. *Journal of Disability Policy Studies, 14*(2), 74–81.

Wallace, J. F. (1995). Creative financing of assistive technology. In K. Flipper, K. Inge, & J. M. Barcus (Eds.), *Assistive technology* (pp. 245–260). Baltimore: Brookes.

Waller, J. A., King, E. M., Nielson, G., & Turkel, H. W. (1969). Alcohol and other factors in California highway fatalities. *Journal of Forensic Science, 14,* 429–444.

Walls, R., & Dowler, D. (1987). Client decision making: Three rehabilitation decisions. *Rehabilitation Counseling Bulletin, 30,* 136–147.

Walls, R., Dowler, D., & Fullmer, S. (1990). Incentives and disincentives to supported employment. In F. Rusch (Ed.), *Supported employment* (pp. 251–269). Sycamore, IL: Sycamore.

Walmsley, S. A. (1978). A life or death issue. *Mental Retardation, 16,* 387–389.

Walz, T., & Boucher, L. A. (2000). Avoiding iron door barriers to the employment of persons with developmental disabilities. In P. D. Blanck (Ed.), *Employment, disability, and the Americans with Disabilities Act* (pp. 432–446). Evanston, IL: Northwestern University Press.

Waterman, J. (1991). Career and life planning: A personal gyroscope in times of change. In J. Kummerow (Ed.), *New directions in career planning and the workplace.* Palo Alto, CA: CPP.

Watson, S. (1988). Importance of cross-cultural counseling in rehabilitation counseling curricula. *Journal of Applied Rehabilitation Counseling, 19*(4), 55–61.

We are a minority in search of civil rights. (1983). *Access Ability, 1*(3), 1–3.

Wechsler, D. (1997). *Wechsler adult intelligence scale–Third edition.* San Antonio, TX: Psychological Corp.

Wechsler, D. (2003). *Wechsler intelligence scale for children* (4th ed.). San Antonio: Harcourt Assessment.

Weed, R. O., & Field, T. F. (2004). *Rehabilitation consultants' handbook* (3rd ed.). Athens, GA: Elliott & Fitzpatrick.

Wehman, P. (1986). Competitive employment in Virginia. In F. Rusch (Ed.), *Competitive employment issues and strategies* (pp. 23–33). Baltimore: Brookes.

Wehman, P. (1992). *Life beyond the classroom: Transition strategies for young people with disabilities.* Baltimore: Brookes.

Wehman, P. (2001). *Life beyond the classroom: Transition strategies for young people with disabilities* (3rd ed.). Baltimore: Brookes.

Wehman, P., & Kregel, J. (1985). A supported work approach to competitive employment of individuals with moderate and severe handicaps. In P. Wehman & J. Hill (Eds.), *Competitive employment for persons with mental retardation* (pp. 20–45). Richmond: Virginia Commonwealth University, Rehabilitation Research and Training Center.

Wehman, P., Kregel, J., & Seyfarth, J. (1985). Employment outlook for young adults with mental retardation. *Rehabilitation Counseling Bulletin, 29,* 90–99.

Weicker, L. (1984). Defining liberty for handicapped Americans. *American Psychologist, 39,* 518–523.

Weinberger, J. (1984). The vocational evaluation of head injured patients. In C. Smith & R. Fry (Eds.), *National forum on issues in vocational assessment* (pp. 250–255). Menomonie: University of Wisconsin–Stout, Materials Development Center.

Weiner, H., Akabas, S., & Sommer, H. (1973). *Mental health care in the world of work.* New York: Association Press.

Weir, R. F. (1983). The government and selective nontreatment of handicapped infants. *New England Journal of Medicine, 309,* 661–663.

Weisberger, B. A. (1975). The paradoxical Doctor Benjamin Rush. *American Heritage Magazine, 27*(1), 40–47, 98–99.

Welfel, E. (1987). A new code of ethics for rehabilitation. *Journal of Applied Rehabilitation Counseling, 22*(1), 9–11.

Welner, S. L. (1998). Screening issues in gynecologic malignancies for women with disabilities: Critical considerations. *Journal of Women's Health, 7,* 281–285.

Welner's Guide to the Care of Women with Disabilities (pp. 9–16). Philadelphia, PA: Lippincott Williams & Wilkins.

Wendell, S. (1989). Towards a feminist theory of disability. *Hypatia, 4,* 104–124.

Wesolek, J., & McFarlane, F. (1992). Vocational assessment and evaluation: Some observations from the past and anticipation of the future. *Vocational Evaluation and Work Adjustment Bulletin, 25*(2), 51–54.

Wesolowski, M. (1981). Self-directed job placement in rehabilitation: A comparative review. *Rehabilitation Counseling Bulletin, 25,* 80–90.

Wessman, H. (1965). Absenteeism, accidents of rehabilitation workers. *Rehabilitation Record, 6*(3), 15–17.

West, J. (1991). The social and policy context of the act. In J. West (Ed.), *The Americans with Disabilities Act: From policy to practice* (pp. 3–24). New York: Milbank Memorial Fund.

Westling, D. L. (1986). *Introduction to mental retardation*. Englewood Cliffs, NJ: Prentice Hall.

What is a disability? (1997, June). In J. Mook (General ed.), *Americans with Disabilities Act: Employee rights & employer obligations* (Release No. 6, Pub. 775, pp. 3-1 to 3-94). New York: Matthew Bender.

What is a "reasonable accommodation"? (1996, June). In J. Mook (General ed.), *Americans with Disabilities Act: Employee rights & employer obligations* (Release No. 5, Pub. 775, pp. 6-1 to 6-103). New York: Matthew Bender.

White House Conference on Handicapped Individuals. (1977). *Awareness papers*. Washington, DC: Department of Health, Education, and Welfare.

White, J. (1986). Longshore and Harbor Workers' Act. In L. J. Deneen & T. A. Hessellund (Eds.), *Counseling the able disabled: Rehabilitation consulting in disability compensation systems* (pp. 131–145). San Francisco: Rehabilitation Publications.

Whitehead, C., Davis, P., & Fisher, M. (1989). The current and future role of rehabilitation facilities in external employment. *Journal of Applied Rehabilitation Counseling, 20*(3), 58–64.

Whitehouse, F. A. (1975). Rehabilitation clinician. *Journal of Rehabilitation, 41*(3), 24–26.

Whitney, M., & Upton, T. (2004). Assistive technology: Unequal access in postsecondary education. *Journal of Applied Rehabilitation Counseling, 35*(1), 23–28.

Whitten, E. B. (1957). The state–federal program of vocational rehabilitation. In H. A. Pattison (Ed.), *The handicapped and their rehabilitation* (pp. 843-856). Springfield, IL: Thomas.

Whitten, E. B. (1973). A crisis year. *Journal of Rehabilitation, 39*(1), 2, 49.

Wilensky, H. L. (1975). *The welfare state and equality: Structural and ideological roots of public expenditures*. Berkeley: University of California Press.

Wilkinson, G. S. (1993). *Wide range achievement test–Third edition*. Wilmington, DE: Wide Range.

Wilkinson, W., & Frieden, L. (2000). Glass ceiling issues in employment of people with disabilities. In P. D. Blanck (Ed.), *Employment, disability, and the Americans with Disabilities Act* (pp. 68–100). Evanston, IL: Northwestern University Press.

Will, M. (1985). Transition: Linking disabled youth to a productive future. *OSERS News in Print, 1*(1), 1.

Williams, C. (1972). Is hiring the handicapped good business? *Journal of Rehabilitation, 38*(2), 30–34.

Williams, I., Petty, D., & Verstegen, D. (1998). The business approach to job development. *Journal of Vocational Rehabilitation, 10,* 23–29.

Williams, J. (1984). A "perky" revolution. *Disabled USA, 4,* 4–5.

Wilms, W. (1984). Vocational education and job success: The employer's view. *Phi Delta Kappan, 65,* 347–350.

Wilson, D. (1963). Foreword. In U. Bhatt (Ed.), *The physically handicapped in India* (pp. v–vi). Bombay, India: Popular Book Depot.

Wilson, K. B. (2000). Predicting vocational rehabilitation acceptance based on race, education, work status and source of support at application. *Rehabilitation Counseling Bulletin, 45*(2), 97–105.

Wilson, K. B., Alston, R. J., Harley, D. A., & Mitchell, N. A. (2002). Predicting VR acceptance based on race, gender, education, work status at application, and primary source of support at application. *Rehabilitation Counseling Bulletin, 45*(3), 132–142.

Wilson, L. M., Livneh, H., & Duchesneau, A. (2002). Disability services in higher education and rehabilitation counseling. *Rehabilitation Education, 16,* 283–293.

Winzer, M. A. (1997). Disability and society—Before the 18th century: Dread and despair. In L. J. Davies (Ed.), *Disability studies reader* (pp. 75–109). New York: Routledge.

Wittenburg, D., Golden, T., & Fishman, M. (2002). Transition options for youth with disabilities: An overview of the programs and policies that affect the transition from school. *Journal of Vocational Rehabilitation, 17,* 195–206.

Wolfe, K. (1999). Responding to a common concern about hiring people with visual impairments: Access to print information. *Journal of Visual Impairment and Blindness, 93,* 110–113.

Wolfensberger, W. (1967). Vocational preparation and occupation. In A. Baumeister (Ed.), *Mental retardation.* Chicago: Aldine.

Wolfensberger, W., & Tullman, S. (1982). A brief outline of the principle of normalization. *Rehabilitation Psychology, 27,* 131–146.

Woodcock, R. W., & Mather, N. (1989). *Woodcock–Johnson tests of cognitive ability: Examiner's manual.* Allen, TX: DLM Teaching Resources.

Woodcock, R. W., McGrew, K. S., & Mather, N. (2001). *Woodcock–Johnson III.* Itaska, IL: Riverside.

Woodrich, F., & Patterson, J. B. (2003). Ethical objectivity in forensic rehabilitation. *International Association of Rehabilitation Professionals Journal (The Rehabilitation Professional), 11,* 41–46.

Workforce Investment Act of 1998, 29 U.S.C. § 794(d) *et seq.*

Wright, B. (1960). *Physical disability: A psychological approach.* New York: Harper & Row.

Wright, B. (1967). Issues in overcoming emotional barriers to adjustment in the handicapped. *Rehabilitation Counseling Bulletin, 11,* 53–59.

Wright, B. (1983). *Physical disability: A psychosocial approach* (2nd ed.). New York: Harper & Row.

Wright, G. (1980). *Total rehabilitation.* Boston: Little, Brown.

Wright, G. N., Leahy, M. J., & Shapson, P. R. (1987). Rehabilitation Skills Inventory: Importance of counselor competencies. *Rehabilitation Counseling Bulletin, 31,* 107–118.

Wright, T. J. (1988). Enhancing the professional preparation of rehabilitation counselors for improved services to ethnic minorities with disabilities. *Journal of Applied Rehabilitation Counseling, 19*(4), 4–10.

Wrye, D. (Director). (1978). *Ice castles* [Motion picture]. United States: Columbia TriStar.

Yelin, E. H. (1991). The recent history and immediate future of employment among persons with disabilities. *Milbank Quarterly 69*(Suppls. 1–2), 129–149.

Yuker, H. (1965). Attitudes as determinants of behavior. *Journal of Rehabilitation, 31,* 15–16.

Yuker, H., Campbell, W., & Block, J. (1960). Selection and placement of the handicapped worker. *Industrial Medicine and Surgery, 29,* 419–421.

Zadny, J., & James, L. (1976). Another view on placement: State of the art. *Studies on Placement Monograph, 1.* Portland, OR: Portland, OR: Portland State University Regional Rehabilitation Research Institute.

Zadny, J., & James, L. (1977). Time spent on placement. *Rehabilitation Counseling Bulletin, 21,* 31–35.

Zadny, J., & James, L. (1978). A survey of job-search patterns among state vocational-rehabilitation clients. *Rehabilitation Counseling Bulletin, 22,* 60–65.

Zadny, J., & James, L. (1979). Job placement in state vocational rehabilitation agencies: A survey of technique. *Rehabilitation Counseling Bulletin, 22,* 361–378.

Zeitzer, I. R., & Duncan, B. (2004). Employment issues for women with disabilities: Opportunities, programs, and outreach efforts. In S. L. Welner & F. Haseltine (Eds.),

Welner's guide to the care of women with disabilities (pp. 9–16). Philadelphia: Lippincott, Williams & Wilkins.

Zola, I. K. (1981). Communication barriers between "the able-bodied" and "the handicapped." *Archives of Physical Medicine and Rehabilitation, 62,* 355–359.

Zuger, R. R. (1971). To place the unplaceable. *Journal of Rehabilitation, 37*(6), 122–123.

Author Index

Aaron, D., 18
Aaron, H. J., 184
Abrams, J., 277
Achenbach, T. M., 173
Acton, N., 89
Ad Hoc Committee of the
  Commission on Practice, 378
Adams, J. E., 99, 106, 109, 111, 113,
  114, 120, 123, 247, 248
Adams-Shollenberger, G. E., 247,
  248
Adelson, R., 445, 447
Adkins, J., 179, 411, 422
Affleck, J. Q., 392
Agich, G., 199
Akabas, S. H., 231, 505, 513, 514,
  515
Akpati, E., 192
Akridge, R., 383
Albertsons Inc. v. Kirkingburg, 104,
  105
Albrecht, G. L., 169, 184
Alexander, L., 62, 161, 173, 380,
  381, 448
Allaire, S., 403, 412
Allan, W. S., 14, 31, 32, 33, 179,
  368, 370, 422
Allen, D., 274
Allen, H., 222, 225
Alliance for Technology Access,
  456
Alston, R. J., 192
Altman, A. H., 411
Altman, B. M., 169, 178, 190
American Association on Mental
  Retardation, 242
American Bankers Association, 119,
  133, 135
American Counseling Association,
  461
American Psychiatric Association,
  101
American Psychological Associa-
  tion, 379, 461
American School Counseling As-
  sociation, 461

American Speech-Language-
  Hearing Association, 379, 448
Ames, T., 226
Anastasi, A., 311, 312, 314, 315
Anderson, C., 393
Anderson, J., 392, 403
Anderson, W., 406, 424
Andrews, H., 224
Angelocci, R., 190
Annino, P., 70
Anthony, W., 230, 231
Area Education Agency 13, 457
Armstrong, A., 446
Arokiasamy, C. V., 167, 176, 178,
  190, 191, 192
Arras, J., 149, 150
Arredondo, P., 199
Arrell, C., 245
Asch, A., 45, 176, 200, 463, 465,
  471, 472, 473, 474, 475, 480
Asch, S. E., 175
Ashby, H., 162
Ashley, J., 248, 249, 250, 253, 254
Asner-Self, K., 410, 514
Asselin, S., 392
Athanasou, J., 227, 229
Athelstan, G., 430
Atkins v. Virginia, 194
Atkins, B., 192, 194
Aubert, V., 175
Avoke, S., 392
Azrin, N., 403, 406, 408, 420, 421

Baillie, B., 239
Baker, E., 374
Baker, P., 145, 425
Baker, R., 303, 304, 374
Balcazar, F., 88, 423
Bangs, S., 82
Baramada, C. H., 468
Barbee, J. R., 407
Baron, R., 233
Bartelo, E., 497
Bartels, E. C., 493
Barth v. Gelb, 114
Basson, R.], 470, 471, 472

Batavia, A., 88, 140, 141
Baum, H., 363
Bayh, B., 56, 60, 62
Beale, A., 245
Beale, J., 115, 116, 125
Beardsley, M., 277
Beauchamp, T., 164, 205
Becker, R. L., 313, 317, 318
Befort, S. F., 107, 108, 111, 112
Bell v. Maryland, 133
Bell, K., 467
Bell, M., 410
Bell, T. J., 192
Bellile, S., 222
Bellini, J., 282, 403, 409
Bender, H. E., 179, 422, 424
Bender, W. N., 250, 254, 256, 257
Benjamin, A., 6, 13, 283, 295
Benjuya, N., 434
Benz, M. R., 464, 465
Berger, K., 393
Berke, J., 439
Berkeley Planning Associates, 380,
  475, 516
Berkman, A. H., 225
Berkowitz, E., 93, 159, 160
Berkowitz, M., 159, 160
Berliner, L., 127
Bernstein, J., 245
Berry, D. B., 222, 478
Berven, N., 232, 320
Besalel, V., 403, 406, 408
Bezyak, J., 178
Bikenbach, J. E., 169
Biklen, D., 178
Bilheimer, E., 444
Biller, E., 302
Bingham, W., 233
Bishop, M., 426
Bissonnette, D., 383, 406, 411, 412,
  418, 419, 422
Black, T. J., 28, 250, 368, 487
Blackford, K. A., 475, 476, 477
Blanch, A., 230
Blanchard, J., 461, 466, 467, 468,
  481

Blanck, P., 88, 114, 436
Blankenship, C., 382
Bleyer, K., 124
Board, M., 25, 27, 32, 43, 50, 58, 59, 125, 128, 139, 496
Bockhoven, J. S., 174
Bogden, R., 178
Bolton, B., 272, 273, 304, 333, 383, 386, 387, 401, 405
Bond, G. R., 238, 239, 240
Bontempo, R., 191
Bonwich, E., 470, 472, 473
Bordieri, J., 232, 320, 328
Borgen, F. H., 313
Bostwick, D., 243, 244
Botterbusch, K., 320, 321, 324
Boucher, L. A., 154, 164
Bowe, F., 50, 56, 60, 61, 169, 176, 180, 189, 190, 199, 217, 220, 444, 456
Bowers, E., 27
Boyle, P., 226
Bracalente, S., 434
Braddock, D. L., 169
Braddy, B., 403
Bradley, P., 311
Bradshaw, B., 383
Brady, B., 277
Brainard, B., 245
Brammell, H., 221, 222
Brandt, E., 429
Branson, R., 190
Branson, W. G., 187
Braun, B. M., 512
Brennan, J., 234
Brickley, M., 246, 248
Brislin, R. W., 191
Brodwin, M. G., 410, 437, 441, 455, 501, 512, 516, 517, 519, 520, 521, 522
Brodwin, S. K., 517, 519, 520
Brolin, D., 247, 248, 323, 324, 375, 386, 391, 395, 403, 407
Bromoge, N., 423
Brooks, N. A., 461
Brostrand, H., 379, 382
Brotherson, M., 451
Brown v. Board of Education, 43
Brown, C., 437
Brown, C. D., 319, 320, 333
Brown, D., 250, 251, 254, 255 449, 456,
Brown, J., 234
Brown, J. A., 506

Brown, P., 393, 412, 420
Brown, S. E., 521
Browning, P., 245, 246
Brubaker, D., 61
Brulle, A. R., 248
Brummer, E., 246
Bruyére, S., 96, 114, 506, 510
Buchanan, A., 201
Buchannan, D., 225
Bulmash, K. J., 175, 176
Burgdorf, R. L., 134, 135
Burk, R., 220, 378
Burke, M., 88, 405
Burkhead, J., 438
Burling, K., 225, 226
Burns, B. J., 240
Burns, E., 4
Bury, M. R., 176
Busby, H., 282
Busse, D., 162
Bussone, A., 370
Butcher, J. N., 311
Butler, S. E., 261, 263
Buzzanell, P. M., 474
Byrd, E. K., 423, 425
Byrd, P. D., 423, 425

Cairl, R. E., 175
Campbell, D., 246, 248
Campbell, J., 121, 122, 387, 388
Campbell, L. R., 179
Campbell, N., 386, 387
Campbell, W., 229
Camus, A., 179, 181
Canon v. Clark, 103
Cape, A. L., 478, 481
Capella, M. E., 192
Caplan, N., 54
Cardoso, E., 437, 441, 455
Carlsen, P., 378
Carlson, D., 472
Carlson, W. L., 178
Carson, G., 23
Carter, S., 10, 444
Cartwright, B. Y., 192
Carty, E. M., 474, 476, 477
Caston, H., 303, 304, 327
Castorena v. Runyon, 123
Cattell, A. K., 311, 312
Cattell, H. E., 311, 312
Cattell, R. B., 311, 312
Centers for Disease Control and Prevention, 467, 468, 469
Certo, N., 248

Chan, F., 178, 269, 271, 279, 362
Chandler, S., 453
Chang, J. C., 469, 479, 481
Chanpong, G. F., 467
Cheatham, H. E., 192
Cheing, G., 178
Chemerinsky, E., 104, 105, 125
Childress, J., 164, 205
Childs, B., 257
Chronister, J., 240
Chubon, R., 270
Church, G., 170, 443
Ciardiello, J., 233
CIL Berkeley, 489, 493
Civil Rights Act of 1964, 44, 67, 105, 123, 124, 134, 141, 189
Clark, C. D., 178
Clark, G. R., 12
Clarke, A., 514
Clowers, M. R., 272
Cogan, F., 402
Cogdal, P., 511
Cohen, C., 149, 150
Cohen, D., 88
Cohen, M., 231
Cohen, R. J., 306, 311, 312, 314
Coil, J. H., 98, 101, 107, 108, 114, 118, 125
Cole, J., 490, 493, 496
Coleman, J. C., 4, 5
Colker, R., 93, 96, 99, 100, 105, 125
Collings v. Longview Fibre Co., 101
Collins, R., 233
Colonna, R., 283
Combs, J., 387
Commager, H. S., 7, 18, 22, 188
Conley, R., 179, 416
Conn, R. A., 190
Connine, T., 225, 443
Conte, L., 352
Convery, J., 100, 118, 133
Cook, A., 430, 467
Cook, A. M., 69, 264, 432, 435, 439
Cook, D., 224, 383,
Cook, J., 230, 240, 265
Cook, T. M., 94, 128
Cooper, R., 432
Coppola, J., 232
Corcoran, P., 497
Cordoso, E., 521
Corrigan, P., 403
Corthell, D., 325, 327

Costello, J., 325, 327
Couch, R. H., 319
Coudrouglou, A., 182
Coulter, D., 242
Coulter, P., 376
Council on Rehabilitation Education, 285, 504, 505, 522
Covey, S., 388, 389
Cramer, E. P., 462
Cramp, J., 370
Crewe, N., 430
Crimando, W., 84, 328, 486
Cronbach, L. J., 51
Cronin, M., 70, 392, 393, 395
Crow, S. H., 321
Crowther, R. E., 240
Crudden, A., 261, 262, 263
Crystal, R. M., 248, 426
Cull, J., 223, 495
Currie-Gross, V., 489
Curry, M. A., 478, 479, 480
Cushman, L., 223
Cutler, F., 305, 310, 322, 326, 327
Cutright, P., 184

D'Amico, R., 392, 395
Dahlstrom, W. G., 311
Dakunchak, P., 370
Dale, J., 183, 186
Dalgin, R. S., 121, 122, 123
Danek, M., 229, 390, 392, 394
Daniels, N., 146, 153
Dankmeyer, C., 377
Darnell, R., 222
Darney, P. D., 471
Davies, L. J., 178
Davis, E. L., 61, 62
Davis, L., 96, 192
Davis, P., 372, 383
Davis, S., 393
Dawis, R., 328, 350
De La Garza, D., 283
Deegan, M. J., 461
Degeneffe, C., 367, 368, 372
DeJong, G., 35, 45, 61, 140, 141, 169, 176, 180, 189, 190, 206, 485, 488, 489, 490, 491
DeLaGarza, D., 410, 516
Delaney, J., 420
DeLoach, C., 165, 229, 230, 471, 474, 485, 488, 490, 495, 496, 497
Dembo, T., 164
Deneen, L. J., 508, 510

Dennin v. Connecticut Interscholastic Athletic Conference, 127
DeOre, J., 160
DePoy, E., 175, 178, 181, 188, 194, 462, 479, 480
Deutsch, A., 3, 4, 6, 7, 14, 169, 170, 171, 172, 173, 174, 178, 179, 188
Deutsch, P. M., 512
Devience, A., 100, 118, 133
Devins, G., 221, 222, 489
DeWitt, J., 430
Dexter, L., 189
Diamond, M., 226
Dietzen, L. L., 238
Dijkers, M., 223
Dileo, D., 372, 424
Dillingham, J., 452, 453
Dispenza, M. L., 106, 110, 113, 117
Ditillo, D., 227
Dixon, G. L., 452, 454
Dodd, J., 282
Dole, R., 159
Domino, G., 312
Domino, M. L., 312
Donnell, C., 280, 351
Donnell, C. M., 511
Doren, B., 464, 465
Doris, J., 20, 21
Dowell, D. A., 232
Dowler, D., 82, 363
Dowling, P. J., 476
Drehmer, D. E., 232
Drew, C., 242, 243
Drey, E. A., 471
Driscoll, J., 232
Droege, R. C., 307, 308, 309
Duchesneau, A., 522
Dumas, L., 256
Duncan, B., 463
Duncan, J., 46
Dunn, D., 255, 322, 323, 404
Dunn, L. M., 5, 11
Durbin, D., 506
Dvonch, P., 176
Dye, T. R., 43, 44
Dziekan, K., 192

Eazell, D. E., 160, 179
Echazabal v. Chevron USA, 120
Eckert, J. M., 485
Edgar, C., 57
Edgar, E., 392
Edgar, E. R., 240
Edmonds, C. D., 96

Eichman, L., 403
Eisengart, S., 283
Eisenman, L., 392, 395
Eldredge, G., 304
Eleventh Institute on Rehabilitation Issues, 393
Ellner, J. R., 179, 422, 424
Emener, W. G., 272, 275, 423
Enders, A., 452, 454
Engelkes, J. R., 402
Enright, M., 352
Erlanger, H. S., 34, 43
Esser, T., 375
Esterson, A., 174
Ettinger, J., 352

Fabian, E., 232, 237, 238, 413, 416, 417, 505
Fafard, M. B., 251
Fagen, T., 176
Faiver, C., 283
Falvo, D., 222, 377
Fanning, P., 248
Farley, R. C., 293, 295, 297, 304, 408
Farr, J. M., 341, 342, 346, 347, 417
Farrow, J., 226
Faulkner, H. U., 24
Fawcett, S., 401, 403, 406
Fay, F., 50, 497
Fearday, F. L., 478, 481
Federal Employees Health Benefits Program, 508
Federal Register, 51, 64, 65, 487
Feinstein, C., 393
Feist-Price, S., 192, 464, 465
Fekete, D. M., 240
Feldblum, C., 55, 99, 106, 111, 115, 117, 118, 119, 124, 141
Fenderson, D. A., 176
Ferguson, B., 391
Field, T., 10, 514, 517, 519
Fielder, J. F., 113
Fielding, G. J., 64, 67
Fields, C., 61, 62
Filkins, L. D., 178
Finch, E., 404, 406
Fine, M., 15, 17, 18, 200, 463, 465, 469, 471, 472, 473, 474, 475, 480
Finn, J., 93, 140
Finucci, J. M., 257
Fischer, J., 282
Fisher, D., 248

Fisher, M., 372
Fishman, M., 390
Fitting, M. D., 190
Fitzgerald, S., 241
Flandez, R., 433
Flannery, W., 124
Flannigan, J., 162
Fleischer, D. Z., 146, 148, 151, 155, 162, 372, 485
Flemmings v. Howard University, 117
Flexer, R. W., 245
Flores, T., 403
Flowers, C., 486, 493
Flynn, R. J., 490
Fogarty, T., 248
Fonosch, G. G., 61
Forbes, W., 486
Ford, J. A., 478
Ford, L., 280, 281, 401
Forness, S. R., 257
Foss, G., 243, 244
Foucault, M., 170, 173, 174, 179
Fowler, C., 200
Franche, R., 514
Francis, F., 15, 423
Frank, A. R., 256
Frank, J., 403, 409
Fraser, K. E., 260
Fraser, R. T., 272
Freed, E., 178
Freeman, H. E., 51
Fried, C., 146, 147
Frieden, L., 155, 166, 490, 493, 496, 499
Friedlander, R., 442
Friedson, E., 175, 190
Frierson, J. G., 102, 103, 104
Fritzche, B., 313, 314, 341
Fry, R., 421
Fuhrer, M., 77
Fullmer, S., 82
Fulton, S. A., 463, 464, 465
Furnas, J. C., 6, 7, 8
Furnham, A., 178

Gagne, C., 241
Gallagher, J., 243
Gallor, S. M., 464, 466
Galvin, D. E., 505, 513
Galvin, J., 445, 451
Ganet, M., 403
Gannaway, T., 10
Garcia, S., 107, 283
Gardner, K., 373, 384

Garland-Thomson, R., 461, 471, 481
Garner, W. E., 274, 276
Garrett, J. F., 3, 125, 126
Garske, G., 240, 274
Gartner, A., 169, 178
Gatens-Robinson, E., 197, 205
Gates, L. B., 505, 515
Gaylord-Ross, R., 392
Gearheart, B., 260, 372, 386
Gearheart, C., 260, 372, 386
Geib, B. B., 254
Geis, H. J., 224
Gelfand, B., 321
Gellman, W., 189
Genova, P. M., 254
Genskow, J. K., 325, 326
Georgia Institute of Technology, 430, 444
Gerber, G., 240
Gerber, P. J., 252
Getch, Y., 393
Gibson, B. B., 431, 432, 433
Gice, J., 318, 321
Gilbert, J. S., 99
Gilbride, D., 404, 405, 407, 410, 412, 417, 425, 505
Gilson, S. F., 175, 178, 181, 188, 194, 462
Glasser, W., 362
Glennen, S., 443
Gliedman, J., 486
Goffman, E., 174, 176
Goldberg, R., 133, 134, 351, 352
Golden, M., 97, 111, 113, 118, 133
Golden, T., 390
Goldenson, R., 373, 376
Goldfine, L., 376
Goldstein, A., 283
Goldston, R., 28, 29
Goldstone, D., 233
Goodwin, L., 270, 271, 280, 401, 405
Gordon, G., 180
Gordon, L., 248
Gordon, W., 222
Gosling, F. G., 173, 174, 175, 188
Gostin, L. O., 122
Gottfredson, G., 341
Gottfredson, L., 352
Gottfredson, L. S., 257
Gough, H. G., 311
Gove, W. R., 174
Governmental Activities Office,

405
Goyette, C., 248
Grady, K. E., 461
Graham, J. R., 311
Graham, L. R., 153
Graham, M., 228
Graham, S., 251
Gray, D., 403, 455
Greenburg, J. C., 120, 121
Greenhouse, L., 104
Greenwood, R., 229, 380, 381, 422, 425
Greer, D., 178
Gregg, C., 225
Gregg, C. H., 225
Gregory, R. J., 307, 308, 309, 384, 385
Grieve, S., 475
Griffin, H., 62, 377
Grimes, J. W., 514
Grissom, J., 304
Grob, G. N., 6, 174, 188
Groce, N., 8, 32
Groff, J. Y., 470
Groth-Marnat, G., 302, 306, 312
Growick, B., 152
Gugerty, J. J., 248, 250, 251, 254
Guice, S., 190
Gulick, E., 224, 225
Guzzardi, L. R., 254
Gwee, A. L., 171

Habeck, R. V., 513, 514
Hagner, D., 326, 370, 372, 424, 505
Hahn, H., 52, 53, 54, 59, 89, 157, 169, 176, 180, 189, 190, 194, 202, 203, 204, 212
Haliker, D., 150
Hall, C., 11, 408, 498
Haller, M. H., 16, 178
Halpern, A., 246, 395, 430
Hamburger, M., 233
Hamilton, K., 176, 217, 219, 220
Hammer, A. L., 313
Hammerman, S., 179
Hanley-Maxwell, C., 289, 413, 414, 505
Hanna, W., 461, 473, 481
Hansen, J. C., 313
Harasymiw, S., 222
Hardman, M., 242
Harley, D. A., 192
Harmon, L. W., 313, 314
Harris v. H & W Contracting Co., 103

Harris, D., 282
Harris, J., 149, 150
Harrison, K., 231
Harrison, T. C., 462
Hart, D., 233, 442
Hartlage, L., 233
Hartman, L. A., 252
Hasazi, S., 248
Hassouneh-Phillips, D., 478, 479, 480
Haubrich, P. A., 251
Haugen, J., 33
Havranek, J. E., 511, 514, 522
Hayward, B., 446
Head, L., 145, 425
Hearne, P. G., 140, 141
Heider, F., 175
Heimbach, J., 489
Hein, S., 347, 351
Hendel, D., 350
Hendricks, D. J., 380
Hennessey, M., 269
Herbert, J. T., 17, 28, 185, 192
Hernandez, B., 88, 423
Hersen, M., 231
Hershenson, D., 218, 219, 269, 270, 283, 352, 362
Hess, H., 233
Hess, J., 239
Hessellund, T. A., 508, 510
Heward, W., 69, 70, 241, 242, 249, 250, 260
Hickey, H., 378
Higgins, E. L., 257, 258, 259
Hill, J., 387
Hill, M., 369
Himler, L., 221
Hindman, D., 148
Hinkebein, J., 252
Hinman, S., 11, 386, 401, 407, 408
Hirsh, A., 380
Hochstedler, E., 180, 181
Hoehne, C., 30, 31
Hoffman, P. R., 323
Hofstadter, R., 7, 18, 19, 21, 22
Hohmann, G., 217
Hoisington, V., 233
Holbrook, S. H., 8, 9, 10, 13
Holcomb, R. L., 178
Holden, J., 233
Holland, J., 313, 314, 315, 316, 341, 346, 347
Honey, S., 422
Hoops, H., 231

Hoppe, M. S., 190
Horiuchi, C., 248
Hosek, S., 461, 466, 467, 468, 481
Hough, J., 467
Howie, J., 205, 206, 208, 210, 211
Howland, C.,
Howland, C. A., 467, 470, 478
Huang, L., 450
Huffaker, B., 405
Hughes, C., 74
Hughes, R. B., 467, 470, 473, 478
Hui, C. H., 191
Hull, K., 45, 62, 67
Hume, K., 236
Humphrey v. Memorial Hospitals Association, 117
Hursh, N., 82, 395
Huss, D. S., 431, 432, 433
Hussey, S. M., 69, 264, 432, 435, 439
Huxley, P., 240
Hylbert, K., Jr., 295
Hylbert, K., Sr., 295

Ianacone, R., 392
ICAN, 442
Illich, I., 190
ILRU Insights, 493
Ince, L., 376, 377
Indices, Inc., 430
Infinitec, 437, 438
Ingelfinger, F. J., 147, 148
Ingraham, K., 240
Institute of Medicine, 431, 435, 444
International Association of Rehabilitation Professionals, 505, 508
Ira, V., 434
Irvin, L., 245

Jackman, M., 190, 191
Jacobs, H., 235, 403
Jaffe, D., 353
James, L., 155, 175, 272, 404, 418, 426
Janikowski, T., 320
Janis, I., 353
Jans, L., 468, 475
Jansen, M. A., 190, 464, 465
Jastak, J., 313, 316, 317
Jastak, S., 310, 313, 316, 317
Jenkins, W., 74, 281, 510
Jessop, D., 423
Johnson, K. L., 521
Johnson, S., 282

Johnson, V., 229, 422, 425
Johnston, M. V., 160, 179
Jome, L., 351
Jones, A., 46, 51, 73,
Jones, E. E., 232
Jones, G. C., 467
Jones, N. L., 62, 99, 100, 113, 119, 133, 134, 137, 139, 194
Jones, R. J., 420, 421
Jones, W., 461
Judge, M., 20
Justesen, T., 452, 454

Kaemmer, B., 311
Kagay, M., 94, 202
Kahle, L. R., 174
Kahn, D. L., 462
Kaiser, J., 63, 334
Kalb, R., 363
Kamieniecki, S., 180, 191
Kanfer, F., 283
Kaplan, A. B., 106, 120, 121
Kaplan, D., 142
Kaplan, H. S., 225
Kaplan, R. M., 307
Kaplan, S. J., 403
Kardashian, S., 235, 403
Karlan, P. S., 112, 113, 116, 117
Kates, N., 239
Katz, K., 384
Katz, L. J., 464, 465
Katz, S., 169
Katzmann, R., 66, 131, 132
Kavale, K. A., 257
Keane, R. M., 506
Keen, L., 104, 105
Keil, E. C., 407
Keim, J., 465
Keith, R. D., 402
Keller, S., 194, 225
Kelley, B., 522
Kelley, R. H., 252
Kellogg, C. E., 306, 307
Kelly, J., 245
Kemp, B. J., 402, 403
Kendall, P., 363
Kennedy, J., 192, 377
Kennedy, T., 194
Kenney, S., 434
Kenny, D., 228
Kerr, N., 57, 223
Kessler, H., 24, 26, 31, 32, 411
Ketz, K., 465
Keynes, J. M., 186, 187

Keys, C., 88, 240, 423
Khanna, N., 464, 465, 466
Kiernan, W. E., 408
Kilb, L., 97
Kilbury, R. F., 485, 488, 490, 492, 493, 494, 495, 498
Kilpatrick, J. J., 155, 156
Kimbro v. Atlantic Richfield Co., 117
King, E. M., 9, 178
Kirchner, K., 513
Kirk, F., 90
Kirk, S., 242
Kirkbride, T., 409, 418, 419, 422
Kirszner, M., 233
Kitchener, K., 205
Kittrie, N., 179, 180
Kivitz, M. S., 12
Klein, H., 233
Kleinfield, S., 162
Kline, M., 233
Knopf, L., 277
Kohler, P., 390
Kokaska, C. J., 169
Kolata, G., 203
Kolek, M., 391
Koller, J., 252
Komisar, C., 442
Kopelman, L. M., 109, 111, 116
Kornblith, A., 363
Kortering, L., 392
Kosciulek, J., 280, 283, 284, 351, 353, 383, 393, 488, 518
Kraepelin, E., 172, 173
Kraus, R., 478
Kregel, J., 244, 413, 414
Kreinbring, R., 235, 403
Kress, M., 513
Kriegal, J., 85
Kriegel, L., 169, 178
Krishnaswami, U., 250, 253, 254, 256
Krueger, D., 223
Kruse, D., 88
Kruz, S. E., 311
Kuehl v. Wal-Mart Stores Inc., 107
Kuehn, M. D., 202
Kues, J., 82
Kunce, J., 232, 252
Kutsch, J., 450, 451

La Forge, J., 190
LaChance v. Duffy's Draft House Inc., 120
Laden, B. F., 476

Lagomarcino, T., 414, 415
Laing, R. D., 174, 176
Lamborn, E., 28, 34
Lancioni, G., 434
Langton, A., 445, 451
Lanhann, J., 228, 229
Lansing, S., 378
LaPlante, M. P., 472
LaRocca, N., 363
LaRue, C., 9, 12, 14, 15, 21, 22
Lassiter, R. S., 27
Latimer, R., 377, 378
LaValley, M., 412
LaVor, M., 46
Lazzaro, J., 435, 436, 437, 438, 440, 444
LC Technologies., 437
Lea, H. C., 178
Leaf, A., 151
Leahy, M. J., 269, 275, 278, 279, 280, 281, 362
Leal, D., 248
Lee, C. C., 191, 192
Lee, G., 240
Lee, M., 98, 99, 107, 108, 142, 260
Lehman, L., 222
Lehtinen, L., 252, 256
Lehtinen-Rogan, L. L., 252
Leichenko, S., 94, 202
Leierer, S., 279, 280, 282, 352
Leins, D., 430
Leja, J. A., 260, 261
LeJeune, B. J., 261
Lemert, E., 174
Lemkau, J. P., 461
Lenihan, J., 10, 12, 13, 14, 30, 185
Lesh, K., 465, 481
Leung, K., 191
Leung, P., 282
Levine, L., 224
Levine, M., 384
Levine, P., 392
Levinson, K., 495
Levitan, S., 159, 160, 179
Levitan, S. A., 31
Levitas, A. S., 170
Leviticus., 177
Levy, C. W., 487
Levy, J., 423
Levy, P., 423
Lewis, F., 386, 401, 407
Lewis, R., 243, 244, 245
Li, L., 478
Li, W., 412

Lichtenstein, S., 393
Lieberman, M., 455
Liebman, R., 517
Lifchez, R., 169, 176, 189, 206, 488
Lillard, B., 383
Limaye, S., 471, 474
Lindberg, A., 378
Lindsey, J., 429
Lindzey, G., 498
Linkowski, D., 393, 410, 514
Lipoff, E., 513
Lipson, J. G., 474, 475, 476, 477
Lissette, A., 478
Little, N., 26, 29, 37, 203, 444, 456
Litton, F., 377, 378
Livneh, H., 522
Lloyd, C., 240
Lo, B., 209
Lock, R., 70, 320, 392
Locke, D. C., 11, 191
Loehlin, J., 498
Lofquist, L., 328, 350
Logan, D., 242
Long, T., 178, 309, 369, 450, 496, 509
Longmore, P. K., 169
Lorber, J., 149, 150, 151
Louis Harris & Associates, 392, 405
Lowenfeld, B., 9
Lubove, R., 19, 20
Luckasson, R., 242
Ludden, L., 341, 347
Luecking, R., 416
Luke, 170
Lustig, D., 280, 347, 351
Lynch, E., 243, 244, 245
Lynch, R. K., 506, 512
Lynch, R. T., 506, 512
Lysaker, P., 410

MacDonald, M. E., 14, 25, 26, 27, 29, 30, 185
Mackelprang, R. W., 188
Mackie v. Runyon, 123
Maddi, S., 498
Maddox, S., 225, 226
Magnes, T., 225
Magnus, E., 463
Maikowski, S., 179
Mainstream, Inc., 63, 125
Maki, D., 225
Maki, D. R., 222, 303
Maley, S., 478
Malikin, D., 183, 243

Mancuso, L., 233, 236
Mangum, G. L., 31
Mann, L., 353
Mann, W., 452, 454, 455
Manosevitz, M., 498
Mansouri, L., 232
Manus, G. I., 190
Marder, C., 392
Marinelli, R., 373, 375
Marini, I., 85, 152, 159
Mark, 170
Mark, L., 82
Marr, J., 385, 386
Marshall, C., 236, 282, 465, 481
Marshall, M., 240
Marshall, R., 31
Martin, J. E., 170, 248, 501
Martin, S. L., 170, 248, 501
Mas, L. O., 512
Maslow, A. H., 498, 499
Mather, N., 250, 309
Mathews, M., 401, 403, 406
Mathot-Buckner, C., 391
Matkin, R. E., 506, 519
Matthew, 170
Matthias, V., 403
May, V. R., 16, 27, 98, 247, 333, 341, 343, 345, 347, 348, 349
Mayall, D., 333, 341, 343, 347, 348, 349
Mayer, T., 224
Mayerson, A., 97
Maze, M., 333
McAlees, D., 304, 325
McAllan, L., 227
McBroom, L. W., 261, 262, 263
McCarron, L. T., 313, 316
McCarthy, H., 279, 280, 282, 352,
McCarthy, M., 472, 473, 474
McCaughrin, W., 416
McClanahan, M., 319
McCoy, L. F., 298
McCray, P., 253
McCuller, G., 367, 369, 384, 385
McDaniel, J., 222
McDaniel, R., 374
McDaniel, R. S., 319
McDavis, R., 199
McDonald, J., 101, 108
McDonnell, J., 391, 392
McDonough, T., 450
McFarlane, F., 325
McFarlane, J., 480
McGowan, J. F., 162

McGrew, J. H., 238, 250, 309
McGrew, K. S., 238, 250, 309
McGurk, S., 240
McHaugh, R., 497
McKay v. Toyota Motor Manufacturing, 98
McMahon, B. T., 178, 179, 241
McManus, L., 85
McNeil, J., 463
McReynolds, C., 240
McWilliams, P., 436
Mead, P., 86
Meager, N., 422
Means, B., 383
Meenan, R., 403
Meisler, N., 240
Meister, R. K., 322
Menchetti, B., 325
Menlove, M., 452, 454
Menz, F., 304, 325
Messer, J., 251, 254
Messinger, S. S., 175
Meyers, G. S., 251, 254
Michaelides, N., 393
Michaels, C., 229
Mikochik, S. L., 93
Miller, D., 410, 514
Miller, J. C., 6
Miller, L. A., 272
Miller, L. D., 238
Miller, R. D., 181
Miller, W., 18
Milligan, T., 383
Millington, M., 410, 425, 514
Milton v. Scrivner Inc, 114, 123
Minch, J., 50
Minkel, J., 450
Minkoff, K., 231
Mirch, M., 378
Mitchell, N. A., 192
Mitchell, T. E., 247, 248
Mngadi, S., 192
Modahl, T., 334
Mohamed v. Marriott International Inc., 116
Monroe, C. H., 263
Moon, M. S., 442
Mooney, W. L., 426
Moore, C. L., 192
Moore, D., 478
Moore, J., 63
Moore, S., 367
Morgan, B., 385, 386
Morison, S. L., 17, 18, 185

Morris, P., 240
Morton, N. W., 306, 307
Moses v. American Nonwovens Inc, 120
Mueller, J., 519
Mueser, K. T., 240
Mulhern, J., 322
Mullen, P. D., 470
Mullen, R. C., 260, 372
Mullins, J. B., 190
Murphy, G., 227, 229
Murphy, J. M., 174
Murphy, K. R., 305, 309, 312, 314
Murphy, P. A., 150
Murphy, S., 362, 370
Murphy v. UPS, 104, 105, 122, 142
Muthard, J. E., 271
Muther, T. J., 106, 109, 110, 113, 114
Muzzio, T., 48, 491

Nadolsky, J., 305, 327
Nagle, K., 391, 392
National Collaborative on Workforce and Disability for Youth, 389, 390
National Council on Disability, 50, 51, 140
National Council on Rehabilitation Education, 504
National Information Center for Children and Youth with Disabilities, 333
National Institute on Deafness and Other Communication Disorders, 440
National Institute on Disability and Rehabilitation Research, 50, 52, 230, 439, 441
National Organization on Disability, 87, 90, 145, 161
National Rehabilitation Information Center, 447
National Women's Health Information Center, 468
Nau, L., 371
Navarro, V., 166
Neath, J., 386
Neely, C. R., 272
Neff, W. S., 322, 323, 324, 383
Neisser, U., 305
Nelson, J., 282
Nelson, R., 304
Nelson, S., 54

Nelson, N., 9, 11, 30, 368
Nemec, P., 231, 241
Neubert, D., 392
Newill, B., 248
Newman, L., 234
Newman, R. D., 417
Newsome, M., 192
Niccoli, S., 222
Nichtern, S., 3, 11, 12, 15
Niese, N., 269
Nikolaou, L., 239
Ninth Institute on Rehabilitation
   Issues, 249
Nitsch, K. E., 490
Noble, J. H., 164, 165, 190
Noll, A., 453, 454
Noonan, B. M., 464, 466
Nordstrom, C., 405
Nosek, M., 77, 467, 469, 470, 471,
   472, 473, 474, 478, 479, 480,
   488, 489, 492
Nowak, L., 159
Nugent, T., 57
Nunnally, J. C., 169

O'Day, B., 30, 261, 262
O'Hara, B., 463
O'Korn, D. W. D., 263, 264, 440
O'Mara, S., 85
O'Toole, R., 387, 388
Oakland County Coordinating
   Council Against Domestic
   Violence, 480
Obermann, C. E., 4, 5, 8, 10, 12,
   14, 15, 17, 24, 25, 26, 33
Office of Technology Assessment,
   159, 447, 452
Oja, P., 467
Okocha, A., 192
Okolo, C., 256
Olick, R. S., 156, 157, 158
Oliva, S., 434
Olshansky, S., 232, 233, 322, 368,
   373
Olsheski, J. A., 513
Ondusko, D., 229
Orcutt, J. D., 175
Orlansky, M., 241, 242
Oschwald, M., 478
Osmond, H., 180
Ososkie, J., 284
Ostwald, S., 282
Ouellette, S. E., 260, 261
Oulvey, E., 240

Overs, R., 382
Owens-Johnson, L., 505

PACER Center, 79, 80, 81
Paciello, M., 436
Palmer, R., 192
Pape, D. A., 303
Parent, W., 369
Parette, H., 451
Parish, S., 169
Parker, J., 277
Parker, R., 283
Parker, R. M., 33, 289, 307, 324,
   325, 410, 516
Parkerson, S., 304
Parry-Jones, W. L., 194
Parsons, T., 175, 180, 380
Pati, G., 67, 179, 411, 422
Patrick, D., 362
Patry, D., 444
Patterson, J. B., 49, 50, 74, 190, 411,
   510, 511, 518
Patterson, C. H., 269
Patton, J., 70, 392
Patton, M. Q., 51
Paul, P., 392
Pauls, T., 403
Peck, B., 409, 418, 419, 422
Peckham, R., 244
Pedersen, P. B., 192
Peerce, L., 162
Pegg, C. H., 28
Pendred, J., 178
Perese, E. F., 468
Perese, K., 468
Perrin, B., 200, 201
Perrucci, R., 174
Peterson, W., 139, 244
Petro, C., 269
Petty, D., 418
Pfeifer, E., 33
Pfeiffer, D., 16, 17, 93, 140, 178,
   217
Pfrommer, M., 455
Phillip, R., 403
Phillips, S., 351
Phillips, S. D., 240
Phillips, S. M., 306
Pimentel, R., 228
Piner, K. E., 174
Pinner, J. I., 411
Poister, T. H., 64, 66, 67
Pollett, S. L., 121
Ponder, R., 235, 403

Poor, C., 401, 420
Pope, A., 429
Popick, B., 34, 35
Porter, D. F., 511
Porter, R., 235
Porter, T. L., 162
Posner, B., 34, 245
Potter, C. G., 493
Potts, B., 403, 404
Poulton, S., 378
Powell, A., 313, 314, 341
Power, P., 290, 294, 302, 303, 305,
   306, 307, 310, 311, 312, 319,
   320, 321, 323, 324, 373, 375
Powers, L. E., 478, 479, 480
Pransky, G. S., 514
Preen, B., 3
Prentke Romich Co., 437, 444
President's Committee on Employ-
   ment of People with Disabilities,
   113, 380, 382
President's Committee on Mental
   Health, 192
Preston, T., 190
Prince, P., 240
Prout, H. T., 303, 311, 312, 313
Pruitt, W. A., 319
Pryor, R. L., 184
Psychological Corporation, 306
Pumo, B., 402, 403
Pumpian, I., 248
Putnam, M., 492

Quatrano, L., 455
Quittner, A., 383

Rabkin, J. G., 173, 174
Ralph, P., 4
Ramm, A., 305, 310, 322, 326, 327
Randolph, A. H., 30, 49
Rappaport, M., 380
Raskind, M., 437, 442, 456
Raskind, M. H., 257, 258, 259
Rawlinson, S., 440
Ray, J. M., 173, 174, 175, 188, 434
Razzano, L., 230, 240, 265
Reagles, S., 229
Redkey, H., 368
Reed, C., 393, 412
Reedy, P., 403
Region V News, 125
Rehab Action, 145, 159
Rehab Brief, 48, 192, 494
Rehabilitation Act Amendments of

1992, 74, 75, 192, 454
Rehabilitation Act Amendments of
    1998, 79, 81, 295, 390
Rehabilitation Act of 1973, 39,
    46, 47, 49, 50, 51, 52, 54, 55,
    58, 60, 64, 67, 73, 75, 79, 89,
    93, 94, 126, 163, 189, 191, 194,
    258, 271, 272, 429, 435, 487,
    503, 516
Rehabilitation Services Administra-
    tion, 36, 50, 78, 159, 376, 377,
    378, 379, 382, 390, 496
Reid, C., 85, 152, 159, 170, 177
RESNA Technical Assistance
    Project, 446, 454
Resources for Rehabilitation, 429,
    437, 439, 440
Reswick, J., 379
Reyes, S. S., 511
Rice, N., 351
Richardson, B. K., 272, 273
Richardson, B. L., 192
Richardson, H., 475
Richter, N. S., 124, 125, 126
Rigdon, L., 494
Riggar, T., 84, 362, 486
Rimmerman, A., 423
Rinne, M., 467
Rintala, D. H., 467
Ripke, B., 237
Risley, B., 30, 31
Risucci, D., 229
Ritchie, H., 436
Robbins, K., 225
Roberson, D., 222
Robert, M., 159, 174, 392
Roberts, L., 485
Roberts, R. R., 272
Roberts, V., 192
*Robinson v. Global Marine Drilling
    Co,* 102, 103
Robinson, H., 241, 242
Robinson, N., 241, 242
Robinson, T. L., 461
Rodgers, B., 182, 186
Roe, C., 248
Roessler, R., 85, 86, 88, 152, 167,
    241, 248, 274, 275, 284, 295,
    303, 304, 340, 349, 363, 383,
    385, 386, 389, 391, 393, 394,
    395, 401, 403, 405, 407, 409,
    412, 418, 420, 421, 488, 505,
    515
Rogan, P., 252, 326

Rogers, J. B., 426
Rogers, J. G., 474, 475, 476, 477
Rogovsky, B., 461, 473, 481
Rollins, C., 282
Rose, G., 410
Rose, M. E., 186
Rosen, M., 12, 370, 373
Rosen, S., 350
Rosenbaum, C., 169
Rosenberg, B., 318, 319
Rosenberg, C., 175
Rosenbloom, A. L., 171
Rosenhan, D. L., 174, 176
Rosenthal, D., 282
Rosenthal, D. A., 178, 513
Rosman, J., 101, 108
Rossi, P. H., 51
Roth, W., 34, 43, 486
Rothman, D. J., 28, 173, 174
Rothstein, L. J., 65
Rowland, S., 408
Roybal, E. R., 179
Rubin, N. M., 248, 249, 250, 253,
    254
Rubin, S. E., 51, 167, 192, 197,
    205, 241, 248, 272, 273, 274,
    275, 276, 277, 282, 284, 293,
    295, 297, 340, 349, 409, 459,
    505, 515
Rucker, T., 351
Rumrill, P., 88, 241, 363, 403, 409,
    412, 420
Rusalem, H., 32, 43, 183, 243
Rusch, F., 74, 248, 416
Rusk, H. A., 32
Russo, N. F., 464, 465
Rutherglen, G., 112, 113, 116, 117
Ryan, C., 401, 403, 406, 407
Ryan, D., 401, 403, 406, 407

Sabornie, E. J., 463, 464, 465
Saccuzzo, D. P., 307
Sade, R., 147, 148
Saks, A., 353
Salkever, D., 389, 394, 395
Salomone, P., 271, 410, 412, 413,
    416
Salsgiver, R. O., 188
Salzberg, C., 367
Samuelson, R., 114
Sand, R., 3, 4, 5, 8, 9, 225, 226
Sandowski, C., 225, 226
Sansing, W. K., 261
Santos, A. B., 240

Sarason, S. B., 20, 21
Satcher, J., 229, 405
Sattler, J. M., 306, 309
Saunders, J., 269, 362
Savickas, M., 341, 352
Sawatzki, B., 232
Sawyer, H., 225, 385, 386
Scales, W., 251, 311, 312, 313
Schaberg, D., 228
Schall, C. M., 106, 108, 109
Schaller, J., 283
Scheff, T., 174, 176
Scheinberg, L., 363
Scheinkmann, N., 375
Scherer, M., 363, 521
Schlachter, G., 452
Schlesinger, A. M., 22, 23, 37
Schlesinger, H. S., 260
Schneider, C., 406, 424
Schrader, B., 455
Schrager, S., 467, 469
Schramm, J., 88, 405
Schriner, K., 88, 363, 425
Schultz, J., 284
Schur, L., 88, 461, 463, 466
Schwartz, G. E., 513
Schwochau, S., 88
Scotch, R. K., 43, 45
Scott, C., 353
Scott, R., 174
Scott, S., 376
Scott, S. S., 258
Scully, S., 513
Scully, S. M., 514
Sehl, R., 402
Seventeenth Institute on Rehabili-
    tation Issues, 429, 430, 450
Seventh Institute on Rehabilitation
    Issues, 496
Seyfarth, J., 244
Shabas, D., 467
Shank, M., 248
Shapiro, A., 178
Shapiro, L. J., 98, 101, 107, 108,
    114, 118, 125
Shapson, P. R., 275, 278
Sharp, W., 242
Shatkin, L., 341, 342, 417
Shaul, S., 476, 477
Shaw, K., 374, 384
Shaw, W. S., 514
Sheffield, J., 405, 409, 419
Sheldon, J., 82
Sheldon, J. R., 83, 84

Sheldon-Wildgen, J., 408
Shelton, R., 147
Shen, R., 440
Sherman, B., 222
Sherman, J., 408
Shervey, J., 403
Shields, D., 88
Shnek, Z., 489
Shontz, F., 217, 226
Shragai, Y., 440
Shrey, D., 82, 83, 85, 395
Shurka, E., 176
Siegel, M., 227
Siegel, S., 392
Siegler, M., 163, 180
Sievanen, H., 467
Sievert, A., 383
Sigelman, C., 430
Siller, J., 176, 221, 222, 223
Silverstein, R., 85, 86
Simon, A., 245
Simpson, A., 235, 403
Simpson, R., 250, 252
Singh, S., 225
Sinick, D., 419, 422
Sitlington, P., 256
Sitlington, P. L., 256
Sixth Institute on Rehabilitation
 Issues, 379
Skinner, B. F., 66, 386
Slappo, J., 464, 465
Slosson, R. L., 306
Smalley, K., 248
Smart, J., 176, 222, 224
Smart, L., 94
Smith v. Kitterman Inc., 98
Smith, R., 24, 25, 26, 27, 98, 99,
 184, 202, 259, 461, 485
Smolkin, D., 321
Social Security Administration, 82,
 83, 84, 85, 87, 262, 511
Sommer, H., 231
Song, C., 88
Spanhel, C., 430
Spaniol, L., 231
Spelkoman, D., 178
Spellane, B., 60
Sperry, J., 496
Spires, H. P., 313, 316
St. Louis Developmental Disabili-
 ties Treatment Center v. Mal-
 lory, 128
Star, T., 437, 441, 455, 521
Stebnicki, M., 282

Steinberg, A. G., 468, 469
Steinbock, R., 209
Stensrud, R., 404, 405, 407, 410,
 412, 417, 425
Stevens, H. A., 190
Stewart, T., 225
Stiker, H. J., 175
Stoddard, S., 468, 475, 492, 493
Stoll, C. S., 175
Stone, C. I., 232
Stone, D. A., 190
Stone, J. B., 225
Stotlar, B., 494, 495
Stotlar, B. J., 485
Straker, M., 383
Strange, H., 171
Straus, R., 35
Strauser, D., 280, 281, 351
Strauser, D. R., 384, 465
Strauss, K. P., 137, 138, 139, 438,
 439
Strickland, C., 245
Strobel, W., 450
Strohmer, D. C., 190, 311, 312, 313
Stubbins, J., 200
Stude, D. W., 422
Stude, E. W., 403, 515, 516
Sue, D., 192, 461, 462
Sue, D. W., 192, 199, 461, 462
Sullivan, V. J., 468
Sulzer-Azaroff, B., 283
Swedlund, N. P., 479, 480
Sweet, E., 280, 281, 401
Swerdlik, M. E., 306
Switzer, M. E., 31, 32, 162
Szasz, T., 169, 174, 176, 179, 180,
 181, 190
Szymanski, E., 74, 289, 352, 362,
 390, 392, 394, 510

Tabor, T., 269
Talbot, H., 161, 162
Tan, E. S., 171
Tarvydas,V., 225
Tashjian, M., 446
Task Force #1, 304
Task Force #2, 321, 322, 324
Taylor, H., 94
Taylor, H. B., 478
Taylor-Gooby, P., 183, 186
Tellegen, A., 311
Ten Hoor, W., 236
Tesolowski, D., 403
Texas Education Agency, 390, 391

Thadani, D., 403
Thierry, J. M., 468
Thomas, J. E., 424, 425
Thomas, J. R., 404
Thomas, L. T., 424, 425
Thomas, R., 31, 34
Thomas, S., 204, 327
Thompson, J., 75
Thoreson, R., 33, 57
Ticket to Work and Work Incen-
 tives Advisory Panel, 86
Tilson, G., 392, 416
Tines, J. J., 248
Tinsley, H., 282
Tishler, H. S., 15, 18, 19, 20
Trach, J., 82
Traustadottir, R., 461, 464, 471,
 472, 474, 481
Travis, M. A., 105
Triandis, H. C., 191
Trieschmann, R., 221, 223, 226,
 491
Trotter, S., 231, 232
Tsang, H., 240
Tucker, B. D., 136
Tucker, B. P., 70, 94, 100, 126, 133,
 134, 137
Tucker, C., 277
Tullman, S., 224
Turkel, H. W, 178
Turnbull, A. P., 248, 249, 250
Turnbull, H. R., 248, 249, 250
Turner, T., 282
Turpin, J., 274
Tyler, A. F., 8, 9, 13
Tyler, L., 169

U.S. Catholic Bishops Conference,
 180, 191
U.S. Census Bureau, 56, 145, 461,
 463, 466
U.S. Commission on Civil Rights,
 5, 55, 56, 59, 60, 62, 63, 67, 68,
 69, 72, 145
U.S. Department of Education, 145
U.S. Department of Justice, 126,
 127, 128, 129, 131, 132, 133,
 134, 136, 137
U.S. Department of Labor, 87, 307,
 308, 319, 333, 341, 347, 377,
 378, 379, 380, 417, 508
U.S. Equal Employment Opportunity Commission, 96
U.S. Food and Drug Administra-

tion, 432
U.S. General Accounting Office, 86
U.S. Workforce, 79
Umansky, L., 169
Umbach, B., 250, 252
Unger, D. D., 179
United Cerebral Palsy Association, 79, 80, 445
University of Washington Center for Technology and Disability Studies, 429, 453
Unterberger, H., 233
Upton, T., 24, 435
Urban Institute, 48, 176
Urbina, S., 311, 312, 314, 315
Uruk, A., 347
Uslan, M., 440
Uusi-Rasi, K., 467

Van Lieshout, R., 421
Vandergoot, D., 409, 410, 412, 425
Vash, C., 38, 54, 202, 217, 224
Vash, C. L., 402, 403
Vatour, J., 391, 393, 395
Veatch, R. M., 152
Vengroff, L., 430
Veron, L., 377, 378
Verstegen, D., 418
Verville, R., 35, 159
Volkli, J., 403
Vontress, C. E., 192
Vuori, I., 467

W. T. Grant Foundation, 392
Wadsworth, J., 200
Wagner, N. N., 30, 171
Waldrop, D. G., 384
Waldrop, J., 145
Walker, G., 165, 485
Walker, S., 192
Wallace, A., 176
Wallace, J., 429, 446
Wallace, J. F., 452
Waller, J. A., 178
Walls, R., 82, 363
Walmsley, S. A., 190

Walz, T., 154, 164
Warren-Marlatt, R., 274
Wasmuth, W., 384
Waterman, J., 351
Waterworth, A., 237
Watson, A., 303, 304, 327
Watson, S., 282
Watson, S. D., 513
Weber, D., 452
Wechsler, D., 242, 250, 305, 306
Weed, R. O., 517, 519
Wehman, P., 244, 245, 247, 248, 369, 387, 391, 413, 414, 415, 416, 446, 453
Weicker, L., 59, 93, 159
Weinberger, J., 334
Weiner, H., 231
Weinreb, H., 467
Weir, R. F., 149
Weisberger, B. A., 6, 13
Weiss, D., 350
Welfel, E., 205
Welner, S. L., 468, 470
Wendell, S., 200, 201, 203, 204, 205, 206, 207
Wesolek, J., 325
Wesolowski, M., 406
Wessman, H., 229
West, J., 69, 72, 93, 516, 520
West, M., 69, 85, 242
Westling, D. L., 242
Whang, P., 403
Wheaton, J. E., 263, 264, 440
White House Conference on Handicapped Individuals, 199
White, D. M., 248
White, J., 509
White, W., 302
Whitehead, C., 372, 374, 375
Whitehouse, F. A., 269, 270
Whitlow, C. B., 384
Whitney, M., 435
Whitten, E. B., 26, 34, 47
Wiggins, E. A., 468
Wilensky, H. L., 184, 185, 186
Wilkins, R., 165, 485
Wilkinson, G. S., 310

Wilkinson, M., 446
Wilkinson, W., 155, 166
Will, M., 153, 156, 291, 292, 297, 390, 453
Williams, C., 229, 423, 425
Williams, I., 418, 419
Williams, J., 441, 444
Williams, J. M., 150
Williams, K., 405
Williams, M., 422
Williams, O., 240,
Wilms, W., 393
Wilson, D., 184
Wilson, K., 395
Wilson, K. B., 192
Wilson, L. M., 522
Winborn, B. B., 402
Wingate, J. A., 248
Winzer, M. A., 169
Witten, B. J., 190, 248, 390
Wittenburg, D., 390, 393, 395
Wolfe, K., 263
Wolfensberger, W., 34, 204, 224
Woodall, H., 430
Woodbridge, M., 450
Woodcock, R. W., 250, 309
Woodrich, F., 49, 50, 511
Woodward, S., 169
Woolverton, M., 450
Wright, B., 170, 175, 176, 187, 189, 190, 217, 218, 224
Wright, G., 192, 278, 368, 370, 401
Wright, G. N., 275
Wright, T., 61
Wright, T. J., 192, 282
Wrye, D., 162

Yelin, E. H., 183
Yuker, H., 189, 229

Zadny, J., 272, 404, 418, 426
Zames, F., 105, 146, 148, 151, 155, 162, 372, 485
Zeitzer, I. R., 463
Zhu, Y., 488
Zola, I. K., 217, 456
Zuger, R. R., 419, 421

Subject Index

ABLEDATA, 446, 454
Abuse Assessment Screen-Disability, 480–481
Accommodation request process, 408–409
Acoustic cue system, 434
Advocacy, 382, 494–495
Affective counseling, 274–275
Air Carriers Access Act of 1986, 72
Albertsons, Inc. v. Kirkingburg, 104, 142
American Charity Movement, 19–20
Americans with Disabilities Act (ADA) (P.L. 101–336),
    93–142, 439, 516–517
  consultation, 516–517
  definition of disability, 96–105
  hearings, 94
  passage, 93
  purposes, 95–96
  rationale, 94–95
  Title I of the ADA, 106–126
    enforcement, 123–126
    essential functions, 106–110
    job application, 117–123
    reasonable accommodation, 110–113
    undue hardship, 113–117
  Title II of the ADA, 126–132
    Subtitle A, 127–131
    reasonable modification, 126
    Subtitle B of Title II, 131–132
    enforcement, 132
  Title III of the ADA, 132–137
    architectural barriers, 134–135
    readily achievable, 134–135
    enforcement, 136
  Title IV of the ADA, 137–139, 439
    dual party relay service, 137–138
    Federal Communications Commission, 138
    enforcement, 138
    TDD, 137–138
  Title V of the ADA, 139–140
Apticom, 333
Architectural and Transportation Barriers Compliance
    Board, 58–59
Arguments for rehabilitation services, 158–164
  balanced approach, 163–164
  cost-benefit ratios, 159–160
  economic argument, 158–161
  moral argument, 162–163
Assistive technology, 379–382, 521–522
  categories, 430
  cognitive-intellectual functioning, 442
  communication, 435–441
  daily living, 443–445
  financing, 451–453
  health maintenance, 441–442
  marketing, 447, 449–450
  mobility and manipulation, 431–434
  problem solving, 450–451
  resources, 445–446, 448–449
  social and recreational activities, 442–443
  training and product service, 456–457
Assistive Technology Act of 1998, 429
Assistive Technology Project , 429
Audiology, 379

Baby Doe case, 149
Balance Sheet, 353, 359–360
Barden-Lafollette Act, 31
Barriers, 464, 479
Bedlam, 5
Behavior management, 386–388
Biotran, 441
Blindness, 440–441
  closed-circuit systems, 440
  optical character recognition, 440
  voice input/output systems, 440–441
Board of Physical Medicine and Rehabilitation, 32
Boston Industrial School for Crippled and Deformed, 14
Brown vs. Board of Education, 43

CAD-CAM System, 441–442
Career perspective, 362–363, 518–519
Centers for independent living, 493–495
Civil rights, 487
Civil Rights Act of 1964, 44
Civil rights for persons with disabilities, 54–67
  Section 501, 56
  Section 502, 56–59
  Section 503, 60
  Section 504, 61–67

Client rights ,495
Client Assistance Projects (CAP), 49–50
Client self-understanding, 353
Commission on Rehabilitation Counselor Certification, 285
COMPASS, 333
Computer, 436–438
　information input, 436–438
　interfaces, 436–438
Consumer involvement, 304
　assistive technology development, 455–456
　rehabilitation planning, 351–352
　vocational evaluation, 304
Consumerism, 488
Consumer movement, 43–45
　civil rights, 43
　Vietnam War protests, 43
Council on Rehabilitation Education (CORE), 285
Counseling, 283
Counselor-client relationship, 281–283
Counselor functions, 269–272
　Clinician, 269–270
　consulting function, 270
　coordinator skills, 270
　counseling and guidance, 271–272
　face-to-face contacts, 272
　mediator, 270
　specialization, 270–271
Counselor interview behavior, 273
　information giving, 273
　information seeking, 273
Crux Model, 339–340
Cultural model, 462

Deafness, 438–441
Deafness early training, 5, 8–9
Demedicalization, 489
Dennin v. Connecticut Interscholastic Athletic Conference, 127
Developmental Disabilities Assistance and Bill of Rights Act (DDA) of 1976 (P.L. 94–103), 68–69
Dictionary of Occupational Titles, 342
Disability definition, 218
　Disability, 3
　Colonial America, 5–7
　Great Depression, 28
　Greek philosophy, 3
　Middle Ages, 4–5
　minority status, 54
　19th-century America, 5–14
　post-Civil War treatment, 15
　Roman philosophy, 3
　World War II, 31–32

Disability management, 513–515
　job-match model, 513
　managed care model, 513
　medical model, 513
　physical rehabilitation model, 513
　services, 514
　work settings, 514–515
Disability statistics, 94, 145–146
Dix, Dorothea, 13–14
Double discrimination/handicaps, 461
Driving aids, 432–433
Down syndrome, 149

Ecological assessment, 324–325
　supported employment application, 324–325
Ecological paradigm, 462
Economic argument, 158–161
Economic condition, 181–187
　demand for labor, 182–183
　government revenue, 183
　Keynesian economics, 186–187
　laissez-faire economics, 184–185
　level of economic development, 184
　level of inflation, 183
　prevailing economic philosophy, 184–187
　socialist economics, 186
　state of economy, 182–183
Employment, 404–406, 463–464
　expectations, 405–406
　inequalities, men vs. women, 463–464
　rights, 404–405
Employers, 421–425
　Concerns, 422–425
　hiring attitudes, 423–425
　partnerships, 421
Engineering, 379
　RESNA Technical Assistance Project, 446
Environmental control, 462
Environments hypothesis, 3
Ethical principles, 205–212
　autonomy, 208–210
　beneficence, 205–207
　justice, 210–212
Eugenics, 15–17
　sterilization, 15–16

Facilities, 367–375
　centers, 370–371
　historical overview, 367–368
　limitations, 372–374
　selecting and using, 374–375
　strengths, 371–372
　workshops, 368–370

The Fair Housing Act Amendments of 1988, 72
Federal Board of Vocational Education, 25, 27
Federal Employers Compensation Act, 508–509
Forensic rehabilitation, 510–511
   expert witness testimony, 510–511

Gallaudet, Thomas, 8–9
Galton, Francis, 15
Ginsberg, Eli, 43
Gladden, W., 18
Golden Era, 32
Greek and Roman attitudes toward disability, 3–4
Group homes, 496
Guide for Occupational Exploration, 346

Handicap, 218
Hauy, Valentin, 9
Hoover, Herbert, 28
Howe, Samuel Gridley, 9–12

Impaired role, 180
Income tax, 23
Independent living, 47–49, 485–498
   comprehensive needs study, 47
   continuum of services, 491, 497–498
   movement, 485–490
   paradigm, 489–490
   service delivery models, 492–497
   services, 491–492, 495
Individualized Education Program (IEP), 70
Individuals with Disabilities Education Improvement
   Act (IDEA), 69–70
Information and referral, 493–494
Information Collection Questions, 296–297
Information Processing Questions, 291–293
Information Processing Summary Form, 328–332,
   353–354
Intake Interview, 294–295
Intelligence tests, 305
   Revised Beta Examination, 306–307
   Slosson Intelligence Test, 306
   Wechsler Adult Intelligence Scale, 305–306
Interest Measures, 313–318
   McCarron-Dial Systems Vocational Exploration
     System, 316
   Reading-Free Vocational Interest Inventory, 317–319
   Self-Directed Search, 314–316, 346–347
   Strong Interest Inventory, 314
   Wide Range Interest-Opinion Test, 316–317
Intermediate Objectives, 361
Internet, 435–436
   accessibility, 435–436
   advantages, 435

   problems, 435
   resources, 446–447
Itard, Jean, 11
Job Accommodation Network, 380–382, 446
   accommodation plans, 381–382
Job analysis, 517
Job application, 406–407
Job aptitudes, 349
Job development, 411–412, 417–422
   strategies, 418–422
Job fairs, 420–421
Job interview training, 407–408
Job satisfaction, 349
Job search, 406
Job seeking skills training, 401–410
   programs, 401–402
   recommended components, 403–410
   supervised practice, 408
   trainer familiarity with world of work, 409–410
Job Task Inventory (JTI), 274–277

Ku Klux Klan, 28

Labor market survey, 518
Learning disabilities, 248–259, 442
   assistive technology, 258–259
   college, 257–258
   definition, 249
   dyscalculia, 249
   dysphasia, 249
   Etiology, 248
   follow-up studies, 256–257
   mixed type, 249
   prevalence, 250
   psychological aspects, 250–252
   pure hyperkinetic type, 249
   pure learning disability type, 249
   rehabilitation potential, 252–259
   social skills, 250–252
   software, 442
   vocational evaluation, 253
Life care planning, 512
Long-term disability insurance, 509–510
Longshore and Harbor Workers' Compensation Act,
   509

Mainstreaming, 44
Medical causes, 171–172
   Hippocrates, 171
   Kraepelin, 172
   Pinel, Phillipp, 173
Medical evaluation, 295–302
Medical model, 462, 513

Melinda Bracken, 298–302, 341, 361
  intake interview summary, 299–300, 341
  intermediate objectives, 361
  medical referral questions, 298
  medical report, 301–302
  outcomes, 361
Minnesota Theory of Work Adjustment, 350
Mental illness, 217–227
  possession, 3
  sanitariums, 4
  societal attitudes, 3–4
  treatment, 13
Mental retardation, 241–248
  AAMR classification system, 242
  AAMR definition, 242
  denial, 243
  employment potential, 244–248
  institutional environment, 244
  job adjustment, 244–245
  prevalence, 242
  psychosocial aspects, 243–244
  rehabilitation potential, 244–248
Minority group model, 54
Moral argument, 162–163
Multicultural counseling, 282–283
Multicultural training, 282
Multiculturalism, 191–193
Murphy v. United Parcel Service, Inc., 104, 142

Naderism, 44
Natural causes, 172–174
19th-century treatment, 7
Nursing, 376

O*NET, 342
Occupational Outlook Handbook, 347
Occupational therapy, 378
On-the-job evaluation, 325
  advantages, 326
  disadvantages, 326–327
Orthotics, 376

Paper-and-pencil measures, 305–318
Penile implant, 226
Pennhurst School and Hospital v. Halderman, 72
Perceived threat, 177–181
  civil commitment procedures, 181
  justification by fear or perceived threat, 179–181
  threat to economic well-being, 178–179
  threat to others, 168
  threat to personal safety, 177–178
  threats to themselves, 179
  threats to the social order, 179
Perkins Institute, 10

Personality tests, 311–313
  16 Personality Factor Questionnaire, 311–312
  California Psychological Inventory, 311–312
  Emotional Problems Scale, 311–313
  Minnesota Multiphasic Personality Inventory, 311–312
Peer counseling, 494
Physical disability, 220–230
  acceptance, 224
  body image, 224
  body beautiful, 224
  coping, 224–225
  reactions, 221–224
  rehabilitation potential, 227–230
  sexuality, 225–227
Physical medicine, 32, 376
Physical therapy, 377
Placement, 410–413, 518–519
  direct intervention, 410–411
  job seeking skills training, 401–410
  selective, 411–413
Planning, 358
  generating a plan, 358–362
  intermediate objectives, 361
  outcomes, 361
Political model, 462
Populists, 22
Post-employment services, 412–413
Private sector rehabilitation, 503–505
  growth factors, 503
  employment opportunities, 504–505
  practitioner skills, 517–521
  services, 503–504
Productivity, 422–423
Professionalization, 190–191
Progressives, 22–24
Prosthetics, 376
Psychiatrics disabilities, 230–239
  assertive community treatment and supported
    employment, 239–241
  employer attitudes, 232–233
  prejudice, 232–233
  psychiatric diagnosis, 231
  social attitudes, 232
  work adjustment problems, 233
  work adjustment training, 233–234
  vocational rehabilitation potential, 232–239
Psychological evaluation, 302–303
Psychological functioning, physical disabilities,
  221–225
  body image, 224
  denial, 221–222
  identification, 221
  passivity, 221
  stages, 223

Physical medicine, 376
Public Law 565, 33–34

Randolph-Sheppard Act, 30
Readily achievable, 134–135
Reagan, Ronald, 71–72
Reasonable accommodations, 110–113, 516, 520
Reasonable modifications, 126
Rehabilitation Act of 1973, 46–67, 89
    consumer involvement, 49–51
    National Institute of Handicapped Research, 52
    program evaluation, 51
    rehabilitation research, 52–54
    Section 501, 56
    Section 502, 56–59
    Section 503, 60
    Section 504, 60–67, 429, 488
    severe disability, 47–48
    Title V of the Rehabilitation Act of 1973, 54–67
Rehabilitation Act Amendments of 1978, 48–49
Rehabilitation Act Amendments of 1986, 73–74
Rehabilitation Act Amendments of 1992, 74–78, 194
    client involvement, 75
    eligibility, 76
    Individualized Written Rehabilitation Program
      (IWRP), 75–76
    interagency collaboration, 77
    Rehabilitation Advisory Councils, 75
    expanded Access to Service, 77
    minority group careers in rehabilitation, 78
Rehabilitation Act of Amendments of 1998, 79–81
Rehabilitation Counselor, 269–285
    cultural encapsulation, 282
    way it should be perspective, 269–271
    way it is perspective, 271–274
    multifaceted role, 274–280
    quality of the counseling relationship, 281–283
    rehabilitation counselor as a counselor, 283–284
    subrole behavior, 273
Rehabilitation Initial Diagnosis and Assessment of Clients (RIDAC), 328, 332–333
Rehabilitation Profession Job Task Inventory, 274–276
Rehabilitation Profession Knowledge Competency
    Inventory, 277
Rehabilitation psychology, 379
Rehabilitation Skills Inventory, 278
Residential programs, 495
    combination programs, 497
    group homes, 496
    long-term, 496
    transitional, 496
Rights or people with disabilities, 145–153
    Baby Doe, 149
    John Hopkins case, 150

    John Lorber, 150
    nontreatment, 150
    right to health care, 146
    right to normal opportunity, 146
Robotics, 433–434
    exoskeleton, 434
    household, 444
Roosevelt, Franklin Delano, 29
Roosevelt, Theodore, 22
Rush, Benjamin, 13
Rusk, Howard, 32

Science of molecular genetics, 156
Self-help movement, 488
Services, 375–384
Sexuality and physical disability, 225–227
Sick role, 180
Situational assessment, 323–324
    advantages, 323
    disadvantages, 323–324
Skill development, 383, 394
Smith-Fess Act, 26–27
Smith-Hughes Act, 25
Social Darwinism, 17–18
Social Gospel Movement, 18–19, 23
Social Security Act of 1935, 29–30
Social Security Act Amendments (1956–72), 34–35
Social Security Disability Insurance program, work
    incentives, 82–84
    continuation of Medicare coverage, 84
    extended period of eligibility, 84
    impairment-related work expenses, 83–84
    trial work period, 83
Socialization, 199
Socialized values, 200–204
    dependency, 200
    devaluation, 202
    employment, 201–202
    independence, 200–201
    productivity, 201–202
    physical appearance, 202–204
    self-sufficiency, 200–201
Social model, 462
Society as cause, 174–175
    perceived responsibility, 175–177
    personal responsibility, 175–176
    societal responsibility, 176–177
Sociocultural milieu, 187–193
    sociocultural trends, 188–193
    sociocultural values, 187–188
Soldier's Rehabilitation Act, 25–26
Sources of job leads, 404
Special education, 20–21
Speech–language pathology, 379

Spencer, Herbert, 17–18
State Federal Program in the 1920s, 26–28
State Federal Program in the 1930s, 29–30
Substance abuse rehabilitation, 515–516
Supernatural causes, 169–171
    demon possession, 169
    divine punishment, 170–171
    healers, 171
Supported employment, 324–325, 413
    Place-train-follow-up model, 415–417
    Train-place-train-follow-up model, 415–417
Sutter v. United Airlines, 104, 142

Terminology, 217–218
    disability, 217–218
    handicap, 217–218
    physical functioning, 219
    vocational handicap, 218–220
    vocational skills, 219
Therapeutic recreation, 482
Ticket to Work and Work Incentives Improvement Act
    of 1999, 85–87
Transferable skills, 519–520
Transition; school-to-work, 388–395, 521
    accountability, 391–392
    definition, 390–391
    process, 392–393
    outcomes, 394–395
    recommendations, 395
    services, 388–390, 393–394
Transportation, 63–67
    ADAPT vs. Skinner, 66
    American Public Transit Association vs. Lewis, 64–65
    Urban Mass Transportation Assistance (UMTA) Act
        of 1964, 64–66

Universal design, 444–445
    principles, 445
Upside-Down Welfarism, 154–155

Veblen, Thorstein, 19
Visual impairments and blindness, 259–264
    definition, 260
    prevalence, 261
    rehabilitation potential, 261–264
Vocational analysis, 339–341
Vocational assessment, 275
Vocational development, 352
    theories, shortcomings, 352

Vocational education, 21–22
Vocational evaluation, 289, 303–305, 517–518
    computer-based, 333–334
    evaluation summary report, 328–332
    flexible approach, 289
    plan, 327
    preparation for, 304
    process, 290–294
    purpose, 303
    report, 327–328
    subobjectives, 289
Vocational handicap, 218–220
Vocational Rehabilitation Act Amendments, 33–36
    1954, 33–34
    1965, 35–36
Voting Accessibility for the Elderly and Handicapped
    Act (1984), 72

Wagner-O'Day Act, 30
Wheelchairs, 431–432
Wilbur, Harvey, 12
Wild boy of Aveyron, 11
Women with disabilities, 465–481
    abuse, 478–481
    health concerns/access, 466–470
    motherhood, 474–478
    safety plans, 480–481
Woodrow Wilson, 37
Wonder drugs, 31
Work adjustment, 350, 384–388
    training, 384–388
Workers Compensation, 23–24
Work Experience Survey, 412
Workforce Investment Act (WIA), 78–81
Work Personality Profile, 386
Work reinforcers, 350
Work samples, 318
    advantages, 321
    disadvantages, 321–322
    JEVS Work Sample System, 319–320
    Singer/Graflex Work Sample, 319
    Tower System, 318–319
    Valpar Component Work Sample, 319–320
    Vocational Information and Evaluation Work
        Samples, 319
    Vocational Interest Temperament Aptitude Systems,
        319
    Wide Range Employment Sample Test, 319
World War II, 31–32

About the Authors

Stanford E. Rubin, professor emeritus, was a professor and coordinator of the Doctor of Rehabilitation Program at the Rehabilitation Institute at Southern Illinois University at Carbondale from 1980 to 2005. Previously, he worked as a senior research scientist at the Arkansas Rehabilitation Research and Training Center and as a counselor at Wright State University. Dr. Rubin has worked in the field of re-habilitation for the past 38 years and has over 100 profes-sional publications. In addition to *Foundations of the Vocational Rehabilitation Process,* Dr. Rubin has coauthored *Case Management and Rehabilitation Counseling* (Roessler & Rubin, 1982, 1992, 1998, 2006) and *Facilitative Management in Rehabilitation Counseling: A Casebook* (Bozarth & Rubin, 1972), as well as coedited *Contemporary Challenges to the Rehabilitation Counseling Profession* (Rubin & Rubin, 1988). He has also authored several widely used, comprehensive in-service training packages for practicing rehabilitation counselors. Dr. Rubin has served as the president of the American Rehabilitation Counseling Association (1982–1983), as a commissioner on the Commission on Rehabilitation Counselor Certification (1980–1986), as a board member of the Foundation for Rehabilitation Education and Research (1995–2000), as the editor of two special issues of professional journals, and on the editorial boards of the *Journal of Applied Rehabilitation Counseling* and *Rehabilitation Education.*

Dr. Rubin has been the recipient of six national research awards from rehabilitation or counseling professional associations. His areas of current interest include rehabilitation philosophy, disability rights issues, case management practices, curriculum design for rehabilitation education, multicultural rehabilitation counseling, the role of the rehabilitation counselor, and survey research methods. Dr. Rubin has also been involved in the development and evaluation of ethics education materials directed at preparing rehabilitation counselors to effectively deal with ethical dilemmas in the case management process.

Richard T. Roessler is a university professor in the Rehabilitation, Human Resources, and Communication Dis-orders Department in the College of Education and Health Professions at the University of Arkansas. He has served as a senior research scientist at the Arkansas Research and Training Center in Vocational Rehabilitation and as co-ordinator of the rehabilitation education program. He has authored or coauthored over 150 journal articles, book chapters, and monographs, as well as four textbooks. *Foundations of the Vocational Rehabilitation Process* and *Case Management and Rehabilitation Counseling* (4th ed.) are widely used in graduate education. He coauthored the first two Richard J. Baker Memorial Monographs published by the Vocational Evaluation and Work Adjustment Association.

Dr. Roessler collaborated in the development of *Life Centered Career Education* (Council for Exceptional Children) and contributed to two Institutes on Rehabilitation Issues study groups. The American Rehabilitation Counseling Association has recognized four research studies in which Dr. Roessler participated. He has also received research and career awards from the College of Education and Health Professions, the Arkansas Alumni Association, the National Council on Rehabilitation Education, and the American Rehabilitation Counseling Association. Dr. Roessler and his colleagues received the Innovative Program Award from the National Association of Student Personnel Administrators (Region IV) for Project Career. Dr. Roessler has coauthored training programs such as Return-to-Work, Occupational Choice Strategy, Vocational Coping Training, Getting Employment Through Interview Training, and the Goal-Setting Module. He has participated in the development of rehabilitation assessments, including the *Work Personality Profile,* the *Employability Maturity Interview,* the *Work Performance Assessment,* and the *Work Experience Survey.* His recent research activities address the employment discrimination experiences and the reasonable accommodation needs of people with severe chronic illnesses such as multiple sclerosis.